Positive Behavior Support

Positive Behavior Support:

Critical Articles on Improving Practice for Individuals with Severe Disabilities

∾

Edited by
Linda M. Bambara, Glen Dunlap,
and Ilene S. Schwartz

(800) 897-3202
www.proedinc.com

(410) 828-8274
www.tash.org

PRO-ED, Inc. and TASH
© 2004

Library of Congress Cataloging-in-Publication Data

Positive behavior support : critical articles on improving practice for individuals with
    severe disabilities / edited by Linda M. Bambara, Glen Dunlap, and Ilene Schwartz.
        p. cm.
        Compilation of articles from two journals.
        Includes bibliographical references.
        ISBN 0-89079-986-5 (pbk.)
        1. People with mental disabilities—Services for. 2. People with mental
disabilities—Behavior modification.   3. People with mental disabilities—Family
relationships. I. Bambara, Linda M., 1952– II. Dunlap, Glen. III. Schwartz, Ilene S.
HV3004.P673   2004   2003066432
362.3'86—dc22   CIP

Positive Behavior Support:
Critical Articles on Improving Practice for Individuals with Severe Disabilities

∽

TABLE OF CONTENTS

Part III. Assessment-Based Interventions

Part IV. Families and Family Support

Part V. Capacity Building

Part VI. Extended Applications: Focus on Systems Change

Preface

~

Support. Understanding. Teaching. Accommodations. Consumer Input. Person-Centered Values. Meaningful Outcomes. When thinking about behavioral interventions, these words historically have not come to mind. They are integral, however, to positive behavior support (PBS), a comprehensive approach for understanding and addressing the needs of individuals with disabilities who engage in challenging behaviors. The primary goal of PBS is not to stop problem behavior from occurring but rather is to create long-lasting change that will have a broad impact on individuals' overall quality of life. PBS is characterized by educational, proactive, and respectful interventions that involve teaching alternative skills to problem behaviors and changing problematic environments. It blends best practices in behavioral technology, educational methods, and ecological systems change with person-centered values in order to achieve outcomes that are meaningful to the individual and to his or her family.

PBS is as much a way of thinking about people and their support as it is an intervention approach. PBS first emerged during the early 1980s, when advocates protested the use of highly punitive or aversive interventions (e.g., electric shock, pinching, forced physical movement, exclusionary time-out) to control the behavior of people with severe disabilities. Advocates drew the proverbial line in the sand, rejecting counterarguments that these interventions could be effective. There was no justification for interventions that use pain, discomfort, or humiliation as a means for changing the behaviors of people with severe disabilities.

The stand against the use of aversives opened doors to alternative approaches and perspectives. From the scientific community, applied behavior analysts literally took functional assessment out of the clinical closet and introduced the technology and its conceptual underpinnings to everyday mainstream settings. Functional assessment tells us that challenging behaviors are not random acts that should be snuffed out, but rather are primitive forms of communication that should be understood. They are purposeful and environmentally determined, and ironically, often provoked by the very conditions designed by professionals to "treat" challenging behaviors. Functional assessment tells us that in order to be truly effective, we must change the conditions that are problematic and trouble-

some to the person and give him or her new ways of controlling and interacting with his or her environment. A simple focus on stopping problem behavior is never the answer.

At the same time, professionals from the disability community introduced person-centered values to mainstream practice. These person-centered values challenge us to see people who engage in very difficult behaviors as deserving of the same compassion, understanding, and treatment we would afford ourselves. Moreover, person-centered values challenge us to put the person's well-being above programmatic needs. Rather than forcing the person to fit in a program that is not working, person-centered values obligate us to stand by the person, do whatever it takes to make accommodations, create new systems of support, and help build a better life.

When advances in applied behavior analysis merged with person-centered values, PBS was born. TASH was the original home of PBS. As an organization dedicated to the welfare of people with severe disabilities, TASH contributed immeasurably to the ideological development, values, and promotion of PBS. Its journal, *JASH,* now called *Research and Practice for Persons with Severe Disabilities* (RPSD), published, and continues to publish, authoritative research and conceptual articles on PBS, with a focus on supporting people with severe disabilities. Indeed, in the late 1980s and early 1990s, *JASH* was one of the few journals bold enough to publish "value-based" intervention research, blending scientific rigor with socially acceptable standards of human dignity and meaningful outcomes.

Since its inception more than 15 years ago, PBS has expanded as an intervention approach designed to support all people with disabilities who present behavioral challenges, not just individuals labeled with severe disabilities. As such, in 1999, PRO-ED, Inc. founded the *Journal of Positive Behavior Interventions* (JPBI). Consistent with the traditions and values of PBS, JPBI's mission is to expand the knowledge and practice of PBS across various disabilities in home, school, and community settings.

In a collaborative venture between *Research and Practice in Severe Disabilities* and the *Journal of Positive Behavior Interventions,* this book contains some of the most exciting and influential articles documenting the history, foundation, and critical features of PBS for people with severe disabilities. Taken together, the selected articles from the two journals trace the historical roots of PBS and provide state-of-the-art discussions and supportive research on how to design meaningful and effective supports for people with severe disabilities and their families.

This book is organized in six sections. The first section lays out the historical, conceptual, and ethical foundations of PBS, beginning with some of the first conceptual articles on the subject ever published, and ending with a contemporary discussion describing its continued evolution and future directions. Although debates about aversive interventions no longer predominate discussions, tensions regarding the blending of science, values, and practice continue to exist.

The second section provides practical information on how to conduct functional assessments in everyday settings. Seminal articles on person-centered planning and the evaluation of meaningful outcomes are also included.

The third section presents empirical and case illustrations of comprehensive, assessment-based interventions for children and adults with severe disabilities in home, school, and community settings. The way that positive behavior supports are individually crafted to address individuals' strengths, needs, preferences, and learning contexts will be of particular interest to readers.

The fourth section emphasizes the family perspective of PBS. These articles highlight family support, family well-being, and family-centered practices in PBS.

In a shifting of the focus beyond the individual, the fifth section deals with capacity-building, or supporting the people who are called upon to implement PBS. Because parents, teachers, and other support staff are the implementers of change, their training and their support are key ingredients for success.

Finally, the last section focuses on the continuing evolution of PBS by highlighting new and exciting directions. Articles in this section illustrate how problem behaviors may be prevented from developing by changing the systems in which people with disabilities live and go to school.

Given the history of the two journals and their continued commitment to the development of positive behavior support, what better source of information on state-of-the art practices in PBS for people with severe disabilities exists? We believe that this book is for anyone who is interested in practical information and research on designing meaningful and effective supports.

Linda M. Bambara
Lehigh University

Glen Dunlap
University of South Florida

Ilene S. Schwartz
University of Washington

PART I
Foundations of Positive Behavior Support

∾

It was not until the mid-1980s that positive behavior support (PBS) began to emerge as a distinct approach for resolving behavioral challenges and enhancing desired lifestyles. At that time, a convergence of human rights activism (including opposition to institutionalization, segregation, and aversive control) and the advancement of new perspectives on educational interventions mandated the development of a different and more humane and values-oriented approach for addressing the needs of individuals whose lives were compromised by the presence of seriously destructive and disruptive behaviors. Since these early beginnings, the description and definition of PBS has been a generative endeavor. The field has expanded dramatically, and its purpose, relevance, and essential features have been continually shaped by its growing constituencies.

This section presents a chronological sequence of pivotal articles representing the vicissitudes of the conceptual and ethical foundations of PBS. The first article in this section, by Horner and his colleagues (1990), sought to define the new field of "nonaversive behavior management" and present a proactive agenda for research and intervention. Although very important contributions had previously established the parameters of PBS (see, e.g., Carr & Durand, 1985; Donnellan, Mirenda, Mesaros, & Fassbender, 1984; Evans & Meyer, 1985; Guess, Helmstetter, Turnbull, & Knowlton, 1987; Meyer & Evans, 1989), this article proposed a definition of PBS and its delineated critical features in a manner that had not yet been achieved.

The next article, by Meyer and Evans (1993), provided a thoughtful consideration of the goals and methodological processes of PBS and, in so doing, helped advance the field in very substantial ways. These authors were among the first to articulate explicitly the need for researchers and practitioners to acknowledge the essential value of meaningful lifestyle outcomes and to ponder the implications of the nature of these outcomes for decisions about research designs and program evaluation. This article has been influential in propelling PBS researchers beyond the strictures of conventional research protocols and toward more person-centered and usable strategies of investigation.

Brown, Gothelf, Guess, and Lehr's article (1998), part of a special section of *JASH* devoted to questions of self-determination, was one of the few early writings to directly address the crucial, difficult, and controversial issue of interpreting the communicative intent of nonconventional expressions by individuals with severe disabilities. As the authors noted, this vital aspect of PBS relates in important ways to the processes of functional assessment and the development of respectful support plans. Because of the fundamental place occupied by self-determination and person-centeredness in the field of PBS, Brown and colleagues contributed needed perspectives that entered into the ongoing challenges of PBS development.

Singer, Gert, and Koegel (1999) focused on the ethical concerns relevant to the use of aversive stimuli to suppress severe challenging behavior. Their philosophical and moral analysis provided an important scholarly perspective on the ethical foundations of PBS.

The article by Carr and his coauthors (2002) may be considered a follow-up article to the article by Horner et al. (1990), in that the authorship is composed of principal collaborators within the Research and Training Center on Positive Behavior Support, the longest-running federally funded project on PBS (1987 to the present). A comparison of the two articles, however, shows how far the field has advanced in a mere dozen years. By 2002, the empirical and practical basis for PBS was well established, and the defining features had come to describe not only parameters of state-of-the-art practice but, arguably, the precepts for a new applied science. Because the article presented a singular exposition of the contemporary state of PBS, JPBI followed its publication with three commentaries, and we reprint these commentaries as the final entries in this section. Bambara (2002), Snell (2002), and Wacker and Berg (2002) offered perspectives on the Carr et al. article and added insights of their own regarding the evolving status of PBS.

As a set, the articles in this section provide a rich sample of the pivotal writings that have defined PBS and established its place in the arena of human services and human supports. The chronological sequence offers an historical perspective on the development of the field and how it has contributed to the lives of individuals with severe disabilities.

—Glen Dunlap

REFERENCES

Carr, E., & Durand, M. (1985). Reducing behavior problems through functional communication training. *Journal of Applied Behavior Analysis, 11,* 459–501.

Donnellan, A. M., Mirenda, P. L., Mesaros, R. A., & Fassbender, L. L. (1984). Analyzing the communicative functions of aberrant behavior. *Journal of the Association for Persons with Severe Handicaps, 9,* 201–212.

Evans, I. M., & Meyer, L. H. (1985). *An educative approach to behavior problems: A practical decision model for interventions with severely handicapped learners.* Baltimore: Brookes.

Guess, D., Helmstetter, E., Turnbull, H. R., & Knowlton, S. (1987). *The use of aversive procedures with persons who are disabled: An historical review and critical analysis.* Seattle: The Association for Persons with Severe Handicaps.

Meyer, L. H., & Evans, I. M. (1989). *Nonaversive intervention for behavior problems: A manual for home and community.* Baltimore: Brookes.

JASH
1990, Vol. 15, No. 3, 125–132

Toward a Technology of "Nonaversive" Behavioral Support

Robert H. Horner
University of Oregon

Glen Dunlap
University of South Florida

Robert L. Koegel
University of California at Santa Barbara

Edward G. Carr
State University of New York at Stony Brook

Wayne Sailor
San Francisco State University

Jacki Anderson
California State University, Hayward

Richard W. Albin and Robert E. O'Neill
University of Oregon

Nonaversive behavior management is an approach to supporting people with undesirable behaviors that integrates technology and values. Although this approach has attracted numerous proponents, more adequate definition and empirical documentation are still needed. This article presents an introduction to the nonaversive approach. Important definitions are suggested, and three fundamental elements are presented: (a) an emerging set of procedures for supporting people with severe challenging behavior; (b) social validation criteria emphasizing personal dignity; and (c) a recommendation for prohibition or restriction of certain strategies. These elements are defined in hopes of stimulating further discussion and empirical analyses of positive behavioral support.

DESCRIPTOR: nonaversives

In recent years, a broad-based movement has emerged in support of nonaversive behavior management. This movement reflects a commitment to the value that people with severe disabilities who exhibit

Preparation of this manuscript was supported in part by the United States Department of Education, Cooperative Agreement G0087C023488. The opinions expressed herein do not necessarily reflect the position or policy of the United States Department of Education, and no official endorsement by the Department should be inferred.

Requests for reprints should be sent to Robert H. Horner, Ph.D., Specialized Training Program, 135 Education Building, University of Oregon, Eugene, Oregon 97403.

challenging behaviors should be treated with the same respect and dignity as all other members of the community (Evans & Meyer, 1985; Gast & Wolery, 1986; LaVigna & Donnellan, 1986; McGee, Menolascino, Hobbs, & Menousek, 1987). It also reflects a concern that many people who perform undesirable behavior have been, and are being, subjected to dehumanizing interventions that are neither ethical nor beneficial (Durand, 1988; Guess, Helmstetter, Turnbull, & Knowlton, 1987). Nonaversive behavior management seeks alternatives to the emphasis on behavioral suppression through aversive contingencies and calls instead for a focus on positive procedures that educate and promote the development of adaptive repertoires (Evans & Meyer, 1985). However, defining the critical elements and empirical basis for the nonaversive approach remains a major challenge (Mulick, in press).

An important feature of the current focus on nonaversive behavior management is that the basic concepts are being promoted from several different perspectives. There is no specific technique or procedure that distinguishes the approach. Rather, different proponents offer not only varying procedural recommendations, but different theories of behavior in its support (Carr, 1988; Donnellan, LaVigna, Negri-Shoultz, & Fassbender, 1988; Durand & Crimmins, 1988; Evans & Meyer, 1985; McGee et al., 1987). This article is a response to these varying presentations of nonaversive behavior management. To begin such a discussion, however, it is necessary define critical terms.

Defining "Aversive" and "Nonaversive"

The term "nonaversive behavior management" is an unfortunate label. In our view, the term is operationally inaccurate, and functionally misdirected. Of greatest concern is the inconsistency between the technical and ethical standards for labeling an event as aversive. Technically, the term "aversive" refers to a class of stimuli that are followed by escape or avoidance responses (Azrin & Holz, 1966; Bandura, 1969; Johnston, 1988; Van Houten, 1983). A slap or an electric shock is aversive if a person moves away or avoids being slapped or shocked. Similarly, a hug or a brussels sprout is aversive if a person consistently moves away from, or avoids it. In many traditional behavioral programs, aversive stimuli are used as punishers in an effort to decrease targeted behaviors.

The problem with the technical definition is that it does not include a clear mechanism for distinguishing *mildly* aversive events from *very* aversive events. It is practically impossible to provide support or instruction that does not include at least some mildly aversive events. Withholding attention, redirecting from preferred (albeit self-injurious) behavior, making a request to perform a new behavior, and delivering instructional prompts all may be aversive to some degree. If the technical definition of "aversive" is applied, there are few teachers or clinicians who could argue that they implement a totally nonaversive approach.

Nonaversive behavior management, however, has developed less as a response to mild, or potentially mild, forms of aversive stimuli, than as an alternative to the use of more extreme aversive events. The ideological use of "aversive" has become synonymous with procedures that involve the delivery of pain, withholding basic human needs, or social humiliation. From an ethical perspective these procedures are viewed as too extreme to be accepted as "treatment" (Guess, 1988).

At present, we do not have an adequate means of assessing operationally the level of aversiveness or intrusiveness of an intervention for a particular individual before its implementation. The result is that nonaversive behavior management is interpreted by some individuals to mean the abolition of all punishers. For others, nonaversive behavior management is associated with rejection of only those punishers that involve pain or physical harm (tissue damage). For still others, a more complex definition of aversive includes presumptions of "physical or emotional distress." A major obstacle to building an effective set of procedures and a coherent support philosophy is the absence of accepted definitions. For the purposes of this article, we will use the term "aversive" in its technical form.

A second, and equally important, reason why the label "nonaversive behavior management" is confusing is that it focuses attention on the negative aspects of this approach. The most important and exciting elements of the nonaversive avenue to behavioral support lie in the emphasis and precision with which positive intervention strategies are used. We anticipate that history will view these contributions as far more important than the rejection of the aversive procedures that currently dominates efforts to define nonaversive behavior management. For this reason, we join many colleagues in preferring the label "positive behavioral support," and will employ it for the remainder of this article.

A major issue for the positive approach to behavior management is the range of different theoretical and methodological banners that fly under the positive flag. Educative programming, positive programming, functional communication training, gentle teaching, functional equivalence programming, and nonaversive behavior management are all variations on the positive approach to providing behavioral support. We view the differences among these, and other variations, as important and constructive aspects of the movement. As with any developing area, time is needed to explore different strategies and options. An important objective at this time is to define different variations and document their effects. Across the array of discussions and descriptions of positive or nonaversive options, however, we believe three main contributions are dominant: (a) the emerging positive technology; (b) an emphasis on social validation and human dignity in determining the appropriateness of behavioral procedures; and (c) the recommendation for prohibition, or severe restriction, of certain classes of behavioral techniques.

An Emerging Technology of Positive Behavioral Support

The first contribution of positive programming is an emphasis on specific procedures for managing severe, challenging behavior in community settings. It is important to recognize that the positive/nonaversive approach will be a hollow contribution if it does not include an effective set of procedures for managing challenging behaviors. At this writing, empirical support for a comprehensive, positive technology is developing but is by no means compelling (Carr, Taylor, Carlson, & Robinson, 1990). There are a number of clinical demonstrations in which positive procedures have been associated with a broad reduction in very severe behaviors (Berkman & Meyer, 1988; Donnellan et al., 1988; Donnellan, LaVigna, Zambito, & Thvedt, 1985; Durand & Kishi, 1987; McGee et al., 1987). In addition, there is a growing literature providing empirically rigorous demonstrations that specific techniques can produce important behavior reduction under experimental conditions (Carr & Durand, 1985; Durand & Carr, 1987; Horner & Albin, 1988; Hunt, Alwell, & Goetz, 1988; Koegel, Koegel, Murphy, & Ryan, 1989; Koegel & Koegel, 1990; Mace et al., 1988; Singer, Singer, & Horner, 1987; Winterling, Dunlap, & O'Neill, 1987).

There is not, however, a data base that allows confidence in the ability of available positive programming technology to respond to all severe behavior challenges. The technology of positive programming is still developing and is just beginning to receive adequate empirical support. Among the different efforts to build this technology, however, we believe there are at least nine common themes that are worthy of acknowledgment and encouragement. These are listed here.

An Emphasis on Lifestyle Change

The positive/nonaversive approach focuses on the lifestyle of the individual, in addition to the frequency, duration, and intensity of the challenging behaviors (Horner, Dunlap, & Koegel, 1988). Behavioral support should result in durable, generalized changes in the way an individual behaves, and these changes should affect the individual's access to community settings, to social contact, and to a greater array of preferred events. Among the most important issues for a technology of behavioral support is recognition that the standards for assessing "success" are changing. An effective behavioral support plan should integrate procedures for building access to activities, places, people, and events in addition to modifying the patterns of specific desirable and undesirable behaviors (Hitzing, 1988; Horner, in press; O'Brien, 1987).

Functional Analysis

Assessing the antecedents and consequences of a behavior has long been advocated in applied behavior analysis (Baer, Wolf, & Risley, 1968; Bandura, 1969; Kanfer & Saslow, 1969; Ullman & Krasner, 1965). The technology of functional analysis is improving, however, and much greater focus is being given to efficient processes for defining when challenging behaviors are likely to occur and what events are likely to be maintaining the behavior (Carr & Durand, 1985; Durand & Carr, 1987; Durand & Crimmins, 1988; Iwata, Dorsey, Slifer, Bauman, & Richman, 1982; Touchette, McDonald, & Langer, 1985). In addition, there is increasing emphasis on building a direct link between the results from a functional analysis and the actual intervention program that is developed (Carr, 1988; Horner & Billingsley, 1988; O'Neill, Horner, Albin, Storey, & Sprague, 1988).

Multicomponent Interventions

The positive approach to behavior management seldom employs a single intervention to address a single challenging behavior. In most cases, interventions involve the simultaneous manipulation of many variables (e.g., Berkman & Meyer, 1988; Durand & Kishi, 1987). Movement of an individual to a more personal, less segregated setting, ignoring minor inappropriate behaviors, providing multiple opportunities for choice making, systematic instruction on new functional behaviors,

increased access to preferred events, and staff training may all be combined into one intervention plan. As part of the focus on lifestyle change, the nonaversive approach often includes complex (multicomponent) interventions that are designed to increase classes of positive behavior and decrease classes of undesirable behavior simultaneously (Koegel & Koegel, 1988).

Manipulation of Ecological and Setting Events

Behavior management has long been associated with manipulation of the events that immediately precede and follow targeted behaviors. An exciting area of growth within the field is the recognition that if broad behavior patterns are to be affected, a greater range of variables must be considered. Various authors (Patterson, 1982; Wahler & Fox, 1981) have advocated expanding the range of variables included in behavioral support plans. These recommendations are beginning to be acknowledged in the support of people with more severe disabilities. Diet, eating schedule, exercise options, sleeping patterns, rapport, noise level, density of housing, and predictability of daily events are being recognized as nontrivial variables in both the quality of a person's life and the extent to which undesirable behaviors are manifested (Bailey, 1987; Kern, Koegel & Dunlap, 1984; Rast, Johnston, Ellinger-Allen, & Drum, 1985). The important issue for practitioners and families is that behavioral support plans are beginning to include practical, basic elements that have great promise for both affecting behavior change and improving the likelihood that positive changes endure.

Emphasis on Antecedent Manipulations

The emerging, positive approaches to behavioral support emphasize the use of antecedent manipulations. This emphasis comes in such forms as (a) modifying events in a setting so that the stimuli eliciting the undesirable behavior are reduced or removed (Touchette et al., 1985) and (b) adding antecedent events that increase the likelihood of positive behaviors (Horner & Albin, 1988; Horner, Day, Sprague, O'Brien & Heathfield, in press). These are not new ideas, but the increased use of functional analysis information permits these approaches to be practical elements in behavioral support plans.

Teaching Adaptive Behavior

Among the most important elements in a nonaversive approach is attention to teaching individuals adaptive ways of obtaining outcomes that they currently achieve through challenging behaviors (Carr, 1988; Evans & Meyer, 1985; LaVigna & Donnellan, 1986). This approach focuses on defining the behavioral "function" of challenging behaviors and teaching the individual socially acceptable ways of achieving that function. Among the most common examples is the teaching of communication skills. There are a growing number of clinical and experimental demonstrations in which the development of communication skills has been associated with the reduction in levels of challenging behaviors (Carr & Durand, 1985, Durand & Carr, 1987; Horner & Budd, 1985; Koegel et al, 1989). Challenging behaviors occur as part of a complex behavioral ecology. By attending to the functions of challenging behaviors, clinicians may be able to identify skill deficits. Focusing on the development of the identified skills may be an effective and efficient approach to decreasing challenging behaviors without the use of intrusive interventions.

Building Environments with Effective Consequences

Positive procedures focus less on the manipulation of consequences than has been typical of behavioral interventions. Nonaversive systems include traditional procedures of consistently rewarding positive behavior and reducing rewards for undesirable behavior. Differential reinforcement of other behavior (DRO) (Luselli, Miles, Evans, & Boyce, 1985; Rose, 1979), differential reinforcement of incompatible behavior (DRI) (Mulick, Schroeder, & Rojahn, 1980; Steen & Zuriff, 1977), and differential reinforcement of alternative behaviors (Alt-R) (Carr, 1988) are cornerstones of all positive behavioral interventions. The positive approach, however, also includes attention to additional consequence variables. One strategy has been to identify a presumed reinforcer that maintains a challenging behavior, and to deliver that reinforcer at a high rate either for desirable behaviors, or noncontingently (LaVigna & Donnellan, 1986).

A second, and more complex, contribution of positive procedures has been to focus on the development of the individual's reinforcement history. People with challenging behaviors who have lived in highly restrictive settings may have very limited reinforcement histories. Very few events function as reinforcers, and the relationship between a person's behavior and positive events is not clear. One approach to this situation is to create a setting in which an array of potentially positive events are made available at a high, predictable rate as long as undesirable behaviors are not performed. The objective is, in part, to allow some of these events to develop into effective reinforcers. Only with the development of effective reinforcers (including social contact with staff) is programmatic success anticipated.

Minimizing the Use of Punishers

Although there is considerable debate about the use of punishers, a general theme of the positive programming approach is that the delivery of punishers for challenging behaviors is not desirable. The most common alternative is to minimize the reinforcement of challenging behaviors, redirect the person to more appropriate behaviors, and combine this procedure with other instructional and environmental manipulations

(Evans & Meyer, 1985; Koegel & Koegel, 1989; LaVigna & Donnellan, 1986; McGee et al., 1987). Many advocates of positive behavior management recognize, however, that a typical array of events (frowns, reprimands, etc.) can be viewed technically as punishers and yet provide critical learning information.

Distinguish Emergency Procedures from Proactive Programming

An effective technology for supporting people with severe challenging behaviors must provide families and staff with specific strategies for responding when these behaviors occur. It is not sufficient simply to recommend how to ignore or avoid undesirable behaviors. Many behaviors place the person with a disability, or others, at such severe social or physical risk that both of these options are unacceptable. It is equally important, however, to recognize that many times the preferred response to dangerous situations is not to deliver a behavioral intervention designed to change the behavior, but just to provide sufficient temporary control to ensure that no one gets hurt. An effective technology of positive behavioral support must include specific procedures for providing support in dangerous situations. It is critical, however, that a clear distinction be made between crisis intervention strategies for infrequent use in emergency situations and ongoing proactive programming designed to produce substantive positive change. Crisis intervention procedures must not be allowed to turn into on-going restraint, or be used as a defense for the absence of effective programming.

The development of a well defined technology of positive behavioral support will take time. There is too little information currently available to assert that positive approaches are capable of solving all behavior problems or documenting that one approach is superior to any other. Both well controlled empirical analyses and less controlled clinical analyses are needed. The objective for the near future should not be to force consensus among those developing positive strategies, but to increase the precision with which a wide array of approaches are evaluated empirically.

Social Validation and the Role of Dignity in Behavioral Support

The second defining element of positive behavioral support is the addition of a social validity standard (Wolf, 1978) for determining the appropriateness of any intervention. Defining the appropriate use of the technology within an ethical context has long been accepted within applied behavior analysis (Kazdin, 1980). Two professional criteria often have been defined. The first is that any behavioral intervention must be justified in balance with the benefit anticipated for the person with disabilities (Irvin & Singer, 1984). Any intervention, no matter how benign, intrudes into a person's life to some degree. The level of intrusiveness should be in proportion to the magnitude of the anticipated gain. The second standard is that clinicians should use the least intrusive intervention option that can logically be expected to be successful in a reasonable time period (Foxx, 1982; Matson & DiLorenzo, 1984). This second standard often has led to guidelines requiring that less intrusive interventions be documented as ineffective before implementing significantly intrusive actions (Foxx, 1982; Katz bill, 1988; Lovaas & Favell, 1987). An important nuance of this standard is that the demand is *not* that all less intrusive interventions be tried, but that all less intrusive strategies that logic and current research indicate *may have an effect* should be attempted.

A positive approach to behavior management fully endorses these traditional criteria. In addition, however, the positive approach adds a "dignity" standard. *Behavioral interventions should maintain and support the personal dignity of the individual.* Procedures that typical members of a community find excessive should be viewed with extreme caution. Because the purpose of behavioral interventions is to assist people in becoming full participants in society, the procedures used to achieve this goal should be within the standards set by society. Requiring behavioral interventions to be socially valid recognizes that it is not just the type of intervention that is important, but also the manner in which that intervention is implemented. By its nature, behavioral technology involves continuous on-site technical and ethical judgement. Even mildly intrusive, or reinforcement-based, interventions can be used in an inhumane, undignified manner that is disrespectful and stigmatizing to the individual with challenging behaviors. As a result, the following are recommended:

1. *The appropriateness of all behavioral interventions should be evaluated in terms of three criteria.* (a) Is the level of intrusiveness logically balanced by the value of the anticipated behavior change for the person with challenging behavior? (b) Is the proposed intervention evaluated by competent professionals as the least intrusive intervention likely to be successful? (c) Is the intervention judged by community members not to be dehumanizing, degrading, or disrespectful to the individual receiving support?

2. *The more intrusive an intervention, the greater the need for continuous public monitoring.* The more intrusive an intervention, the more important it is that members of the community (e.g., human rights committee) both approve the written plan for the intervention *and observe the plan being implemented.* Written descriptions and the labels applied to behavioral intervention strategies can be ambiguous. Repeated direct observation of the intervention implementation by community members is critical for maintaining the social validity of more intrusive interventions.

3. *The more intrusive an intervention. the greater the*

need for procedural regulation. The greater the social or physical intrusiveness of an intervention, the more appropriate are procedural regulations that restrict (a) who may use the intervention, (b) when the intervention may be used, and (c) the conditions for monitoring the intervention. For example, such interventions as overcorrection, psychotropic medications, or time out may be used with minimal intrusiveness, or they may involve severe social and physical restriction. While it would be inappropriate to eliminate all forms of these interventions, it is appropriate for regulatory agencies to specify restrictions defining when more restrictive forms may be used, and to limit the use of these forms by people who do not have adequate training in the implementation of effective, ethical interventions (Lovaas & Favell, 1987; Van Houten et al., 1988).

Recommendations to Prohibit or Restrict Classes of Behavioral Interventions

The most hotly debated element of positive programming has been the recommendations that aversive behavioral procedures be banned or restricted (Iwata, 1988; Matson & Taras, 1989; Mulick, in press). At one extreme has been a call that all interventions that (a) deliver physical pain, (b) result in harm (medical attention), or (c) are judged to be disrespectful or dehumanizing should be legally and morally prohibited. Multiple recommendations to this effect have been made in texts (Donnellan et al., 1988; Evans & Meyer, 1985; LaVigna & Donnellan, 1986; McGee et al, 1987), newsletters (Sobsey, 1987), resolutions by professional organizations (TASH, AAMR, ASA), and proposed state regulations/laws (Katz bill, 1988). In response has been the argument that in a small number of severe situations it is more immoral to withhold an effective, though painful, intervention (e.g., electric shock), or to use less effective interventions that require extended time to be effective, than to use a painful yet immediately effective procedure (Mulick, in press). Of equal importance, it has been argued that to impose prohibitions on a science as young and ill-defined as behavioral support is damaging to the development of practical, effective procedures.

The debate surrounding the prohibition or restriction of interventions that use severe, aversive stimuli will not be settled soon. An unfortunate aspect of the debate is that it focuses attention away from the more important contributions of positive behavioral support in developing technology and social validation standards. The positive aspects of the debate are that (a) it is forcing an in depth evaluation of acceptable, professional procedures, and (b) it is adding a strong voice from families and consumers of behavioral support in addition to the longstanding discussions of clinicians and ethicists. In addition, there is a growing acceptance within the field that the use of aversive stimuli must be regulated (either by professional organizations or by legal mandate). Lovaas and Favell (1987), for example, have provided a set of guidelines for using aversive stimuli that precludes use of these procedures in all but the most extremely unusual situations, and then only by a very small number of very well trained and monitored clinicians. The functional difference between the professional guidelines recommended by Lovaas and Favell (1987) and a total prohibition of all procedures that involve pain or harm is minimal in terms of the number of people who would receive aversive stimuli. Clearly, the time has come for limiting the use of stimuli and procedures that are painful, damaging, and dehumanizing. The debate should be not on whether to limit our use of the most severe forms of behavioral intervention, but on *how* that limitation should occur.

A consistent message for families, teachers, and community service providers is that positive programming is the expected technology. The routine use of procedures that deliver pain (shock, pinching, slaps), procedures that result in harm (bruises, cuts, broken bones), and procedures that are disrespectful or dehumanizing (facial sprays, shaving cream in mouth, foul smells) are no longer acceptable. Families, teachers, and community service personnel should turn toward (a) developing competence in the technology of positive programming and (b) addressing internal policies and procedures to prevent the abuse of severe, intrusive procedures.

The resolution to the debate surrounding the use of aversive stimuli is to develop and rigorously document positive support procedures that produce consistent, rapid, durable, generalized changes in challenging behaviors while facilitating the development of broad lifestyle changes. This is a tall order, but there must be effective strategies for creating alternatives to the use of behavioral procedures that are painful, harmful, or dehumanizing. The critical question is how to do this and to ensure that all individuals gain access to the best, most humane, most effective support possible. The marriage of ideology and science must be in the delivery of effective, positive alternatives.

Summary

This article describes aspects of positive behavioral support. Our effort has been to further define this technology and emphasize three main elements: (a) an emerging set of procedures, (b) the addition of social validation standards for acceptability, and (c) the prohibition or regulation of procedures viewed as excessively aversive or disrespectful. Through these three elements, positive behavioral support is an integration of technology and values. At this time, the values are more well defined than the technology. Our hope is to refocus attention on the discussion, analysis, and application of those powerful positive procedures that will be critical for raising positive behavioral support from

a debated approach to the established technology in our field.

References

Azrin, N. H., & Holz, W. C. (1966). Punishment. In W. R. Honig (Ed.), *Operant behavior: Areas of research and application*, (pp. 380–447). New Jersey: Prentice Hall.

Baer, D. M., Wolf, M. M., & Risley, T. R. (1968). Some current dimensions of applied behavior analysis. *Journal of Applied Behavior Analysis, 1*, 91–97.

Bailey, J. S. (1987). *Functional analysis.* Presented at ABA Symposium, Nashville, TN.

Bandura, A. (1969). *Principles of behavior modification.* New York: Holt, Rinehart, and Winston.

Berkman, K. A., & Meyer, L. H. (1988). Alternative strategies and multiple outcomes in the remediation of severe self-injury: Going "all out" nonaversively. *Journal of The Association for Persons with Severe Handicaps, 13*, 76–86.

Carr, E. G. (1988). Functional equivalence as a mechanism of response generalization. In R. H. Horner, G. Dunlap, & R. L. Koegel (Eds.), *Generalization and maintenance: Life-style changes in applied settings.* (pp. 221–241) Baltimore: Paul H. Brookes.

Carr, E. G., & Durand, V. M. (1985). Reducing behavior problems through functional communication training. *Journal of Applied Behavior Analysis, 18*, 111–126.

Carr, E. G., Taylor, J. C., Carlson, J. I., & Robinson, S. (in press). Reinforcement and stimulus-based treatments for severe behavior problems in developmental disabilities. *Proceedings of the Consensus Conference on the Treatment of Severe Behavior Problems and Developmental Disabilities.* Washington, D.C.: National Institute of Health.

Donnellan, A. M., La Vigna, G. W., Negri-Shoultz, N., & Fassbender, L. L.(1988). *Progress without punishment: Effective approaches for learners with behavior problems.* New York: Teachers College Press, Columbia University.

Donnellan, A. M., La Vigna, G. W., Zambito, J., & Thvedt, J. (1985). A time limited intensive intervention program model to support community placement for persons with severe behavior problems. *Journal of The Association for Persons with Severe Handicaps, 10*, 123–131.

Durand, V. M. (1988). Towards acceptable and effective intervention for severe behavior problems. In R. H. Horner & G. Dunlap (Eds.), *Behavior management and community integration for individuals with developmental disabilities and severe behavior problems* (pp. 83–96). Eugene: Specialized Training Program, University of Oregon.

Durand, V. M. & Carr, E. G. (1987). Social influences on "self-stimulatory" behavior: Analysis and treatment application. *Journal of Applied Behavior Analysis, 20*, 119–132.

Durand, V. M., & Crimmins, D. M. (1988). Identifying the variables maintaining self-injurious behaviors. *Journal of Autism & Developmental Disorders, 18*(1), 99–117.

Durand, V. M., & Kishi, G. (1987). Reducing severe behavior problems among persons with dual sensory impairments: An evaluation of a technical assistance model. *Journal of The Association for Persons with Severe Handicaps, 12*, 2–10.

Evans, I. M., & Meyer, L. H. (1985). *An educative approach to behavior problems: A practical decision model for interventions with severely handicapped learners.* Baltimore: Paul H. Brookes.

Foxx, R. M. (1982). *Decreasing behaviors of severely retarded and autistic persons.* Champaign, IL: Research Press.

Gast, D. L. & Wolery, M. (1986). Severe maladaptive behaviors. In M. E. Snell, (Ed.), *Systematic instruction of persons with severe handicaps* (3rd ed.) (pp. 300–332). Columbus, OH: Merrill Publishing.

Guess, D. (1988). Problems and issues pertaining to the transmission of behavior management technologies from researchers to practitioners. In R. H. Horner & G. Dunlap (Eds.) *Behavior management and community integration for individuals with developmental disabilities and severe behavior problems* (pp. 19–46). Eugene: Specialized Training Program, University of Oregon.

Guess, D., Helmstetter, E., Turnbull, H. R., & Knowlton, S. (1987). *Use of aversive procedures with persons who are disabled: An historical review and critical analysis.* Seattle: The Association for Persons with Severe Handicaps.

Hitzing, W. (1988). *Community support for people with challenging behaviors.* Presentation at Oregon Developmental Disabilities Conference, Eugene.

Horner, R. H. (in press). The future of applied behavior analysis for people with severe disabilities. In L. Meyer, C. Peck, & L. Brown, (Eds.), *Critical issues in the lives of people with severe disabilities.* Baltimore: Paul H. Brookes.

Horner, R. H., & Albin, R. W. (1988, September). *Functional Analysis.* Presentation at the Research and Training Center on Community-Referenced, Nonaversive Behavior Management National Conference, Santa Barbara, CA.

Horner, R. H., & Billingsley, F. F. (1988). The effect of competing behavior on the generalization and maintenance of adaptive behavior in applied settings. In R. H. Horner, G. Dunlap, & R. L. Koegel (Eds.), *Generalization and maintenance: Life-style changes in applied settings* (pp. 197–220). Baltimore: Paul H. Brookes.

Horner, R. H., & Budd, C. M. (1985). Teaching manual sign language to a nonverbal student: Generalization of sign use and collateral reduction of maladaptive behavior. *Education and Training of the Mentally Retarded, 20,* 39–47.

Horner, R. H., Day, M., Sprague, J., O'Brien, M., Heathfield, L. T. (in press). The effects of interspersed requests on challenging behavior during instruction. *Journal of Applied Behavior Analysis.*

Horner, R. H., Dunlap, G., & Koegel, R. L. (1988). *Generalization and maintenance: Life-style changes in applied settings.* Baltimore: Paul H. Brookes.

Hunt, P., Alwell, M., & Goetz, L. (1988). Acquisition of conversation skills and the reduction of inappropriate social interaction behaviors. *Journal of The Association for Persons with Severe Handicaps, 13,* 20–27.

Irvin, L. K., & Singer, G. S. (1984). *Human rights review manual.* Eugene: Oregon Research Institute.

Iwata, B. A. (1988). The development and adoption of controversial default technologies. *The Behavior Analyst, 11,* 149–157.

Iwata, B. A., Dorsey, M. F., Slifer, J., Bauman, K. E., & Richman, G. S. (1982). Toward a functional analysis of self-injury. *Analysis and Intervention in Developmental Disabilities 2,* 3–20.

Johnston, J. M. (1988). Regulating the delivery of behavioral technology. In R. H. Horner & G. Dunlap (Eds.) *Behavior management and community integration for individuals with developmental disabilities and severe behavior problems* (pp. 6–18). Eugene: Specialized Training Program, University of Oregon.

Kanfer, F. H., & Saslow, G. (1969). Behavioral diagnosis. In C. M. Franks (Ed.), *Behavior therapy: Appraisal and status* (pp 417–444). New York: McGraw-Hill.

Katz bill, State of California Proposed Legislation, AB520, 1988.

Kazdin, A. E. (1980). *Behavior modification in applied settings (2nd ed.).* Homewood, IL: Dorsey Press.

Kern, L., Koegel, R. L., & Dunlap, G. (1984). The influence of vigorous vs. mild exercise on autistic stereotyped behaviors. *Journal of Autism and Developmental Disorders, 14,* 57–67.

Koegel, R. L., & Koegel, L. K. (1988). Generalized responsivity and pivotal behaviors. In R. H. Horner, G. Dunlap, & R. L. Koegel (Eds.), *Generalization and maintenance: Life-style changes in applied settings* (pp. 41–66). Baltimore: Paul H. Brookes.

Koegel, R. L., & Koegel, L. K. (1989). Community-referenced research on self-stimulation. In E. Cipani (Ed.), *The treatment of severe behavior disorders: Behavior analysis approaches* (pp. 129–150). American Association on Mental Retardation, Washington, D.C.

Koegel, R. L., & Koegel, L. K. (1990). Extended reductions in stereotypic behavior of students with autism through a self-management treatment program package. *Journal of Applied Behavior Analysis, 23,* 119–127.

Koegel, R. L., Koegel, L. K., Murphy, C., & Ryan, C. (1989). *Assessing the effect of different teaching paradigms on disruptive behavior.* Manuscript submitted for publication.

LaVigna, G. W., & Donnellan, A. M. (1986). *Alternatives to punishment: Solving behavior problems with non-aversive strategies.* New York: Irvington Publishers.

Lovaas, O. I., & Favell, J. E. (1987). Protection for clients undergoing aversive/restrictive interventions. *Education and Treatment of Children, 10,* 311–325.

Luselli, J. K., Miles, E., Evans, T. P., & Boyce, D. A. (1985). Reinforcement control of severe dysfunctional behavior of blind, multihandicapped students. *American Journal of Mental Deficiency, 90,* 328–334.

Mace, F. C., Hock, M. L., Lalli, J. S., West, B. J., Belfiore, P., Pinter, E., & Brown, D. K (1988). Behavioral momentum in the treatment of noncompliance. *Journal of Applied Behavior Analysis, 21,* 123–141.

Matson, J. L. & DiLorenzo, T. M. (1984). *Punishment and its alternatives: A new perspective for behavior modification* (Vol. 13). New York: Springer Publishing.

Matson, J. L, & Taras, M. E. (1989). A 20 year review of punishment and alternative methods to treat problem behaviors in developmentally delayed persons. *Research in Developmental Disabilities, 10,* 85–104.

McGee, J. J., Menolascino, F. J., Hobbs, D. C., & Menousek, P. E. (1987). *Gentle teaching: A non-aversive approach to helping persons with mental retardation.* New York: Human Sciences Press.

Mulick, J. A. (in press). The ideology and science of punishment in mental retardation. *American Journal on Mental Retardation.*

Mulick, J. A., Schroeder, S. R., Rojahn, J. (1980). Chronic rumination and vomiting: A comparison of four treatment procedures. *Journal of Autism and Developmental Disorders, 10,* 203–213.

O'Brien, J. (1987). A guide to lifestyle planning: Using the Activities Catalog to integrate services and natural support systems. In B. Wilcox and G. T. Bellamy (Eds.), *A comprehensive guide to The Activities Catalog* (pp. 175–189). Baltimore: Paul H. Brookes.

O'Neill, R. E., Horner, R. H., Albin, R. W., Storey, K., & Sprague, J. (1988). *Manual for the functional analysis of challenging behaviors.* Unpublished manuscript. Eugene: Specialized Training Program, University of Oregon.

Patterson, G. R. (1982). *Coercive family process.* Eugene, OR: Castalia Publishing.

Rast, J., Johnston, J. M., Ellinger-Allen, J. A., & Drum, C. (1985). Effects of nutritional and mechanical properties of food on ruminative behavior. *Journal of the Experimental Analysis of Behavior 44,* 195–206.

Rose, T. L. (1979). Reducing self-injurious behavior by differentially reinforcing other behaviors. *The American Association for the Education of the Severely/Profoundly Handicapped 4,* 179–186.

Singer, G. H. S., Singer, J., & Horner, R. H. (1987). Using

pretask requests to increase the probability of compliance for students with severe disabilities. *Journal of The Association for Persons with Severe Handicaps, 12*, 287–291.

Sobsey, D. (1987, November). Non-aversive behavior management: The verdict is in. News & Notes, *American Association on Mental Retardation* newsletter

Steen, P. L., & Zuriff, G. E. (1977). The use of relaxation in the treatment of self-injurious behavior. *Journal of Behavior Therapy and Experimental Psychiatry, 18*, 447–448.

Touchette, P., McDonald, R., & Langer, S. (1985). A scatter plot for identifying stimulus control of problem behavior. *Journal of Applied Behavior Analysis, 18*, 343–351.

Ullman, L. P., & Krasner, L. (Eds.). (1965). *Case studies in behavior modification.* New York: Holt, Rinehart & Winston.

Van Houten, R. (1983). Punishment: From the animal laboratory to the applied setting. In S. Axelrod and J. Apsche (Eds.), *The effects of punishment on human behavior,* (pp. 13–44). New York: Academic Press.

Van Houten, R., Axelrod, S., Bailey, J. S., Favell, J. E., Foxx, R. M., Iwata, B. A., & Lovaas, O. I. (1988). The right to effective behavioral treatment. *The Behavior Analyst, 11*(2), 111–114.

Wahler, R. G., & Fox, J. J. (1981). Setting events in applied behavior analysis: Toward a conceptual and methodological expansion. *Journal of Applied Behavior Analysis, 14*, 327–338.

Winterling, V., Dunlap, G., & O'Neill, R. (1987). The influence of task variation on the aberrant behavior of autistic students. *Education and Treatment of Children, 10*, 105–119.

Wolf, M. M. (1978). Social validity: The case for subjective measurement or how applied behavior analysis is finding its heart. *Journal of Applied Behavior Analysis, 11*, 203–214.

Received: February 8, 1990
Final Acceptance: April 11, 1990
Editor in Charge: John Nietupski

JASH
1993, Vol. 18, No. 4, 224–234

Science and Practice in Behavioral Intervention: Meaningful Outcomes, Research Validity, and Usable Knowledge

Luanna H. Meyer
Syracuse University

Ian M. Evans
State University of New York at Binghamton

Many professional journals publish research reports of interventions for persons with developmental disabilities which traditionally have been expected to fulfill two quite different functions. First, this research literature is the scientific data base to support the validity of recommended most promising practices. Second, these same reports are expected to be a source of information to guide the efforts of practitioners to implement those most promising practices. In a parallel fashion, the experimental method has been used both to test intervention hypotheses in research studies and as an evaluation model for practitioners in evaluating applications in typical settings. This paper explores the extent to which it is reasonable or practical to expect conventional experimental methodologies and research reports to perform this dual purpose. Recommendations are made for research and practice that require multiple perspectives and approaches better suited to a human science.

DESCRIPTORS: philosophy of science, methodology, challenging behavior, intervention practices

There is a compelling need for new directions in the mutual interdependence of science and practice that go beyond traditional notions about research and evaluation, narrow definitions of what are valid contributions to knowledge, and singular views of the function and form of the published literature to both document what we know and guide what we should do. In this paper, the literature on intervening with challenging behavior will be used to illustrate the issues involved. The ongoing controversy regarding appropriate and effective interventions reveals discussion occurring at entirely different levels by proponents of the various approaches. Among those who adhere most closely to the tradition of "technical rationality" (Schon, 1983), the choice of

an intervention is a scientific one in which ". . . specialized scientific knowledge [is applied] to specific cases and circumstances with the objective of solving particular problems" (Kirk & Kutchins, 1992, p. 23). Alternatively, those who approach the debate from the perspective of values, advocacy, and civil rights (TASH, 1986) see the application of such scientific principles and practices as secondary to societal decisions about how people will be treated; this perspective adheres to the Kantian tradition of the categorical imperative (i.e., where the end never justifies the means; Popper, 1959). Intersections of these two juxtaposed points of view can be seen in the social validity or social acceptability literature on the one hand (generally reflecting the scientific perspective—see, for example, Miltenberger, Suda, Lennox, & Lindeman, 1991) and the clinical-experimental literature on nonaversive intervention strategies on the other (generally reflecting the values base perspective—see, for example, Guess, Helmstetter, Turnbull, & Knowlton, 1986; Meyer & Evans, 1989).

We submit that this debate and the controversy surrounding the choice of interventions and models of services for persons with disabilities is but one example of a major paradigm crisis in an applied science. Our theme is not novel: Skrtic (1991) has recently expanded on these same issues that he and others have been discussing in regard to the inclusion of students with disabilities into general education settings (see, for example, Bogdan & Kugelmass, 1984; Meyer, 1991; Skrtic, 1986; Voeltz & Evans, 1983). The present purpose, however, is to illustrate what may eventually become a significant philosophical revision with examples from the clinical intervention literature on challenging behaviors—where the consequences of failing to reach a working consensus have become negative for all involved. A second intent is to suggest positive new directions for research in practice that are more responsive to theoretical and scientific issues.

Such broader issues are being increasingly referenced in the applied sciences. In the words of Hoshmand and Polkinghorne (1992):

Requests for reprints should be sent to Luanna H. Meyer, School of Education, Syracuse University, 805 South Crouse Avenue, Syracuse, NY 13244-2280.

In our judgment, an alternative conception of the science-practice relationship is needed that emphasizes the mutuality of science and practice, in which psychological science as a human practice and psychological practice as a human science inform each other . . . We propose a more radical effort of integration whereby the *processes* of knowledge in the two domains [science and practice] are considered under a new conception of psychology as a human science of practice (pp. 55, 57).

Thus, at the same time the aversives controversy has raged in the field of developmental disabilities, there has been occurring a thorough reexamination of the traditional criteria for scientific respectability and the adequacy of scientific proof as relating to professional activities, national policies, and service standards. This reconstruction has been occurring quietly in a number of seemingly unrelated quarters and now represents a substantial counterweight to the presumptions that have been prominent within applied behavior analysis for approximately 30 years. Our objective is to examine some of the new directions in which this trend might be leading the discipline. Because interventions for persons with severe disabilities have been essentially synchronous with the field of applied behavior analysis, the implications for researchers and research consumers (*JASH*'s readership) should be far-reaching (see also Kaiser, 1992).

Constructing a Knowledge Base for Intervention

The knowledge base for intervening with challenging behaviors is constructed through empirical research and clinical practice. Confidence in the validity of a particular approach to solving behavior problems has been dependent upon the existence of a research literature demonstrating a functional relationship between the application of those specialized principles and positive behavior change. Kirk and Kutchins (1992) have emphasized the depth of any profession's wish for scientific respectability: ". . . among the hallmarks of many professions is the claim that their practitioners will consciously and carefully apply specialized scientific knowledge to specific cases and circumstances with the objective of solving particular problems" (p. 23).

Almost all the behavioral scientists who work in the area of severe disabilities endorse the spirit of technical rationality. This perspective is so strong that the clinical judgments of those who might be regarded as "experts" in the field—who must act and make recommendations in areas where precise evidence on validated practices does not yet exist—are viewed as behaving outside the realm of science. There is little recognition of a valid role for the reflective practitioner or for expert judgment in theory development and clinical practice (see Carr &

Kemmis, 1986; Ewert, 1991), according to such views of science.

What Is Valid Science?

What exactly is the empirical data base on challenging behaviors that would be regarded as validated according to this technical rationality perspective? The published studies of interventions to remediate challenging behaviors in persons with developmental disabilities number in the hundreds (see Schlosser & Goetze, 1992). They illustrate the application of a variety of methods for decreasing challenging behaviors and, in some instances, replacing them with alternative skills. All the reports tend to follow the same general format that has long been advocated in applied behavior analysis—the single-subject or small group controlled experiment with emphasis on documenting both the specific methods and the results obtained according to the accepted conventions of design and measurement (e.g., Barlow & Hersen, 1984). Typically, this approach would be regarded as "quantitative," whether involving single-subject or nomothetic evaluation of an experimental intervention in contrast to results obtained in a non-treatment control condition.

Other paradigms for contributing to our knowledge base, such as interpretive or "qualitative" (Bogdan & Biklen, 1992), case study (Yin, 1989), or critical theory research (Carr & Kemmis, 1986), have not enjoyed widespread acceptance in the behavioral literature. Evidence of the status hierarchy accorded different paradigms can be found in virtually every listing of author publication guidelines in the major, peer-reviewed journals that publish research on developmental disabilities in psychology (e.g., *Journal of Applied Behavior Analysis, Journal of Consulting and Clinical Psychology*), special education (e.g., *Journal of Special Education*), and interdisciplinary fields (e.g., *The Journal of The Association for Persons with Severe Handicaps, American Journal on Mental Retardation*). These guidelines specify the experiment as "the" scientifically valid method acceptable for publication consideration and suggest formats such as a Brief Report or refer authors to a lower status "practitioner" journal as the appropriate dissemination outlet for case studies or qualitative reports. Another illustration of this status hierarchy can be found in a critique of Berkman and Meyer's (1988) report of a successful intervention with an adult man with severe disabilities and self-injurious behavior. Linscheid and Landau (1993) note that these authors "admit" that theirs was a case study and not a controlled experiment. Replying, Meyer and Berkman (1993) emphasize the positive features of a case study approach and make no apology for using a methodology different from that favored by their critics.

Experimental methodologies, in actuality, are not neutral but are closely tied to shared philosophical assumptions of a scholarly community (Kurtines,

Azmitia, & Alvarez, 1992). For example, certain laboratory procedures that were popularized by Skinner for studying animal learning became established as the only legitimate research strategies. Thus, applied behavior analysis, far from being an open, scientific system, has become restricted by its potentially powerful but narrow techniques with the concept of technology favored by those who see noninvasive interventions as simply the extension of nonpunishment principles of operant behavior (e.g., Horner et al., 1990). Researchers operating within this behavioral paradigm may fail to incorporate or even to recognize alternative approaches as they individually accumulate a knowledge base that references only self-generated information sources (Staats, 1981). The recent special issue of the *Journal of Applied Behavior Analysis* on the education crisis illustrates this insularity. Throughout the articles in this special issue, applied behavior analysis is repeatedly credited with having made the only significant contributions to our understanding of teaching and learning. Innovations such as cooperative learning, interdisciplinary teaching, and natural language instruction (e.g., MacIver & Epstein, 1991; Tharp & Gallimore, 1988), which have been validated through methodoligically sound nomothetic educational research, are nowhere referenced.

Empirical research should automatically self-correct theoretical constructs and thus enhance and elaborate theory. However, because of the restrictive model of empirical correctness in applied behavior analysis (Schwartz, 1986), theory development in behavioral intervention has lagged seriously behind. Of special relevance for intervention design are such legitimate but neglected behavioral concepts as: (a) a person's repertoire is complex and consists of interrelated hierarchies of skills; (b) deficit environments (whether the result of institutionalization or the attempt to create a controlled experiment) further restrict the skills that can be supported; and (c) affective dimensions such as emotion, motivation, and stress must be incorporated into our understandings of persons (Eifert & Evans, 1990; Staats, 1988). Important concepts from cognitive science, learning and memory, self-regulation, developmental research, and so on, have been explicitly excluded from applied behavior analysis on prespecified grounds regarding which constructs and research approaches are legitimate. This is exactly as Kuhn (1970) asserted happens when a scientific community acquires and becomes committed to a paradigm, so that discrepant information is excluded from consideration as long as possible to avoid reform of a basic paradigm (see also Guess, Turnbull, & Helmstetter, 1990; and Skrtic, 1991).

Implementation of formal research. Schwartz and Baer (1991) discuss the related issue of *social invalidity*—the deliberate or unconscious actions by direct service providers and/or the client to fail to implement the planned intervention. Whenever the practitioner or family member has reservations regarding the relevance of an intervention, the feasibility of carrying out such an intervention in one's own setting, or generally dislikes the intervention strategy for any reason, practices actually used may not be those supported by the research literature. The literature on the acceptability of particular intervention techniques is an example of efforts to determine the conditions under which a procedure will be approved or disapproved for use with persons with disabilities. This literature examines the reactions of various relevant constituencies (staff, parents, and consumers) to techniques that are controversial, such as aversives (see, for example, Miltenberger et al., 1991).

Interestingly, those who support the use of aversive interventions to address challenging behavior have now recognized this policy problem and have recommended increased attention to public relations:

In a more explicit political vein, we have not done a very good job of integrating effectively with the larger group of professionals who constitute the power structure in developmental disabilities. Just one behavior analyst in even a moderately powerful position in a state agency office may sometimes be more valuable than a number of behavior analysts working in service facilities ... behavior analysis is not as well represented in the academic, state, and federal power structure of developmental disabilities as it must be to avoid inappropriately constraining regulations and to achieve its long term goals. (Johnston, 1991, p. 194)

Another set of circumstances has had an unintended collateral effect upon both research and practice. The evolution of modern communications is the context for this effect. Rapid, engaging, and seemingly uniquely suited to today's consumer, the "sound bite" and "human interest story" may well be preferred as the source of information and attitudes over an hour of difficult reading in an experimentally oriented journal. Television journalism reaches millions of people who have never and will never look at *JASH* or any other publication in developmental disabilities or applied behavior analysis—and many of these people have a family member or friend with a developmental disability. Consumers and advocates are now in a position of influence over the choices made on behalf of persons with disabilities. Educated, politically influential, and articulate parents can adapt to due process guarantees and force once powerful bureaucracies and elite professional groups to implement something they want for their children. We continue to promote our professional journals as the source of these good ideas for these parents and advocates (Kaiser, 1992). But the kinds of empirical detail and responsible caution that our scientific data base requires is not likely to excite the same kinds of allegiances as the treatments that will make a good story to "60 Minutes" or "20/20" or *Time* magazine. Will we succeed in convincing the consumer that the slow and careful way of science is preferable to the flashy promises of miracle cures through our traditional ways of knowing and sharing what we know?

What Is Valid Practice?

A relatively narrow empirical orientation is also evident among practitioners working in school and community settings. Special education teachers, therapists, psychologists, and other professionals who have no intention of conducting or publishing research reports about their ongoing interventions are expected to be conversant with the research literature. Their preservice training programs generally include information and practice on experimental research design (e.g., single subject), graphing, and data analysis. After graduation, teachers and other clinicians are expected to become consumers of the research literature—to read *JASH* and other journals as their primary source of "most promising practices." Finally, to evaluate the success of their day-to-day direct service efforts, they are admonished to adopt in their classrooms, community settings, and family homes the very same data collection and experimental analysis methods utilized by researchers in the published literature (Browder, 1991; O'Neill, Horner, Albin, Storey, & Sprague, 1990).

The adequacy of the knowledge base for practitioners. In the early days of applied behavior analysis, behavior problems were addressed through efforts to decrease and eliminate specific target behaviors (e.g., Lovaas & Bucher, 1974). The need to describe behavior objectively as a prerequisite to any modification efforts has led to a consistent focus upon precision (Sidman, 1960). However, this admirable emphasis has also left us with an unfortunate legacy. Descriptions of behavior in reliably measurable terms has sometimes resulted in reports of what could be characterized as trivial outcomes, for instance, monitoring such minor motor topographies as "hand movements to head." Clearly, such responses could have serious negative consequences if self-injury were the result, but topographically reported outcomes fail to communicate extent of injury, the person's affective state, or the purpose of the behavior. We have neglected, in the behavioral intervention literature, to monitor and report changes in the *reasons* we cared about the behavior in the first place.

This neglect was illustrated in a meta-analysis of 403 intervention studies published in 18 major journals across a 12-year period of time (Scotti, Evans, Meyer, & Walker, 1991). Scotti et al. (1991) evaluated the empirical evidence using two statistical measures of intervention effectiveness—one, a measure of the improvement in comparison to baseline data and the other, the degree to which the behavior was absolutely

suppressed. The findings failed to support several widespread assumptions regarding the standards of practice followed by researchers in the conduct of an intervention research study. If, for example, the published intervention report gives no information about a functional analysis prior to treatment, to what extent is it an appropriate validation of that treatment? If the report includes no attempt to "program for generalization"—now recognized as critical to long-term behavior change (Horner, Dunlap, & Koegel, 1988)—how legitimate is that scientific exemplar? Can the accumulation of dozens and even hundreds of studies that themselves violate various precepts of our best standards of practice result in a believable empirical data base? Indeed, Scotti et al. (1991) were able to rate only 44 of the 403 studies as "highly effective" based upon the two effectiveness statistics, and results were not generally impressive across the remaining studies.

The kinds of outcomes reported in the literature reviewed are even more disappointing. For example, the literature on self-injurious behavior, although recent, is still predominantly comprised of data on discrete instances of head-hitting or self-biting and says little about whether the person in the study learned to do anything else, became socially more proficient, developed new and more positive interpersonal relationships (such as friendships), or was considered to be happier after the intervention. Such literature could never be expected to guide practitioners or family members who accepted responsibility for outcomes such as making friends and having a better lifestyle as sequelae to decreases in behavior such as hand-to-head movements. Moreover, this literature could hardly be expected to generate enthusiastic support from family members, teachers, psychologists, and others confronted with the very real consequences of such a behavior on a day-to-day basis.

Conceptualizing and documenting positive changes in intervention goals such as personal fulfillment, self-determination, happiness, friendships, and even contributions to the social good, will, no doubt, be difficult (Evans, 1993). But these are the outcomes that matter, and should become the goals of intervention if persons with disabilities are to become full participants in their family, community, and culture. For too long the focus of intervention has been the highly discrete behaviors that observers are trained to discriminate from the ongoing flow of events. For the future, the focus of intervention efforts might be better directed toward the kinds of outcomes that we seek for ourselves, know when we see them, and would generally regard as universally good. Indeed, if the behavior changes achieved are so insignificant that we need graphs to see them and must explain why they are good to the child's parents, they may be of little consequence for the daily lifestyle of the individual involved. It is ironic that single-subject graphs of specific behaviors were rightly welcomed in behavior modification as a vast improvement over outcomes expressed as group averages of artificial test scores. Yet it is the need for outcome measures to truly represent the criteria of interest that should predominate, not the need to conform to an increasingly technical measurement technique (baselines) in which much professional time has been invested. It is easy to understand why outcome measures that are interpretable only by other professionals will not elicit the kind of enthusiasm and advocacy that will be generated by an article in the popular press that tells a story of personal achievement.

The impact of this research on practice. As already contended in the previous section, research does not typically have its intended impact on practice. Treatments developed in research settings often cannot be implemented in more typical educational and clinical contexts. Obvious reasons include the lack of resources available to the clinical researcher in typical classrooms, clinical facilities, or family environments. The published study may also fail to describe the intervention in sufficient detail to allow replication by a practitioner. Finally, an idiosyncratic development in the behavior modification literature in particular has been the focus of interest upon the specific treatment—so much so that the general setting in which the intervention was assessed receives little attention or description in published reports (Scotti et al., 1991). Many of the early behavioral interventions took place in specialized, segregated, often institutional settings, where the requisite degree of experimental control could be guaranteed. Background activities, experiences, and opportunities for the "subject" were often nonexistent or were so limited that they could be ignored. As other principles began to shape classrooms and school programs in complex ways (none of them incompatible with broad, behavioral principles per se), these ecological or general "quality of life" factors became as important, if not more so, than the specific intervention strategies.

Researchers might have adapted to this increased interest in the value of background variables by incorporating such circumstances and conditions into the design of their experiments. Thus, favored interventions might be adapted and expanded by behavior analysts so as to be useful and practical in integrated and community settings. Instead, it would appear that this literature largely continues to ignore these new ecosystems. Well-known scholars persist in validating interventions in specialized settings. This research practice has remained despite the widespread movement of children with severe disabilities into their neighborhood public schools. The ecosystem of a regular classroom or community job site is so dramatically different from a university laboratory school, institution, or sheltered workshop, that it becomes difficult to imagine how any

research findings based on segregated and specialized circumstances could be relevant to the new reality for the growing majority of individuals on whose behalf such research receives public and professional support.

The research community has so resisted its own movement into nonsheltered real world environments and situations that separate technologies and a dissemination and technical assistance industry have been constructed to address disappointing effectiveness. Thus, people with severe disabilities who are taught positive behavior in a controlled environment but who continue to exhibit the behavior problem in a community environment, are perceived as having "failed to transfer" so that "generalization training" may be required. Or, if an individual exhibited a skill for the research staff yet fails to maintain gains over time, the direct service personnel may be described as being poorly trained, having inadequate resources, or being noncompliant. To remedy such occurrences, interventions may be watered down, complex ideas made elementary, and strategies communicated on the basis of their formal procedure rather than on the principles that originally shaped them. Time-out is one of the best examples of this, when a reasonably useful principle of restricting access to reinforcement became translated in countless settings into physical battles between angry, fearful, and generally out-of-control students and their frustrated and emotionally stressed teachers, paraprofessionals, and parents.

Of course, social analysts have warned for some time that individual research studies seldom influence policy makers and typical service delivery practices (Baumeister, 1981). At the level of everyday practice, it is simply not the case that parents, teachers, and other clinicians follow the swelling scientific literature. We have all had experiences similar to the one described recently by Meyer (see Meyer & Evans, 1993) in which a program described in a supermarket-type popular magazine was held up by a parent as evidence that a particular approach would cure her child with autism. Professional experts' ideas about evidence are not easily explained, nor is it easy to tell a parent why the promise of an instant cure in the popular media should be less compelling than the carefully reasoned and cautiously promoted innovation from the latest issue of a professional journal—especially when the method is difficult to interpret, probably undoable in the real world, and reported in the oftentimes turgid and dispassionate style of the typical scientific report.

Alternative Research-on-Practice Approaches

In this section, we propose several partial solutions or, more modestly, moves in new directions to redeem ourselves. In making these proposals, we have been influenced greatly by social scientists such as Baumeister (1981), Hoshmand and Polkinghorne (1992), Habermas (Ewert, 1991), and Tharp (1981).

The Value of Multiple Research Methodologies

First, researchers should consider the relevant and necessary contributions from multiple perspectives and approaches (Guess, 1990). Ours has been a limited methodology, driven by the somewhat insular world view of operant metatheory (Schwartz, 1986), and we must make room for alternative research methodologies. Researchers may well choose to develop substantial competence in the use of a particular methodology, but at the same time, could become at least an intelligent consumer of as many alternative methodologies as possible. One consequence of failing to appreciate the value of different methodologies is a "research self-righteousness," wherein proponents of particular methodologies not only restrict their own work to one chosen approach, but actively denigrate other approaches. This has already happened in the aversives-nonaversives controversy, such that scholars who identify themselves as being proponents of aversives believe they represent science and regard the opponents of aversives as non-scientists (Guess et al., 1990; Yuskauskas, 1992). Intolerance can also be seen in the qualitative-quantitative "debate," in which supporters of two different approaches alternatively accuse one another of various inadequacies (Meyer, 1991).

Over a decade ago, Tharp (1981) eloquently and simply stated the value of multiple ways of knowing, and the history of science is rich with varied approaches to discovery, understanding, and hypothesis testing (e.g., Ewert, 1991; Hoshmand & Polkinghorne, 1992; Popper, 1959; Staats, 1988). A comprehensive reading of this literature also reveals a certain working consensus that different methodologies are well suited to different stages in the production of new knowledge and the validation of most promising practices (see Ewert, 1991, for a thorough discussion of the social scientist Habermas' framework for the production of new knowledge). To give one example, a single-subject "experiment" may provide empirical support for objective behavior change, but a qualitative study may be required to explore the interpretations and understandings of family members to determine whether that behavior change was clinically significant. Additionally, if the behavior change was deemed clinically insignificant, reflective problem-solving and critical theory might be needed to generate new directions to achieve the kinds of outcomes desired for the social good. Ewert (1991) describes this final "emancipatory" critical theory development as the sometimes deliberate and sometimes evolutionary process that results in the achievement of practices and outcomes that reflect a society's values base. Thus, discovering that the empirical literature does not lead us to a successful strategy to intervene with serious challenging behavior in typical school

settings would not preclude future efforts to find such a strategy. The critical theory process described by Habermas demands instead that we continue to pursue directions that are valued by a society (Ewert, 1991). Our point here is to emphasize that respectable social scientists have long regarded various kinds of knowledge production as valid, and short-sighted allegiance to one or another methodology is not supported by the history of science. Another valuable contribution of multiple methodological perspectives is that such a framework allows for the integration of values, practices, policies, and science—rather than placing these notions in conflict with one another.

Publication Standards and Ecological Validity

Texts in the conduct of behavior modification research methodology state explicit guidelines for the design of interventions, yet researchers fail to emulate the very same standards of practice advocated for practitioners (Scotti et al., 1991). Indeed, this lack of rigor in the scientific journals may well explain many of the contradictory findings and limited outcomes now evident in the published literature on challenging behavior. It seems improbable that the accumulation of even more research reports—each of which violates different aspects of longstanding precepts of research standards even within a well-articulated single-subject research approach—can result in the resolution of remaining needs. Journal publication standards should require greater adherence to these basic features (see Table 1 for a listing of criteria that might be applied to ensure such standards of practice).

In addition, however, our research literature will be relevant to the tasks confronting families, teachers, and other community agency personnel only if the reported "validated strategies" were successful in circumstances resembling the real life settings of people with disabilities. This journal included the following criteria of "educational validity" for publication considerations in its editorial guidelines beginning in 1986:

Educational Validity: JASH emphasizes ecological and educational validity in the content of the journal. Applied research conducted in actual service delivery and community environments is likely to be more relevant to our readers than research conducted in highly artificial and controlled settings. Reports of validated interventions should also strive to meet three criteria for educational validity: (1) a demonstration of behavior change associated with the intervention or independent variable/s; (2) why and how the behavior change is meaningful; and (3) a description of the program strategies used which is replicable, along with documentation that implementation of those strategies was reliable (*Editorial Policy and Author Guidelines*).

Table 1
Essential Information for Published Intervention Research*

1. Participant characteristics
   a. Age
   b. Gender
   c. Level of functioning
   d. Diagnostic characteristics
   e. Adaptive behavior measure
   f. Verbal/communication skills
2. Treatment setting characteristics
   a. Degree of integration/segregation
   b. Age-appropriateness of daily lifestyle and placement features
   c. Evidence of active educational/habilitative program
   d. Information on significant social relationships for participant
3. Treatment history
   a. Evidence on previous treatments/results
   b. History of functional analysis of behavior
   c. Medication history
   d. Level of intrusiveness in prior treatments
   e. Standards of practice procedures/human rights review
4. Assessment of behavior changes
   a. Functional analysis of behavior
   b. Baseline description and observable definition of behavior
   c. Delineation of desired (meaningful) outcomes and their measurement
   d. Anticipated collateral/side effects and their measurement
5. Intervention design and follow-up
   a. Replicable description of intervention
   b. Replicable description of needed resources and staff development
   c. Written intervention plan
   d. Documentation of integrity of intervention
   e. Sufficient baseline/intervention phase data reported to allow calculation of effectiveness statistics
   f. Evidence of generalization and maintenance
   g. Follow-up of one year or more

* These features are adapted from suggestions made in Scotti et al. (1991).

The basic premise behind this requirement of ecological validity for applied research is that practices cannot be of much value for an applied science (i.e., to schools, homes, and other community environments delivering services to persons with disabilities) if they were validated in the presence of ingredients and resources that differ from the real world in significant ways. Thus, laboratory or university-affiliated schools where unrealistic staff supports and external resources are embedded in the research effort have an unfair advantage over the typical neighborhood public school setting attempting to replicate the results of that research.

Conducting research in artificially restrictive settings presents further threats to the ecological validity of our data base. Attempts to isolate experimentally "the" treatment component responsible for desired behavior change often involve restricting someone's program or life experiences in order to avoid possible confounding effects of unintended (independent) variables. While such efforts to protect the internal validity of an experiment may appear to be scientifically correct, the re-

sultant "validated practice" again will have little external validity. Real world environments do not dish out treatments in simple nonconfounded dosages. Trying to do so in experimental studies will not only require that the participant (a person with a disability) is restricted in his/her life experiences but will also guarantee that the intervention can never be replicated by real life practitioners working in typical service delivery and community environments. We urge researchers to move their "research laboratories" to demographically representative, reality-based sites that not only look like but indeed are the kinds of settings expected to use the strategies investigated. Where researchers choose instead to carry out their initial studies in the laboratory, the results of their efforts should not be disseminated to practitioners until there has been movement through a phase of research on the implementation of their recommended strategies in such real life settings (Meyer & Evans, 1993). Interventions developed in uncommon settings may have little to no relevance to the interventions needed and usable in typical settings. Guess (1990) also urged implementation research for an additional reason. Unless research is exposed to the scrutiny of implementation in typical settings, the strategies developed in the laboratory or other restrictive environment may be socially invalid and unacceptable in average contexts—regardless of whether or not they are doable.

Finally, an expansion of our methodological acceptance to include a variety of research approaches will also allow researchers to address meaningful outcomes in a variety of ways. We find it telling that the only long-term outcome studies to date of successful interventions with persons who exhibit severe self-injury are essentially case studies—not traditional single-subject designs or large group comparisons (e.g., Berkman & Meyer, 1988; Foxx & Dufrense, 1984; Meyer & Berkman, 1993). This statement presupposes, of course, that the definition of "success" includes long-term follow-up and evidence of an improved quality of life, as well as documented reduction in a specific self-injurious behavior. We have argued elsewhere that single-subject designs, including the multiple baseline design (Meyer, Evans, Wuerch, & Brennan, 1985), are poorly suited to demonstrations of meaningful outcomes. For the very same reasons that such designs require careful specification of quantifiable behavior change as a function of experimental manipulations, reports using them typically involve inconsequential behaviors or measures that defy assignment of significance to behavior change. Behavioral reports rarely use readily available "indirect" measures (such as trips to the emergency room, number of sutures, and so on) or "affective" measures (a shift in mood from anger to happiness), despite these possibly being more indicative of significant and clinically meaningful progress. Even statistically significant changes in frequencies of discrete behaviors may not matter much if the caregivers or families of the individual do not regard those changes as clinically significant (Voeltz & Evans, 1983).

The behavioral intervention literature in the 10 years since we published our paper on educational validity has not offered any convincing evidence that conventional research designs will solve important problems. Instead, this literature continues to report short-term changes under experimental conditions of primarily trivial behaviors. We think, for example, that what the field really needs now is detailed case study information on a variety of individuals who once exhibited severe challenging behaviors—not simply stereotyped behaviors or temper tantrums, but serious self-injury and aggression—who can be found years later living, working, and recreating in the community. Both our applied science researchers and practitioners would derive better ideas for future research and helpful procedures by such case studies.

The Need for Alternative Communication Formats

We have suggested that a new set of circumstances has had an unexpected collateral effect on professional practices. The context for this effect is modern telecommunications and more than one generation educated through the mass media. Further, with desktop publishing and popularized presses widely available, "face validity" takes on a new meaning as something that makes a dramatic story and can sway opinion in a way that university researchers can only begin to imagine. Indeed, the seductiveness of the modern media has reached a point where expert status may be accorded to the researcher who appears on the most talk shows or television news magazines—and the peer-reviewed journal article may become little more than back-up scholarly window dressing, rather than the major vehicle of scientific sharing and accumulation of knowledge. A major new task of applied science must be the development of strategies to speak effectively and responsibly to the people whom we expect to value our wisdom and our services. We should do this not to protect our scholarly status but to ensure that shared criteria for evaluation do remain in evidence.

Certain suggestions regarding important directions are offered as illustrations only. The major principle is to diminish the presumption that "good" science can be equated with studies that fail to meet the needs of practitioners and policy makers. Those who still remember the call in the 1960s for scholarship to become "relevant" will realize that this is not a new need, but perhaps one that can now be better realized with the new research and dissemination methodologies available today.

Research on practice. One strategy would be to encourage scientific journals to have regular issues or sections of each issue that are devoted to the data concerned with the practical application of various interventions validated in empirical reports. This is slightly different from interpretations of research (once called "Tips for Teachers," for example) that one might find in professional newsletters or research digests. Of course, such digests are probably valuable, since there are numerous surveys suggesting that even the best scientifically trained practitioners stop reading the research journals once they are involved in full-time practical work. Digests that are reviewed for scientific respectability and then written by professional writers with good communication skills are particularly useful, such as the *Harvard Mental Health Newsletter*, which collects and interprets research findings from various sources.

Our proposal would be also to explore novel formats for existing scientific journals—with articles that include elements of both the scientific report and newsletter stories. Scientific journals might have sections devoted to research on issues of practice and implementation of most promising practices. Examples would be: (a) articles written in collaboration with practitioners who would discuss the empirically observed problems or subtleties involved in implementing a particular procedure; (b) studies of practitioner behavior and natural ecosystems examining the standards of implementation; and (c) outcome research in which the intervention was carried out by typical providers in typical settings.

Action research. There is growing interest in the social sciences in models generally referred to as action research, in which the purpose is not an effort to validate an intervention per se but rather a collaborative effort by a team of researchers that always involves the constituents or practitioners as researchers to solve a particular problem across a period of time (Bolster, 1983; Lewin, 1946). These might be longstanding collaboratives, such as the school-university partnerships that have been established in some communities to address the need to prevent school failure. Typically, such a partnership never has as its goal the validation of the one effective strategy to solve a complex need such as school dropout. Instead, the collaborative problem-solving effort will be a dynamic one that changes and adapts for the complex array of student needs, teacher and school resources, and specific set of circumstances in a variety of "cases." The purpose of a report on such an action research project would be to describe the workings of the partnership and how collaborative problem-solving has been applied to address significant service delivery needs. Specific examples would be included that might give the reader new ideas for his/her own situation, but the major focus would be upon implementation issues rather than a specific intervention.

Conclusion

Ultimately, what is needed is recognition that ours is a human science. It is both practical and appropriate to acknowledge that human behavior does not necessarily follow the same law-like relationships that were believed to be universally evident in the physical world. Chaos theory has already modified similar beliefs in the natural sciences (see Gleick, 1987). Nor should intervention decisions be seen as strictly technical problems or necessarily based upon the most effective path to achieve a desired end. Fischer (1980) argued that the best course of action is the course supported by the best reasons (p. 89). As Ewert (1991) noted, for example, educational decisions cannot occur in a vacuum, but must take into consideration a background of political, professional, and public interests. Sometimes, the most efficient course of action is not permitted in human situations. Carr and Kemmis (1985) acknowledge the impact of moral constraints on applying what we know about what works. Apple (1972) cautions us to recognize that any innovation involves "... making profound ethical decisions about a group of other human beings" (p. 12). Perhaps Habermas' greatest contribution to social science theory is the acknowledgment of the value of both empiricism and values in the evolution of future science and practice. The traditional experiment or quantitative approach can tell us what will happen when we intervene. The traditional interpretive or qualitative approach can tell us what people think about that change and whether it matters to them. Both are important. Without the experiment, we cannot be certain that something works (particularly when beliefs are so powerful that they can obscure reality); without listening to the participants, we cannot be certain that we understand the consequences of what was done.

> Whereas empirical and interpretive social sciences describe the world as it is, critical theory tries to understand why the social world is the way it is and, through that process of critique, strives to know how it should be. Underlying the process of critique is the concept that existing social structures and beliefs are socially constructed and therefore can be transformed through social action. Rational action within this paradigm has evaluative and expressive dimensions. The evaluative dimension includes: interpreting the nature of wants and needs of self and others, in terms of culturally established standards of value; and adopting a reflective attitude toward the standards of value to critically determine the adequacy of the existing standards of value. (Ewert, 1991, p. 356)

Thus, a human science must incorporate both analytic and interpretive information, but these are viewed as part of the process of science in support of social structures that contribute to the human good. Critical social science also requires that empirical data be continuously evaluated against our values and beliefs. Indeed, the purpose of a human science could be viewed as an evaluation of the adequacy of our practices for achieving our values. Where discrepancies exist, this broader perspective would compel critical examination of both our practices and our values. Either might need to be changed. But the continuous interplay between intervention outcomes, understandings of those outcomes by the participants, and what we value as a culture is an essential condition of social science.

In his elegant discussion of many of these issues, Skrtic (1991) has pointed out that persons advocating an objectivist, functionalist paradigm simply reject perspectives from a holistic, subjectivist worldview—and vice versa, a problem of incomprehensibility. In this paper, although we have had to present certain perspectives from postmodernist philosophies of applied science, we have attempted to steer clear of the merely philosophical issues and to give practical examples and illustrations of the consequences of doing science and practice in certain ways. The conventional model of objectivist science clearly dominates our field, with its system of experimental journals, standards for research, peer review based on agreed-upon criteria—such as those embodied in this journal. It is unlikely that the dominant paradigm will surrender to an alternative conception of knowledge. Personally, we doubt the value or wisdom of such a surrender and believe that paradigm substitution alone will do little to help us with the complex task ahead. It may very well hurt if this results in the loss or devaluation of certain admittedly powerful strategies that have helped to bring us to this state of paradigm crisis precisely because we now know what is possible. We are not among those who believe, for example, that serious challenging behavior will disappear simply by providing a person who is self-injurious with an outstanding educational program, community acceptance, and friends. We believe that these should be the context for any intervention attempt, but, in our experience, systematic behavioral intervention will still be needed and applied behavior analysis has contributed in great measure much of the detail of that intervention.

What we have tried to suggest are a number of practical and pragmatic strategies to *expand* the pursuit of useful knowledge within the essential guidelines of conventional science. Proposals for meaningful collaboration in the human sciences would help keep knowledge unified. In the physical and biological sciences, as well as in psychology and education, there are interesting and important expansions of knowledge and understanding. Philosophies of social advocacy and deconstruction that would have us denigrate traditional science do little to advance practical intellectualism or improve opportunities and services for our constituents. But the continued insularity of a human science that clings stubbornly to the paradox of research that is separate from practice will almost certainly lead to its extinction.

References

Apple, M. W. (1972). Adequacy of systems management procedures in education. *Journal of Educational Research, 68*(9), 10–18.

Baumeister, A. A. (1981). Mental retardation policy and research: The unfulfilled promise. *American Journal of Mental Deficiency, 85*, 445–456.

Berkman, K. A., & Meyer, L. H. (1988). Alternative strategies and multiple outcomes in the remediation of severe self-injury: Going "all out" nonaversively. *Journal of The Association for Persons with Severe Handicaps, 13*, 76–88.

Bogdan, R., & Biklen, S. (1992). *Qualitative research for education* (2nd ed.) Boston, MA: Allyn & Bacon.

Bogdan, R., & Kugelmass, J. (1984). Case studies of mainstreaming: A symbolic interactionist approach to special schooling. In L. Barton & S. Tomlinson (Eds.), *Special education and social interests* (pp. 173–191). London: Croon-Helm.

Bolster, A. S. (1983). Toward a more effective model of research on teaching. *Harvard Educational Review, 53*, 294–308.

Browder, D. M. (1991). *Assessment of individuals with severe disabilities: An applied behavior approach to life skills assessment* (2nd ed.) Baltimore: Paul H. Brookes.

Carr, W., & Kemmis, S. (1986). *Becoming critical: Education, knowledge and action research.* London: Falmer Press.

Eifert, G. H., & Evans, I. M. (Eds.). (1990). *Unifying behavior therapy: Contributions of paradigmatic behaviorism.* New York: Springer.

Evans, I. M. (1993). Constructional perspectives in clinical assessment. *Psychological Assessment, 5*, 264–272.

Ewert, G. D. (1991). Habermas and education: A comprehensive overview of the influence of Habermas in educational literature. *Review of Educational Research, 61*, 345–378.

Fischer, F. (1980). *Politics, values, and public policy—The problem of methodology.* Boulder, CO: Westview.

Foxx, R. M., & Dufrense, D. (1984). "Harry": The use of physical restraint as a reinforcer, timeout from restraint, and fading restraint in treating a self-injurious man. *Analysis and Intervention in Developmental Disabilities, 4*, 1–13.

Gleick, J. (1987). *Chaos: Making a new science.* New York: Penguin Books.

Guess, D. (1990). Transmission of behavior management technologies from researchers to practitioners: A need for professional self-evaluation. In A. C. Repp & N. N. Singh (Eds.), *Perspectives on the use of nonaversive and aversive interventions for persons with developmental disabilities* (pp. 157–172). Sycamore, IL: Sycamore.

Guess, D., Helmstetter, E., Turnbull, H. R. III, & Knowlton, S. (1986). *Use of aversive procedures with persons who are disabled: An historical review and critical analysis* (Monograph). Seattle: The Association for Persons with Severe Handicaps.

Guess, D., Turnbull, H. D., & Helmstetter, E. (1990). Science, paradigms, and values: A response to Mulick. *American Journal on Mental Retardation, 95*, 157–163.

Horner, R. H., Dunlap, G., & Koegel, R. L. (Eds.). (1988). *Generalization and maintenance: Lifestyle changes in applied settings.* Baltimore: Paul H. Brookes.

Horner, R. H., Dunlap, G., Koegel, R. L., Carr, E. G., Sailor, W., Anderson, J., Albin, R. W., & O'Neill, R. E. (1990). Toward a technology of "nonaversive" behavioral support. *Journal of The Association for Persons with Severe Handicaps, 15*, 125–132.

Hoshmand, L. T., & Polkinghorne, D. E. (1992). Redefining the science-practice relationship and professional training. *American Psychologist, 47*, 55–66.

Johnston, J. M. (1991). What can behavior analysis learn from the aversives controversy? *The Behavior Analyst, 14*, 187–196.

Kaiser, A. P. (1992). Is *JASH* fulfilling its purpose? *Journal of The Association for Persons with Severe Handicaps, 17*, 1–2.

Kirk, S. A., & Kutchins, H. (1992). *The selling of DSM: The rhetoric of science in psychiatry.* New York: Aldine De Gruyter.

Kuhn, T. (1970). *The structure of scientific revolutions* (2nd ed.). Chicago: University of Chicago Press.

Kurtines, W. M., Azmitia, M., & Alvarez, M. (1992). Science, values, and rationality: Philosophy of science from a critical co-constructivist perspective. In W. M. Kurtines, M. Azmitia, & J. L. Gewirtz (Eds.), *The role of values in psychology and human development* (pp. 3–29). New York: John Wiley & Sons.

Lewin, K. (1946). Action research and minority problems. *Journal of Social Issues, 2*, 34–46.

Linscheid, T. R., & Landau, R. J. (1993). Going "all out" pharmacologically?: A re-examination of Berkman and Meyer's *Alternative strategies and multiple outcomes in the remediation of severe self-injury: Going all-out nonaversively. Mental Retardation, 31*(1), 1–6.

Lovaas, O. I., & Bucher, B. D. (1974). *Perspectives in behavior modification with deviant children.* Englewood Cliffs, NJ: Prentice-Hall.

MacIver, D. J., & Epstein, J. L. (1991). Responsive practices in the middle grades: Teacher teams, advisory groups, remedial instruction, and school transition programs. *American Journal of Education, 99*, 587–622.

Meyer, L. H. (1991). Advocacy, research, and typical practices: A call for the reduction of discrepancies between what is and what ought to be and how to get there. In L. H. Meyer, C. A. Peck, & L. Brown (Eds.), *Critical issues in the lives of people with severe disabilities* (pp. 629–640). Baltimore: Paul H. Brookes.

Meyer, L. H., & Berkman, K. A. (1993). What's straw and what's real: A reply to Linscheid and Landau. *Mental Retardation, 31*(1), 7–14.

Meyer, L. H., & Evans, I. M. (1989). *Nonaversive intervention for behavior problems: A manual for home and community.* Baltimore: Paul H. Brookes.

Meyer, L. H., & Evans, I. M. (1993). Meaningful outcomes in behavioral intervention: Evaluating positive approaches to the remediation of challenging behaviors. In J. Reichle & D. P. Wacker (Eds.), *Communicative approaches to the management of challenging behavior* (pp. 407–428). Baltimore: Paul H. Brookes.

Meyer, L. H., Evans, I. M., Wuerch, B. B., & Brennan, J. M. (1985). Monitoring the collateral effects of leisure skills instruction: A case study in multiple-baseline methodology. *Behaviour Research and Therapy, 23*, 127–138.

Miltenberger, R. G., Suda, K. T., Lennox, D. B., & Lindeman, D. P. (1991). Assessing the acceptability of behavioral treatments to persons with mental retardation. *American Journal on Mental Retardation, 96*, 291–298.

O'Neill, R. E., Horner, R. H., Albin, R. W., Storey, K., & Sprague, J. R. (1990). *Functional analysis of problem behavior: A practical assessment guide.* Sycamore, IL: Sycamore.

Popper, K. R. (1959). *The logic of scientific discovery.* New York: Harper & Row.

Schlosser, R. W., & Goetze, H. (1992). Effectiveness and treatment validity of interventions addressing self-injurious behavior: From narrative reviews to meta-analyses. In K. Gadow (Ed.), *Advances in learning and behavioral disabilities: A research annual* (Vol 7). Greenwich, CT: JAI Press.

Schon, D. (1983). *The reflective practitioner: How professionals think in action*. New York: Basic Books.

Schwartz, B. (1986). *The battle for human nature: Science, morality and modern life*. New York: W. W. Norton & Co.

Schwartz, I. S., & Baer, D. M. (1991). Social validity assessments: Is current practice state of the art? *Journal of Applied Behavior Analysis, 24*, 189–204.

Scotti, J. R., Evans, I. M., Meyer, L. H., & Walker, P. (1991). A meta-analysis of intervention research with problem behavior: Treatment validity and standards of practice. *American Journal on Mental Retardation, 96*, 233–256.

Sidman, M. (1960). *Tactics of scientific research*. New York: Basic Books.

Skrtic, T. M. (1986). The crisis in special education knowledge: A perspective on perspective. *Focus on Exceptional Children, 18*(7), 1–16.

Skrtic, T. M. (1991). *Behind special education: A critical analysis of professional culture and school organization*. Denver: Love Publishing Co.

Staats, A. W. (1981). Paradigmatic behaviorism, unified theory, unified theory construction methods, and the *zeitgeist* of separatism. *American Psychologist, 36*, 240–256.

Staats, A. W. (1988). Paradigmatic behaviorism, unified positivism, and paradigmatic behavior therapies. In D. B. Fishman, F. Rotger, & C. M. Franks (Eds.), *Paradigms in behavioral therapy: Present and promise* (pp. 211–253). New York: Springer.

Tharp, R. G. (1981). The metamethodology of research and development. *Educational Perspectives, 20*, 42–48.

Tharp, R. G., & Gallimore, R. (1988). *Rousing minds to life: Teaching, learning, and schooling in social context*. Cambridge, England: Cambridge University Press.

The Association for Persons with Severe Handicaps. (1986). *Resolution on the cessation of intrusive interventions* (originally adopted October 1981, Revised November 1986). Seattle, WA: TASH.

Voeltz, L. M., & Evans, I. M. (1983). Educational validity: Procedures to evaluate outcomes in programs for severely handicapped learners. *Journal of The Association for Persons with Severe Handicaps, 8*, 3–15.

Yin, R. (1989). *Case study research: Design and methods* (rev. ed.). Beverly Hills: Sage.

Yuskauskas, A. (1992). *Perspectives on changing treatment approaches for persons with developmental disabilities: Conflict within a discipline*, Unpublished doctoral dissertation, Syracuse University, Syracuse, NY.

Received: October 21, 1992
Final Acceptance: February 5, 1993
Editor in Charge: James W. Halle

JASH
1998, Vol. 23, No. 1, 17–26

Self-Determination for Individuals With the Most Severe Disabilities: Moving Beyond Chimera[1]

Fredda Brown
Queens College, City University of New York

Carole R. Gothelf
Jewish Guild for the Blind

Doug Guess
University of Kansas

Donna H. Lehr
Boston University

Individuals with the most severe disabilities may be unsuccessful in effecting changes in their environment for various reasons. Because of limitations in cognitive and expressive language skills, their attempts at communicating may be overlooked or misunderstood, or may be knowingly or inadvertently obstructed. Consequently, self-determination is often dependent on our interpretation of what people with the most severe disabilities are communicating. This article explores the implications of making interpretations, the need for such interpretations, and the dangers. Current progress in supporting and promoting self-determination are acknowledged. It is suggested that although these procedures may be intended to increase self-determination, they do not automatically do so. In fact, they may function to limit self-determination. Strategies and methodologies must be critically evaluated to ensure that such efforts reflect the tenets and spirit of self-determination.

DESCRIPTORS: functional assessment, preference assessment, quality of life, self-determination, positive behavior supports

Education provides the means for individuals to shape, mold, and define the nature of their personal social experience. Without education, people may not know what to ask for, they may ask for the wrong things, they may ask in ineffective ways, or they may not ask at all (Pumpian, 1996; Wehmeyer, 1996). These individuals are caught in a conundrum that induces a diminished quality of life.

Changing views of disability in our society have created a new vision of outcomes for individuals with severe disabilities, one in which each individual is empowered to pursue an individually determined satisfying life (Gothelf & Brown, in press; Wehmeyer, 1996). The challenge is how to support individuals with the most severe disabilities to be self-determining, in light of the higher order cognitive processes suggested in most definitions.

Various definitions of self-determination have been suggested. Wehmeyer (1996) defined self-determination as acting as "the primary causal agent in one's life and making choices and decisions regarding one's quality of life free from undue external influence or interference." Furthermore, Wehmeyer suggests that self-determined individuals reflect the four characteristics of autonomy, self-regulation, psychological empowerment, and self-realization. Ward (1988) viewed self-determination as the attitudes, abilities, and skills that allow a person to define personal goals and to take initiative in reaching these goals. Perhaps the most insightful definition of self-determination comes from Michael Kennedy, who notes that "... self-determination is different for each person, depending on the person's circumstances and what his or her disabilities are. For me, self-determination is not physical independence."

These ideas—education, self-determination, and rights of individuals—may seem commonplace or even simple until we apply them to complicated people in complex circumstances. Then we realize that even simple ideas are difficult to implement in real-life situations. Gothelf and Brown (in press) note that:

---

[1]According to Webster's (1992) dictionary, "chimera" is a groundless or impracticable conception or fancy. The Microsoft Word Thesaurus (1992) includes synonyms for chimera such as anything unsubstantial, fantasy, fluff, bubble, bauble, and trivia.

Address correspondence and requests for reprints to Fredda Brown, 90 Bryant Avenue, F6B, White Plains, NY 10605.

strategies that are developed to teach and support the development of self-determination in individuals with severe disabilities are often basic and concrete, even though the concept of self-determination is as complex as is human behavior, and far from concrete. Thus educators or families are sometimes in the position of *interpreting, guessing* or *hypothesizing* what the individual is attempting to communicate (p. 5).

This article will explore the implications of making interpretations, the need for such interpretations, and the dangers. We will probe our assumptions about what we think people are telling us and about the tools we use to support self-determined communicative behavior in people with profound disabilities. We will wrestle with the questions: (1) Can we justly support people with profound disabilities to say what they really mean to say without exerting our influence or imposing our values? and (2) How can we hear people clearly and respond fittingly? Finally, we will discuss current efforts to promote self-determination. We suggest that although these procedures were initially developed to support the tenet of self-determination, we must continually review our implementation efforts to ensure that they indeed meet our expectations.

Communication and Self-Determination

The development of communicative competence goes hand in hand with the development of self-determination (Williams, 1991). Communication is essential to growth, providing people with a degree of control and autonomy in their daily lives (Siegel-Causey & Guess, 1988). Intentional communication may be the most basic form of self-determination and is meaningful only if the environment responds (Malette et al., 1992). Halle (1987) suggested that spontaneity is the most important function of language, as spontaneous communication is the means by which individuals transmit messages to appropriately exert control over what is happening to them.

Ordinary people in the mainstream of society regularly tell us what they want. Although they speak in plain everyday language they still may not get what they thought they were asking for. This may be for several reasons. Perhaps we think we *know better* and give them what we think they really *should* want. Or perhaps we may have heard what they said, but we may interpret it to mean something else. Or, we may not have heard them clearly because we were not listening closely enough. Thus, a "mainstreamed" individual's self-determination can be thwarted in various ways. Depending on skills, personal resources, and power, individuals may or may not be able to successfully overcome the situation and eventually get what they want, or they may be stuck with our erroneous, albeit well-meaning, response. Chadsey-Rusch, Drasgow, Re-

inoehl, and Halle (1993) note that, "effective communication is essential to our quality of life: it allows us to make choices, seek information, make our desires known, engage in interactions, and form relationships with others" (p. 177).

Most of our experiences have taught us that reasons to communicate, exercise one's initiative, indicate choices, and shape events occur throughout the course of the day. Experiences, commodities, and people that spark one's interest, desire, dislike, or avoidance represent uncontrived opportunities to be acknowledged and in a sense require us to learn to effectively respond and appropriately express our wants and needs. The act of self-determination and the nature of communicative interaction are entirely natural in such an enriched world. Our communicative interactions influence the environment which in turn responds in accordance with the intent of the communication (Gothelf & Brown, 1996; Rowland, 1996; Rowland & Schweigert, 1993; Siegel-Causey & Ernst, 1989).

The self-determined individual has personal resources, power, skills, and varied and interesting life experiences. Many individuals with severe disabilities have little access and participation in any of these events or conditions. Their self-determination is often wholly dependent on our interpretation and our interpretation is dependent on whether we listened, whether we are willing to give them what they asked for, and whether we acted in good faith or attempted to "put one over on them." Our ability and willingness to listen and interpret and respond appropriately is based on our values.

Many of us are driven by the belief that by simply uncovering opportunities in the daily routine in which self-initiated behavior and choice making can be fostered, we can provide individuals with the most severe disabilities with a powerful motivation to use appropriate communication and thus be more self-determining (Brown, 1991; Brown, Belz, Corsi, & Wennig, 1993; Brown & Gothelf, 1996; Gothelf, Crimmins, Mercer, & Finocchiaro, 1994). We may, for instance, teach students communicative responses that facilitate self-determination, such as spontaneously requesting help. However, unless the individual truly wants help, it cannot be considered self-determination; they have only learned to make a response under the conditions in which we taught them (Chadsey-Rusch et al., 1993). In addition, without participation in interesting routines and activities, there will be little to communicate about, and without power and personal resources, there is little recourse when life is "out of control."

It has been acknowledged that some problem behaviors may be an individual's communicative attempts to take some control of their environment (Carr & Durand, 1985; Durand, 1990; Dyer, Dunlap, & Winterling, 1990; Meyer & Evans, 1989); in other words, to achieve some level of self-determination. These behaviors are frequently effective in controlling the environment. Current trends in positive behavior supports encourage interventionists to respect the "message" of self-determination and instead of reducing the problem behavior (i.e., reducing the attempts to be self-determining) to teach the individual an alternative and more appropriate way to express that self-determination. The crux of the positive behavior support movement is listening to the individual's attempt at communication and control and supporting the individual to achieve his or her desired outcomes.

But what about the individuals whose behaviors are not successful in effecting changes in the environment; individuals whose messages are "quiet" and difficult to hear versus the "loud" message given through severe problem behavior? Individuals with profound multiple disabilities, profound levels of cognitive impairments, and those with deaf-blindness may be attempting to control their world. In fact, we must assume that they are doing so (Brown & Gothelf, 1996); their way of communicating, however, may be "quiet." Their attempts at communicating are thus easily overlooked and may be knowingly or inadvertently obstructed. Our intention may be to support their communication but we may not for several reasons. For example, a person who has severe oral-motor problems and little expressive communication must rely on the "intuition" of others who assist him or her to eat lunch to provide assistance in a preferred way. As she turns her head away to protest the food presented to her, her teacher does not acknowledge the protest but instead uses a "least to most" prompting strategy to facilitate her taking the food off the spoon. The teacher moves down the prompting hierarchy to teach her to eat and to help her learn to compensate for her oral-motor problems. The student's attempts at protest remain unnoticed and thus are ineffective. The inability to produce communicative behavior that can be understood by others represents one of the most frustrating experiences imaginable (Reichle, Mirenda, Locke, Piche, & Johnson, 1992). Roger Ebert, the noted movie critic, states in his 1995 review of the movie *Smoke* (Ebert, 1995) that ". . . of all the handicaps in life, the worst must be the inability to express how you feel."

If we truly believe that through communicating choice, individuals can affect their environment and satisfy their desires, we must ask the following questions to evaluate this commitment:

1. Are we prepared to recognize all the opportunities for individuals with the most severe disabilities—individuals who may appear unresponsive to most stimuli—to communicate choice, engage in self-selected activities, and become more in control of their lives, even if these choices are not convenient or are inconsistent with the outcomes that we have designed?

2. When faced with the person who appears unresponsive—the person whose spontaneous form of communication is limited and not reliably understood across communication partners—are we assuming the controlling posture of a competent, all-knowing professional who must teach certain operationally defined aspects of self-determination according to individualized education plan objectives, rather than empowering an individual to shape his or her own life?

3. In interpreting people's communication are we ever guilty of the fundamentally dishonest attribution of assigning the word choice to an act as a politically correct interpretation rather than acknowledging that the individual needs help in developing the communicative behaviors that would allow the individual to be truly self-determining?

Depending on Other's Interpretations of Communication

Effective communication is dependent on skills on the part of both communication partners, the sender and receiver. Even when communication occurs between competent communicators, misunderstandings can occur. "Communication requires that one partner's behavior [sic] is noticed by another, who understands the message and responds accordingly so that the first partner is satisfied" (Butterfield & Arthur, 1995). When the sender has limited ability to communicate clear messages and limited ability to seek clarification, the message may be misunderstood. Individuals with profound cognitive and physical disabilities and/or deaf-blindness may not develop expressive language skills beyond those of a young child (Haring & Breen, 1989). Furthermore, the presence of physical disabilities may result in a restricted range of gestures and facial expression. This seriously limits the ways in which the individual can use his or her body to communicate. The normal sensory channels may be ineffective or completely cut off. The individual cannot see the facial expressions of others to learn how to use their own face to better communicate and may have limited access to the facial expressions, gestures, or words of others as feedback for his or her own attempts to develop language. These individuals may not be able to physically use their hands for sign language communication and there may be underlying cognitive reasons for the absence of spontaneously produced manual signs.

Consequently, interpretation of an individual's communicative intent is largely dependent on the sensitivity and skills of the receiver (Butterfield & Arthur, 1995) who forms hypotheses about what the sender means. Caregivers and teachers rely on their own interpretation of an individual's nonsymbolic, idiosyncratic, inconsistent, or self-selected modes of communication (e.g., vocalizations, gestures, and facial expressions)

(Downing & Siegel-Causey, 1988). They are continually trying to discover what event, internal state, need, or desire caused the expression. For example, an individual may cry for many different reasons: he or she may want to be left alone, he or she may want their position changed, he or she may want attention, or he or she may want to go into another room. Such expressions of communication are very limiting, inefficient, extremely difficult to correctly interpret, and generally frustrating to both communication partners.

The danger of relying on other than direct communication with the sender was the basis for controversy concerning the validity of facilitated communication (FC). FC refers to an alternative communication system that involves a communication partner (facilitator) who provides physical and emotional support to a person with a severe communication impairment as he or she types on a keyboard or points to symbols (Biklen, 1990; Biklen, Saha, & Kliewer, 1995). This method has been met with both unqualified acceptance by those who believe that FC has given a voice to individuals who have never meaningfully communicated, as well as extreme criticism by those who question the validity of the communication system. The controversy concerns the issue of whose words are really being communicated; the person with the disabilities or the facilitator. Research has been published demonstrating that it was facilitators who were communicating, not the individual (e.g., Eberlin, McConnachie, Abel, & Volpe, 1993; Wheeler, Jacobson, Paglieri, & Schwartz, 1993). Other research demonstrates and supports the validity of FC (e.g., Cardinal, Hanson, & Wakeham, 1996; Olney, 1995; Sheehan & Matuozzi, 1996; Vasquez, 1994). Controversy still remains. Green and Shane (1994) note that several "harms" could occur when FC authorship is not substantiated, including: suppression and denial of authentic communication by the individual; inappropriate educational treatment; expectations for outcomes that are not realistic resulting in a negative impact on the parents, facilitators, and others; and intense pressure on facilitators to produce "success."

Similar issues, however, have not been raised in regard to attributing certain "messages" to individuals with significant disabilities based on observation of behavior. Families, advocates, and educators are often in the position of making such judgments about the intent of behaviors, especially problem behaviors. However, these judgments about the message the individual would be giving if he were able to communicate in a more articulate manner are made based on personal preferences and perceptions about what is desirable and what quality of life means. Just as there is concern that the facilitator (in the case of FC) may be inadvertently communicating for the person, the educator or behavior analyst may inadvertently misinterpret mes-

sages. Olney (1995) states that, "reading another person, or understanding the intent and meaning of an individual's communication, is a complex process." When we make an interpretation of an individual's message of self-determination, we too are in danger of suppressing or overlooking the individual's real message by making inappropriate educational decisions regarding curriculum and exerting undue pressure on supporters to produce "successful" self-determination.

In response to the dangers of misinterpretation of messages, Biklen, Saha, and Kliewer (1995) designed a communication portfolio to reflect the various ways that each student may be communicating. In this approach, teachers collect cumulative information to authenticate each student's communication. A similar type of assessment methodology may be helpful in our quest to "hear" each individual as they make their quiet attempts at self-determination.

Perceptual Congruence

Communication messages are received and interpreted within the framework of shared meaning (Kaiser & Goetz, 1993). Each receiver's own personal knowledge and experiences serve to assign meaning to the message. But what if the receiver's knowledge and experience are so different from the sender's that they are not aware of the possible intent of the sender's message? Grandin (1995) states that, "The symbols [used by some individuals with autism] are harder to understand and often appear to be totally unrelated to the thing they represent. For example, French toast may mean 'happy' if the child was happy while eating it." A logical hypothesis to form when a child says "French toast" is that this is what they want. Acting on that hypothesis would not serve as a satisfactory act of communication to the sender who meant something quite different.

A receiver's ability to interpret messages can be enhanced by increasing the amount of information the receiver has about the sender or about the experiences of the sender. Lehr and Macurdy (1994) acknowledged the importance of this in their research on individuals with special health care needs. They were concerned about the sensitive administration of procedures such as tracheostomy suctioning, tube feeding, and catheterization care to individuals who are unable to communicate information about the care they receive. They recognized that few health care service providers have an understanding of what the procedure might feel like—most have never been tube fed, suctioned, or catheterized. In an effort to increase the care provider's ability to "read" the children's communication about the administration of the health care procedures they received, the authors interviewed individuals who were able to describe what it feels like physically to be the recipient of special health care procedures.

Sacks (1995) notes the importance of Temple Grandin's book, *Thinking in Pictures,* in which she describes her life with autism in "... providing a bridge between our world and hers, and allowing us a glimpse into a quite other sort of mind" (Sacks, 1995, p. 16). Books by Grandin (1995), Grandin and Scariano (1986) and Williams (1992 and 1994), another author with autism, give persons charged with responsibility for interpreting communication an increased understanding of the possible meaning of a communication, and perhaps an awareness that we may not always be understanding the true intent of a communication. For example, failure to comply with a direct request may not be a deliberate act of defiance, but rather a misunderstanding of a direct statement (Williams, 1992); refusal to wear particular clothes might be due to the fact that the clothing feels like sand paper to the individual (Grandin, 1986); withdrawal from a hug, a powerful act of communication, might be because the individual being hugged does not associate that act with affection, but instead experiences pain (Williams, 1992). The receiver's misunderstandings may result in inappropriate actions and decisions (e.g., Johnny withdraws from my hugs, so he does not enjoy spending time with me; I will reduce the amount of time I spend with him).

A number of new and exciting strategies have been developed to guide teams to develop visions and individualized, preferred lifestyles for individuals with severe disabilities. These strategies have had a major impact on the development of individualized lifestyles, especially for individuals who may not be able to easily communicate their own desires. For example, the Mc-Gill Action Planning System (Forest & Lusthaus, 1989), PATH (Pearpoint, O'Brien, & Forest, 1993), and Personal Futures Planning (Mount & Zwernik, 1988) began as a search for ways to understand the experience of people with disabilities and work with them and their friends and families to change that experience for the better (O'Brien, O'Brien, & Mount, in press). At the foundation of these strategies is the circle of family members, friends, service providers, and the focus person coming together to describe a vision of a quality life in the community for the focus person (Malette et al., 1992). When input from the target individual is not readily accessible, others must take the responsibility for developing the vision and subsequent action plan for the individual. This vision and plan will therefore be largely based on the standards and perceptions of the circle members. This process represents a dramatic step in the development of services for individuals with the most severe disabilities. However, as Grandin (1986) and Williams (1992) cautioned, individuals who do not share the same perceptual reality may have different visions of quality life than the individual with disabilities. O'Brien, O'Brien, and Mount (in press) also remind us that deep relationships with the focus person

are critical if we are to develop plans that are congruent with the person's vision.

Current Efforts in Increasing Self-Determination

The motivation to increase self-determination is reflected in the increasing availability of literature, funded grants in the area, and in the mission statements of state and private agencies (Brown & Gothelf, 1996). Several practices have evolved that focus on increasing self-determination in individuals who because of their level of communication, cognitive, physical, and/or behavioral impairments are at risk for living lives devoid of personal control. Two such practices include the use of preference assessments and positive behavioral supports. Although these two practices have been successfully used to support individuals with severe disabilities to achieve more self-determined and individualized lifestyles, it is crucial that we continue to critically analyze these efforts. The following sections examine the use of preference assessments and positive behavioral supports as they contribute to the development of self-determination, but also raise red flags to signal the danger zones that exist when such procedures are implemented without reflection and reference to self-determination.

Use of Preference Assessments

Various choice and preference assessment methodologies have been used to assist in the determination of preferences in individuals with severe and profound disabilities. Green et al. (1988) suggested two purposes to assessing preferred stimuli. First, this assessment process allows us to systematically determine preferred stimuli that can be added to the natural routines of an individual's life. Support personnel could then arrange or alter the environment to increase the consumer's satisfaction and happiness (Green, Gardner, & Reid, 1997). Second, these assessments may provide information that can be used to improve the effectiveness of training programs by increasing the likelihood of using stimuli that have reinforcing value.

The first purpose described by Green et al. (1988) supports the use of preference assessment data to increase noncontingent access to preferred stimuli. Using assessment information in this way reflects the ambition of many nondisabled individuals who strive to have noncontingent reinforcement in their lives as frequently as possible (e.g., movies and dinner on Saturday night, summer vacations, and music). Having the freedom to "eat too many donuts and take a nap" (Bannerman, Sheldon, Sherman, & Harchik, 1990), if these were reinforcing stimuli to an individual, also represents noncontingent reinforcement that nondisabled adults assume as part of their daily routine, yet is often denied to individuals with disabilities in the name of habilitation. Newton, Ard, and Horner (1993) suggest that we focus future research on the degree to which an individual's daily activities consist of the preferences that have been identified in preference assessments.

Preference assessments can be used to increase goals that are consistent with self-determination. Kennedy and Haring (1993) taught students to use a microswitch communication system to request a change in recreational stimuli during social interactions with nondisabled peers. This goal was achieved by first assessing preferred stimuli and then teaching the student to press a microswitch that activated a tape recorded message requesting a change in the stimuli. Students were taught to use this system to influence interactions with their nondisabled peers. Kennedy and Haring (1993) found that two of the four students in the study were more engaged in interactions when they chose when to change the stimuli, one student was more engaged when their nondisabled peer controlled the stimuli, and one student did not demonstrate any difference in interactions under the two conditions. The researchers suggest that instruction include not only assessment of preference, but also the provision of a mechanism for the students to control the presentation of preferred stimuli.

Although many such efforts effectively support and enhance self-determination for individuals with severe disabilities, using preference assessment does not in itself ensure that the goal of self-determination will be achieved. If not used with the goal of increasing an individual's control over his or her environment, assessment information may instead restrict self-determination. Researchers must pay careful attention not only to the goals of the assessment process, but to issues in the methodology of the assessment. The methodology of the assessment process must be examined to ensure that it identifies and is based on the range of preferences that would be meaningful for an individual. If the stimuli being assessed in the protocols are ones that are neither preferred nor representative of the breadth of potentially reinforcing stimuli that are available to people who participate in naturally occurring daily routines in the community, then its validity must be questioned. For example, Pace, Ivanic, Edwards, Iwata, and Page (1985) and Fisher et al. (1992) used a set of 16 stimuli, with two stimuli from each of eight categories: (1) visual (mirror and light), (2) auditory (music and beep), (3) olfactory (coffee grounds and hibiscus flowers), (4) edible (juice and graham cracker), (5) temperature (heat pad and ice pack), (6) vestibule (swing and rocking chair), (7) social (clap and hug), and (8) tactile (vibrator and fan). Derby et al. (1995) conducted a forced-choice assessment by using stimuli that include a ball, vibrator, radio, stuffed animals, pop-up toys, and block sorters. The types of stimuli that may have more impact on a person's performance and quality of life are not included in these examples of assessment protocols

(e.g., control of daily events, outdoor activities, being with preferred people, and having free access to a refrigerator).

Other efforts, however, have expanded the array of stimuli and reference the stimuli to activities that reflect typical home and community activities enjoyed by nondisabled individuals. For example, Newton et al. (1993) used the Resident Life-Style Inventory (Kennedy, Horner, Newton, & Kanda, 1990) to determine whether staff members could correctly predict broad activity preferences of participants with severe disabilities. Resident Life-Style Inventory includes stimuli such as: accompanying staff on business, preparing meals, receiving or writing a letter, maintaining wardrobe, receiving or making phone calls, and going to a sit down restaurant.

The methodology used by Newton et al. (1993) reflects many important elements that contribute to the validity of the information derived from the assessment. For example, staff who knew the individual well, as opposed to a researcher, presented the activities that were being assessed; assessments were completed in the individual's home, as opposed to a training room; and staff determined the response modes that were typical for each individual, as opposed to a predetermined motor response. These elements are critical to the validity and usefulness of the information derived from the assessment methodology.

The progress we have made in the area of preference assessment is commendable. The information derived from preference assessments that are referenced to the community especially hold great promise for the support of self-determination. Determining the preferences of an individual, however, is only the beginning and in itself does not ensure that the effort is supportive of self-determination.

Positive Behavior Supports

During the past decade, major efforts have been directed toward the research and development of an approach to reduce challenging behavior among persons with disabilities by using only positive nonaversive strategies and support (Horner et al., 1990; Koegel, Koegel, & Dunlap, 1996). Impetus for the positive behavior support approach followed intense debate in the field of developmental disabilities over the use and effectiveness of behavior procedures that used punishers to reduce unwanted behaviors among persons with disabilities (Guess, Helmstetter, Turnbull, & Knowlton, 1986; Repp & Singh, 1990). Also at issue was a concern that application of aversive procedures to persons with disabilities was neither ethical nor consistent with humane practices (Guess, 1990). This involved practices that not only produced physical pain, but were psychologically humiliating, personally stigmatizing, and generally unacceptable to the wider community of persons without disabilities.

Positive behavior support is an emerging comprehensive empirically derived technology with an emphasis on building skills in inclusive settings (Anderson, Russo, Dunlap, & Albin, 1996; Sailor, 1996). It provides procedures for analyzing the communicative functions of disruptive behavior (Donnellan, Mirenda, Mesaros, & Fassbender, 1984), as well as systematic approaches for teaching both symbolic (Carr et al., 1994; Reichle, York, & Sigafoos, 1991) and nonsymbolic (Siegel-Causey & Guess, 1989) communicative skills as potential replacements for these behaviors. Other interventions include self-regulatory social skill instruction, relaxation techniques, priming, and opportunities for expression of preferences and choices (Dunlap et al., 1994; Dyer, Dunlap, & Winterling, 1990). Comprehensive strategies are provided for identifying and assessing ecological factors and conditions that influence normalized living opportunities (and choices) and procedures for using these assessments to enhance the present and future lifestyles of persons with challenging behavior (Horner et al., 1990; Koegel, et al., 1996).

The positive behavior support approach has led us away from reliance on consequence approaches and placed greater emphasis on how antecedent events and lifestyle variables contribute to the development of problem behaviors. Gothelf and Brown (in press) state that positive behavior supports focus on dimensions that are attributed to the development of self-determination and that have had a positive impact on the assessment, intervention, and evaluation phases of behavior change for individuals with severe disabilities. The process of *functional assessment* includes an examination of a wide range of variables that may contribute to the presence of the problem behavior; many of these variables are related to the individual's lifestyle and lead to an examination of issues related to self-determination. An *intervention* plan is then developed based on the results of the functional assessment and typically including multiple components (Lucyshyn, Horner, & Ben, 1996), many of which relate to changing an individual's lifestyle, arranging the environment to allow the student more control of daily events, and teaching the individual skills that would support this increased control over daily and long-term events (Gothelf & Brown, in press). Finally, the *evaluation* phase of positive supports encourages looking at qualitative outcomes of behavior change rather than at narrow quantitative measures of a single target behavior (Haring & Breen, 1989; Meyer & Evans, 1989; Meyer & Janney, 1989).

Although positive behavior supports provide a significant contribution to the development of self-determination for individuals with challenging behavior, we must reflect on the potential dangers that exist when this approach is operationalized without regard to the tenets of self-determination.

Positive behavior supports are founded, in part, on the traditional assumptions of applied behavior analysis, excluding, of course, the use of aversive procedures. Although attention is now directed to the significant impact of living, learning, and working environments on the behavior of persons with challenging behavior, some elements of the positive support plan are likely to be based on reinforcement approaches that have existed since the late 1960s. The challenge is to ensure that the systematic use of external "rewards," when imposed by persons in positions of authority and power, are consistent with the more philosophically derived concepts of choice, self-determination, and self-advocacy. Drawing heavily from the published literature on normal child development and general education, Kohn (1993) asserts that the problems associated with punishers are equivalent to the problems presented by the use of externally applied reinforcers. Kohn suggests that both methods control people through temporary obedience and that both are detrimental to long-term learning and healthy emotional development. Similar issues can be raised concerning the use of positive reinforcement programs that are designed to increase skills when these skills are nonpreferred or represent tasks that hold little social validity. For example, increasing the behaviors of following a one-step instruction such as "stand up," placing pegs in a pegboard, or stacking blocks (Paclawsky & Vollmer, 1995) may not represent skills that the individual would choose to increase.

Professionals who practice positive behavior supports depend on the use of functional assessment to determine the maintaining variables, including lifestyle variables, associated with a problem behavior. But not all professionals who conduct functional assessment practice positive behavior supports. How the data from a functional assessment are used is at issue. Similar to issues in preference assessments, data can be used to take more control of the individual, rather than providing the individual with more control. For example, if functional analysis reveals that an individual's problem behavior is positively reinforced by attention, the interventionist can either: (1) identify ways to increase the noncontingent attention received by the individual and teach the individual how to elicit attention in an appropriate way or (2) use social interaction and attention as a positive reinforcer contingent on appropriate behaviors and withhold attention contingent on inappropriate behaviors. Which strategy is used will be determined by the values and philosophy of the interventionist.

Differential reinforcement paradigms represent a major class of interventions that use positive reinforcement to reduce problem behavior and thus present similar challenges to self-determination. For example, differential reinforcement of other behaviors requires the application of a reinforcer contingent on the absence of the target problem behavior for a specific interval of time. Although judicious use of this strategy would include a functional assessment of the problem behavior (Alberto & Troutman, 1993; Schloss & Smith, 1994), there is no requirement to assess the function or communicative intent of the behavior (e.g., attention seeking and avoidance of nonpreferred tasks). If the communicative intent of the problem behavior is not addressed, then an individual's effort to be communicative or self-determining is likely to be thwarted as "communications" are targeted for extinction without replacement.

Conclusions

It is with some hesitation that we raise many of the issues in this article. The reluctance is in the danger of being misunderstood; this report in no way intends to diminish the importance and success of the great efforts that have been made in recent years to increase opportunities for self-determination for many individuals with severe disabilities. The purpose of this report is to acknowledge and raise a red flag to signal the danger zones that exist in our current efforts. We must not be satisfied with our progress and believe that because we offer choices within the context of daily routines that our work is done. We must not be too cavalier in our confidence that certain procedures (e.g., preference assessments and positive supports) automatically result in the support of self-determination.

Few, if any, people are completely autonomous, and few of us would choose to meet all of our daily living demands independently and without the assistance and support of others: autonomy includes interdependence of families and others with whom we interact (Pumpian, 1996; Wehmeyer, 1996). Educational and behavioral interventions should acknowledge this interdependence and focus on supporting people with severe disabilities to become more autonomous within the context of interdependence. The development of educational objectives is one educational practice that should be critically examined; objectives should more meaningfully reflect how students can increase control of their activities and experiences, affect their environment, and with dignity partake in the interdependence that other citizens enjoy.

We as professionals have become glib in discussing self-determination. We use the right words and take the politically correct postures. However, we need to go further, much further. We need to undertake a critical self-examination to ensure that not only do we say the right things, but that we believe them, and not only that we believe them, but there we are truly and effectively putting them into practice.

References

Alberto, P. A., & Troutman, A. C. (1993). *Applied behavior analysis for teachers.* (4th Edition). Columbus, OH: Charles E. Merrill.

Anderson, J., Russo, A., Dunlap, G., & Albin, R. (1996). A team training model for building the capacity to provide positive behavioral supports in inclusive settings. In L. Koegel, R. Koegel, & G. Dunlap (Eds.). *Positive behavioral support* (pp. 467–490). Baltimore: Paul H. Brookes.

Bannerman, D. J., Sheldon, J. B., Sherman, J. A., & Harchik, A. E. (1990). Balancing the right to habilitation with the right to personal liberties: The rights of people with developmental disabilities to eat too many donuts and take a nap. *Journal of Applied Behavior Analysis, 23,* 79–89.

Biklen, D. (1990). Communication unbound: Autism and praxis. *Harvard Educational Review, 60,* 291–314.

Biklen, D., Saha, N., & Kliewer, C. (1995). How teachers confirm the authorship of facilitated communication: A portfolio approach. *Journal of The Association for Persons With Severe Handicaps, 20,* 45–56.

Brown, F. (1991). Creative daily scheduling: A non-intrusive approach to challenging behaviors in community residences. *Journal of the Association for Persons With Severe Handicaps, 16,* 75–84.

Brown, F., Belz, P., Corsi, L., & Wenig, B. (1993). Choice diversity for people with severe disabilities. *Education and Training in Mental Retardation, 28,* 318–326.

Brown, F., & Gothelf, C. R. (1996). Community life for all individuals. In D. Lehr & F. Brown (Eds.). *People with disabilities who challenge the system* (pp. 175–188). Baltimore: Paul H. Brookes.

Brown, F., & Gothelf, C. R. (1996). Self-determination for all individuals. In D. Lehr & F. Brown (Eds.). *People with disabilities who challenge the system* (pp. 335–354). Baltimore: Paul H. Brookes.

Butterfield, N., & Arthur, M. (1995). Shifting the focus: Emerging priorities in communication programming for students with a severe intellectual disability. *Education and Training in Mental Retardation and Developmental Disabilities, 30,* 41–50.

Cardinal, D. N., Hanson, D., & Wakeham, J. (1996). Investigation of authorship in facilitated communication. *Mental Retardation, 34*(4), 231–242.

Carr, E. G., & Durand, V. M. (1985). Reducing behavior problems through functional communication training. *Journal of Applied Behavior Analysis, 26,* 111–126.

Carr, E. G., Levin, L., McConnachie, G., Carlson, J., Kemp, D., & Smith, C. (1994). *Communication-based intervention for problem behavior.* Baltimore: Paul H. Brookes.

Chadsey-Rusch, J., Drasgow, E., Reinoehl, B., & Halle, J. (1993). Using general-case instruction to teach spontaneous and generalized requests for assistance to learners with severe disabilities. *Journal of The Association for Persons with Severe Handicaps, 18,* 177–187.

Derby, K. M., Wacker, D. P., Andelman, M., Berg, W., Drew, J., Asmus, J., Prouty, A., & Laffey, P. (1995). Two measures of preference during forced-choice assessments. *Journal of Applied Behavior Analysis, 28,* 345–346.

Donnellan, A., Mirenda, P., Mesaros, R., & Fassbender, L. (1984). Analyzing the communicative functions of aberrant behavior. *Journal of The Association for Persons with Severe Handicaps, 9,* 201–212.

Downing, J. E., & Siegel-Causey, E. (1988). Enhancing the nonsymbolic communicative behavior of children with multiple impairments. *Language, Speech and Hearing Services in School, 19,* 338–348.

Dunlap, G., DePerczel, M., Clarke, S., Wilson, D., Wrights, S., White, R., & Gomez, A. (1994). Choice making to promote adaptive behavior for students with emotional and behavioral challenges. *Journal of Applied Behavior Analysis, 27,* 505–518.

Durand, V. M. (1990). *Severe behavior problems: A functional communication training approach.* New York: Guilford Press.

Dyer, K., Dunlap, G., & Winterling, V. (1990). Effects of

choice making on the serious problem behaviors of students with severe handicaps. *Journal of Applied Behavior Analysis, 23,* 515–524.

Eberlen, M., McConnachie, G., Abel, S., & Volpe, L. (1993). Facilitated communication: A failure to replicate the phenomenon. *Journal of Autism and Developmental Disorders, 23,* 507–530.

Ebert, R. (1995). *Smoke* (September 16). Chicago Sun Times.

Fisher, W., Piazza, C. C., Bowman, L. G., Hagopian, L. P., Owens, J. C., & Slevin, I. (1992). A comparison of two approaches for identifying reinforcers for persons with severe to profound disabilities. *Journal of Applied Behavior Analysis, 25,* 491–498.

Forest, M., & Lusthaus, E. (1989). Promoting educational equality for all students: Circles and maps. In S. Stainback, W. Stainback, & M. Forest (Eds.). *Educating all students in the mainstream of regular education* (pp. 43–57). Baltimore: Paul H. Brookes.

Gothelf, C. R., & Brown, F. (1996). Instructional support for self-determination in individuals with profound disabilities who are deaf-blind. In D. Lehr & F. Brown (Eds.). *People with disabilities who challenge the system* (pp. 355–378). Baltimore: Paul H. Brookes.

Gothelf, C. R., & Brown, F. (in press). Participation in the education process: Students with severe disabilities. In M. L. Wehmeyer & D. J. Sands (Eds.). *Making it happen: Student involvement in educational planning, decision-making and instruction.* Baltimore: Paul H. Brookes.

Gothelf, C. R., Crimmins, D. B., Mercer, C. A., & Finocchiaro, P. A. (1994). Teaching choice-making skills to students who are deaf-blind. *Teaching Exceptional Children, 26,* 13–15.

Grandin, T. (1995). *Thinking in pictures.* New York: Vintage Press.

Grandin, T., & Scariano, M. (1986). *Emergence: Labeled autistic.* New York: Warner Press.

Green, C. W., Gardner, S. M., & Reid, D. H. (1997). Increasing indices of happiness among people with profound multiple disabilities: A program replication and component analysis. *Journal of Applied Behavior Analysis, 30,* 217–228.

Green, C. W., Reid, D. H., White, L. K., Halford, R. C., Brittain, D. P., & Gardner, S. M. (1988). Identifying reinforcers for persons with profound handicaps: Staff opinion versus systematic assessment of preferences. *Journal of Applied Behavior Analysis, 21,* 31–43.

Green, G., & Shane, H. C. Science, reason, and facilitated communication. (1994). *Journal of The Association for Persons with Severe Handicaps, 19,* 151–172.

Guess, D. (1990). Transmission of behavior management technologies from researchers to practitioners: A need for professional self-evaluation. In A. Repp & N. Singh (Eds.). *Perspectives on the use of nonaversive and aversive interventions for persons with developmental disabilities* (pp. 157–172). Sycamore, IL: Sycamore.

Guess, D., Helmstetter, E., Turnbull, H. R., & Knowlton, S. (1986). *Use of aversive procedures with persons who are disabled: An historical review and critical analysis* (monograph 2). Seattle: The Association for Persons with Severe Handicaps.

Halle, J. (1987). Teaching language in the natural environment: An analysis of spontaneity. *Journal of The Association for Persons with Severe Handicaps, 12,* 28–37.

Haring, T. G., & Breen, C. (1989). Units of analysis of social interaction outcomes in supported education. *Journal of The Association for Persons with Severe Handicaps, 14,* 255–262.

Horner, R., Dunlap, G., Koegel, R., Carr, E., Sailor, W., Anderson, J., Albin, R., & O'Neill, R. (1990). Toward a technology of "nonaversive" behavioral support. *Journal of*

The Association for Persons with Severe Handicaps, 15, 125–132.

Kaiser, A., & Goetz, L. (1993). Enhancing communication with persons labeled severely disabled. *Journal of The Association for Persons with Severe Handicaps, 18,* 137–142.

Kennedy, C. H., & Haring, T. G. (1993). Teaching choice making during social interactions to students with profound multiple disabilities. *Journal of Applied Behavior Analysis, 26,* 63–76.

Kennedy, C. H., Horner, R. H., Newton, J. S., & Kanda, E. (1990). Measuring the activity patterns of adults with severe disabilities using the Resident Lifestyle Inventory. *Journal of The Association for Persons with Severe Handicaps, 15,* 79–85.

Koegel, L., Koegel, R., & Dunlap, G. (1996). *Positive behavioral support.* Baltimore: Paul H. Brookes.

Kohn, A. (1993). *Punished by rewards.* Boston: Houghton Mifflin.

Lehr, D. H., & Macurdy, S. (1994). *What does it feel like? Understanding the impact of special health care need procedures.* Paper presented at the conference of The Association for Persons with Severe Handicaps, San Francisco, CA.

Lucyshyn, J. J., Horner, R. H., & Ben, K. R. (1996). Positive behavioral support with families. *TASH Newsletter, 22*(7), 31–33.

Malette, P., Mirenda, P., Kandbor, T., Jones, P., Bunz, T., & Rogow, S. (1992). Application of a lifestyle development process for persons with severe intellectual disabilities: A case study report. *Journal of The Association for Persons with Severe Handicaps, 17,* 179–191.

Meyer, L. H., & Evans, I. M. (1989). *Nonaversive interventions for behavior problems: A manual for home and community.* Baltimore: Paul H. Brookes.

Meyer, L. H., & Janney, R. (1989). User-friendly measures of meaningful outcomes: Evaluating behavioral interventions. *Journal of The Association for Persons with Severe Handicaps, 14,* 263–270.

Microsoft Word, Version 2.0c. (1992). Seattle: Microsoft Corporation.

Mount, B., & Zwernik, K. (1988). *It's never too early, it's never too late: A booklet about personal futures planning.* St. Paul Metropolitan Council.

Newton, J. S., Ard, W. R. Jr., & Horner, R. H. (1993). Validating predicted activity preferences of individuals with severe disabilities. *Journal of Applied Behavior Analysis, 26,* 239–245.

O'Brien, C. L., O'Brien, J., & Mount, B. (in press). Person-centered planning has arrived . . . or has it? *Mental Retardation.*

Olney, M. (1995). Reading between the lines: A case study on facilitated communication. *Journal of The Association for Persons with Severe Handicaps, 20*(1), 57–65.

Pace, G. M., Ivancic, M. T., Edwards, G. L., Iwata, B. A., & Page, T. J. (1985). Assessment of stimulus preference and reinforcer value with profoundly retarded individuals. *Journal of Applied Behavior Analysis, 18,* 249–255.

Paclawskyj, T. R., & Vollmer, T. R. (1995). Reinforcer assessment for children with developmental disabilities and visual impairments. *Journal of Applied Behavior Analysis, 28,* 219–224.

Pearpoint, J., O'Brien, J., & Forest, M. (1993). *PATH: Planning alternative tomorrows with hope. A workbook for planning possible positive futures.* Toronto: Inclusion Press.

Pumpian, I. (1996). Foreword. In D. J. Sands & M. L. Wehmeyer (Eds.). *Self-determination across the life span: Independence and choice for people with disabilities.* Baltimore: Paul H. Brookes.

Reichle, J., Mirenda, P., Locke, P., Piche, L., & Johnson, R. A. (1992). Beginning augmentative communication systems. In

S. F. Warren & J. Reichle (Eds.). *Causes and effects in communication and language intervention* (Volume 1, pp. 131–156). Baltimore: Paul H. Brookes.

Reichle, J., York, J., & Eynon, D. (1989). Influence of indicating preferences for initiating, maintaining, and terminating interactions. In F. Brown & D. H. Lehr (Eds.). *Persons with profound disabilities: Issues and practices* (pp. 191–212). Baltimore: Paul H. Brookes.

Reichle, J., York, J., & Sigafoos, J. (1991). *Implementing augmentative and alternative communication: Strategies for learners with severe disabilities.* Baltimore: Paul H. Brookes.

Repp, A., & Singh, N. (Eds.). (1990). *Perspectives on the use of nonaversive and aversive interventions for persons with developmental disabilities.* Sycamore, IL: Sycamore.

Robertson, R., & Combs, A. (1995). *Chaos theory in psychology and the life sciences.* Mahwah, NJ: Lawrence Erlbaum Associates.

Rowland, C. (1996). *Communication skill matrix.* Unpublished manuscript. Portland: Oregon Health Sciences University.

Rowland, C., & Schweigert, P. (1993). Analyzing the communication environment to increase functional communication. *Journal of The Association for Persons with Severe Handicaps, 18,* 161–177.

Sacks, O. (1995). *An anthropologist on Mars.* New York: Alfred A. Knopf.

Schloss, P. J., & Smith, M. A. (1994). *Applied behavior analysis in the classroom.* Boston: Allyn & Bacon.

Sheehan, C. M., & Matuozzi, R. T. (1996). Investigation of the validity of facilitated communication through the disclosure of unknown information. *Mental Retardation, 34*(2), 94–107.

Siegel-Causey, E., & Ernst, B. (1989). Theoretical orientation and research in nonsymbolic development. In E. Siegel-Causey & D. Guess (Eds.). *Enhancing nonsymbolic communication interactions among learners with severe disabilities* (pp. 17–51). Baltimore: Paul H. Brookes.

Siegel-Causey, E., & Guess, D. (1988). *Enhancing interactions between service providers and individuals who are severely multiply disabled: Strategies for developing communication.* Lawrence, KS: University of Kansas.

Siegel-Causey, E., & Guess, D. (1989). *Enhancing nonsymbolic communication interactions among learners with severe disabilities.* Baltimore: Paul H. Brookes.

Stremel, K. (1994). Expressive communication. *FOCUS FLYER: Mississippi services for individuals who are deafblind* (no. 4). Hattiesburg, MS: University of Southern Mississippi.

Vasquez, C. (1994). A multi-task controlled evaluation of facilitated communication. *Journal of Autism and Developmental Disorders, 24,* 369–379.

Ward, M. J. (1988). *The many facets of self-determination: Transition summary, 2* (ERIC document no. 305805). Washington, DC: U.S. Department of Education.

Webster's Dictionary. (1992). New York: Pamco.

Wehmeyer, M. L. (1996). Self-determination as an educational outcome: Why is it important to children, youths, and adults with disabilities? In D. J. Sands & M. L. Wehmeyer (Eds.). *Self-determination across the life span: Independence and choice for people with disabilities* (pp. 17–36). Baltimore: Paul H. Brookes.

Wehmeyer, M., Kelchner, K., & Richards, S. (1996). Essential characteristics of self-determined behavior of individuals with mental retardation. *American Journal on Mental Retardation, 100,* 632–642.

Wheeler, D., Jacobson, J., Paglieri, R., & Schwartz, A. (1993). An experimental assessment of facilitated communication. *Mental Retardation, 31,* 49–60.

Williams, R. (1991). Choices, communication, and control: A call for expanding them in the lives of people with severe disabilities. In L. Meyer, C., Peck, & L. Brown (Eds.). *Critical issues in the lives of people with severe disabilities* (pp. 543–544). Baltimore: Paul H. Brookes.

Williams, D. (1992). *Nobody nowhere.* New York: Avon Books.

Williams, D. (1994). *Somebody somewhere.* New York: Times Books.

Received: August 18, 1997
Final Acceptance: February 23, 1998
Editor in Charge: Carolyn Hughes

A Moral Framework for Analyzing the Controversy Over Aversive Behavioral Interventions for People with Severe Mental Retardation

George H. S. Singer
University of California at Santa Barbara

Bernard Gert
Dartmouth College and Dartmouth Medical School

Robert L. Koegel
University of California at Santa Barbara

Abstract: This article applies a systematic analysis of everyday moral decision making to the controversy surrounding the use of aversive treatments for people with severe mental retardation. The authors' aim is to provide a framework for analyzing the issue, and they take a position against the use of aversive procedures. The analysis adds some new ideas to the debate. It provides a definition of aversive procedures based upon common moral rules. The concept of protection by the moral rules is discussed and the case made that people with severe mental retardation deserve the protection of the moral rules and that this right is historically new and tenous. The importance of symbols of dehumanization is discussed in light of this tenous condition. The idea of moral agency is applied in order to clarify the kinds of societal sanctions that are and are not appropriate when a person with severe mental retardation violates a moral rule. The authors argue that data are always relevant to moral decision making and that a mounting body of evidence indicates that nonaversive alternatives are available and can replace aversive procedures in all but a very small number of highly unusual cases.

The purpose of this article is to provide a framework from a philosophical perspective for examining the issues concerning the use of aversive methods in treating dangerous aggressive or self-injurious behavior in people with severe mental retardation. Two of the authors of this article are social scientists and one is a moral philosopher. Many researchers in the social sciences and philosophers of social science believe that science does not take place in a moral vacuum and that values often shape the questions we ask, the methods we employ, and the interpretations we give to our findings (Root, 1993). Just as research evidence must be carefully gathered and analyzed, values statements are likely to be most useful in application and most persuasive if they go well beyond slogans or bare assertion and instead present logical and empirical evidence in their development.

One purpose of this article is to add a thorough ethical analysis to the contemporary debate about aversive treatments for persons with severe cognitive disabilities. We contrast two points of view by referring to proponents of aversive versus proponents of nonaversive interventions. This structure is deliberately oversimplified for pur-

poses of clarity. We recognize that the arguments in this article are not simply a matter of "us versus them," but a matter of presenting a framework for professionals on both sides to analyze this issue. This article draws on a contemporary analysis of morality (Gert, 1996, 1998; Gert, Culver, & Glouser, 1997). Gert's justification of common morality aims to make explicit the thinking that lies behind everyday moral thinking and ethical decision making. It does not attempt to establish a new or different morality, but rather to explicate the presuppositions that underlie common moral discourse. In this article we are primarily concerned with decision making involving typical, widely accepted moral rules. These rules are familiar to any reader: Do not kill, do not cause pain, do not disable, do not deprive of freedom, do not deprive of pleasure, do not deceive, keep your promise, do not cheat, obey the law, and do your duty. In this article we refer to these rules as *commonplace moral rules*.

Gert (1996, 1998; Gert et al., 1997), unlike most philosophers, has provided a detailed account of the kind of decision making that people commonly employ in deciding when one of these rules can be justifiably violated, including those situations in which the rules conflict with one another. He has identified certain features of moral reasoning such as the idea that moral rules apply impartially to all who are granted the protection of morality. Gert's justification of these moral rules incorporates aspects of both deontological and consequentialist theories, but in this article we are not concerned with rival philosophical theories of moral justification. Rather we use Gert's description of common moral reasoning. This description makes clear that the moral rules are known to all who are judged by them and that it is never irrational for someone to guide his or her conduct by these rules. Gert's account of common morality also includes an analysis of the morally relevant features that enter into ethical decision making. Although we argue strongly for one position in the debate over aversive treatments, our most important goal is to provide a framework for the discussion so that all the relevant features of any moral decision are considered in the debate.

One of the central features of Gert's account of our common morality is that evidence about the consequences of one's action, although not the only relevant feature, is always relevant in making particular ethical decisions and this evidence is never trumped by reference to some absolutist position concerning morality, rights, or values. Thus, actual moral disagreements are often a matter of differential weighing of evidence, but never one in which the evidence about consequences, available alternatives, and so on is simply irrelevant. It is our hope to steer the debate away from discussion stopping moral claims to either the right to freedom from harm or the right to effective treatment; the appeal to such presumed rights tends to overshadow consideration of relevant evidence. Although most of our arguments are not new, they are presented in a new conceptual framework, which leads us to consider some new aspects of the issue.

The debate over the use of aversive behavioral procedures is an argument about a moral issue. In Gert's account, morality is an informal public system applying to all rational persons who govern behavior that affects others; and it includes what are commonly known as the moral rules, ideals, and virtues and has the lessening of harm as its goal (Gert, 1998). The common moral rules are used to judge people who are moral agents. These individuals must know that others do not want to have any of the five kinds of harm—death, pain, loss of ability, loss of freedom, or loss of pleasure—inflicted on them. These five harms are meant to represent everything that all rational persons want to avoid; the centrality of these harms is shown by the fact that all diseases, disorders, or maladies involve suffering one of these harms, or an increased risk of suffering one of them. To be a moral agent a person must also have the volitional capacity to control urges to harm oneself or another. Moral agents are subject to moral judgments and societal sanctions (e.g., fines, required service, imprisonment, the death penalty) for breaking the shared moral rules. When we refer to such societal sanctions in this article, we are not endorsing them as ways to punish offenders but simply describing the present state of affairs.

We define the term *punishment* in a nontechnical sense. Used in this way it does not mean anything that reduces the probability of a behavior occurring. Instead, we use the term to mean unusual punishers involving infliction of four of the five categories of harm: pain, temporary but significant loss of ability, prolonged loss of freedom, and prolonged loss of pleasure. These unusual methods risk the danger of dehumanizing their recipients, and thus encourage the infliction of even greater harms. Examples of such procedures include, but are not limited to electric shock, certain overcorrection procedures that require the people who implement the procedure to overpower the recipient, prolonged time-out, administration of noxious substances, chemical restraints that deprive the person of alertness and ability to learn, helmets that administer white noise and water spray, hitting and slapping, and so on.

Moral Agents and Rules

We address three major issues about morality and the debate over aversive treatment, along with a set of questions that follow from one of the issues. A first major question concerns who is a moral agent. People are assumed to be moral agents and thus subject to moral judgments if they can understand that others do not want harms done to them. That is, they understand that others do not want to be killed, disabled, hurt, deprived of freedom, or deprived of pleasure. Historically, the question of who is a moral agent has also been a major source of ethical controversy. It is, for example, an essential focus of concern regarding the appropriateness of imprisonment and capital punishment for people with mild mental retardation and the controversy over the insanity defense.

Second, a common source of ethical controversy is the question of who should be protected by the moral rules. No one, for example, believes that the moral rules apply to bacteria. But there is considerable debate over whether they apply to animals and fertilized human eggs. We argue that this issue is settled in regard to persons with severe mental retardation. They are protected by the moral rules, but this protection is historically recent and still tenuous.

A third question specific to the debate over aversive treatment asks whether there is adequate justification for violating some moral rules in order to treat severe problem behavior. In order to systematically address this third question, we examine the appropriate morally relevant features of the controversy. These features are specified in Gert's discussion of the justification of violations of the moral rules. Most moral arguments about aversive treatment focus on what counts as an adequate justification for violating moral rules that prohibit intentionally inflicting harm on a person. No moral rules are absolute; all can be justifiably violated under appropriate circumstances. In examining whether a particular violation of a moral rule is justified, all the morally relevant features must be considered.

In summary, some moral issues focus on who is a moral agent, some on who should be protected by the moral rules, and some on whether there is an adequate justification for violating a moral rule prohibiting intentionally inflicted harm in the circumstances under consideration. In addressing the third question regarding justification, the morally relevant features are examined in turn. We address those morally relevant features that Gert has identified that relate to aversive treatment.

ARE PEOPLE WITH SEVERE MENTAL RETARDATION MORAL AGENTS?

The question of whether people with severe mental retardation who are aggressive or self-injurious should be held morally accountable generates some important confusion because typically we excuse people with severe mental retardation from normal legal sanctions and moral blame for violating the moral rules. Persons with severe mental retardation are normally not considered to be moral agents from a legal perspective. To be a moral agent one must understand that other people do not want to have any of the five harms inflicted on them. A moral agent also must have sufficient volitional control to be able to act on this knowledge. People with severe mental retardation are assumed not to have a sufficient understanding of the moral rules such that they can be held accountable in the normal fashion for transgressions. Alternatively, in some cases, these individuals may not have sufficient volitional control to act on their knowledge. If a person with severe mental retardation hits a co-worker, we normally do not call the police and have that person charged with assault. We excuse people with severe cognitive disabilities from moral blame and subsequent societal sanctions because, in most cases, they are not moral agents in the normal sense of having the understanding that others do not want to have harms perpetrated against them and in the sense of having full volitional capacity to inhibit harmful behavior. By contrast, persons with mild cognitive disabilities are considered full moral agents and are punished for transgression even to the extent of capital punishment. We do not endorse this state of affairs but simply describe it. We believe it is important to recognize that to say someone is not a moral agent is not a pejorative statement; it is simply a description that this particular person either does not have the understanding or the volitional control to prevent himself or herself from doing harm. We usually view children in this way and do not consider it a negative judgment on them.

But because persons are not moral agents does not mean that they are not protected by the moral rules. For example, we normally do not judge 3-year-old children or severely mentally ill people in the way that we judge moral agents. We do not imprison 3-year-olds for hurting other people. But we do safeguard children with the protection of the moral rules. It is not acceptable to hurt children, people with mental retardation, and people with mental illness because they lack a full understanding of what morality requires. Because we excuse people with severe mental retardation from normal punishment for what is usually considered to be immoral behavior does not in turn mean that we are excused from treating them as members of the class of people who are protected by the moral rules but who are not subject to normal societal punishment if they break the rules. Their difficulties in understanding normal social and moral rules should lead civilized society to treat people with severe mental retardation with the full protection of the moral rules and to provide extraordinary efforts to give them opportunity to learn appropriate behavior and to protect them from unethical treatment. Although such people are excused from typical social sanctions such as fines and imprisonment, we should try to educate them about the moral rules and how to behave consistently with them.

WHO IS PROTECTED BY THE MORAL RULES?

Historically, arguments over who should be protected by the moral rules have been the center of major social movements. This argument was an important feature of such major social reforms as the granting of civil rights to members of all social classes after the American and French Revolutions, the abolition of slavery, and the granting of voting and property rights to women. It has required lengthy and massive societal change to extend the protection of the moral rules to people in Western societies who were slaves, members of ethnic minorities, females, poor people, children, and homosexuals. The philosophical view that all moral agents are protected has played a positive role in most of these movements. However, the similar sounding but very different philosophical position that only moral agents are protected is regarded by most as far too restrictive, for it excludes young children and adult human beings who lack the intellectual or volitional capacity to be moral agents. Whether people with severe mental retardation are protected by the common morality is central to the debate about the use of aversives. This question of who should be protected by the moral rules when applied to persons with severe mental retardation has become inappropriately linked with the first issue: whether they should be considered moral agents.

The question of whether people with mental retardation deserve the protection of the moral rules is settled for the most part. However, because the nature of the social agreement has only recently been to provide this group with normal moral protections, a brutal history still shades contemporary controversies. It has not been long since the major governmental policy response to persons with severe mental retardation was to place them in large institutions, where they were often treated more poorly than prized animals (Blatt, 1973; Ferguson, 1994); that is, they were treated as if they did not have the equal protection of the moral rules. As recently as the 1940s people with disabilities were displayed in carnivals for public amusement (Bogdan, 1986). Within the past two decades numerous court decisions and settlements have provided ample evidence of continuing disregard for the basic well-being of many people residing in institutions as well as poorly run community residences (*Milonas v. Williams*, 1982; *Youngberg v. Romeo*, 1982). The protection of the moral rules is tenuous for this group of human beings in the United States and in many other parts of the world. Consequently, many who are familiar with the circumstances of persons with severe mental retardation believe that vigilance is required to safeguard their rights to be protected by the moral rules. A history of exclusion from equal protection of the moral rules gives cause for extra care and concern about the treatment of formerly excluded persons. Much of the argument concerning the use of aversive treatment procedures for persons with severe mental retardation is a proxy for an argument about whether they have the equal protection of the moral rules or, on the contrary, whether they deserve exceptional safeguards as a protected class. Those who advocate for the use of aversive procedures are vulnerable to the assertion that they do not believe persons with severe mental retardation have the equal protection of the moral rules. For example, the use of strange-looking helmets that administer automatic electric shocks can lead to perceptions that devalue people with severe disabilities. Devaluation has historically exposed people to further harm. Proponents of aversive methods in institutional settings—whether private or public—although typically having good intentions, may appear to give little regard for the importance of the historical mistreatment of persons with severe mental retardation in such settings. Thus the language and context from which proponents of aversive procedures launch their arguments are often laden with symbols of an older order in which persons with severe mental retardation were not given the equal protection of the moral rules. This does not mean that these professionals are immoral or that they do not act with concern and in good faith. Simply, the failure to recognize the danger that devaluation imposes is an important problem.

Opponents of aversive procedures appear in many instances to argue for this larger question when they actually address the narrower issues surrounding aversive procedures. Whether people with severe disabilities should be equally protected by the moral rules is the underlying issue in the statement that they should not be subjected to dehumanizing treatments (The Association for Persons with Severe Handicaps, 1991). We believe that this argument should be openly acknowledged. The argument is as follows: In the recent past, persons with severe mental retardation were often treated worse than some animals. They were not impartially protected by the moral rules. Because of this long-standing history of mistreatment, they deserve extraordinary vigilance in the protection of their rights. Given their tenuous status as persons protected by the moral rules, we believe that it is extremely important to safeguard against weakly justified violation of the moral rules or the application of any symbols that communicate dehumanization. Consequently, it may be even more difficult to justify aversive treatments that imply devaluation because devalued persons are vulnerable to further losses of protection of the moral rules.

Note that this argument draws on empirical evidence in that our assertion that people with severe mental retardation have been dehumanized and are at risk of dehumanization can be substantiated with historical documents and contemporary evidence about living conditions in poorly run care settings. Historical evidence is one valid source of data to support an ethical argument. Photographs of how people were treated in institutions, records of investigative bodies, and evidence provided in legal suits are valid sources of data regarding this claim (Trent, 1994). Similarly, the argument that associating people with severe disabilities with devaluing symbols (such as cattle prods or electric helmets) places them at risk of being devalued is an empirically verifiable claim. Recent studies of social perception suggest that aversive treatments can be associated with negative public perceptions of persons with disabilities (Bihm & Sigelman, 1991). At the same time, it is likely that untreated severe problem behavior are also associated with public social rejection and thus alternatives to aversive treatments must be effective (Bihm, Sigelman, & Westbrook, 1997).

IS THERE JUSTIFICATION FOR VIOLATING SOME MORAL RULES?

Gert (1996, 1998; Gert et al., 1997) identified certain features of situations in which the breaking of a moral rule is considered relevant to ethical decision making. Gert argues that these morally relevant features, such as the amount of harm suffered, are the only features of the situation that matter in a moral decision. In the following discussion we list the questions, the answers to which are morally relevant features, and apply these features to the controversy over aversive treatments. We highlight the way that different perspectives give different weight to supporting evidence. In this article we do not use all the morally relevant features that Gert identified but instead focus on eight features that are most applicable for this issue.

What Moral Rules Are Being Violated? By definition, aversive treatment interventions involve intentionally inflicting pain, depriving of ability, depriving of freedom, or depriving of pleasure. Which of these moral rules is being violated is relevant to the justification.

Aversive treatments are often, although not always, recommended as a way to deal with serious aggressive or self-injurious behavior. Aggression toward others and self represents violation of moral rules, although we do not view the people with severe mental retardation as morally culpable. No one seriously argues that people with severe mental retardation should be allowed to hurt others or themselves. To do so would deny the victims of aggression the protection of the common moral rules. Rather, the argument centers on whether inflicting pain or deprivation is justifiable as a way to stop or reduce extreme aberrant behavior.

What Harms Are Caused and What Harms Are Being Prevented by the Violation? Gert (1998) argued that in addition to specifying the kinds of harms, one must include their severity, the length of time they will be suffered, and their probability of occurrence.

What Harms Are Caused by the Violation? Two classes of harms are caused by using aversive procedures: harms to the individual person with mental retardation and harms to the class of people with mental retardation. Harms to the individual involve either infliction of pain, temporary disabling, restriction of liberty, or deprivation of pleasure. Some of the controversy over the use of aversives focuses on the severity of the potential harm that aversive treatments entail. Proponents of aversive treatment argue that administration of the treatments is usually carefully controlled and when they are carefully controlled, the treatments are not as severe as the harms that the targeted person usually inflicts on himself or herself or others. Again, both these arguments are open to empirical challenge. The first claim unfortunately often cannot be supported in many of the applied settings where people with severe mental retardation live, work, and go to school (Horner, 1990).

Often the people who are responsible for the application of aversive procedures are not highly trained, nor are they closely supervised. Most people with severe mental retardation are supervised in living and work settings by people who often have very limited training and infrequent supervision (Horner, 1990). When they are given license to use painful stimuli or prolonged deprivation as a form of treatment, there is always danger that the treatment procedure will be misused. Such "procedural drift," or failure to ensure treatment fidelity, is commonplace

(Hastings & Remington, 1994). The risk of workers losing their tempers, forgetting the procedures, or deciding on their own to intensify the pain or deprivation is great. Again, these assertions could be empirically verified or challenged through case histories, court records, and direct observations studies.

In regard to the second assertion, that aversive stimuli or deprivation can be kept at a relatively low level, empirical evidence from analogue animal studies—as well as case studies of people—indicates that one of the dangers of using aversives is the potential that the recipient can habituate to the aversive stimuli or to the periods of deprivation. Thus, Azrin and Holz (1966) recommended that punishment begin with high levels of stimulation and never be applied incrementally. When habituation occurs, it becomes necessary to increase the intensity of the electric shock or prolong the period of deprivation. As the intensity or duration of the treatment increases, risks of unplanned harm also increase. Increased intensity and duration may expose the person to the risk of injury and, in some tragic instances, to disability or even death. The risks involved in using procedures such as electric shock, prolonged locked time-out, disabling doses of drugs, or enforced aversive overcorrection are not trivial.

The second category of harms involves the larger class of people with severe mental retardation and, perhaps, people with other disabilities. These risks to the larger group of people have been discussed earlier. If violation of some moral rules were to be commonplace against some people with severe mental retardation, there is risk that they will be extended to other people with this disability because the protections against harm are historically new and fragile. Some might argue that a decision to use painful interventions should be focused solely on the one case in point, and not on the larger class. However, moral questions are, by their nature, public questions and have to be regarded as if they initiate a policy that applies to all similar cases (Gert, 1998).

A counterargument is that failure to effectively treat a person with severe aberrant behavior problems can also lead to the creation of negative attitudes toward a class of people. For example, assaultive or otherwise offensive behavior by mentally ill homeless people may cause an increase in negative attitudes about homeless people and people with mental illness (Mechanic & Rochefort, 1990). Similarly, a person with severe mental retardation who is assaultive or self-injurious may stimulate negative attitudes about people with mental retardation if the transgressor is not provided adequate treatment. Both sides in this debate would agree that adequate treatment is necessary. The argument then moves to the issue of whether there are effective nonaversive methods available that can be used in integrated community settings.

A growing body of empirical evidence indicates that there are nonaversive alternatives for addressing even the most serious behavior problems in people with severe cognitive disabilities (Carr et al., in press; Carr et al., 1994, Horner et al. 1996; Koegel, Koegel & Dunlap, 1996). This evidence includes peer-reviewed studies of the following severe problem behaviors:

- self-injury (Durand, 1993; Durand & Kishi, 1987; Horner, Day, & Day, 1997; Kennedy & Souza, 1995; Lerman, Iwata, Smith, & Vollmer, 1994; Saunders, Saunders, Brewer, & Roach, 1996; Sigafoos, Penned, & Versluis, 1996),
- aggression (Bowman, Fisher, Thompson, & Piazza, 1997; Carr & Durand, 1985; Durand, 1993; Dyer, Dunlap, Winterling, 1990; Horner, Day, Sprague, O'Brien, & Heathfield, 1991; Knapczyk, 1988; Steed, Bigelow, Huynen, & Lutzker, 1995),
- property destruction (Hanley, Piazza, & Fisher, 1997), and
- severe noncompliance (Ducharme, Popynick, Pontes, & Steele, 1996).

Nonaversive interventions have been applied successfully to treat challenging behavior in a variety of settings, including

- public schools (Dunlap, Kern-Dunlap, Clarke, & Robbins, 1991; Durand & Carr, 1992; Karsh, Repp, Dahlquist, & Munk, 1995; Kehle, Clark, Jenson, & Wampold, 1986; Knapczyk, 1988),
- home and community settings with family members (Ducharme, Pontes, Guger, & Crozier, 1994; Lucyshn, Albin, & Nixon, 1997; Sanders & Plant, 1989),
- employment settings (Kemp & Carr, 1995; Smith & Coleman, 1986) and
- a dentist's office (Maguire, Lange, Scherling, & Grow, 1996).

Nonaversive methods have been effective for people with all levels of mental retardation as well as for people with multiple disabilities (e.g., Vollmer, Iwata, Smith, & Rodgers, 1992) and autism (e.g., Koegel, Camarata, & Koegel, 1994). The studies referenced here represent only a small part of a large body of research that affirms the efficacy of nonaversive alternatives to aversive procedures (Carr et al., in press).

What Harms Are Being Prevented by the Violation? This question focuses on prevention of possible harms in the future. The prevention of future self-injury or future assault is the usual aim of aversive treatment. In our clinical experience we have found that aversives are often initiated when a person is threatened with expulsion from a community program. Aversives are applied as a final effort to prevent expulsion or further restriction of the person's freedom. The rule of rescue takes effect; that is, well-meaning interventionists resort to extreme measures

in order to prevent the harms involved in expulsion from a program or institutionalization. Of course, there are other alternatives such as giving the program the resources, staff, and skills to manage the person with nonaversive procedures. Numerous community programs around the United States now follow such a policy. Nonetheless, proponents of nonaversives must acknowledge that an increase in institutionalization of people with severe behavior problems would be a highly undesirable outcome of reform efforts. Already, severe behavior problems are one of the major reasons for institutionalization and out-of-home placement of individuals with mental retardation (Blacher, 1994). Thus any effort to promote more humane treatment of people with severe mental retardation must work to change the current structure of services, which set the context for many behavioral treatment decisions.

The severity of future harms is a relevant factor. For example, in some rare instances, one more instance of self-injury is likely to lead to permanent blindness in a child who has already destroyed one eye. Or an individual may have been so assaultive in the past that a staff member or fellow resident may have been severely injured. Certainly, treatment methods must ensure the safety of the recipients as well as the people around them. However, in almost all cases there is no reason safety cannot be provided while nonaversive treatments are used. Proponents of aversives often believe that all other realistic options have been exhausted or that aversives will work quickly and will thereby eliminate the danger. In our experience, implementation of the full array of effective nonaversive alternatives is, in fact, rarely tried and rarely carried out well. The claim that powerful nonaversive procedures have been fully tried should always be subjected to very careful scrutiny as it is an easy claim to make in the face of dangerous behavior but a difficult claim to validate. In fairness, it is important to point out that many nonaversive methods, although empirically validated, are new; this is one reason the full array of alternatives is sometimes not used. In addition to data derived from direct observation of the problem behaviors, one must know a good deal about the fidelity of implementation of the failed methods as well as the environmental opportunities available to the person in order for that person to develop new adaptive responses and to come under the influence of a variety of reinforcers. Furthermore, there is little evidence to support the notion that aversive procedures are quicker or expose all parties to less danger than nonaversives. The most violent of individuals with severe disabilities may require specialized settings where skilled and intensive levels of staffing are provided in order to ensure everyone's safety. There is an emerging body of evidence that such settings can be provided in the community without resorting to congregate care institutions (Horner et al., 1996; Koegel et al., 1996).

Those who argue for the exhaustive and exclusive use of nonaversive measures must acknowledge that in the most severe cases, the safety procedures that are required to protect the persons with disabilities and the people around them may involve brief restriction of liberty. Temporary and brief physical restraints and emergency isolation may be needed in dangerous cases. Although these usually are not recommended as treatment procedures per se but rather as emergency responses to prevent harm, they are infliction of harms. These measures should be openly acknowledged as harms and they should be justified by addressing the same questions about morally relevant features. Although using these methods as emergency procedures rather than as standard treatments changes their moral status, it does not relieve the practitioner of the duty to justify their use.

Are There Alternatives to the Violation That Do Not Involve Violating a Moral Rule? and Are There Alternatives That Involve a Lesser Violation of the Moral Rule? A considerable body of research has demonstrated that many severe problem behaviors can be treated effectively with nonaversive measures (Carr et. al., in press; Koegel, Koegel, & Dunlap, 1996). Nonetheless, only recently have researchers demonstrated that these methods can be effective with some of the most intractable cases of the most violent or destructive behaviors. Until recently, people with mental retardation with the most dangerous behavior problems typically have been confined to institutions. There have been only sporadic data-based reports of community-based treatment for people with the most challenging behavioral problems. This situation is gradually changing. One significant example comes from Horner and his colleagues (1996), who published longitudinal data on a group of individuals who clearly would qualify as representative of the most difficult-to-treat population. The individuals studied all had long-standing behavior problems that involved seriously dangerous behavior, including aggression that caused numerous staff injuries, self-injury that led to permanent tissue damage, and dangerous running away behavior that led to police involvement. All these individuals had been provided with years of unsuccessful treatment, and all had been subjected to deprivation of their liberty and deprivation from normal pleasures available in community settings. Several had histories of aversive treatments that had been ineffective. Data were collected in the institution prior to placement in specialized community programs and subsequent data tracked changes in their problem behaviors over a 2-year period. Horner et al. (1996) also compared indicators of the quality of life of these individuals in institutional and community settings. Individuals in the community treatment setting had much more enriched lives in terms of social contacts and normal activities. Importantly, the authors also presented data on injuries to staff involved

in providing nonaversive treatments. Injuries to staff, bystanders, and self must be considered morally relevant features in making treatment decisions. They are rarely reported in the treatment literature. This omission in the literature is serious, given that it focuses on a significant morally relevant feature.

Thereafter, Horner et al. (1996) showed that, with sufficient support, people with even the most dangerous problem behaviors can be treated in community settings where they have access to typical activities and where they receive effective nonaversive treatment. For the most difficult cases, these programs are costly and may require staff ratios as high as 2:1. Nonetheless, it was reported that these individuals were slightly less expensive to serve in the community than in institutional settings that necessarily require more restrictions on liberty (Knobbe, Carey, Rhodes, & Horner, 1995).

The finding that people with severe disabilities who have a long history of dangerous behavior can be treated in community settings with nonaversive methods is of major importance. A basic principle in ethical decision making is that when less harmful means are available, they should take precedence over the use of more harmful means. Although ethical arguments and legal arguments are not always equivalent, in this area there is substantial agreement. This principle has been recognized in legal cases regarding penal, medical, and behavioral interventions, where it is known as the principle of the least restrictive alternative. In the case *Shelton v. Tucker* (1960) the Supreme Court ruled that even though a government purpose is reasonable, it can not be achieved by means that widely stifle liberties if it can be achieved through a means that has a lesser negative impact. This principle has been extended by the courts to treatments such as psychotropic medications. In *Rennie v. Klien* (1978) the court ruled on behalf of a resident of a psychiatric hospital who refused to take a medication. The court said:

> As a final consideration, many courts and commentators have employed the concept of least restrictive alternatives in regard to the choice of custodial setting. The court feels that this concept should be extended to the choice of medications (*Rennie v. Klien*, 1978).

Thus the notion that the least restrictive alternative should be used when a choice is available is not only a part of common moral reasoning but also of legal precedent in regard to treatment. There is now a growing body of evidence indicating that people with severe problem behaviors can be treated in settings that are less restrictive than institutions, and with means that are less restrictive or less harmful than aversive methods.

What Are the Relevant Desires of the Person Toward Whom the Rule Is Being Violated? This question is primarily useful in addressing moral violations that are aimed at people who have complex verbal behavior and can express it in the form of desires. For example, physicians consider the desires of a person who refuses extreme life support measures when they are making moral decisions about treatment. In these instances it is often possible to simply ask the person what he or she is thinking or to refer to written instructions or verbal directives that the person made previously. The issue of relevant beliefs is more complex in regard to people with severe cognitive disabilities who may not be able to express complex verbal statements. The fact that they do not have the ability to explain verbally their relevant beliefs entrains important consequences: We rely on surrogates to make decisions on their behalf and we are obliged to provide every available means to permit the persons to express their beliefs or the functional equivalent of beliefs.

Because the problem behaviors are dangerous and the treatment procedures involve a potential trade-off of serious risks and unknown benefits, the principle of informed consent is widely applied to the use of behavioral treatments for severe aberrant behavior. Elsewhere we have urged that full informed consent plus procedural due process should be required for any aversive behavioral treatment in public schools (Singer & Irvin, 1987). The process of obtaining informed consent from a surrogate decision maker requires at least some minimal level of discussion about the morally relevant feature of the decision. We believe, however, that the minimal level of informed consent is not sufficient when proposed treatment involves administering of painful stimuli, prolonged deprivation of liberty, or prolonged deprivation of pleasure, as in decisions to use long periods of seclusion or to remove someone from the community. Because such interventions involve the intentional infliction of significant harm, they require procedural safeguards greater than those required of decisions that do not involve violation of the moral rules (Singer & Irvin, 1987).

Further, parental consent per se is not sufficient in such instances. In *Milonas v. Williams* (1982) the court ruled that parental consent was necessary but not sufficient to authorize aversive procedures for children with emotional and behavioral problems. According to the court, parental consent was not a sufficient rationale to waive constitutionally guaranteed liberties. In this case the procedures involved prolonged seclusion, physical punishment including pulling hair, and required polygraph tests. Following this line of reasoning, we believe that the consent of surrogate decision makers for people with severe cognitive disabilities is necessary, but not a sufficient reason to justify aversive treatments.

Testimonials about the value of aversives and consent to use them are not sufficient evidence or sufficient reason to violate the moral rules when alternative treatments are available. To illustrate this point, consider a case of a medical treatment that involves surgery for a serious disease.

Suppose a new medication is discovered that treats the disease without requiring surgery. This medication has no known side effects and is effective in almost all cases. Suppose someone brings a child who has the disease to the hospital and demands surgery. When the physician asks why surgery is preferred, the adult answers that he has talked to others who liked the surgery and he doesn't trust medications because other medicines had previously been ineffective. Normally, this rationale would not be sufficient to expose the child to the dangers of surgery when a less dangerous means of effective treatment is available. Similarly, surrogate consent to aversive behavioral treatments when effective nonaversive measures are available should not be sufficient reason, in itself, to justify a violation of the moral rules against inflicting pain, restricting liberty, or depriving of pleasure.

Although it is not clear at present that the knowledge base on nonaversive procedures would support a total cessation of all aversives, it would be in the rarest and most unusual circumstances that an aversive approach would have merit in comparison to positive behavioral support. Ideally, we would like to see a complete cessation of the use of aversive procedures and the establishment of enriched community-based settings where individuals with severe disabilities and the most severe forms of challenging behavior receive intensive positive behavioral supports as a long-term commitment. History would suggest that this is not likely to come to pass on a large scale soon. What of the interim? We call for research and development of new legal mechanisms for reviewing aversive treatments for persons with disabilities. We believe that the present system of protections with its reliance on local human subject committees is insufficient and should be supplemented by requiring updated information about nonaversive alternatives.

Does the Person Violating the Moral Rule Have a Duty to Violate Some Moral Rules with Regard to the Person Toward Whom the Rule Is Being Violated Independent of the Latter's Consent? Precedent for this question comes from several areas. For example, physicians are held to have a special duty that allows violation of moral rules in regard to some patients. That is, medical law states the conditions under which a physician may seek to override a patient's or parent's wishes regarding treatment or nontreatment.

This feature also accounts for the facts that we allow parents to punish children when the same action in response to the same behavior, if done by a stranger, would usually not be viewed as permissible. It also accounts for the fact that we permit police to use force against some people.

Our argument is that the relationship between behaviorally trained professionals and persons with severe cognitive disabilities is not so clear-cut as to readily grant that a professional has the option to violate the moral rules prohibiting intentionally causing harm. In order to make this case it is necessary to examine the reasons certain professions are granted unusual authority as well as the contexts in which these professionals work.

Society governs the power to violate moral rules. In medicine, the right to deliberately surgically cut into another person is regulated via laws surrounding licensure and through professional societies by means of certifications. Except in emergencies, or when a patient is not competent to give consent, however, this cannot be done without the valid consent of the patient. The right to make complex moral decisions is jealously guarded by the medical profession. But this authority has also been restricted in some areas so that some decisions are routinely turned over to the courts or ethics boards, as in cases in which parents refuse a treatment that a physician deems necessary for a child. Nonetheless, with regard to patients who do not understand and thus can't give informed consent, many life-and-death decisions are made by physicians on their own, sometimes with the oversight of other medical professionals. Psychologists have sought and won similar license to make treatment decisions that may involve infliction of pain or deprivation of liberty. In some circumstances such as state-operated congregate care institutions, some oversight by a human rights review committee is required (*Wyatt v. Stickney,* 1972). In most community settings, with the exception of those states that have passed legislation limiting the use of aversive procedures, decisions about the use of aversive methods are left to the judgment of a licensed psychologist or other authorized persons such as a behaviorally trained special educator. The power to make decisions about and oversee these procedures has been jealously guarded by professional societies, as is any societal grant of authority to the professions.

To return to the question: Does a licensed psychologist or a certified special education teacher have a special relationship such that they have a duty to violate some common moral rules without the person's consent? Any response to this question must be highly qualified. As with physicians, such a duty can be the case only under certain circumstances, as described in this article. The answer is also highly qualified, in part, by the current nature of the knowledge that psychologists and educators hold and the limitations of the environments in which they often work. A body of theory, empirically substantiated findings, and skills is not commonly available to the general public and is the basis for a profession's claim to hold this kind of moral grant of decision-making power. A prerequisite for the grant of authority to use aversives or for a physician to operate on a person is a period of education, training, and supervised practice. It is assumed that these experiences then equip the professional with abilities that are uniquely held by persons with the specialized training.

Is the knowledge held by those with behavioral education and training such that they should be authorized to inflict pain or use other unusual means that are normally immoral when they judge it to be needed? The problem with an unqualified yes answer to this question is that the knowledge base regarding aversives and the methodology for deciding when to use them is ambiguous for the former and subject to severe constraints for the later. The basic infrahuman research on punishment is full of evidence for both the efficacy and the undesirable effects of aversive stimuli (Azrin & Holz, 1966; Azrin, Hutchinson, & Hake, 1967). Findings regarding reduction of targeted behaviors are counterbalanced by indications of undesirable effects: habituation entraining increased intensity or duration of the painful stimuli, induced anxiety and fear responses, and reduction in the reinforcing properties of stimuli. In regard to humans with mental retardation, there is evidence that procedures such as electric shock, aversive overcorrection procedures, and exclusionary time-out can reduce problem behaviors (O'Brien, 1989). However, there is little evidence that these methods are durable and generalizable. Further, there is clinical evidence that these procedures often fail to work, are implemented for long periods of time, involve progressively more severe applications of pain or prolonged periods of deprivation, are highly vulnerable to procedural drift, and may generate negative public attitudes toward the person being treated (Hastings and Remington, 1994; Schopler, 1986).

Applied behavior analysis is an idiomethic science. In research, it relies on an analysis of single subjects. Although there is some recourse to accumulated evidence over many subjects, however, the individualized focus of behavior analysis takes precedence. When enough data from individual analyses have accumulated, a kind of nomomethic validity arises for a procedure. For example, there are enough single-subject studies of the effect of praise on verbal children for the profession to conclude that praise is likely to be an important reinforcer for most children with a verbal repertoire, although there is also evidence that it is not effective as a reinforcer for some children. When there is no clear consensus regarding interpretation of findings, it is doubtful that any general, nomothetic conclusions and guidelines can be drawn, and thus the analysis of a specific individual's behavior must remain the major basis for decision making. Thus, behavior analysts must experiment with different interventions and measure their impact. They must decide when one intervention is no longer worth pursuing and another should be tried in its place. There is little guidance in the way of either formal published knowledge or clinical knowledge to know when to abandon one approach and advance along the continuum toward the use of aversives. Here we are asked to trust the training and experience of the designated professional behaviorist (Van Houten et al., 1988). Such decision making, however, is rarely simply a matter of reading the data and deciding that it "tells" the practitioner that it is time to abandon an exclusively nonaversive regimen and begin delivering painful or highly unpleasant events. The decision making must be informed by current knowledge, constrained by ethical and legal restrictions, and limited by the social and environmental context. Current knowledge includes a body of evidence suggesting the effectiveness of positive behavioral interventions with even the most severe problem behaviors. We believe that this evidence is such that it outweighs the body of research on the efficacy of aversives except, perhaps, in very rare instances.

Contemporary knowledge does not clearly support the use of aversives over nonaversives. An up-to-date, knowledgeable professional is unlikely to have authority based on research evidence that aversive treatments are a preferrable choice except, perhaps, in extremely rare instances. Professionals cannot inflict serious harm on a person with severe cognitive disabilities whose behavior violates common moral rules unless they know that there are no effective options that involve less infliction of harm. However, the present professional knowledge base does not provide evidence that aversives are more effective than nonaversive alternatives. Furthermore, the professional ethics of psychology and special education demand that professionals use the least harmful and least restrictive effective methods available.

The ability of professionals is often constrained by the context in which many people with severe mental retardation live. Prominent researchers have urged a recognition of the importance of the overall context in which a person lives and his or her lifestyle (e.g., Meyer & Evans, 1989; Thompson, Robinson, Dietrich, & Farris, 1996). Horner et al. (1996) explained that giving their clients access to many different reinforcing events that were available only in a community and in programs that allowed for flexible and individualized scheduling of these events were essential features of their behavioral treatment regimen. That is, the treatment required giving people a life full of stimulating and reinforcing activities. Such a background of activities and exposure to a variety of environments and events is rarely possible for people who live in large congregate care facilities and other restrictive environments. The context can be so constrained that a full sampling of a person's preferences and means of obtaining them is, in most cases, severely limited and can provide little evidence about what kinds of reinforcers and ways of obtaining them ought to be the focus of treatment. A professional working in one environment may have a whole array of events and activities available, whereas another in a restrictive setting may have only a few options for activities, events, social interactions, and other potential reinforcers. It is particularly in these restricted settings that we should be reluctant to grant a professional the sole authority to decide when to use aversive treatments. The more restricted the setting, the more there is a need to qualify the professional's decision making authority in respect to breaking the moral rules.

In conclusion, the answer to this fifth question in Gert's system does not yield the ready grant of authority to use aversive treatment that some in the professions desire. We do not mean to suggest that well-trained professionals who are knowledgeable and up-to-date on empirically validated treatments do not posess knowledge that makes them more qualified than others to make treatment decisions. We do, however, believe that those who know the current empirical literature will find that they do not have an empirical basis for using aversives when there is mounting evidence that nonaversive methods are equally effective in treating severe maladaptive behavior. Thus our answer to Gert's question is that the very knowledge base that creates a special relationship now indicates that intentional infliction of serious harm is not needed because, with the exception of an extremely small number of cases, treatments that involve much less harm or no harm at all are now available. There is no convincing evidence that aversive methods are the treatment of choice for severe maladaptive behavior in this population. Furthermore, consideration of this question points out the need to provide more enriched and less restricted places of treatment for this group of people so that professionals can use the full array of treatment methods in supportive contexts.

What Goods (Including Kind, Severity, Probability, Duration, and Distribution) Are Being Promoted by the Violation? Thus far Gert's morally relevant questions about a decision have been concerned with harms. In this next question, we are urged to look at what goods (e.g., benefits) may accrue apart from the prevention of harm. This morally relevant feature of ethical decision making primarily applies to questions of government action but, Gert argues (1998, p. 144), it is also relevant when the previous feature, the existence of a duty to violate a moral rule, applies.

Sometimes severe problem behaviors can be said to reduce opportunities for the person to learn or exhibit previously acquired adaptive responses. Sometimes suppression of the problem behavior leads to an apparently spontaneous improvement in other unprogrammed skills. Consequently, in some cases a behavioral intervention that decelerates problem behavior may set the stage for the emergence of previously masked skills. It may also open doors for the person by allowing him or her access to previously restricted settings and activities. In a few cases these benefits have been shown to endure (Foxx, 1990). However, the fact that some benefits may accrue from treating aberrant behavior does not imply that these ends justify any means. Once again, if these positive effects can be achieved through less harmful means, these less harmful methods must be used.

Is the Rule Being Violated Toward People Because They Have Violated a Moral Rule Unjustifiably or with Weak Justification? This question focuses on whether the person of concern has already committed an act that violates a moral rule without justification or that is weakly justified. In technical terms, this question focuses attention on the consequences of harmful behavior. It returns us again to the argument that people with severe cognitive disabilities are not considered to be moral agents. The attention to justification is a normal feature of moral discourse. For example, a person who actively plans to rob a clothing store by gathering a weapon, drawing a map, and planning a way to break and enter the store is considered to have committed a morally different act than a person who forgets to pay for items and leaves the store. We usually, however, do not attach moral significance to the challenging behavior of people with severe disabilities.

When we analyze the behavior of people with severe disabilities we try to understand the possible causes of problem behavior, but we do not typically concern ourselves with whether a behavior is morally justified. A functional analysis may allow us to understand that a particular behavior functions to terminate a situation in which a student is asked to perform a task that is not preferred. This kind of understanding renders behavior that previously may have seemed random or inexplicable to become understandable. But this kind of understanding, as important as it is, is not the same as determining whether the behavior was morally justified.

The fact that we do not consider people with severe mental retardation to be moral agents has practical significance. It is important to prevent a sense of moral outrage against a person with severe disabilities who does harm. A moralistic response to severe aberrant behavior is undesirable because there is danger that people who feel moral outrage may retaliate, punish, and assign moral condemnation. For example, it takes an unusual and highly trained person to remain calm or at least not angry in the face of dangerous behavior. Granting a person license to inflict pain or deprivation risks involving the person in escalating coercive interactions. Introducing aversives into a treatment setting risks establishing moral outrage as a common attitude among minimally trained staff members. Treatment personnels' behavioral standards can drift so that they may come to overlook or condone retaliatory behavior associated with a sense of moral outrage.

Which approach to treatment—aversive or nonaversive—is most likely to set the stage for people to act on inappropriate feelings of moral outrage? Consider, for example, an aggressive person who hurts another person with disabilities in a group home. Nonprofessional staff members, understandably, might be very angry, but well-trained staff know they cannot act on their anger when they intervene with the violent person. If they are given sanction, however, to hurt or lock up the aggressor, the likelihood that anger and moral outrage may become con-fused with technical procedure could be great. By contrast, if staff members are trained in less intrusive ways of changing behavior, their temporary feelings of anger and outrage are less likely to have a ready outlet. Energy can be directed toward the positive intervention with little risk of confusion between the interventionist's incorrect judgments and consequent feelings of moral outrage and their intervention procedures.

Is the Situation an Emergency That No Person Is Likely to Plan to Be In? This morally relevant question casts light on the issue of emergency procedures applied during positive behavioral interventions as an interim backup strategy for extremely challenging behavior. Gert (1996, 1998; Gert et al., 1997) claims that emergency conditions must be so unusual that no one is likely to anticipate and plan action in response to the situation. A hypothetical example may help to clarify this point: Say a staff person is driving to a clinic a person who experiences autism. On the way, a violent storm envelopes them. The car is caught in a flash flood and washed off the road. Because of the danger of drowning, the staff person pulls the other young man out of the car. The young man with autism becomes so frightened that he runs toward the freeway to escape. He is a large person, and when the staff person tries to stop him, the young man pushes him out of the way and resumes running. The staff person then tackles him. Unfortunately, when the young man falls, he hits his head on a stone and is injured.

It is likely that most people would not attach moral blame to the staff person's actions. The situation is so unexpected and the danger so dire that his action seems to be all that he could reasonably do to prevent greater injury. Imagine, however, that the group home is located in a region where flash floods happen predictably every spring. That is, the situation goes from a condition that is extremely unusual to one that can be anticipated and planned for. In these circumstances, the staff person or the group home administration might be held accountable for failing to prepare a staff person for such a predictable event.

In regard to positive behavioral support, people who use aversive emergency procedures that are part of a formal or an informal plan are not excused from violating a moral rule simply because the procedure has been designated as an emergency. If it can be planned for, it is not excused from moral scrutiny and possible blame. A program that uses emergency procedures that are otherwise labeled aversive is not excused from providing safeguards against the misuse of these methods. We share the concern of other commentators that emergency procedures must be carefully scrutinized so that they do not become a backdoor way for aversive procedures to reappear (Horner et al., 1990). This concern is not trivial given the fact that procedural drift, or failure to ensure treatment fidelity, has been a common concern about programs that intervene with people with challenging behavior (Schopler, 1986). In short, if an emergency procedure is one that would normally be considered aversive, it remains an aversive procedure, regardless of how it is labeled. Thus some emergency procedures are likely to require the same kinds of scrutiny (e.g., informed consent, periodic human rights review, thorough staff training and supervision, expert monitoring) in schools, places of residence, workplaces, and other community settings (Singer & Irvin, 1987).

Conclusion

In summary, we have argued that although people with severe mental retardation are not subject to normal punishment or moral blame because they may not understand that others do not want to have the moral rules violated against them, they still deserve the full protection of the moral rules. They, like other minority groups in many societies, have historically been subjected to mistreatment. They are commonly still exposed to abusive or neglectful treatment. This special vulnerability places a duty on society to be especially vigilant in protecting them from harm and in not treating them with methods that entail devaluation because they have been historically vulnerable to dehumanizing treatment. Devaluation raises the risk of further harms being inflicted. Evidence that people with the most severe behavior problems can be treated in community settings with nonaversive methods now exists, and therefore the situation in regard to use of aversives is fundamentally changed. By the widely recognized principle that it is necessary to use the least dangerous and least restrictive alternative, it is now the duty of those who work with people with severe disabilities to try these methods and eschew more painful, more restrictive, or more dehumanizing methods. Positive behavioral methods are more likely to promote collateral benefits, and they are less likely to set the stage for people to act out of misplaced moral indignation. Thus, based on an ethical analysis, we call for the creation of enriched community environments that provide nonaversive treatments and positive behavioral supports as a long-term commitment.

ABOUT THE AUTHORS

George H. S. Singer, PhD, is a professor of education at the Graduate School of Education, University of California at Santa Barbara. His current interests include research and interventions to support families of people with disabilities, instructional interventions for students with severe disabilities, ethical issues in special education, and history of mental retardation. Bernard Gert, PhD, is the Stone Professor of Intellectual and Moral Philosophy at Dartmouth College. His work focuses on his original account of moral thinking and the application of this account to medical, psychiatric, and social issues. His work has been influential in such areas as genetics research and the development of the DSM-IV as well as the field of moral philosophy. Robert L. Koegel, PhD, is the director of the Autism Research Center and Clinic at the University of California at Santa Barbara. Address: George H. S. Singer, Graduate School of Education, University of California at Santa Barbara, Santa Barbara, CA 93106.

REFERENCES

The Association for Persons with Severe Handicaps. (1991). Resolution on the cessation of intrusive interventions, 1986 revision. In L. H. Meyers, C. A. Peck, & L. Brown (Eds.), *Critical issues in the lives of people with severe disabilities.* Baltimore: Brookes.

Azrin, N. H., & Holz, W. C. (1966). Punishment. In W. K. Honig (Ed.), *Operant behavior: Areas of research and application* (pp. 380–447). New York: Appleton-Century-Crofts.

Azrin, N. H., Hutchinson, R. R., & Hake, D. F. (1967). Attack, avoidance, and escape reactions to aversive shock. *Journal of the Experimental Analysis of Behavior, 10*(2), 131–148.

Bihm, E. M., & Sigelman, C. K. (1991). Effects of behavioral treatment, treatment setting, and client IQ on person to person perception. *Basic and Applied Social Psychology, 12,* 341–355.

Bihm, E. M., Sigelman, C. K., & Westbrook, J. P. (1997). Social implications of behavioral interventions for persons with mental retardation. *American Journal on Mental Retardation, 101,* 567–578.

Blacher, J. (1994). Placement and its consequences. In J. Blacher (Ed.), *When there's no place like home: Options for children living apart from their natural families* (pp. 213–244). Baltimore: Brookes.

Blatt, B. (1973). *Souls in extremis: An anthology on victims and victimizers.* Boston: Allyn & Bacon.

Bogdan, R. C. (1986). Exhibiting mentally retarded people for amusement and profit, 1850–1940. *American Journal of Mental Deficiency, 91*(2) 120–126.

Bowman, L. G., Fisher, W. W., Thompson, R. H., & Piazza, C. C. (1997). On the relation of mands and the function of destructive behavior. *Journal of Applied Behavior Analysis, 30,* 251–265.

Carr, E. G., & Durand, V. M. (1985). Reducing behavior problems through functional communication training. *Journal of Applied Behavior Analysis, 18*(2), 111–126.

Carr, E. G., Horner, R. H., Turnbull, A. P., Marquis, J. E., Magito McLaughlin, D., McAtee, M. L., Smith, C. E., Anderson Ryan, K., Ruef, M. B., & Doolabh, A. (in press). *Positive behavior support in people with developmental disabilities: A research synthesis.*[Monograph]. Washington, DC: American Association on Mental Retardation.

Carr, E. G., Levin, L., McConnachie, G., Carlson, J. I., Kemp, D. C., and Smith, C. E. (1994). *Communication based intervention for problem behavior: A user's guide for producing positive change.* Baltimore: Brookes

Ducharme, J. M., Pontes, E., Guger, S., & Crozier, K. (1994). Errorless compliance to parental requests: II. Increasing clinical practicality through abbreviation of treatment parameters. *Behavior Therapy, 25,* 469–487.

Ducharme, J. M., Popynick, M., Pontes, E., & Steele, S. (1996). Errorless compliance to parental requests III: Group parent training with parent observational data and long-term follow-up. *Behavior Therapy, 27,* 353–372.

Dunlap, G., Kern-Dunlap, L., Clarke, S., & Robbins, F. R. (1991). Functional assessment, curricular revision, and severe behavior problems. Special issue: Social validity: Multiple perspectives. *Journal of Applied Behavior Analysis, 24,* 387–397.

Durand, V. M. (1993). Functional communication training using assistive devices: Effects on challenging behavior and affect. *Augmentative & Alternative Communication, 9,* 168–176.

Ferguson, P. M. (1994). *Abandoned to their fate: Social policy and practice toward severely retarded people in America, 1820–1920.* Philadelphia: Temple University Press.

Foxx, R. M. (1990). "Harry": A ten year follow-up of the successful treatment of a self-injurious man. *Research in Developmental Disabilities, 11*(1), 67–76.

Gert, B. (Ed.). (1996). *Morality and the new genetics: A guide for students and health care providers.* Boston: Jones and Barlett.

Gert, B. (1998). *Morality: Its nature and justification.* New York: Oxford University Press.

Gert. B., Culver, C. M., & Clouser, K. D. (1997). *Bioethics: A return to fundamentals.* New York: Oxford University Press.

Guess, D., Turnbull, H. R., & Helmstetter, E. (1990). Science, paradigms, and values: A response to Mulick. *American Journal on Mental Retardation, 95*(2), 157–163.

Hanley, G. P., Piazza, C. C., & Fisher, W. W. (1997). Noncontingent presentation of attention and alternative stimuli in the treatment of attention-maintained destructive behavior. *Journal of Applied Behavior Analysis, 30,* 229–237.

Hastings, R. P., & Remington, B. (1994). Rules of engagement: Toward an analysis of staff responses to challenging behavior. *Research in Developmental Disabilities, 15*(4), 279–298.

Horner, R. (1990). Ideology, technology, and typical community settings: Use of severe aversive stimuli. *American Journal on Mental Retardation, 95*(2), 166–168.

Horner, R. H., & Albin, R. W. (1988). Research on general-case procedures for learners with severe disabilities. Special issue: Direct instruction: A general case for teaching the general case. *Education and Treatment of Children, 11*(4), 375–388.

Horner, R., Close, D., Fredericks, H. D., O'Neill, R., Albin, R., Sprague, J., Kennedy, C., Flannery, K. B., & Tuesday-Heathfield, L. (1996). Supported living for people with profound disabilities and severe problem behaviors. In D. Lehr & F. Brown (Eds.), *People with disabilities who challenge the system* (pp. 209–242). Baltimore: Brookes.

Horner, R. H., Day, H. M., Sprague, J. R., O'Brien, M., &Heathfield, L. T. (1991). Interspersed requests: A nonaversive procedure for reducing aggression and self-injury during instruction. *Journal of Applied Behavior Analysis, 24,* 265–278.

Horner, R. H., Dunlap, G., Koegel, R. L., Carr, E. G., Sailor, W., Andersen, J., Albin, R. W., & O'Neill, R. E. (1990). Toward a technology of "nonaversive" behavioral support. *Journal of the Association for Persons with Severe Handicaps, 15*(3), 125–132.

Karsh, K. G., Repp, A. C., Dahlquist, C. M., & Munk, D. (1995). In vivo functional assessment and multi-element interventions for problem behaviors of students with disabilities in classroom settings. Special issue: Tom Haring memorial issue. *Journal of Behavioral Education, 5*(2), 189–210.

Kehle, T. J., Clark, E., Jenson, W. R., & Wampold, B. E. (1986). Effectiveness of self-observation with behavior disordered elementary school children. *School Psychology Review, 15*(2), 289–295.

Kemp, D. C., & Carr, E. G. (1995). Reduction of severe problem behavior in community employment using an hypothesis-driven multicomponent intervention approach. *Journal of the Association for Persons with Severe Handicaps, 20,* 229–247.

Kennedy, C. H., & Souza, G. (1995). Functional analysis and treatment of eye poking. *Journal of Applied Behavior Analysis, 28*(1), 27–37.

Knapczyk, D. R. (1988). Reducing aggressive behaviors in special and regular class settings by training alternative social responses. *Behavioral Disorders, 14*(1), 27–39.

Knobbe, C. A., Carey, S. P., Rhodes, L., & Horner, R. H. (1995). Benefit–cost analysis of community residential versus institutional services for adults with severe mental retardation and challenging behaviors. *American Journal on Mental Retardation, 99*(5), 533–541.

Koegel, R. L., Camarata, S. M., & Koegel, L. K. (1994). Aggression and noncompliance: Behavior modification through naturalistic language remediation. In J. L. Matson (Ed.), *Autism in children and adults: Etiology, assessment, and intervention* (pp. 165–180). Pacific Grove, CA: Brooks/Cole.

Koegel, R. L., Koegel, L. K., & Dunlap G. (1996). *Positive behavioral support: including people with difficult behavior in the community.* Baltimore: Brookes.

Lerman, D. C., Iwata, B. A., Smith, R. G., & Vollmer, T. R. (1994). Restraint fading and the development of alternative behaviour in the treatment of self-restraint and self-injury. *Journal of Intellectual Disability Research, 38*(2), 135–148.

Lucyshyn, J. M., Albin, R. W., & Nixon, C. D. (1997). Embedding comprehensive behavioral support in family ecology: An experimental, single case analysis. *Journal of Consulting and Clinical Psychology, 65,* 241–251.

Maguire, K. B., Lange, B., Scherling, M., & Grow, R. (1996). The use of rehearsal and positive reinforcement in the dental treatment of uncooperative patients with mental retardation. *Journal of Developmental and Physical Disabilities, 8,* 167-177.

Mechanic, D., & Rochefort, D. A. (1990). Deinstitutionalization: An appraisal of reform. *Annual Review of Sociology, 16,* 301–327.

Meyer, L. H., & Evans, I. M. (1989). *Nonaversive intervention for behavior problems: A manual for home and community.* Baltimore: Brookes.

Milonas v. Williams, 691 F.2d 931 (1982).

O'Brien, F. (1989). The punishment of people with developmental disabilities. In E. Cipani (Ed.), *The treatment of severe behavior disorders* (pp. 37–58). Washington, DC: American Association on Mental Retardation.

Rennie v. Klein, 452 U.S. 920 (1978).

Root, M. (1993). *Philosophy of social science: The methods, ideals, and politics of social inquiry.* Oxford, England: Blackwell.

Sanders, M. R., & Plant, K. (1989). Programming for generalization to high and low risk parenting situations in families with oppositional developmentally disabled preschoolers. *Behavior Modification, 13,* 283–305.

Saunders, R. R., Saunders, M. D., Brewer, A., & Roach, T. (1996). Reduction of self-injury in two adolescents with profound retardation by the establishment of a supported routine. *Behavioral Interventions, 11*(2), 59–86.

Schopler, E. (1986). Treatment abuse and its reduction. *Journal of Autism and Developmental Disorders, 16*(2), 99–104.

Shelton v. Tucker, 364 U.S. 479 (1960).

Sigafoos, J., Penned, D., & Versluis, J. (1996). Naturalistic assessment leading to effective treatment of self-injury in a young boy with multiple disabilities. *Education and Treatment of Children, 19*(2), 101–123.

Singer, G. H. S., & Irvin, L. K. (1987). Human rights review of intrusive behavioral treatments for students with severe handicaps. *Exceptional Children, 54*(1), 46–52.

Smith, M. D., & Coleman, D. (1986). Managing the behavior of adults with autism in the job setting. *Journal of Autism & Developmental Disorders, 16*(2), 145–154.

Steed, S. E., Bigelow, K. M., Huynen, K. B., & Lutzker, J. R. (1995). The effects of planned activities training, low-demand schedule, and reinforcement sampling on adults with developmental disabilities who exhibit challenging behaviors. *Journal of Developmental and Physical Disabilities, 7*(4), 303–316.

Thompson, T., Robinson, J., Dietrich, M., & Farris, M. (1996). Interdependence of architectural features and program variables in community residences for people with mental retardation. *American Journal on Mental Retardation, 101*(3), 315–327.

Trent, J. (1994). *Inventing the feeble mind: A history of mental retardation in the United States.* Berkeley: University of California Press.

Van Houten, R., Axelrod, S., Bailey, J. S., Favell, J. E., Foxx, R. M., Iwata, B., & Lovass, O. I. (1988). The right to effective behavioral treatment. *Journal of Applied Behavior Analysis, 21,* 381–384.

Vollmer, T. R., Iwata, B. A., Smith, R. G., & Rodgers, T. A. (1992). Reduction of multiple aberrant behaviors and concurrent development of self-care skills with differential reinforcement. *Research in Developmental Disabilities, 13,* 287–299.

Wyatt v. Stickney, 344 F.Supp. 387 (1982).

Youngberg v. Romeo, 451 U.S. 982 (1982).

Action Editor: Glen Dunlap

Positive Behavior Support:

Evolution of an Applied Science

Edward G. Carr
*State University of New York at
Stony Brook and Developmental
Disabilities Institute*

Glen Dunlap
University of South Florida

Robert H. Horner
University of Oregon

Robert L. Koegel
University of California at Santa Barbara

**Ann P. Turnbull and
Wayne Sailor**
University of Kansas

Jacki L. Anderson
California State University, Hayward

Richard W. Albin
University of Oregon

Lynn Kern Koegel
University of California at Santa Barbara

Lise Fox
University of South Florida

Abstract: Positive behavior support (PBS) is an applied science that uses educational and systems change methods (environmental redesign) to enhance quality of life and minimize problem behavior. PBS initially evolved within the field of developmental disabilities and emerged from three major sources: applied behavior analysis, the normalization/inclusion movement, and person-centered values. Although elements of PBS can be found in other approaches, its uniqueness lies in the fact that it integrates the following critical features into a cohesive whole: comprehensive lifestyle change, a lifespan perspective, ecological validity, stakeholder participation, social validity, systems change and multicomponent intervention, emphasis on prevention, flexibility in scientific practices, and multiple theoretical perspectives. These characteristics are likely to produce future evolution of PBS with respect to assessment practices, intervention strategies, training, and extension to new populations. The approach reflects a more general trend in the social sciences and education away from pathology-based models to a new positive model that stresses personal competence and environmental integrity.

The fourfold purpose of this article is to (a) provide a definition of the evolving applied science of positive behavior support (PBS); (b) describe the background sources from which PBS has emerged; (c) give an overview of the critical features that, collectively, differentiate PBS from other approaches; and (d) articulate a vision for the future of PBS.

Definition

PBS is an applied science that uses educational methods to expand an individual's behavior repertoire and systems change methods to redesign an individual's living environment to first enhance the individual's quality of life and, second, to minimize his or her problem behavior (Carr, Horner, et al., 1999; Koegel, Koegel, & Dunlap, 1996). *Positive behavior* includes all those skills that increase the likelihood of success and personal satisfaction in normative academic, work, social, recreational, community, and family settings. Support encompasses all those educational methods that can be used to teach, strengthen, and expand positive behavior and all those systems change methods that can be used to increase opportunities for the display of positive behavior. The primary goal of PBS is to help an individual change his or her lifestyle in a direction that gives all relevant stakeholders (e.g., teachers, employers, parents, friends, and the target person him- or herself) the opportunity to perceive and to enjoy an improved quality of life. An important but secondary goal of PBS is to render problem behavior irrelevant, inefficient, and ineffective by helping an individual achieve his or her goals in a socially acceptable manner, thus reducing, or eliminating altogether, episodes of problem behavior.

Background Sources Related to Philosophy and Practice

PBS emerged from three major sources: (a) applied behavior analysis, (b) the normalization/inclusion movement, and (c) person-centered values.

APPLIED BEHAVIOR ANALYSIS

Applied behavior analysis is the systematic extension of the principles of operant psychology to problems and issues of social importance (Baer, Wolf, & Risley, 1968). Were it not for the past 35 years of research in applied behavior analysis, PBS could not have come into existence. Applied behavior analysis has made two major contributions to PBS. First, it has provided one element of a conceptual framework relevant to behavior change. Second, and equally important, it has provided a number of assessment and intervention strategies.

PBS is indebted to applied behavior analysis for the notion of the three-term contingency (stimulus-response-reinforcing consequence), the concepts of setting event and establishing operations, and the notions of stimulus control, generalization, and maintenance (Chance, 1998; Miltenberger, 1997). These and other concepts have served as a critical springboard for the elaboration and development of PBS.

Functional analysis, an assessment strategy that originated in applied behavior analysis, is an experimental method for determining the motivation (purpose) of a variety of socially significant behaviors, thereby facilitating intervention planning designed to change behavior in a desirable direction (Carr, 1977; Iwata, Dorsey, Slifer, Bauman, & Richman, 1982). The detailed elaboration of empirical methodologies, emphasizing the ongoing, direct measurement of behavior, is one of the enduring contributions of applied behavior analysis.

Applied behavior analysis helped develop educational methods such as shaping, fading, chaining, prompting, and reinforcement contingencies as well as a wide array of procedures for reducing problem behavior (Sulzer-Azaroff & Mayer, 1991). PBS has not only incorporated the elements of applied behavior analysis just described; it has

also evolved beyond the parent discipline to assume its own identity. This identity is strongly influenced by the realities of conducting research and intervention in natural community settings that necessitate changes in assessment methods, intervention strategies, and the definition of what constitutes a successful outcome (Carr, 1997). These themes are an important focus of this article.

NORMALIZATION/INCLUSION MOVEMENT

Philosophically, PBS subscribes to the principle and ideal of normalization, namely, that people with disabilities should live in the same settings as others and have access to the same opportunities as others (in terms of home, school, work, recreation, and social life). The principle of normalization rests, most critically, on the idea of social role valorization, namely, that the ultimate goal is to ensure that people who are in danger of being devalued are helped to assume valued social roles, thereby increasing the likelihood that they will be accorded respect from others and will receive an equitable share of existing resources (Wolfensberger, 1983).

The normalization principle leads naturally to the principle of inclusion. During the past 150 years, the United States has been characterized by an ever-increasing emphasis on the extension of individual rights to formally disenfranchised groups, thereby facilitating the inclusion of those groups in mainstream society. The upward inclusion trajectory began with the women's suffrage/women's rights movement that occurred from 1848 through 1920 (Buechler, 1990), continued with the civil rights movement of the late 1950s and early 1960s (Solomon, 1989), and has most recently focused on the movement emphasizing the rights of individuals with disabilities that evolved during the 1970s and 1980s (Gilhool, 1989). The inclusion movement for people with disabilities continues to this day. In the educational arena, it embodies the trend toward placing students with disabilities in general education classrooms (Bricker, 1995) as opposed to segregated, special education facilities and, most significantly, changing systems so that specialized school support becomes fully integrated and coordinated with the general education program in neighborhood schools (Sailor, 1996). Inclusion in normalized settings extends beyond education. For example, in the vocational sphere, it involves replacing sheltered workshops with supported employment. Inclusion also involves replacing group homes and other congregate facilities with supported living arrangements (in which one chooses one's housemates and the neighborhood in which one wishes to live) and replacing artificial social and recreational opportunities (e.g., social groups for people with disabilities) with those emphasizing participation with people who may not have disabilities (e.g., membership in religious groups, community gyms, and social and ethnic clubs).

PERSON-CENTERED VALUES

The PBS philosophy embraces the idea that while humanistic values should not replace empiricism, these values should inform empiricism. Science tells us *how* we can change things, but values tell us *what* is worth changing (Carr, 1996). Guided by this precept, PBS represents a melding of values and technology in that strategies are judged not only with respect to efficacy (a technological criterion) but also with respect to their ability to enhance personal dignity and opportunities for choice (a values criterion). Thus, the approach eschews the use of strategies that members of the community judge to be dehumanizing or degrading (Horner et al., 1990).

Three interrelated processes serve as the vehicle for implementing the values perspective just described: person-centered planning, self-determination, and the wraparound approach.

Person-centered planning (Kincaid, 1996; O'Brien, Mount, & O'Brien, 1991; Smull & Harrison, 1992; Vandercook, York, & Forest, 1989) is a process for identifying goals and implementing intervention plans. It stands in sharp contrast to traditional program-centered planning, in which individuals with disabilities are provided with those preexisting services that a particular agency or institution has available. In person-centered planning, the specific needs and goals of the individual drive the creation of new service matrices that are carefully tailored to address the unique characteristics of the individual. Specific individual needs are considered within the context of normalization and inclusion, alluded to earlier, to produce an intervention plan that emphasizes community participation, meaningful social relationships, enhanced opportunities for choice, creation of roles that engender respect from others, and continued development of personal competencies.

Because person-centered planning seeks to empower individuals with disabilities, it almost invariably leads to a focus on the issue of *self-determination*. Self-determination is a multidimensional construct that includes but is not limited to process elements involving choice and decision making, problem solving, personal goal setting, self-management, self-instruction, and self-advocacy (Wehmeyer, 1999; Wehmeyer, Kelchner, & Richards, 1996). People with disabilities are often told what they can do, with whom they can do it, and where, when, and how they can do it. In contrast, enhancing the process of self-determination involves changing systems and redesigning environments with a view to minimizing external (often coercive) influences and making the person with disabilities the primary causal agent in his or her own life. The end point of this process can be an enhancement of lifestyle with respect to employment, living situation, friendships, and personal satisfaction (Bambara, Cole, & Koger, 1998; Wehmeyer & Schwartz, 1997). These outcomes represent

some of the defining features of PBS discussed later in this article.

Recently, discussion in the literature has concerned the rapidly accelerating convergence between the core philosophy and methods represented by PBS and a process referred to as *wraparound* (Clark & Hieneman, 1999). Wraparound incorporates person-centered planning in its emphasis on developing support plans that are needs-driven rather than service-driven. Ultimately, such planning has an impact on the entire family system. The approach is buttressed by flexible, noncategorical funding. Wraparound also incorporates a self-determination philosophy in its reliance on a support team whose membership is balanced between experts on the one hand and the individual with disabilities, family members, and advocates on the other, all of whom help identify and act on the individual's needs with a view to empowering that individual (Eber, 1997; VanDenBerg & Grealish, 1998). It reflects person-centered values in its emphasis on assessing strengths rather than deficits and problems. The approach focuses on meeting a person's needs in critical life domain areas such as family, living situation, financial, educational/vocational, social/recreational, behavioral/emotional, psychological, health, legal, cultural, and safety (VanDenBerg & Grealish, 1998). The guiding hypothesis is that if an individual's needs are met, then quality of life will improve, and problem behavior will be reduced or eliminated altogether. This hypothesis, of course, is also one of the defining assumptions behind positive behavior support.

Critical Features

The background sources related to the philosophy and practice of PBS have helped create an evolving applied science whose critical features, collectively, differentiate it from other approaches. As noted, some of these features can be found in other approaches as well and have been scattered throughout the literature of the past 15 years. However, what makes PBS unique is its emphasis on integrating, into a cohesive whole, the nine characteristics described next.

COMPREHENSIVE LIFESTYLE CHANGE AND QUALITY OF LIFE

The sine qua non of PBS is its focus on assisting individuals to achieve comprehensive lifestyle change with a view to improving quality of life not only for persons with disabilities but also for those who support them. When applied to larger organizational units such as schools (Sugai et al., 2000), the focus of PBS is on assisting the unit to achieve broad changes that facilitate more positive outcomes for all participants. In this light, the reduction of challenging behaviors per se is viewed as an important secondary goal that is of value principally because of its facilitative effect on producing meaningful lifestyle and cultural changes that are stable and enduring.

A truly comprehensive approach to lifestyle change addresses the multiple dimensions that define quality of life (Hughes, Hwang, Kim, Eisenman, & Killian, 1995), which include improvements in social relationships (e.g., friendship formation), personal satisfaction (e.g., self-confidence, happiness), employment (e.g., productivity, job prestige, good job match), self-determination (e.g., personal control, choice of living arrangements, independence), recreation and leisure (e.g., adequate opportunities, good quality of activities), community adjustment (e.g., domestic skills, survival skills), and community integration (e.g., mobility, opportunities for participation in community activities, school inclusion). Although not every intervention attempted need be comprehensive, the cumulative impact of many interventions over time should be.

In sum, the definition of outcome success now emphasizes improvements in family life, jobs, community inclusion, supported living, expanding social relationships, and personal satisfaction and de-emphasizes the focus on problem behavior (Risley, 1996; Ruef, Turnbull, Turnbull, & Poston, 1999; Turnbull & Ruef, 1997). The important units of analysis concern the person's daily routines, schedules, and social interactions. Problem behavior is of note to the extent that it interferes with achieving positive results with respect to these molar variables. However, the primary intervention strategy involves rearranging the environment to enhance lifestyle and improve quality of life rather than operating directly on reducing problem behavior per se.

LIFE SPAN PERSPECTIVE

Comprehensive lifestyle change does not typically occur within a compressed time frame. Therefore, another critical feature of PBS is that it has a life span perspective. Efforts to achieve meaningful change often take years (Nickels, 1996; Turnbull & Turnbull, 1999). Successfully assisting an individual to make transitions from preschool to elementary and high school, and then to the workplace and supported living, requires a life span perspective, which views intervention as a never-ending systemic process that evolves as different challenges arise during different stages of life (Turnbull, 1988; Vandercook et al., 1989). When one follows an individual over many years in changing life circumstances, deficient environments and deficient adaptive skills will almost certainly continue to emerge and be identified. Therefore, new PBS strategies may have to be added and old ones modified. With few exceptions, most research published to date has been characterized by short-term approaches (Carr, Horner, et al., 1999). Further, maintenance has often been defined as durable success following inter-

vention cessation (Carr et al., 1990). Yet, as noted, in a truly comprehensive PBS approach, intervention never ends and follow-up is measured in decades, not months. In sum, a life span perspective has become the new standard for maintenance, a fact that is evident in person-centered planning approaches that address the individual's needs and challenges over a period of many years (Kincaid, 1996; Turnbull & Turnbull, 1999; Vandercook et al., 1989).

The focus on comprehensive lifestyle change and life span perspective leads to three additional important features of PBS: ecological validity, stakeholder participation, and social validity.

ECOLOGICAL VALIDITY

Much previous research has focused on the microanalysis of cause-and-effect processes in analog situations, that is, on issues related to internal validity. Although it is true that there is no viable science without internal validity, it is equally true that there is no viable practice without external validity. PBS is not intended to be a laboratory-based demonstration or analog but, rather, a strategy for dealing with quality-of-life issues in natural community contexts. Although there is a continuing emphasis on issues related to internal validity, the main focus of the PBS approach concerns how applicable the science is to real-life settings, in other words, its ecological validity (Dunlap, Fox, Vaughn, Bucy, & Clarke, 1997; Meyer & Evans, 1993).

Internal validity is best demonstrated in situations in which one is able to enhance experimental control. Frequently, these situations are characterized by the involvement of atypical intervention agents such as researchers and psychologists (i.e., intervention agents who would not normally be expected to be the primary support people in community settings), working in atypical settings such as clinics and institutions, carrying out brief intervention sessions that often last only 10 to 15 minutes, in highly circumscribed venues (e.g., only one situation out of the many that may be associated with behavior challenges; Carr, Horner, et al., 1999). However, this approach is inconsistent with the PBS emphasis on normalization and inclusion in natural community contexts. Therefore, PBS entails balancing a concern with internal validity with the realities of conducting research and practice in complex naturalistic contexts in order to achieve ecological validity as well. Thus, the evolution of PBS is toward an approach that involves typical intervention agents (e.g., parents, teachers, job coaches) supporting individuals in typical settings (e.g., the home, the neighborhood, the school, the workplace) for protracted periods of time in all relevant venues (and not just those that lend themselves to good experimental control). This constellation of features defines the ecological validity dimension of PBS.

STAKEHOLDER PARTICIPATION

Traditionally, the field has embraced models of assessment and intervention that have been expert-driven rather than consumer-driven. Thus, behavior analysts, for example, have functioned as experts, defining the issues, selecting and designing interventions, and enlisting the aid of consumers (e.g., parents and teachers) in implementing strategies. The PBS approach, in contrast, has emphasized that consumers are not helpers but, rather, function as active participants and collaborators with professionals in a process of reciprocal information exchange. All members of the support team who are relevant stakeholders (e.g., parents, siblings, neighbors, teachers, job coaches, friends, roommates, and the person with disabilities) participate as partners to build the vision, methods, and success criteria pertinent to defining quality of life for everyone concerned.

This type of collaboration between professionals, researchers, and stakeholders has been called for by policymakers for many years (Lloyd, Weintraub, & Safer, 1997; Malouf & Schiller, 1995). Recently, such thinking has led to an increased emphasis on the notion of partnerships (Meyer, Park, Grenot-Scheyer, Schwartz, & Harry, 1998; Turnbull, Friesen, & Ramirez, 1998) and has produced a model that views researchers, professionals, and stakeholders as collaborators (Browder, 1997; Lawson & Sailor, in press; Nietupski, Hamre-Nietupski, Curtin, & Shrikanth, 1997; Reichle, 1997; Sailor, in press). Thus, the detailed knowledge that families have of the strengths, needs, and challenges of the person with disabilities becomes the cornerstone for collaborative planning, which yields a program of comprehensive family support (Albin, Lucyshyn, Horner, & Flannery, 1996; Lucyshyn, Albin, & Nixon, 1997; Turnbull & Turnbull, 1999; Vaughn, Dunlap, Fox, Clarke, & Bucy, 1997). Likewise, this model has been extended to other stakeholders such as job coaches and other employees at worksites (Park, Gonsier-Gerdin, Hoffman, Whaley, & Yount, 1998) as well as teachers and administrators in neighborhood schools (Salisbury, Wilson, & Palombaro, 1998).

In sum, stakeholders have evolved from a passive role in which they are instructed by an expert, to an active role in which they (a) provide valuable qualitative perspectives for assessment purposes; (b) determine whether proposed intervention strategies are relevant for all the challenging situations that need to be dealt with; (c) evaluate whether the approach taken is practical in that it meshes well (Albin et al., 1996) with the values, needs, and organizational structures related to the individual with disabilities and his or her support network; and (d) define what outcomes are likely to improve the general quality of life and enhance the individual's personal satisfaction. An egalitarian approach toward stakeholder participation has become a normative feature of PBS.

SOCIAL VALIDITY

Long ago, applied behavior analysts rejected the idea that interventions ought to be evaluated solely in terms of their objective effectiveness (Wolf, 1978). This notion has been taken up by PBS practitioners and amplified (Carr, Horner, et al., 1999). Specifically, there is an understanding that interventions should also be evaluated in terms of their practicality (e.g., Can typical support people carry out the strategy?), their desirability (e.g., Do typical support people perceive the interventions to be worthy of implementation?), their goodness of fit (e.g., Do stakeholders agree that the strategies are appropriate for the specific context in which they are to be implemented?), their subjective effectiveness with respect to problem behavior (e.g., Do the relevant stakeholders perceive that the problem behavior has been reduced to an acceptable level?), and their subjective effectiveness with respect to quality of life (e.g., Do relevant stakeholders perceive the strategies implemented to have made a meaningful difference in the lifestyle of the individual involved in terms of increasing opportunities to live, work, go to school, recreate, and socialize with typical peers and significant others in typical community settings?).

A synthesis of the experimental literature published between 1985 and 1996 (Carr, Horner, et al., 1999) indicated that these criteria for social validity have not been a prime focus for applied behavior analysis investigators until recently. Not surprisingly, then, there has been, among those committed to a PBS approach, a growing movement emphasizing the centrality of social validity in the design and implementation of service provision and remediation efforts (Dennis, Williams, Giangreco, & Cloninger, 1993; Hughes et al., 1995; Risley, 1996; Sands, Kozleski, & Goodwin, 1991; Schalock, 1990, 1996; Turnbull & Turnbull, 1999). The movement toward social validity is, of course, one logical consequence of the PBS focus on lifestyle change, life span perspective, ecological validity, and stakeholder participation already discussed.

SYSTEMS CHANGE AND MULTICOMPONENT INTERVENTION

One of the central messages of PBS is that, in providing support, we should focus our efforts on fixing problem contexts, not problem behavior. Behavior change is not simply the result of applying specific techniques to specific challenges. The best technology will fail if it is applied in an uncooperative or disorganized context. This principle has made efforts at systems change one of the defining features of PBS.

Meaningful change is possible only if systems are restructured in a manner that enables change to occur and be sustained. It is necessary that stakeholders share a common vision, that support persons be adequately trained, that incentives be in place to motivate people to alter their approach to problem solving, that resources (temporal, physical, and human) be made available to facilitate change, and that an action plan be created that defines roles, responsibilities, monitoring, and methods to be used to correct new or ongoing deficiencies (Knoster, Villa, & Thousand, 2000).

A systemic perspective rejects the notion that practitioner effectiveness depends solely on identifying a key critical intervention that can turn the tide. For decades, applied behavior analysts have prided themselves on the publication of many successful research demonstrations that involve the application of single interventions. These demonstrations have made for great science but ineffective practice. A comprehensive approach involving multicomponent intervention is necessary to change the many facets of an individual's living context that are problematic (Horner & Carr, 1997). This conclusion was rendered inevitable by the incontrovertible evidence provided by applied behavior analysis that, for any given individual, behavior challenges are likely to be dependent on multiple functional and structural variables whose influence demands a multidimensional remediation strategy built on the assessment information (Bambara & Knoster, 1998; Carr, Carlson, Langdon, Magito McLaughlin, & Yarbrough, 1998; O'Neill et al., 1997). This multicomponent, systems change perspective is very much in evidence throughout the PBS field, whether it be in the home (Clarke, Dunlap, & Vaughn, 1999; Koegel, Koegel, Kellegrew, & Mullen, 1996; Turnbull & Turnbull, 1999), school (Sailor, 1996), workplace (Kemp & Carr, 1995), or community (Anderson, Russo, Dunlap, & Albin, 1996; Carr & Carlson, 1993; Carr, Levin, et al., 1999).

EMPHASIS ON PREVENTION

The PBS approach has helped give birth to what is, arguably, one of the greatest paradoxes in the field of developmental disabilities, namely, the notion that the best time to intervene on problem behavior is when the behavior is not occurring. Intervention takes place in the absence of problem behavior so that such behavior can be prevented from occurring again. The proactive nature of PBS stands in sharp contrast to traditional approaches, which have emphasized the use of aversive procedures that address problem behaviors with reactive, crisis-driven strategies (Carr, Robinson, & Palumbo, 1990).

The political context for the emphasis on prevention that characterizes PBS comes from legislation such as the Individuals with Disabilities Act (IDEA; 1997), which makes prevention and early intervention high priorities for professionals who deal with serious behavior challenges. This issue is part of a larger debate concerning how best to con-

ceptualize approaches to prevention (Albee, 1996, 1998). The methodological context for the emphasis on prevention is inherent in the definition of PBS given at the beginning of this article, namely, that the approach focuses on skill building and environmental design as the two vehicles for producing desirable change.

The proactive skill-building aspect of PBS is seen, for example, in strategies that seek to prevent the recurrence of problem behavior by strengthening communicative competence (e.g., Carr & Durand, 1985) and self-management skills (e.g., Gardner, Cole, Berry, & Nowinski, 1983; Koegel, Koegel, Hurley, & Frea, 1992). The proactive environmental design aspect of PBS is seen, for example, in strategies that seek to prevent the recurrence of problem behavior by enhancing opportunities for choice making (e.g., Dunlap et al., 1994), modifying the setting events that alter the valence of reinforcers for significant behaviors (e.g., Horner, Day, & Day, 1997), and restructuring curricula (e.g., Dunlap, Kern-Dunlap, Clarke, & Robbins, 1991). Indeed, the focus on environmental design as a proactive strategy follows logically from the systems change aspect of PBS discussed earlier. Specifically, staff development, provision of incentives, resource allocation, and construction of action plans represent systemic variables whose design and implementation take place not at the moment that problem behavior is occurring but rather in a coordinated proactive fashion intended to minimize the likelihood of future episodes of problem behavior.

FLEXIBILITY WITH RESPECT TO SCIENTIFIC PRACTICES

The main tradition from which PBS emerged is applied behavior analysis. That tradition has embraced the idea that the gold standard for research methodology is the experiment and that the data of greatest import are those derived from direct observation (Baer, Wolf, & Risley, 1987). Yet, that same tradition has spawned thoughtful discussion as to whether the demonstration of causality through repeated manipulation of independent variables across time is the only acceptable methodology, or whether methods involving correlational analyses, naturalistic observations, and case studies might also produce useful and important information (Risley, 1999). Likewise, there has been a call for researchers to adopt greater flexibility in their definition of what constitutes acceptable data, moving the discussion beyond the parameters of direct observation to consider the acceptability of qualitative data, ratings, interviews, questionnaires, logs, and self-report (Schwartz & Olswang, 1996).

By adhering rigidly to laboratory-based criteria of excellence, we are in danger of putting ourselves in the position of learning more and more about less and less. That is, we run the risk of addressing only those topics that readily lend themselves to our preferred investigational techniques, ignoring other topics that prove too messy or ambiguous (Kunkel, 1987; Risley, 1999). As we move our research from more controlled situations such as laboratories, clinics, and institutional settings to less controlled situations such as community-based schools, homes, and job sites, it becomes apparent that both pragmatic and validity concerns demand flexibility in scientific practices.

One pragmatic concern involves the issue of assessment. Exemplary assessment has often been equated with functional analysis, an approach involving the experimental manipulation of putatively critical variables with a view to identifying those factors responsible for controlling the behaviors of interest. Although functional analysis has proven to be a powerful and elegant tool for demonstrating causal relationships, it has most often been used by atypical intervention agents (e.g., researchers) operating in atypical settings (e.g., institutions) in highly circumscribed venues over short periods of time (Carr, Horner, et al., 1999). A recent survey of 300 practitioners noted that more informal assessment procedures, including many that are not based on direct observation, were the methods of choice; functional analysis was used by only a small minority of the study sample (Desrochers, Hile, & Williams-Moseley, 1997). Practitioners felt that an inability to control complex naturalistic variables and insufficient time to conduct elaborate assessments made functional analysis an impractical and, therefore, seldom used method in community settings. The lack of feasibility is particularly striking when one considers that the comprehensive assessment of problem behavior for even a few individuals living in the community often identifies hundreds of situations associated with diverse behavior challenges (Carr et al., 1994). A detailed functional analysis of all relevant situations would, in this case, be not just daunting but impossible. Further, conducting even a small number of functional analyses in the community is often not possible because of ethical considerations. For example, one could not manipulate variables in a supermarket in order to study the frequency with which an individual destroys property and attacks other customers.

Validity concerns arise from the issue of intervention. From a purely scientific perspective, the ideal intervention experiment is one in which a single variable is manipulated and all others are held constant. This methodology allows one to ascribe causality to the single variable being manipulated. In contrast, if several variables were to be manipulated at the same time, the experiment would be inconclusive due to confounds. There is in fact a wealth of literature demonstrating the causal impact of single interventions. While such information is useful in the initial development of a science, an exclusive reliance on pure experimentation impedes application. Specifically, in the community, one must deal with multiple interacting variables embedded in complex systems. That is why PBS intervention is almost always multicomponent in nature

(e.g., Carr, Horner, et al., 1999; Horner et al., 1996; Vaughn et al., 1997). The irony is that if one adheres strictly to laboratory criteria of excellence, then what is considered to be optimal practice (multicomponent intervention) is bad science (a confounded demonstration); if one adheres strictly to pragmatic criteria of excellence, then what is considered optimal science (single variable intervention) is bad practice. A rational approach to this dilemma is to recognize that both laboratory and pragmatic criteria must be part of a truly applied science. Scientific practices must be varied and flexible enough to accommodate the analysis of pragmatic effectiveness (by studying multicomponent interventions) and the analysis of causal mechanisms and basic processes (through single variable experimentation or studies that systematically dismantle intervention packages into their components).

In sum, PBS has evolved into a science that respects the realities of conducting research in complex community settings while incorporating the fruits of research conducted within the tradition represented by formal experimentation. For this reason, PBS research methodology is flexible in encouraging correlational analyses, naturalistic observations, and case studies in addition to experiments. Likewise, the PBS definition of acceptable data includes qualitative measures, ratings, interviews, questionnaires, logs, and self-report in addition to direct observation. The type of data may vary but the expectation remains that a systematic data source will be used to evaluate and guide intervention.

MULTIPLE THEORETICAL PERSPECTIVES

As noted earlier, applied behavior analysis and its accompanying operant conceptual framework have played a major role in shaping the development of PBS. However, as PBS has continued to evolve, it has drawn, increasingly, on other theoretical perspectives as well.

The strongly interrelated fields of systems analysis, ecological psychology, environmental psychology, and community psychology have made significant contributions to PBS. Strikingly, at a conceptual level, the ecological paradigm is isomorphic with PBS in several respects: It deals with units larger than the individual (i.e., systems), it emphasizes natural settings rather than institutions or clinics as being most appropriate for carrying out research and intervention studies (i.e., it emphasizes ecological validity), and it views research as comprising an ongoing collaboration between scientists and stakeholders. The confluence of these ideas has led to three theoretical principles that have long characterized community psychology and the related fields referred to earlier (Levine & Perkins, 1987), principles that have now become dominant motifs within PBS as well.

The first principle embodies the idea that since people in community settings are interdependent, clinically significant change occurs in social systems and not just in individuals. This notion, a major theme in ecological systems theory (Bronfenbrenner, 1989), manifests itself in PBS with the idea that the focus of intervention must be on changing problem context, not problem behavior. We must move beyond blaming the victim (e.g., certain people have problems that must be "treated") to holding societal contexts accountable (e.g., certain people live in deficient environments that must be redesigned). The second principle embodies the idea that producing change is not simply a matter of implementing specific techniques; rather, change involves the reallocation of resources such as time, money, and political power. Thus, administrative support, interagency collaboration, funding mechanisms, and commonality of mission philosophy are critical variables in the change equation (Dunlap et al., 2000; Knoster et al., 2000; Sailor, 1996). The third principle embodies the idea that an individual's behavior, appropriate or inappropriate, is the result of a continuous process of adaptation reflecting the interface between competence (a property of individuals) and context (a property of environments). Therefore, a successful intervention must modulate the goodness of fit between competence and context (see Albin et al., 1996, for a recent formulation of this idea). This goal is achievable by promoting skill development (a competence variable) in an integrated fashion with environmental redesign (a context variable). Exemplary intervention must involve multicomponent systems change, which, as noted earlier, constitutes the heart of PBS.

Another important aspect of systems change theory relates to the fact that many societies, including our own, are multicultural in nature. Family systems, for example, are characterized by considerable cultural heterogeneity. Effectiveness of community-based research and services therefore depends on knowledge of this heterogeneity. Thus, adherents of PBS have welcomed and are influenced by the theoretical perspectives inherent in cultural psychology, anthropology, and sociology. Cultural variables can have a profound influence on values, communication, interpersonal behavior, and social perception (Matsumoto, 1996). If one is not knowledgeable about these influences and sensitive to them, then the most well-intentioned and best-designed interventions may nonetheless fail. Although no culture is totally homogeneous with respect to goals, every culture deems certain goals to be normative and desirable. In illustration, for many who work with families, a common goal is to make a child autonomous and self-reliant. This choice of goals reflects the premium that Western cultures place on independence. In contrast, many Asian cultures (e.g., the Japanese culture) place a premium on interdependence, that is, on belongingness, dependency, and reciprocity (Weisz, Rothbaum, & Blackburn, 1984); an emphasis on autonomy and self-reliance per se is seen as a sign of selfishness and immaturity. Also, in Western culture, seeking help for social and emotional problems is seen as rational and constructive, whereas in traditional Chinese culture, it is seen as shameful; only when problems are somaticized (e.g., "his strange behavior reflects an underlying 'liver' problem") is it permissible to seek help (Kleinman, 1980). These two examples make clear that cultural insensitivity on the part of intervention agents would likely produce noncompliance or outright avoidance if Asian families were involved. For this reason, attention must be paid to assessing, from a cultural perspective, differences pertaining to family structure and childrearing practices, family perceptions and attitudes, and language and communication styles (Lynch, 1998). In sum, the systemic, community-based, multicultural aspects of PBS lead naturally to a consideration of multiple theoretical perspectives that, in turn, guide the continued evolution of this approach.

A Vision of the Future

The continued evolution of PBS along the lines that we have discussed is likely to lead to substantive changes in at least four areas: (a) assessment practices, (b) intervention strategies, (c) training, and (d) extension to new populations.

ASSESSMENT PRACTICES

The focus on quality-of-life issues, life span perspectives, stakeholder participation, and systems change necessitates a greater reliance on alternative approaches to assessment. The traditional approach to assessment has tended to be microanalytic in nature, emphasizing the analysis of the effects of specific antecedent and consequent stimuli on discrete topographies of behavior. Current developments within PBS suggest that although the microanalytic approach will be retained, a greater emphasis will be placed on an emerging macroanalytic approach that relies on focus groups, expansion of the unit of analysis, evolution of user-friendly measures, and delineation of molar dependent variables.

Since PBS is community based, the relevant stakeholder constituency is diverse and includes not only practitioners but also administrators, policymakers, families, friends, individuals with disabilities, and teachers. Therefore, focus groups and other sources of multiperspective, narrative-discursive data are needed to assess and identify the full array of stakeholder priorities, the structural and organizational barriers to success, feasibility of proposed solutions, and effective packaging of change strategies (Ruef et al., 1999). This systemic approach to assessment moves the field beyond a sole consideration of discrete behaviors to a consideration of what interested parties have to say about their vision and values, incentives for problem solving, resource allocation, and the infrastructure of available supports (Knoster et al., 2000). Discursive-narrative methodologies are inherent in both the personal futures planning and wraparound approaches discussed earlier (e.g., Kincaid, 1996; Eber, 1997), and it is likely that these approaches to the assessment of personal as well as systemic needs will become preferred and more prevalent in the future.

The systems orientation of PBS is another factor leading to changes in assessment practices. Specifically, the traditional emphasis on the behavior of individuals as the unit of analysis is being broadened to include larger units. This movement reflects greater sensitivity to issues that have long been the concern of professionals in the fields of school and educational psychology. For example, in schools, adherents of PBS have expanded the unit of analysis to capture group behavior at the level of entire classrooms and, even further, at the level of entire buildings (Lewis & Sugai, 1999; Sugai et al., 2000; Warren et al., in press). In taking PBS "to scale," researchers and practitioners are attempting to address the practical realities of carrying out assessment at a systemwide level, often involving hundreds, and sometimes thousands, of children. In this context, it is not possible to study behavior, one child at a time, using traditional assessment strategies. Thus, the development of assessment tools that measure changes in these expanded units of analysis is an important future direction for the field.

Because PBS involves the participation of diverse stakeholders who must function in complex community systems, traditional assessments involving the use of formal functional analysis are generally not workable. We articulated this point earlier, in the discussion of flexibility in scientific practices, and noted the ever-increasing reliance of practitioners on qualitative measures, ratings, interviews, questionnaires, and the like. An important issue for the future of PBS is whether these diverse assessment measures have a degree of validity that permits effective intervention planning. Some recent data (Yarbrough & Carr, 2000) suggested that identifying the parameters within which user-friendly assessments, such as those based on interviews, for example, show convergent validity with more formal assessments, such as those based on functional analysis, is a complicated issue that the field will have to address. We need to develop a set of decision rules and procedures for determining when user-friendly, pragmatic assessment tools are valid and can therefore be employed by practitioners who do not have the time, the control, or perhaps even the training to carry out experimental (functional) analyses. PBS will only reach its full potential when new assessment tools are developed that do not depend on the availability of a small group of highly trained and often unavailable experts.

Finally, the emphasis of PBS on quality-of-life issues and life span perspectives requires that the scope of assessment be expanded to include molar dependent variables (Carr et al., 1998). Traditionally, the main focus has been on causal analyses involving the influence of discrete antecedent and consequent stimuli on well-defined, temporally circumscribed units of behavior. The PBS focus not only includes this type of analysis but also includes assessments related to the influence of broad contextual variables operating over protracted periods of time. Therefore, molar assessments must be developed to capture the effects of systemic changes related to friendship networks (e.g., sociometric analysis), vocational placement (e.g., work productivity, work satisfaction), living environments (e.g., autonomy, self-determination), educational arrangements (e.g., social acceptance, self-esteem, academic competence), and leisure situations (e.g., consumer satisfaction). The use of assessment strategies related to molar dependent variables is essential if we are to fully understand the impact of systems changes on quality of life over time.

In sum, the future is likely to see changes with respect to the who, where, how, and what of assessment: who (e.g., focus groups and key stakeholders, not just experts, will play an increasing role), where (e.g., schoolwide settings, not just individual tutorial situations), how (e.g., user-friendly indirect assessments, not just formal experimental analyses), and what (e.g., sociometric analysis, not just discrete social behaviors).

INTERVENTION STRATEGIES

Because intervention is linked directly to assessment within the PBS framework, there will also be changes in the who, where, what, and when of intervention. With respect to "who," for more than three decades, researchers, psychologists, and other experts have implemented intervention. Yet, the PBS emphasis on ecological validity necessitates a movement toward natural supports in the community, that is, typical intervention agents. Although the recent increase in the involvement of parents and teachers represents a constructive step in this direction, it is not enough. Most people have a broad network of social supports that includes siblings, friends, grandparents, neighbors, and others whose involvement in intervention has rarely been tapped. The participation of this extended circle of people as active intervention agents in socially supportive roles is likely to become an important feature of PBS.

With respect to "where," the traditional approach has emphasized laboratory, clinic, and segregated institutional settings. Again, however, ecological validity concerns are pressing the field of PBS to carry out interventions in naturalistic, community-based settings. Home, school, and workplace represent a good beginning, but they constitute only a small portion of the universe of possibilities. The future will see the extension of this approach to settings that most of us experience, including restaurants, movie theaters, sports venues, churches and synagogues, social clubs, and vacation places. Expanding the variety and breadth of intervention agents and settings will be a sign that PBS has matured to the highest level of ecological validity.

The focus on comprehensive lifestyle change and quality-of-life issues will drive the field toward a reconceptualization of the "what" of intervention. Thus, in the past, the question has often been, "What intervention (singular) is most appropriate for dealing with a particular problem?" It has become clear, however, that the multidimensional nature of quality of life requires, in turn, a multicomponent (plural) approach to intervention. Further, the components are not necessarily discrete intervention procedures in the traditional sense. For example, extinction (a discrete procedure) may be one component; however, environmental redesign, including architectural variables, social systems, sequences of daily routines, respite care, resource allocation, and development of support networks, may also be involved even though they are not the type of discrete intervention variables that have dominated the field for many years. There will be a greater concentration of effort designed to identify these molar variables and create decision rules regarding how best to combine multiple components into a comprehensive package that addresses the needs of people with disabilities as well as their families and friends.

The PBS focus on prevention will also influence the "when" of intervention. As noted, PBS is an approach in which intervention and support strategies are implemented in a proactive fashion with a view to reducing future occurrences of behavior challenges. Recently, for example, functional communication training has been used with young children to prevent the emergence of serious problem behavior (Reeve & Carr, 2000). There is a clear need to extend this type of demonstration. Specifically, we should be able to identify, early on, the multiple deficiencies in skills and environments that eventually lead to problem behavior and result in a poor quality of life. When these risk factors are better explicated, we will be in a position to teach carefully selected and delineated skills as well as to design living environments proactively before any behavior challenges manifest themselves. In this manner, the direction of the field will be changed from its traditional focus on problems and difficulties to a new positive focus on building on an individual's strengths and creating living environments that support a high quality of life.

TRAINING

Several critical features of the PBS approach ensure that there will be innovations in the who, where, and what of training. There is likely to be continued movement away from an emphasis on simply training experts in university settings who subsequently go out into the field to instruct others. Instead, there will be a movement toward training interprofessional teams, often including parents, that re-

flects the PBS focus on stakeholder participation. At one level, this trend will involve a collaborative relationship between expert professionals on the one hand and parents, teachers, residential and work support staff, and childcare providers on the other. Collaboration will occur with respect to case formulation, goal setting, intervention selection, and ongoing programmatic change made within a collegial and egalitarian model of operation that would eventually extend to administrative staff and, ultimately, lead to interagency collaboration (Anderson et al., 1996). Thus, training will be viewed not simply as a transfer of strategic information from experts to providers but rather as a process of mutual education involving capacity building that ultimately results in systems change as opposed to narrowly defined changes for a particular individual.

The future should see a de-emphasis on lecture formats carried out within the confines of university settings and formal workshops, and a greater emphasis on on-site education. That is, the PBS emphasis on ecological validity will require that the training of professionals, families, and direct service providers take place in typical settings in neighborhood schools, work sites, community residences, and other locations in the community (e.g., restaurants, shopping malls, theaters). Meaningful training involves in vivo problem solving within real-life contexts occurring for time durations sufficient to produce trainee competence (Anderson et al., 1996). It is likely that these situational training innovations will be greatly enhanced by creative use of new information technologies, including CD-ROM and online, Web-based instructional methods (Sailor et al., in press).

Because of the critical PBS feature of systems change, it will no longer be sufficient to train people to master a laundry list of specific intervention techniques (e.g., extinction, prompting, reinforcement); rather, people will also need to know how to deal with the systems in which intervention strategies are embedded and how to integrate technology within broader support infrastructures and networks. Thus, the content of training will also have to include knowledge of administrative issues, funding mechanisms, mission and philosophies, and interagency collaboration (Dunlap et al., 2000).

EXTENSION TO NEW POPULATIONS

PBS has made many valuable contributions to improving the quality of life of people with developmental disabilities. It is not surprising, therefore, that there is a mistaken perception that the approach is applicable primarily to this population. In fact, there is growing evidence that PBS is undergoing a rapid extension to other populations as well. Already, the application of PBS has expanded to include people with traumatic brain injury (Singer, Glang, & Williams, 1996; Ylvisaker & Feeney, 1998), typically developing children with school discipline problems (Burke &

Burke, 1999; Lewis & Sugai, 1999; Sugai et al., 2000; Warren et al., in press), and children and youth with emotional and behavioral disorders (Dunlap & Childs, 1996; Dunlap, Clarke, & Steiner, 1999; Kern, Childs, Dunlap, Clarke, & Falk, 1994). The extension of PBS represents part of a larger movement in the social sciences and education away from traditional models that have emphasized pathology and toward a new positive model that emphasizes "a science of positive subjective experience, positive individual traits, and positive institutions" (Seligman & Csikszentmihalyi, 2000b, p. 5) with a view to improving quality of life and preventing behavior problems (Seligman & Csikszentmihalyi, 2000a).

ABOUT THE AUTHORS

Edward G. Carr, PhD, is leading professor in the Department of Psychology at the State University of New York at Stony Brook. His research interests include community integration, systems change, family support, and problem behavior. Glen Dunlap, PhD, is a professor of child and family studies and special education at the University of South Florida. Glen also serves as director of the Division of Applied Research and Educational Support, an organization composed of research, training, and demonstration projects. Glen's primary interests are in positive behavior support, early intervention, and family support. Robert H. Horner, PhD, is a professor of special education in the College of Education at the University of Oregon. His primary research interests are applied behavior analysis, positive behavior support, severe disabilities, functional behavioral assessment, and instructional technology. Robert L. Koegel, PhD, is director of the Autism Research and Training Center, professor in the Counseling/Clinical/School Psychology program and professor in special education, disabilities, and risk studies at the University of California, Santa Barbara. Ann P. Turnbull, EdD, is the co-director of the Beach Center and professor in the Department of Special Education at The University of Kansas. Her major research area focuses on the conceptualization and measurement of family quality-of-life outcomes. Wayne Sailor, PhD, is a professor in the Department of Special Education at the University of Kansas, a senior scientist with the Beach Center on Disability, Life Span Institute, University of Kansas, and a courtesy professor with the Department of Human Development and Family Life, University of Kansas. His interests are full integration of students with severe disabilities through school restructuring processes and service integration strategies for health, social, and educational services for all children at the school site. Jacki L. Anderson, PhD, is a professor of special education in the Department of Educational Psychology at California State University at Hayward and coordinator of credential and master's degree programs in the area of moderate/severe disabilities. She is also co-training coordinator of the Rehabilitation Research and Training Center on Positive Behavioral Support. Her interests include inclusion, positive behavioral supports, and effective instruction for individuals with moderate/severe disabilities. Richard W. Albin, PhD, is a senior research associate/associate professor in the special education area of the College of Education at the University of Oregon. His professional interests include positive behavior support, developmental disabilities, and applied research methods. Lynn Kern Koegel, PhD, is clinic director of the Autism Research and Training Center at the Gevirtz Graduate School of Education, University of California, Santa Barbara. Lise Fox, PhD, is an associate professor in the Department of Child and Family Studies of the Louis de la Parte Florida Mental Health Institute at the University of South Florida. Her publications and research interests include supporting young children with disabilities and challenging behavior in developmentally appropriate environments, positive behavior support, and family support. Address: Edward Carr, Dept. of Psychology, State University of New York, Stony Brook, NY 11794-2500.

AUTHORS' NOTE

Preparation of this article was supported by Cooperative Agreement H133B98005 from the National Institute on Disabilities and Rehabilitation Research, Rehabilitation Research and Training Center on Positive Behavioral Support.

REFERENCES

Albee, G. W. (1996). Revolutions and counterrevolutions in prevention. *American Psychologist, 51*, 1130–1133.

Albee, G. W. (1998). The politics of primary prevention. *The Journal of Primary Prevention, 19*, 117–127.

Albin, R. W., Lucyshyn, J. M., Horner, R. H., & Flannery, K. B. (1996). Contextual fit for behavior support plans. In L. K. Koegel, R. L. Koegel, & G. Dunlap (Eds.), *Positive behavioral support* (pp. 81–98). Baltimore: Brookes.

Anderson, J. L., Russo, A., Dunlap, G., & Albin, R. W. (1996). A team training model for building the capacity to provide positive behavior supports in inclusive settings. In L. K. Koegel, R. L. Koegel, & G. Dunlap (Eds.), *Positive behavioral support* (pp. 467–490). Baltimore: Brookes.

Baer, D. M., Wolf, M. M., & Risley, T. R. (1968). Some current dimensions of applied behavior analysis. *Journal of Applied Behavior Analysis, 1*, 91–97.

Baer, D. M., Wolf, M. M., & Risley, T. R. (1987). Some still-current dimensions of applied behavior analysis. *Journal of Applied Behavior Analysis, 20*, 313–327.

Bambara, L., & Knoster, T. (1998). Designing positive behavior support plans. *Innovations* (No. 13). Washington, DC: American Association on Mental Retardation.

Bambara, L. M., Cole, C. L., & Koger, F. (1998). Translating self-determination concepts into support for adults with severe disabilities. *Journal of the Association for Persons with Severe Handicaps, 23*, 27–37.

Bricker, D. (1995). The challenge of inclusion. *Journal of Early Intervention, 19*, 179–194.

Bronfenbrenner, U. (1989). Ecological systems theory. In R. Vasta (Ed.), *Annals of child development* (Vol. 6, pp. 187–249). Greenwich, CT: JAI Press.

Browder, D. M. (1997). Educating students with severe disabilities: Enhancing the conversation between research and practice. *The Journal of Special Education, 31*, 137–144.

Buechler, S. M. (1990). *Women's movements in the United States: Woman suffrage, equal rights, and beyond.* New Brunwick, NJ: Rutgers University Press.

Burke, M. D., & Burke, S. H. (Eds.). (1999). Focus: Discipline and school safety, Part 2 [Special issue]. *Effective School Practices, 17*(4).

Carr, E. G. (1977). The motivation of self-injurious behavior: A review of some hypotheses. *Psychological Bulletin, 84,* 800–816.

Carr, E. G. (1996). The transfiguration of behavior analysis: Strategies for survival. *Journal of Behavioral Education, 6,* 263–270.

Carr, E. G. (1997). The evolution of applied behavior analysis into positive behavior support. *Journal of the Association for Persons with Severe Handicaps, 22,* 208–209.

Carr, E. G., & Carlson, J. I. (1993). Reduction of severe behavior problems in the community through a multicomponent treatment approach. *Journal of Applied Behavior Analysis, 26,* 157–172.

Carr, E. G., Carlson, J. I., Langdon, N. A., Magito-McLaughlin, D., & Yarbrough, S. C. (1998). Two perspectives on antecedent control: Molecular and molar. In J. K. Luiselli & M. J. Cameron (Eds.), *Antecedent control: Innovative approaches to behavioral support* (pp. 3–28). Baltimore: Brookes.

Carr, E. G., & Durand, V. M. (1985). Reducing behavior problems through functional communication training. *Journal of Applied Behavior Analysis, 18,* 111–126.

Carr, E. G., Horner, R. H., Turnbull, A. P., Marquis, J., Magito-McLaughlin, D., McAtee, M. L., Smith, C. E., Anderson-Ryan, K., Ruef, M. B., & Doolabh, A. (1999). *Positive behavior support for people with developmental disabilities: A research synthesis.* Washington, DC: American Association on Mental Retardation.

Carr, E. G., Levin, L., McConnachie, G., Carlson, J. I., Kemp, D. C., & Smith, C. E. (1994). *Communication-based intervention for problem behavior: A user's guide for producing positive change.* Baltimore: Brookes.

Carr, E. G., Levin, L., McConnachie, G., Carlson, J. I., Kemp, D. C., Smith, C. E., & Magito McLaughlin, D. (1999). Comprehensive multisituational intervention for problem behavior in the community: Long-term maintenance and social validation. *Journal of Positive Behavior Interventions, 1,* 5–25.

Carr, E. G., Robinson, S., Taylor, J. C., & Carlson, J. I. (1990). *Positive approaches to the treatment of severe behavior problems in persons with developmental disabilities: A review and analysis of reinforcement and stimulus-based procedures.* Seattle: The Association for Persons with Severe Handicaps, 4.

Chance, P. (1998). *First course in applied behavior analysis.* Pacific Grove, CA: Brooks/Cole.

Clark, H. B., & Hieneman, M. (1999). Comparing the wraparound process to positive behavioral support: What we can learn. *Journal of Positive Behavior Interventions, 1,* 183–186.

Clarke, S., Dunlap, G., & Vaughn, B. (1999). Family-centered, assessment-based intervention to improve behavior during an early morning routine. *Journal of Positive Behavior Interventions, 1,* 235–241.

Dennis, R. E., Williams, W., Giangreco, M. F., & Cloninger, C. J. (1993). Quality of life as a context for planning and evaluation of services for people with disabilities. *Exceptional Children, 59,* 499–512.

Desrochers, M. N., Hile, M. G., & Williams-Moseley, T. L. (1997). Survey of functional assessment procedures used with individuals who display mental retardation and severe problem behaviors. *American Journal on Mental Retardation, 101,* 535–546.

Dunlap, G., & Childs, K. E. (1996). Intervention research and behavioral disorders: An analysis of studies from 1980 to 1993. *Behavioral Disorders, 21,* 125–136.

Dunlap, G., Clarke, S., & Steiner, M. (1999). Intervention research in behavioral and developmental disabilities:1980 to 1997. *Journal of Positive Behavior Interventions, 1,* 170–180.

Dunlap, G., dePerczel, M., Clarke, S., Wilson, D., Wright, S., White, R., & Gomez, A. (1994). Choice making and proactive behavioral support for students with emotional and behavioral challenges. *Journal of Applied Behavior Analysis, 27,* 505–518.

Dunlap, G., Fox, L., Vaughn, B. J., Bucy, M., & Clarke, S. (1997). In quest of meaningful perspectives and outcomes: A response to five commentaries. *Journal of the Association for Persons with Severe Handicaps, 22,* 221–223.

Dunlap, G., Hieneman, M., Knoster, T., Fox, L., Anderson, J., & Albin, R. W. (2000). Essential elements of inservice training in positive behavior support. *Journal of Positive Behavior Interventions , 2,* 22–32.

Dunlap, G., Kern-Dunlap, L., Clarke, S., & Robbins, F. R. (1991). Functional assessment, curricular revision, and severe behavior problems. *Journal of Applied Behavior Analysis, 24,* 387–397.

Eber, L. (1997). Improving school-based behavioral intervention through the wraparound process. *Reaching Today's Youth, 1,* 32–36.

Gardner, W. I., Cole, C. L., Berry, D. L., & Nowinski, J. M. (1983). Reduction of disruptive behaviors in mentally retarded adults: A self-management approach. *Behavior Modification, 7,* 76–96.

Gilhool, T. K. (1989). The right to an effective education: From Brown to PL 94-142 and beyond. In D. Lipsky & A. Gartner (Eds.), *Beyond separate education: Quality education for all* (pp. 243–253). Baltimore: Brookes.

Horner, R. H., & Carr, E. G. (1997). Behavioral support for students with severe disabilities: Functional assessment and comprehensive intervention. *Journal of Special Education, 31,* 84–104.

Horner, R. H., Close, D. W., Fredericks, H. D. B., O'Neill, R. E., Albin, R. W., Sprague, J. R., Kennedy, C. H., Flannery, K. B., & Heathfield, L. T. (1996). Supported living for people with profound disabilities and severe problem behaviors. In D. H. Lehr & F. Brown (Eds.), *People with disabilities who challenge the system* (pp. 209–240). Baltimore: Brookes.

Horner, R. H., Day, H. M., & Day, J. R. (1997). Using neutralizing routines to reduce problem behaviors. *Journal of Applied Behavior Analysis, 30,* 601–614.

Horner, R. H., Dunlap, G., Koegel, R. L., Carr, E. G., Sailor, W., Anderson, J., et al. (1990). Toward a technology of "nonaversive" behavioral support. *Journal of the Association for Persons with Severe Handicaps, 15,* 125–132.

Hughes, C., Hwang, B., Kim, J. H., Eisenman, L. T., & Killian, D. J. (1995). Quality of life in applied research: A review and analysis of empirical measures. *American Journal on Mental Retardation, 99,* 623–641.

Individuals with Disabilities Education Act Amendments of 1997, 20 U.S.C. § 1401 (26).

Iwata, B. A., Dorsey, M. F., Slifer, K. J., Bauman, K. E., & Richman, G. S. (1982). Toward a functional analysis of self-injury. *Analysis and Intervention in Developmental Disabilities, 2,* 3–20.

Kemp, D. C., & Carr, E. G. (1995). Reduction of severe problem behavior in community employment using an hypothesis-driven multicomponent intervention approach. *Journal of the Association for Persons with Severe Handicaps, 20,* 229–247.

Kern, L., Childs, K. E., Dunlap, G., Clarke, S., & Falk, G. D. (1994). Using assessment-based curricular intervention to improve the classroom behavior of a student with emotional and behavioral challenges. *Journal of Applied Behavior Analysis, 27,* 7–19.

Kincaid, D. (1996). Person-centered planning. In L. K. Koegel, R. L. Koegel, & G. Dunlap (Eds.), *Positive behavioral support.* Baltimore: Brookes.

Kleinman, A. (1980). *Patients and healers in the context of culture.* Berkeley: University of California Press.

Knoster, T. P., Villa, R. A., & Thousand, J. S. (2000). A framework for thinking about systems change. In R. A. Villa & J. S. Thousand (Eds.), *Restructuring for caring and effective education* (pp. 93–128). Baltimore: Brookes.

Koegel, L. K., Koegel, R. L., & Dunlap, G. (1996). *Positive behavioral support.* Baltimore: Brookes.

Koegel, L. K., Koegel, R. L., Hurley, C., & Frea, W. D. (1992). Improving social skills and disruptive behavior in children with autism through self-management. *Journal of Applied Behavior Analysis, 25,* 341–353.

Koegel, L. K., Koegel, R. L., Kellegrew, D., & Mullen, K. (1996). Parent education for prevention and reduction of severe problem behaviors. In L. K. Koegel, R. L. Koegel, & G. Dunlap (Eds.), *Positive behavioral support* (pp. 3–30). Baltimore: Brookes.

Kunkel, J. H. (1987). The future of *JABA:* A comment. *Journal of Applied Behavior Analysis, 20,* 329–333.

Lawson, H., & Sailor, W. (in press). Integrating services, collaborating, and developing connections with schools. *Focus on Exceptional Children.*

Levine, M., & Perkins, D. V. (1987). *Principles of community psychology: Perspectives and applications.* New York: Oxford University Press.

Lewis, T. J., & Sugai, G. (1999). Effective behavior support: A systems approach to proactive schoolwide management. *Focus on Exceptional Children, 31,* 1–24.

Lloyd, J. W., Weintraub, F. J., & Safer, N. D. (1997). A bridge between research and practice: Building consensus. *Exceptional Children, 63,* 535–538.

Lucyshyn, J. M., Albin, R. W., & Nixon, C. D. (1997). Embedding comprehensive behavioral support in family ecology: An experimental, single-case analysis. *Journal of Consulting and Clinical Psychology, 65,* 241–251.

Lynch, E. W. (1998). Developing cross-cultural competence. In E. W. Lynch & M. J. Hanson (Eds.), *Developing cross-cultural competence* (pp. 47–86). Baltimore: Brookes.

Malouf, D. B., & Schiller, E. P. (1995). Practice and research in special education. *Exceptional Children, 61,* 414–424.

Matsumoto, D. (1996). *Culture and psychology.* Pacific Grove, CA: Brooks/Cole.

Meyer, L. H., & Evans, I. M. (1993). Science and practice in behavioral intervention: Meaningful outcomes, research validity, and usable knowledge. *Journal of the Association for Persons with Severe Handicaps, 18,* 224–234.

Meyer, L. H., Park, H. S., Grenot-Scheyer, M., Schwartz, I., & Harry, B. (1998). Participatory Action Research as a model for conducting family research. *The Journal of the Association for Persons with Severe Handicaps, 23,* 165–177.

Miltenberger, R. (1997). *Behavior modification: Principles and procedures.* Pacific Grove, CA: Brooks/Cole.

Nickels, C. (1996). A gift from Alex—The art of belonging: Strategies for academic and social inclusion. In L. K. Koegel, R. L. Koegel, & G. Dunlap (Eds.), *Positive behavioral support* (pp. 123–144). Baltimore: Brookes.

Nietupski, J., Hamre-Nietupski, S., Curtin, S., & Shrikanth, K. (1997). A review of curricular research in severe disabilities from 1976 to 1995 in six selected journals. *The Journal of Special Education, 31,* 36–55.

O'Brien, J., Mount, B., & O'Brien, C. (1991). *Framework for accomplishment: Personal profile.* Decatur, GA: Responsive Systems Associates.

O'Neill, R. E., Horner, R. H., Albin, R. W., Sprague, J. R., Storey, K., & Newton, J. S. (1997). *Functional assessment and program development for problem behavior.* Pacific Grove, CA: Brooks/Cole.

Park, H.-S., Gonsier-Gerdin, J., Hoffman, S., Whaley, S., & Yount, M. (1998). Applying the Participatory Action Research model to the study of social inclusion at worksites. *The Journal of the Association for Persons with Severe Handicaps, 23,* 189–202.

Reeve, C. E., & Carr, E. G. (2000). Prevention of severe problem behavior in children with developmental disorders. *Journal of Positive Behavior Interventions, 2,* 144–160.

Reichle, J. (1997). Communication intervention with persons who have severe disabilities. *The Journal of Special Education, 31,* 110–134.

Risley, T. (1996). Get a life! In L. K. Koegel, R. L. Koegel, & G. Dunlap (Eds.), *Positive behavioral support* (pp. 425–437). Baltimore: Brookes.

Risley, T. R. (1999). Foreword: Positive behavioral support and applied behavior analysis. In E. G. Carr, R. H. Horner, A. P. Turnbull, J. G. Marquis, D. Magito-McLaughlin, M. L. McAtee, C. E. Smith, K. Anderson-Ryan, M. B. Ruef, & A. Doolabh, *Positive behavior support for people with disabilities: A research synthesis.* Washington, DC: American Association on Mental Retardation.

Ruef, M. B., Turnbull, A. P., Turnbull, H. R., & Poston, D. (1999). Perspectives of five stakeholder groups: Challenging behavior of individuals with mental retardation and/or autism. *Journal of Positive Behavior Interventions, 1,* 43–58.

Sailor, W. (1996). New structures and systems change for comprehensive positive behavioral support. In L. K. Koegel, R. L. Koegel, & G. Dunlap (Eds.), *Positive behavioral support* (pp. 163–206). Baltimore: Brookes.

Sailor, W. (in press). Federal devolution policy, school/community partnerships, and inclusion: Some common themes. In W. Sailor (Ed.), *Inclusive education and school/community partnerships.* New York: Teachers College Press.

Sailor, W., Scott, T. M., Nelson, C. M., Freeman, R., Smith, C., Britten, J., & McCart, A. (in press). Using information technology to prepare personnel to implement functional behavioral assessment and positive behavioral support. *Exceptionality.*

Salisbury, C. L., Wilson, L. L., & Palombaro, M. M. (1998). Promoting inclusive schooling practices through practitioner directed inquiry. *The Journal of the Association for Persons with Severe Handicaps, 23,* 223–237.

Sands, D. J., Kozleski, E. B., & Goodwin, L. D. (1991). Whose needs are we meeting? Results of a consumer satisfaction survey of persons with developmental disabilities in Colorado. *Research in Developmental Disabilities, 12,* 297–314.

Schalock, R. L. (Ed.). (1990). *Quality of life: Vol. 1. Conceptualization and measurement.* Washington, DC: American Association on Mental Retardation.

Schalock, R. L. (Ed.). (1996). *Quality of life: Perspectives and issues.* Washington, DC: American Association on Mental Retardation.

Schwartz, I. S., & Olswang, L. B. (1996). Evaluating child behavior change in natural settings: Exploring alternative strategies for data collection. *Topics in Early Childhood Special Education, 16,* 82–101.

Seligman, M. E. P., & Csikszentmihalyi, M. (Eds.). (2000a). Happiness, excellence, and optimal human functioning [Special issue]. *American Psychologist, 55*(1).

Seligman, M. E. P., & Csikszentmihalyi, M. (2000b). Positive psychology: An introduction. *American Psychologist, 55,* 5–14.

Singer, G. H. S., Glang, A., & Williams, J. M. (1996). *Children with acquired brain injury.* Baltimore: Brookes.

Smull, M. W., & Harrison, S. B. (1992). *Supporting people with severe retardation in the community.* Alexandria, VA: National Association of State Mental Retardation Program Directors.

Soloman, I. D. (1989). *Feminism and black activism in contemporary America: An ideological assessment.* Hartford, CT: Greenwood Press.

Sugai, G., Horner, R. H., Dunlap, G., Hieneman, M., Lewis, T. J., Nelson, C. M., Scott, T., Liaupsin, C., Sailor, W., Turnbull, A. P., Turnbull, H. R., & Wickham, D. (2000). Applying positive behavior support and functional behavior assessment in schools. *Journal of Positive Behavior Interventions, 2,* 131–143.

Sulzer-Azaroff, B., & Mayer, G. R. (1991). *Behavior analysis for lasting change.* Fort Worth, TX: Holt, Rinehart & Winston.

Turnbull, A. P. (1988). The challenge of providing comprehensive support to families. *Education and Training in Mental Retardation, 23,* 261–272.

Turnbull, A. P., Friesen, B., & Ramirez, C. (1998). Participatory Action Research as a model of conducting family research. *Journal of the Association for Persons with Severe Handicaps, 23,* 178–188.

Turnbull, A. P., & Ruef, M. (1997). Family perspectives on inclusive lifestyle issues for people with problem behavior. *Exceptional Children, 63,* 211–227.

Turnbull, A. P., & Turnbull, H. R. (1999). Comprehensive lifestyle support for adults with challenging behavior: From rhetoric to reality. *Education and Training in Mental Retardation and Developmental Disabilities, 34,* 373–394.

VanDenBerg, J. E., & Grealish, E. M. (1998). *The wraparound process training manual.* Pittsburgh, PA: The Community Partnerships Group.

Vandercook, T., York, J., & Forest, M. (1989). The McGill action planning systems (MAPS): A strategy for building the vision. *Journal of the Association for Persons with Severe Handicaps, 14,* 205–215.

Vaughn, B. J., Dunlap, G., Fox, L., Clarke, S., & Bucy, M. (1997). Parent-professional partnership in behavioral support: A case study of community-based intervention. *Journal of the Association for Persons with Severe Handicaps, 22,* 185–197.

Warren, J. S., Edmonson, H. M., Turnbull, A. P., Sailor, W., Wickham, D., Griggs, P., & Beech, S. E. (in press). School-wide application of Positive Behavioral Supports: Implementation and preliminary evaluation of PBS in an urban middle school. *Journal of Educational Psychology.*

Wehmeyer, M. L. (1999). A functional model of self-determination: Describing development and implementing instruction. *Focus on Autism and Other Developmental Disabilities, 14,* 53–61.

Wehmeyer, M. L., Kelchner, K., & Richards, S. (1996). Essential characteristics of self-determined behavior of individuals with mental retardation. *American Journal on Mental Retardation, 100,* 632–642.

Wehmeyer, M., & Schwartz, M. (1997). Self-determination and positive adult outcomes: A follow-up study of youth with mental retardation or learning disabilities. *Exceptional Children, 63,* 245–255.

Weisz, J. R., Rothbaum, F. M., & Blackburn, T. C. (1984). Standing out and standing in: The psychology of control in America and Japan. *American Psychologist, 39,* 955–969.

Wolf, M. M. (1978). Social validity: The case for subjective measurement, or how applied behavior analysis is finding its heart. *Journal of Applied Behavior Analysis, 11,* 203–214.

Wolfensberger, W. (1983). Social role valorization: A proposed new term for the principle of normalization. *Mental Retardation, 21,* 234–239.

Yarbrough, S. C., & Carr, E. G. (2000). Some relationships between informant assessment and functional analysis of problem behavior. *American Journal on Mental Retardation, 105,* 130–151.

Ylvisaker, M., & Feeney, T. J. (1998). *Collaborative brain injury intervention: Positive everyday routines.* San Diego: Singular Publishing Group.

Action Editor: Glen Dunlap

Are You a Behaviorist or a Bonder?

Smashing Artificial Dichotomies and Entering Into a Dialogue of Shared Knowledge and Multiple Perspectives

Linda M. Bambara
Lehigh University

Few articles excite me as much as the one written by Carr and colleagues (this issue). Because I have been involved, at least peripherally, in the positive behavior support (PBS) movement since its inception, their article gave me pause to celebrate the movement's evolution and reflect on my own personal journey through the process. What excited me most about this article was the continued meshing, refinement, and expansion of ideas from diverse philosophical and theoretical perspectives. This marks a new chapter in the evolution of PBS, one that will continue to shape the broader paradigm shift in human services and education.

But Are You a Behaviorist or a Bonder?

As I read the article, I couldn't help but reflect on the new dichotomy that emerged soon after the aversives debate died down (Durand, 1990). As described by Carr and his esteemed colleagues, PBS is influenced by two main sources, applied behavior analysis (the behaviorists) and the inclusion/person-centered planning movement (the bonders). Although it is clear that proponents from both camps were interested in supporting people with difficult behavior through positive means, each group clung to its own tradition when advocating an approach. The behavioral approach, rooted in positivism, is characterized by systematic assessment and precise interventions that can be objectified, operationalized, measured, and applied to other individuals with similar problems. The person-centered approach, which is often affiliated with interpretivist or qualitative research traditions, focuses on broader systemic interventions that are uniquely tailored to the individual and discovered not by objective assessments but through personal, intimate knowledge of the person offered by family members, friends, and staff who know the

person best (ergo, the bonders). The distinction between the two orientations bred tension, and people either quickly joined camps or were labeled by their affiliations. "But where do you belong, Linda?" I've been asked. What could I say? I liked the precision of the behavioral orientation. For example, once a hypothesis statement had been formulated, I could systematically change each variable that contributed to problem behavior. This was very exciting, but I was also strongly influenced by people like Herb Lovett. Lovett's views (1996) on the importance of forming genuine interpersonal relationships with the people we support and really listening to what people communicate through their words and actions, as a replacement to functional assessment (heresy to those who believe only in measurable and objective assessment), opened doors for me, despite the fact that his harsh criticisms and lack of appreciation of behaviorism infuriated me at times. Understanding the contributions of multiple perspectives, I often lived in both worlds, borrowing the best from each orientation. However, as anyone who has taken a middle-of-the-road position can attest, this existence was not comfortable. I feared being ostracized by my colleagues, both old and newfound friends, and I could easily have become roadkill to the traffic on both sides.

I've recently reconciled my pluralist stance, but nevertheless found the article personally freeing. I took delight in knowing that my colleagues, who shared similar histories and background with me, were traveling similar paths, opening themselves to diverse ideas and even hinting at accepting different ways of knowing (more on that later). Although previous papers written by the same authors (e.g., Horner et al., 1990; Koegel, Koegel, & Dunlap, 1996) acknowledged the multiple influences of PBS, it remained largely behavioral and technological. This article, however, takes a bold leap in a new direction by blurring the boundaries around the major sources of influences and embracing multiple theoretical perspectives in social sciences and human services. As stated by the authors, PBS is emerging as an entity in its own right. For me, it means that I need no longer live in multiple worlds, but in one that allows and encourages me to be open to a variety of perspectives.

Toward the Acceptance of Diverse Thought

The evolution of PBS can be attributed to the broader postpositivist, or even postmodernist, social science movements that emphasize new paradigms for acquiring knowledge. However, staying close to home, I believe that person-centered values were chiefly responsible for opening our thoughts to supporting people with challenging behaviors.

Among the many values that person-centered planning has brought to the field, two are central to this discussion. The first is seeing and accepting people with disabilities as us, which serves to break down the objective and distant, "I–thou" researcher–subject relationship, and embrace a more empathic "we" point of view. Heron (as cited in Lincoln & Guba, 1985) argued that researchers should not define one model of behavior for themselves and a different one for their subjects. Seeing people with disabilities as people first, and not just as recipients of our services, led us to the axiom that they should be treated as we would treat ourselves and that they, like us, deserve a good quality life, just as we want for ourselves. But I believe that, more than this, seeing people with disabilities as us has hastened and broadened our search for understanding the complex influences that affect problem behaviors. During person-centered planning meetings, for example, facilitators often engage team members in perspective-taking activities, in which participants are asked to figuratively walk in another person's shoes and try to see life from his or her perspective. One could imagine a facilitator asking, "If you had a headache, and were unable to talk, and you were directed to keep working, how might you respond?" Or, "If you had a history of being abused in an institution, and, while living in the community, you experienced countless years of staff turnover, how might you perceive, and thereby respond to, new staff?" In my own research (Bambara, Gomez, Koger, Lohrmann-O'Rourke, & Xin, in press), staff participants reported that it was not until they attempted to understand the person from their own experiences that they became open to the myriad of factors that could be contributing to problem behaviors. Such an understanding led them to consider multiple variables that they had previously been unable to see.

Of course, this makes a lot of sense. When asked to explain influences on our own behavior, we are quick to identify multiple sources, some internal, some external, some historical, some systemic, and so forth. Further, we acknowledge that in our own lives, more than one source can influence our action at any one time. The grand "ah-ha" for our field is that if these things are true for us, then why are they not for people with disabilities? Suddenly, reinforcement theory (e.g., all behaviors function to escape or obtain something), compelling as it is, provides a woefully inadequate explanation for all human behavior. Human behavior is simply more complex than that. Although applied behavior analysts are exploring contextual variables (i.e., establishing operations), our values have pushed us even further to consider the impact of lifestyle variables (e.g., social relationships, opportunities for control, living arrangements) on people's behavior and general well-being.

Making a commitment to keeping the person with disabilities at the center of our work is the second person-centered value that has revolutionized our field. Superseding an allegiance to any methodological or theoretical orientation, our commitment is to the person, discovering and meeting the individual's needs and preferences. This commitment fundamentally requires us to let go of preconceived notions about what is the best intervention, because best can only be determined by what is effective in one person's life, contributes to his or her happiness (i.e., quality-of-life outcomes), and fits with that person's social–cultural milieu. On a broader research scale, this commitment obligates us to seek other theoretical explanations and methods of inquiry when our pet tradition fails to adequately address the complexities of real-life problems. Rather than become complacent with the limitations of any one tradition, we are motivated by a broader social purpose of producing meaningful outcomes for people. We can do this only by opening ourselves to new perspectives. After all, no one theory adequately explains the complexity of the human condition, and theories are only mental frameworks we generate to help explain that which we seek to understand. They are malleable and should be used flexibly.

Not Knowing Leads to Open Inquiry

To be honest, these ideas make my head swim. For those who believe that the accumulation of knowledge must proceed in an orderly fashion within a well-defined discipline, this discussion about multiple perspectives, as well as the newly defined characteristics of PBS, which seems to borrow a little of this and that (e.g., systems theory, community psychology, applied behavior analysis, and person-centered values, seems, well, chaotic. From my perspective, it is refreshingly chaotic, because it represents an admission of how much we don't know (yet) about the multiple and multidirectional layers of influence that could affect problem behavior and what is truly needed to promote meaningful outcomes. The good news is that in addition to person-centered values, the humble admission of not knowing lends itself to open inquiry, really listening to different views, and ultimately sharing knowledge that will lead to meaningful and effective supports (Edgar, in press).

To broaden our perspective, we must be sure to invite many into the conversation. Forming partnerships with the very people who will be affected by positive behavior support (e.g., people with disabilities, families, educators, service providers) is essential to developing authentic and meaningful supports. To underscore an important point made by Carr and colleagues, true partnering involves viewing stakeholders as co-collaborators in setting the agenda for research and practice, and not just as social validators for interventions designed by researchers. To discover what is truly meaningful, researchers must take the time to understand stakeholders' experiences and needs from their perspective and then tackle these issues head-on rather than shy away from those perceived to be too messy or difficult to investigate systematically.

Recently, for example, I conducted a 2-day workshop on functional assessment for behavior support specialists from the Philadelphia region. Although I was prepared to teach them all I knew about the strategies and tools for functional assessment, I was unprepared for most of their questions on how to make functional assessment *really work* for them. The behavior support specialists were more interested in the social process, or how to enlist and maintain the support of others, than in the assessment tools; social process, in their view, would determine whether or not they were able to do their jobs. They wanted to know, for instance, how to engage teachers in functional assessment interviewing when teachers are biased by their motivation to remove children with problem behavior from their classrooms. They wanted to know how they could get group-home support staff to record data when staff members perceive data collection as unnecessarily burdensome and not terribly useful. They wanted to know how to bring team members to a concensus when each one has a different interpretation of the causes of problem behavior and selects a different intervention. At one time, I might have dismissed their questions as mere complaints. I thought, "Hey, it's my job to give you research-based information on how to assess problem behaviors. It's your job to figure out what you need to do to make it work in your settings." However, it is my job, our job as researchers, to figure out with stakeholders why these concerns exist and what we can do about them if we are truly committed to effecting change. We can begin by trying to understand the behavior support specialists' experiences and exploring the vast literature on group dynamics and teamwork from the point of view of counseling psychology and organizational management (e.g., Larson & LaFastso, 1989; Yalom, 1995). Whatever the approach, it is clear to me that I can no longer "silo" my thinking but rather must think holistically about problems.

Inviting others also means encouraging social scientists and scholars from other disciplines and research traditions to join the conversation. Despite talk of diversity, the current PBS conversation is being held within a relatively small group of reformed behaviorists, myself included. Not that there is anything wrong with this, but holding a conversation among only like-minded people does seem to limit how quickly we are able to discover and assimilate new concepts and practices. I am also mindful that scholars from other traditions may decline the invitation in fear of criticism or of abandoning their own most cherished assumptions. This provides all the more reason to take an empathetic stance (i.e., listening to understand) to create an atmosphere of open discussion, even if we do not ultimately agree.

One conversation that would benefit from the views of other social scholars is the discussion of how to broaden the current PBS definition of an applied science to accept multiple ways of knowing. Although Carr et al. persuasively argue for the acceptance of flexible experimental methods and nonexperimental data sources, their implied definition of science as the operational framework for accumulating knowledge is deeply rooted in positivism, which holds that truth can be achieved by identifying causal relations among variables through scientific methods (i.e., experimentation). A long-held assumption of many positivists is that science is the only way of informing practice. However, this assumption is rapidly changing, particularly in light of recent developments in PBS and other social science movements. As implied throughout the article by Carr et al. (this issue) and as argued by other social scholars (e.g., Edgar, in press), social practice (i.e., the support for people with challenging behaviors) must be informed not only by scientific methods, but also by moral, ethical, and societal values and decision making, information that is not gleaned through traditional scientific practice. Further, as suggested by the authors, given the complex nature of natural influences on human behavior, it is impossible to isolate relevant variables in most situations. This leads to what qualitative researchers, who conduct research only in natural settings, have accepted all along—that entities are in a constant state of simultaneous and mutual shaping, making linear cause-and-effect predictions impossible and an unlikely outcome of science (Lincoln & Guba, 1985). For this reason, qualitative researchers emphasize understanding, not prediction and control, as a way to offer plausible explanations for relations that might exist.

By inviting other scholars into the conversation, the evolving PBS definition might be encouraged by a more inclusive view of "applied science" to ensure that we go beyond just flexing our experimental methods in natural settings. From my perspective, an applied science is one that is informed by both values and rigorous inquiry, that serves multiple purposes (i.e., to predict, to discover, and to understand), and that embraces information from various research traditions as credible sources. I believe that this is what Carr and colleagues are trying to say. Inviting others into the conversation can help to make this more inclusive view of science more explicit.

Summary

So, are you a behaviorist or a bonder, or an organizational theorist, an ecological psychologist, a community psychologist, a systems analyst, or a cultural anthropologist? Are you a single-subject, large *N*, or interpretivist researcher? Do you ascribe to positivist, postpositivist, natural inquiry, or postmodernist assumptions? I don't know. What I do know is that I am committed to figuring out how to provide respectful and dignified supports for people with disabilities who engage in challenging behaviors, supports that will ultimately result in meaningful outcomes for these people and their families. In the final analysis, this is what positive behavior support is all about.

ABOUT THE AUTHOR

Linda M. Bambara, EdD, is an associate professor of special education at Lehigh University. Her current research interests include teaming aspects of positive behavior support, self-determination (e.g., choice and self-management), and community inclusion for adults with developmental disabilities. Address: Linda M. Bambara, College of Education, 111 Research Dr., Lehigh University, Bethlehem, PA 18015.

REFERENCES

Bambara, L. M., Gomez, O., Koger, F., Lohrmann-O'Rourke, S., & Xin, Y. (in press). More than techniques: Team members' experiences and perspectives on implementing positive supports for adults with severe challenging behaviors. *Journal of the Association for Persons with Severe Handicaps.*

Durand, M. V. (1990). The "aversives" debate is over: And now the work begins. *Journal of the Association for Persons with Severe Handicaps, 15,* 140–141.

Edgar, E. (in press). Knowing when we don't know. *Journal of the Assoication for Persons with Severe Handicaps.*

Horner, R. H., Dunlap, G., Koegel, R. L., Carr, E. G., Sailor, W., Anderson, J., Albin, R. W., & O'Neill, R. E. (1990). Toward a technology of "nonaversive" behavioral support. *Journal of the Association for Persons with Severe Handicaps, 15,* 125–132.

Koegel, L. K., Koegel, R. L., & Dunlap, G. (1996). *Positive behavioral support.* Baltimore: Brookes.

Larson, C. E., & LaFasto, F. M. J. (1989). *Teamwork: What must go right/what can go wrong.* Newbury Park, CA: Sage.

Lincoln, Y. S., & Guba, E. G. (1985). *Naturalist inquiry.* Newbury Park, CA: Sage.

Lovett, H. (1996). *Learning to listen: Positive approaches and people with difficult behaviors.* Baltimore: Brookes.

Yalom, I. D. (1995). *The theory and practice of group psychotherapy* (4th ed.). New York: Basic Books.

Action Editor: Glen Dunlap

Strengthening the Focus on Problem Contexts

Martha E. Snell
University of Virginia

Let me start this review by recalling an incident from several months ago that involved Nicky, a 5-year-old child with developmental disabilities. When one of my graduate students confessed that she thought it best to forego a thorough functional assessment of Nicky's aggression, I was disappointed. She proposed that she would instead rely on all she knew about Nicky and go ahead and teach him how to play without hurting others or perseverating on the same play theme, characteristics of his play that drove peers away. This student had listened carefully when Nicky's mom said,

> I want Nicky to learn how to play with other kids, to be with them, to enjoy them, and them him. I don't want to keep focusing on his hitting. Hitting is not his biggest problem. It's his isolation, his quality of life.

Nicky was full of energy, sometimes too full, and struggling to be a valued member of his kindergarten class and his neighborhood. Why the disappointment on my part? Did I believe that my student would not be completing the assignment with adequate rigor? I guess so.

In their provocative article, Carr and his nine colleagues (this issue) examine the evolving features of positive behavior support (PBS). Nicky's case is highly compatible with their ideas. For example, Nicky's mom was a central stakeholder who knew Nicky better than anyone else did. Her views were critical to a successful intervention—how lucky my student was that she was so assertive! Her priority was to bring about improvements in Nicky's lifestyle that would benefit all while secondarily rendering the problem behavior ineffective. For her, improvements in Nicky's play and social relationships formed the path to improve his quality of life. Nicky's mom asked the student to trust all the observations this student had previously made, as well as her perspective and the team's previous conversations regarding Nicky's problems and needs. Defining and observing had already taken place, even though no data had been graphed. The functions that aggressive behavior served for Nicky had been consistently indicated by observations, teacher notes, and team reports—all acceptable data. Aggression most often produced escape from the frustration of cooperative play to playing alone, but hitting, tackling, squeezing, and yelling also yielded desired tangibles; these behaviors frequently guaranteed Nicky his toy of choice! It was time to improve the play skills Nicky used so unsuccessfully and expand data gathering to observation of play skills and peer interaction.

The PBS plan that followed involved many components. It started with having the graduate student teach several key play skills; then, with success, play groups were to be shifted to include several hardy classmates who liked Nicky. His mom would recruit a play group that would include Nicky during the upcoming summer. The school team members wanted to see videotapes of his emerging social skills so they too could learn. Nicky's mom and other team members would add IEP objectives to continue this growth and build peer support. The team knew they needed to adapt his curriculum and instruction so he could be more successful learning early academics in school. They needed to address multiple contexts for change, multiple intervention agents, and plan for the long term, not just the graduate student's semester of involvement. Nicky was the person at the center of planning. His PBS represented "a melding of values and technology in that strategies are judged not only with respect to efficacy (a technological criterion) but also with respect to their ability to enhance personal dignity and opportunities for choice (a values criterion)" (Carr et al., this issue).

Journal of Positive Behavior Interventions

Volume 4, Number 1, Winter 2002, pages 21–24

I have been given the luxury of discussing any of the issues raised by Carr et al. that I found interesting, important, or controversial. As I read the article, I moved around in my seat, muttered out loud, underlined key points, wrote notes in the margins, and generated a list of things to add to my fall class, all behaviors of someone reading something exciting! Thus, in the following pages I will set forth without difficulty several of the points made by Carr and his colleagues and add my comments.

Carr and his colleagues emphasize, "One of the central messages of PBS is that, in providing support, we should focus our efforts on fixing problem contexts, not problem behavior." Why has it taken so long to understand that systems change is the primary name of the game? Defining, measuring, and intervening with systems—agencies, schools, and families—is certainly more taxing to the behavioral technology than tackling precise behaviors of individuals. Yet, we have all experienced less-than-adequate results when schools, vocational programs, or community mental health agencies—the contexts for PBS—are disorganized, uncooperative, or resistant. Recently, I faced this firsthand with a graduate student when we were asked to consult with a nearby school to assist with a 9-year-old whose injurious behavior to self and others over a period of 4 years had reached a point of great concern. This boy had evolved from being one member of a typical class to being the sole member of a special class with oodles of staff coming and going! His aggressive behavior had occurred everywhere, so he was removed from the fourth grade classroom, music and art, school bus, recess with others, and all but the side table in the cafeteria early in the lunch period. Unfortunately, while implementing a comprehensive functional assessment and engaging the team in designing a PBS plan, my student and I failed to note that most of the school staff had given up, and the principal was just waiting to transfer this child to the "autism class." The school did not want this little boy anymore, even with our promise of a strong PBS plan. Expanding and strengthening his continued inclusion in a neighborhood school by asking for more resources was not on the agenda, but it should have been. Had we put more energy into team building (including the principal and central office), identifying ways to mentor school staff over the long term, exploring approaches for funding with the school system, appealing to the school's stated values for inclusion, and sharing our enthusiasm for positive change, the problem context might have yielded to change and become a context that welcomed the embedding of a broader set of intervention strategies.

In short, "a systemic perspective rejects the notion that practitioner effectiveness depends solely on identifying a key critical intervention that can turn the tide" (Carr et al., this issue). The days when a simple functional assessment followed by teaching a single replacement phrase (e.g., saying "Break" when tasks are too hard, nonfunctional, or boring) are over. It is debatable if these interventions ever produced any lasting positive effects. Interventions must involve multiple components that address all the relevant factors of the individual's behavior (the problem behavior and function and the skill needs and preferences) and the context (setting, agency or school, family, and community).

Carr and his colleagues emphasized prevention: "The PBS approach has helped give birth to what is, arguably, one of the greatest paradoxes in the field of developmental disabilities, namely, the notion that the best time to intervene in problem behavior is when the behavior is not occurring" (this issue). Many of us "oldsters" who started our careers in residential settings in the 1960s remember the traditional mantra of behavioral practices: "Reinforce *any* nonproblem behavior when it occurs to increase its occurrence, but be sure to deliver the planned and approved consequences immediately and consistently to decrease the target problem behavior." While these practices seemed to work some of the time, many of us never viewed an opportunity for generalization outside the institution or even stayed long enough to check on the long-term effects of intervention. We did not think in terms of quality of life, but focused on a declining graph. The problem behavior was the signal for us to take planned action, to implement the behavior modification plan, while nonproblem behavior was our signal that it was safe to focus on other things. The written plan was designed to reduce problem behavior in the target individual; the plan less often had categories for building skills and shaping replacement behaviors, and rarely had categories for expanding the person's "best times," improving and extending the activities and contexts, creating opportunities for choice, or making system changes (staff training, values building, exploring funding to increase supports).

This notion of intervening when the problem behavior is not occurring is a simple but powerful addition to our thinking. Our new mantra is to be alert for the times when no problem behavior is occurring and to actively create more "windows of opportunity" without problem behavior when teaching is the focus. Sometimes PBS plans require staff training to transform our thinking, and temporary support so the skill-building plans are triggered when things are calm. But when team members invest together in the design of the skill training details of a PBS plan and take time to monitor learning, their attention more readily shifts to these windows of opportunity.

While the operant framework was the foundation for PBS, there are several other theoretical perspectives that together characterize this evolving approach. Carr and colleagues describe several perspectives, each of which warrant comment. First, "the focus of intervention must be on changing problem context, not problem behavior" (this issue). Based on Bronfenbrenner's (1989) ecological systems theory, which has become an important element of community psychology, people and the environments in which they function are seen as interdependent, with the potential for mutual support. Thus, it is both logical and necessary to assess the individual and each context where problem behavior occurs and to design support and change strategies that address this interrelationship: "Producing change is not simply a matter of implementing specific techniques; rather, change involves the reallocation of resources such as time, money, and political power" (Carr et al., this issue). Team members will find that they need a broader repertoire of intervention strategies, including those that change the contextual resources affecting staff (time, training, role), activities, schedules, team planning and support, budget allocation, and agency politics. Aiming to change a person's behavior with little consideration for the context is no longer acceptable.

Closely related is the principle that "an individual's behavior, appropriate or inappropriate, is the result of a continuous process of adaptation reflecting the interface between competence and context . . . successful intervention must modulate the goodness of fit between competence and context . . . must involve multicomponent systems change" (Carr et al., this issue). This interdependency between an individual's competence and the context has always existed; we have just failed to let it influence our planning. The individual, not the setting, has been held responsible both for the problem and for change. As teams plan and monitor PBS programs, this interdependency between the target individual and the target contexts must be acknowledged.

These characteristics of PBS have the following implications:

- Collaborative team composition and communication must be extended to include those from each relevant context who wield the power.
- Young teachers (and other inexperienced direct care staff) must have knowledge of collaborative teaming and systems change strategies. They need mentors to boost their confidence and success in implementing context assessment and system change strategies.
- Agency evaluations, such as accreditation procedures, should assess agency characteristics that are linked to the behavior of those an agency serves. Parents, students/clients, and friends are fundamental sources of information in these evaluation and reform efforts.

This principle of systems change also raises several ongoing concerns. If we focus mainly on systems change, will we neglect or slow down individual change? Can we do a more effective job of equipping young beginning professionals with the skills needed to change systems? Should organizations be restructured so beginning staff are not isolated but integrated into supportive teams? Do we understand adequately the psychology of motivating change in systems and the people involved? Can there be adequate systems change without involving the courts more?

Another important issue Carr and his colleagues raise is that the multicultural element of systems change theory is often ignored: "If one is not knowledgeable about these [multicultural] influences and sensitive to them, then the most well-intentioned and best-designed interventions may nonetheless fail" (this issue). How many times have we heard this, yet how many staff members with concerns about their students'/clients' problem behavior actually operationalize this principle? At the pre- and in-service phases of teacher training and staff development, we tend to cover multiculturalism in several lectures or one obligatory course. But because coverage may not yield understanding or heartfelt acceptance, the principle is rarely integrated into routine planning processes. This principle suggests several essential refinements in the PBS process:

- Accurate cultural knowledge will be allowed to shape PBS planning so that team members will both value the culture of the student or client (and the family) and understand how influential culture can be to the goals, methods of assessment, intervention approaches, and approaches for monitoring outcomes.
- Multiculturalism will be incorporated into PBS planning, which will require (a) that all team members learn to take several perspectives (one familiar and the other unfamiliar) at the same time, and (b) that they work to balance PBS plans to reflect not only the heritage and beliefs of a family but also the realities of "majority" contexts.
- Family members will be given a more dominant voice that team members listen to.

Recently, I read the book *The Spirit Catches You and You Fall Down*, by Anne Fadiman (1997). The author relates 9 years of culture gap between a Hmong family with a daughter who has epilepsy and the U.S. doctors who treated her. The reader is taken back and forth between two vastly divergent views on how to regard and treat epilepsy, that of the Hmong culture and that of U.S. medicine. The task facing the reader is to understand two groups of people who do not understand each other and to discover what might have been done differently to improve the outcomes. Such an exercise is one that we all must experience if we are to become multicultural thinkers.

This fall I will again teach a course on PBS. Carr and his colleagues have raised the bar for me and for others in this position, but I am not surprised about what must be added to make this course more complete. At the same time, we need to rethink our approach to teaching in university settings. Perhaps the notion of systems change should be applied to our traditional ways of building staff skills in PBS via lectures, readings, written assignments, and tests. Learning must involve taking in content that is then actively manipulated until it is understood, that is applied repeatedly in realistic simulations and then in reality, and whose applications are evaluated, revised, and reapplied until successful. We must pay attention to both our students' skill maintenance over the long term and their generalization across settings. Finally, instruction must extend beyond the competencies involved in using the behavioral technology required for PBS to embrace the many facets of collaboration that will make or break successful PBS. Instruction should address extending team membership to those in agency positions of power and to family members and student/client friends, establishing common team values, determining ground rules, practicing cultural sensitivity, promoting active member participation, using methods to find common ground and to negotiate, problem solving, reaching consensus, and designing, implementing, and improving team-generated plans for changing the context. The task lies ahead of us.

ABOUT THE AUTHOR

Martha E. Snell, PhD, is a professor of education in the Curry School of Education at the University of Virginia. She serves as coordinator of the special education program and directs graduate degree programs in severe disabilities and early childhood special education. Her current interests include the inclusion of individuals with disabilities in general education, teacher collaboration, modification of schoolwork, behavior support, and prelinguistic communication. Address: Martha E. Snell, University of Virginia, Curry School of Education, 405 Emmet St., Room 234 Ruffner Hall, Charlottesville, VA 22903.

REFERENCES

Bronfenbrenner, U. (1989). Ecological systems theory. In R. Vasta (Ed.), *Annals of child development* (Vol. 6, pp. 187–249). Greenwich, CT: JAI Press.
Fadiman, A. (1997). *The spirit catches you and you fall down: A Hmong child, her American doctors, and the collision of two cultures.* New York: Farrar, Straus, & Giroux.

Action Editor: Glen Dunlap

PBS as a Service Delivery System

~

David P. Wacker and Wendy K. Berg

The University of Iowa

Carr et al. (this issue) describe positive behavior support (PBS) and make the argument that PBS is currently an applied science. They argue that the methods used by PBS have evolved beyond applied behavior analysis because the current scientific methods used by behavior analysts are inadequate for meeting the challenges of inclusion, normalization, and other highly desirable outcomes. A major supposition of these authors appears to be that the blending of philosophical guidelines with selected assessment and intervention processes constitutes an applied science that is distinct from behavior analysis. Although we believe that there is much to admire about the goals of PBS, we do not view it as constituting a science. In this commentary, we describe (a) our concerns with characterizing PBS as a science, (b) some potentially troubling issues regarding the blending of philosophy with science, and (c) our perspective on the past and future of PBS.

Is PBS a Science?

The authors state that PBS is an applied science. We are not sure that any definition of science could be used to categorize PBS as an applied science that is distinguishable from the scientific methods from which it is derived, such as those of applied behavior analysis or social psychology. The authors have attempted to merge philosophies, findings, and practices from several related disciplines, but this does not necessarily constitute the evolution of a science. Instead, it appears to constitute the evolution of a service delivery system that is based, at least in part, on scientifically obtained results.

As stated by Carr and colleagues, the goals of PBS are to assist the individual to develop a lifestyle that gives the individual and the people who are important to that individual the opportunity "to perceive and to enjoy an improved quality of life" and "to render problem behavior irrelevant, inefficient, and ineffective." The authors may be in a unique position to achieve these outcomes, but however worthy these goals may be, they do not match the goals and activities typically ascribed to science. We reviewed various descriptions of science and found the descriptions of scientific practice to be very consistent. Whereas the goals of PBS are to obtain preidentified outcomes for the individual, the goals of science are to observe events and to identify lawful relationships between those events (Vadum & Rankin, 1998). Scientists study events that are observable and testable (Johnston & Pennypacker, 1993; McReynolds & Kearn, 1983) and rely on data that are objective, reliable, and quantifiable (Poling, Methot, & LeSage, 1995) to draw conclusions about relationships between those events. The outcome of scientific methods is the development of scientific laws to explain observed relationships between events. These laws are tested and refined over time and eventually may be discarded or used to develop better services, practices, or procedures.

Many of the studies conducted within the framework of PBS undoubtedly follow the procedures outlined in descriptions of scientific methodology. To the degree that these studies test observable events with data that are objective, reliable, and quantifiable, and use procedures that are replicable, they will meet the requirements of science and will in all likelihood advance our knowledge of behavior analysis or systems change models.

However, it is unclear that the outcomes specified by the authors and the processes selected to obtain those outcomes will be manipulated as independent variables whose effects are to be studied or if they are outcomes or integral components of the PBS model that will remain constant. For example, Carr et al. state that PBS is based on humanistic values and that these values prescribe components such as the use of person-centered planning, self-determination, and the wraparound approach as processes to achieve the goals of PBS. The scientific method may not be relevant for evaluating either the values or the derived processes of the PBS model. This is not necessarily a shortcoming of PBS, but the emphasis on using predetermined components and processes to achieve predetermined goals suggests that PBS is not a science because it is not based on the scientific method. Although all scientists work within a framework of values regarding what constitutes worthy avenues of research and acceptable procedures, the PBS model dictates not only the outcomes to be achieved but the processes to be followed (i.e., person-centered planning, self-determination, and the wraparound approach) in achieving those outcomes.

Our view is that PBS is not a science but, instead, a service delivery model. As a service delivery model, it functions in much the same manner as community-based training of functional skills and the supported employment models. The outcomes achieved by existing practice failed to realize the goals of instruction that were considered to be ideal (and obtainable) by some caregivers and service providers. In the best-case scenarios, the positive outcomes achieved with these models far exceeded any outcomes achieved with preexisting models. In addition, topics of interest to parents, practitioners, and researchers changed as a direct function of concerns and questions that occurred in the new intervention contexts. For example, issues related to generalization and maintenance were often encountered as youth with disabilities worked in a larger variety of job locations. Some of these investigations involved social psychology studies (e.g., how workers with disabilities were perceived by coworkers), and some involved operant analyses of stimulus control. Some results were obtained first in highly controlled settings, whereas others were obtained directly in community contexts. These results, in turn, led to further investigation and refinement of the scientific disciplines most closely associated with the service delivery model. In operant research, for example, novel methods for promoting generalization (e.g., general-case instruction) were developed from existing methodologies (e.g., sufficient exemplars). In this way, both service (e.g., community-based instruction and supported employment) and science (e.g., applied behavior analysis concepts related to stimulus control) evolved.

However, even with this evolution, the service models associated with community-based instruction and supported employment were not new sciences. They were (and are) exemplary service delivery systems that blended information from a wide array of disciplines. We agreed with most of the goals of community-based instruction and supported employment, and, as applied behavior analysts, we actively sought to provide needed data through our research programs that could be used, for example, to facilitate successful job matches. Our main point here is that even though our dependent variables evolved from steps completed on a task analysis to monthly income, our methods for changing the dependent variables were based on operant mechanisms.

We question the validity, or even the value, of labeling PBS as a science. Over time, and with further clarification

and refinement, we believe that PBS may evolve into an exemplary service system that is replicable across distinct service teams. We believe that many of the effective interventions for behaviors such as self-injury will be applications and extensions of operant procedures. We have no doubt or concern that these procedures will be blended into multicomponent packages that are quite complex. It is a desirable evolution to change the way procedures are delivered in the community, but this does not constitute an evolution of the science. It is an evolution of the way the science is applied in particular contexts.

Blending Philosophical Guidelines with Selected Assessment and Intervention Practices

Carr and colleagues describe PBS as emerging from three sources: (a) applied behavior analysis, (b) the normalization/inclusion movement, and (c) person-centered values. Of these sources, one is scientific (applied behavior analysis) and two are philosophical. One provides specific procedures that can be tested and refuted, and two provide guidelines that cannot be tested. Thus, the science that underlies PBS is behavior analysis, although information from related disciplines such as social psychology is also evident in the PBS model. This blending of science with philosophy is not unique to PBS. In our outpatient clinics, for example, we are trained in person-centered values and largely agree with this concept. We also are strongly supportive of full inclusion and normalization. The authors are quite correct in suggesting that behavior analysis does not specify particular behavioral goals in applied contexts. These goals are largely determined by philosophical orientation and standards. What behavior analysis provides is a methodology for understanding and predicting target behaviors in given contexts based on operant mechanisms.

Our philosophical orientation has led us to use operant principles to improve child behavior in home settings. This is why we conduct most of our research in parent homes and outpatient clinics. These are not tightly controlled environments selected based on our desire for internal validity. We selected these settings because of our desire to facilitate normalized family interactions. We rely on operant principles to guide assessment and intervention in these settings, and we have needed to adjust standard assessment and intervention to better match the contexts within which we work. In a few cases, our adjustments have, we hope, advanced the science of applied behavior analysis. This, however, will be determined by peer review, as is the case in all sciences. Regardless of whether our peers determine that our results have advanced science, we continue to work in the contexts that are socially meaningful to us and to the families we serve. We have chosen how best to put our science into practice. That choice is not based on science alone, but also on the philosophical guidelines we have chosen to follow. The methods we use, which are based on science, are replicable and arguable. Our philosophy is only arguable. The blending of science and philosophy is perhaps a necessary step for most applied researchers, but it is not a sufficient step for describing the practice as constituting a new science. Instead, it describes the service model we employ to deliver the procedures developed via scientific analysis. Thus, the blending of philosophy and science is not, in our view, the evolution of a science. It is, instead, the evolution of a service delivery system. The scientific components of that system are replicable and will likely change, given empirical evaluation. The philosophical components are not testable, but they also will continue to change as new philosophies emerge. It would be a mistake to believe that current philosophy will remain unchanged over time. What appears to be "true" today may not be true in the future.

PBS: The Past and the Future

To suggest that PBS is not a science is not to say that it is without merit. Existing service delivery systems are often inadequate and fail to properly support individuals and families. We have been impressed by the outcomes achieved by the developers of PBS, and we support their desire to evolve their service delivery system.

As researchers in applied behavior analysis, Carr and his colleagues have contributed notable studies on stimulus control, reinforcement, and functional analysis. Our treatment of choice is functional communication training, and these authors were largely responsible for developing that set of procedures. Many of the most creative and notable advances in reinforcement-based treatment (and generalization) have been provided by this team of researchers. Many of these advances began as tightly controlled studies that involved microscopic analyses of response–reinforcer relations. The positive results of these studies made it seem reasonable to design and conduct large-scale demonstration studies, which often required that different units of analysis be tested. Thus, it is precisely because of researchers such as Carr and colleagues that the goals of PBS may become a reality. We hope that they continue to pursue the goals outlined in their article and that they are able to design effective service plans for those who need them.

There is little to gain in criticizing the methodologies and the professionals who continue to advance our more basic understanding of response–reinforcer relations. As mentioned earlier, studies conducted in tightly controlled situations have provided much of the basis for PBS, and it seems likely that similar studies will contribute relevant information to PBS in the future. For example, in recent years, much has been learned about the benefits and potential disadvantages of fixed-time (noncontingent) schedules of reinforcement. We are learning, for example, that fixed-time schedules can decrease problem behavior but not necessarily inhibit the learning of adaptive behavior. We hope that service providers will apply and extend these findings to other situations, such as all-day school programs. If successful application does occur, one reason for this success will be the results from the controlled studies that suggested this possibility.

Many of the studies in journals, such as the *Journal of Applied Behavior Analysis,* can be considered to be bridge studies, studies that bridge the gap between basic and applied science. These studies are important because they offer the first tightly controlled demonstrations of how a behavioral mechanism might influence human behavior. They are of necessity tightly controlled, because the goal is to learn more about the mechanism and its influence on human behavior. One purpose of these studies is to provide a base of knowledge that others can apply in novel or more extensive ways. Thus, these studies form part of the history upon which innovative service systems can be based, both now and in the future.

As future applications occur, it may not be necessary to study a mechanism in the manner used in the bridge studies, but it seems critical to study the conditions that are necessary for effective application. Otherwise, others will have difficulty replicating, expanding, or troubleshooting the service delivery model. Our suggestion for researchers interested in PBS is to evaluate those conditions that can be shown to be necessary for effective delivery of important services. If, for example, we can implement a schoolwide reinforcement program (as opposed to a schoolwide punishment program) that significantly reduces aggressive behavior, then we need to specify under what conditions that program will be most effective. Although the initial demonstrations may be largely descriptive or correlational, it is important to follow these studies with ones that tell others why the services were effective. Otherwise, limited replication may occur. If it is believed that success is achieved largely because of philosophical commitment, then causal or "why" studies must focus on systems that share procedures but deliver those procedures in different manners because of their philosophical perspectives.

Overall, we do not believe it is sufficient to describe a highly complex model and provide case examples demonstrating that it can be successful. This is a necessary step but not a sufficient one to suggest evolution of either a science or a service delivery model. Instead, we believe that studies are needed to explain why a model worked (under what conditions) and that specify the active components of the model.

Finally, we hope that in the future, PBS continues to emphasize the individual rather than some construct related to the "average" student. Models can be based on one individual at a time. We have elected to pursue our areas of research because individuals were not responding optimally to "average" group-based treatment. Once a service delivery system has evolved sufficiently for large-scale replication, at least a few individuals will not respond positively to that system. Applied behavior analysts will likely be among the first to work with those individuals and will probably begin by conducting tightly controlled, internally valid studies. To us, that will be a good initial step for advancing both our science and the application of that science in the future. Thus, while groups such as Carr et al. are conducting important, large-scale demonstration and replication projects, we will be working with individuals. We believe that both approaches are valid and that an exciting reciprocal relationship can be created between groups that are addressing socially relevant problems from similar perspectives but with different methods. That approach to our future would be more fruitful than one in which each group argues that their approach is somehow the "best."

Summary

We congratulate this extraordinary team on being among the first to implement and study large-scale programs for children with significant needs. Procedures developed by applied behavior analysts can have substantial, durable, and large-scale effects when delivered properly within ongoing service systems. This approach represents a natural evolution from basic studies that developed a behavioral mechanism, to bridge studies that first evaluated the mechanism in human behavior, to tightly controlled field studies, to large-scale application studies. These large-scale application studies are not common, but they constitute an important test of an applied science.

ABOUT THE AUTHORS

David P. Wacker, PhD, is a professor of pediatric psychology and special education at the University of Iowa. His primary research interests are with young children who display challenging behavior at home. Wendy K. Berg, MA, is an investigator on two research grants funded by the National Institutes of Health. Her research interests include the influence of competing stimuli on response allocation and the use of concurrent operant procedures in assessment. Address: David P. Wacker, 251 Center for Disabilities and Development, 100 Hawkins Dr., The University of Iowa, Iowa City, IA 52242-1011; e-mail: david-wacker@uiowa.edu

REFERENCES

Johnston, J. M., & Pennypacker, H. S. (1993). *Strategies and tactics of behavioral research.* Hillsdale, NJ: Erlbaum.

McReynolds, L., & Kearn, K. (1983). *Single subject experimental design in communication disorders.* Baltimore: University Park Press.

Poling, A., Methot, L., & LeSage, M. (1995). *Fundamentals of behavior analytic research.* New York: Plenum.

Vadum, A., & Rankin, N. (1998). *Psychological research: Methods for discovery and validation.* Boston: McGraw-Hill.

Action Editor: Robert L. Koegel

PART II
Assessment:

Functional Assessment, Person-Centered Planning, and Meaningful Outcomes

❧

Assessment, the process of gathering information, guides the supports we select and tells us whether our interventions efforts are making a difference. With specific regard to positive behavior support (PBS), we assess to know the person—learn about who the person is, what the person's interests and preferences are, and what dreams the person and his or her family might have for the future. We assess to understand reasons for problem behavior, from both micro (immediate environment) and macro (lifestyle) perspectives. Furthermore, we assess to determine the extent to which PBS has resulted in outcomes that are meaningful to the person and his or her family.

The collection of articles in this section capture all forms of assessment relevant to PBS. Functional assessment focuses on understanding the environmental determinants of problem behavior. Specifically, functional assessment asks the following question: *What events or conditions evoke problem behavior, and what purpose or function does problem behavior serve for the person under these circumstances?* In what is now a classic article, Lennon and Miltenberger (1989) described the basic strategies for conducting a functional assessment. Their description of the various assessment methods and the advantages and limitations of each are still pertinent today. Building on this foundation, Knoster (2000) and Scott and Nelson (1999) illustrated how these assessment methods may be used in typical school and classroom settings. Moreover, these articles place functional assessment within the overall framework for designing individualized support plans, beginning with gathering information through functional assessment, moving on to

formulating specific hypotheses about the reasons for problem behavior, and, finally, designing support plans that link back to the assessment information.

Durand et al.'s (1989) study on reinforcer assessment tells us why conducting a functional assessment is critical for effective supports. Through a series of single-case analyses with 14 students with severe disabilities, Durand et al. demonstrated unequivocally that when interventions are designed to help the student achieve the same outcome (function) as provided by the problem behavior but through alternative means, that problem behavior can be reduced. When interventions ignore what the learner is trying to achieve through problem behavior, however, those interventions will be ineffective, and in some cases, occurrences of the behavior will actually increase.

In addition to functional assessments, lifestyle assessments are needed to ensure that PBS is focused on achieving a quality life. Person-centered planning methods such as MAPS, described by Vandercook, York, and Johnson (1989), and the Lifestyle Development Process, described by Mallette and colleagues (1992), offer both assessment and planning approaches for designing quality lifestyles in inclusive school and community settings.

This section ends with an article by Meyer and Janney (1989). If the goal of PBS is to foster meaningful outcomes, how should intervention success be judged and evaluated? Meyer and Janney have offered evaluative criteria and user-friendly ways of measuring success.

—Linda M. Bambara

JASH
1989, Vol. 14, No. 4, 304-311

Conducting a Functional Assessment of Problem Behavior in Applied Settings

David B. Lennox and Raymond G. Miltenberger
New Medico Associates
North Dakota State University

Researchers have recently called for a greater emphasis on the use of functional assessment procedures in the selection of treatment strategies for problem behavior in persons with mental retardation. In applied settings there are several methods available for conducting a functional assessment. This article identifies and describes three methods that have been used in applied behavior analysis research: informant assessment (e.g., behavioral interviews, rating scales, and questionnaires), direct observation assessment, and experimental analysis. Although experimental analysis provides the most conclusive information regarding controlling variables for a behavior problem, less rigorous methods of assessment also yield important information with which to select and evaluate treatment strategies. This article reviews the strengths and weaknesses of each functional assessment method and provides a case example to illustrate the use of the various assessment procedures.

DESCRIPTORS: applied behavior analysis, behavioral assessment, behavior management, excess behavior, functional analysis, functional assessment, interviewing, A-B-C assessment

The treatment of problem behavior in children and adults with mental retardation has received considerable attention over the last 20 years. There is an abundance of treatment research available for practitioners to consider when making treatment decisions (e.g., Bailey, Shook, Iwata, Reid, & Repp, 1986; Barrett, 1986; Lennox, Miltenberger, Spengler, & Erfanian, 1988; Lundervold & Bourland, 1988; Matson & Taras, 1989). However, determining the most appropriate treatment for a given individual remains a complex and often difficult process, requiring consideration of a variety of issues (Lovaas & Favell, 1987; Lennox & Miltenberger, in press).

We thank Kathleen Wright for conceptual contributions to an earlier draft of this manuscript.

Requests for reprints should be sent to David Lennox, Highwatch Rehabilitation Center, P.O. Box 99, Center Ossipee, NH 03814.

It is widely accepted that an important step in the treatment selection process is determining the variables occasioning and maintaining the target behavior. The term *functional assessment* denotes the identification of antecedent and consequent events, temporally contiguous to the behavior, which occasion and maintain the behavior. A functional assessment may involve the manipulation of antecedent and consequent variables or a more naturalistic assessment in which variables are not manipulated. Iwata, Dorsey, Slifer, Bauman, and Richman (1982a) and Axelrod (1987) have used the term *functional analysis* to refer specifically to the manipulation of potential controlling variables. Presumably, an understanding of the controlling variables, achieved through a functional assessment of the problem behavior, will lead to the selection of more effective treatments (Axelrod, 1987; Demchak & Halle, 1985; Durand, 1987; Iwata et al., 1982a; Lennox & Miltenberger, in press; Repp, Felce, & Barton, 1988; Touchette, MacDonald, & Langer, 1985). In particular, knowledge of controlling variables has been shown to aid in developing treatment procedures in at least three ways. First, a functional assessment may identify the reinforcing consequences of the target behavior, which can then lead a practitioner to eliminate or prevent their occurrence following the behavior (Carr, Newsom, & Binkoff, 1980; Rincover, Cook, Peoples, & Packard, 1979). Second, a functional assessment may identify antecedent conditions that evoke the target behavior. By either removing these conditions or altering their characteristics (Horner, 1980; Weeks & Gaylord-Ross, 1981), the behavior can be prevented. Finally, functional assessment information may aid the practitioner in identifying more appropriate but functionally equivalent (i.e., resulting in the same reinforcing consequences) alternatives to the target behavior (Carr & Durand, 1985; Durand & Carr, 1987; Favell, McGimsey, & Schnell, 1982). Reliance on such functionally based strategies as these may preclude the use of more restrictive, punishment-based procedures (Axelrod, 1987; LaVigna & Donnellan, 1986).

Although direct empirical evidence for the validity of functionally based treatment procedures is sparse (e.g., Repp et al., 1988; Steege, Wacker, Berg, Cigrand, & Cooper, 1989), several studies provide strong supporting evidence (e.g., Carr & Durand, 1985; Carr et al., 1980; Day, Rea, Schussler, Larson, & Johnson, 1988; Durand & Carr, 1987; Gaylord-Ross, Weeks, & Lipner, 1980; Solnick, Rincover, & Peterson, 1977). In addition, applied behavior analysts have recently called for more emphasis on a prior functional assessment when devising procedures to decrease problem behavior (Durand, 1987; Lennox et al., 1988). It is unfortunate that few published treatment studies report the use of a functional assessment strategy prior to treatment selection (Deitz, 1978; Durand, 1987; Haynes, 1987; Lennox et al., 1988; Lundervold, & Bourland, 1988).

There could be many reasons for this significant omission. One may be the apparently "established" practice of treatment selection based simply on the direction of behavior change desired, rather than on the control of a particular set of contingencies. For example, if the intent is to decrease the frequency of a problem behavior, a practitioner might select a treatment designed to be decelerative or suppressive in function, but not necessarily related to the controlling variables of the target behavior. This strategy of treatment selection is facilitated by the publication of articles or chapters reviewing specific treatments (e.g., Browder & Shapiro, 1985; Lennox et al., 1988; Miltenberger & Fuqua, 1981) or problem behaviors (e.g., LaGrow & Repp, 1984; Gorman-Smith & Matson, 1985; Matson & Gorman-Smith, 1986). In addition, some authors have published "inventories" of treatment procedures classified by outcome (e.g., "procedures which decrease behavior," Martin & Pear, 1983; Sulzer & Mayer, 1972), and some recommend particular behavior-treatment combinations (e.g., Lennox et al., 1988).

Failing to conduct a functional assessment of problem behavior prior to treatment selection presents some risks. One of the most apparent risks involves exposing a client to an ineffective treatment regimen which, at minimum, delays the use of potentially effective treatment procedures (Romanczyk, Kistner, & Plienis, 1982). A treatment procedure selected without the benefit of a functional assessment also may adversely affect the client through counter-therapeutic effects on the target behavior (e.g., Lennox et al., 1988; Solnick et al., 1977) or unnecessary exposure to aversive and restrictive procedures (LaVigna & Donnellan, 1986).

This article provides a review of methods for conducting a functional assessment of aberrant behavior in applied settings. The functional assessment methods described are classified according to the sophistication or rigor of the functional assessment involved, although they also differ according to the environment in which they are typically conducted. The first category includes behavioral interviews, rating scales, and questionnaires, which rely on the reporting of an informant (e.g., teacher, staff, parent) who knows the client. The second category involves direct observation which produces a descriptive or A-B-C assessment. The final type of assessment involves the experimental manipulation (functional analysis) of variables hypothesized to be related to the problem.

Informant Assessment

Behavioral interviews. The behavioral interview procedure frequently is used to obtain a functional assessment of problem behavior (Haynes & Jensen, 1979; Swan & McDonald, 1978). It is designed to obtain the informant's (teacher, staff, or parent) report of a particular behavior and its related variables (Bergan, 1977; Cone, 1987; O'Leary & Wilson, 1986). A complete interview should contain questions about the topography of the behavior problem, antecedent events, consequent events, and other information to determine the variables maintaining behavior and to select appropriate treatment procedures (Iwata, Wong, Reardon, Dorsey, & Lau, 1982b; Miltenberger & Fuqua, 1985; Miltenberger & Veltum, 1988).

In certain cases, the behavioral interview may be the practitioner's main source of assessment information. However, it is more likely to be part of a more thorough assessment process that may include direct observation, self-monitoring, rating scales, and/or other assessment procedures (Cone, 1987; O'Leary & Wilson, 1986). For example, the practitioner may interview the informant about the client's behavior problem and, based on the information obtained, develop a data collection system for teachers, parents, or staff to use to directly observe and record the behavior and maintaining variables of the client. In addition, after an initial interview a practitioner may direct the client to record his or her own behavior and the antecedents and consequences of the behavior in the classroom (or other applied setting).

The behavioral interview is a useful tool for obtaining the initial information on which to base further assessment (Morganstern, 1976). However, there are limitations to what may be accomplished in the interview. The interview does not allow direct access to the behavior (or its controlling variables) in question; it is, therefore, an indirect or ex-post facto method of data collection accompanied by problems inherent in such indirect measures, including faulty recollection of events, observer bias, and observer expectations (Kazdin, 1980). The interview should be merely the starting point in the functional assessment process, leading to more objective or rigorous methods that allow a more complete assessment.

The most useful type of behavioral interview is structured specifically to obtain the information needed to functionally assess the problem behavior. The interview formats used by Iwata et al. (1982b) for child management clients and Miltenberger and Veltum (1988) for general outpatient clients exemplify the degree of structure that is desirable for obtaining specific information on controlling contingencies. In each of these interview formats, the informant answers a number of open-ended and closed-ended questions, with each question addressing a different content area relevant to understanding the problem.

Behavioral rating scales, checklists, and questionnaires. The use of behavioral rating scales, checklists, and questionnaires is another highly structured method for obtaining functional assessment information. These instruments provide questions that, when answered by the informant, help pinpoint the function of a behavior problem. For example, answers to each of the 16 questions on the Motivation Assessment Scale (Durand & Crimmins, 1988) provide information useful for determining whether the behavior problem is reinforced by attention, tangibles, escape/avoidance, or sensory stimulation. Similarly, Donnellan, Mirenda, Mesaros, and Fassbender (1984) developed an instrument designed to determine the communicative function of problem behaviors. A range of communicative functions (different ways a behavior may be reinforced by the actions of another person) is provided, and staff check those that apply to the behavior problem in question. Finally, Evans and Meyer (1985) developed a questionnaire with 15 open- and closed-ended questions that provide insight into the function of the behavior and other information needed to formulate appropriate, functionally based treatments.

The degree of structure in these and similar instruments is useful when trying to obtain specific information from staff, teachers, and parents regarding the behavior of a client. It is important to note, however, that such instruments produce ex-post facto information similar to behavioral interviews. As such, this information is a product of the informant's memory of events and may, therefore, be influenced by lack of relevant exposure to the behavioral events in question, forgetting, expectations or demand characteristics, or by the informant's idiosyncratic interpretation of events. Keeping this in mind, the practitioner should look for consistency among informants' reports and between interview information and the results of these assessment instruments. The practitioner should realize that information from informants is valuable but can be limited, and that the best information on controlling variables is derived from directly observing the target behavior under specified antecedent and consequent conditions. Two such methods for completing a functional assessment will follow.

Direct Observation Assessment

A second method for identifying the controlling variables of a target behavior involves an assessment based on direct observation. Two types of direct observation include the use of a scatterplot to record temporal patterns in the problem behavior (Touchette et al., 1985) and an antecedent-behavior-consequence (A-B-C) assessment (Cooper, Heron, & Heward, 1987).

Scatterplot assessment. The scatterplot assessment method described by Touchette et al. (1985) involves plotting the time of each occurrence of the target behavior on a grid, with time of day on the ordinate and consecutive days on the abscissa. The result is a scatterplot in which differentially higher rates of behavior are represented by darker notations on the temporal grid. As repeated observations are plotted on the grid, correlations between one or more recording times and differential rates of behavior become more evident. The practitioner can then conduct further A-B-C assessments during the specific time periods in which the scatterplot shows the behavior to be most probable. Although the scatterplot strategy fails to specifically identify potential controlling variables and provides only a rough representation of rate, it is relatively easy to use and to interpret, and narrows the field of analysis so that the A-B-C assessment can be conducted more efficiently.

A-B-C assessment. The A-B-C assessment (Cooper et al., 1987), attempts to directly evaluate the immediate antecedent and consequent events surrounding the target behavior and, subsequently, to determine the extent to which specific events may be related to the occurrence of the behavior. An A-B-C assessment is accomplished through recorded descriptive accounts of directly observed behavior and temporally related environmental events and is conducted during the initial assessment process (Bijou, Peterson, & Ault, 1968; Cooper et al., 1987; Kazdin, 1980).

Although a practitioner cannot conclude that a causal relationship exists between the behavior and recorded events (because no variables are actually manipulated), the data may reflect a correlational relationship leading to hypotheses about controlling variables. As Kazdin (1980) pointed out, it is likely that a frequently emitted undesirable behavior is being maintained by environmental events, presumably those which are temporally close to the behavior. If this is indeed the case, an A-B-C assessment conducted over the course of several observation periods would reflect such a relationship between the behavior and events that consistently preceded or followed it. Once identified, a treatment regimen that involved the manipulation of these antecedent and/or consequent environmental variables would likely lead to a change in the behavior. For example, Repp et al. (1988) demonstrated that treatments based on A-B-C assessments were more effective than treatments not based on prior functional assessments.

When deciding to use an A-B-C assessment, a practitioner should consider several issues. First, although extensive training is probably not required to gather the requisite descriptive data, the resulting assessment depends entirely on the accuracy of these descriptive accounts by the observer. Thus, it is important for the observer to be aware of the critically concise temporal parameters involved in an A-B-C recording procedure. It is our experience that observers, without at least initial detailed instruction, often record global environmental stimulus events that are far removed from the target behavior being recorded. Furthermore, interpretations or judgmental narratives of the events often are provided instead of objective recordings, seriously compromising the integrity of the resulting assessment. Thus, the observer must be trained not to infer motivation or intention, but to describe events clearly and accurately.

Cooper et al. (1987) provided extensive guidelines for conducting an A-B-C assessment. For example, they suggested that observers (a) use shorthand or abbreviations for the observed events to facilitate recording; (b) report only actions (events) that are seen or heard, thus limiting inferences or interpretations; (c) record events that occur immediately before and after each response; (d) record the estimated duration of each behavioral event; (e) carry out the observation over several days; (f) observe as unobtrusively as possible; and (g) use a form or data sheet designed specifically for A-B-C information. By following these guidelines a practitioner should achieve a useful picture of variables likely to be controlling the target behavior.

We would suggest that an even more rigorous A-B-C assessment may be conducted that does not rely solely on descriptive reports but also on further direct observation of the events described in the descriptive reports. In such an assessment the practitioner would first collect the descriptive reports of the antecedents and consequences generated by observers and then develop a direct observation system in which these events are observed and recorded in much the same way the target behavior may be recorded, for example, in an interval recording method (Bailey & Bostow, 1979). In this way, the frequency of occurrence of specific environmental events, as well as their temporal relation to the target behavior, would not only be described, but also quantified. Mace and Lalli (1989) reported the use of this type of A-B-C assessment, and Alessi and Kaye (1983) approximated this recommendation by providing specific consequent codes, each of which represented a teacher or peer reaction to the occurrence of a problem behavior by the target student.

Experimental Analysis

The final method for conducting a functional assessment involves experimental manipulation of controlling variables and, as such, constitutes a functional analysis (Axelrod, 1987; Iwata et al., 1982a). By recording behavioral changes associated with the introduction and repeated presentation of various antecedent and consequent events, a practitioner can determine which variables are functionally related to the target behavior. Such control of potential maintaining variables is difficult to attain in the natural environment and often requires that the practitioner arrange an analogue en-

vironment in which the contingencies are essentially contrived but closely approximate those operating in the natural environment. Once the controlling variables are identified in the analogue situation, the practitioner can then manipulate functionally similar contingencies found in the natural environment in an effort to decrease the problem behavior.

Experimental methods have been used only recently for identifying functional relationships between particular environmental events and behavior. In a functional analysis of self-injury, Iwata et al., (1982a) exposed persons with mental retardation to each of four different conditions using an alternating treatments design (Barlow & Hayes, 1979). These conditions consisted of (a) a contingent social disapproval condition to assess the role of positive reinforcement, in which each instance of self-injury was followed by attention in the form of social disapproval or concern; (b) an escape condition, in which academic demands were withdrawn following each occurrence of self-injury to assess the role of escape (negative reinforcement); (c) an alone condition, in which the client was alone in a room with no stimulating objects or activities to evaluate the possible self-stimulatory function of the behavior; and (d) unstructured play with no demands and frequent, noncontingent attention as a control condition. After repeated observations of clients exposed to each of these four conditions in a controlled, analogue environment, these researchers were able to identify which of the contingencies were differentially associated with the occurrence of high rates of self-injury and to conclude with some confidence that a functional relationship existed. For example, if the client consistently exhibited the highest level of self-injury in the social disapproval condition, one would conclude that attention was the variable that was most likely maintaining the self-injurious behavior. Mace, Page, Ivancic, and O'Brien (1986) reported a similar analysis of aggression and disruption, as did Scotti and Schulman (1987) for the analysis of muscle tics. In these cases the determination of the controlling variables for each of the behaviors resulted in selection of effective treatments.

Another method of conducting an experimental analysis was reported by Durand and Carr (1987), in which an extended reversal design (Barlow & Hersen, 1984) was used to assess the function of variables hypothesized to be associated with problem behavior in a classroom setting. After repeatedly exposing students to sequential phases of easy or difficult tasks and low or high attention, the authors were able to identify the controlling variables for stereotypies (e.g., escape from aversive situations) by comparing the differential rates of the behavior under each condition. The subsequent implementation of a communication training program was successful in teaching students to appropriately request assistance. The behavior of requesting assistance was functionally equivalent to the target behavior, and its increase, therefore, resulted in substantial decreases in the target behavior. Similar findings have been reported by Gaylord-Ross et al. (1980) and Weeks and Gaylord-Ross (1981).

Although it should be apparent that the experimental analysis provides more conclusive data regarding controlling variables, there are possible disadvantages with conducting such an analysis. One disadvantage is that the analogue environment typically arranged for an experimental analysis may not permit naturalistic observation (Iwata et al., 1982a), resulting in concerns for assessment artifacts and treatment generalization. In fact, Evans and Meyer (1985) and LaVigna and Donnellan (1986) have suggested that such analogue analysis procedures may not be ecologically valid. In other words, it is possible that the variables operating in the analogue situation are not the same variables responsible for the behavior in the natural environment. It is, therefore, important that the analogue environment simulate events occurring in the natural setting as closely as possible. Recently, however, researchers have suggested that experimental analyses of client problem behaviors may be conducted in more naturalistic settings such as the classroom (Sasso & Reimers, 1988) or in outclinic settings with parents present (Cooper, 1989).

A second potential disadvantage with experimental analysis procedures is the possibility of multiple treatment interference, which jeopardizes the integrity of the condition in effect at any point during the analysis. Multiple treatment interference (McGonigle, Rojahn, Dixon, & Strain, 1987), a confounding of one experimental phase caused by the presence of other phases during an alternating-treatments regimen or the carryover effects associated with the sequentially presented conditions of a reversal design, can present concerns, but these can be minimized by counterbalancing the order of treatments and/or through the use of longer inter-component intervals (McGonigle et al., 1987).

A third possible disadvantage is that the time required to conduct an extended experimental analysis can delay the implementation of potentially effective interventions. However, the additional time may increase the degree of confidence in the treatment because of the increased rigor of the analysis. Finally, it may be difficult or impractical in many applied settings (e.g., in classroom or outpatient clinical settings) to arrange the conditions necessary to conduct an experimental analysis. Limitations in staff, time, or facilities may, in many cases, preclude the possibility of such a rigorous analysis. Recently, however, Cooper (1989), Steege (1989), and Wacker, Reimers, Cooper, Northup, and Donn (1988) demonstrated that such an experimental analysis of controlling variables for child behavior problems can be successfully carried out in a relatively brief period of

time (one 90-min session) in an outpatient child behavior management clinic. Future research should investigate the possibility of conducting experimental analyses in other applied settings and investigate the treatment utility of such analyses (Hayes, Nelson, & Jarrett, 1987).

Summary

One of the primary ways in which behavior analysis differs from other approaches to the treatment of problem behavior is in its greater emphasis on *functional* rather than *topographical* analyses of behavior (Catania, 1984). Because of this focus and because failure to conduct a functional assessment may delay an effective treatment procedure or expose the client to an unnecessarily restrictive treatment procedure, it is critical that we delineate the methods for conducting a functional assessment of problem behavior. This paper outlines three methods for conducting a functional assessment of problem behavior. These methods comprise a hierarchy based on empirical integrity and rigor, with the informant assessment at the lowest level, the direct observation assessment at the intermediate level, and the experimental analysis at the highest level.

As discussed above, the exigencies of the applied setting in which the practitioner works and/or the need for a rapid reduction of the behavior (as in cases where the target behavior is extremely dangerous to the client or others) may preclude the practitioner from obtaining higher level (more rigorous) functional assessment data. However, the most rigorous or highest level of assessment should be the goal of any behavioral assessment of problem behavior. This does not mean that less rigorous assessments should be neglected, nor that data obtained from such assessments are not valid. They can, and often do, provide valuable information for selecting the most effective intervention for the reduction of a target behavior. Certainly the use of behavioral interviews and rating scales to identify treatments is preferred over treatment selection without the benefit of any functional assessment. The value of less rigorous methods is enhanced, however, when multiple methods are used and when each suggests the same controlling variables are operating for the target behavior. This congruence should then lead to even more confident treatment selection. In the following case example, we provide an illustration of how the use of the various functional assessment methods leads to treatment selection.

Case Example

Tommy was a 22-year-old man with severe mental retardation. He exhibited independent dressing and hygiene skills, but had no discernible vocal communication skills. He was reported to have a rudimentary signing repertoire, but this had not been observed in his new workshop setting. Although Tommy engaged in mild property destruction and aggression, the primary concern was his severe self-injury characterized by face-slapping and wrist-biting. A group interview with staff at the workshop where the problem primarily occurred initiated the functional assessment of Tommy's self-injurious behavior. Staff interviews revealed that Tommy's self-injury was somewhat episodic, occurring in "spurts" of 10 to 15 responses throughout the day. In addition, some staff believed that Tommy became upset and engaged in self-injury whenever he was taught a new task.

To supplement the information from staff interviews, the Motivation Assessment Scale was administered to Tommy's workshop supervisor and to two other shop staff. Although the responses varied somewhat, results from all three suggested that Tommy's self-injurious responding was more likely to occur in instructional situations when demands were placed on him.

Following the interviews and use of the Motivation Assessment Scale, staff were instructed in the use of a scatterplot assessment to determine temporal patterns in the behavior. The scatterplot confirmed that higher rates of self-injury were present during Tommy's scheduled 1:1 training sessions each day.

Given these data, two additional assessment procedures were implemented. Instruction was provided to staff for anecdotally recording the antecedents and consequences of each self-injurious episode utilizing a standard A-B-C data sheet. Since all indications, thus far, suggested that self-injury occurred only in instructional situations, these observations were conducted only during 1:1 training sessions.

We also decided to conduct a brief experimental analysis within the workshop setting. Tommy was exposed to three randomly sequenced conditions that were commonly encountered during his working day. Each condition was presented three times for 5 min. In the first condition, a new 3-piece sorting task was presented during which graduated guidance and reinforcement were terminated for 30 s if self-injury occurred (to assess an escape/avoidance relationship). During the second condition, Tommy was left alone with a familiar sorting task, which he had previously mastered, and staff provided "calming" and reassurance following any self-injurious responses (to assess the role of contingent social attention). During the third condition, Tommy was allowed to sit alone at his work table with no task present to assess the possible self-stimulatory nature of the behavior.

The data collected during these latter assessment procedures (A-B-C and experimental) were consistent with earlier information, suggesting that the self-injury was motivated by the termination of new tasks (negative reinforcement). The descriptive account showed that the majority of self-injurious responses were preceded by the presentation of a new task and were followed closely by termination of the training session. The experimental analysis further confirmed these findings. During the new task condition, Tommy engaged in almost continuous self-injury, in most cases, preventing the presentation of additional training trials. With the onset of the familiar task/social attention condition, self-injury occurred but decelerated rapidly as the condition progressed. Finally, during the alone condition, self-injury was nonexistent.

All assessment procedures produced consistent results, showing that Tommy's self-injury was maintained by negative reinforcement—the termination of new training tasks. With this information, a program could be developed that addressed the function of the behavior (Sasso & Reimers, 1988). The program for Tommy included two critical components: one to teach a new communication skill that was functionally equivalent to self-injury (Carr & Durand, 1985) and a second component to eliminate the negative reinforcement for the self-injury (Repp et al., 1988). First, during the next several sessions, Tommy was prompted to sign "break" following the presentation of a new task trial. The materials and instruction were then removed for 15 s. Gradually, less prompting to request a break was provided until Tommy signed independently. The second component of Tommy's program included extinction of self-injury, whereby he was guided through the completion of any trial during which he emitted self-injury so that the behavior did not result in escape from the task. These procedures resulted in elimination of the behavior in a relatively short period of time.

This case example illustrates the importance of functional assessment information for the selection of effective treatment procedures. In Tommy's case, the functional assessment procedures produced a clear picture of the variables occasioning and maintaining the problem behavior. Treatment procedures were then developed to specifically address the function of the behavior. Without this assessment information, treatment for Tommy may have been much different and possibly, much less effective. In general (as in this case), a prior functional assessment will facilitate the selection of the most appropriate treatment(s) and, therefore, must be the first step in the treatment selection process.

References

Alessi, G. J., & Kaye, J. H. (1983). *Behavioral assessment for school psychologists.* (Available from National Association of School Psychologists, P.O. Box 184, Kent, OH 44240.)

Axelrod, S. (1987). Functional and structural analyses of behavior: Approaches leading to reduced use of punishment procedures? *Research in Developmental Disabilities, 8,* 165–178.

Bailey, J. S., & Bostow, D. E. (1979). *A handbook of research methods in applied behavior analysis.* Tallahassee, FL: Copy Grafix.

Bailey, J., Shook, J., Iwata, B., Reid, D., & Repp, A. (1986). Behavior analysis in developmental disabilities: *Journal of Applied Behavior Analysis, Reprint Series, 1,* 1968–1985.

Barlow, D. H., & Hayes, S. C. (1979). Alternating treatments design: One strategy for comparing the effects of two treatments in a single subject. *Journal of Applied Behavior Analysis, 12,* 199–210.

Barlow, D. H., & Hersen, M. (1984). *Single-case experimental designs: Strategies for studying behavior change.* New York: Pergamon.

Barrett, R. P. (1986). *Severe behavior disorders in the mentally retarded: Non-drug approaches to treatment.* New York: Plenum.

Bergan, J. R. (1977). *Behavioral consultation.* Columbus, OH: Merrill.

Bijou, S. W., Peterson, R. F., & Ault, M. H. (1968). A method to integrate descriptive and experimental field studies at the level of data and empirical concepts. *Journal of Applied Behavior Analysis, 1,* 175–191.

Browder, D. M., & Shapiro, E. S. (1985). Applications of self-management to individuals with severe handicaps: A review. *Journal of The Association for Persons with Severe Handicaps, 4,* 11–13.

Carr, E. G., & Durand, V. M. (1985). Reducing behavior problems through functional communication training. *Journal of Applied Behavior Analysis, 18,* 111–126.

Carr, E. G., Newsom, C. D., & Binkoff, J. A. (1980). Escape as a factor in the aggressive behavior of two retarded children. *Journal of Applied Behavior Analysis, 13,* 101–117.

Catania, A. C. (1984). *Learning* (2nd ed.). Englewood Cliffs, NJ: Prentice-Hall.

Cone, J. D. (1987). Behavioral assessment with children and adolescents. In M. Hersen & V. B. Van Hasselt (Eds.), *Behavior therapy with children and adolescents: A clinical approach* (pp. 29–49). New York: Wiley.

Cooper, J. O., Heron, T. E., & Heward, W. L. (1987). *Applied behavior analysis.* Columbus, OH: Merrill.

Cooper, L. J. (1989, May). Functional analysis of conduct disorders in an outclinic setting. In D. Wacker (Chair), *Functional analysis of severe behavior problems: Recent applications and novel approaches.* Symposium presented at the 15th Annual Conference of the Association for Behavior Analysis, Milwaukee, WI.

Day, R. M., Rea, J. A., Schussler, N. G., Larson, S. E., & Johnson, W. L. (1988). A functionally based approach to the treatment of self-injurious behavior. *Behavior Modification, 12,* 565–589.

Deitz, S. M. (1978). Current status of applied behavior analysis. *American Psychologist, 33,* 805–814.

Demchak, J. A., & Halle, J. W. (1985). Motivational assessment: A potential means of enhancing treatment success of self-injurious individuals. *Education and Training of the Mentally Retarded, 20,* 25–38.

Donnellan, A. M., Mirenda, P. L., Mesaros, R. A., & Fassbender, L. L. (1984). Analyzing the communicative functions of aberrant behavior. *Journal of The Association for Persons with Severe Handicaps, 9,* 201–212.

Durand, V. M. (1987). "Look Homeward Angel": A call to return to our (functional) roots. *Behavior Analyst, 10,* 299–302.

Durand, V. M., & Carr, E. G. (1987). Social influences on "self-stimulatory" behavior: Analysis and treatment application. *Journal of Applied Behavior Analysis, 20,* 119–132.

Durand, V. M., & Crimmins, D. B. (1988). Identifying the variables maintaining self-injurious behavior. *Journal of Autism and Developmental Disorders, 18,* 99–117.

Evans, I. A., & Meyer, L. (1985). *An educative approach to problem behaviors: A practical decision model for interventions with severely handicapped learners.* Baltimore: Paul H. Brookes.

Favell, J. E., McGimsey, J. F., & Schnell, R. M. (1982). Treatment of self-injury by providing alternate sensory activities. *Analysis and Intervention in Developmental Disabilities, 2,* 83–104.

Gaylord-Ross, R., Weeks, M., & Lipner, C. (1980). An analysis of antecedent, response, and consequent events in the treatment of self-injurious behavior. *Education and Training of the Mentally Retarded, 15,* 35–42.

Gorman-Smith, D., & Matson, J. (1985). A review of treatment research for self-injurious and stereotypic responding. *Journal of Mental Deficiency Research, 29,* 295–308.

Hayes, S. C., Nelson, R. O., & Jarrett, R. B. (1987). The treatment utility of assessment: A functional approach to evaluating assessment quality. *American Psychologist, 42,* 963–974.

Haynes, S. N. (1987). The design of intervention programs. In R. O. Nelson & S. C. Hayes (Eds.), *Conceptual foundations of behavioral assessment* (pp. 386–429). New York: Guilford.

Haynes, S. N., & Jensen, B. J. (1979). The interview as a behavioral assessment instrument. *Behavioral Assessment, 1,* 97–106.

Horner, R. D. (1980). The effects of an environmental enrichment program on the behavior of institutionalized profoundly retarded children. *Journal of Applied Behavior Analysis, 13,* 473–491.

Iwata, B. A., Dorsey, M. F., Slifer, K. J., Bauman, K. E., & Richman, G. S. (1982). Toward a functional analysis of self-injury. *Analysis and Intervention in Developmental Disabilities, 2,* 3–20.

Iwata, B. A., Wong, S. E., Reardon, M. M., Dorsey, M. F., & Lau, M. M. (1982). Assessment and training of clinical interviewing skills: Analogue analysis and field replication. *Journal of Applied Behavior Analysis, 15,* 191–204.

Kazdin, A. E. (1980). *Behavior modification in applied settings.* Homewood, IL: Dorsey.

LaGrow, S., & Repp, A. (1984). Stereotypic responding: A review of intervention research. *American Journal of Mental Deficiency, 88,* 595–609.

LaVigna, G. D., & Donnellan, A. (1986). *Alternatives to punishment: Solving behavior problems with non-aversive strategies.* New York: Irvington.

Lennox, D. B., & Miltenberger, R. G. (in press). On the conceptualization of treatment acceptability. *Education and Training in Mental Retardation.*

Lennox, D. B., Miltenberger, R. G., Spengler, P., & Erfanian, N. (1988). Decelerative treatment practices: A review of five years of the literature on mental retardation. *American Journal on Mental Retardation, 92,* 492–501.

Lovaas, O. I., & Favell, J. E. (1987). Protection for clients undergoing aversive/restrictive interventions. *Education and Treatment of Children, 10,* 311–325.

Lundervold, D., & Bourland, G. (1988). Quantitative analysis of treatment of aggression, self-injury, and property destruction. *Behavior Modification, 12,* 590–617.

Mace, F. C., & Lalli, J. (1989, May). Linking descriptive and experimental analysis in the treatment of aberrant behavior. In D. Wacker (Chair), *Functional analysis of severe behavior problems: Recent applications and novel approaches.* Symposium presented at the 15th Annual Conference of the Association for Behavior Analysis, Milwaukee, WI.

Mace, C. F., Page, T. J., Ivancic, M. T., & O'Brien, S. (1986). Analysis of environmental determinants of aggression and disruption in mentally retarded children. *Applied Research in Mental Retardation, 7,* 203–221.

Martin, G., & Pear, J. (1983). *Behavior modification: What it is and how to do it.* Englewoods Cliffs, NJ: Prentice-Hall.

Matson, J., & Gorman-Smith, D. (1986). A review of treatment research for aggressive and disruptive behavior in the mentally retarded. *Applied Research in Mental Retardation, 7,* 95–103.

Matson, J. L., & Taras, M. E. (1989). A 20-year review of punishment and alternative methods to treat behavior problems in developmentally delayed persons. *Research in Developmental Disabilities, 10,* 85–104.

McGonigle, J. J., Rojahn, J., Dixon, J., & Strain, P. S. (1987). Multiple treatment interference in the alternating treatments design as a function of the intercomponent interval length. *Journal of Applied Behavior Analysis, 20,* 171–178.

Miltenberger, R. G., & Fuqua, R. W. (1981). Overcorrection: Review and critical analysis. *Behavior Analyst, 4,* 123–141.

Miltenberger, R. G., & Fuqua, R. W. (1985). Evaluation of a training manual for the acquisition of behavioral assessment interviewing skills. *Journal of Applied Behavior Analysis, 18,* 323–328.

Miltenberger, R. G., & Veltum, L. (1988). Evaluation of an instructions and modeling procedure for training behavioral assessment interviewing. *Journal of Behavior Therapy and Experimental Psychiatry, 19,* 31–41.

Morganstern, K. P. (1976). Behavioral interviewing: The initial stages of assessment. In M. Hersen & A. Bellack (Eds.), *Behavioral assessment: A practical handbook* (pp. 51–76). New York: Pergamon.

O'Leary, K. D., & Wilson, G. T. (1986). *Behavior therapy: Application and outcome.* Englewood Cliffs, NJ: Prentice-Hall.

Repp, A., Felce, D., & Barton, L. (1988). Basing the treatment of stereotypic and self-injurious behavior on hypotheses of their causes. *Journal of Applied Behavior Analysis, 21,* 281–290.

Rincover, A., Cook, R., Peoples, A., & Packard, D. (1979). Sensory extinction and sensory reinforcement principles for programming multiple adaptive behavior change. *Journal of Applied Behavior Analysis, 12,* 221–233.

Romanczyk, R., Kistner, J. S., & Plienis, A. (1982). Self-stimulatory and self-injurious behavior: Etiology and treatment. In J. Steffen & P. Karoly (Eds.), *Advances in child behavior analysis and therapy* (pp. 189–254). Lexington, MA: Lexington Books.

Sasso, G. M., & Reimers, T. M. (1988). Assessing the functional properties of behavior: Implications and applications for the classroom. *Focus on Autistic Behavior, 3,* 1–15.

Scotti, J. R., & Schulman, D. E. (1987, May). *A functional analysis of a tic disorder.* Paper presented at the 13th annual convention of the Association for Behavior Analysis, Nashville, TN.

Solnick, J. V., Rincover, A., & Peterson, C. R. (1977). Some determinants of the reinforcing and punishing effects of time-out. *Journal of Applied Behavior Analysis, 10,* 415–424.

Steege, M., Wacker, D., Berg, W., Cigrand, K., & Cooper, L. (1989). The use of behavioral assessment to prescribe and evaluate treatments for severely handicapped children. *Journal of Applied Behavior Analysis, 22,* 23–33.

Steege, M. W. (1989, May). Functional analysis of self-injurious behavior in an outclinic setting. In D. Wacker (Chair), *Functional analysis of severe behavior problems: Recent applications and novel approaches.* Symposium presented at the 15th Annual Conference of the Association for Behavior Analysis, Milwaukee, WI.

Sulzer, B., & Mayer, G. R. (1972). *Behavior modification procedures for school personnel.* New York: Holt, Rinehart and Winston.

Swan, G. E., & McDonald, M. L. (1978). Behavior therapy in practice: A national survey of behavior therapists. *Behavior Therapy, 9,* 799–807.

Touchette, P. E., MacDonald, R. F., & Langer, S. N. (1985). A scatter plot for identifying stimulus control of problem behavior. *Journal of Applied Behavior Analysis, 18,* 343–351.

Wacker, D., Reimers, T., Cooper, L., Northup, J., & Donn, L. (1988, November). *Child behavior management: Assessment and therapy in a tertiary care setting.* Paper presented at the Fall Conference of the Minnesota Association for Behavior Analysis, Minneapolis, MN.

Weeks, M., & Gaylord-Ross, R. (1981). Task difficulty and aberrant behavior in severely handicapped students. *Journal of Applied Behavior Analysis, 14,* 449–463.

Received: March 7, 1989
Final Acceptance: May 1, 1989
Editor in Charge: David P. Wacker

JASH
2000, Vol. 25, No. 4, 201–211

Practical Application of Functional Behavioral Assessment in Schools

Timothy P. Knoster
Central Susquehanna Intermediate Unit, Lewisburg, PA

Individualized Educational Program (IEP) teams working with students who have disabilities and a history of problem behavior that impedes their learning or that of others have the responsibility to develop their capacity to conduct functional behavioral assessments that lead to the delivery of effective behavior intervention plans. This article provides guidance to school-based teams that should prove useful to practitioners and families. In particular, this article highlights (a) the necessary components of a functional behavioral assessment, (b) a decision making framework concerning the selection of assessment and intervention procedures to be used at school, and (c) a description of one practical functional behavioral assessment tool—the Initial Line of Inquiry—that has been employed by school-based teams.

DESCRIPTORS: intervention, problem behavior, functional behavior

School-based teams have the responsibility of conducting functional behavioral assessments (FBAs) and designing and implementing effective behavior intervention plans as stipulated in the Individuals with Disabilities Education Act (IDEA). In particular, Section 615(k)(B)(i) of the law states: "If the local education agency did not conduct a functional behavioral assessment and implement a behavioral intervention plan for such child before the behavior that resulted in the suspension described in subparagraph (A), the agency shall convene an [Individualized Education Plan] IEP meeting to develop an assessment plan to address that behavior." Further, Section 615 (k)(B)(ii) states: "If the child already has a behavioral intervention plan, the IEP Team shall review the plan and modify it, as necessary, to address the behavior."

The task of conducting an FBA in light of these and other IEP-related requirements under IDEA can appear overwhelming for educators and parents unfamiliar with the assessment and intervention design process. A student-centered, team approach is necessary to

meet the requirements of the law. One goal of IEP teams is to provide effective intervention to ensure that students with problem behavior benefit from their educational programs. The IEP team should include representatives in addition to professionals from the environments in which the child interacts and receives support (Rainforth & York-Barr, 1997). For example, the IEP team should include people who know the child well, individuals who will implement the intervention plan, and those who will live with the results of intervention and support (e.g., teachers, para-professionals, and other agency staff, family members, and the student). A team approach is consistent with the legal requirements of the IDEA and can best ensure that students will derive reasonable benefit from their educational program.

To realize the potential of FBAs, student-centered teams need to understand what it means to conduct an FBA, be familiar with the array of tools and processes that are available, know that these tools and processes occur along a continuum of resource intensity and empirical rigor, and develop a process for selecting relevant tools and processes at given points along this continuum. The purpose of this article is to provide school-based teams with guidance as to how to integrate efficient methods of conducting FBAs within the context of a team decision-making process that results in the development and implementation of a student-centered plan of intervention and support.

What Is an FBA?

An FBA is a problem-solving framework that leads to intervention (Knoster & McCurdy, in press; Repp, Karsh, Munk, & Dahlquist, 1995; Tilly et al., 1998). The process of coming to an understanding about why students engage in problem behavior and how student behavior relates to the environment is referred to as functional behavioral assessment (Tilly et al., 1998). The purpose of FBA is to gather both broad and specific information in order to better understand the reasons for a student's behavior. In particular, Bambara and Knoster (1995, 1998) note that FBA can provide a student-centered team (e.g., an IEP team) with information about why a given student engages in problem behavior, when the student is most and least likely to engage in the behavior of concern, and under what conditions the student is more likely to be successful (e.g.,

Address all correspondence and requests for reprints to Timothy P. Knoster, Division of Applied Research and Educational Support (DARES), Department of Child and Family Studies (CFS), Louis de la Parte Florida Mental Health Institute (FMHI), University of South Florida (USF), 13301 Bruce B. Downs Blvd., MCH2113A, Tampa, FL 33612-3807. E-mail: knoster@fmhi.usf.edu performance of expected behavior and absence of problem behavior). After gathering information, the student's educational team develops hypotheses as a result of the assessment. Hypotheses are simply a set of propositions set forth by the student's team as possible explanations for the occurrence of problem behavior (Evans & Meyer, 1985; Meyer & Evans, 1989). Hypotheses serve a number of purposes. They summarize assessment results, offer explanations for the student's problem behavior, and guide the development of a behavior intervention plan.

Completing an FBA requires more than simple descriptions of the student's problem behavior, such as "Tommy is screaming." Although it is important for the team to note that Tommy is screaming, simply describing Tommy's action does not provide sufficient information to design an effective intervention plan. Tommy's educational team must be concerned with not only Tommy's screaming (i.e., frequency and duration), but also *why* he is screaming (i.e., function) and the conditions under which he is most and least likely to scream (context). To illustrate, screaming in response to pain or fear may look and sound the same but serve a different function than screaming to gain attention from someone. The point is that two instances of the same behavior can look and sound identical while serving different purposes in different situations for the same student (Bambara & Knoster, 1995; Durand, 1990; Lalli & Casey, 1996; O'Neill et al., 1997; Smith, Iwata,

Vollmer, & Zarcone, 1993). Acquiring this broader understanding of why, and under what circumstances, a student engages in problem behavior is critical to designing successful interventions.

A Decision Making Framework for Schools

In order for any assessment to be useful, it must lead to the design of an intervention that will be successful. Table 1 provides examples of approaches to gathering information in conducting FBAs. The tools and procedures represent an array of approaches that can be implemented in typical school settings (e.g., simple interview techniques and direct observational procedures). Information generated through the use of these tools and procedures can be used to design effective behavior support plans.

There are three common approaches to systematically collecting functional assessment information related to student problem behavior (Anderson, Freeman, Mullen, & Scotti, 1999; O'Neill et al., 1997; Tilly, Knoster, & Ikeda, 2000). The first approach is referred to as informant methods; it involves talking with the student who presents the problem behavior and with people who have direct contact with, and knowledge of, the student. The second approach is direct observation, which requires systematic observation of the student within typical routines and settings over time. Typically, school-based teams that employ either, or a combina-

Table 1
Continuum of Effective Tools and Procedures for Typical School Settings

Difficulty of behavioral problem	Level of information gathering	Examples of tools/procedures
Low	Intuitive decision making	Teacher's extemporaneous decision making in the ebb and flow of daily routines Teacher reflection devoid of a systematic process Teacher discussions devoid of a framework/protocol
	Informant methods	Informal Hypothesis Generation (Meyer & Evans, 1989) Person Centered Assessment (Mount & Zwernick, 1988; O'Brien & Lyle, 1987; Vandercook, York, & Forest, 1989) Functional Assessment Interview (O'Neill et al., 1997) Social Network Analysis (Kennedy, Horner, & Newton, 1990) Quality of Life Survey (Kincaid et al., 1997) Motivation Assessment Scale (Durand & Crimmins, 1988) Quality of Life Cue Questions (Anderson, Mesaros, & Neary, 1991) Positive Environment Checklist (Albin, Horner, & O'Neill, 1993) Interaction Observation Form (Albin et al., 1993) Curriculum Activity Profile (Foster-Johnson, Ferro, & Dunlap, 1991) Communication Interview Format (Schuler, Peck, Tomlinson, & Theimer, 1984) Initial Line of Inquiry (Knoster & Llewellyn, 1997, 1998) Anecdotal Record Review
High	Direct observation	A-B-C (SORKC) Analysis (Kanfer & Saslow, 1969; Reese, Howard, & Reese, 1977) Scatterplots (Touchette, MacDonald, & Langer, 1985) Functional Analysis Observation Form (O'Neill, Horner, Albin, Storey, & Sprague, 1990) Behavior Maps (Bijou, Peterson, & Ault, 1968; Ittelson, Rivlin, & Proschansky, 1976)

tion of, these two approaches will derive sufficient information from which to formulate hypotheses.

In addition to these two approaches, there is a third approach known as experimental analysis (i.e., analog functional analysis; Iwata, Dorsey, Slifer, Bauman, & Richman, 1994/1982). In many cases, it may not be necessary to conduct an experimental analysis, particularly if the results of less intrusive and more time efficient methods (e.g., informant methods or direct observation) yield plausible explanations for student problem behavior (O'Neill et al., 1997). In this method, specific variables that are hypothesized as being related to the occurrence or nonoccurrence of the student's problem behavior are systematically manipulated to test the team's hypotheses (Repp et al., 1995). Experimental analysis has the advantage of demonstrating, with a higher degree of confidence, the relations between environmental events and problem behavior (Bijou et al., 1968; Sasso et al., 1992). However, conducting such analyses in typical school settings is problematic due to resource implications including time and expertise of staff. Therefore, experimental analysis is not depicted in Table 1 as a common approach to gathering information in schools. Experimental analysis may serve as the last option for a small number of student-centered teams when other procedures have proven inconclusive.

The process of FBA can be best understood as a continuum of integrated assessment procedures that may involve an array of data collection tools and procedures (Tilly et al., 1998, 2000). In determining the amount of resources and degree of precision in the intervention design process (e.g., informant methods, direct observation, or a combination of informant methods and direct observation), student-centered teams should make decisions on a case-by-case basis. Specifically, decisions should be made in relation to the need for immediate behavior change (e.g., urgent behaviors, such as self-injury, vs. excessive behaviors that reflect normal deviance; Meyer & Evans, 1989) and should consider the school's resource and capacity implications (e.g., time availability and information gathering expertise of staff). Accelerating through this continuum toward conducting a comprehensive experimental analysis for an excessive behavior (e.g., a student occasionally pushing other children on the playground), prior to employing less intensive and more efficient methods (i.e., informant methods and, if warranted, direct observation), would represent an overly intrusive and costly approach to intervention.

FBA is a problem-solving framework. It is critical to note when matching the intensity and precision of assessment procedures to problem behavior that no matter which specific procedures are used, the same decision-making processes are employed. In other words, the thinking process does not change, although the

level of precision needed in the data collection and subsequent intervention will vary.

Most mild problem behaviors can be efficiently addressed (e.g., occasional aggressive actions such as pushing other children on the playground) through informant methods. Teachers and significant others may be asked about the setting, circumstances, and consequences surrounding the student's aggressive acts. On the other hand, an educational team confronted with a student who engages in extreme problem behavior (e.g., self-injury including head banging and face slapping in multiple settings) will likely need to employ informant methods (e.g., in-depth interviews) along with more resource intensive systematic behavioral observations across settings and time. In addition, this team may also need to conduct a comprehensive record review. This may result in a medical assessment concerning physical health factors (e.g., history of inner ear infections) that may be contributing to the student's self-injury (LaVigna & Donnellan, 1986; O'Neill et al., 1997). Further, the team may conduct this record review within the context of a person-centered planning process.

Person-centered planning describes a range of techniques for identifying a person's wants and needs (Kincaid, 1996). It involves the facilitation of the support team (which should involve the person to be supported) in learning more about the person and that person's family. Further, the process highlights planning for a more positive future as defined by the person, the person's family, and other members of the support team. Person-centered planning includes Lifestyle Planning (O'Brien, 1987; O'Brien & Lyle, 1987), Personal Futures Planning (Mount, 1987; Mount & Zwernick, 1988), the McGill Action Planning System (Forest & Lusthaus, 1987; Vandercook et al., 1989), Framework for Accomplishment/Personal Profile (O'Brien, Mount, & O'Brien, 1991), and Essential Lifestyle Planning (Smull & Harrison, 1992).

It is important for student-centered teams to allocate resources that will best match the severity of the problem. It is also important to understand that teams will conduct FBAs at various "points of entry:" To illustrate, a team may be confronted with a first-grade student whose off-task behavior has become increasingly problematic during general academic instruction to the point that the teacher will begin to use a simple checklist to record student on- and off-task behavior (FBA at the screening and general education level). An educational team may initiate an FBA as part of a full and individual evaluation for eligibility for special education services in response to a third-grade student's persistent tantrums and peer hitting (FBA as a part of an evaluation for special education). An IEP team may initiate an FBA to design a behavior intervention plan for a sixth-grade student with significant disabilities who has not previously required a behavior intervention plan (FBA as a part of IEP development). And a final example is an IEP team that may initiate a comprehensive FBA as a result of disciplinary proceedings (i.e., conducting a manifestation determination as delineated in the IDEA) for an eighth-grade student with an IEP (FBA in response to disciplinary matters that may impact on educational placement).

Given the approaches to gathering information and the varying points of entry for educational teams in conducting FBAs, it is important that student-centered teams identify and use appropriate information gathering and intervention design techniques (Tilly et al., 2000). Therefore, student-centered teams must carefully consider the cost and potential impact of intervention from the perspective of all relevant parties. Specifically, student-centered teams should consider the efficiency and use of human resources at school, as well as any potential adverse effect that the selected information gathering and intervention procedures may have on the student and others in the setting of concern. Teams should proceed in a less to more intrusive manner based on student and parent preferences coupled with the success rate of previous assessment and intervention procedures employed. In the instance of failure of interventions that were based on less rigorous FBA procedures, such as the use of simple surveys and record reviews, the use of more intensive methods, such as repeated direct observations using a structured protocol, should be considered.

Specific FBA Components

Gathering broad information. Once a student-centered team decides to systematically move beyond intuitive decision-making (e.g., extemporaneous decision making in the classroom by the teacher as to how to respond to the occurrence of problem behavior), the first step in the FBA is to gather broad contextual information about the student: skills and abilities, preferences and interests, general health, and quality of life. This information is helpful not only to increase understanding about why the student engages in problem behavior, but also to develop effective intervention plans that are tailored to the student's preferences, needs, and life circumstances (Bambara & Knoster, 1995, 1998).

When gathering broad information, school teams should consider how to build on current student strengths in each area assessed. Conversely, the team should also take into account how negative influences (e.g., academic deficits, boredom with curriculum, history of failure at school) or the absence of positive factors may be contributing to the problem behavior. In addition, teams should consider whether problem behaviors are related to illness or pain (e.g., a cold, fatigue), sensory problems, poor dietary or sleep habits, or clinical mental health issues (e.g., depression). It is also important to gather information about the student's quality of life.

Gathering specific information. In the second stage of the FBA, the team gathers specific information that will pinpoint the conditions that are regularly associated with occurrence and nonoccurrence of problem behavior. Additionally, the team gathers information to identify the function or purpose of the student's behavior. Specifically, the team asks three questions: When is the student most and least likely to engage in problem behavior? What specific events appear to be contributing to the problem situation? What function does the problem behavior serve for the student?

A Practical Place To Start

In order to realize the potential of FBA, school-based teams need a practical place to start the assessment process that teachers will find acceptable and useful (Lohrmann-O'Rourke, Knoster, & Llewellyn, 1999). The logistical constraints and pressures typically present in schools when responding to student problem behavior (e.g., resources and time vs. urgency and degree of need) and the comprehensive nature of FBA can be unnerving to educators who are just becoming aware of the legal requirements under the IDEA or who are learning about the assessment-intervention process.

To provide educational teams with a practical FBA process, Knoster and Llewellyn (1997) developed the Initial Line of Inquiry (ILI). The ILI is an initial screening process for identifying, analyzing, and addressing student problem behavior. It can serve as a starting point for conducting an initial systematic assessment of a student's problem behavior (Lohrman-O'Rourke et al., 1999). The tool is designed for use within the context of team planning, making it a good fit within the existing IEP structure delineated in IDEA 1997. The author and colleagues associated with the *Tri-State Consortium on Positive Behavior Support* have utilized the ILI with student-centered teams across urban, suburban, and rural settings in a number of states.

The ILI is an informant method (team interview) that serves as a screening tool for identifying patterns of student behavior. Interviews can serve as valuable tools for contextualizing problem behavior, identifying associated environmental variables, and eliminating variables not associated with the student's problem behavior. There is evidence to suggest that the reliability (interrater) and validity (criterion-related) of behavioral interviewing is adequate, with the exception of interviews conducted with children (Gresham, 1984). The psychometric qualities of behavioral interviews generally improve with training and structure (Bergan, 1977; Bergan & Kratochwill, 1990; Bergan & Tombari, 1975). However, like other indirect measures, behavioral interviews rely on subjective impressions of others that can be influenced by events (Horner & Carr, 1997).

A facilitator conducts the ILI within the context of a

team meeting. The team's facilitator can be either an internal (e.g., school psychologist or guidance counselor) or external (e.g., consultant) member of the team. Core team members include people who know the student well, as well as the individual student, whenever feasible. In addition to being an efficient method of collecting interview information because a number of team members are interviewed simultaneously, the process can also yield additional information not obtainable through independent individual interviews (e.g., one team member's comments may trigger reflection and additional comment by other team members). The team facilitator is typically well versed in assessment and intervention. Therefore, the ILI can serve as a valuable vehicle for helping student-centered teams understand the behavior of concern from a functional perspective and lead to more effective intervention strategies.

To promote communication among team members, user friendly terminology is used in place of more traditional terms (e.g., the term *fast trigger* is used to refer to antecedents associated with the problem behavior). Using a flip chart or chalkboard, the facilitator publicly records relevant information for all members to view (Table 2). The facilitator serves as a scribe and inter-

preter for emerging patterns in the team's discussion leading to the development of hypotheses. The ILI typically takes approximately 60 minutes to conduct. At the end of the meeting, the team will have generated specific and global hypotheses concerning the student and his/her behavior.

As can be seen in Table 2, broad information is gathered on student strengths and setting events (slow triggers). Specific information emerges through team discussion relevant to the problem behavior, antecedents (fast triggers), actual consequences, and perceived function(s). As can be noted in Leonard's example, valuable insight regarding intervention and support can be learned as a result of gathering broad and specific information. In Leonard's example, gaining an appreciation of how quality of life factors (e.g., father passing away coupled with Leonard's age, his affection for Mr. Jones, Leonard's self-perception of himself, and his lack of relationships with peers) interact with the operational details of his routines at school (e.g., when presented with work he perceives as too hard to successfully complete, verbal instructions not paired with pictures/symbols, and independent seatwork of longer than 5 minutes duration) logically leads Leonard's team

Table 2
Initial Line of Inquiry for Leonard

Slow trigger (setting events)	Fast trigger (antecedents)	Problem behavior(s)	Perceived function(s)	Actual consequence(s)
• Leonard's father passed away 3 years ago as a result of an automobile accident. • He has chronic allergies that are particularly bad in the spring. • No real close friends or peers. • Low self-esteem (he describes himself as a geek). • Limited sight word vocabulary. • Poor organizational and planning skills. • Diagnosed as having significant language delays and mental retardation.	• When presented with work he thinks is too hard (or will take too long). • Verbal instructions when not paired with pictures/symbols. • Independent tasks longer than 5 minutes. • When other students in general education settings finish work/task before him (other kids get "choice" time). • When corrected by adults in front of peers (particularly in general education settings such as shop and homeroom).	• Invading the physical space of others (sometimes pushing when ignored). • Destroying materials in class. • Verbal outbursts. • Off task/out of seat (high levels of roaming around).	• Attention from others. • Help from others to make tasks/work easier (including teacher). • Avoidance of tasks he believes he cannot complete successfully to avoid vailure in front of peers.	• Redirection hierarchy: Eye contact Verbal Name on board Sent to office • Gains attention and/or help from others. • Avoids tasks/work he believes he cannot complete. • Tasks are made easier or terminated. • Some kids in both special and general education settings laugh at him (others get increasingly angry with some typical students telling him to "knock it off").

Student Strengths: Interested in social relationships with same-aged peers (15 years). Leonard enjoys playing video games and listening to music on his portable CD. He is verbal, but also uses pictures/symbols to communicate. Leonard lives at home with his mother and younger sister, Alice (9 years old). He is a typical 15-year-old in appearance (5 ft 10 in./150 lb) and enjoys physical activities. He receives a significant portion of his educational program in a self-contained special education program for students with significant cognitive disabilities. He also attends his local public school and participates in some general education settings. He really likes his homeroom teacher (Mr. Jones) who is also the basketball coach at school. Leonard has been making progress toward goals/objectives on his IEP. With support, he has experienced some success in his scheduled general education settings.

to generate hypotheses that facilitate the design of intervention and support systems.

Generating Hypotheses

Once relevant information has been gathered through the FBA, the student-centered team is ready to develop hypothesis statements. Hypothesis statements summarize assessment results by offering a logical explanation for problem behavior (O'Neill et al., 1997; Tilly et al., 1998, 2000). As a result of reflecting both the function of and factors that are identified as contributing to the student's problem behavior, these hypotheses guide the development of intervention plans. Interventions based on hypotheses that are developed as a part of an FBA are more likely to lead to durable, positive behavior change (Carr et al., 1999; Dunlap & Kern, 1996; Iwata et al., 1994; Repp et al., 1995; Scotti, Evans, Meyer, & Walker, 1991). Specific and global hypotheses serve as the foundation from which interventions are designed (Bambara & Knoster, 1995, 1998).

Specific Hypothesis

A specific hypothesis synthesizes the specific information gathered during the assessment (Dunlap et al., 2000). Specific hypotheses explain why a problem behavior occurs by describing fast and slow triggers (i.e., antecedents and setting events) regularly associated with the problem behavior and identifying possible function(s). Specific hypotheses consist of three component statements (O'Neill & Reichle, 1993): (a) When this happens (a description of specific antecedents and settings events associated with the problem behavior), (b) the student does this (a description of the problem behavior), and (c) in order to get that (a description of the perceived functions of the problem behavior). These three component statements are linked to create the specific hypothesis. An example of a specific hypothesis for Leonard is presented in Table 3.

Global Hypothesis

Specific hypotheses are essential for building effective intervention plans as they provide the student-centered team with operational details as to both the antecedent and settings events commonly associated with, and the perceived function of, the problem behavior. Understanding antecedent and setting events aids in the identification and selection of preventative strategies (e.g., in Leonard's example, minimizing the use of independent seatwork when his allergies are bothering him). Understanding the function of the problem behavior is essential in identifying and teaching socially acceptable alternative skills (e.g., teaching Leonard to communicate through more socially acceptable ways that he does not feel well and needs a break from independent tasks).

As important as specific hypotheses are to intervention design, they alone cannot provide a comprehensive

Table 3
An Example of Specific and Global Hypotheses for Leonard

Specific Hypothesis Statement

When Leonard is presented with instructions of more than a few words that are not paired with pictures/symbols, with work he perceives as too difficult to successfully complete or will take too long (i.e., 5 minutes of independent work), and/or when his allergies are bothering him, he disrupts the classroom with verbal outbursts, leaves his seat and roams around, tears up materials (e.g., papers), or invades the physical space of staff/peers (sometimes he pushes the person when ignored) in order to gain attention/help.

Global Hypothesis

Leonard is a 15-year-old student identified as having a significant language delay and mental retardation. He is interested in social relationships with peers and enjoys playing video games and listening to music. Leonard is able to functionally communicate through limited verbal statements and use of pictures and symbols. He greatly enjoys physical activities. He appears capable of handling social interactions given support in the form of pictures/symbol systems. His greatest difficulties have been increasingly noted in both general and special education settings, with the most concern in shop class. As Leonard attends his local public school, he is familiar with some students at school, but indicates that he does not really "fit in" or have close friends. Leonard lives with his mother and younger sister, Alice. His father passed away 3 years ago as a result of a car crash. He particularly likes his homeroom teacher (Mr. Jones, who is also the basketball coach) and has communicated the same to his mother at home.

understanding of the complexity of conditions that might be adversely influencing a student's behavior. For example, in addition to the information provided in Leonard's specific hypothesis, some team members may have learned through record reviews and interviews that Leonard's father had been killed in a car accident and that Leonard has increasingly been expressing to his mother how lonely he feels.

Therefore, the student-centered team should also formulate a global hypothesis summarizing relevant contextual information gathered through the assessment (Bambara & Knoster, 1995, 1998). A global hypothesis describes broad influences related to the student's skills, health, preferences, daily routines, and overall quality of life. In effect, a global hypothesis provides a broader, contextual explanation for why the events identified in the specific hypothesis are problematic for the student. Specific and global hypotheses provide valuable information in response to which student-centered teams can logically link interventions and support systems.

As shown in Table 3, important information is contained in both the specific and global hypotheses for Leonard. In particular, Leonard's support team should not only develop preventative interventions based on their specific hypothesis, but also should take into account the broader information associated with Leonard's quality of life and well-being in designing supportive interventions (e.g., the fact that he is a 15-year-old who tragically lost his father a few years ago and is increasingly expressing feelings of loneliness).

Designing the Support Plan

Effective support plans consist of multiple interventions and support strategies. A comprehensive plan for intervention is sometimes referred to as a multi-component plan. This is a technical way of saying that the team is going to do a number of different things within a close time proximity in an agreed upon manner. Comprehensive plans include preventative, teaching, and reactive types of strategies. Comprehensive plans include antecedent and setting event modifications, teaching alternative skills, consequence strategies, and lifestyle interventions (Bambara & Knoster, 1995, 1998; Dunlap et al., 2000; Meyer & Evans, 1989; Tilly et al., 1998). Each of these four component areas work together to contribute to meaningful outcomes that can be durable over time.

Once hypotheses have been developed, a structured process should be used to identify and select supportive strategies and interventions (Knoster, 1998, 1999). In particular, the student-centered team may proceed in the following manner. First, teams may brainstorm possible interventions with the goal of generating the greatest number of possible interventions within a set time frame (5–10 minutes). Second, teams may seek clarification of particular items that emerge through brainstorming by having the team member who initially offered the idea describe it if other members need clarification. Third, teams may discuss the appropriateness of interventions identified through brainstorming in relation to the hypotheses and feasibility of implementation within typical routines and settings. Fourth, teams may prioritize interventions in light of this discussion by placing numbers next to each intervention prioritized (e.g., 1 = the highest priority). Next, top priority strategies may be selected and the types of support that team members will need to implement the selected interventions may be identified (e.g., materials, on-site technical assistance, flexible scheduling). Finally, the selected interventions and supports are documented in the student's support plan and/or IEP. This six step process may be repeated for each strategy (i.e., antecedent and setting event strategies, teaching alternative skills, consequence strategies, and lifestyle intervention).

Although the use of hypotheses should increase the likelihood of success, it is unlikely that any one intervention will be sufficient by itself with students who have extensive histories of problem behavior (Horner & Day, 1991; Horner, Day, & Day, 1997). Student-centered teams should design comprehensive plans involving multiple intervention strategies.

Preventative strategies can have a powerful and fast effect on a student's behavior. In Leonard's case, this could include the teacher(s) minimizing the use of verbal instructions not paired with pictures/symbols, limiting independent work to no longer than 5 minutes, and lessening demands on days when his allergies are making him feel ill. However, it is unlikely that teachers will be in a position to completely engineer the entire school day for any one student. Additionally, even if this were possible, it would not be desirable as students are not being taught new skills to enable them to function independently. Therefore, it is necessary to combine the use of preventative strategies with teaching alternative skills (Meyer & Evans, 1989).

Alternative skill instruction can be classified into a few domains (Bambara, Mitchell-Kvacky, & Iacobelli, 1994; Dunlap & Kern, 1996; Meyer & Evans, 1989; O'Neill & Reichle, 1993). Bambara and Knoster (1995, 1998) describe these domains as teaching replacement skills, general skills, and coping and tolerance skills. Replacement skills operate as a one-for-one substitute for the student that will serve the exact same function as the problem behavior. In Leonard's case, this entails having him cue the teacher that he needs help to successfully complete the assignment. General skills are broad skills that constructively alter problem situations and help to prevent the need for problem behavior. For Leonard, this means helping him to more effectively communicate in multiple settings. Students learn coping and tolerance skills to employ when they are faced with difficult situations. For Leonard, this could mean teaching him how to self-monitor his allergies as well as to use problem-solving techniques during stressful situations.

It is necessary for student-centered teams to employ consequence interventions in concert with antecedent/setting event modifications and the teaching of alternative skills. For example, a child's teacher may use consequence strategies to reinforce the acquisition and use of alternative skills. In Leonard's case, this could simply include the teacher responding to his cues (hand raising) for assistance to increase success on assignments. In another example, a child's teacher might provide negative feedback to reduce the effectiveness of problem behavior should it continue to occur. For Leonard, this might include the use of verbal redirections and loss of privileges for disruptive behavior. The goal of consequence strategies is to teach students that using alternative skills is a better way (i.e., more acceptable, more effective, and more efficient; Horner & Day, 1991) to achieve desired results than is the problem behavior. For a student-centered team concerned about a child with a history of significant behavioral challenges, consequence interventions may also be used to de-escalate crisis situations and protect the child and their family, staff, and property from harm. A four-step approach should be considered by student-centered teams in developing crisis management plans. First, carefully define what constitutes a crisis. Second, describe the intervention procedures and assign who will implement them. Third, identify resources needed to implement the plan (such as calling another adult for help). Finally, agree on procedures for documenting and reporting the use of the crisis management plan. Crisis management plans should be developed to address the escalation, eruption, and de-escalation phases of crisis and should not be used as the sole approach to addressing a student's problem behavior (Bambara & Knoster, 1995, 1998; Meyer & Evans, 1989).

Finally, lifestyle intervention and support should be designed and implemented by the student-centered team in conjunction with the other previously described approaches. Lifestyle refers to the typical ebb and flow of daily life across routines and settings. Lifestyle interventions and support will be most directly aligned with global hypotheses and contribute to long-term prevention of problem behavior through general improvement in the student's quality of life (e.g., friends, access to events or activities of interest, personal choice, and power over age appropriate life decisions). In Leonard's case, lifestyle intervention could employ strategies to increase his participation in extracurricular activities with peers in conjunction with using Mr. Jones (his homeroom teacher whom he likes) as a mentor. Lifestyle interventions and support are important for three reasons. First, dissatisfaction with their circumstances may likely contribute to students' problem behavior. Second, students are more likely to learn new social skills in contexts that are enjoyable and desired. Lastly, lifestyle interventions allow for ongoing, long term support for students as they grow and develop.

Individualized plans of intervention and support are uniquely tailored to each child's needs, preferences, and long-range goals (Hansen, 1999). Comprehensive intervention will reflect a multi-component approach to prevention and intervention. Effective support plans consider the perspective of the students and their families and the feasibility of interventions in the plan (i.e., contextual fit; Albin, Lucyshyn, Horner, & Flannery, 1996). This is accomplished by involving the students, their families, and staff members in designing interventions and support to best ensure a good fit across settings and routines.

Monitoring Student Progress

Effective intervention and support focus not only on behavior change, but on enhancing a student's overall quality of life (Bambara & Knoster, 1995, 1998; Knoster et al., 2000; Meyer & Evans, 1993). Meaningful outcomes include lifestyle improvements such as participating in community life, gaining and maintaining satisfying relationships, expressing personal preferences and making choices, and developing personal competencies (Meyer & Evans, 1989). Such improvements in quality of life are facilitated by establishing a

positive long-range vision with the students and their families and mobilizing natural support systems through effective teamwork (Kincaid, 1996).

School-based teams are required to monitor student progress. Deciding what information to collect and analyze will be guided by the specific goals in the student's behavior intervention plan in the IEP. Assessment procedures employed during the initial FBA may be used to monitor student progress (e.g., informant procedures may be used to monitor outcomes). In Leonard's case, progress monitoring might involve periodically interviewing (or surveying) team members regarding Leonard's progress. Progress is defined as the increased use of socially acceptable alternative skills (e.g., replacement skills, general skills, and coping and tolerance skills) and the reduction in problem behavior (Bambara & Knoster, 1995, 1998). Leonard's progress may include his successful use of cueing techniques (raising hand for teacher assistance), improvement in general communication skills, and self-monitoring of allergies. Reductions in disruptive behavior (e.g., verbal outbursts, materials destruction, out of seat/roaming around in the classroom, and/or invading the physical space of others) are also evidence of progress. Teams will likely monitor these outcomes over time and across different situations (e.g., different classrooms, in the community, at home). School-based teams may also measure broader results that emerge through lifestyle interventions (Janney & Snell, 2000; Meyer & Janney, 1989; Risley, 1996; Turnbull & Turnbull, 1996). This may include assessing positive side effects of support (e.g., increased participation in community events), measuring improvements in health and well-being (e.g., decreased need for psychotropic medications, fewer bruises), and measuring child, family, and staff satisfaction with the process and results of intervention (Meyer & Evans, 1989, 1993).

In addition to determining what information to collect and how to collect it, the school-based team selects the person who will be responsible for gathering the information. This is particularly important for students who receive services and programs from more than one child-serving system (e.g., a combination of local school services and county mental health programs). In particular, the team should answer the following questions: Who will collect what pieces of information and in which settings? Who will be responsible for summarizing and displaying the information? When and how often will information be collected? Who will meet, when, and how often to review and discuss the displayed information for decision making?

Once consensus has been reached concerning information gathering, using this information to make the best educational and therapeutic decisions is critical for long-term success. Based on the analysis of the information collected, the school-based team will determine whether to reevaluate components of the plan, strengthen support strategies, or expand the plan beyond its current scope (Bambara & Knoster, 1998).

Facilitating Implementation

To implement the most current techniques in FBA practice in schools, teachers and administrators will require support to successfully integrate a new system of operation (Weigle, 1997). It is important that student-centered teams address environmental inhibitors that may impede their ability to adequately conduct FBAs and implement comprehensive support plans. One important step in the process is to establish commitment from key decision makers at the school. An efficient way of accomplishing this is for the student-centered team to establish communication links that result in addressing the concerns of each team member. It is important to enlist and support team members who are committed to the student. It is also wise to identify and address the most urgent needs of these team members (e.g., providing someone to whom they can relate their story, lending a shoulder to cry on, and assisting with on site technical assistance and training as warranted). All team members should participate in conducting the FBA and in designing and implementing the behavior support plan. They should also be engaged in monitoring the effect of the interventions and modifying the support plan as warranted. In Leonard's case, monitoring could involve ensuring that the selected interventions fit the typical routines and settings at school in a way that does not adversely impact the education of other students. Additionally, it is important to develop action plans to address areas of concern of team members (e.g., altering the student's and/or teacher's daily schedule at school) and to attend to communication issues that arise during the team's problem-solving process.

Based on the experiences of this author and colleagues associated with the *Tri-State Consortium on Positive Behavior Support*, the practical application of FBA in schools is inextricably linked with engaging the relevant stakeholders in the process. The ultimate challenge for school-based teams is to develop the capacity to collaboratively problem solve issues of mutual concern among all team members.

Summary

School-based teams have the responsibility to develop their capacity to conduct FBAs that lead to the delivery of effective behavior intervention plans. In short, FBA is a problem-solving framework that leads to the design of interventions that have a high likelihood of success. Teams must develop the capacity to employ effective intervention design procedures in response to student problem behavior. Specifically, the resources and precision used in designing and implementing interventions (e.g., FBA tools and procedures) should be commensurate with the seriousness of the problem behavior and the team's previous behavior support activities. This is important in terms of both intrusiveness to the student, family, and school, and resource management in school programs. It is particularly important that the student and the people who know the student best (e.g., teachers, family members) serve as the primary informants when conducting FBAs. A variety of informant methods and direct observational procedures exist along a continuum from which school-based teams can select and employ methods for gathering information.

The framework presented in this article is conducive to supporting student-centered teams in schools to provide comprehensive behavior support. The author and collaborating colleagues have experience in schools in many states that indicates clearly that the approach described is both efficient and effective in achieving meaningful change for students, families, and practitioners. For example, the described framework has been employed with hundreds of student-centered teams within Pennsylvania, Virginia, and West Virginia through activities of the Tri-State Consortium on Positive Behavior Support (a federally funded Outreach Project by the U.S. Department of Education Office of Special Education Programs). Consumer and team satisfaction measures concerning student behavior change, support in terms of contextual fit, and impact on the quality of life of students and their families provide evidence of both the feasibility and effectiveness of this approach.

To illustrate, 77 student-centered teams supported through the Tri-State Consortium responded to post-assessment surveys concerning student behavior change, their experiences, and satisfaction. They consistently reported reductions in problem behavior and increases in the acquisition and use of socially-acceptable alternative skills. Further, they indicated moderate to high levels of improvement in the quality of life of students following implementation of an individualized support plan. For example, 94% of respondents indicated that students' participation in school and community activities had improved. Further, 95% of respondents indicated that the students' relationships with peers, teachers, and other family members had improved. In addition, 93% of team members indicated improvement in the students' general health and well-being. Finally, 89% of team members reported that the interventions and support systems employed by their respective teams were efficient and had little to no adverse impact on typical routines at school.

This article describes a practical approach to conducting FBAs in schools that can lead to effective and efficient intervention and support for students with problem behavior. Lastly, and perhaps most importantly, this approach can be successfully implemented by student-centered teams in typical public school settings.

References

Albin, R. W., Horner R. H., & O'Neill, R. E. (1993). *Proactive behavioral support: Structuring and assessing environments.* Unpublished manuscript, University of Oregon, Eugene.

Albin, R. W., Lucyshyn, J. M., Horner, R. H., & Flannery, K. B. (1996). Contextual fit for behavior support plans. In L. K. Koegel, R. L., Koegel, & G. Dunlap (Eds.), *Positive behavioral support: Including people with difficult behavior in the community* (pp. 82–98). Baltimore: Paul H. Brookes.

Anderson, C. M., Freeman, K. A., Mullen, K. B., & Scotti, J. R. (1999). The School Consultation Project. In J. R. Scotti & L. H. Meyer (Eds.), *Behavioral intervention: Principles, models and practices* (pp. 319–337). Baltimore: Paul H. Brookes.

Anderson, J. L., Mesaros, R. A., & Neary, T. (1991). *Community referenced nonaversive behavior management trainers manual.* Washington, DC: National Institute on Disability and Rehabilitation Research.

Bambara, L. M., & Knoster, T. (1995). *Guidelines: Effective behavioral support.* Harrisburg: Pennsylvania Department of Education, Bureau of Special Education.

Bambara, L. M., & Knoster, T. (1998). *Designing positive behavior support plans.* Washington, DC: American Association on Mental Retardation.

Bambara, L. M., Mitchell-Kvacky, N. A., & Iacobelli, S. (1994). Positive behavioral support for students with severe disabilities: An emerging multicomponent approach for addressing challenging behaviors. *School Psychology Review, 23,* 263–278.

Bergan, J. R. (1977). *Behavioral consultation.* Columbus, OH: Merril.

Bergan, J. R., & Kratochwill, T. R. (1990). *Behavioral consultation and therapy.* New York: Plenum.

Bergan, J. R., & Tombari, M. L. (1975). The analysis of verbal interactions occurring during consultation. *Journal of School Psychology, 13,* 209–226.

Bijou, S. W., Peterson, R. F., & Ault, M. H. (1968). A method to integrate descriptive and experimental field studies at the level of data and empirical concepts. *Journal of Applied Behavior Analysis, 1,* 175–191.

Carr, E. G., Horner, R. H., Turnbull, A. P., Marquis, J. G., McLaughlin, D. D., McAtee, M. L., Smith, C. E., Ryan, K. A., Ruef, M. B., & Doolabh, A. (1999). *Positive behavior support for people with developmental disabilities: A research synthesis.* Washington, DC: American Association on Mental Retardation.

Dunlap, G., Hieneman, M., Knoster, T., Fox, L., Anderson, J., & Albin, R. W. (2000). Inservice training in positive behavior support: Issues and essential elements. *Journal of Positive Behavior Interventions, 2,* 22–32.

Dunlap, G., & Kern, L. (1996). Modifying instructional activities to promote desirable behavior: A conceptual and practical framework. *School Psychology Quarterly, 11,* 297–312.

Durand, V. M. (1990). *Severe behavior problems: A functional communication training approach.* New York: Guilford.

Durand, V. M., & Crimmins, D. B. (1988). Identifying variables maintaining self-injurious behavior. *Journal of Autism and Developmental Disorders, 18,* 99–117.

Evans, I. M., & Meyer, L. H. (1985). *An educative approach to behavior problems: A practical decision model for interventions with severely handicapped learners.* Baltimore: Paul H. Brookes.

Forest, M., & Lusthaus, E. (1987). The kaleidoscope: Challenge to the cascade. In M. Forest (Ed.), *More education/integration* (pp. 1–16). Downsview, Canada: G. Allan Roeher Institute.

Foster-Johnson, L., Ferro, J., & Dunlap, G. (1991). *Curricular activity profile.* Tampa: Florida Mental Health Institute, University of South Florida.

Gresham, F. (1984). Behavioral interviews in school psychology: Issues in psychometric adequacy and research. *School Psychology Review, 13,* 17–25.

Hansen, M. (1999). *Writing effective treatment plans: The Pennsylvania CASSP model.* Harrisburg: Pennsylvania CASSP Training and Technical Assistance Institute, Department of Education.

Horner, R. H., & Carr, E. G. (1997). Behavioral support for students with severe disabilities: Functional assessment and comprehensive intervention. *The Journal of Special Education, 31,* 84–104.

Horner, R. H., & Day, H. M. (1991). The effects of response efficiency on functionally equivalent competing behaviors. *Journal of Applied Behavior Analysis, 24,* 719-732.

Horner, R. H., Day, H. M., & Day, J. R. (1997). Using neutralizing routines to reduce problem behaviors. *Journal of Applied Behavior Analysis, 30,* 601-614.

Ittelson, W. H., Rivlin, L. G., & Proschansky, H. M. (1976). The use of behavioral maps in environmental psychology. In H. M. Proschansky, W. H. Ittelson, & L. G. Rivlin (Eds.), *Environmental psychology: People and their physical setting.* New York: Holt, Rinehart & Winston.

Iwata, B., Dorsey, M. F., Slifer, K. J., Bauman, K. E., & Richman, G. S. (1994). Toward a functional analysis of self-injury. *Journal of Applied Behavior Analysis, 27,* 197–209. (Reprinted from *Analysis and Intervention in Developmental Disabilities, 2,* 3–20, 1982)

Iwata, B. A., Pace, G. M., Dorsey, M. F., Zarcone, J. R., Vollmer, T. R., Smith, R. G., Rodgers, T. A., Lerman, D. C., Shore, B. A., Mazaleski, J. L., Goh, H. L., Cowdrey, G. E., Kalsher, M. J., McCosh, K. C., & Willis, K. D. (1994). The functions of self-injurious behavior: An experimental-epidemiological analysis. *Journal of Applied Behavior Analysis, 27,* 215–240.

Janney, R., & Snell, M. E. (2000). *Behavioral support.* Baltimore: Paul H. Brookes.

Kanfer, F. H., & Saslow, G. (1969). Behavioral diagnosis. In C. M. Franks (Ed.), *Behavior therapy: Appraisal and status* (pp. 417–444). New York: McGraw-Hill.

Kennedy, C. H., Horner, R. H., & Newton, J. S. (1990). The social networks and activity patterns of adults with severe disabilities: A correlational analysis. *Journal of The Association for Persons with Severe Handicaps, 15,* 86–90.

Kincaid, D. (1996). Person-centered planning. In L. Kern-Koegle, R. L. Koegle, & G. Dunlap (Eds.), *Positive behavioral support: Including people with difficult behavior in the community* (pp. 439–465). Baltimore: Paul H. Brookes.

Kincaid, D., Shannon, P., Knoster, T., McFarland, J., Schall, C., Malatchi, A., & Brinkley, J. (1997). *Quality of life survey.* (Available from the Tri-State Consortium on Positive Behavior Support by contacting the Florida Mental Health Institute at the University of South Florida-DARES, 13301 Bruce B. Downs Blvd., Tampa, FL. 33612-3807).

Knoster, T. (1998, Spring). Positive behavior support in schools. *Tri-State Consortium on Positive Behavior Support Newsletter, 1,* 1–3.

Knoster, T. (1999). Effective support for students with dual diagnoses who have histories of challenging behavior at school. Journal of Positive Approaches, 2, 15–20.

Knoster, T., Kincaid, D., McFarland, J., Schall, C., Malatchi, A., Shannon, P., Hazelgrove, J., Brinkley, J., & Harrower, J. (2000). Effectively educating students with problem behavior: A summary of outreach by the Tri-State Consortium on Positive Behavior support. *TASH Newsletter, 26,* 25–28.

Knoster, T., & Llewellyn, G. (1997). *Screening for an understanding of student problem behavior: An initial line of in-*

quiry. Harrisburg: Pennsylvania Department of Education, Instructional Support System of Pennsylvania.

Knoster, T., & Llewellyn, G. (1998). *Screening for an understanding of student problem behavior: An initial line of inquiry* (2nd ed.). Harrisburg: Pennsylvania Department of Education, Instructional Support System of Pennsylvania.

Knoster, T., & McCurdy, B. (in press). Best practices in functional behavioral assessment. In A. Thomas & J. Grimes (Eds.), *Best practices in school psychology* (Vol. 4). Washington, DC: National Association of School Psychologists.

Lalli, J. S., & Casey, S. D. (1996). Treatment of multiply controlled problem behavior. *Journal of Applied Behavior Analysis, 29,* 391–396.

LaVigna, G. W., & Donnellan, A. M. (1986). *Alternatives to punishment: Solving behavior problems with non-aversive strategies.* New York: Irvington.

Lohrmann-O'Rourke, S., Knoster, T., & Llewellyn, G. (1999). Screening for understanding: An initial line of inquiry for school-based settings. *Journal of Positive Behavior Interventions, 1,* 35–42.

Meyer, L. H., & Evans, I. M. (1989). *Nonaversive intervention for behavior problems: A manual for home and community.* Baltimore: Paul H. Brookes.

Meyer, L. H., & Evans, I. M. (1993). Meaningful outcomes in behavioral intervention: Evaluating positive approaches to the remediation of challenging behaviors. In J. Reichle & D. P. Wacker (Eds.), *Communication and language intervention series: Vol. 3. Communicative alternatives to challenging behavior: Integrating functional assessment and intervention strategies* (pp. 407–428). Baltimore: Paul H. Brookes.

Meyer, L., & Janney, R. (1989). User-friendly measures of meaningful outcomes: Evaluating behavioral interventions. *Journal of The Association for Persons with Severe Handicaps, 14,* 263–270.

Mount, B. (1987). *Personal futures planning: Finding directions for change* (Doctoral dissertation, University of Georgia, 1987). Ann Arbor, MI: UMI Dissertation Information Service.

Mount, B., & Zwernick, K. (1988*). It's never too early. It's never too late: A booklet about personal futures planning.* St. Paul, MN: Metropolitan Council.

O'Brien, J. (1987). A guide to lifestyle planning: Using The Activities Catalog to integrate services and natural support systems. In B. Wilcox & G. T. Bellamy (Eds.), *A comprehensive guide to The Activities Catalog: An alternative curriculum for youth and adults with severe disabilities* (pp. 175–189). Baltimore: Paul H. Brookes.

O'Brien, J., & Lyle, C. (1987). *Framework for accomplishment.* Decatur, GA: Responsive Systems Associates.

O'Brien, J., Mount, B., & O'Brien, C. (1991). *Framework for accomplishment: Personal profile.* Decatur, GA: Responsive Systems Associates.

O'Neill, R. E., Horner, R. H., Albin, R. W., Sprague, J. R., Storey, K., & Newton, J. S. (1997). *Functional assessment and program development for problem behaviors: A practical handbook.* Pacific Grove, CA: Brooks/Cole.

O'Neill, R. E., Horner, R. H., Albin, R. W., Storey, K., & Sprague, J. R. (1990). *Functional analysis of problem behavior: A practical assessment guide.* Sycamore, IL: Sycamore.

O'Neill, R., & Reichle, J. (1993). Addressing socially motivated challenging behaviors and establishing communicative alternatives: Basics of a general-case approach. In J. Reichle & D. P. Wacker (Eds.), *Communicative alternatives to challenging behavior: Integrating functional assessment and intervention strategies* (pp. 135–173). Baltimore: Paul H. Brookes.

Rainforth, B., & York-Barr, J. (1997). *Collaborative teams for students with severe disabilities: Integrating therapy and educational services* (2nd ed.). Baltimore: Paul H. Brookes.

Reese, E. P., Howard, J. S., & Reese, T. W. (1977). *Human behavior: An experimental analysis and its applications.* Dubuque, IA: Brown.

Repp, A. C., Karsh, K. G., Munk, D., & Dahlquist, C. M. (1995). Hypothesis-based interventions: A theory of clinical decision making. In W. O'Donohue & L. Krasner (Eds.), *Theories of behavior therapy: Exploring behavior change* (pp. 585–608). Washington, DC: American Psychological Association.

Risley, T. (1996). Get a life! In L. K. Koegel, R. L. Koegel, & G. Dunlap (Eds.), *Positive behavioral support: Including people with difficult behavior in the community* (pp. 425–437). Baltimore: Paul H. Brookes.

Sasso, G. M., Reimers, T. M., Cooper, L. J., Wacker, D., Berg, W., Steege, M., Kelly, L., & Allaire, A. (1992). Use of descriptive and experimental analyses to identify the functional properties of aberrant behavior in school settings. *Journal of Applied Behavior Analysis, 25,* 809–821.

Schuler, A. L., Peck, C. A., Tomlinson, C. D., & Theimer, R. K. (1984). Communication interview. In C. A. Peck, C. Schuler, R. K. Tomlinson, T. Theimer, T. Haring, & M. Semmel (Eds.), *The social competence curriculum project: A guide to instructional programming for social and communicative interactions* (pp. 43–62). Santa Barbara: University of California at Santa Barbara.

Scotti, J. R., Evans, I. M., Meyer, L. H., & Walker, P. (1991). A meta-analysis of intervention research with problem behavior: Treatment validity and standards of practice. *American Journal on Mental Retardation, 96,* 233–256.

Smith, R. G., Iwata, B. A., Vollmer, T. R., & Zarcone, J. R. (1993). Experimental analysis and treatment of multiply controlled self-injury. *Journal of Applied Behavior Analysis, 26,* 183–196.

Smull, M. W., & Harrison, S. B. (1992). *Supporting people with severe retardation in the community.* Alexandria, VA: National Association of State Mental Retardation Program Directors.

Tilly, W. D., Knoster, T. P., & Ikeda, J. J. (2000). Functional behavioral assessment: Strategies for positive behavior support. In C. Telzrow & M. Tankersley & (Eds.), *IDEA amendments of 1997: Practice guidelines for school-based teams* (pp. 151–198). Bethesda, MD: National Association of School Psychologists Publications.

Tilly, W. D., Knoster, T. P., Kovaleski, J., Bambara, L., Dunlap, G., & Kincaid, D. (1998). *Functional behavioral assessment: Policy development in light of emerging research and practice.* Alexandria, VA: National Association of State Directors of Special Education.

Touchette, P. E., MacDonald, R. F., & Langer, S. N. (1985). A scatter plot for identifying stimulus control of problem behavior. *Journal of Applied Behavior Analysis, 18,* 343–351.

Turnbull, A. P., & Turnbull, H. R. (1996). Group action planning as a strategy for providing comprehensive family support. In L. K. Koegel, R. L. Koegel, & G. Dunlap (Eds.), *Positive behavior support: Including people with difficult behavior in the community* (pp. 99–114). Baltimore: Paul H. Brookes.

Vandercook, T., York, J., & Forest, M. (1989). The McGill Action Planning System (MAPS): A strategy for building the vision. *Journal of The Association for Persons with Severe Handicaps, 14,* 205–215.

Weigle, K. L. (1997). Positive behavior support as a model for promoting educational inclusion. *Journal of The Association for Persons with Severe Handicaps, 22,* 36–48.

Article received: April 4, 2000
Final acceptance: November 15, 2000
Editor in charge: Joseph R. Scotti

Using Functional Behavioral Assessment to Develop Effective Intervention Plans:

Practical Classroom Applications

Terrance M. Scott
University of Kentucky

C. Michael Nelson
University of Kentucky

Abstract: Functional behavioral assessment was mandated in the Individuals with Disabilities Education Act (IDEA) Amendments of 1997 as a behavioral evaluation for students who display behaviors that are likely to result in school exclusion. Functional behavioral assessment is not intended to be used solely as a reaction to chronic and serious behaviors. Rather, functional behavioral assessment is most effective when used proactively at the first display of challenging behaviors by students. Through case examples, this article presents step-by-step procedures for conducting functional behavioral assessment and developing effective intervention plans for students in public school classrooms.

For many years, functional assessment has been advocated as an effective approach to behavioral assessment by professionals who work in the area of low-incidence disabilities and with students who exhibit serious behavior problems (Carr & Durand, 1985; Day, Horner, & O'Neill, 1994; Bijou, Peterson, & Ault, 1968; Foster-Johnson & Dunlap, 1993; Repp, Felce, & Barton, 1988). The 1997 amendments to the IDEA now mandate functional behavioral assessment for those students with disabilities who exhibit behaviors leading to a change in school placement or that constitute a pattern of misbehavior (P.L. 105-17, § 615 (K)1.B.i). Functional behavioral assessment is a systematic method of assessing the purpose or function of a student's behavior in relation to its context (i.e., environment) so that appropriate interventions can be designed to meet the unique needs of the student. The great benefit of functional assessment is the ability to assist in developing proactive (i.e., preventative), positive, individualized behavior support plans for students with challenging behaviors. Unfortunately, current public attitudes and school discipline policies (e.g., zero tolerance for undesired behavior) threaten to effectively negate the proactive benefits of functional behavioral assessment. Given a climate in which *any* misbehavior is regarded as an occasion for punishment and exclusion from school, it is imperative that educators who believe that children should learn appropriate social behaviors as well as academic skills become highly competent in conducting functional behavioral assessments and developing functional intervention plans.

School personnel must rush to learn why, when, and how a functional behavioral assessment should be implemented. However, simple awareness of such procedures is insufficient to make a positive difference. To be effective, schools must embrace the concept of functional assessment as a common routine whose procedures are adopted, supported, and equally shared across the school. The purpose of this article is to present a simplified, step-by-step example of functional behavioral assessment and its role in developing effective behavior support plans in public school settings. This article is in no way exhaustive of this topic, but it does present a comprehensive picture of functional assessment and individualized intervention that is designed to provide school-based personnel with an understanding of the subject and a set of practical guidelines.

Why Did He Do That?

As the students enter the classroom after recess, Jeremy goes quietly to his desk and takes his seat. The teacher reminds the class that it is time for oral reading. Jeremy, who lately has been more and more difficult in Ms. Fluster's language arts class, puts his head down on his desk and buries it deep within his folded arms. Two of Jeremy's peers, Randy and Susan, approach and, in quiet and consoling voices, gently inquire about his problem. Jeremy sighs loudly but refuses to bring his head up. Randy returns to his seat while Susan continues to console Jeremy and prod him regarding the nature of his problems. After several minutes, the teacher directs all the students to take their seats to begin oral reading time. Susan leaves Jeremy's side and returns to her desk. The teacher calls on the first student, who then begins reading aloud. A couple of minutes pass and then Jeremy, while continuing to conceal his head in his arms, loudly pounds his fist several times on the desktop. Other students gasp in the wake of the sudden disruptive noise and then a few quietly giggle. Ms. Fluster approaches Jeremy and, in a whisper, asks him if he would like to talk to her about anything that might be bothering him. Head remaining buried, Jeremy says nothing, and after several seconds the teacher turns and calls on a new student to continue reading aloud. Shortly thereafter, Jeremy again pounds his fist on the desk. Ms. Fluster has noticed that lately Jeremy has been increasingly moody and reluctant to comply with her requests. Believing that the best strategy is based on firm discipline, from across the room she commands loudly that Jeremy go to the hallway for 5 minutes and come back ready to read. With the students' eyes glued to his every move, Jeremy stands up quietly and without warning capsizes his desk so that its contents scatter for several feet around and then storms across the room. As he reaches the door, Ms. Fluster orders Jeremy to go to the principal's office.

What's wrong with Jeremy and what can we do about it? Is he emotionally disturbed or is he just having a bad day? Would the answers to these questions assist us in preventing future exhibitions of these problem behaviors? Similarly, would knowing that Jeremy has been identified as having a disability give us the information necessary to develop an appropriate intervention strategy? These broad labels for behavior may help us communicate about a student, but they provide us with little information for intervention.

Too often we struggle with asking what is wrong with the *student*, focusing on behavior management problems rather than the student's needs and overlooking the *behavior* itself. What if we change our focus and question the function that misbehavior serves in meeting a student's individual needs? For example, suppose that Jeremy cannot read, hates the embarrassment he suffers from lack of ability to read during reading class, and repeatedly engages in misbehavior so that he will be removed? If this in fact is the case, misbehavior serves a very adaptive function for Jeremy—it helps him to escape a very aversive situation. Furthermore, knowing this to be true, we can predict that Jeremy's problems will occur whenever he is put in a position where it is likely that he will be asked to read in the company of his peers, because of the consequence. But what if we found that Jeremy could read and that reading

did not predict misbehavior? What if we now learn that Jeremy misbehaves because he gets attention from his teachers and peers? Again, the misbehavior can be seen to be adaptive for Jeremy in that it allows him to access the attention that he desires. Furthermore, Jeremy's misbehaviors again are predictable, because their occurrence is based on the availability of attention.

Either of these explanations of behavior typically might be associated with students who have been identified by such broad labels as *emotionally disturbed, socially maladjusted,* or the like. However, effective intervention is dependent upon knowledge of the function of behavior and how that behavior is both prompted and reinforced by the environment. For example, suppose we could determine that escape from reading was the function of Jeremy's misbehavior (i.e., negative reinforcement)? Under these circumstances, interventions such as time-out and planned ignoring likely would be counterproductive, in that they predictably would allow misbehavior to serve the function of escape from reading. Similarly, were we to determine that access to attention was the function of Jeremy's misbehavior, any extra help, lectures, or attention from teachers or peers following misbehavior would likely be counterproductive, because these responses predictably would allow misbehavior to serve the function of accessing attention. The vast majority of student behaviors can be categorized as serving one of two functions: to access or to avoid/escape some object or event (e.g., talking out to get the teacher's attention, sleeping to avoid math, hitting another student to escape his or her taunting). Of course, all people are unique, and the function of a given behavior may be quite different for each person or situation. Moreover, any given problem behavior may serve different functions, depending on the context in which it occurs. For example, Jeremy's behavior may serve to avoid the embarrassment of reading in front of his peers, whereas in math the same behavior pattern may occur because it predictably results in sympathetic attention from peers or the teacher.

Effective intervention for any student behavior depends on our ability to determine the function of that behavior and create alternative contexts to avoid the problem and to teach desirable replacement behaviors that serve the same function. For example, if Jeremy's behavior was maintained by escape from oral reading, we might allow him to read orally to the teacher in private instead of in front of peers. By providing Jeremy with opportunities to read orally in private, we have created a context in which escape is no longer necessary. If, on the other hand, his behavior proves to be maintained by peer attention, we might instruct peers to ignore him when he displays such behavior, or follow episodes of noncompliance with a brief time-out. At the same time, we could teach him more appropriate ways to solicit peer attention. In either case, we can plan a response to his undesired behavior that involves making the misbehavior less likely to access that function. We also would teach him a replacement behavior that is desirable and that serves the same function for him as the misbehavior. Other examples of interventions based on the function of behavior include teaching a student to raise her hand instead of calling out to gain teacher attention, allowing a student to escape part of a class by completing a specified lesson that has been designed to improve his ability to perform, or reconfiguring a class so that peer scrutiny is minimized. The interventions in these examples are functional because they are based on the function of misbehavior. They include an instructional component that allows the student to access the outcomes of problem behavior through desired behavior, and they involve the creation of situations that prevent or remove the reinforcing consequences of misbehavior.

Once we establish the function of a behavior, we can design interventions that teach behaviors that help the student meet individual needs in a more desirable manner. That is, the student achieves the desired outcomes of his or her problem behavior through behaviors that are more acceptable to the environment. The question, then, is how to go about determining the function of a student's behavior. Functional behavioral assessment serves this purpose and is a method for identifying the predictors (recurring antecedents and/or consequences) of specific behaviors. This information is then used to develop and teach a replacement behavior and to reduce the frequency or severity of the problem behavior.

Functional Assessment Procedure

The three main outcomes of a functional assessment are (a) the development of a concrete definition of the problem behavior(s), (b) one or more predictions regarding when and under what conditions the problem behavior occurs, and (c) identification of the function that a behavior serves in meeting the needs of the individual (O'Neill et al., 1997). The remainder of this article presents case examples to demonstrate a step-by-step procedure for performing a functional behavioral assessment and developing individualized interventions for students in typical public school settings.

CASE EXAMPLES

Amy is a third-grade student who does well academically but who has some serious social deficits. Specifically, her teacher describes her as "impulsive and aggressive." She has been referred to the principal on several occasions for fighting or otherwise being involved in physical altercations with others. Amy has been suspended 4 days during the current school year, continues to have difficulty with peers, and is frequently restrained by adults as a consequence.

Jay is a seventh-grade student who rarely completes his work and whose teacher describes him as being "bizarre and scattered." Jay exhibits an array of disruptive behaviors in the classroom, including loud and (apparently) purposeful flatulence, sticking pencils up his nose, and licking his desk. He has been sent to the counselor several times during the current year but continues to engage in disruptive behaviors.

STEP 1: ASSESS THE STUDENT'S BEHAVIOR

Assessment of the student's behavior is the first step in the process. Initial assessment involves informal conversations, questionnaires, checklists, and structured interviews with key persons who have contact with the individual student (e.g., teachers, parents) and can offer insights into the predictability of behavior. For example, instruments such as the Motivation Assessment Scale (Durand & Crimmins, 1992) and the Problem Behavior Questionnaire (Lewis, Scott, & Sugai, 1994) are simple paper-and-pencil methods of assessing the likelihood of problem behavior under a variety of contextual circumstances. These instruments provide information that may be used to direct the timing and location of more direct assessments.

When asking Amy's other teachers about her behavior, we find that similar behaviors are seen in all but one class. In that one class, Amy works either by herself or with a small group of peers with whom she enjoys a close relationship. Her worst behaviors tend to occur in math class, where she is mixed with a group of older students who regularly harass her.

Similar questioning of Jay's teachers reveals that his behaviors typically occur during only two of his classes. Both of these settings involve a high degree of independent seat work wherein the students work with little interaction with the teacher. Jay's academic performance also is extremely poor in these classes.

As previously indicated, one result of a functional behavioral assessment is a definition of specific problem behavior. Although in a broad sense behavioral difficulties initiate the functional assessment process, specific, concrete behaviors are defined after observational assessments have been performed. In general, behaviors are defined by their physical characteristics (what they look like) and at least one of the following: how often they occur, how long they occur, when/where they occur, and/or the intensity with which they occur (i.e., measurable characteristics such as distance, loudness, etc.).

Given the behavior of Amy and Jay, a likely question is "*Why* do these students engage in such behavior?" First, we must define their behaviors by describing the physical characteristics and context in an observable and measurable way. For Amy, her teachers' descriptions define her problem behavior as physically striking other students during verbal altercations. In Jay's case, informal questioning leads to defining his problem behavior as unsolicited noises and gestures that cause other students to look away from their assigned tasks. In both cases, the behavior is defined in terms of the conditions or context under which it occurs. This contextual information is critical to the development of a reliable definition and influences the timing and location of further, more direct observations.

Whether in the preferred form of a structured antecedent-behavior-consequence (ABC) assessment, or in less reliable anecdotal notes, or in simple repeated observations with mental notes, direct observation is crucial to providing information that is key to determining behavioral function. In general, the more detailed and descriptive the functional assessment data, the more efficient the process of determining behavioral function. All functional behavioral assessment procedures are concerned with analyses of problem behavior in the context (i.e., in relation to all persons, physical stimuli, and events) of environmental antecedents and consequences. In other words, the focus is on determining what environmental events predict and maintain the student's problem behavior. Structured assessment procedures (e.g., ABC assessment) more reliably capture not only those events that surround behaviors but also those events occurring prior to and after occasions when the problem behavior is absent. These subtleties, although observable, often are beyond the discrimination of the casual observer, even when the observer is specifically thinking in terms of functional behavioral assessment. Completed ABC assessments for Amy and Jay are presented in Figures 1 and 2.

STEP 2: PROPOSE A HYPOTHESIS

The second outcome of a functional behavioral assessment is development of a hypothesis regarding the function of the misbehavior. This hypothesis concerns the relationship between observable and measurable antecedent and consequence variables that predictably occur in the presence of the target behavior. As previously noted, the more structured the functional assessment, the easier it will be to accurately identify antecedent predictors and maintaining consequences. Repetitive patterns where similar antecedent and/or consequent events are paired with target behavior represent clues regarding events that may predict and/or explain the existence of behavior.

When behavior is observed, recurring antecedent or consequent events probably will not be identical. Rather, it is likely that several specific and individual events will occur, each of which differs from the others in some manner. Key to identifying antecedent predictor and maintaining consequent variables is the identification of events that have some common elements.

Although in this example we have defined the behavior in which Amy is engaging and know that teachers have responded to it by physically restraining her, up to this point we cannot demonstrate whether the function of her behavior is to gain teacher attention, to escape an aversive peer interaction, or both. Using antecedent and consequent variables identified from her ABC assessment (see Figure 1), we may hypothesize that the behavior serves the function of terminating an aversive event (e.g., verbal insult), in that it brought a quick end to the aversive situation. We saw that, at times, the teacher approached and inquired whether she could be of assistance and Amy turned her away. Drawing on observations along these same lines, we may hypothesize that teacher attention is not a controlling factor.

However, each instance of the target behavior was preceded by a verbal exchange with the recipient of Amy's aggression. Although none of the exchanges were exactly the same, each one could be classified as an "insult" of sorts. This observed connection between antecedent and behavior is a hypothesized predictor. We can state this observation in the hypothesis "Amy physically strikes out at others when she is verbally insulted."

From Jay's functional behavioral assessment (see Figure 2), we could predict from the recurring sequence of events that he is unlikely to act in a disruptive manner when peer attention is unavailable. However, we might guess that the mere proximity of peers is a stimulus that will bring about disruptive behaviors from Jay (in expectation of peer attention).

In Jay's example, each instance of disruptive behavior was followed by a reaction from his peers. At times they just looked at him; at other times they laughed or yelled in anger. Although no two peer reactions are exactly the same, each one can be classified as "attention" in that peers are directing their attention toward Jay. Thus, the consequent variable "peer attention" is identified as part of the hypothesis: "Jay engages in disruptive behaviors because his peers provide him with consequent attention."

In these examples, we formulated hypotheses about behavior and both antecedents and consequences—in isolation. In reality, predictable sequences of behavior are made up of all three components: antecedents, behaviors, and consequences. However, it is not always possible to identify all the subtle pieces of this puzzle from a simple and limited number of observations. The relationship between behavior and antecedent/consequent variables is one that will require repeated measures over time.

STEP 3: ASSESS THE VALIDITY OF THE HYPOTHESIS

Simply assessing the correspondence between behavior and environmental variables from historical observations gives us valuable information but does not necessarily demonstrate a causal connection. It merely hypothesizes (i.e., provides an informed best guess), based on observations, that certain stimulus events may predict behavior. To demonstrate the validity of our hypothesis, we must make

Functional Assessment Form

Name: Amy   Date: 6-1-99

Setting Information:
Free time in the classroom, at a table with several others working on art project.

Antecedents	Behavior	Consequences
1st student "Give me the tape"	"No, I'm using it"	"You don't need it"
✓	"I'm keeping it"	"You're ugly"
✓	slugs peer in chest	teacher restrains for 2 minutes
teacher debriefs, tells her to return to work	begins gluing	none
2 students approach and stare at Amy	"let me see that," grabs from hand	students move closer
"Don't hit our friend again!"	looks up, then continues working, "whatever"	"Or we'll kill you"
✓	ignores	"You better listen!"
✓	ignores	1st student: "Your Momma is fat"
✓	jumps up and throws glue at student who spoke	Teacher comes over and Asks, "What's up?"
✓	"nothing"	T: "Get busy"
1st student: "I'll get you for that"	ignores	2nd student threatens with a clenched fist
✓	I'm telling the teacher	2nd student: "Sh** head!"
✓	dives over table and chokes student who spoke	teacher intervenes

✓ = prior consequence also serves as antecedent
0 = no discernible antecedent/consequence

Figure 1. Functional assessment for Amy.

Functional Assessment Form

Name: Jay   Date: 6-1-99

Setting Information:
General education Math class

Antecedents	Behavior	Consequences
T: "Get out your math books"	licks math book and says "Mmm, I love math"	Students all turn and look, teacher ignores
lesson commences	works on assignment for 5 minutes, then slumps and looks around room.	T: "Jay, please get busy"
✓	sticks pencils up nose, says "Yes sir!" with a salute	Peers look and laugh, T ignores.
0	works several minutes, completes half of assignment.	T: "Nice job, Jay!"
T: "Jay, what did you get on Number 37?"	"7"	T: "Correct," goes to next student, no peer attention
0	works for a couple of minutes	0
teacher continues to question students aloud	raises hand	T: "Yes, Jay?"
✓	grins, loud flatulence	Peers: "Ugggg!"
✓	"Oops, excuse me" (laughing)	Peers threaten to kill him for stinking up the room
T: "What's your question?"	"Uh, I forgot"	0
0	smiles, gets back to work	0

✓ = prior consequence also serves as antecedent
0 = no discernible antecedent/consequence

Figure 2. Functional assessment for Jay.

future predictions that changes in the antecedent and consequent variable(s) will result in predictable changes in the target behavior. Note that the statements developed in response to functional behavioral assessments for Amy and Jay make such predictions. We predicted that Amy would be aggressive when insulted and that Jay would act in a bizarre manner when he receives consequent attention. Both of these predictions can be monitored for validation.

In Amy's case, it is theoretically possible to have students approach and make different types of statements to her. We would then predict, based on our hypothesized behavioral chain, that she will react with physical aggression whenever that statement is insulting *and* that she will not react with physical aggression whenever that statement is not insulting. For ethical reasons, however, we cannot intentionally allow peers to insult Amy or potentially put themselves in harm's way. But the hypothesis can be verified by carefully monitoring the frequency of physical aggression under conditions in which name-calling is experimentally controlled. If her aggressive behavior is unrelated to peer statements, we would expect to see aggressive acts occur randomly and without relation to whether insulting statements were made. Suppose that, when we manipulated peer comments, we found that only the controlled absence of insults predicted long periods of positive, aggression-free behavior. In this case, we would have verified the function of Amy's behavior as escape from insult-laden peer interactions.

For Jay, we conduct systematic observations in both the presence and absence of predictor variables (peer availability). When Jay is involved in one-on-one settings with adults, we can observe the frequency of disruptive behavior. If we were to instruct the class (during Jay's absence) not to attend to Jay's behavior during class, we might predict that Jay's bizarre behaviors will not be present when the class is not available, because he knows that peer attention is not available. With the class present but not attending to his bizarre behavior, we would predict that the frequency of target behaviors would eventually decrease. We can assume that our predictions are correct if Jay does not engage in disruptive behaviors when peer attention is not available. Thus, the function of Jay's undesirable behavior would be confirmed as access to peer attention.

Once an antecedent and/or consequent variable has been validated, the function of a behavior can be determined and the stage is set for designing intervention. However, a behavior may serve different functions in different contexts. For instance, Jay's disruptive behavior might terminate aversive interactions with adults in one setting but gain attention from peers in others. Therefore, the function of any given behavior can be identified only in relation to specific contexts and circumstances.

Although the most powerful manner of validating a hypothesis is to systematically manipulate antecedent and consequent variables, in the scope of a complex placement such as a classroom, systematic manipulations can not be feasible. In such instances, simple direct observations can be used. Although not as robust as manipulations, systematic observations of consistent patterns of predictable behavior can confirm a hypothesis and be used to create effective behavior intervention plans. When a hypothesis does not prove accurate, it must be reformulated and retested in an ongoing process that ends only with the validation of the hypothesis. At this point we would say that we have identified the "function" of behavior in that we know what purpose it serves—to access reinforcement or avoid aversives—under specific circumstances.

STEP 4: DESIGN AN INTERVENTION

Knowing what variables predict an undesirable student behavior provides the information necessary to intervene. The basic rule of thumb is that we want to replace the undesirable behavior with a desirable behavior that can serve the same function for the student. Contexts and circumstances that formerly predicted misbehavior must now, via instruction, predict appropriate behavior. To accomplish this we need to (a) select an appropriate functional replacement behavior, (b) directly teach that behavior, and (c) facilitate access to the same functional outcome for the student. Once the function of a problem behavior has been identified, we can ask, "How can I arrange for the student to achieve his or her desired outcome by performing a desirable behavior?" The answer to this question helps to identify a replacement behavior.

Note that it may be necessary to modify our immediate goals so that the replacement behavior will serve the same function as the target behavior. For example, if the function of a behavior is to escape or avoid an academic task, we may have to teach a replacement behavior that *temporarily* will serve this function (e.g., raising a hand and asking to be excused, as opposed to creating a disturbance in the classroom). With the temporary replacement behavior established, we can begin modifying instructional tasks to make them less difficult and provide reinforcement to the student for each successive approximation toward the longer-term objective.

Although the student can receive the same functional outcome via the identified replacement behavior, the student likely will not engage in replacement behaviors without instruction, because his or her undesirable behaviors have served that function over a period of time and will not be easily abandoned. For example, if a student characteristically has screamed to get the teacher's attention, we can teach that student to raise his or her hand, but, because the screaming is easy, immediate, and historically effective, it is not likely to automatically be abandoned in favor of hand raising. The replacement behavior must be negotiated with the student, and through direct instruction he or she should be taught how and when to exhibit it. Introduction of replacement behavior requires a general rule and rationale. It must both describe when that behavior is appropriate (rule) and what the consequences for that behavior will be (rationale). Once the replacement behavior has been introduced, it must be taught using the array of techniques available to maximize the potential for success. That is, we must model the replacement behavior for the student, allow opportunities for guided practice, and gradually fade out supports until the student demonstrates mastery. The key to the instruction process is providing the minimum amount of support necessary to teach the behavior while precluding failure.

Even after instruction, students are not likely to automatically replace functionally undesirable behaviors. The initial demonstration and eventual maintenance of replacement behaviors will depend on the student's perception of his or her effectiveness in meeting his or her needs. Because of this, the student will initially require prompting and guidance to ensure that he or she is undertaking the replacement behaviors at the appropriate time and in the appropriate manner. This process can be considered a further component of instruction, in that it is calculated to ensure student success.

Of course, the student's perception of how successful the replacement behavior is will depend on its consequences. If a replacement behavior does not meet the student's needs (e.g., raising one's hand to gain attention fails to result in an effective outcome), that behavior will not persist. Instead, the undesirable behavior, which historically has been very reliable in meeting those needs, will continue to occur. It is crucial that demonstrations of replacement behaviors be associated with serving the same functional needs as the undesirable behavior. For this reason, initial replacement behaviors need to be simple, guided with prompts, and immediately reinforced when observed.

Over time, replacement behaviors can be shaped toward more sophisticated responses and/or longer duration (e.g., delaying teacher attention in response to raised hand). Initially, however, we must focus on facilitating any successful demonstration of replacement behavior and providing immediate reinforcement—using reinforcers that provide the same function as the misbehavior. Table 1 presents a few generic examples of functional replacement behaviors and their relative benefits over target behaviors.

Returning to Jay's example, we determined the function of his behavior to be access to peer attention. We now can ask what we would like Jay to do instead of engaging in bizarre behaviors to gain attention. We might decide that we will ask Jay to complete all of his assignments without disruption (our goal), in return for giving him 5 minutes to tell jokes in front of the class (his goal of "accessing peer attention"). We thus have identified a functional replacement behavior (completing assigned tasks) that has been designed to allow Jay to meet his needs for peer attention via more acceptable social behaviors. Now we must introduce this behavior to Jay. We tell him that during class time (rule), if he can perform the identified replacement behavior, we will see that he is allowed to spend 5 minutes telling jokes in front of the class. The rationale for Jay is set up in our discussion of his ability to complete his work and, most important, to Jay, his access to peer attention without interruption. Table 2 presents alternate setting events (*distal antecedents*), antecedents, and consequences for problem and replacement behavior pathways for Amy and Jay, along with some possible intervention strategies to be used at each stage.

Despite our best hopes and efforts, we cannot simply assume that Jay now will complete his assignments immediately. Although he may be very motivated by the potential to spend time in front of the class, his long-standing

Table 1. Functional Replacement Behaviors and Their Benefit

Predictor	Undesirable behavior	Replacement behavior	Function of both behaviors	Benefit of replacement behavior
Addition problems with regrouping	Screams until thrown out of class	Raises hand to get assistance	Escape frustration	More math completed and less screaming
Lineup	Pushes peers and ends up at front of line	Doesn't touch anyone and is allowed to be the first one in line	Access first spot in line	No physical aggression in line
Reading groups	Refuses directions to read and ends up sitting alone at desk	Is allowed to sit and play at desk after reading a predetermined number of pages	Escape from reading/ access playing at desk	Student now gets some reading instruction
Robert	When Robert is near, student engages in off-task behavior to get Robert's attention	Completes all assigned tasks and earns time to play alone with Robert	Access to Robert's attention	Student remains on task and completes assigned tasks

pattern of undesirable behavior may be difficult to break. Furthermore, if we have the expectation that Jay will perform the replacement behavior without systematic instruction and reinforcement and that his probable failure likely will reduce his motivation to make further attempts at replacing a behavior that, although undesirable, has been very successful for him. To ensure success, we might teach Jay our expectations, give him a lot of prompting and guidance, set attainable goals, and provide immediate and frequent reinforcement for engaging in the replacement behavior. As Jay becomes successful at meeting his needs with the replacement behavior, he will become increasingly likely to maintain that behavior in lieu of the undesirable behavior. Still, replacement behaviors will be maintained only when they are more efficient, effective, and relevant than problem behaviors.

STEP 5: FACILITATE ACQUISITION OF REPLACEMENT BEHAVIORS

Even as we identify functional replacement behaviors and facilitate the student's success through instruction, events will occur in the environment that may hasten the return of undesirable behaviors by making those responses easier, or more efficient, in meeting the student's needs. To facilitate the performance of desired responses under conditions that have been highly predictive of undesired behaviors, alterations in the environment to mask or minimize those conditions may be necessary.

Arranging the classroom and/or positioning students to avoid the potential for disruption is the simplest method of manipulating the environment. Careful functional assessment of student behavior may indicate specific times, circumstances, or placements that predict problem behavior. Arrangements such as increasing space between students' desks, providing sufficient areas for moving from one setting to another, and removing problematic or otherwise distracting stimuli can help to preclude predictable patterns of undesirable behavior.

Returning to our examples, if we know that verbal insults predict Amy's aggressive behaviors, preventing insults to the greatest extent possible will serve to facilitate success for Amy. For example, the teacher might physically place Amy in an area of the classroom where she is less likely to encounter those students who are likely to call her names. Or, the teacher might speak with the other students and offer reinforcement contingent upon appropriate conversations (without name-calling and insults) for all students in the class. In each case, Amy's teacher designs an environment that facilitates Amy's success. Of course, at some point the teacher will need to gradually fade out the artificial environmental conditions while continuing to prompt and reinforce desired behavior. A history of success, facilitated by the teacher's environmental arrangements, will likely heighten Amy's confidence in her ability to succeed with each new and increasingly more natural condition.

STEP 6: COLLECT DATA ON INTERVENTION EFFECTIVENESS

For the teacher, caregiver, or therapist, the purpose of ongoing data collection is to determine the effectiveness of an intervention. Without regular and continual measurement of student outcomes, the interventionist has no systematic way of knowing whether a given intervention is effective in changing behavior. Accurate data collection requires (a) concrete and observable definitions of behaviors, settings, and contexts; (b) an individualized recording system; and (c) the ability to gain fluency through practice prior to application.

Table 2. Sample Pathways and Possible Interventions for Amy and Jay

Event	Problem pathway	Replacement pathway	Possible interventions
Amy			
Setting event	Peer altercation	Peer altercation	Teach problem-solving skills
Antecedent	Verbal insult	Verbal insult	Use prompts and cues
Behavior	Physical aggression	Move away or tell teacher	Teach anger management skills
Consequence	Escape altercation	Escape altercation and access teacher reinforcement	Provide reinforcement for appropriate behavior and response cost for inappropriate behavior
Jay			
Setting event	Classroom setting	Classroom setting	Use group contingency
Antecedent	Peer holds class attention	Peer holds class attention	Use prompts and cues
Behavior	Disruptive sounds and actions	Raise hand and make appropriate comment	Teach student to access peer attention in positive manner
Consequence	Peer attention	Peer attention	Provide praise along with student attention and have peers ignore inappropriate behavior under group contingency

Note. *Format adapted from Horner and Billingsley, 1988, and O'Neill et al., 1997.*

Key to using behavioral data effectively is the ability to monitor student progress on a regular basis. In general, the more time spent monitoring a student's behavior, the more accurately the data will reflect actual behavior. For example, because Jay's behavior in our example was classroom oriented (disruptive of classroom routines), it would be sufficient to collect data only in classroom settings and contexts. However, in Amy's example, undesired behavior occurs in response to insults, which may take place in any setting or context. In this case, Amy's behavior should be monitored across school settings. Although we know from informal questioning that there are contexts in which her target behavior is more likely to occur, monitoring by many teachers and across locations and times may be necessary. In Amy's case, staff need only report any observed incidents of physical aggression by Amy.

STEP 7: ALTER OR CONTINUE THE INTERVENTION

When interventions are successful (behaviors change in a desired direction), there typically is little question as to what should be done. Successful interventions are continued until criterion levels are met, at which time the criteria for successful performance are raised, prompts are faded, and/or more advanced skills are targeted. Practitioners are not so certain regarding when to determine that a program is not a success and what to do in response to these circumstances.

Success should not be judged in a subjective and capricious manner; rather, determinants of successful programming should be defined prior to intervention. Teachers should set clearly defined goals and objectives for student success and short-term timelines within which teachable components of that skill should be demonstrated at criterion levels. When students do not meet the short-term goals, teachers must reassess their interventions by looking at data patterns and reanalyzing the functional assessment data. At that point, it may be determined that the intervention should (a) continue with an abbreviated timeline for evaluating outcomes; (b) be altered by adding or deleting prompts, changing the criteria for acceptable performance, redefining the target behavior, changing reinforcers, and/or moving back to teach an unmastered prerequisite skill; or (c) be abandoned in favor of a new intervention that is believed to be more reasonably calculated to facilitate student success.

Summary and Conclusions

The premise of functional behavioral assessment is the assumption that behavior occurs predictably and that the ability to identify the specific predictors of problem behavior allows for the development of maximally effective intervention plans. The success of functional behavioral assessment depends on its proactive use—facilitating and predicting desired behavior rather than merely reacting to undesired behavior. In addition, success rests on the practitioner's ability to continually assess student behavior, monitor student progress, and continue, alter, or abandon interventions according to their success.

The mandate contained in the reauthorization of the IDEA aside, teachers have not only the ability but also the responsibility to teach and reinforce behaviors that are predictive of success in life. Although students are responsible for their own behavior, teachers are responsible for teaching appropriate behavior and for supporting students to correct undesired behavior. As functionally equivalent behaviors are taught, students must receive feedback for engaging in desired behavior with even greater frequency than is regularly received for undesirable behavior (e.g., minimum 4-to-1 ratio). Teachers can facilitate such positive interactions by arranging environments to maximize the probability of success. These procedures work best when applied consistently by all school personnel as a component of a planned system of support.

ABOUT THE AUTHORS

Terrance M. Scott, PhD, is an assistant in the Department of Special Education and Rehabilitation Counseling at the University of Kentucky. He has worked in both residential and school settings with children displaying seriously challenging behaviors. **C. Michael Nelson,** *EdD, is a professor in the Department of Special Education and Rehabilitation Counseling at the University of Kentucky. He has been involved with students in correctional, residential, and school settings. Current interests of both authors include effective assessment, prevention, and intervention for students with behavioral disabilities. Address: Terrance M. Scott, 229 Taylor Education Building, University of Kentucky, Lexington, KY 40506-0001.*

AUTHORS' NOTES

1. *Preparation of this article was supported in part by the U.S. Department of Education Office of Special Education and Rehabilitation Services, Special Projects Program, Grant No. H324M80076.*
2. *The authors would like to thank George Sugai, Rob Horner, and Ann Turnbull for their thoughts in preparation of this article.*

REFERENCES

Bijou, S. W., Peterson, R. F., & Ault, M. H. (1968). A method to integrate descriptive and experimental field st\udies at the level of data and empirical concepts. *Journal of Applied Behavior Analysis, 1,* 175–191.

Carr, E. G., & Durand, V. M. (1985). Reducing behavior problems through functional communication training. *Journal of Applied Behavior Analysis, 18,* 111–126.

Day, H. M., Horner, R. H., & O'Neill, R. E. (1994). Multiple functions of problem behaviors: Assessment and intervention. *Journal of Applied Behavior Analysis, 27,* 279–289.

Durand, V. M., & Crimmins, D. B. (1992). *The motivation assessment scale.* Topeka, KS: Monaco.

Foster-Johnson, L., & Dunlap, G. (1993). Using functional assessment to develop effective, individualized interventions for challenging behaviors. *Teaching Exceptional Children, 25,* 44–50.

Horner, R. H., & Billingsley, F. F. (1988). The effect of competing behavior on the generalization and maintenance of adaptive behavior in applied settings. In R. H. Horner, G. Dunlap, & R. L. Koegel (Eds.), *Generalization and maintenance: Lifestyle changes in applied settings* (pp. 197–220). Baltimore: Brookes.

Individuals with Disabilities Act Amendments of 1997, 20 U.S.C. § 1400 *et seq.*

Lewis, T. J., Scott, T. M., & Sugai, G. M. (1994). The problem behavior questionnaire: A teacher-based instrument to develop functional hypotheses of problem behavior in general education classrooms. *Diagnostique, 19,* 103–115.

O'Neill, R. E., Horner, R. W., Albin, R. W., Sprague, J. R., Storey, K., & Newton, J. S. (1997). *Functional assessment and program development for problem behavior: A practical handbook* (2nd ed.). Pacific Grove, CA: Brooks/Cole.

Repp, A. C., Felce, D., & Barton, L. E. (1988). Basing the treatment of stereotypic and self-injurious behaviors on hypotheses of their causes. *Journal of Applied Behavior Analysis, 21,* 281–289.

Action Editor: Tim Knoster

JASH
1989, Vol. 14, No. 2, 113–126

Reinforcer Assessment I: Using Problem Behavior to Select Reinforcers

V. Mark Durand
State University of New York at Albany

Daniel B. Crimmins
Mental Retardation Institute

Marie Caulfield and Jill Taylor
State University of New York at Stony Brook

We tested the hypothesis that knowledge of the variables controlling problem behavior could be used to select reinforcers. Students with severe developmental disabilities who exhibited frequent aggression, self-injury, and/or tantrums participated in the study. One group (N = 7) was assessed to engage in problem behavior maintained by social attention, and the second group (N = 7) was assessed to engage in problem behavior maintained by escape from unpleasant situations. A combined multiple baseline and alternating treatments design demonstrated that (a) praise was a reinforcer for the group with attention-maintained behavior and appeared to serve as a punisher for the students with escape-maintained behavior, (b) a procedural "time-out" was a reinforcer for the latter group, and (c) problem behavior was lowest when students with attention-maintained problem behavior were praised and students with escape-maintained problem behavior received the procedural time-out. This study suggests that stimuli that are functionally related to problem behavior (e.g., social attention, escape from tasks) can be used effectively as reinforcers. These findings further emphasize the need to individually select reinforcers because, for some individuals, a presumably positive consequence such as social praise can serve as a punisher.

DESCRIPTORS: aggression, assessment, excess be-

havior, functional analysis, generalization, motivation, nonaversives, reinforcement, self-injurious behavior

It is generally recognized that stimuli that serve as reinforcers differ among individuals, across settings, and over time. In other words, what may serve as a reinforcer for one person may be neutral or aversive for another person. In addition, what is reinforcing to a student in one setting may not be reinforcing in a different setting or at a different time. Given the deficits in communication skills often exhibited by persons with severe developmental disabilities, how then can we select effective reinforcers?

Several methods of selecting reinforcers exist, including intuitive selective procedures (e.g., Mullins & Rincover, 1985), reinforcer surveys (e.g., Atkinson et al., 1984), systematic pretesting of stimuli (e.g., Green et al., 1988; Pace, Ivancic, Edwards, Iwata, & Page, 1985), and choice procedures (e.g., Dyer, 1987). An additional procedure involves observing student behavior outside of structured settings. Researchers have relied on Premack's (1959) reinforcement principle that high probability behavior can reinforce low probability behavior (e.g., Allen & Iwata, 1980; Koegel, Dyer, & Bell, 1987; Osborne, 1969).

A second principle noted by Premack (1959), and more relevant to the present study, is that "reinforcement results when an R of a lower independent rate coincides, within temporal limits, with the stimuli governing the occurrence of an R of a higher independent rate" (p. 219). In other words, any behavior that is occurring at a low rate can be reinforced by *the stimuli associated with high-rate behavior.* These reinforcement principles suggest that not only may high-rate behavior itself serve as a reinforcer but the associated stimuli should function as reinforcers also. To find reinforcers, therefore, one approach might be to look at the behavior repertoire of a student and find the variables maintaining frequently occurring behavior.

Problematic behavior (e.g., aggression, self-injury, and stereotyped behavior) is one class of high-rate be-

Support for this research was provided by Grant G008720211 from the U.S. Department of Education.

We wish to thank the teachers of Parsons Child and Family Center and O. D. Heck Developmental Center for their assistance. Additionally, we acknowledge the tremendous efforts of Pat Geary of the Parsons Child and Family Center and the numerous undergraduate research assistants who have helped us complete this project. We also thank David H. Barlow for his comments on the manuscript.

Correspondence regarding this manuscript, data on MAS scores for each student, and requests for reprints should be sent to V. Mark Durand, PhD, Department of Psychology, State University of New York, 1400 Washington Avenue, Albany, NY 12222.

havior upon which a substantial body of research exists. Recent work points to a number of specific variables that appear to maintain problem behavior, including adult attention (e.g., Lovaas, Freitag, Gold, & Kassorla, 1965), task difficulty (e.g., Weeks & Gaylord-Ross, 1981), sensory consequences (e.g., Rincover, 1978), and tangible consequences (e.g., Durand & Crimmins, 1988).

An integration of the literature on reinforcer selection and the literature on the variables controlling problem behavior (following the reasoning outlined by Premack [1959]) leads to the following hypothesis: Variables that maintain an individual's frequent problem behavior should be capable of serving as reinforcing stimuli for that person. In other words, identifying the variables controlling the problem behavior of an individual should point to important classes of reinforcers.

This study tested this hypothesis with 14 students who exhibited frequent problem behavior. Half of the students had problem behavior assessed to be maintained by attention, and a second group displayed problem behavior assessed to be maintained by escape from academic tasks. We hypothesized that social praise would serve as a reinforcer for students with attention-maintained behavior problems and that removing attention and task materials (time-out) would serve as a reinforcer for students with escape-maintained problem behavior. This study is the first in a series of investigations using information on problem behavior to assess reinforcers.

Method

Participants and Setting

The participants in this study were 14 students with severe developmental disorders. The groups were similar on measures of chronological age, mental age (Leiter International Performance Scale), receptive language age (Peabody Picture Vocabulary Test), DSM-III diagnosis, and medication use (see Table 1).

The students attended segregated schools, and sessions were conducted in the students' classrooms. The student was seated at a table with the task materials in front. An experimenter sat at the table across from the student, and a research assistant recorded the sessions with a portable video camera.

Procedures and Design

Overview. We compared two consequences (i.e., social praise and a procedural time-out) as task reinforcers using an alternating treatments design (Barlow & Hayes, 1979) with a multiple baseline across participants (Baer, Wolf, & Risley, 1968). We assessed both task performance and problem behavior for students in each group to determine the differential effects of using these consequences on their behavior. Additionally, a *functional manipulation* (described below) was introduced following the initial experimental sessions to assess for mul-

tiple-treatment interference (Barlow & Hersen, 1984; Sidman, 1960). Each student participated in 10-min sessions of each experimental condition, with two or three sessions per day. When multiple sessions were run on the same day, there was a 5- to 10-min break between sessions.

Preassessment. Each participant was required to complete a receptive labeling task. This task was used because it appeared in some form in each student's IEP, and it allowed for direct comparison of performance across students. Task stimuli were taken from pictures adapted from the Peabody Picture Vocabulary Test (i.e., not the actual PPVT pictures themselves). A pool of items was selected for each student during the preassessment phase such that the student could respond correctly approximately 50% of the time. This level of responding was selected so that decrements in responding could be observed as a function of differing conditions, and so the task would be sufficiently difficult to be challenging to the student.

Reinforcer assessment. Students were initially selected to participate in this study if they exhibited frequent problematic behavior maintained by either social attention or escape from unpleasant situations. Teachers from two schools were polled to identify students who engaged in frequent behavior problems (e.g., self-injurious behavior, aggression, tantrums). Thirty-six potential participants were identified. The teachers of these students then were administered the Motivation Assessment Scale (MAS) (Durand & Crimmins, 1988) to determine the variables presumably maintaining their problem behavior.

The MAS is a 16-item questionnaire that requests information about the situations in which problem behavior is likely to occur. Respondents are asked to rate the likelihood of the target behavior occurring in these situations on a 7-point Likert-type scale (i.e., from "never" to "always"). Initial studies using this scale have shown it to have adequate interrater and test-retest reliability and validity (Durand & Crimmins, 1988; Durand & Kishi, 1987). The MAS was used in this study because of the practical advantages of using this scale with teachers and parents over more complex observational procedures.

Scores from two administrations of the MAS were used to select students with problem behavior maintained by social attention and students with problem behavior maintained by escape. Students with the highest scores on the MAS for two or more maintaining variables that were either the same or within .25 points were not included in this study. The selection procedure was deemed necessary in order to observe the effects on students with "extreme" scores, although it should be noted that this could limit the generality of the results. Seven students who scored highest on those MAS questions assessing the role of social attention and seven

Table 1
Description of Participants

Participants	Chronological age (months)	Mental age (months)	Language age (months)	DSM-III diagnosis	Behavior topography	Medication
Attention group						
Ed	94	44	18	Autism	Aggression	None
Pat	98	65	7	Autism	Tantrums	Mellaril
Rae	282	43	28	Autism	Self-injury	Mellaril
Jim	199	41	40	Perv. DD	Aggression	Mellaril
Gary	203	60	60	Perv. DD	Tantrums	None
Jeff	188	30	12	Perv. DD	Tantrums	None
Hal	194	48	36	Perv. DD	Tantrums	Benadryl
Escape group						
Tim	163	55	43	Perv. DD	Aggression	None
Mia	292	53	28	Autism	Tantrums	Mellaril
Mike	240	21	18	Autism	Self-injury	Mellaril
Nan	167	25	20	Autism	Tantrums	None
Dan	123	86	60	Autism	Self-injury	None
Bob	172	25	20	Autism	Self-injury	Mellaril
Ray	234	36	30	Autism	Aggression	Mellaril

students whose highest scores were on the escape-related questions were selected to participate in the experimental portion of this study.

The persons carrying out the experimental procedures were undergraduates with experience working with persons with severe disabilities and who were naive to the results of the MAS administrations and the experimental hypotheses.

Baseline. These sessions were identical for all students and involved requiring them to complete the receptive labeling task. This task was not "functional" for the students, but it allowed us to control for variables such as complexity and variation which may have confounded our results. Stimuli for the tasks were taken from a pool of approximately 100 pictures individually selected for each student during the preassessment phase. Multiple copies of these pictures were produced and four pictures were pasted on approximately 100 cards (20 cm × 20 cm). The experimenter would present one of these cards and then would ask the student to point to one of the four pictures (e.g., "Point to the 'Stop' sign"). The experimenter recorded correct and incorrect responses continuously during the task, and substituted simple or more complex cards to ensure that responding remained at approximately 50% correct. When a student correctly responded to a picture five consecutive times, this picture was replaced with a more difficult card, and the experimenter recorded a replacement.

Each correct and incorrect response on the task was followed by brief statements (i.e., "That's right" or "That's not right") presented in a neutral tone of voice. If a student did not respond to the task for more than 10 s, then the request to point to the picture was repeated, also in a neutral tone of voice. Instances of problem behavior that were not deemed physically harmful to the student or others were ignored. More

severe problems were blocked by the experimenter, and the task was resumed after the student stopped engaging in that behavior. Experimenters were instructed to stop the session if there was a potential for serious harm to the student or others; however, no sessions were discontinued during the study.

Baseline sessions were introduced to conform to a multiple baseline across participants. Following baseline, alternating sessions (in a random order within each experimental phase) of Praise and Time-Out were conducted.

Praise. Sessions during this condition were identical to baseline except that each correct response was followed by approximately 7 s of enthusiastic praise. This praise included saying phrases such as "Good!," "Good work!," and "Nice job!," in addition to smiles, hugs, and pats on the back by the experimenter. This type of enthusiastic praise is consistent with the use of social praise typically recommended for reinforcing correct responses in persons with severe disabilities (e.g., Lovaas, 1981), although the duration (7 s) may be longer than is usual. This longer duration was designed to be comparable to the duration of the time-out manipulation used in the next condition.

Time-out. These sessions involved a change in the consequence used for correct responses: When a student correctly pointed to a labeled picture, the experimenter would say in a neutral voice, "That's right," and then remove the task materials and turn away from the student for approximately 7 s. After this period of time-out, the experimenter would turn back to the student and resume the task.

Functional manipulation. Carryover effects from one treatment (e.g., praise) to another (e.g., time-out) is a potential problem when using an alternating treatments design. For example, is the effect of praising a student due to the praise alone, or because in the previous session she or he received time-out as a consequence? To assess for possible multiple treatment interference, we modified the strength of one of the treatments to assess for any effect on the other treatment. For those students whose behavior was affected by the time-out manipulation (i.e., reduced task performance), we reduced the duration of the time-out during this phase (i.e., Reduced "Time-Out") from 7 s to approximately 2 to 3 s. The duration of praise for these students remained unchanged. For those students who were affected by the praise manipulation (i.e., reduced task performance), we reduced the duration of praise from 7 s to 2 to 3 s and kept the time-out duration constant at 7 s. We would consider multiple treatment interference to be a factor if, for example, when we reduced the duration of praise, the student's behavior also changed substantially in the time-out condition.

Similarly, multiple treatment interference would be considered to be present if, when we reduced the time-out duration, behavior also changed in the praise condition. No multiple treatment interference would be present if a change in one condition (e.g., praise) had little effect on student behavior in a second condition (e.g., time-out). Fourteen to 16 sessions of the functional manipulation were conducted for each student (i.e., Reduced "Time-Out" or Reduced "Praise"), followed by 20 sessions of that condition which had the most beneficial effect on each student's behavior (i.e., maintained task performance and reduced problem behavior). It is important to point out that this last condition would not fully answer the question of treatment interference, because we are interested in the effects of *both* interventions on all of the students.

Response Definitions and Observer Agreement

All responses were recorded using a continuous 10-s interval procedure, and all data were collected from the videotapes made of each session. Undergraduate psychology majors (not the same persons who carried out the experimental sessions) who were naive to the experimental hypotheses observed the tapes and recorded all responses.

Correct responses for the receptive labeling task were scored if the student pointed to the picture labeled by the experimenter. An incorrect response was scored if the student pointed to a different picture, and no response was scored if the student failed to respond within 10 s. The number of pictures replaced during each session was recorded also as a task acquisition measure. The recorded problem behavior consisted of the high-rate behavior identified by the student's teacher that was rated on the MAS. Three categories of problem behavior were identified and defined as follows: *Aggression* was defined as anytime the student hit, pushed, scratched, bit, or pulled the hair of another person. *Self-*

injurious behavior was defined as anytime a student hit his or her head with his or her hand, banged his or her head on some object, or bit any part of his or her body. *Tantrums* were defined as anytime a student screamed, fell to the floor, or otherwise disrupted a session.

Praise was defined as the enthusiastic approval of a student's response through verbal statements (e.g., "Good!," "Good work!," "Nice job!"), smiles, hugs, and pats on the back. Time-out was defined as the experimenter's removal of the task materials from the table and turning away from the student.

Observer agreement was assessed covertly for 100% of the sessions by trained undergraduate observers. Training was conducted prior to this study until observers reached a criterion of 75% agreement on all responses with a standard observer (an undergraduate with prior observer experience). Observer records were compared on an interval-by-interval basis. Agreement scores were computed as the number of agreements divided by the number of agreements plus disagreements. The mean occurrence agreement score was 77% or higher for all students and response categories (range 77 to 100%). The mean nonoccurrence agreement score was 73% or higher for all students and response categories (range 73 to 100%). Table 2 describes these data.

Results

Independent Variable Manipulation

The percentage of intervals of praise and time-out were each 0% during baseline. During all Praise conditions, the mean percentage of intervals of praise was 59% (range 40 to 72%) and 0% for time-out. Conversely, during all Time-Out conditions, the mean percentage of intervals of praise was 0% and was 54% (range 37 to 69%) for time-out. These data confirm the integrity of the independent variable manipulation; no instances of praise occurred during time-out sessions, no instances of time-out occurred during praise sessions, and relatively high levels of each consequence occurred during their respective conditions.

Problem Behavior Data

For the group who exhibited behavior maintained by attention (Figure 1), baseline levels of problem behavior varied greatly (mean 30.7%, range 0 to 95%). For example, one student (Gary) exhibited no instances of problematic behavior during baseline, and a second student (Rae) engaged in high, stable rates of problem behavior (mean 88%). The effect of the Praise condition on problem behavior for these students involved either little change from baseline (Ed, Jim, Gary, and Jeff), or a decline in the frequency of problem behavior (Pat, Rae, and Hal) and, as a group, declined to a mean percentage of approximately 11.7% (range 0 to 80%) from baseline levels (30.7%) during the initial intervention, and was approximately 5.9% (range 0 to 55%) during "Praise" Only.

Table 2
Observer Agreement Data for Experimental Phases

Experimental measures	Experimental phases			
	Baseline (%)	Intervention (%)	Functional manipulation (%)	Intervention alone (%)
Praise				
Occurrence	0	99.6(96–100)[a]	99.3(95–100)	99.3(95–100)
Nonoccurrence	100(–)	97.2(89–100)	95.6(85–100)	98.6(85–100)
Timeout				
Occurrence	0	99.6(95–100)	98.9(95–100)	100(–)
Nonoccurrence	100(–)	96.6(90–100)	96.5(91–100)	98.9(90–100)
Percentage correct	98.0(92–100)	97.8(91–100)	97.0(90–100)	97.5(90–100)
Picture replacements	99.6(98–100)	100(–)	99.8(98–100)	100(–)
Problem behavior				
Occurrence	84.7(75–100)	84.3(73–97)	82.3(75–95)	77.0(73–91)
Nonoccurrence	76.8(71–100)	77.0(70–100)	75.4(69–100)	73.3(67–100)

[a] Range in parentheses.

Time-Out, however, had the opposite effect on the problem behavior of these students. Problem behavior either remained consistent with baseline responding (Pat, Rae, Jim, and Hal) or increased from baseline (Ed, Gary, and Jeff) and, as a group, increased to a mean of approximately 45.2% (range 0 to 100%) from baseline levels (30.7%). Time-out, as occurred with task performance, had a detrimental effect on these students' rates of problem behavior.

Baseline levels of problematic behavior also varied for the group of students with escape-maintained problem behavior (Figure 2), with a mean percentage of intervals of 11.5% (range 0 to 52%). Participation in the Praise condition resulted in a general increase in the frequency of problem behavior exhibited by this group (mean 22.6%, range 0 to 77%) over baseline, although Time-Out produced either no change (Mia, Nan, and Ray) or a reduction in problem behavior (Tim, Mike, Dan, and Bob), averaging 2.2% (range 0 to 17%). In contrast to the students with attention-maintained problem behavior, this latter group of students were better behaved during the Time-Out sessions and engaged in relatively more behavior problems during Praise conditions. The positive results with time-out were replicated in the "Time-Out" Only condition (mean 1.8%, range 0 to 13%).

Task Performance Data

A mean of 52.7 trials per session were conducted across all of the conditions (range 10 to 136), with fewer trials conducted during sessions with high frequencies of problem behavior (e.g., with Rae, Pat, Hal, and Tim). Figure 3 represents the data for the students with problem behavior assessed to be maintained by social attention. As expected, task performance for each student approximated 50% correct for baseline (mean 48.7%, range 42 to 55%). During Praise sessions, the perform-

ance of this group was maintained at approximately 50% correct (mean 49.2%, range 35 to 55%). However, during Time-Out, task performance for the group fell to a mean of 13.7% (range 0 to 47%). Similar results were observed for this group during the "Praise" Only conditions (data on all functional manipulation sessions are described in a separate section below). Task performance was maintained at approximately 50% correct during all Praise sessions (mean 48.8%, range 40 to 55%).

Figure 4 illustrates the effects of the manipulations on the task performance of the students with problem behavior maintained by escape. Again, baseline performance approximated 50% correct responding (mean 49.1%, range 35 to 57%). However, the response of this group to the experimental manipulations was opposite that of the first group. Task performance was maintained at approximately 50% correct during the Time-Out condition (mean 48.8%, range 40 to 55%), but was reduced to 15.1% correct during Praise sessions (range 0 to 55%). The mean levels of responding were similar during "Time-Out" Only, averaging 49.2% (range 35 to 55%). These data are consistent with our predictions that students with attention-maintained behavior problems would prefer praise, and that students with escape-maintained behavior problems would prefer time-out.

When a student reached criterion on a particular picture (i.e., responded correctly to a picture five consecutive times), this picture was replaced with a more difficult picture. Figures 5 and 6 show the cumulative number of acquired pictures replaced in each session for each experimental condition. For each student, more pictures were acquired in the preferred reinforcer condition (mean 15.8, range 6 to 37) than in the nonpreferred reinforcer condition (mean 0.8, range 0 to 3).

We further analyzed the task performance data by assessing the percentage of inaccurate responses in the

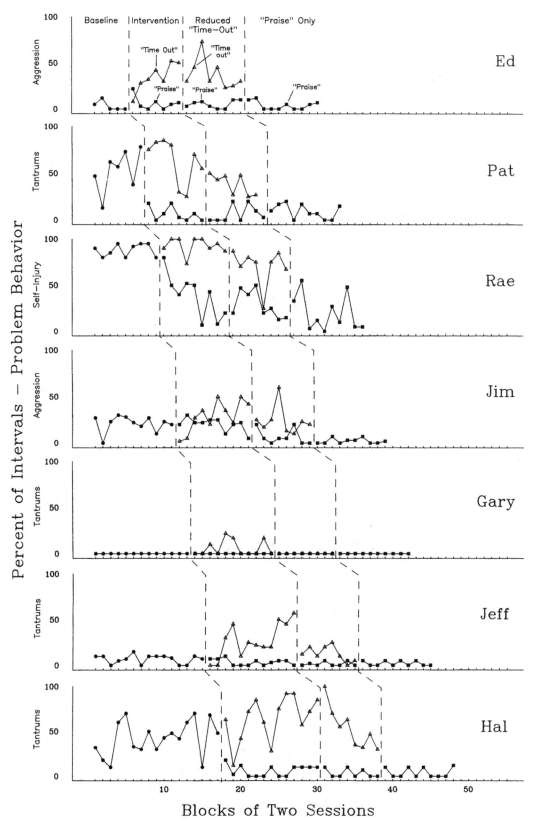

Figure 1. Percentage of intervals of problem behavior for students with attention-maintained behavior problems. Each point represents data from two sessions.

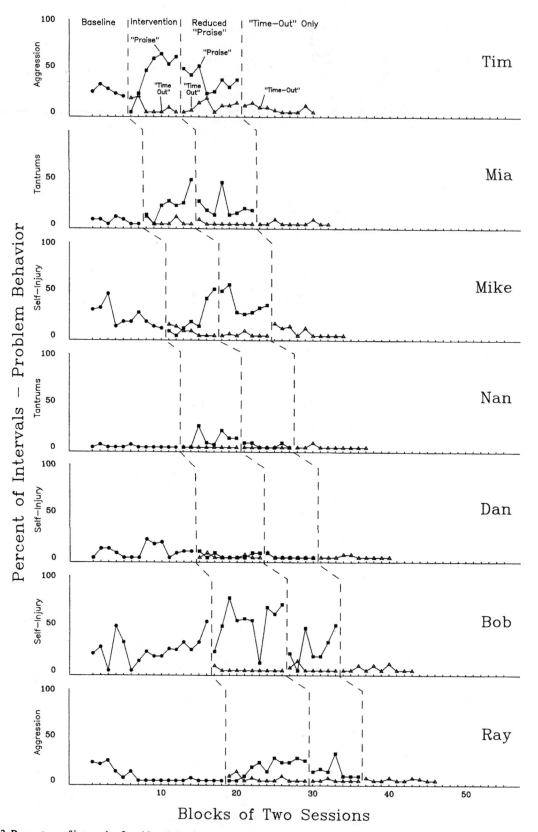

Figure 2. Percentage of intervals of problem behavior for students with escape-maintained behavior problems. Each point represents data from two sessions.

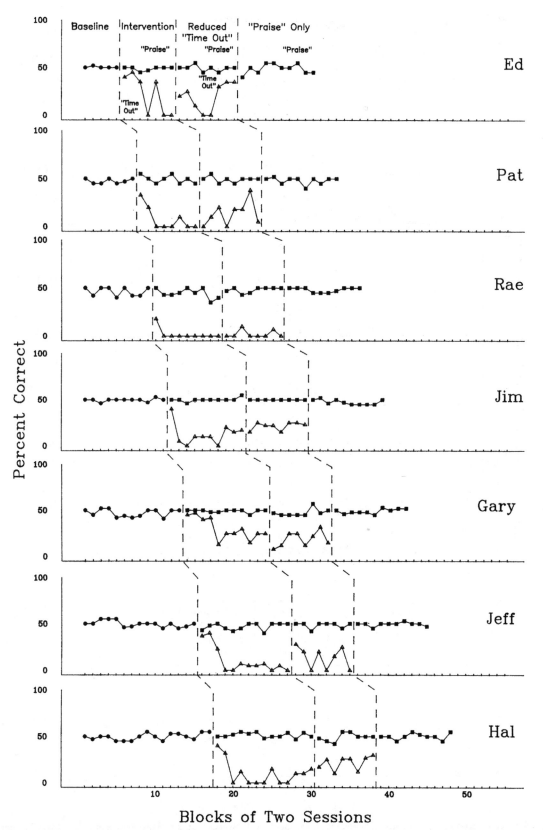

Figure 3. Percentage correct on receptive labeling task for students with attention-maintained problem behavior. Each point represents data from two sessions.

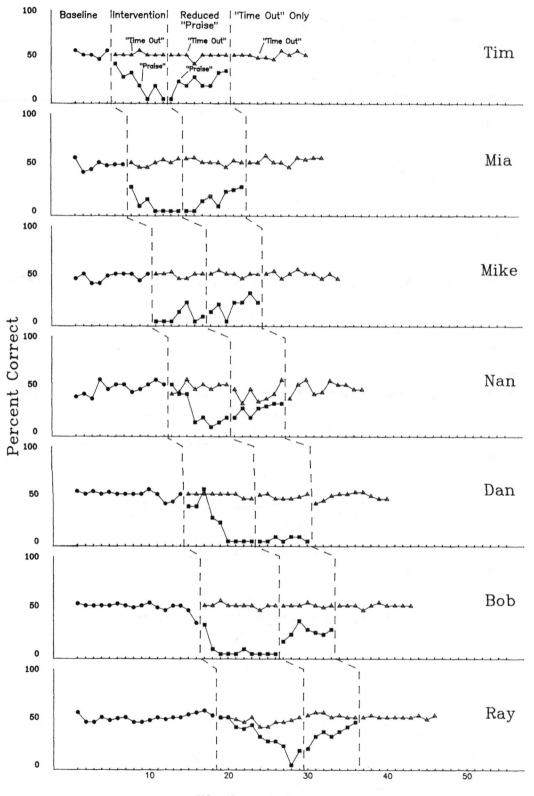

Figure 4. Percentage correct on receptive labeling task for students with escape-maintained problem behavior. Each point represents data from two sessions.

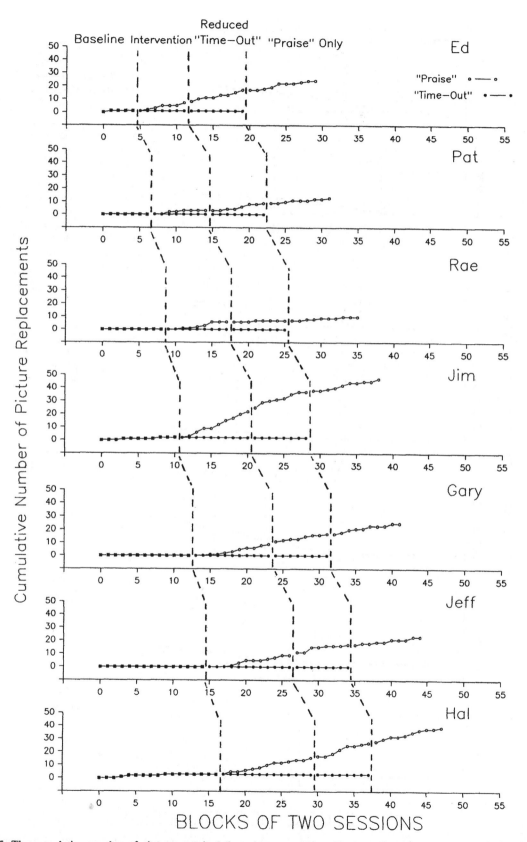

Figure 5. The cumulative number of pictures acquired (i.e., pictures reaching criterion) for students with attention-maintained behavior problems. Each point represents data from two sessions.

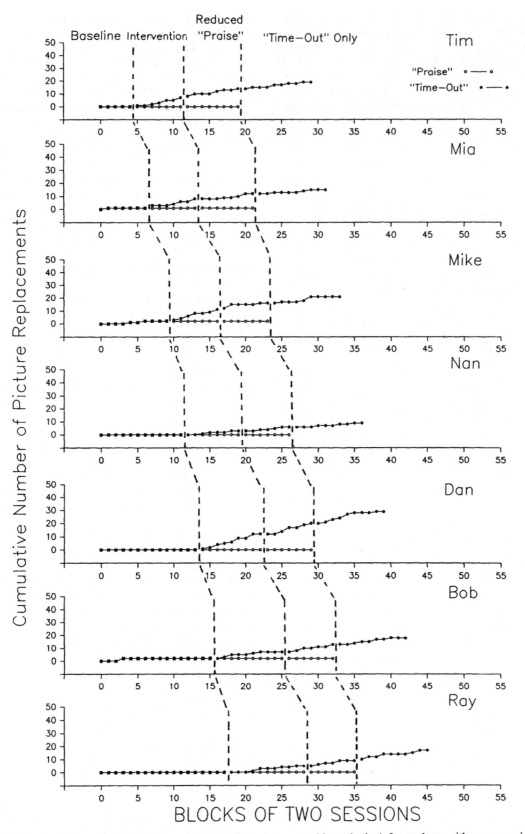

Figure 6. The cumulative number of pictures acquired (i.e., pictures reaching criterion) for students with escape-maintained behavior problems. Each point represents data from two sessions.

nonpreferred condition that involved pointing to the wrong picture versus not responding within 10 s. For 11 students, the majority of inaccurate responses were due to their not responding within the 10 s. For this group, a mean of 74.6% of the incorrect responses were because of no response to a request. This may be attributed to their engaging in problem behavior during this time. The majority of incorrect responding for three students involved pointing to the wrong picture (Dan, mean 72%; Gary, 58%; Tim, 86%). Given that they responded correctly to these pictures in the other condition, it appeared that these students may have been responding incorrectly to avoid the task consequence.

Functional Manipulation

We constructed the functional manipulation to assess for multiple treatment interference. For the group with problem behavior maintained by attention, reducing the duration of the time-out consequence had a positive impact on task performance for some of the students during Time-Out sessions (mean 15.8%, range 0 to 38%) when compared with the initial intervention, but little subsequent change in percentage correct was observed during Praise sessions (mean 48.9%, range 42 to 57%). Similarly, reducing time-out duration tended to reduce levels of problematic behavior during Time-Out sessions (mean 38.2%, range 0 to 100%) when compared with initial intervention; however, no concurrent changes were recorded for problem behavior during Praise sessions (mean 7.5%, range 0 to 47%).

The data on the functional manipulation for the group with escape-maintained behavior problems parallels those of the previous group. Reducing the duration of praise positively impacted on task performance (mean 18.5%, range 0 to 45%) and, to a lesser extent, problem behavior (mean 17.9%, range 0 to 55%) during Praise sessions; however, there appeared to be little carryover effect on Time-Out sessions for task performance (mean 48.5%, range 30 to 55%) or problem behavior (mean 1.6%, range 0 to 15%). The data from both groups suggest that there was little multiple treatment interference using the alternating treatments design, and that the observed effects can be interpreted more confidently as attributable to the separate influences of praise and time-out on students' behavior.

Discussion

We found that the variables controlling a student's frequent problematic behavior could be used to select reinforcers. For students with problem behavior maintained by social attention, praise was an effective reinforcer, and, when praise was used as a task consequence, several students engaged in less problematic behavior. In contrast, students with escape-maintained problem behavior responded adversely to social praise. Task performance declined sharply when these students were praised for correct responses, and several students sub-

sequently engaged in more behavior problems. For this latter group of students, removing attention and task materials (a procedural time-out) actually served as a reinforcer, and most were better behaved during these sessions. These results point to a method of selecting reinforcers that may be especially meaningful for those who work with students who have difficulty communicating.

This study represents an integration of Premack's (1959) reinforcement principles with the literature on the functional analysis of problem behavior. It should be noted that we have adapted the work of Premack in a way that differs from previous applications. This study explored how the *variables associated with high-rate behavior* can be used as reinforcers for low-rate behavior. This difference is particularly important in the present study, because it would be problematic to use behaviors such as self-injury, aggression, or tantrums as reinforcers.

However, this departure in the use of Premack's work goes beyond practical difficulties for students such as the ones described in this study. If the variables associated with a particular high-rate behavior are not considered in a reinforcement analysis, attempting to use this behavior as a reinforcer may be unsuccessful. For example, suppose an individual, if left alone, almost always walks to a chair in a room and pages through a magazine. Now suppose, as we have occasionally observed, that when we attempt to use access to the magazine as a reinforcer, it is not effective in increasing the probability of a targeted behavior. How can we explain this failure? One factor important to this issue is that the act of looking at a magazine can be controlled by a number of stimuli, including the attention paid to the student by others during this activity, escaping from work demands, or the visual input from the pictures. If, for example, the accompanying social attention maintained looking at the magazine, and now when we use it as a task consequence we do not also provide positive social attention, then we could predict that this high-rate behavior (i.e., looking at a magazine) would not serve as a reinforcer. It is information on the *function* of high-rate behavior that should be used when selecting reinforcers.

Previous research has shown that for some students, under certain stimulus conditions, "time-out" can serve as a reinforcer. For example, Solnick, Rincover, and Peterson (1977) observed that time-out resulted in increases in problem behavior for one student. When the "time-in" environment was enriched, time-out subsequently served to reduce problem behavior. Others have used analogous paradigms based on negative reinforcement procedures to change behavior, including escape from being held (Powers & Thorwarth, 1985), avoiding overcorrection (Foxx, 1977), and switching to high-difficulty tasks (Sailor, Guess, Rutherford, & Baer,

1968). Conversely, Herbert et al. (1973) observed that for some of their students, parental attention served to punish appropriate behavior. The present study suggests one way of predicting when and for whom certain stimuli will be reinforcing and when they may serve as a punisher.

Readers should note that the effects of these interventions were assessed only for brief periods, and it remains to be studied whether these procedures would be effective in more natural settings across a student's day. And, despite the positive findings observed in previous research and in this study, relying *exclusively* on time-out (or any other negative reinforcement procedure) as a task consequence for students with escape-maintained problem behavior is not a preferred method of intervention. Although there are behaviors that are routinely maintained through negative reinforcement (e.g., asking for a break from work, requesting assistance with difficult tasks, asking to leave anxiety-provoking situations), the removal of attention as a consequence for appropriate behavior will not be duplicated frequently outside of the teaching environment, especially for socially related skills such as communication. And, because generalization and maintenance of such skills depend, in part, on the effectiveness of these social consequences to reinforce desired behavior, using the removal of social attention to teach new responses may inhibit performance in extra training settings. However, in those instances where teaching is problematic (e.g., because of frequent escape behavior), this study points to the use of a procedural time-out as an effective first effort to promote skill acquisition. Our ongoing work in this area involves the pairing of social attention with time-out in an attempt to establish social attention as a reinforcer for individuals who have traditionally avoided social interactions.

An additional finding from this study was that the students exhibited fewer problematic behaviors when they were exposed to reinforcers. One explanation for this may be that because task performance was successful in eliciting these reinforcers, the students did not also have to engage in their problematic behavior to obtain the same reinforcers. The students with attention-maintained behavior problems could get access to social attention through correct task responses, and, similarly, the students with escape-maintained problem behavior could escape social attention and task demands through correct responding. This is consistent with previous treatment research, which demonstrated that teaching a functionally equivalent alternative response could successfully reduce severe self-injury, aggression, and other stereotyped behaviors (e.g., Carr & Durand, 1985; Durand & Carr, 1987; Durand & Crimmins, 1987; Durand & Kishi, 1987; Horner & Budd, 1985). Correct task responding appeared to have

served as a functionally equivalent response to the students' problematic behavior in the present study.

It is also important to understand why students engaged in *more* problem behavior during certain conditions. For students with attention-getting problem behavior, using time-out may have elicited these behaviors because this contingency resulted in less attention, thereby serving as a discriminative stimulus for attention-getting behavior (in this case, problem behavior). Analogously, for students with escape-maintained problem behavior, praise may have signaled the continued presence of an adult (with continued social interaction and no apparent break in the ongoing task), thereby serving as a discriminative stimulus for escape-maintained behavior. For this latter group, it would be important to individually assess the variables eliciting problem behavior (e.g., continued social interaction, continued presentation of difficult tasks). Increasing praise would be contraindicated (at least initially) for students who were escaping from social interaction.

Future work on reinforcer assessment should take a number of directions. In addition to replicating these findings, we need to expand our analysis to include students who exhibit problem behavior maintained by variables other than social attention and escape (e.g., behaviors maintained by their tangible or sensory consequences). There is also a need to adapt this work for students who are typically considered difficult to motivate, but who do not engage in frequent behavior problems. This approach to reinforcer assessment may be a valuable addition to our technology of habilitation, particularly for students who have historically proven difficult to teach.

References

Allen, L. D., & Iwata, B. A. (1980). Reinforcing exercise maintenance: Using existing high-rate activities. *Behavior Modification, 4,* 337–354.

Atkinson, R. P., Jenson, W. R., Rovner, L., Cameron, S., Van Wagenen, L., & Petersen, B. P. (1984). Validation of the autism reinforcer checklist for children. *Journal of Autism and Developmental Disorders, 14,* 429–433.

Baer, D. M., Wolf, M. M., & Risley, T. R. (1968). Some current dimensions of applied behavior analysis. *Journal of Applied Behavior Analysis, 1,* 91–97.

Barlow, D. H., & Hayes, S. C. (1979). Alternating treatments design: One strategy for comparing the effects of two treatments in a single subject. *Journal of Applied Behavior Analysis, 12,* 199–210.

Barlow, D. H., & Hersen, M. (1984). *Single case experimental designs* (2nd ed.). New York: Pergamon.

Carr, E. G., & Durand, V. M. (1985). Reducing behavior problems through functional communication training. *Journal of Applied Behavior Analysis, 18,* 111–126.

Durand, V. M., & Carr, E. G. (1987). Social influences on "self-stimulatory" behavior: Analysis and treatment application. *Journal of Applied Behavior Analysis, 20,* 119–132.

Durand, V. M., & Crimmins, D. B. (1987). Assessment and treatment of psychotic speech in an autistic child. *Journal of Autism and Developmental Disorders, 17,* 17–28.

Durand, V. M., & Crimmins, D. B. (1988). Identifying the

variables maintaining self-injurious behavior. *Journal of Autism and Developmental Disorders, 18,* 99–117.

Durand, V. M., & Kishi, G. (1987). Reducing severe behavior problems among persons with dual sensory impairments: An evaluation of a technical assistance model. *Journal of The Association for Persons with Severe Handicaps, 12,* 2–10.

Dyer, K. (1987). The competition of autistic stereotyped behavior with usual and specially assessed reinforcers. *Research in Developmental Disabilities, 8,* 607–626.

Foxx, R. M. (1977). Attention training: The use of overcorrection avoidance to increase the eye contact of autistic and retarded children. *Journal of Applied Behavior Analysis, 10,* 489–499.

Green, C. W., Reid, D. H., White, L. K., Halford, R. C., Brittain, D. P., & Gardner, S. M. (1988). Identifying reinforcers for persons with profound handicaps: Staff opinion versus systematic assessment of preferences. *Journal of Applied Behavior Analysis, 21,* 31–43.

Herbert, E. W., Pinkston, E. M., Hayden, M. L., Sajwaj, T. E., Pinkston, S., Cordua, G., & Jackson, C. (1973). Aversive effects of differential parental attention. *Journal of Applied Behavior Analysis, 6,* 15–30.

Horner, R. H., & Budd, C. M. (1985). Acquisition of manual sign use: Collateral reduction of maladaptive behavior, and factors limiting generalization. *Education and Training of the Mentally Retarded, 20,* 39–47.

Koegel, R. L., Dyer, K., & Bell, L. K. (1987). The influence of child-preferred activities on autistic children's social behavior. *Journal of Applied Behavior Analysis, 20,* 243–252.

Lovaas, O. I. (1981). *Teaching developmentally disabled children: The Me book.* Baltimore: University Park Press.

Lovaas, O. I., Freitag, G., Gold, V. J., & Kassorla, I. C. (1965). Experimental studies in childhood schizophrenia: Analysis of self-destructive behavior. *Journal of Experimental Child Psychology, 2,* 67–84.

Mullins, M., & Rincover, A. (1985). Comparing autistic and normal children along dimensions of reinforcement maximization, stimulus sampling, and responsiveness to extinction. *Journal of Experimental Child Psychology, 40,* 350–374.

Osborne, J. G. (1969). Free-time as a reinforcer in the management of classroom behavior. *Journal of Applied Behavior Analysis, 2,* 113–118.

Pace, G., Ivancic, M., Edwards, G., Iwata, B., & Page, T. (1985). Assessment of stimulus preferences and reinforcer values with profoundly retarded individuals. *Journal of Applied Behavior Analysis, 18,* 249–255.

Powers, M. D., & Thorwarth, C. A. (1985). The effect of negative reinforcement on tolerance of physical contact in a preschool autistic child. *Journal of Clinical Child Psychology, 14,* 299–303.

Premack, D. (1959). Toward empirical behavior laws I.: Positive reinforcement. *Psychological Review, 66,* 219–233.

Rincover, A. (1978). Sensory extinction: A procedure for eliminating self-stimulatory behavior in psychotic children. *Journal of Abnormal Child Psychology, 6,* 299–310.

Sailor, W., Guess, D., Rutherford, G., & Baer, D. M. (1968). Control of tantrum behavior by operant techniques during experimental verbal training. *Journal of Applied Behavior Analysis, 1,* 237–243.

Sidman, M. (1960). *Tactics of scientific research: Evaluating experimental data in psychology.* New York: Basic Books.

Solnick, J. V., Rincover, A., & Peterson, C. R. (1977). Some determinants of the reinforcing and punishing effects of timeout. *Journal of Applied Behavior Analysis, 10,* 415–424.

Weeks, M., & Gaylord-Ross, R. (1981). Task difficulty and aberrant behavior in severely handicapped students. *Journal of Applied Behavior Analysis, 14,* 449–463.

Received: November 14, 1988
Final Acceptance: January 4, 1989
Editor in Charge: Robert H. Horner

JASH
1989, Vol. 14, No. 3, 205–215

The McGill Action Planning System (MAPS): A Strategy for Building the Vision

Terri Vandercook and Jennifer York
University of Minnesota

Marsha Forest
Centre for Integrated Education

The McGill Action Planning System (MAPS) is a planning process that places primary emphasis on the integral involvement of learners with disabilities in the school community (i.e., regular classes and other typical school environments and activities). The seven key questions that comprise the MAPS process provide a structure that assists teams of adults and children to creatively dream, scheme, plan, and produce results that will further the inclusion of individual children with labels into the activities, routines, and environments of their same-age peers in their school community. This article provides a detailed description of the MAPS process, including the structure used, content covered, and the underlying assumptions of the process. An example of MAPS planning for an elementary age child with severe disabilities is provided, along with suggested modifications that have been used for secondary age students. The final discussion addresses practical considerations for using MAPS, including how it complements an ecological approach to curriculum development and areas requiring further development and evaluation.

DESCRIPTORS: friendship, integration, least restrictive environment, mainstreaming, nonhandicapped peers, peer relationships, teaming

The growing number of interpersonal relationships of people with disabilities and their peers who are not

labeled and increasing demonstrations of normalized life in the community have led to two major innovations in education and human services individualized planning processes for children, youth, and adults with disabilities. First, planning sessions are evolving to focus on creating visions of an integrated life and determining ways to realize the visions (Mount, 1987; O'Brien & Lyle, 1987). This is in direct contrast to old models of planning that were based on a deficit orientation (Hammill & Bartel, 1975; Salvia & Ysseldyke, 1985). Second, friends, neighbors, and family members are assuming key roles in the planning processes (Forest & Lusthaus, 1987; Mount & Zwernik, 1988; O'Brien, 1987). These are the individuals who can provide both continuity and support throughout an individual's life. Three formalized planning processes have emerged that embrace a futures and vision orientation and the integral involvement of friends, family members, and others who care about and are involved in the life of an individual with disabilities.

The "Lifestyle Planning" process was developed by O'Brien and Lyle (O'Brien & Lyle, 1987; O'Brien, 1987). Lifestyle planning moves service providers, family members, and friends of the individual for whom the planning is occurring through three planning activities: (a) describing a desirable future for the individual, (b) delineating a schedule of activities and supports necessary to move toward that desired outcome, and (c) accepting responsibility for using available resources and dealing with the reality of those resources and supports which are not available. The basic questions addressed by lifestyle planning center around five outcomes identified as essential for achieving an acceptable quality of life. These outcomes are referred to as accomplishments (O'Brien, 1987; Mount & Zwernik, 1988) and include community presence, choice, competence, respect, and community participation. Thus, the basic questions addressed with the lifestyle planning process are: "How can we identify constructive actions that will improve the quality of life experiences for a particular individual? How can we increase that individual's community presence, choice, competence, respect, and community participation?" (O'Brien, 1987, p. 178).

We wish to acknowledge Catherine Fleetham and the circle of caring people who participated in her MAPS planning sessions. Also, we thank the students and staff at the Roseville Area Middle School for including secondary age students with severe disabilities into their school community. They fill us with hope!

Development of this paper was supported in part by the Minnesota Integrated Education Technical Assistance Project (Grant 37010-57613) and the Least Restrictive Environment Project (Grant G008630347-88). The opinions expressed herein do not necessarily reflect the position or policy of the Minnesota Department of Education or the United States Department of Education, and no official endorsement should be inferred.

Requests for reprints should be sent to Terri Vandercook, University of Minnesota, Institute on Community Integration, 6 Pattee Hall, 150 Pillsbury Dr. SE, Minneapolis, MN 55455.

The "Personal Futures Planning" model (Mount, 1987; Mount & Zwernik, 1988) is a second futures-oriented process and is drawn directly from the lifestyle planning framework. Lifestyle planning and personal futures planning have been used most often for adults with disabilities and focus on their presence and participation at home, at work, and in the general community.

A third process, the McGill Action Planning System (MAPS)[1], (Forest & Lusthaus, 1987) is a planning process that places primary emphasis on the inclusion, participation, and learning of students with disabilities in regular education classes and other integrated school settings. MAPS is a way to operationalize the assertion that all children belong in a school community and to promote the establishment of relationships with others in the school community. Communities are built upon relationships. Relationships develop through longitudinal interactions that occur when sharing common places and experiences over time. Relationships are not only one of the most valid markers for measuring a person's quality of life, they are also viewed as serving a function in social and cognitive development (Lewis, 1982). According to Hartup (1985), they are the context in which basic competencies emerge. Second, they are resources. Relationships are used to protect an individual from stress, as well as to assist in problem solving (Erickson, 1976; Goodnow, 1984). Supportive and interdependent relationships are essential for the community involvement of persons with disabilities (Edgerton, 1967; McCord, 1983; Morreau, Novak, & Sigelman, 1980). Many persons with severe disabilities will never be able to function independently in the wide range of typical home, school, and community environments experienced daily. They will be dependent upon the willingness and skill of those who surround them to provide the support necessary for their maximum participation in much the same way that each of us is dependent on others in our home, work, and community endeavors (Strully & Strully, 1985). By having the opportunity to learn and grow up together, peers who do not have identified disabilities will establish the willingness and competencies to facilitate the participation of peers with disabilities (Johnson & Meyer, 1985; Meyer, McQuarter, & Kishi, 1985).

Assumptions of the MAPS Process

The assumptions underlying and guiding the MAPS process include (a) integration, (b) individualization, (c)

teamwork and collaboration, and (d) flexibility. The first assumption asserts that all individuals, including those with identified disabilities, should be educated in typical school and community environments, including regular classes, and should be provided with the necessary adaptations and supports to make this possible. Ongoing interactions with and proximity to peers who do not have labels is essential and preparatory for both those students who are labeled and those who are not. Use of segregated places for instruction must be minimized. Instead, special supports should be provided in regular education environments used by all students. Second, the assumption of individualization recognizes that each learner has unique abilities, interests, and needs. The ultimate goal of the MAPS process is to develop a plan that will meet an individual student's needs in regular education settings. Strategies and adaptations for successful integration are individualized also. Third, teamwork is essential to plan and implement the inclusion of learners with high needs (i.e., those with labels of moderate to profound disabilities) in regular education environments. MAPS capitalizes on the creative problem-solving abilities of adults and children who know and care about the individual for whom the planning is to occur. Through collaborative teamwork, the benefits of group problem solving can be realized. Flexibility, the final assumption in the MAPS process, is necessary, as even the most thoughtfully designed strategies and plans sometimes are not successful and need revision. False starts should be anticipated and a commitment made to ongoing problem solving and change as needed. Initial objectives for student involvement in regular classes and the supports necessary to achieve individualized objectives may need to be modified after the students actually participate in regular classes. Changes may also need to be made as team members acquire more expertise in the area of regular class integration. The saying that "What *is* can be better and what *is best* is fluid" (Association for Retarded Citizens Suburban, 1988, p. 1), captures nicely the essence of flexibility.

The MAPS Process

The team includes the individual, family members, friends, and both regular and special education personnel. Given the current reality of learners with high needs being based in special education classrooms, the special education professionals are likely to know the child better than regular education personnel. The regular educators, however, are the experts on the goals, activities, and routines that occur in regular classes. Both are important participants. The inclusion of typical peers in the planning process is an essential and unique feature of MAPS. The children provide a necessary and fresh perspective on the needs of their peer with a disability related to involvement in regular classes. They

---

[1] A video depicting the MAPS process, "With a Little Help From My friends," is available for teams interested in learning more about the process. Write to the Centre for Integrated Education, Frontier College, 35 Jackes Avenue, Toronto, Ontario, Canada, M4T1E2, or Expectations Unlimited, P.O. Box 655, Niwot, CO 80544.

also serve a key role in supporting their peer with high needs in regular activities and settings. Typical peers help other team members to realize that the vision and dream of being an accepted and valued member of the school community and the larger community can be a reality if children have the opportunity to grow and learn together.

Because the involvement of peers who know and care about the individual is an essential feature of the MAPS process, the planning should not occur until the student with disabilities has been a member of the regular education community, so that friends without disabilities can be identified and their involvement recruited. Peers typically are identified by the classroom teacher, based upon interest as demonstrated by the amount of interaction and time spent with the student. At least two, and preferably three to five classmates have been involved in the planning. In a MAPS session in which only one friend was involved, the friend was uncomfortable participating, given the size of the group and the disproportionate number of adults. For very young children (kindergarten and first grade), classmate involvement might be limited to certain questions or the planning broken down into smaller segments (e.g., three 1-hour sessions versus one 3-hour time block). The MAPS planning typically occurs in one or two sessions. A minimum of 3 hours should be allotted to work through the process. Addressing the questions that compose the MAPS process, however, will be an ongoing activity for the educational team. The seven key questions are not carved in stone, and the facilitator may choose to address the questions in a different order or eliminate a question if the information generated seems redundant.

The participants are arranged in a half circle, with the facilitator positioned at the open end of the circle. The information and ideas generated during the process are recorded on large chart paper, which serves as a communication check during the session and as a permanent record when the planning is finished. The facilitator can also serve the role of recorder, or an additional person can serve in that capacity. The facilitator needs to be a person who is committed to building an integrated school community in which the individual is valued and provided the support necessary to be a member of the class with same-age peers. The facilitator needs good listening skills and an ability to facilitate interaction among team members in such a way that they challenge one another to broaden their visions of community and also make practical suggestions regarding the support and adaptations necessary to meet the needs of the individual in regular class settings and other typical school and nonschool environments. The facilitator must be comfortable interacting with both the adults and the children and able to elicit input from all participants. The best planning will occur for the individual with disabilities when input is gathered from all participants and conversation is not dominated by a select few. The importance of *each* person's contribution should be clearly communicated by the facilitator before the planning begins. The seven key questions and a final reflection which compose the MAPS process are delineated and discussed below.

What is the individual's history?

Aside from the individual for whom the planning is occurring, family members are the most important members of the circle because they typically know the individual better than anyone else. Because of this, family members, and the individual to the greatest extent possible, are asked to spend a few minutes talking about the individual's history, including some of the key milestones in the persons's life.

What is your dream for the individual?

This question is intended to get people to think about their vision for the individual's future. They are encouraged to think about what they want and what they think the person would want for his or her future. This vision should not be based solely on current realities. Dreams can become reality if there is a shared vision and commitment to strive for that vision. In the realm of dreams, the only certainty is that if we can't dream it, we won't achieve it. The dream question forces the team to think about the direction in which the individual is heading. This allows concrete plans to be made for realizing the vision. This is not to say, however, that the vision or the plans for achieving the dream are set in concrete. The visions and resulting expectations will be challenged continually as more is learned about how to facilitate inclusion in the school community and as positive outcomes are realized. Depending upon the age of the individual, it may be difficult to think about the dream for the individual as an adult. If that is a problem, team members can be encouraged to think about the person 5 years from the present time or perhaps when the individual is of high school age. The important factor is not how far into the future the vision projects but simply that a dream exists for an integrated future, thereby providing direction and goals to strive toward.

What is your nightmare?

This is a very difficult question to ask the parents of any child, yet an extremely important one. Parents frequently relate the nightmare as a vision of their child being alone. The nightmare presents the situation that the members of the individual's team and others who care for him or her must work very hard to keep from happening.

Who is the individual?

Everyone in the circle participates in responding to this question. The participants are asked to think of words that describe the individual; that is, what comes to mind when they think of the person? There are no right or wrong words. Participants take turns going around the circle until all thoughts have been expressed. Participants can pass if nothing comes to mind when it is their turn to supply a descriptor. When the list is complete, the facilitator asks certain people to identify the three words from the list that they feel best describe the individual. Frequently, family members and peers are asked to identify key descriptors.

What are the individual's strengths, gifts, and abilities?

So often when educational teams get together, they dwell upon the things that the individual cannot do, as opposed to identifying and building upon the strengths and abilities of the individual. The facilitator asks the participants to review the list describing the individual as a way to identify some of his or her strengths and unique gifts. In addition, they are instructed to think about what the individual can do, what he or she likes to do, and what he or she does well.

What are the individual's needs?

This question provides an opportunity for all the team members to identify needs from each of their unique perspectives. When the list of needs is complete, family, friends, and educators are asked to prioritize the identified needs.

What would the individual's ideal day at school look like and what must be done to make it happen?

MAPS is a process intended to assist teams to plan for the full integration of students with high needs into regular age-appropriate classes. Frequently, attention to this question begins by outlining a school day for same-age peers who do not have labels. Next, the team begins to develop strategies for meeting the needs identified in the previous question in the context of the regular education day. Finally, initial planning occurs for the supports needed to achieve successful integration. As learners reach middle and high school age, the ideal school day will include instruction in both regular education and a variety of community instruction sites (e.g., home, work sites, stores, and recreation settings).

MAPS . . . in a word

The last request by the facilitator provides an opportunity for feedback specifically related to the process itself and, as such, should always be included. The facilitator asks each person to describe, in one word, the MAPS process. The adjectives supplied by team members are usually very positive and affirming of the process and the time they have spent planning together. However, this is also an opportunity to share impressions or feelings that may not be completely positive. A regular class teacher once put forth the word "pressure" when asked to describe MAPS in a word and then went

on to explain that she considered herself a 'Type A' personality and, as a result, was feeling that all of the wonderful ideas generated during the process should be implemented right away. This provided the opportunity for other team members to assure the teacher that it was not their intent for everything to be in place by the end of the week. Together the team immediately prioritized actions to be initiated, identified persons responsible, and established reasonable timelines for implementation.

Catherine's MAPS

An example of the MAPS planning process is provided here in an attempt to clarify and enrich the previous description of the process. Catherine is a 9-year-old child who attends a regular elementary school in a metropolitan school district. Catherine has received the majority of her educational program in a self-contained special education class. As part of a school district mini-grant project designed to increase the integration of students with severe disabilities into their school community, Catherine increased the time she spent with her third grade same-age peers in typical school settings. For the most part, this was the result of what Biklen (1987) describes as the "teacher deals approach" to integration. This approach typically involves a special education teacher establishing informal relationships with regular educators as a basis for increasing the inclusion of students with disabilities in regular class settings. Toward the end of the school year, Catherine's educational team committed itself to participation in the MAPS process in an effort to plan more systematically how to further Catherine's integration with her third grade peers. The process described here represents the team's initial formal attention to include Catherine in regular third grade life. Since this initial planning and subsequent implementation, much more has been done as the team learned together and saw positive outcomes for Catherine and her peers. Specifically, the conclusion reached by the majority of Catherine's team was that her needs were *not* being met most appropriately with a model of "partial" membership in the regular classroom. As a result, Catherine's team is now in the process of planning for her full membership in the regular classroom with individually designed special education support services provided in regular education environments. The MAPS process has generally been used with children who are established and full-time members of a regular class, and that certainly is the most desirable circumstance.

For Catherine's MAPS, the team included Catherine, her mom (Diane) and 10-year-old brother (John), three third grade friends (Jessica, Julie, Amy), her third grade classroom teacher (Metta), special education teacher (Mary), speech and language teacher (Rebecca), teaching assistant (Carol), and occupational therapist (Sharon). The third grade teacher and peers already knew Catherine because of her involvement in some of their class activities throughout the school year. The facilitator and the team met after school on each of two days and worked their way through the questions that compose the MAPS process. The first planning session began by having everyone in attendance introduce themselves and state their relationship with Catherine. Name tags were used to help the facilitator and team members remember names. Following is a summary of the discussion and information generated related to Catherine for each specific question in the MAPS process.

What is Catherine's history?

Catherine's mom, Diane, identified the members of Catherine's family and then continued by sharing major events in Catherine's history. Catherine experienced a normal delivery and birth. At approximately 15 months she began losing some skills and was later diagnosed as having Rett Syndrome. Catherine went to a developmental achievement center when she was 18 months old, and Diane recalled how strange it seemed to be sending someone so young off to "school." When the time came for Catherine's transition to the public school system, Diane was advised by a number of people to send Catherine to the special school for students with severe disabilities so that she could receive the services necessary to meet her intensive needs. From Diane's perspective, the problem with that option was that the school served only students with disabilities. Diane wanted Catherine to be around regular education students so that she could learn from them and have the opportunity to get to know them. As a result of her convictions, Diane pursued alternative settings, and Catherine was placed in a self-contained special education class within a regular elementary school in her local school district.

What is your dream for Catherine as an adult?

Diane's dream for Catherine as an adult was to see her live with friends that she cared about and who cared about her. Catherine's friend Julie saw her doing math in sixth grade, and another friend Jessica was hoping that maybe they could be the friends that live with Catherine when she grows up. Rebecca, the speech teacher, envisioned Catherine in high school having the opportunity to go out after school for pizza with friends, selecting a song on the juke box, and placing her own order. John's dream for Catherine included a cure for Rett Syndrome and the two of them going to concerts and movies together. A consistent theme throughout the dream discussion was Catherine's involvement with family and peers who do not have disabilities.

What is your nightmare?

Diane's nightmare was that Catherine would be alone.

Who is Catherine?

Catherine's team generated an extensive list of descriptors: giggly, funny, endearing, charming, wiggly, drools, loved, sister, enjoyable, book lover, likes people, likes outdoors, chair tipper, likes to touch things, likes vegetables, salad, McDLTs, baked potatoes, bran, and applesauce, smiles, nice, shining eyes, Anne Murray fan, messy, excited, likes to be held, loving, beautiful, likes to look at faces, likes bright colors, likes to be read to, likes new clothes, and a friend.

What are Catherine's strengths, gifts, and abilities?

Catherine's planning team identified the following strengths, gifts, and abilities: touches faces in books, plays bongo drums, can walk, very social, which endears her to others, cooperative attitude, great personality, lets you know what she wants and likes, likes to tease, recognizes and remembers people, love of music, "holds" the guitar (will place her hand on the neck when assisted), has good friends, really tries, interested in a lot of things around her, spending quality time with third grade. (One of the most valuable aspects of the MAPS process is evident in reviewing the responses to this question and the previous questions, which reveal a positive view of the person and highly valued unique characteristics. Such a positive orientation assists in designing a hopeful future.)

What are Catherine's needs?

Because this was the last question that could be covered during the first MAPS session, the discussion was opened up for general response from all of those present, instead of going person by person. The list generated was then rewritten on a large sheet of paper and served as the starting point for the second meeting. At the next meeting, family, friends, and educators were asked to identify the needs from the list that they considered priorities and to add any needs they thought were missing. Beginning the second session in this fashion helped the group to focus on Catherine's needs and have them clearly in mind before addressing the next and final question about what Catherine's ideal day would look like. Priority needs identified by family members, friends, and educators are listed in Table 1. Other needs which were identified but not listed as priorities by any group included: (a) help with basic needs such as dressing and eating, (b) an advocate, (c) to do "Mousercize" (the friends explained that Mousercize was an activity in physical education class that would be good for Catherine because of the movement and that she would like it because of the music), and (d) a strong support system outside the family.

Table 1
Catherine's Priority Needs Identified by Family, Friends, and Educators

Family	Friends	Educators
For others to know she is not helpless	More friends	More friends
Music and time to listen to it	Support to get more places and learn things there	Support to get more places and learn things there
Affection	A lot of opportunity to walk and use her hands	A lot of opportunity to walk and use her hands
To be with people	As an adult, to live in a small home with friends in a community where she is accepted	Opportunity to let people know what she wants and a way to communicate that with more people
To change environments and surroundings often	Teachers to accept her	To increase the opportunity and skill to make more choices
Healthy foods	To learn to hang onto the book when a friend is reading with her	Affection
		People to know how to: deal with her seizures, help her stand up, and accept and deal with her drooling

Table 2
Tuesday Morning Schedule for Catherine: Moving Toward the Ideal School Day

Time	Catherine's day (current)	3rd grade day (current)	Possibilities for change (proposed)
9:00–9:30	Take off coat Use restroom Adaptive P.E.	Pledge of Allegiance Seat work directions Spelling	Breakfast (could eat with nondisabled peers if school arrival coincided)
9:30–10:00	Breakfast Work on lip closure, holding the spoon, choosing objects she wants	Reading Group I Others do seat work, write stories, read silently	Switch center (in 3rd grade reading) Transition to center, reaching, touching picture, activating tape player
10:00–10:45	Switch center Transition to center, reaching, touching picture, activating tape player using microswitch (leisure activity)	Physical education (10:00–10:20) Mousercize, Exercise Express, Use restroom Reading Group II (10:25–10:45)	Physical education (with 3rd grade) Skills related to maintaining ambulation and mobility (weight shifting, balance reactions, strength exercise) Cooperation with peer partner Rest time
10:45–11:10	Reading Group III (with 3rd grade) Makes transition to floor, responds to greeting from peer, reaches for peer's hand, holds onto book, looks at book, closes book, makes transition to standing	Reading Group III	Maintain current activity with 3rd grade
11:10–11:30	Library (with 3rd grade) Return book, choose book, look at it, check it out, return to class	Library	Maintain current activity with 3rd grade

What would Catherine's ideal day at school look like and what must be done to make it happen?

Because the MAPS sessions for Catherine occurred in late March and early April, the planning was viewed as merely an initial opportunity to begin creatively planning to meet Catherine's needs in regular education settings with her third grade peers. As was noted earlier, the initial planning resulted in only partial inclusion into the third grade. After one year of partial integration, however, the team consensus was that partial integration was not meeting Catherine's needs. Plans for full inclusion are now underway.

The initial planning, which resulted in only partial inclusion of Catherine with her third grade peers, was facilitated by delineating the activities engaged in by the third graders and those engaged in by Catherine during her school day. The two schedules of activities and the list of priority needs identified previously were displayed side by side. By doing so, brainstorming about how Catherine could have more of her needs met in the same settings as her third grade peers was facilitated. Table 2 presents a format for organizing the two schedules and developing a list of possible changes. Please note that time ran out for the second MAPS session before the entire school day could be addressed. With the activities of the third grade students during each time period delineated, the team began to discuss ways for Catherine to participate in each activity, and initial goals and objectives were identified. After Catherine had a chance to participate in the third grade activities, the team was able to finalize priorities for instruction and develop instructional strategies. The instructional programs developed for Catherine in regular classes specified skills to be learned, antecedent instructional procedures, reinforcement and error correction procedures, and criteria for change in procedures. Data probes were carried out by the special education personnel on Catherine's team, including the speech and language teacher, occupational therapist, special education teacher, and teaching assistant. Adaptations in the form of personal assistance, materials adaptations, and changes in curricular goals for regular class activities were necessary for Catherine and are likely to be necessary to some extent for the inclusion and learning of each student with high needs in regular class settings.

The sheet of paper which depicted the priority needs for Catherine identified by her family, friends, and teachers was kept in view throughout the planning sessions. This provided a way for the group to validate suggested activities and to remember identified needs. In developing the day of possibilities for more inclusion with peers, identified needs were addressed:

1. for others to know that Catherine is not helpless
2. to be with people
3. for affection
4. to change environments and surroundings often
5. for more friends
6. for support to get more places and learn things there
7. to walk and use her hands
8. for teachers to accept her
9. to learn to hang onto a book when a friend is reading with her
10. to let people know what she wants and a way to communicate that with more people
11. to increase the opportunity and skill to make more choices
12. for others to learn how to deal with her seizures, help her stand up, and accept and deal with her drooling

The largest change made in Catherine's Tuesday morning schedule was a switch from physical education in an adaptive physical education class to attending a regular third grade physical education class in which the activity is movement to music. The third grade P.E. period is 20 min long and occurs 5 days a week. This class was considered a particularly good match for Catherine because she thoroughly enjoys music and needs to have a lot of opportunities to move. The occupational therapist agreed to make time in her

schedule to go to P.E. with Catherine 3 times each week to assist in the development of an exercise routine for Catherine that would meet her physical needs. It was also decided that a classroom assistant would learn the routine from the occupational therapist and be available to provide support on the other 2 days. The third grade teacher added P.E. Assistant to the list of classroom honors, so that there would be a peer partner for Catherine during P.E. who would act as a mentor for her during that time.

For reading class, the speech therapist agreed to assess the possibility of using a switch to activate music or a storybook tape in the third grade classroom while the first reading group is in session and the other children are doing seatwork, silent reading, or writing. Catherine and a peer could use headphones to listen to the tapes, and the peer could help Catherine to activate the switch to maintain the activity. In addition to the needs addressed by the activity of learning to activate a switch (music and time to listen to it, use of her hands, opportunity to let people know what she wants, opportunity and skill to make more choices), instruction on this activity in the third grade would address additional needs (i.e., the opportunity for Catherine to be with more people and to gain more friends, for others to learn that Catherine is not helpless, to learn how to deal with her seizures, help her stand up, and accept and deal with her drooling).

MAPS ... in a word

The last request of the facilitator was to ask everyone to describe in a word what they thought of the MAPS process. The following list of descriptors was generated: fun, creative, exciting, radical, awesome, overwhelming, fantastic, joyful, great, helpful, enthusiastic, cooperative, enlightening, and hopeful. Use of the words radical and overwhelming in this context need clarification. Radical was the word supplied by Catherine's 10-year-old brother John. It was not intended to convey "revolutionary" or "extreme" as defined in the dictionary, but rather, "excellent," "terrific," "great." Overwhelming was the word supplied by Catherine's mom. Her intention was not to convey a sense of the dream being too large and unrealistic, but, rather, a sense of overpowering understanding, love, and commitment by all members of the team to Catherine and her right and ability to be an important member of her school community.

MAPS Modifications for a Secondary Age Student

There are both programmatic and logistical differences between elementary and secondary schooling which result in several modifications of the MAPS process. Programmatically, students with disabilities begin spending part of their school day in off-campus community instructional sites (e.g., stores, work sites).

Furthermore, increasing emphasis is placed on transition to adulthood. Logistical changes result from the regular education departmentalization by curricular areas instead of by grades. Students change classes and teachers every period of the day instead of remaining largely in one class with one teacher and a constant set of classmates. Two practical implications of these changes from elementary to secondary programs for MAPS are (a) determining which regular education teachers and classmates should be involved in the MAPS process and (b) planning for participation in both regular classes and community instructional sites, with an increasing focus on transition to adulthood.

The time of year during which MAPS occurs and the ways in which specific regular educators have been involved with the student will influence who participates. If MAPS planning occurs in the spring of the year, planning will focus in part on the next school year's educational program, as well as on developing a vision for transition to adulthood. To participate in the discussion regarding the student's gifts, strengths, talents, and needs, regular educators must have some history of interaction with the student. Teachers who have had the student in their classes, therefore, would be invited. To assist in selecting and planning for involvement in future regular classes, knowledge of regular education course offerings is required. The student's grade level dean, counselor, or assistant principal might be involved for this purpose. It is often difficult to schedule MAPS so all the regular educators involved with the student can participate. Scheduling must allow those who have taken a special interest in the student to be included.

For students with disabilities who have grown up and attended regular classes with classmates who do not have disabilities throughout their elementary years, determining which of the peers should be involved in MAPS is easy. By the time they reach secondary school, friendships already have been established. For students whose inclusion in regular classes and school life is just beginning at the secondary level, identifying peers to be involved is more difficult. The relationships established among elementary students that frequently are sustained through secondary years do not exist for students with disabilities who were not integrated during elementary years. Particularly in these situations, the MAPS process should be scheduled only after the student with disabilities has been a regular class member for at least several weeks. This will allow peers who take an interest in the student to be identified. Another consideration in determining peers for involvement, at both elementary and secondary levels, is to identify neighborhood peers.

Given the increased emphasis on community-based instruction at the secondary level and on transition planning to adulthood, the following question modifications based on the Personal Future's Planning model have been used (Mount, 1987; Mount & Zwernik, 1988). In responding to the "dreams" question, part of the discussion can be directed at developing a vision of life in early adulthood by asking: At age 21, where will the individual live and work? What will these places be like? What will he or she do there? What community places will he or she use? Who will he or she spend time with? As students near age 18, the final question of the MAPS process can be modified to ask: What would the individual's ideal day look like? MAPS participants can outline a day in the life of the person after graduation. The purpose of these modifications is to structure the discussion to create a vision of an integrated life in adulthood which can serve as the basis for identifying priorities to address in the remaining years of public school education. The resulting plan for a secondary age student is a school day which includes instruction in both regular class and community environments. This is in contrast to planning for elementary students in which the result is typically a school day of full inclusion in regular classes with classmates without disabilities. The longitudinal proximity to a relatively constant group of classmates during the elementary years should facilitate the development of stable relationships in secondary years.

Portions of a MAPS session for Ed, a secondary age student, using the modifications described above, are provided in Table 3. Only the modified sections are included. Table 4 presents a projected day for Ed postgraduation. There were several interesting outcomes of this process. First, the initial discussion related to "Where will Ed live?" focused on remaining at home with his family. As the discussion progressed, the vision changed to focus on living in a supported apartment complex that has a variety of leisure facilities. Second, in brainstorming employment possibilities, the initial discussion centered on service industry options that were considered current realities and then shifted to a focus on work that capitalized on Ed's interests and strengths. As a result, jobs involving caring for animals or delivering mail in a large office building, which matched Ed's love of animals and his pleasant and social nature, were considered. Finally, after outlining a day in Ed's life postgraduation, team members remarked that priority instructional environments and activities could be identified easily from the outlined day and from other information generated during the MAPS session. They also felt hopeful and inspired about the "nice life" that Ed could continue to lead.

Although the MAPS process has resulted in many positive outcomes for children with disabilities and their friends, families, and educational team members, numerous questions have been raised related to the pragmatics of implementation and the need to empirically validate, socially and educationally, both short- and long-term outcomes.

Table 3
The Dream for Ed as an Adult

Where will Ed live? . . . What will it be like?
  Living at home with his family
  Thinking about alternative living arrangements
  Spend weekends and summers away from family
  Living at home—possibly having his own area within parents' home, maybe with a roommate (e.g., apartment in basement)
  Living close to his family
  Friends will visit and he will visit others
  More independence
  Close to shopping area
  On a bus line
  Close to recreation/leisure areas
  Has a pet
  Apartment with complete facilities: swimming, food service hobbies, recreation, etc.

Where will Ed work? . . . What will it be like?
  Washing dishes—loading/unloading dishwasher
  Zoo—take care of animals
  Cleaning business (motels, apartments)
  Lots of people around—lots of action, activity going on
  Co-workers to assist . . . work as a member of a team
  Close to bus line
  Car pool member
  Action job. Somewhere he can move around, possibly outside (e.g., deliver newspapers or deliver mail in office building)
  Day care center
  A job with routine
  Large company

What community environments will Ed use?
  YMCA recreation areas
  Health club
  Community education . . . after work activities
  Church social groups
  Public transportation
  Pizza place
  Dances
  Cattle company
  Kellogg club
  Fast-food restaurants
  Shopping areas
  Laundromat
  Sporting events—Twins games
  State fair

Who will Ed be around?
  Co-workers
  Friends the same age
  Family
  Neighbors
  Opportunities for dating
  Support staff
  Salespeople, waitresses, waiters
  Club members/staff
  Roommate
  Sports team—co-ed league
  Strangers
  Supervisor

MAPS and IEPs

When considering use of the MAPS process, teams frequently ask: "How does MAPS relate to an environ-mentally referenced approach to Individualized Educational Plan (IEP) development?" The MAPS process complements IEP development in at least two ways. First, in most instances, engaging in the process results in a clearer sense of mission and a greater sense of teamwork. Collaborative teamwork facilitates well designed and implemented IEPs. Second, the MAPS process is particularly useful in assisting teams to identify priority environments and activities and to identify student needs that can be addressed in those settings. An environmentally referenced curricular approach (Brown et al., 1979; Falvey, 1986; Nietupski & Hamre-Nietupski, 1987) is merely expanded to include referencing regular education environments and activities, in addition to domestic, recreation/leisure, community, and vocational environments. Traditionally, the community domain has been defined in terms of general community functioning such as participation in stores, restaurants, banks, post offices, and other service environments. If an individual is of school age, however, the primary community environment is the school. The community domain, therefore, might be better conceptualized as consisting of two principal divisions, the general community and the school community. Learner participation in both the general and school communities must receive attention in the IEP development and implementation process. Part of the MAPS process delineates regular school environments and activities. Specific IEP goals and objectives are derived from assessing the abilities of the student in regular classes and other typical school and community environments. See York and Vandercook (in press) for a strategy that can be used in designing an integrated education through the IEP process. Included are specific examples of skills targeted for instruction in regular classes and related IEP goals and objectives.

Another frequent inquiry is: How often do we do MAPS, especially since it takes so long? A logical time to use the MAPS process is as part of required 3-year re-evaluations or, at the very least, at crucial transition points in each learner's educational career (e.g., preschool to elementary school, middle to high school, high school to adulthood).

Future Directions

The MAPS process has been used by the authors and their associates with over 200 school-age children with moderate to profound disabilities in 50 school communities. To date, the outcomes delineated with regard to MAPS planning has been anecdotal in nature. An empirical basis for the educational validity of the MAPS process has yet to be established. Factors that warrant study include (a) the utility of the process from the perspective of various team members (i.e., parents, administrators, classroom teachers, special education teachers, related services personnel, and classmates); (b)

Table 4
An Ideal Day in Ed's Life at Age 21

What will Ed's weekdays look like?

Ed lives in a high rise apartment building with a roommate and a pet bird. He has a job as a courier in a company. He has an overseer.

MONDAY

6:30–7:00	Gets up to first alarm	12:30–2:00	Back to work
	Showers/grooms, "mousses" his hair	2:00–2:15	Break
	Dresses in the clothes he chose the night before		Stops in restroom
	Takes his medication		Joins co-workers
7:00	Prepares breakfast for himself		Looks at magazine, newspapers (sports page)
	Eats, listens to radio (music)	2:15–4:00	Back to work
	Cleans up kitchen, loads dishwasher	4:00–4:30	Gets ready to go home
	Feeds the pet		Goes to the restroom
	Brushes his teeth		Goes to the bus stop
	Gets ready for work	5:00–6:00	Arrives at home
	Gets his money		Prepares supper with roommate
7:30	Takes the elevator to lobby		Does chores—vacuums, makes bed, and so on
	Goes to bus stop	6:00–6:30	Eats supper
	Meets a friend to ride with	6:30	Cleans kitchen
7:40	Boards bus		Watches TV, listens to radio
8:00	Starts work	7:00–9:00	Plays in softball game with people from work
	Makes rounds as courier (delivering mail) with co-worker		Dad is the coach
	Greets people		Family is there to watch and cheer
10:00–10:15	Break	9:00–9:30	Partakes of refreshments with team members (no coach)
	"Talks" to people in break room	9:30–10:30	Rides home with a friend
	Gets refreshments		Calls mom ("checks in")
	Uses bathroom		Chooses clothes for next day
10:15–12:00	Back at work—same routine		Grooms
12:00–12:30	Lunch break		Says his prayers
	Goes to restroom (cleans up for lunch)		Covers the bird cage
	Goes to cafeteria to purchase his lunch		Watches the news, listens for weather report
	Eats with a group of people (not the same everyday)	10:30	Goes to bed
	Goes for a walk		Sets alarm
	Makes plans for evenings with friends		
	Stops in restroom		

"What a Nice Life"

short-term impact in the school and general community; and (c) long-term impact such as longitudinal relationships with peers and participation in typical school and community activities.

Summary

For integrated education to be successful, several aspects of current educational services will necessarily change. Special education personnel and resources will change the focus of their service from one of educating children in separate environments to one of providing support and instruction in regular classrooms and other typical school environments. Regular educators will begin to include all children in their classes. Administrators will provide leadership and support building personnel to build integrated school communities in which collaborative teamwork develops among all educators.

MAPS is an affirmative process that capitalizes on the resources of classmates without disabilities and on family members and educational service providers to plan for the inclusion of children and youth with disabilities into regular school life. The process can assist regular and special educators to merge resources in the quest to build integrated school communities of benefit to all. MAPS is not intended to be beneficial only for those students with high needs. All children benefit by learning together. Learning to accept and value diversity is a lesson that all members of the school community must learn if we truly want our communities to be places where each individual is valued and belongs. We believe preliminary implementation of the process has yielded many positive outcomes. Continued use, refinement, and study of the process will yield valuable information regarding the pragmatics of implementation in educational systems and long-term outcomes for individuals with disabilities.

References

Association for Retarded Citizens Suburban. (1988). *Strategic plan for ARC Suburban.* Burnsville, MN.

Biklen, D. (1987). In pursuit of integration. In M. S. Berres & P. Knoblock (Eds.), *Program models for mainstreaming:*

Integrating students with moderate to severe disabilities (pp. 19–39). Rockville, MD: Aspen.

Brown, L., Branston, M. B., Hamre-Nietupski, S., Pumpian, I., Certo, N., & Grunewald, L. (1979). A strategy for developing chronological age appropriate and functional curricular content for severely handicapped adolescents and young adults. *Journal of Special Education, 13*(1), 81–90.

Edgerton, R. B. (1967). *The cloak of competence: Stigmas in the lives of the mentally retarded.* Berkeley: University of California Press.

Erickson, K. T. (1976). *Everything in its path: Destruction of community in the Buffalo Creek flood.* New York: Simon & Schuster.

Falvey, M. (1986). *Community-based curriculum: Instructional strategies for students with severe handicaps.* Baltimore: Paul H. Brookes.

Forest, M. (Ed.). (1987). *More education/integration.* Downsview, Ontario: G. Allan Roeher Institute.

Forest, M., & Lusthaus, E. (1987). The kaleidoscope. Challenge to the cascade. In M. Forest (Ed.), *More Education/Integration* (pp. 1–16). Downsview, Ontario: G. Allan Roeher Institute.

Goodnow, J. J. (1984). Some lifelong everyday forms of intelligent behavior: Organizing and reorganizing. In R. Sternberg & R. Wagner (Eds.), *Practical intelligence: Origins of competence in the everyday world* (pp. 143–162). Cambridge, MA: Cambridge University Press.

Hammill, D. D., & Bartel, N. R. (Eds.). (1975). *Teaching children with learning and behavior problems.* Boston: Allyn and Bacon.

Hartup, W. W. (1985). Relationships and their significance in cognitive development. In R. A. Hinde, J. Stevenson-Hinde, & A. N. Perret-Clermont (Eds.), *Social relationships and cognitive development* (pp. 66–82). New York: Oxford University Press.

Johnson, R. F., & Meyer, L. (1985). Program design and research to normalize peer interactions. In M. P. Brady & P. L. Gunter (Eds.), *Integrating moderately and severely handicapped learners* (pp. 79–101). Springfield, IL: Charles C Thomas.

Lewis, M. (1982). The social network systems model: Toward a theory of social development. In T. M. Fields, A. Huston, H. C. Quay, L. Trowl, & E. Finely (Eds.), *A review of human development* (pp. 180–214). New York: Wiley Interscience.

McCord, W. T. (1983). The outcome of normalization: Strengthened bonds between handicapped persons and their communities. *Education and Training of the Mentally Retarded, 18*, 153–157.

Meyer, L. H., McQuarter, R. J., & Kishi, G. S. (1985). Assessing and teaching social interaction skills. In S. Stainback & W. Stainback (Eds.), *Integration of students with severe handicaps into regular schools* (pp. 66–86). Reston, VA: The Council for Exceptional Children.

Morreau, F. A., Novak, A. R., & Sigelman, C. K. (1980). Physical and social integration of developmentally disabled individuals into the community. In A. R. Novak & L. W. Heal (Eds.), *Integration of developmentally disabled individuals into the community* (pp. 91–103). Baltimore: Paul H. Brookes.

Mount, B. (1987). Personal futures planning: Finding directions for change (Doctoral dissertation, University of Georgia). Ann Arbor, MI: *UMI Dissertation Information Service.*

Mount, B., & Zwernik, K. (1988). *It's never too early, it's never too late.* St. Paul, MN: Metropolitan Council, Publication No. 421-88-109.

Nietupski, J. A., & Hamre-Nietupski, S. M. (1987). An ecological approach to curriculum development. In L. Goetz, D. Guess, & K. Stremel-Campbell (Eds.), *Innovative program design for individuals with dual sensory impairments* (pp. 225–253). Baltimore: Paul H. Brookes.

O'Brien, J. (1987). A guide to life-style planning. In B. Wilcox & G. T. Bellamy (Eds.), *A comprehensive guide to The Activities Catalog.* Baltimore: Paul H. Brookes.

O'Brien, J., & Lyle, C. (1987). *Framework for accomplishment.* Decatur, GA: Responsive Systems Associates.

Salvia, J., & Ysseldyke, J. E. (1985). *Assessment in special and remedial education.* Boston: Houghton Mifflin.

Strully, J., & Strully, C. (1985). Friendship and our children. *Journal of The Association for Persons with Severe Handicaps, 10*, 224–227.

York, J., & Vandercook, T. (in press). Designing an integrated education learners with severe disabilities through the IEP process. *Teaching Exceptional Children.*

Received: November 28, 1988
Final Acceptance: June 21, 1989
Editor in Charge: Robert H. Horner

JASH
1992, Vol. 17, No. 3, 179–191

Application of a Lifestyle Development Process for Persons with Severe Intellectual Disabilities: A Case Study Report

Paul Malette
University of British Columbia
and
CBI Consultants, Ltd., Vancouver, BC

Pat Mirenda
University of Nebraska–Lincoln[1]

Tracy Kandborg
CBI Consultants, Ltd., Vancouver, BC

Peter Jones
Simon Fraser University, Burnaby, BC

Tia Bunz
Madison (Wisconsin) Metropolitan School District

Sally Rogow
University of British Columbia

This report summarizes the results of four data-based case studies that examined the efficacy of the Lifestyle Development Process (LDP) for persons with severe disabilities. The process involves five steps, described in detail in the paper. The planning process was implemented by means of a consultant model, and involved planning meetings, on-site visits, in-service training, problem solving, written program planning, and demonstrations of instructional techniques. The consulting teams were composed of educational and behavioral consultants. Four persons with severe disabilities and challenging behaviors were participants. These individuals resided in four communities in the Province of British Columbia, and received consultative services from 1989 through 1991. All four individuals engaged in a greater number of preferred, integrated activities during the mid- and posttests than at baseline. Their social networks and program quality scores also showed various degrees of improvement. The behavior problems that were reported at the referral stage were substantially reduced at the posttest for all individuals. These results are discussed in relation to previous research in the areas of lifestyle planning and behavior management. Problems in implementing the process by means of a consultant model are also discussed, and areas for future research are identified.

DESCRIPTORS: behavior management, communication training, community integration, friendship, individualized instruction, lifestyle planning, quality of life, participation

This report was completed in partial fulfillment of the requirements for a Master of Arts degree at the University of British Columbia by the first author. The authors are grateful to the individuals, families, and service providers who allowed their stories to be told and who contributed to the data collection process.

Reprint requests should be sent to Paul Malette, CBI Consultants, Ltd., 4573 West 11th Street, Vancouver, British Columbia V6R 2M5 Canada.

[1] Beginning September 1, 1992, Pat Mirenda will be employed by CBI Consultants, Ltd., in Vancouver, British Columbia, Canada.

Planning processes for persons with severe disabilities have increasingly emphasized the importance of concepts such as full inclusion, community presence and participation, and choice making (Brown et al., 1983, 1991; Guess, Benson, & Siegel-Causey, 1985). A number of planning models have been introduced in this regard, including "Lifestyle Planning" (O'Brien & Lyle, 1987), "Personal Futures Planning" (PFP) (Mount, 1987; Mount & Zwernik, 1988), and the "McGill Action Planning System" (MAPS) (Vandercook, York, & Forest, 1989). These models are based on the principle that collaborative efforts by family members, friends, and service providers are necessary if quality lifestyles are to be achieved for individuals with disabilities (O'Brien & Lyle, 1987).

Despite the widespread use of these models, almost no empirical data are available to document the outcomes and effectiveness of these three approaches. One exception is the work of Mount (1987), who compared the outcomes achieved for six individuals with intellectual disabilities through the PFP process with those achieved for six control participants through the traditional individualized program plan (IPP) process. She found that, whereas none of the IPP participants showed evidence of significant lifestyle changes over a 1-year period, two of the six individuals in the PFP group did experience such outcomes. It was unclear, however, the extent to which these changes could be directly attributed to the PFP process per se. In addition, Vandercook et al. (1989) provided detailed anecdotal histories documenting the changes that occurred in the lives of several individuals who were involved in the MAPS process.

The purpose of the present report is to describe a fourth planning model, the "Lifestyle Development Process (LDP)," that incorporates the values and many of the procedures of its predecessors. In addition, interventions based on current "best practices" in the fields of behavioral, communication, and instructional programming are utilized. The LDP incorporates outcome measures to evaluate changes in the target individual's social and activity patterns and to evaluate intervention effectiveness.

Method

Participants

This report focuses on two children and two adults with severe intellectual disabilities who were referred for LDP consultative services by a school, government agency, adult service provider, or family member. All four participants received services in their home districts by two or more members of the consulting team.

Laura. Laura was a 34-year-old woman who lived with her parents in a small seaside community in British Columbia. Laura had severe intellectual disabilities and dual sensory impairments (cataracts and profound hearing loss) secondary to rubella syndrome. Laura received instruction either in her home or in segregated school facilities until she reached the age of 21. After this, she remained at home with her parents most of the time, except for a 1-year period when she was placed in a sheltered workshop in her community. This placement was terminated because the workshop staff and Laura's family agreed that it did not meet her needs. Shortly thereafter, she was referred to the consulting team by

her parents and her social worker. The main concerns at the time of referral were Laura's lack of effective communication skills, her excessive ritualistic/stereotypic behaviors, and her need for meaningful community participation and/or employment.

At the time of referral, Laura had no speech, but used approximately 25–30 Blissymbols (Hehner, 1980), written words, gestures, and vocalizations for communication. She was reported by her caregivers to enjoy a range of home and community activities, including going to the post office, swimming, folding laundry, and a variety of other domestic and leisure activities. She mastered the steps of various routines easily. However, when delays or interruptions occurred, she became agitated and reverted to ritualistic behaviors, such as tracing and retracing her steps for hours at a time. In addition, she frequently stayed up for much of the night engaged in these behaviors, and then was too tired or disinterested to engage in many activities the next day. Once she started her rituals, she refused to accept further instruction or mediation. Thorazine (chlorpromazine) 60 mg/day for "depression," and Noctec (choral hydrate) as necessary at night for sleep had been prescribed by her physician, but were not administered consistently by her caregivers.

Bob. Bob was a 53-year-old man with severe intellectual disabilities who lived in a large provincial institution for 40 years. He left the institution in May, 1989, when it was permanently closed. At this time, Bob moved into a supported duplex apartment in a large urban center, with a male roommate who also moved from the institution. Although Bob's family was contacted by service providers, they did not wish to be involved in planning. Bob had no friends or acquaintances outside of the institution. Bob was referred to the consulting team by his community service provider, who provided vocational and residential services to persons with intellectual disabilities.

Bob's abilities were quite limited; according to the staff in his home, he was able to dress, eat, and drink independently but required assistance with all other self-care routines. He had never participated in regular domestic, vocational, or leisure routines and thus had few skills in these areas. He required systematic instruction with many repetitions in order to master new tasks or routines. Bob did not speak and did not show evidence of an accurate "yes/no" response; he communicated primarily through a few simple gestures (e.g., pointing and reaching toward desired items), with considerable support from staff. His preferences were limited to walking outdoors, eating, and picking up small objects. Bob had a "collection" of many such items (e.g., a bottle cap, a plastic stacking ring), and always carried at least one of them in his hands at all times. This restricted his ability to participate without assistance in a range of activities; furthermore, if one of his items was misplaced or lost, Bob yelled, screamed, and turned over furniture until it was found. Frequently, these behaviors occurred at night, when Bob usually took "inventory" of his items and often discovered that one was missing. He was then likely to be awake for hours, screaming, yelling, pounding on the bedroom walls, and urinating and defecating on the floor. In fact, it was these behavioral excesses that were the main reason for Bob's referral to the LDP team. In January 1990, Bob was taking Artane (trihexphenidyl), 4 mg/day; Colace (docusate sodium), 240 mg/day; Mellaril (thioridazine), 200 mg/day; and Noctec (chloral hydrate), 1000 mg if needed at bedtime.

Susan. Susan was a 7-year-old girl with autism and a seizure disorder who lived at home with her natural family. At the time of intervention, she was taking Depakene (valproic acid) and Frisium (clobazam) twice daily for her seizures, which were under good control. She attended an integrated preschool program from 1985 to 1986, and was then placed in a segregated school for her first 2 years of elementary education. At that point, Susan's mother requested that Susan be placed in her neighborhood school in a regular Grade 3 class. This request was granted by school district officials, who then contacted the consulting team in the spring of 1990 to request assistance in developing a transition and curricular plan for Susan.

At the time of referral, Susan had an expressive vocabulary of approximately 40–50 spoken words (e.g., *sit here, come, mom, yes, no*); she did not show evidence of echolalia. Observations and teacher reports indicated that she was quite adept at processing and using visual information, and that she had difficulty following complex verbal instructions. She liked to be in control of her environment and functioned better when she could anticipate upcoming events and routines. Her favorite activities were swimming, listening to music, looking at books, riding in a bus or car, playing lotto and other matching games, and looking at pictures. She disliked waiting, new activities, not knowing what was expected of her, large groups, physical education, and academic work in general. Susan's academic skills were very limited; she could not read, write, or count. At school, she exhibited a number of "resistant" behaviors, including scratching, pinching, and "flopping to the ground" prior to a scheduled activity. These behaviors were of considerable concern to the school staff and her family, and substantially prevented Susan from participating in many classroom routines.

Carol. Carol was an 8-year-old girl with Sanfilippo syndrome, also known as mucopolysaccharidosis III (MPS III). This syndrome is a progressive, degenerative neurological disorder that causes rapid deterioration of language, self-care, behavioral, and other skills. It is ultimately fatal, although some individuals with the syndrome have been known to live into their late 20s or 30s. Carol had developed normally until October, 1989, and had participated in a regular school curriculum as a kindergartner during the 1988–1989 school year. In October, 1989, it was observed that her language and self-care skills were rapidly deteriorating, and that she was becoming hyperactive and increasingly aggressive toward her peers. Within 2 months, she lost the ability to speak and did not appear to understand what was said to her. Her gait became unsteady, although she was still able to walk. He family sought medical assistance and a diagnosis of Sanfilippo syndrome was made. Concurrently, the feasibility of maintaining Carol at home and at school was raised by the school and medical staff involved with her care. Because of aggressive and screaming behaviors, a decision was made to remove Carol from her neighborhood school and place her in a self-contained soundproof room with padding on the walls in an elementary school across town. A referral to the consulting team was initiated in November, 1989, by Carol's social worker and her parents. The family sought guidance in the areas of curriculum planning, behavior management, environmental management, communication strategies, and general "survival" skills. The situation was described as urgent.

At the time of her referral, Carol had no speech, no ability to respond to "yes/no" questions, and no apparent receptive language abilities. Her parents and school staff agreed that she could not identify the members of her family by name, follow simple commands, or make accurate choices between two objects or pictures when presented with a verbal label. She required substantial assistance with all self-care routines, and had "lost" all of her previous academic skills (e.g., reading, writing, drawing, counting). Although her gait was quite ataxic, she was still able to walk unassisted; in fact, one of her favorite activities was running freely outdoors. She slept no more than 4 hr per night and was extremely hyperactive when awake, engaging in frequent episodes of screaming and tantruming. She required constant attention because of her aggressive behavior, especially toward her younger sister and other, smaller children. She took no regular medications.

Procedures

Two separate consulting teams provided services to the children and adults described in this report. The adult team consisted of a speech-language pathologist, three behavior consultants, and one instructional consultant. The children's team consisted of two education/behavior consultants. After a referral to the consulting agency had been initiated by a social worker, parent, or service provider, an initial planning meeting was convened with all relevant parties. During this meeting, the consultants explained the values, assumptions, procedures, and strategies incorporated by the Lifestyle Development Process. In addition, they emphasized that their role would be to assist in developing an appropriate action plan and related interventions, not to supplant the traditional roles of the service delivery or educational staff (Janney & Meyer, 1990). If all of the relevant parties agreed to participate, the LDP was implemented.

Written inventories, field observations, interviews with family and service providers, record reviews, and videotape analyses were used during Step 1 of the LDP to gather baseline information about each participant's preferences, activity patterns, daily and weekly schedules, communication and behavioral skills, medication history, learning strengths and weaknesses, and other relevant factors. During intervention, a variety of data collection systems that were "user friendly" (Janney & Meyer, 1990) were used by direct care staff. These included daily written logs and detailed "critical incident" reports that were completed whenever property destruction or aggression against other people occurred. Daily frequency and duration data were collected for all behaviors of concern, and data on skill acquisition were collected via monthly probe trials. The time of implementation for the participants in this report ranged from 4 to 16 months, depending on individual needs and circumstances. During this time, one or more consultants met with the service providers and/or families on a variable schedule, initially once or more each week and decreasing gradually to once a month or less. Basically, there were five steps and three evaluation measures involved in the LDP, as described in the sections that follow.

Basic Steps of the LDP

Step 1: Vision planning. Similar to processes used in PFP (Mount & Zwernik, 1988) and related models (e.g., MAPS), this step of the LDP assisted family members, friends, neighbors, service providers, and others to describe their vision of a quality life in the community for the target individual. Whenever possible, the target individual was included in this step of the process as well. During this step, information was obtained concerning the target individual's: (a) background and history; (b) current daily and weekly schedule; (c) current program placement; (d) current social and friendship network; (e) behavioral, communication, and/or skill excesses and/or deficits, and the current intervention approaches to each of these; and (f) primary caregiver skills and attitudes. The individual's current daily and weekly schedules were compiled and compared to those of a typical, nondisabled peer (i.e., a nondisabled individual of the same age, gender, and cultural background as the target individual). The discrepancies between the two were identified and documented as baseline information, along with other evaluation measures that will be described in a subsequent section.

Step 2: Assessing and remediating barriers to participation. This step involved a process for assessing and remediating service delivery or other barriers that were interfering with the target individual's ability to participate in integrated school or community settings. Such barriers included, for example, restrictive staff or administrative attitudes, a lack of integrated vocational or recreational options, insufficient funding or staff supports, and differences of opinion regarding values and meaningful outcomes. Once potential barriers were identified, a variety of strategies were used to attempt to remediate them, as part of what Gallessich (1985) referred to as "social/political consultation" (p. 417). In all cases, a variety of research and literature review articles that addressed the barrier(s) of concern were provided to the relevant service providers. In some cases, videotaped case studies of persons who had been assisted, through the LDP process, to move from very restrictive to integrated school or vocational placements were used to illustrate the process to service providers. In other cases, negotiating strategies based on the principles of "game theory" (Zagare, 1984), in which "win-win" solutions are the ultimate goal, were developed and applied. When this was the case, meetings were held with administrators and/or key service providers who had authority over and control of the factors creating specific barriers. On occasion, recognized experts were asked to provide input at these meetings, which continued to be held until the major participation barriers had been removed. If it became clear that barrier resolution was impossible, the LDP process was terminated and the service providers were assisted to locate another consultation resource.

Step 3: Assembling meaningful routines and schedules. This step emphasized identification of the capacities, strengths, and preferences of the target individual. Service providers were taught to identify where and with whom the individual wanted to live, work, relax, and spend leisure time. They were also taught to analyze the person's daily schedule in light of his or her learning strengths, learning styles, and capacities. These activities involved the target individual as well as the key people who knew him or her best. Planning meetings, informal home and community-based interviews, and observations were used to gather the required information. The result of this step was the development of daily and weekly schedules that included goals and objectives related to where and with whom the person would live, work, go to school, and spend leisure time. Typically, mid-intervention evaluation data were collected after the implementation of Step 3; for the four participants described in this report, this occurred within 5–9 months of baseline.

Step 4: Developing specific intervention strategies. One of the ways in which the LDP differs from more traditional intervention procedures is that specific intervention programs to address behavioral, communication, and/or skill deficits are not instituted until participation barriers have been remediated (Step 2) and meaningful lifestyle changes have been instituted (Step 3). In Step 4, programs and staff training were provided in areas such as: (a) functional analysis of behavior and application of nonaversive behavior management strategies (Durand, 1990; LaVigna & Donnellan, 1986; O'Neill, Horner, Albin, Storey, & Sprague, 1990); (b) augmentative and alternative communication assessment and intervention techniques (Mirenda, Iacono, & Williams, 1990); and/or (c) systematic instructional strategies (Snell, 1987), as needed. Of course, the strategies implemented during this step depended on the target individual's needs and the goals that were during established during Step 1.

Step 5: Evaluating effectiveness and developing a monitoring system. During this final step, the target individual's daily and weekly schedules were reviewed to determine the extent to which they reflected the goals, objectives, and intervention strategies identified in the preceding steps. This review also evaluated the extent to which the lifestyle discrepancies identified in Step 1 had been eliminated. Postintervention data were collected as a component of Step 5.

Measurement of Intervention Effectiveness

Three empirically validated measures were utilized to evaluate intervention effectiveness related to lifestyle changes.

The Resident Lifestyle Inventory (RLI). The RLI (Wilcox & Bellamy, 1987) is a 17-page interview form that requires approximately 45 min to administer and provides information on 144 different leisure and personal management activities taken from listings in *The Activities Catalogue* (Newton et al., 1987). Specifically, the RLI measures (a) the types of activities that are performed by the target individual during a 1-month period, (b) how often each activity occurs, (c) where each activity typically occurs, (d) which activities are preferred, and (e) the level of support needed for participation by the target individual. One of the consultants collected the information for the RLI from each target individual and at least two additional persons who had daily contact with the individual during the intervention and for at least 6 months prior to its initiation. For Laura, the informants were her mother, father, and a day program worker; for Bob, they were two key residential/day program providers; for Susan, they were her mother, father, teacher, and a teacher's aide; and for Carol, they were her mother, father, a teacher's aide, and a child care worker. All RLI interviews were conducted in the target individuals' homes or schools. The RLI was administered during Steps 1 and 3 and following Step 5 of the LDP for Laura, Bob, and Carol. Because the duration of Susan's intervention was quite short, her RLI data were collected during Step 1 and after Step 5 only.

Kennedy, Horner, Newton, and Kanda (1990) reported that the RLI has moderate to high congruent validity when compared with a similar valid, reliable instrument, the Valued Outcomes Information System (VOIS) (Newton et al., 1988). Pearson product-moment correlations between variables measured with the RLI and the VOIS ranged from $r = .564$ to $r = .812$, indicating that it is a valid means of gathering information about activity patterns. In addition, Kennedy et al. (1990) found the RLI to have moderate to high test-retest reliability, with mean percentage agreements ranging from 75.5 to 93.3 over an average time interval of 3.6 days. Finally, a social validation assessment of the RLI indicated that direct support staff and program managers perceived it as useful in preparing the content of individual program plans and in facilitating the choices and preferences of residents (Kennedy et al., 1990).

Social Network Analysis Form (SNAF). The SNAF (Kennedy, Horner, & Newton, 1990; Kennedy et al., 1990) is a three-page form used in a 15–30-min interview to gather information about the social network of a person with disabilities. It elicits information about (a) the persons who are socially important in the life of the target individual, and (b) the types and frequencies of activities in which persons in the social network typically engage with the individual. The SNAF was administered to the same individuals and at the same time intervals used for the RLI. Kanda (1989) reported that the overall test-retest reliability of the SNAF across individuals ranged from .60 to 1.0 (median = .83).

Program Quality Indicators (PQI) checklist. The PQI checklist (Meyer, Eichinger, & Park-Lee, 1987) contains 123 items that represent the "most promising practices" in educational programs for persons with severe disabilities, as gleaned from a literature review and survey of nationally recognized experts in the field. It can be used to assess the content of individualized education plan (IEP) goals and objectives, and many items are also applicable to IPP analyses. Selected items from the PQI checklist were administered by the first author during Step 1 and following Step 5 of the LDP for all four participants. For the two adult participants (Laura and Bob), Section 6 of the PQI (Facilities and Resources) and several individual items in other sections were omitted because they specifically addressed school-based issues, which were not relevant. In addition, several items were omitted because adequate information was not available from the service providers. For Carol and Susan, the items deleted from the PQI were all related to secondary school issues that did not directly affect the quality of their programs (e.g., Item 5: "the program philosophy emphasizes the goals of competitive and/or supported employment in integrated, community work placements"). The informants for the PQI were the key support staff and program coordinators for Laura and Bob, and the classroom teachers for Susan and Carol.

Meyer et al. (1987) reported validation data for the PQI that indicated that, with the exception of nine items, all of the checklist statements were assigned ratings of 13 or more on a 20-point scale on which 0 = not a consideration, 10 = undecided, and 20 = very important consideration by a group of 254 parents and professionals in the field. In general, these findings provide support for the social validity of the PQI.

Interventions

Laura. The initial "vision planning" meeting for Laura (Step 1) was held in September, 1988, and was attended by two members of the consulting team, Laura, her parents, her social worker, and a friend. Baseline RLI, SNAF, and PQI data were collected at this time, and the following goals were identified: (a) to involve Laura in meaningful employment, (b) to help Laura develop relationships in the community, (c) to develop Laura's communication skills, (d) to increase Laura's participation in exercise activities, and (e) to reduce Laura's ritualistic/stereotypic behaviors. The major components of Laura's intervention (LDP Steps 2–4) are summarized in Table 1.

Interviews with relevant persons and direct observations of Laura's daily activities revealed a number of barriers to community participation. The major barrier was that Laura received services through a provider with whom her parents had substantive philosophical disagreements. The provider believed that Laura should be placed in a specialized group home for other persons with dual sensory impairments that was located in a community far from her family; Laura and her family wanted her to continue to live in her natural home, in the community where she grew up. Thus, during Step

2, a variety of published research articles, as well as videotaped case studies of similar individuals who were successfully living and working in the community, were used to explain a community-based program philosophy to Laura's social worker and service provider. Eventually, they agreed that a work and recreational plan would be attempted for Laura in her own community, with the assistance of a different provider who was receptive to delivering integrated adult services. Over the next several months, the consultants assisted Laura's parents in training the new service provider to provide individualized services to Laura.

During Step 3, the consultants assessed Laura's strengths and needs in a range of community, recreational, and vocational environments. Together with her parents and new service provider, they revised her daily schedule to reflect more of the goals identified during vision planning. Although her activity pattern and social network gradually expanded, Laura continued to experience frequent communication breakdowns and ritualistic behavior. Thus, in Step 4, the consultants assisted her service providers to conduct functional analyses of her behavior (O'Neill et al., 1990) and to assess her current communication capabilities in detail (Mirenda et al., 1990). Based on these analyses, a multielement intervention plan was designed that incorporated (a) functional communication training (Durand, 1990); (b) a pictorial calender and time management system (Rowland & Schweigert, 1990); (c) systematic task analyses to teach new skills (Snell, 1987); and (d) videotapes and written teaching strategies for staff training. These interventions were implemented over the subsequent 12-month period.

Bob. Bob's "vision planning" meeting (Step 1) was conducted in March, 1990, and involved the consulting

Table 1
Major Intervention Components for Case Study Participants

Name	Intervention components	
Laura	Change in service provider Change in daily/weekly schedule Functional communication training Pictorial schedule and expanded communication system	Task analyses of new skills Staff training Ongoing data collection and feedback
Bob	Six-month preference assessment Part-time paid employment Small toy program (multielement)	Calendar box Choice-making program Ongoing data collection and feedback
Susan	Staff and family consultation Pictorial schedule Curricular adaptations Lotto games during recess with peers Shorter activities	Small group instruction/cooperative learning Functional, community-based instruction Communication/conversation programs Choice of nap at midday Ongoing data collection and evaluation
Carol	Resolution of philosophical differences Increased child care worker support Change in daily/weekly schedule Inclusion of preferred activities Circle of friends intervention Task analyses and instructional programs	Real object schedule Ecological interventions Teaching functional communication skills Choice-making intervention Reintegration into regular classroom Ongoing data collection and evaluation

team and his key service providers. Baseline data were collected at this time, and the following goals were identified: (a) to identify his strengths and preferences; (b) to develop a comprehensive, integrated daily and weekly schedule based on his strengths and preferences; (c) to increase the size of his social network; and (d) to reduce the frequency and intensity of his behavioral outbursts.

The primary components of Bob's intervention are summarized in Table 1. Bob's service provider already incorporated many of the standards that are considered to be "best practices," and no significant service delivery barriers to participation were identified during Step 2. Therefore, during Step 3, the focus shifted to exploring a wide variety of new activities with Bob, in order to assess his preferences and strengths. Over the next 6 months, a number of Bob's personal strengths and preferences started to emerge.

Despite Step 3 activities, Bob's placement in his supported apartment was in jeopardy because of socially unacceptable behaviors that kept his neighbors up at night and resulted in property destruction. Thus, Step 4 involved an extensive functional analysis of his behavior (O'Neill et al., 1990), followed by multiple ecological and instructional programs (Snell, 1987) designed to (a) minimize the likelihood that one of his small toys would be misplaced, (b) help Bob manage his anxiety when this did occur, and (c) teach him functional alternatives to carrying the toys around. He was also provided with a "calendar box" to represent his daily schedule, and began to use real object symbols to make choices (Rowland & Schweigert, 1990). These programs were instituted over a 7-month period.

Susan. An initial "vision planning" meeting (Step 1) was held at Susan's school in October, 1990, and was attended by Susan's mother, the school team, the school principal, and the consulting team. Susan's classmates did not attend the meeting; rather, the school staff decided to elicit information from them in a less formal context. Baseline data were collected from observations and from parent and teacher interviews, and the school team and Susan's mother agreed on the following goals: (a) to help Susan make friends, (b) to help Susan enjoy and participate in classroom activities, and (c) to enable Susan to acquire new skills at school.

The primary components of Susan's intervention are summarized in Table 1. An assessment of participation barriers (Step 2) failed to reveal any overt, systemic problems in this area. The school team expressed positive attitudes toward the process of integration, and Susan was not pulled out of the classroom for any portion of the day. However, there were discrepancies between the expectations of Susan's family and the school staff, largely because her frequent resistive behavior at school was in contrast to her behavior at home, where she willingly engaged in a variety of activities.

When examining Susan's schedule during Steps 3 and 4, the consultants and the school team hypothesized that her apparent dislike of school, as reflected in her refusal to participate in most classroom activities, was related to her current curriculum and how it was presented to her. It also appeared that Susan's classmates tended to remain at a distance from her because of her behavioral outbursts. Thus, adjustments to her classroom schedule were instituted concurrently with a multielement intervention that was designed to address the behavioral, curricular, and social concerns simultaneously. The components of this intervention included numerous schedule, curricular, and instructional adaptations, as summarized in Table 1. Communication strategies such as teaching her to ask for a break at the first signs of agitation (Durand, 1990), teaching her peers to recognize and respond to gestural signals of distress, and teaching both Susan and her classmates to initiate conversations using a photograph book (Hunt, Alwell, & Goetz, 1988) were also implemented. Finally, the team noted that Susan usually slept in the classroom between the hours of 10:00 and 11:00 a.m. It was hypothesized that this was related to her seizure disorder and the medication schedule that was required to keep the seizures under control. Susan was offered the choice of sleeping in a designated area at the back of the class at this hour. These interventions were instituted over a 4-month period.

Carol. An initial "vision planning" meeting (Step 1) was held at Carol's home in November, 1989. The meeting was attended by the consultants, Carol's parents, and her sister, and focused on identifying Carol's existing and desired future schedule of activities. The following goals were established at that time: (a) to provide Carol with the supports necessary for her to participate in preferred activities, and (b) to provide Carol's family with the supports needed for them to keep her at home and function as a relatively "normal" family.

A summary of the major components of Carol's intervention is provided in Table 1. Because of the rapidly degenerative nature of her illness, numerous professionals were involved in planning for her future, including her parents, two provincial consultants, three LDP consultants, and her physician. During Step 2, numerous barriers to participation were identified, including a recommendation to institutionalize Carol and a recommendation for one-to-one day care (Nidiffer & Kelly, 1983). The LDP consultants, Carol's family, and the social service agency providers felt that Carol should be supported in whatever manner would be necessary to reintegrate her into her previous network of friends in her neighborhood school. These discrepant opinions required a series of meetings between November 1989, and March 1990, among the parents and professionals involved, as well as additional experts in the area of integration, to negotiate and resolve the differences. Written materials, videotaped case studies, and meetings with recognized experts in the field were used during this portion of the consultation. The school district stated that, if it could be demonstrated that integrated activities were mutually beneficial to Carol and her peers over the upcoming summer months, Carol could begin reintegration into the regular school system in September, 1990.

In June, 1990, two additional summer program staff were hired and trained to provide support to Carol for 8 hr each day. Together with Carol's parents and the consultants, they initiated Step 3 by planning a schedule that contained numerous unrestricted "high-energy" activities that Carol seemed to enjoy. "Low"- or "moderate"-energy activities that she preferred were also planned regularly, including taking baths and buying yogurt at the store. In addition, Carol's parents compiled a list of Carol's old friends from her neighborhood school, and contacted the parents of five of these children to discuss reuniting her with her peers, some of whom thought that Carol had died. All five parents agreed to have their children participate in activities with Carol. Subsequently, meetings were held with the children to solicit their ideas for involving Carol in a range of motivating activities and to share with them strategies for managing her aggression. The "circle of friends" and MAPS processes (Vandercook et al., 1989) were used to structure these meetings and to enlist the involvement of Carol's peers. At least daily activities with these peers were instituted over the summer months.

After her participation in integrated activities had markedly increased, Carol still required almost total assistance to engage in these activities. Therefore, during Step 4, instructional interventions were developed to teach Carol a variety of functional skills. Carol's service providers were taught to develop task analyses and to systematically fade and shape their instructional cues (Billingsley & Romer, 1983). Ecological strategies such as placing safety locks on cupboards were also incorporated in the plan. Real object symbols were used to signal the beginning of each activity, and to allow Carol to make choices among activities (Rowland & Schweigert, 1990). Carol's peers were taught to shake her hand when she approached them; this strategy seemed to interrupt her aggression, which seemed to function, in part, as a greeting behavior.

A meeting was held in September, 1990, with Carol's school team, after the Step 4 interventions had been in place for 1 month. An itinerant teacher had been hired to provide one-to-one instruction to Carol in the self-contained classroom she had used during the previous year. However, after reviewing the summer progress reports and videotapes of Carol and her friends, the school team agreed to reenroll Carol in her neighborhood school. All of those involved agreed that Carol required a slow transition to an integrated school environment; thus, lunch, recess, and gym were identified as the initial integration points. The remainder of Carol's day was to be spent in the community.

Results

Laura

Table 2 summarizes the baseline, mid-intervention, and postintervention evaluation data for Laura. The baseline review of Laura's daily and weekly schedules revealed numerous discrepancies between the goals identified and Laura's existing lifestyle. For example, although she had engaged in 101 activities during the baseline month, only 39 of these occurred in the community. She was unemployed and exercised infrequently. Her social network consisted of two friends, four paid staff, and five family members; most of her activities occurred with the latter group of people. Only 32% of the PQIs were evident in Laura's overall program. During much of the day, Laura engaged in 2–3-hr episodes of pacing back and fourth in repetitive patterns that could not be interrupted without screaming, tantruming, and aggression.

By May, 1989, when mid-intervention data were collected, the total number of activities in which Laura engaged during the month prior to data collection had increased by more than 300% over baseline; and the total number of preferred community activities had almost doubled. Her social network had expanded to include a neighbor and a co-worker with whom she occasionally socialized outside of work.

In June, 1990, 16 months after the initial referral, RLI data for Laura indicated that 35 of the 36 different activities in which she regularly engaged were preferred by her. A total of 84 preferred community activities had been performed during the preceding month. Socially, Laura's SNAF scores indicated that three new persons outside of her paid and family circles had been added to her social network (one friend, one neighbor, and one co-worker). The overall PQI score for her program was 72%.

Bob

Table 3 summarizes the baseline, mid-intervention, and postintervention evaluation data for Bob. Examination of Bob's initial assessment data in March, 1990, revealed that, in general, his existing lifestyle was quite varied and balanced. For example, 201 community activities were documented for Bob during the baseline period; however, all of these were performed with paid staff members. One of Bob's neighbors was the only unpaid person in Bob's life.

The mid-intervention measures collected in August, 1990, indicated that Bob was participating in several

Table 2
Baseline, Mid-intervention, and Postintervention Scores for Laura

Measure	Baseline (9/88)	Mid (5/89)	Post (6/90)
RLI (total category sum scores)			
Number of activities	101	360	286
Number of different activities	24	31	36
Number of preferred different activities	17	28	35
Number of preferred community activities	39	77	84
SNAF (total category sum scores)			
Number of people paid to provide service	4	1	2
Number of activities with paid people	24	60	55
Number of friends	2	2	3
Number of activities with friends	8	8	10
Number of neighbors/others	0	1	1
Number of activities with neighbors/others	0	1	4
Number of family members	5	5	5
Number of activities with family members	53	50	50
Number of co-workers	0	1	1
Number of activities with co-workers	0	4	4
PQI checklist (percentage of items in evidence/area)			
Program philosophy (items 1–18)	28%		81%
Program design and opportunities for learning (items 19–27, 33, 34, 36)	38%		73%
Systematic instruction and performance evaluation (items 41–64)	42%		60%
IPP development and parent participation (items 65–84)	25%		80%
Staff development and team collaboration (items 85, 86, 89, 90, 95, 96, 101)	21%		71%
Overall percentage of PQI items evident in IPP	32%		72%

Table 3
Baseline, Mid-intervention, and Postintervention Scores for Bob

Measure	Baseline (3/90)	Mid (8/90)	Post (3/91)
RLI (total category sum scores)			
Number of activities	220	267	385
Number of different activities	22	22	32
Number of preferred different activities	19	22	32
Number of preferred community activities	201	250	224
SNAF (total category sum scores)			
Number of people paid to provide service	4	4	4
Number of activities with paid people	220	267	385
Number of friends	0	0	0
Number of activities with friends	0	0	0
Number of neighbors/others	1	2	3
Number of activities with neighbors/others	1	16	24
Number of family members	0	0	0
Number of activities with family members	0	0	0
Number of co-workers	0	0	0
Number of activities with co-workers	0	0	0
PQI checklist (percentage of items in evidence/area)			
Program philosophy (items 1–18)	94%		100%
Program design and opportunities for learning (items 19–27, 33, 34, 36)	69%		88%
Systematic instruction and performance evaluation (items 41–64)	64%		79%
IPP development and parent participation (items 65–84)	64%		88%
Staff development and team collaboration (items 85, 86, 89, 90, 95, 96, 101)	57%		78%
Overall percentage of PQI items evident in IPP	71%		85%

additional preferred activities, both at home and in the community. In addition, the SNAF scores reflect a slight increase in Bob's social network and an increase in the number of activities he performed with unpaid people from 1 (baseline) to 16.

In March, 1991, Bob's RLI scores indicated that he had engaged in a total of 32 different activities during the previous month, all of which were preferred by him. Over half of these were functional household routines;

this represented a substantive increase over baseline, when he engaged in no activities of this type. He accessed the community 224 times during this month, which represented a slight increase over baseline. Bob's SNAF scores indicated that his social network consisted of four paid staff and three neighbors who had befriended him. However, he had engaged in 24 activities with these neighbors during the previous month, a marked increase compared to his baseline rate of 1 activity. The PQI score for Bob's program was 85%, representing an increase of 14 percentage points over baseline.

Susan

Table 4 summarizes the baseline and postintervention evaluation data for Susan. A review of Susan's baseline schedule in October, 1990, revealed that it was essentially identical to that of her classmates. She had participated in a total of 405 activities during the previous month; of these, 143 were integrated community or school activities. She participated in 45 different activities; however, fewer than half of these were preferred by her, and the majority of the nonpreferred activities took place in school. Susan's social network outside of her family and paid staff consisted of five children in her class who consistently greeted her in the morning and played with her in the playground. Susan did not have any friends visit her home during the baseline period.

Five months later, the data showed evidence of gains in all three of Susan's goal areas. She had participated in 38 different and 316 total preferred activities during the previous month, representing over a 200% increase in this category over baseline. The increase was attributed to the fact that Susan was participating in 80% of all classroom activities (compared with 20% at baseline). Susan's social network of friends from school had increased from six to eight children. She engaged in 146 total activities with these friends, including after-school visits to her house, "sleep overs," and birthday parties. The PQI score for her program had increased from 68% to 81%.

Carol

Table 5 summarizes the baseline, mid-intervention, and postintervention evaluation data for Carol. In November, 1989, examination of Carol's baseline daily and weekly schedules revealed that she had engaged in only 11 different activities during the preceding month, and that her only community-based activity was an occasional walk in the neighborhood, which she enjoyed. The majority of Carol's time was spent in a self-contained classroom with a one-to-one teaching aide and in home activities with her parents and sister. Carol's entire social network consisted of her family and paid instructional or child care worker staff, including trained respite care staff who provided services to Carol outside of her home for one weekend each month. Her PQI score was 43% at this time.

Nine months later (in August, 1990), mid-intervention data were collected. Carol had participated in a total of 90 preferred community activities during the previous month, representing almost a 500% increase over baseline. Thirty of these activities were performed with one or more of the five friends with whom Carol interacted over the summer months.

By February, 1991, when consultant input was formally terminated, substantive progress had been made in both of the goal areas. Carol had engaged in 63 integrated community and school activities during the previous month. These included her regular gym class, recess, lunch, and swimming with two peers from her school at a nearby pool. She had eight friends and participated in 15 activities with them during the preceding month; this represented an increase over baseline

Table 4
Baseline and Postintervention Scores for Susan

Measure	Baseline (10/90)	Post (3/91)
RLI (total category sum scores)		
Number of activities	405	562
Number of different activities	45	53
Number of preferred different activities	20	38
Number of preferred community activities	143	316
SNAF (total category sum scores)		
Number of people paid to provide service	4	4
Number of activities with paid people	21	21
Number of friends	6	8
Number of activities with friends	120	146
Number of neighbors/others	0	0
Number of activities with neighbors/others	0	0
Number of family members	3	3
Number of activities with family members	125	140
PQI checklist (percentage of items in evidence/area)		
Program philosophy (items 1–5, 7–18)	76%	94%
Program design and opportunities for learning (items 19, 20, 23–25, 27–40)	80%	93%
Systematic instruction and performance evaluation (items 41–64)	56%	70%
IPP development and parent participation (items 65–75, 77–79, 81–84)	47%	66%
Staff development and team collaboration (items 85–89, 93–95, 98, 100–104)	66%	77%
Facilities and resources (items 105–113, 115, 118, 119, 121–123)	86%	86%
Overall percentage of PQI items evident in IEP	68%	81%

Table 5
Baseline, Mid-intervention, and Postintervention Scores for Carol

Measure	Baseline (11/89)	Mid (8/90)	Post (2/91)
RLI (total category sum scores)			
Number of activities	172	391	295
Number of different activities	11	21	18
Number of preferred different activities	6	19	16
Number of preferred community activities	19	90	63
SNAF (total category sum scores)			
Number of people paid to provide service	2	9	9
Number of activities with paid people	80	190	165
Number of friends	0	5	8
Number of activities with friends	0	30	15
Number of neighbors/others	0	0	0
Number of activities with neighbors/others	0	0	0
Number of family members	3	5	3
Number of activities with family members	92	152	130
PQI checklist (percentage of items in evidence/area)			
Program philosophy (items 1–5, 7–18)	41%		65%
Program design and opportunities for learning (items 19, 20, 23–25, 27–40)	38%		63%
Systematic instruction and performance evaluation (items 41–64)	47%		60%
IPP development and parent participation (items 65–75, 77–79, 81–84)	25%		70%
Staff development and team collaboration (items 85–89, 93–95, 98, 100–104)	50%		55%
Facilities and resources (items 105–113, 115, 118, 119, 121–123)	57%		62%
Overall percentage of PQI items evident in IEP	43%		63%

but a decrease over the mid-intervention data, which were collected during the summer when Carol and her friends had daily contact. Carol's program was given a PQI score of 63% at this time, reflecting an improvement of 20% over baseline.

Discussion

This report extends the previous literature on lifestyle planning models for persons with severe disabilities. The results suggested that, to varying degrees, the Lifestyle Development Process had a positive impact on the activity patterns and social networks of the four individuals who participated in the case studies. All four participants were engaged in a greater number of integrated activities during the mid- and postintervention periods, compared with baseline. Three of the four participants experienced gains of more than 200% in the number of preferred, integrated activities they performed at the end of the intervention period. The two adults in this study were engaged in the first integrated work opportunities of their lives. The two children participated to various degrees in regular classroom activities in their neighborhood schools. Finally, all four participants experienced at least slight increases in their unpaid social networks, and performed a greater number of integrated activities with people who were not paid to spend time with them. This extends the data reported by Mount (1987) concerning the development of lifestyle plans that are based on individuals' strengths and capacities rather than their deficits.

Although it is not possible to attribute causation in the context of a case study report, all four participants showed evidence of improved behavior and communication skills over the course of the LDP intervention. At postintervention, Laura's expressive vocabulary had increased by 20 Blissymbols, she had learned to write the names of people in her social network, and she experienced considerably fewer communication breakdowns. Finally, Laura was independent in most of her daily activities and routines, and her stereotypic/ritualistic behaviors had been reduced substantially. Bob still required more than minimal support to complete all activities, except for garbage collection and bathing, He was sleeping through the night most of the time, and his destructive behavior had decreased dramatically in both frequency and intensity. He was able to engage in several regular activities without holding his small items. In addition, Bob was beginning to initiate activities independently using real object symbols. Susan's resistant behaviors had decreased markedly, and her aggression had been reduced substantially. Carol's aggressive behaviors were no longer of major concern at home or in school. Her family had established numerous routines and support mechanisms in the community, and her home placement was no longer in jeopardy, despite the fact that her physical condition continued to deteriorate.

The participants also acquired a number of age-appropriate and functional skills in home, work, and community settings. Improvement in these areas continued for all four participants even after the formal LDP consultation was completed. Laura now folds laundry on a volunteer basis at a local intermediate care facility 2 days each week, and paints with a friend in a local store 1 day per week. In recent months, her ritualistic behavior has increased somewhat over its postintervention level. Her mother believes that this is due to boredom, and additional community activities, including formal literacy instruction, are being arranged to remediate this. Bob now shares a duplex apartment in a suburban neighborhood with a nondisabled male roommate, and is looking for a new, full-time employment opportunity, having worked in the recycling business for 3 years. Susan is a fully integrated participant in a regular Grade 3 classroom, has several friends who play with her regularly after school, and has developed considerable spontaneous speech over the past year. Finally, Carol also attends Grade 3 with her nondisabled classmates, who have formed a strong support system for her. Although her health continues to deteriorate, she enjoys school and continues to access the community on a regular basis.

The data also suggest a number of areas that require increased attention. In particular, a lack of substantive change in the social network scores for the two adult participants suggests that additional, systematic attention needs to be paid to this area. The importance of a rich social life for persons with disabilities has only recently emerged as a component of program planning, probably because little empirical information is available to guide families, service providers, and researchers in this area (Kennedy, Horner, & Newton, 1990). In addition, Barrera (1986) suggested that neither the service delivery system nor the community as a whole has a clear understanding of what defines a "social life," much less how to measure the extent to which it occurs. Although Susan's social network seemed to increase without direct interventions aimed at this goal, Carol's circumstances required quite deliberate activities in this regard. However, building networks for Bob and Laura remained a challenge. Perhaps direct, systematic interventions for these two individuals might have helped to increase their networks beyond the few friends and acquaintances they acquired during intervention.

All four participants' programs reflected an increase in the number of validated "most promising practices" on the PQI during postintervention data collection. The overall percentage gains from pre- to posttest ranged from 13% to 43%. The lowest pretest scores were reported in the most segregated programs (Laura's and Carol's), which is consistent with the findings of Hunt, Goetz, and Anderson (1986) regarding the impact of integrated placements on the quality of program plans. It should be noted, however, that the overall percentage of program quality indicators during the posttest ranged from 63% to 85%, indicating that even the "best" program in this area (Bob's) failed to reflect all of the desired best practices. Specific analyses of the deficiencies at this point might enable staff to determine the

relative importance of each and to plan related interventions, as necessary.

The results of this report must be interpreted cautiously in light of several factors. The most important of these is that, because of the multielement nature of the LDP intervention, no experimental or causal documentation is available. In addition, in order for a participant to be included in this report, all of the steps of his or her LDP had to be completed. Since completion was substantially dependent on the ability of service providers and families to commit to and carry out the process, selection bias may limit the degree to which the findings can be generalized. Also, the small sample size further limits generalizability. In an attempt to limit these shortcomings, data were collected in four separate locations that represented four different program placements along the LRE continuum. In addition, a number of data collection techniques such as videotaping, frequency and duration recording, direct observations, and interviews were used to control experimenter bias (Borg & Gall, 1989). Finally, extensive placement and program histories were compiled, and data collection occurred at predetermined intervals that coincided with specific steps of the LDP, in order to minimize the effects of outside influences on the results.

Future research efforts are needed to establish norms for instruments such as the RLI and SNAF, so that planners and researchers can evaluate the extent to which the activity patterns and social networks of individuals with severe disabilities resemble those of same-age peers without disabilities. Future research should also involve assessment of the functional relationships between multielement planning and support models and their outcomes. Finally, research is needed to identify strategies for conducting lifestyle planning for individuals who receive services in highly restrictive programs such as day activity centers and large sheltered workshops.

References

Barrera, M. (1986). Distinctions between social support concepts, measures, and models. *American Journal of Community Psychology, 14,* 413–445.

Billingsley, F. F., & Romer, L. T. (1983). Response prompting and the transfer of stimulus control: Methods, research, and a conceptual framework. *Journal of the Association for Persons with Severe Handicaps, 8,* 3–12.

Borg, W. R., & Gall, M. D. (1989). *Educational research.* New York: Longman.

Brown, L., Nisbet, J., Ford, A., Sweet, M., Shiraga, B., York, J., & Loomis, R. (1983). The critical need for nonschool instruction in educational programs for severely handicapped students. *Journal of the Association for Persons with Severe Handicaps, 8,* 71–77.

Brown, L., Schwarz, P., Udvari-Solner, A., Kampschroer, E., Johnson, F., Jorgensen, J., & Gruenewald, L. (1991). How much time should students with severe intellectual disabilities spend in regular education classrooms and elsewhere? *Journal of the Association for Persons with Severe Handicaps, 16,* 39–47.

Durand, V. M. (1990). *Severe behavior problems: A functional communication training approach.* New York: Guilford Press.

Gallessich, J. (1985). Toward a meta-theory of consultation. *Counseling Psychologist, 13,* 410–425.

Guess, D., Benson, H., & Siegel-Causey, E. (1985). Concepts and issues related to choicemaking and autonomy among persons with severe disabilities. *Journal of the Association for Persons with Severe Handicaps, 10,* 79–86.

Hehner, B. (1980). *Blissymbols for use.* Toronto, Ontario: Blissymbolics Communication Institute.

Hunt, P., Alwell, M., & Goetz, L. (1988). Acquisition of conversation skills and the reduction of inappropriate social interaction behaviors. *Journal of the Association for Persons with Severe Handicaps, 13,* 20–27.

Hunt, P., Goetz, L., & Anderson, J. (1986). The quality of IEP objectives associated with placement on integrated versus segregated school sites. *Journal of the Association for Persons with Severe Handicaps, 11,* 125–130.

Janney, R. E., & Meyer, L. H. (1990). A consultant model to support integrated educational services for students with severe disabilities and challenging behaviors. *Journal of the Association for Persons with Severe Handicaps, 15,* 186–199.

Kanda, E. (1989). *Comparisons of social networks and activity patterns of high school students with severe handicaps and recent high school graduates with severe handicaps.* Unpublished Master's thesis, University of Oregon.

Kennedy, C. H., Horner, R. H., & Newton, S. J. (1990). The social networks and activity patterns of adults with severe disabilities: A correlational analysis. *Journal of the Association for Persons with Severe Handicaps, 15,* 86–90.

Kennedy, C. H., Horner, R. H., Newton, S. J., & Kanda, E. (1990). Measuring the activity patterns of adults with severe disabilities using the Resident Lifestyle Inventory. *Journal of the Association for Persons with Severe Handicaps, 15,* 79–85.

LaVigna, G. W., & Donnellan, A. M. (1986). *Alternatives to punishment: Solving behavior problems with non-aversive strategies.* New York: Irvington.

Meyer, L. H., Eichinger, J., & Park-Lee, S. (1987). A validation of program quality indicators in educational services for students with severe disabilities. *Journal of the Association for Persons with Severe Handicaps, 12,* 251–263.

Mirenda, P., Iacono, T., & Williams, R. (1990). Communication options for persons with severe and profound disabilities: State of the art and future directions. *Journal of the Association for Persons with Severe Handicaps, 15,* 3–21.

Mount, B. (1987). *Personal futures planning: Finding directions for change.* Unpublished doctoral dissertation, University of Georgia.

Mount, B., & Zwernik, K. (1988). *It's never too early, it's never too late* (Publication No. 421-88-109). St. Paul, MN: Metropolitan Council.

Newton, J., Bellamy, G. T., Honer, R., Boles, S., LeBaron, N., & Bennett, A. (1987). Using *The Activities Catalogue* in residential programs for individuals with severe disabilities. In B. Wilcox & G. T. Bellamy (Eds.), *A comprehensive guide to The Activities Catalogue: An alternative curriculum for youth and adults with severe disabilities* (pp. 125–153). Baltimore: Paul H. Brookes.

Newton, J., Stoner, S., Bellamy, G. T., Boles, S., Horner, R., LeBaron, N., Romer, L., Romer, M., & Schlesinger, D. (1988). *Valued Outcomes Information Systems (VOIS) operations manual.* Eugene: University of Oregon, Center on Human Development.

Nidiffer, F. D., & Kelly, T. E. (1983). Developmental and degenerative patterns associated with Sanfilippo syndrome. *Journal of Mental Deficiency, 27,* 185–203.

O'Brien, J., & Lyle, C. (1987). *Framework for accomplishment.* Decatur, GA: Responsive Systems Associates.

O'Neill, R., Horner, R., Albin, R., Storey, K., & Sprague, J. (1990). *Functional analysis of behavior: A practical assessment guide.* Sycamore, IL: Sycamore Publishing.

Rowland, C., & Schweigert, P. (1990). *Tangible symbol systems: Symbolic communication for individuals with multisensory impairments.* Tucson, AZ: Communication Skill Builders.

Snell, M. (1987). *Systematic instruction of persons with severe handicaps* (3rd ed.). Columbus, OH: Merrill.

Vandercook, T., York, J., & Forest, M. (1989). The McGill Action Planning System (MAPS): A strategy for building the vision. *Journal of the Association for Persons with Severe Handicaps, 14,* 202–215.

Wilcox, B., & Bellamy, T. (1987). *A comprehensive guide to The Activities Catalog: An alternative curriculum for youth and adults with severe disabilities.* Baltimore: Paul H. Brookes.

Zagare, F. (1984). *Game theory: Concepts and application.* London: Sage Publications.

Received: February 4, 1992
Final Acceptance: June 19, 1992
Editor in Charge: Lori Goetz

JASH
1989, Vol. 14, No. 4, 263–270

User-Friendly Measures of Meaningful Outcomes: Evaluating Behavioral Interventions

Luanna Meyer and Rachel Janney
Syracuse University

This article describes principles and practices of data collection to evaluate the attainment of meaningful outcomes in educational services for students with severe disabilities and serious behavior problems. In contrast to a limited outcome such as a temporary change in one target behavior in a controlled clinical setting, an expanded definition of effectiveness would require evidence of a range of more meaningful outcomes for child, school, family, and community. Several user-friendly measures to document such outcomes are described, which were field-tested in an educational consultation project serving students with severe disabilities and challenging behaviors in integrated schools. The article concludes with a discussion of the advantages of an emphasis upon both meaningful outcomes and the use of measurement strategies that blend well and have high utility for typical schools while simultaneously increasing programmatic rigor and general school responsibility for what happens to students.

DESCRIPTORS: applied behavior analysis, assessment, behavioral assessment, behavioral management, data collection, decision-making, educational validity, excess behavior, functional analysis, research evaluation

Introduction

Children and youth with severe behavior problems may well represent the greatest challenge to the design and implementation of supported education in neighborhood schools (Janney & Meyer, in press; Meyer & Evans, 1986). Whereas virtually all other students with severe disabilities may be attending integrated public school programs with their nondisabled age peers, local educational agencies continue to refer students who

exhibit behaviors such as severe aggression, self-injury, and disruptive behaviors to segregated day or residential programs (Elmquist, 1989; Janney & Meyer, in press). In fact, interventionists and school district personnel alike may maintain a commitment to handicapped-only service delivery for these students, despite the absence of substantive evaluation data regarding the efficacy of a continuum model that proposes to eliminate problem behaviors in the context of separate programs before returning students to the public schools (Elmquist, 1989; Evans & Meyer, 1985; Meyer & Evans, 1989). Meyer and Evans (1989) specifically critiqued the validity of this segregation-elimination-integration continuum on theoretical and practical grounds; they emphasized the importance of typical schools and community environments to the habilation process for students with severe excess behaviors. First, because challenging behaviors are generally functional and are emitted by the student to achieve some purpose, it is most useful to view such behaviors as skill deficits. For example, a student who is self-injurious during instruction may engage in this behavior because the task is too difficult and he or she lacks the appropriate skills to communicate this difficulty in any other way (Durand & Crimmins, 1988). If such behaviors do have specific functions, the most effective intervention strategy logically would involve teaching the appropriate positive replacement skills to students; schools are the appropriate places to address these educational needs. Second, regular education environments offer various motivational and contextual advantages over segregated ones (Evans & Meyer, 1985; Meyer & Evans, 1989). For example, typical peers can provide both appropriate models of positive behavior and a context of peer relationships and friendships to support the development and use of such positive behaviors.

To date, there are few demonstrations of successful efforts to remediate severely challenging behaviors in typical school and community settings. Donnellan, LaVigna, Zambito, and Thvedt (1985) reported the results of a consultation-mediated intervention effort to support children in community residential placement, including both the natural home and group homes.

This work was supported in part by Contract G00-86-300358, awarded to Syracuse University by the Office of Special Education Programs, U.S. Department of Education. It does not necessarily reflect the position or policies of the U.S. Department of Education, and no official endorsement should be inferred.

Requests for reprints should be sent to Luanna H. Meyer, PhD, Division of Special Education and Rehabilitation, Syracuse University, 805 South Crouse Ave., Syracuse, NY 13244-2280.

They documented changes across time in both the frequency of each child's targeted problem behaviors and positive placement outcomes; the children remained at home rather than being referred to more restrictive settings. Durand and Kishi (1987) demonstrated the effectiveness of teaching alternative replacement skills through a consultation and technical assistance service provided to teachers working with students with dual sensory impairments. Although their work was carried out in handicapped-only residential schools, they were able to relate long-term maintenance of original improvements in the children's behaviors to staff commitments to improving the quality of curricular opportunities in general, in addition to changing the original referral behaviors. Most recently, Janney and Meyer (in press) reported the results of educational consultation services designed to support students with the most challenging behaviors in their neighborhood schools and regular education environments in several school districts in central New York. Their evaluation model requires data on the referral problem behaviors of individual students as well as a variety of outcome measures, including educational placement at follow-up (i.e., whether the student remained in a regular education setting or was referred to a segregated placement during the subsequent school year).

A Paradox

Paradoxically, the evaluation of interventions to address the behavioral needs of students with severe disabilities has been simplistic in focus as well as intrusive in practice for both the teacher and student. The appearance of simplicity comes from a clear focus in the behavioral intervention literature upon documenting changes in specific referral or target behavior problems. A "treatment" is judged successful if the following conditions are met: (a) a behavior problem is described that is clearly in need of reduction or elimination; (b) this behavior is defined in observable terms, and a baseline rate or duration is measured so that post-intervention changes can be evaluated; (c) a described intervention is designed to reduce or eliminate the problem behavior, ideally based upon the results of a functional analysis of the behavior along with clinical judgment that the intervention selected is appropriate for that behavior and that student; (d) the intervention is systematically applied in some way that allows the interventionist to decide whether it is associated with significant behavior change; and (e) there is evidence that the intervention associated with the desired reduction in the problem behavior is reported as a successful outcome. Lennox, Miltenberger, Spengler, and Erfanian (1988) used these criteria in their extensive review of this literature, but were also critical of the relatively narrow focus upon only short-term behavior change in limited contexts. They called for "more indices of effec-

tiveness" such as long-term follow-up and evidence of stimulus and response generalization.

Earlier, Voeltz and Evans (1983) critiqued this failure to document more meaningful outcomes in behavioral intervention efforts and suggested that both the above sequence of clinical practice and our dominant paradigm of how to demonstrate experimental control were partly responsible. The extensive literature review reported by Voeltz and Evans (1982) and updated by Evans, Meyer, Kurkjian, and Kishi (1988) clearly documented the continuing narrow focus on changes in only the referral target behavior in the published literature, despite widespread theoretical support for and growing anecdotal information regarding unintended collateral (positive) and side (negative) effects. Voeltz and Evans (1983) argued that the dominant research paradigm apparently is failing to provide for such phenomena in the design and evaluation of intervention studies. Assuming a compelling interest in maximizing positive outcomes and minimizing negative ones on behalf of children and youth with the most severe disabilities, the continued absence of more systematic efforts to achieve multiple and meaningful outcomes is difficult to understand or justify. As long as our notions of what constitutes "effectiveness" are restricted to demonstrations of experimental control over single target behaviors in treatment environments, both science and practice can be regarded as contributing to the restrictions placed upon the lives of persons with severe disabilities.

In their defense of a positivist behavioral approach, Test, Spooner, and Cooke (1987) maintained that the current emphasis upon issues of generalization and maintenance did address concerns about the meaningfulness of behavior change efforts. In response, Evans and Meyer (1987) repeated that the need to limit outside sources of influences as potentially confounding variables in order to demonstrate treatment validity could be regarded as contributing to the continued segregation and isolation of the students involved. Because the model requires compelling evidence of the effects of a specific intervention strategy upon a single referral target behavior, the multiplicity of variables present in typical environments sometimes are seen as a threat to the internal validity of an experiment. Attempts to address this issue by systematically moving or introducing the student to typical environments and situations *later* to demonstrate maintenance or generalization of behavior change can be similarly viewed as an intrusion of the demands of science upon the experiences of children and educational practices. An alternative perspective would be one in which our values about meaningful outcomes drive research and practice, and might involve the discovery and use of alternative scientific paradigms, if necessary, rather than continuing to allow methodology to dictate the opportunities made available to real people with disabilities. Such alternative scientific paradigms would need to work in typical, complex, integrated environments, and would incorporate both the possibility of multiple "treatments" (sources of influence over a child's behavior) and the expectation of multiple positive outcomes (upon the child and his or her caregivers) as desirable features (see, for example, the review by Jacob, 1987).

A Partial Solution

Meyer and Evans (1989) summarized various outcomes that might be regarded as meaningful and could be measured or documented in different ways. We have adapted this list for school settings, and Table 1 summarizes nine possible outcomes that might be monitored and strategies that could be used to document each of these outcomes. This list includes the more traditional data collection strategies recommended for use by both teachers and researchers; use of these techniques alone can restrict both the intervention practices of teachers and other clinicians as well as the instructional opportunities made available to students. In the next section we present a brief overview of the use of such measures by teachers in programs for students with severe disabilities.

Teacher Data Collection Practices and Needs

Obviously, teachers must make instructional decisions about their students' performance and progress based upon analyzing regularly collected objective data. Recommended data collection practices for use by teachers have historically not differed greatly from those used by researchers in the published intervention literature (Browder, 1987; Snell & Smith, 1983). Snell and Smith (1983) stated that ". . . the teacher selects suitable data collection procedures and devises recording sheets to assess the student's pretreatment of baseline performance" (p. 88), and added, "Behavior measurement is arduous, and data-based analyses are complex" (p. 88). Perhaps it is not surprising, then, that even teachers who are well trained in data collection and the analysis of those data apparently cease to use those skills shortly after they become teachers (Burney & Shores, 1979; Haring, Liberty, & White, 1980).

So how do teachers make decisions? Grigg, Snell, and Lloyd (1989) found that teachers not only reported using their "intuition" to make instructional decisions, but tended to discount the validity of the kinds of objective and graphic representations of student performance recommended in teacher education programs. Fisher and Lindsey-Walters (1987) surveyed teachers nationally and found a similar pattern of teacher doubt regarding the value of such data; they reported that teachers described such data collection techniques as "unreliable" as well as "demanding and difficult to manage." Although it is conceivable that teachers are justified in their apparent rejection of behavioral observation data collection techniques, there is contrary evidence that teachers do make better decisions when those decisions are based upon data (see Farlow & Snell, 1989, for a careful discussion of these issues). Perhaps what is needed are data collection strategies for teachers that are not so arduous nor so difficult to manage in real classrooms that teachers either cannot or will not use them. Furthermore, those strategies must be more reflective of multiple outcome possibilities than the more traditional frequency measures focused upon isolated targets.

Although it is perhaps axiomatic that data collection can be demanding, we would also maintain that it is appropriate to consider the demands of the environment in addition to the demands of science in the design of alternative techniques that might better meet the needs of both schools and children. In the remainder of this paper, four data collection techniques will be described and illustrated. We have found these techniques to be particularly useful for teachers, who have willingly used them in the evaluation of educational consultation services to address the needs of students with serious behavior problems in integrated schools (for a summary of the outcomes for students served by this effort, see Janney and Meyer, in press). Each of these techniques is a measure of student behavior and experiences that is quantifiable and thus allows for change comparisons across time and situations. Equally important, each is "user-friendly" in the sense that the documentation process does not interrupt the flow of instruction or intervention in the classroom, requires minimal time to complete, and allows professionals and paraprofessionals to share both their objective and subjective observations.

User-Friendly Measurement Tools

Schedule of Student Activities

A diary of student activities completed by program staff before, during, and after the intervention can be used to document broad changes in the nature of the student's school day and staff perceptions of the behavior change. As depicted in Figure 1, this is essentially an expanded weekly schedule, including time by types of activities, grouping arrangements, staff assignments, how much of the day is integrated, and a success rating for each time period (each activity is rated as "usually successful," "usually unsuccessful," or "success varies"). In our experience, the school day of students with severe disabilities and challenging behaviors often is characterized by a lack of integrated school and community learning opportunities, a high frequency of one-to-one instruction, and many daily activities that are persistently scheduled and attempted even though the result is usually unsuccessful. At the conclusion of an intervention, we would hope to find that the student's day

Table 1
Behavioral Intervention in Children and Youth: Meaningful Outcomes[a]

Outcome	Examples	How measured/documented
Improvement in target behavior (reduction of excess)	Decrease in frequency of head banging to near zero levels	Frequency counts of hits recorded in *Daily Logs* (see Figure 2) *Incident Records* (see Figure 3)
	Decrease in tantrums	Same as above
	Decrease in operant vomiting behavior	Weight gain Quantity measures
Acquisition of replacement skills and behaviors	Asking for help rather than head banging	Frequency counts of requests for help
	Asking for a break rather than tantrumming	Frequency counts of requests for breaks
	Playing video games rather than engaging in hand flapping	Time spent in arcade; game tokens used; time clocked on school microcomputer
Acquisition of general self-control strategies to support behavior change	Using an anger control technique in circumstances associated with aggression	Observed use of cassette player with headphones Observed movement to another room location or seat when "disliked" peer is close by
	Using a calendar and picture schedule to predict and better cope with changes in routine (transitions, cancelled preferred events, absence of preferred people, etc.)	Correct reply if asked "What class is next?" Spontaneous interest in calendar and daily schedule (as recorded in *Daily Logs*)
	Learning zone discrimination behaviors for masturbation	Self-initiated and appropriate private times (family report)
Positive collateral effects and absence of negative side effects	Increased peer interactions as aggression declines	Participation in small group activities that were previously impossible
	Decrease in skin irritations as hand mouthing decreases	Red and flaky skin becomes more normal in appearance
Reduced need for and use of medical services and crisis management, for student and/or others	Decrease in cuts due to head banging that requires sutures	Medical/hospital records
	Decrease in staff injuries due to aggression	Worker's compensation and health insurance records and claims; decrease in staff complaints to principal
	Decrease in medication prescribed to control behavior	Reduction and elimination of dosages
	Decrease in emergency hospitalizations and use of crisis management	Medical/hospital records *Incident Records*
Less restrictive placements and greater participation in integrated school experiences	Attends regular school rather than special school	Student placement records
	Spends more time in regular classes rather than in self-contained special class	Changes in student schedule (see Figure 1)
	Participates in group experiences (social and academic) with typical peers	Changes in student schedule and staff "success" ratings (see Figure 1)
Subjective quality-of-life improvement: happiness, satisfaction, choices, and control	More smiling, less anxiety/sadness/crying/anger, and general positive affect	Observation and reports
	More student choice and control	Rating scale on choices/control and record of opportunities
	General motivation to participate in daily activities	*Daily Log* ratings (see Figure 2)
Perceptions of improvement by teachers/family/significant others	Family is pleased with behavior change	Communications from home to school
	Teachers are pleased with behavior change	Fewer complaints, end to requests for placements elsewhere, positive comments to home and school administration
	Child problems disappear as a school concern	School and district records involving child problems; nature of IEP; agenda of meetings; "reputation" of child at school
Expanded social relationships and informal support networks	Increased participation in school activities and play with peers	Activity records and informal observations at lunch, on the playground, etc.
	Fading of once-needed one-to-one staff assignment to student	Staffing changes; reduced need for staff presence and/or proximity Trusted to play alone with peers under typical general school supervision
	Friendships	Does child have friends? Observed friendship patterns and play
	Increased involvement of general school staff in support for child	Offers of assistance/involvement from general school staff and regular education personnel

[a] Adapted and reprinted with permission from Meyer and Evans (1989), pp. 154–155.

STUDENT SCHEDULE

STUDENT: _____   STAFF: _____   _____   _____
                                              name/role   name/role   name/role

SCHOOL: _____

                                              _____   _____   _____
DATE: _____   name/role   name/role   name/role

Time	Monday	Tuesday	Wednesday	Thursday	Friday	1:1 independent small group large group	Staff	+ = Usually Successful − = Usually Unsuccessful v = Varies	✓ If Integrated

Figure 1. Student schedule.

includes more integrated learning opportunities, fewer one-to-one staff assignments, more varied instructional groupings, and a greater proportion of the student's daily activities rated "successful."

This schedule should be completed at a team meeting at baseline and after any ecological modifications such as changes in the duration or order of activities, the addition or deletion of activities from the student's schedule, and changes in staff assignments or grouping arrangements. It should also be completed at the end of the intervention (or school year) and at follow up. A simple bar graph showing the percentage change in each variable could then be constructed.

Daily Log

A narrative Daily Log (see Figure 2) can be useful for problem solving the design of an intervention and as a strategy to systematically accumulate information to be used in day-to-day decision making. We recommend that the Daily Log be completed twice weekly by the staffperson who knows the student best. The dates for completing the log should be determined ahead of

Figure 2. Daily log.

time—preferably on a rotating schedule so that the log is not completed on the same two days each week. It should be completed whether or not behavior problems occurred on the designated day.

Some training may be required to ensure that the information recorded on the Daily Log is reliable and useful. One training strategy would be for all staff members to complete the Daily Log during a baseline of at least five days, and then hold brief team meetings after school to discuss and compare their observations. Periodic reliability checks also should be conducted; two staff members should complete a Daily Log and then compare notes with one another.

Incident Record

A more detailed Incident Record (see Figure 3) should be completed following the occurrence of more serious behaviors such as an incident of serious self-injurious or otherwise destructive behavior. It should be completed by the staffperson most directly involved in the incident. This record is useful for required documentation of the use of a crisis management procedure, for problem solving and decision making regarding the intervention and the crisis management procedure, and to document overall changes in the frequency of serious incidents. This Incident Record incorporates both objective information that may help in conducting a functional analysis and also subjective thoughts about why the incident might have occurred and how it might have been prevented. Objective information would include a description of the antecedents (the date and time, activity taking place, who else was present, and so on), the behavior itself (its topography, duration, and intensity), and any consequences that followed the behavior and which may be maintaining the behavior. Both these data and the subjective observations of the staffperson can be used in problem solving regarding intervention planning, implementation, and evaluation.

Use of the Incident Record may also require some staff training using the approach described above for the Daily Log. Again, two or more staff members periodically should complete written records of the same incident as a reliability check (see Meyer and Evans, 1989, for more information).

Skill Acquisition and Excess Behavior Record

Documentation of the acquisition of alternative skills being taught to replace excess behaviors can be achieved through weekly probe trials of relevant instructional programs. In order to determine whether meaningful behavior change has occurred, instruction—and data collection—must occur across relevant situations, persons, and environments. If these data reveal that a skill is used appropriately in one context but not in another, the teacher has information that is important for designing the needed modifications and adaptations of the program. In addition to the need to collect data in *context*, the teacher may need to monitor more than one excess behavior at a time. This is particularly crucial to ensure that both positive and negative collateral effects are being monitored whenever the teacher believes that several behaviors are related in some way. Evans and Meyer (1985) provided an example of a data collection measure to monitor more than one behavior in the context of instruction (see Figure 4).

Community-based instruction and group activities

INCIDENT RECORD

COMPLETED BY _____

STUDENT _____ ACTIVITY TAKING PLACE _____

WHERE _____ DATE/DAY OF WEEK _____ TIME _____

STAFF PRESENT WHEN INCIDENT OCCURRED _____

STUDENTS PRESENT WHEN INCIDENT OCCURRED _____

1. Describe what happened just before behavior occurred: (Was the student prompted? Was a staff person attending to the student? Was the student alone? Etc.)

2. Describe what the student did and what happened through the incident: (How intense was the behavior? How long did it last? Etc.)

3. Describe what happened to the student immediately after the incident: (include any "consequences" deliberately applied and also those that occurred without planning. Did people gather around? Did task demands stop? Did people get excited or stay calm? Etc.)

4. Why do you think the incident occurred?

5. How do you think the behavior could have been prevented or handled differently?

Figure 3. Incident record.

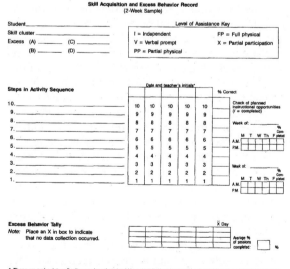

Figure 4. Skill acquisition and excess behavior record. (Reprinted with permission from Evans and Meyer (1985), p. 203.)

do not allow for the use of a measure such as this on a continuous basis. Rather than attempting to collect these data continuously, we believe that periodic probes can adequately support or refute teacher "intuitions" (i.e., good clinical judgments) as to whether a program is working. Thus, using a measure such as this once a week or so should be sufficient if the major purpose of these data is instructional problem solving or developing hypotheses regarding side effects associated with an intervention effort.

Summary

There is a need for intervention and measurement methods that are practical and which allow for the documentation of empirically and socially valid outcomes. The teacher's interest is less in demonstrating that an intervention was responsible for a change in behavior than in gathering information that can be used in ongoing decision making and problem solving. Teachers require measurement systems that are useful in formative program evaluation; competent instructional decision making is ongoing and does not occur only upon completion of a program. Teachers also need evidence that the outcomes associated with their efforts are meaningful for the students themselves.

The kinds of trial-by-trial data collection practices required in conventional single-subject research are not practical for educators supporting students in typical schools and classrooms. They interrupt the flow of instruction in natural contexts and do not reflect the multiple outcomes essential to the meaningful changes mentioned above. A data collection system should be designed around instructional requirements, not vice-versa!

Thus, the requirements of a system designed to evaluate multiple behavioral outcomes are to (a) demonstrate decreases in target excess behaviors as a function of the intervention; (b) demonstrate acquisition of replacement skills and other related behaviors as a function of the intervention; (c) demonstrate behavior change across relevant situations, persons, and environments; (d) not interrupt the flow of instruction and activities in natural contexts; (e) make the kinds of technical and time demands that allow for use by existing program staff (both professional and paraprofessional); and (f) provide information about how significant others perceive the behavior change (i.e., the behavior change can be perceived and valued by others who can make a difference to the child's life and experiences).

The data collection strategies described here do not address or solve all of these measurement needs. In fact, much additional experimental work is needed to identify and validate the variety of measures that would do so. However, it is essential that our efforts not be constrained by continued exclusive allegiance to strategies that are designed to measure only limited outcomes, on the one hand, or simply won't be used by teachers, on the other. As Tharp (1981) observed, there are "many ways of knowing"—both for teachers and for researchers. We need to be more creative and open to alternative paradigms and techniques to address the important issues emphasized by our values.

References

Browder, D. M. (1987). *Assessment of individuals with severe handicaps: An applied behavior approach to life skills.* Baltimore: Paul H. Brookes.

Burney, J. P., & Shores, R. E. (1979). A study of relationships between instructional planning and pupil behavior. *Journal of Special Education Technology, 2*(3), 16–25.

Donnellan, A. M., LaVigna, G. W., Zambito, J., & Thvedt, J. (1985). A time-limited intensive intervention program model to support community placement for persons with severe behavior problems. *Journal of The Association for Persons with Severe Handicaps, 9*, 201–212.

Durand, V. M., & Crimmins, D. B. (1988). Identifying the variables maintaining self-injurious behavior. *Journal of Autism and Developmental Disorders, 18*, 99–117.

Durand, V. M., & Kishi, G. S. (1987). Reducing severe behavior problems among persons with dual sensory impairments: An evaluation of a technical assistance model. *Journal of The Association of Persons with Severe Handicaps, 12*, 2–10.

Elmquist, D. L. (1989). *Features of effectiveness of residential treatment centers for adolescents with behavioral disorders: A literature review.* Logan: Utah State University Department of Special Education.

Evans, I. M., & Meyer, L. H. (1985). *An educative approach to behavior problems: A practical decision model for interventions with severely handicapped learners.* Baltimore: Paul H. Brookes.

Evans, I. M., & Meyer, L. H. (1987). Moving to educational validity: A reply to Test, Spooner, and Cooke. *Journal of The Association for Persons with Severe Handicaps, 12*, 103–106.

Evans, I. M., Meyer, L. H., Kurkjian, J., & Kishi, G. S. (1988). An evaluation of behavioral interrelationships in child behavior therapy. In J. C. Witt, S. N. Elliott, & F. N. Gresham (Eds.), *Handbook of behavior therapy in education* (pp. 189–215). New York: Plenum Press.

Farlow, L. J., & Snell, M. E. (1989). Teacher use of student performance data to make instructional decisions: Practices in programs for students with moderate to profound disabilities. *Journal of The Association for Persons with Severe Handicaps, 14*, 13–22.

Fisher, M., & Lindsey-Walters, S. (1987, October). *A survey report of various types of data collection procedures used by teachers and their strengths and weaknesses.* Paper presented at the annual conference of The Association for Persons with Severe Handicaps, Chicago.

Grigg, N. C., Snell, M. E., & Lloyd, B. H. (1989). Visual analysis of student evaluation data: A qualitative analysis of teacher decision-making. *Journal of The Association for Persons with Severe Handicaps, 14*, 23–32.

Haring, N. G., Liberty, K. A., & White, O. R. (1980). Rules for data-based strategy decisions in instructional programs. In W. Sailor, B. Wilcox, & L. Brown (Eds.), *Methods of instruction for severely handicapped children* (pp. 159–192). Baltimore: Paul H. Brookes.

Jacob, E. (1987). Qualitative research traditions: A review. *Review of Educational Research, 57*, 1–50.

Janney, R. E., & Meyer, L. H. (in press). Educational consultation to support home school services for students with severe disabilities and challenging behaviors. *Journal of The Association for Persons with Severe Handicaps.*

Lennox, D. B., Miltenberger, R. G., Spengler, P., & Erfanian, N. (1988). Decelerative treatment practices with persons who have mental retardation: A review of five years of the literature. *American Journal on Mental Retardation, 92,* 492–501.

Meyer, L. H., & Evans, I. M. (1986). Modification of excess behavior: An adaptive and functional approach for educational and community contexts. In R. H. Horner, L. H. Meyer, & H. D. B. Fredericks (Eds.), *Education of learners with severe handicaps: Exemplary service strategies* (pp. 315–350). Baltimore: Paul H. Brookes.

Meyer, L. H., & Evans, I. M. (1989). *Non-aversive intervention for behavior problems: A manual for home and community.* Baltimore: Paul H. Brookes.

Snell, M. E., & Smith, D. D. (1983). Developing the IEP: Selecting and assessing skills. In M. E. Snell (Ed.), *Systematic instruction of the moderately and severely handicapped, 2nd edition* (pp. 76–112). Columbus, OH: Charles E. Merrill.

Test, D. W., Spooner, F., & Cooke, N. L. (1987). Educational validity revisited. *Journal of The Association for Persons with Severe Handicaps, 12,* 96–102.

Tharp, R. G. (1981). The metamethodology of research and development. *Educational Perspectives, 20,* 42–48.

Voeltz, L. M., & Evans, I. M. (1982). Behavioral interrelationships in child behavior therapy. *Behavioral Assessment, 4,* 131–165.

Voeltz, L. M., & Evans, I. M. (1983). Educational validity: Procedures to evaluate outcomes in programs for severely handicapped learners. *Journal of The Association of the Severely Handicapped, 8*(1), 3–15.

Received: June 8, 1989
Final Acceptance: August 29, 1989
Editor in Charge: David P. Wacker

PART III
Assessment-Based Interventions

One of the hallmarks of positive behavior support (PBS) is the close linkage of assessment with the development of strategies for reducing challenging behaviors and improving quality of life. These strategies include comprehensive intervention options such as teaching alternative behaviors, changing antecedents, and changing consequences. Assessment is the process of gathering information to assist in answering a question. The studies included in this section all begin with careful assessments focusing on answering the question of what is motivating and maintaining the challenging behavior of interest. They then link the results of the assessment with creative and effective solutions that have positive outcomes for people with disabilities and their families, showing that accurate and comprehensive assessments are key. The articles in this section demonstrate how assessments can be linked to interventions to reduce problem behaviors and improve the quality of life of people with disabilities and their families. This two-step process of assessment and intervention has become standard practice in working with people with severe disabilities.

The article by Lucyshyn, Olson, and Horner (1995) reported on the change in the quality of life of a young woman with severe disabilities as she made the transition from an institution to her own home in the community. It described the process of collecting assessment information to identify the participant's challenges, needs, and strengths and documented the supports and services that were put in place to help her succeed and flourish in the community. The article by Kemp and Carr (1995) described the process of turning assessment information into hypotheses that can be used to inform interventions. This step is essential for developing support plans that meet the unique needs of individuals with severe disabilities who demonstrate challenging behavior. The authors also expanded the application of PBS by conducting the assessments and intervention in an employment setting.

As PBS has become more commonplace, the procedures have become more sophisticated and well defined. This is demonstrated in the articles by Carr et al. (1999) and Clarke, Worcester, Dunlap, Murray, and Bradley-Klug (2002). These articles provide examples of assessments that were directly linked to effective interventions across settings and assessment strategies. The article by Carr and his colleagues also reported social validity measures and maintenance of behavior change over time—both critical elements that will enhance the adoption of educational innovations.

The three articles by Koegel, Stiebel, and Koegel (1998); Clarke, Dunlap, and Vaughan (1999); and Durand (2002) demonstrated the use of PBS during typical family routines in typical places. Using PBS technology to decrease aggression toward siblings, improve the morning routine, and decrease sleep problems directly affected the quality of life experienced by people with disabilities and their families.

Finally, the article by Dunlap and Fox (1999), combined the principle of family centeredness, a hallmark of early intervention, with PBS. This integration marked the inclusion of families as true partners in the PBS process and exemplified how the application of PBS could be extended by working effectively with multiple stakeholders and diverse providers and consumers.

—Ilene S. Schwartz

Family-Centered, Assessment-Based Intervention to Improve Behavior During an Early Morning Routine

Shelley Clarke
University of South Florida

Glen Dunlap
University of South Florida

Bobbie Vaughn
University of South Florida

Abstract: This article presents a demonstration of assessment-based intervention conducted in a family context to improve the responding of a boy with Asperger syndrome during the early morning routine of getting dressed and ready for school. Following a process of functional assessment, we developed a multicomponent intervention package, which was implemented by the boy's mother. We used a reversal design to demonstrate the effectiveness of the intervention package. The results showed that the intervention produced a substantial reduction of problem behaviors, higher levels of on-task responding, and a clear decrease in the length of time required to complete the morning routine. This empirical analysis provides another demonstration of the efficacy of a family-centered approach of assessment-based positive interventions in natural family contexts.

Although a growing volume of research literature has documented the efficacy of positive behavior support (Carr et al., in press), most of the research has been conducted in relatively structured settings such as classrooms and clinics. In recent years, however, a number of studies have broadened the database to include support programs implemented by typical intervention agents in less controlled home and community contexts (Carr & Carlson, 1993; Carr et al., 1999; Vaughn, Clarke, & Dunlap, 1997). An important feature of these studies is the use of findings from functional assessments carried out in natural environments to develop interventions that are then implemented in the same environments. When functional assessments are conducted in this manner and the interventions are developed in partnership with those who will be responsible for implementation, it is likely that the interventions will be conducted with increased consistency and fidelity (Albin, Lucyshyn, Horner, & Flannery, 1996). This emphasis on ecological validity and partnership is considered to be an important factor in the continuing development of positive behavior support (Dunlap, Fox, Vaughn, Bucy, & Clarke, 1997).

The involvement of families in the process of behavior support has been described as being of special importance because of the amount of time that families spend with their children and because of the tremendous reciprocal influences that characterize parent–child interactions (Dunlap & Fox, 1996; Koegel, Koegel, Kellegrew, & Mullen, 1996). Researchers have recently begun to look closely at the process of involving parents in the development of behavior support strategies for use in home and community settings (e.g., Lucyshyn, Albin, & Nixon, 1997; Vaughn, Dunlap, Fox, Clarke, & Bucy, 1997). These studies have found encouraging outcomes in the child's behavior and the functioning of the family system.

A characteristic of family-centered positive behavior support is that the interventions and data collection focus on routines as a unit of analysis. For example, Lucyshyn et al. (1997) examined a mealtime routine in the home as an initial focus of assessment and intervention. Vaughn, Dunlap, and associates (1997) centered their efforts on three family-selected community routines—shopping in a grocery store, eating in a fast-food restaurant, and banking in a drive-through facility. Vaughn, Clarke, and Dunlap (1997) worked with a family in the context of a fast-food restaurant routine, as well as a home-toileting routine. Family lives are improved substantially when interventions are able to modify regularly occurring routines characterized by highly disruptive, frequent, intense problem behavior so that they become peaceful and even enjoyable opportunities for family interaction (e.g., Fox, Vaughn, Dunlap, & Bucy, 1997).

In this article, we describe another demonstration of assessment-based, family-centered positive behavior support. In this case, a family's life was disrupted by significant problems associated with a child's failure to complete a morning "get ready for school" routine. To correct the problems and help build a smoother and more agreeable routine, we worked with the family to assess the variables contributing to the difficulties and design an appropriate intervention that would fit the family's lifestyle.

Method

PARTICIPANTS AND SETTING

John was a 10-year-old boy who had recently been diagnosed with Asperger syndrome. He was in the fifth grade at the time of the study and was enrolled in a classroom for students with speech and language difficulties. Academically, he was on grade level in most subjects, with the exception of reading, in which he was described as having particular problems in comprehending abstractions. Although his social interactions were inconsistent, John was able to carry out age-appropriate conversations and could communicate his preferences without difficulty. John often exhibited problem behavior when he was given demands or time lines to complete an activity. At such times, he would often run out of a room, use perseverative speech, and/or engage in crying and tantrums. John's family included his mother, Maureen; his father; two younger brothers, ages 5 and 8; and his grandmother, who resided in another city but stayed with John's family during regular visits of 2 to 3 months.

John's family requested assistance from our university-based research group, which investigates family-centered behavior support. In accordance with our usual operations (e.g., Vaughn et al., 1997), we established a team. It included all members of John's immediate family, his grandmother, and two consultants from our research group. The team was involved in developing all steps of the assessment and intervention process. The study was conducted in the family's home during the daily morning routine. This routine was selected for intervention by Maureen because it was associated with significant behavior problems and disruptions to the family's interactions. The routine consisted of John's getting out of bed when instructed, using the bathroom, getting dressed, brushing his hair, and coming out to the breakfast area fully dressed.

ASSESSMENT

After establishing the team and identifying the target routine, we initiated a functional assessment. The assessment included interviews using a variation of the Functional As-

sessment Interview (O'Neill et al., 1997). Interviews were conducted with John's parents, his grandmother, and his brothers and with John himself. With some family members (including John), the interviews were abbreviated and focused primarily on information regarding John's preferences and the times and circumstances during which problems did and did not occur. With Maureen, the interview included detailed questions about the types of programs or strategies that had been successful with John in the past. Direct observations were conducted by a consultant during different routines throughout the day, and especially during the morning routine, which began at approximately 6:00 a.m.

The assessment process confirmed the reports of morning difficulties and revealed several variables that needed to be addressed in generating an intervention for John. All family members reported that John's problem behavior threw off the family routine. It was recounted by family members, and observed many times, that John failed to get dressed in the morning when instructed; instead, he played with his pet hamsters, ran around the house, or watched the Weather Channel on television. When the school bus came to pick him up an hour later, his mother would either have to rush him out of the house without his shoes on or drive him to school. During times when John exhibited problem behavior, it was observed that he cooperated only in allowing Maureen to dress him in the living room area. On these occurrences, John became agitated and displayed problem behavior that included yelling, repetitive speech, and stomping his feet.

The morning routine consisted of six specific steps:

1. getting out of bed;
2. going to the bathroom;
3. changing from pajamas to underwear;
4. putting on pants, shirt, socks, and shoes;
5. brushing hair;
6. walking out to the breakfast table in the kitchen.

This routine required that John have the ability to complete each dressing step independently. The observations raised questions about his ability to do the steps of the routine without assistance. Most days, John would only put on his pants and shirt by himself and required Maureen's assistance in putting on his socks and shoes. His ability to tie his own shoes independently and fluently was unclear. When he attempted to put on his socks, he would get frustrated by the effort it took, throw his shoes across the room, leave the area, refuse to continue dressing, and/ or engage in other, unrelated activities.

During the interview with Maureen, she reported specific strategies that had been successful in the past with John. One was the use of a visual schedule or chart to help him see what came next. Although this was something that John had used at school to help him understand the day's sequences, there were no schedules currently in place at school or home. Maureen also stated that visual cues were more effective than verbal requests in getting John to respond.

The assessment process also included obtaining information from John, who was asked to report his preferences for certain types of activities and reinforcers. His favorite activities were playing with his hamsters, landscaping, mowing the lawn, and playing with bubble machines. He stated that he liked "to do things by myself" and enjoyed being able to choose from a number of different activities.

HYPOTHESIS DEVELOPMENT

The data from the interviews and observations confirmed what had been reported by different family members. The information allowed the team to develop hypotheses regarding the function of John's behavior during the morning routine. It appeared as though the function of John's problem behavior was to escape from his morning dressing routine and engage in other activities that operated as competing reinforcers (Horner & Billingsley, 1988). It seemed that the routine was difficult and frustrating for John in some respects and that it was preferable to him to spend time with his favored activities than to attempt to complete the routine. The team generated three hypothesis statements relevant to intervention. They postulated that John would be more successful and exhibit less problem behavior during his morning routine if (a) a visual chart of the steps of the routine was provided to help him comprehend and appreciate his progress; (b) adjustments were made to his dressing requirements so that the routine would be less difficult to complete independently; and (c) an opportunity was provided following the completion of the routine for John to choose a preferred activity reinforcer. To test these hypotheses, we conducted three informal probe sessions over three days. During each day, Maureen implemented one of the components to assess how John would respond, as well as to determine if the components were convenient and easy to implement. The results of the probes went well, and John's behavior improved noticeably. After the team observed that the components appeared to have a positive effect and were easy to implement, a package intervention that included all the components was implemented.

INTERVENTION

Consistent with the hypotheses, the intervention package included three general components: A visual chart was provided, John's clothing arrangements were modified, and a reinforcement contingency was provided.

Maureen started the intervention session by introducing a chart with pictures and written words depicting the routine (MacDuff, Krantz, & McClannahan, 1993; Vaughn & Horner, 1995). This allowed John to see each step that was required for getting out of bed and dressing. The chart was a laminated sheet of paper with each step represented by a picture attached by Velcro™. When John finished with each step, he could remove the picture of the represented step. Once all the pictures were removed, he would walk out to the breakfast area and show his mother that all pictures were removed from the chart, and Maureen would praise him.

In addition, modifications were made to John's clothing that allowed him to complete his dressing routine more successfully. Because John had difficulty tying his shoes, Maureen purchased shoe laces that he did not need tie, but only needed to pull to tighten. She also changed the type of socks that John wore to anklets so that it would require less effort to put them on. The team also decided that it would be more appropriate for John to get dressed in his bedroom, where his clothes and shoes could be laid in a specific area for easy access. Maureen completed all modifications and arrangement of materials before she instructed John to get out of bed. These modifications also allowed Maureen to intermittently check on John and praise him throughout the routine.

The third intervention component included a choice chart that was developed so that John could pick preferred reinforcers once he finished the dressing routine. When he completed all of the steps, John took the choice chart with him to the breakfast area, selected a picture of his preferred activity (e.g., toy), and traded the picture for the selected reinforcer after he ate breakfast. To control for possible satiation, the array of reinforcers was changed once a week based on his preferences.

DATA COLLECTION AND EXPERIMENTAL DESIGN

The experimental design for this controlled case study consisted of four phases: (a) baseline, which consisted of typical preintervention interactions, (b) the initial intervention phase, (c) two days of withdrawal, in which the intervention components were withdrawn and the baseline conditions were in place, and (d) a return to intervention for 4 additional days. All sessions were videotaped using a hand-held camcorder and scored at a later time using a 10-second continuous interval system. Videotaping and data collection were initiated when Maureen initially instructed John that it was time to get dressed and continued until all steps of the task were completed or the school bus came. Data collection occurred approximately twice a week, when the consultant went to the house in the morning (approximately 6:00 a.m.). A research assistant helped to videotape and score tapes for interobserver agreement. Formal collection of baseline data was not initiated until the consultants (with videocamera) had been present during the morning routine during several sessions to develop rapport, obtain assessments, and establish some familiarity.

DEPENDENT MEASURES AND RELIABILITY

Two dependent, non-exclusive measures (i.e., it was possible for both to be scored during a single interval) were assessed. The first was the percentage of intervals with disruptive behavior exhibited during the dressing routine. Disruptive behavior consisted of any occurrence of the following: leaving the dressing area, using materials inappropriately (throwing things or destroying property), running around the house without clothing, crying/tantrumming, and noncompliance, which was defined as not responding to an instruction or prompt within 5 seconds.

The second dependent measure was engagement in the routine. Engagement was defined as being on task and following the sequence of the routine or specific task appropriately. Engagement was scored if John was on task for at least 70% of an interval, as determined by observer judgment (see Vaughn, Clarke, & Dunlap, 1997)

In addition to disruptive behavior and engagement, the length of time it took for John to complete the routine was also documented. The length of the morning routine was determined by calculating the total number of 10-second intervals that passed from the time that Maureen gave the initial instruction to the time that John completed all steps of the routine or was taken to the school bus.

Interobserver agreement was determined for 47% of the sessions. Agreement averaged 99% (range = 91%–100%) for occurrences of disruptive behavior and 99% (range = 96%–100%) for intervals with engagement.

Agreement for the length of the dressing routine was calculated by comparing the number of 10-second intervals that were independently marked for each session by the data collectors. Interobserver agreement for length of session was calculated for 47% of the sessions with 100% agreement.

In addition to direct observation measures, a 10-item questionnaire was completed by Maureen after each session immediately following the completion of all steps of the routine. All questions were scored on a 1-to-5 rating scale, with four questions reflecting John's behavior and six questions concentrating on the strategies used during each session of the routine. The questionnaire took an average of 1 minute to complete with all but the two initial intervention sessions rated.

Results and Discussion

Figure 1 represents the percentage of intervals in each phase during which John was engaged, as well as when he exhibited disruptive behavior during the morning routine. The data on engagement show how each condition influenced John's appropriate participation in the morning routine. The mean percentage of intervals of engagement during the baseline and withdrawal phases was 25%. Engagement rose to an average of 80% during the intervention phases.

For disruptive behavior, the percentage of intervals averaged 68% during the baseline and withdrawal condi-

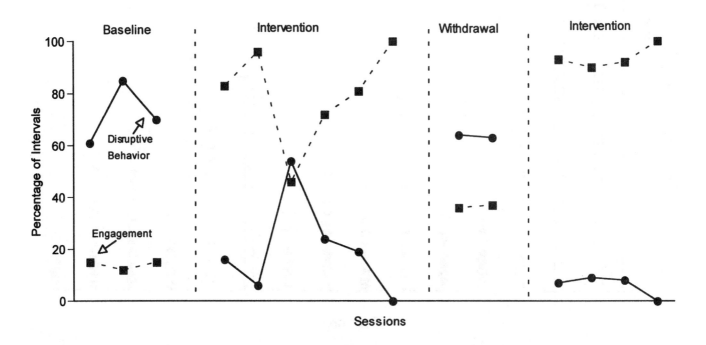

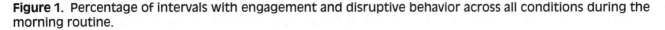

Figure 1. Percentage of intervals with engagement and disruptive behavior across all conditions during the morning routine.

tions, but only 13% during the intervention conditions. The unusual elevation in disruptive behavior and diminished engagement reflected in the third data point of the first intervention condition may be attributed to the fact that a change from standard to daylight savings time occurred on that morning. Unlike on previous days, when this particular session was initiated, it was still dark outside. John resisted beginning the routine (i.e., he stayed in bed), but once out of bed, he dressed immediately and continued his morning routine appropriately. After that day, John's wake-up time was adjusted so that Maureen started the routine 10 minutes later in the morning. As the days progressed and it started getting light earlier, John's wake-up time was adjusted again.

Figure 2 depicts the data collected for the duration of the routine. The average duration during baseline and the withdrawal sessions was 27 minutes and 5 seconds, compared with an average duration of 10 minutes 50 seconds during the intervention phases. These data reflect a considerable reduction in the time it took John to get out of bed and get dressed. This was associated with similar reductions in the family's aggravation, an extended time to eat breakfast, and additional opportunities for John to play with preferred materials.

Table 1 presents the 10 questionnaire items, the anchors for each of the 5-point rating scales, and the mean ratings by Maureen for each condition of the study. Although these data need to be considered in the context of Maureen's being the intervention agent and a principal member of the behavior support team, they are nevertheless encouraging in that Maureen's perceptions were generally (although not completely) consistent with the direct observation data shown in Figure 1. One of the more important messages from these data is that Maureen characterized the procedures as easy to implement and believed that they would work well in other routines. Indeed, in conversations subsequent to the study, Maureen described how she and her family used parallel strategies to facilitate homework and bathing routines for John. She also adapted components of the intervention to fit in the daily routines of John's siblings.

In terms of contributions to our field, the significance of this case report lies not in the uniqueness of the intervention procedures nor in the amplitude of the effects. Rather, we view the importance of the current data in terms of the growing body of empirical testimony that supports the use of parent-professional collaborations to develop effective interventions for use in the ongoing con-

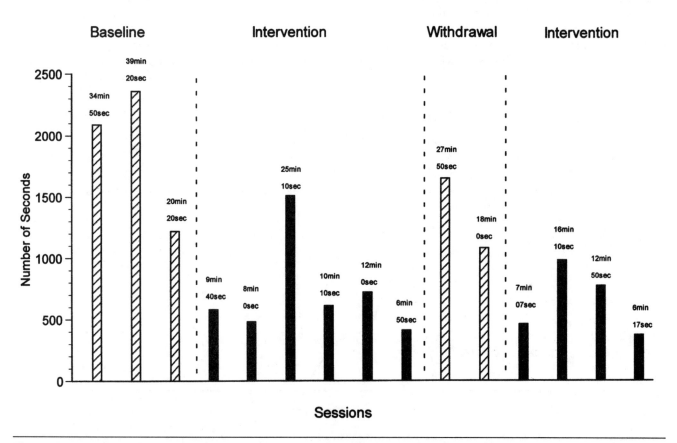

Figure 2. Length of time in seconds to complete all steps of morning routine. Striped bars indicate baseline and withdrawal sessions. Solid bars represent sessions occurring during intervention conditions.

Table 1. Mean Ratings on Questionnaire Items

Question	Rating scale	Baseline (*M*)	Intervention 1 (*M*)	Withdrawal (*M*)	Intervention 2 (*M*)
1. In this activity my child's behavior was _____	1. Very difficult to manage 3. Somewhat manageable	2.3	4	2.3	4
2. Overall in the past week, my child's behavior in this activity was _____	5. Very easy to manage	2	4	3	3.3
3. Communicating with my child during this activity _____	1. Did not work well 3. Worked so–so	2	4	3	5
4. The way the activity was organized _____	5. Worked well	1	5	3	5
5. The way I handled my child's behavior in this activity _____		2.3	5	4	5
6. The intervention strategies used in the morning activity _____	1. Work poorly 3. Work sometimes	2	5	3	5
7. I feel like these strategies will _____ in other activities	5. Work well	2	5	3	5
8. In this activity my child's participation (looking, listening, trying steps) _____	1. Did not happen at all 3. Happened sometimes 5. Happened in all steps of activity	2.3	4	3	3.3
9. In this activity my child communicated _____	1. Nothing 3. Occasionally 5. Throughout	2	4	3	4
10. I feel like I can do this activity on my own	1. Not at all 3. Sometimes 5. All the time	4	5	5	5

texts of families' lives. In one sense, the present experience can be seen as augmenting this database by adding an early morning routine in a family home and by focusing on the behavior of a boy with Asperger syndrome. Similarly, the current study can be seen as a systematic replication of assessment-based, family-centered intervention that relies on the processes and technical foundation of positive behavior support. Many more replications and extensions will be useful as we seek to establish this approach as one capable of offering meaningful and enduring benefits to the many children and families in need.

ABOUT THE AUTHORS

*Shelley Clarke, MA, state certified behavior analyst, is a research coordinator in the Division of Applied Research and Educational Support at the Louis de la Parte Florida Mental Health Institute at the University of South Florida. For the past 10 years, she has been involved in conducting applied research with a variety of populations. **Glen Dunlap**, PhD, is director of the Division of Applied Research and Educational Support and a professor of Child and Family Studies at the Louis de la Parte Florida Mental Health Institute at the University of South Florida. Dr. Dunlap also serves as principal investigator for the Rehabilitation Research and Training Center on Positive Behavioral Support. **Bobbie Vaughn**, PhD, is an assistant professor in the Division of Applied Research and Educational Support in the Department of Child and Family Studies at the Louis de la Parte Florida Mental Health Institute. She also directs a 3-year federally funded National Institute on Disability and Rehabilitation Research (NIDRR) project supporting underserved families who have children with developmental disabilities and challenging behavior. Address: Glen Dunlap, Division of Applied Research and Educational Support, Department of Child and Family Studies, Louis de la Parte Florida Mental Health Institute, University of South Florida, 13301 Bruce B. Downs Blvd., Tampa, FL 33612.*

AUTHORS' NOTES

1. This research was supported by Field-Initiated Research Grant No. H133G60119 and RRTC Grant No. H133B980005 from the National Institute on Disability and Rehabilitation Research (U.S. Department of Education). However, no official endorsement by any supporting agency should be inferred.
2. Appreciation is extended to all members of the participating family and to Merili Wyatte and Lilliane Reyes for assisting with data collection.

REFERENCES

Albin, R. W., Lucyshyn, J. M., Horner, R. H., & Flannery, K. B. (1996). Contextual fit for behavior support plans. In L.K. Koegel, R.L. Koegel, & G. Dunlap (Eds.), *Positive behavioral support: Including people with difficult behavior in the community* (pp. 81–98). Baltimore: Brookes.

Carr, E. G., & Carlson, J. I. (1993). Reduction of severe behavior problems in the community using a multicomponent treatment approach. *Journal of Applied Behavior Analysis, 26*, 157–172.

Carr, E. G., Horner, R.H ., Turnbull, A. P., Marquis, J., Magito McLaughlin, D., McAtee, M. L., Smith, C. E., Anderson Ryan, K., Ruef, M. B., & Doolabh, A. (in press). *Positive behavior support as an approach for dealing with problem behavior in people with developmental disabilities.* AAMR Monograph.

Carr, E. G., Levin, L., McGonnachie, G., Carlson, J., Kemp, D., Smith, C. E., & Magito McLaughlin, D. (1999). Comprehensive multisituational intervention for problem behavior in the community: Long-term maintenance and social validation. *Journal of Positive Behavior Interventions, 1*, 5–25.

Dunlap, G., & Fox, L. (1996). Early intervention and serious problem behaviors: A comprehensive approach. In L. K. Koegel, R. L. Koegel, & G. Dunlap (Eds.), *Positive behavioral support: Including people with difficult behavior in the community* (pp. 3–50). Baltimore: Brookes.

Dunlap, G., Fox, L., Vaughn, B. J., Bucy, M., & Clarke, S. (1997). In quest of meaningful perspectives and outcomes: A response to five commentaries. *Journal of the Association for Persons with Severe Handicaps, 22*, 221–223.

Fox, L., Vaughn, B. J., Dunlap, G., & Bucy, M. (1997). Parent–professional partnership in behavioral support: A quantitative analysis of one family's experience. *Journal of the Association for Persons with Severe Handicaps, 22*, 198–207.

Horner, R. H., & Billingsley, F. (1988). The effect of competing behavior on the generalization and maintenance of adaptive behavior in applied settings. In R. H. Horner, G. Dunlap, & R. L. Koegel (Eds.), *Generalization and maintenance: Lifestyle changes in applied settings* (pp. 197–220). Baltimore: Brookes.

Koegel, L. K., Koegel, R. L., Kellegrew, D., & Mullen, K. (1996). Parent education for prevention and reduction of severe problem behaviors. In L. K. Koegel, R. L. Koegel, & G. Dunlap (Eds.), *Positive behavioral support: Including people with difficult behavior in the community* (pp. 3–30). Baltimore: Brookes.

Lucyshyn, J. M., Albin, R. W., & Nixon, C. D. (1997). Embedding comprehensive behavioral support in family ecology: An experimental, single-case analysis. *Journal of Consulting and Clinical Psychology, 65*, 241–251.

MacDuff, G. S., Krantz, P. J., & McClannahan, L. E. (1993). Teaching children with autism to use photographic activity schedules: Maintenance and generalization of complex response chains. *Journal of Applied Behavior Analysis, 26*, 89–97.

O'Neill, R. E., Horner, R. H., Albin, R. W., Storey, K., Sprague, J. R., & Newton, J. S. (1997). *Functional assessment and program development for problem behavior: A practical handbook.* Pacific Grove, CA: Brooks/Cole.

Vaughn, B., Clarke, S., & Dunlap, G. (1997). Assessment-based interventions for severe behavior problems in a natural family context. *Journal of Applied Behavior Analysis, 30*, 713–716.

Vaughn, B. J., Dunlap, G., Fox, L., Clarke, S., & Bucy, M. (1997). Parent-professional partnership in behavioral support: A case study of community-based intervention. *Journal of the Association for Persons with Severe Handicaps, 22*, 185–197.

Vaughn, B. J., & Horner, R. (1995). Effects of concrete versus verbal choice systems on problem behavior. *Augmentative and Alternative Communication, 11*, 89–92.

Action Editor: Robert L. Koegel

JASH
1995, Vol. 20, No. 4, 229–247

Reduction of Severe Problem Behavior in Community Employment Using an Hypothesis-Driven Multicomponent Intervention Approach

Duane C. Kemp and Edward G. Carr
State University of New York at Stony Brook
and
Developmental Disabilities Institute

Individuals with severe problem behavior typically are excluded from integration efforts involving community employment. This study examined one strategy for reducing severe problem behavior in an employment situation. The strategy involved three factors: (a) interventions were chosen based on hypotheses about the maintaining variables for the problem behavior (hypothesis-driven model); (b) a multicomponent intervention package was used that included some combination of functional communication training, building rapport, making choices, embedding demands, and building tolerance for delay of reinforcement; and (c) measures of latency to problem behavior and percentage of work steps completed were used instead of the more traditional measure of frequency. The results demonstrated both an increase in the time spent in the employment situation without problem behavior and increases in completion of work steps to maximum. Social validation of these results was provided by employment site management. The value of this strategy for addressing the obstacles to assessment, measurement, and intervention for severe problem behavior in community employment situations was discussed.

This investigation was supported in part by grants G0087C0234, H133G20098, and H133B20004 from the U.S. Department of Education, National Institute on Disability and Rehabilitation Research. In addition, this investigation was supported in part by the Developmental Disabilities Institute Foundation Grant, "Communication-Based Treatment of Severe Problem Behavior in Community Employment Situations."

We thank Martin Hamburg, Executive Director, Developmental Disabilities Institute, for his generous support, and Diana Lynne Robinson, the job coach, for her tireless efforts. We also thank Rob Horner for his constructive criticism.

Address all correspondence to Edward G. Carr, Department of Psychology, State University of New York, Stony Brook, NY 11794-2500

DESCRIPTORS: aggression, challenging behavior, community-based activities, developmental disabilities, functional assessment, positive behavioral support, self-injurious behavior, supported employment

The basis for supported employment services for persons with developmental disabilities can be found 20 years ago in the principle of normalization. This principle holds service delivery to a standard of culturally normal environments and contingencies (Nirje, 1969; Wolfensberger, 1972). In his review of the service delivery systems of that period, however, Whitehead (1979) stated that although more than 200,000 adults with severe disabilities were being served in sheltered workshops, more than 6,000,000 others were not receiving services. Further, although sheltered workshops were purported to be transitional placements, the only individuals to "graduate" to competitive employment were those who did not require skills training.

Federal legislation (i.e., The Rehabilitation Act of 1973, The Competitive Employment and Training Act, The Job Training Partnership Act, The 1984 Amendments to the Education of the Handicapped Act, The Developmental Disabilities Assistance and Bill of Rights Act of 1984, and the Rehabilitation Act Amendments of 1986) has continued to promote the employment of individuals with severe disabilities. The two decades of research that have accompanied this legislation have focused on several issues related to supported employment including cost-benefit analyses (Hill, Wehman, Kregel, Banks, & Metzler, 1987), implementation (Nisbet & Hagner, 1988), and conversion from sheltered employment to supported employment (Wehman & Kregel, 1985). Productivity and collateral social skills have been identified as critical elements for the acquisition and retention of jobs (Martin, Rusch, Lagomarcino, & Chadsey-Rusch, 1986). Analyses of the social skills necessary for vocational success and identification of the inappropriate social behavior leading to job separation are numerous (Hanley-Maxwell, Rusch, Chadsey-Rusch, & Renzaglia, 1986; Martin et al., 1986). The published literature on intervention for severe problem behavior (e.g., property destruction, aggression, tantrums, and self-injury) in community vocational settings, however, virtually has been nonexistent (see Hughes & Rusch, in press; Ponthieu, Jones, Williamson, & Beaird, 1994; Rusch & Hughes, 1989; Smith & Coleman, 1986). Smith (1990), investigating intervention for behavior problems in continuing employment, suggested that individuals with autism who exhibit severe problem behavior are at risk for segregation and institutionalization. Job placement is unlikely. These facts recommend redress of severe problem behavior as a necessary element in promoting normalization in the area of employment. This focus constitutes the major purpose of this study.

Recent reviews and analyses of the literature suggest that problem behavior in community settings requires multifaceted intervention (Carr, Robinson, Taylor, & Carlson, 1990; Haring & Kennedy, 1990; Horner et al., 1990; Iwata, Vollmer, & Zarcone, 1990). Intervention likely will consist of the manipulation of a number of variables (e.g., Durand & Kishi, 1987) and include a simultaneous increase in specific classes of adaptive behavior and decrease in classes of maladaptive behavior (Koegel & Koegel, 1988). One purpose of this study, therefore, was to present a method by which this multifaceted intervention may be derived. Specifically, an hypothesis-driven model was adopted (Repp, Felce, & Barton, 1988; Repp & Karsh, 1990) in which the antecedents and consequences of each problem situation were examined and used to form hypotheses concerning the variables maintaining problem behavior in each instance. Specific intervention procedures were then chosen based on these hypotheses. This method represents an extension of our earlier work on intervention for problem behavior in other community settings such as supermarkets (Carr & Carlson, 1993). However, because a single study in one setting (i.e., the supermarket) cannot establish the generality of an intervention, we felt that it was important to test the efficacy of our community-based methodology in a significantly different situation, namely, the workplace. This goal, then, represented an additional contribution of this study.

Intervention for severe problem behavior in the community presents difficulties not faced by intervention conducted in university laboratories, private homes, or segregated schools. Aggression, self-injury, and destructive behavior are not well tolerated by parents and other caregivers, especially when the person with the disability is an adult. Members of the community often argue that a person who exhibits aggressive, self-injurious, or destructive behavior should not be at liberty in the community (Smith, 1990). Lack of public tolerance requires that the investigator measure problem behavior using alternatives to the traditional measures of frequency, rate, duration, and time sampling. Thus, the goal of the present study was not only to assist individuals to complete work without displaying severe problem behavior, but also to demonstrate the usefulness, in the evaluation process, of alternative measures that included latency to problem behavior and percentage of work steps completed.

Method

Participants and Setting

Participants (hereafter known as employees) were selected on the basis of objective data maintained by group home and day-service staff working in an agency serving persons in whom developmental disabilities had been diagnosed. The first three adults who met the following criteria were included in the present study: (a) reports of frequent severe problem behavior requiring their removal from community settings and prohibiting current activities in the community; (b) the problem behavior included aggression or self-injury possibly accompanied by property destruction and tantrums; (c) high severity of problem behavior documented by the occurrence of physical restraint or medical attention; (d) exclusion from participation in the agency's Supported Employment Program because of severe problem behavior; and (e) documentation of some communication abilities in the form of speech, sign language, or use of picture communication symbols.

Bill was 28 years of age; Maggie was 30; and Michael was 26. The staff physician had diagnosed each as autistic and mentally retarded. Additionally, each had a test composite score (IQ) of less than 36 points on the Stanford-Binet Intelligence Scale: Fourth Edition that was interpreted by the psychology staff to indicate severe mental retardation. Bill had no articulate speech; rather, he communicated his basic needs through a small number of signs (American Sign Language) and picture communication symbols (Mayer-Johnson, 1985). Maggie spoke in short phrases, generally two or three words in length. Michael could articulate a half-dozen words and, in addition, used a small number of picture communication symbols to communicate. Each responded correctly when simple one-step verbal directions were presented. Through actions or spoken affirmations (i.e., "yes" or "okay"), each indicated his or her willingness to accompany the job coach and leave the current day-service site.

Sessions were conducted in one of two greenhouses located in the community. The first was located near the agency's day-service facility, and was staffed by a manager, several assistants, and workers without developmental disabilities. Workers with developmental disabilities were employed in the ratio of two per worker without disability. This served as the training site. The second greenhouse served as the generalization setting and was located nearby on the grounds of a community golf course. It had the same staffing pattern as the training site. The employees of this study constituted the only workers with developmental disabilities during their shifts and were either matched or outnumbered by workers without disability. Each greenhouse served walk-in customers and, therefore, required employees to have contact with the general public. Importantly, the presence of paid employees, job coaches, and the availability of half-time or better positions meant that each greenhouse possessed those features associated with competitive supported employment.

It is critical to note that we had a prior relationship with each of the greenhouses. Specifically, for a period of 8 months prior to this study, we had successfully introduced several people with disabilities into the greenhouse workforce. Although these individuals did not have severe problem behavior, their success made the management willing to consider the inclusion of other individuals who did.

One job coach served as the intervention agent for all three employees under the direct supervision of the first author. The job coach was a 32-year-old woman who was employed previously by the agency in the capacity of Employment Specialist for one and one-half years. Prior to that position, she was a student teacher at an elementary school and a tutor for a young man with autism. She received 16 hr of training in the Strategies for Crisis Intervention and Prevention course mandated by the Office of Mental Retardation and Developmental Disabilities in New York (OMRDD, NY). This training included the use of physical interventions to control severe problem behavior.

Procedures

Staff interview. The range of potential maintaining variables for the severe problem behavior of each prospective employee was narrowed to guide subsequent assessment (hypothesis formation) and intervention. Group home and day-service staff were asked to provide their hypotheses as to the maintaining variables through a functional assessment interview (O'Neill, Horner, Albin, Storey, & Sprague, 1990). The interview process (described in detail by O'Neill et al., 1990, Appendix B), although technically not a functional analysis in that functional relationships were not documented, provided descriptions of the target behaviors, identified predictive antecedent factors, and indicated potential maintaining consequences. The staff's hypotheses regarding maintaining consequences were consistent for all three employees selected: severe problem behavior was a function of either escape from aversive stimuli (negative reinforcement) or receipt of tangible reinforcement.

Baseline and assessment. Two or three sessions were distributed across each workday in the training greenhouse. Once a stable baseline was established in the training greenhouse, three sessions were conducted across two consecutive days by the job coach in the generalization greenhouse for comparison. In both greenhouses, each individual was returned to the nearby day-service site upon completion of each session. By keeping the sessions brief, we avoided a situation in which regular greenhouse staff would witness protracted bouts of problem behavior, a circumstance that would have undermined their continued cooperation.

Each session consisted of planting using the 10-step task analysis shown in Table 1. Development of this task analysis followed the criteria of Haring and Kennedy (1988) in their evaluation of task-analytic research. Consequently, we monitored the specific task steps correctly completed and the specific prompts given for each step. The educational procedures used were those generally employed by the agency's job coaches when providing instruction in the community. Each step provided a discriminative stimulus consisting of a verbal prompt presented by the staff and a relevant environmental cue. The discriminative stimulus for step 1 (i.e., "gather supplies") consisted of the direct verbal prompt "Let's get our supplies" and the environmental cue of the presence of the materials on the supply table. If the employee made a correct response to the discriminative stimulus within 5 sec, the job coach presented positive feedback relevant to the step completed (e.g., "Great! Now we're ready to plant"). If the employee made an incorrect response (e.g., picked up a potted plant) or no response at all, the job coach implemented the sequence of prompts until a correct response was made or the session was terminated due to problem behavior. Each prompt was implemented only if the preceding prompt failed to evoke the correct response. The sequence of prompts was: (a) provide negative feedback and repeat the verbal cue (e.g., "No, we don't need that. Let's get our supplies"); (b) provide a gestural prompt and repeat the verbal cue (e.g., pointing to the supplies while saying "Let's get our supplies"); and (c) provide a physical prompt and repeat the verbal cue (e.g., placing a hand on the employee's elbow and gently guiding the arm while saying "Let's get our supplies").

Three criteria were used to terminate baseline sessions: (a) 15 min had elapsed; (b) all 10 steps of the planting sequence were completed; or (c) target problem behavior occurred. The 15-min time period was chosen based on the industrial rate for the planting sequence (i.e., the duration of task completion by a worker without disability) with additional time for prompting and behavioral intervention. Observations on other jobsites and interviews with employers and job coaches indicated that different termination crite-

Table 1
Planting Task Sequence

Step	Discriminative stimulus (cue)	Correct response
1. Gather supplies	Nonverbal: Material present on supply table. Verbal: "Let's get our supplies."	Places trowel, sand, pots, hole punch, bowl, and bag on work table.
2. Fill pot ¾ with soil.	Nonverbal: Empty pot. Verbal: "Fill the pot to the line, please."	Fills pot with potting soil to drawn line.
3. Press holes into soil.	Nonverbal: ¾-filled pot. Verbal: "Punch holes in the soil, please."	Punches holes in five places. Puts to one side.
4. Mix seeds with sand.	Nonverbal: Holes in soil Verbal: "Mix the seeds with sand, please."	Pours seeds and sand into bowl. Mixes.
5. Put mixture into holes.	Nonverbal: Prepared bowl. Verbal: "Put the mixture in the holes, please."	Fills punched holes with seed and sand mixture.
6. Fill last ¼ of pot.	Nonverbal: Seeded pot. Verbal: "Fill the pot, please."	Adds potting soil to pot until full.
7. Press firmly on soil.	Nonverbal: Filled pot. Verbal: "Press the soil, please."	Compacts and flattens top of soil.
8. Soak soil with water.	Nonverbal: Compacted pot. Verbal: "Water the soil, please."	Wets soil with spray from wand and lets drain.
9. Place in ziplock bag.	Nonverbal: Pot with wet soil. Verbal: "Put the pot in the bag, please."	Places pot sitting upright in ziplock bag. Closes.
10. Clean work area.	Nonverbal: Bagged pot. Verbal: "Let's clean up."	Replaces pots, sand, trowel, bowl, hole punch, and bags.

ria were needed depending on the severity of problem behavior. Aggression and destructive behavior to glass (including ceramics) were target problem behaviors for which a single occurrence could not be tolerated. Therefore, a single occurrence of aggression (i.e., hitting, kicking, biting, scratching, striking the head against another's head, tearing another's clothing, or pulling another's hair) or destructive behavior to glass objects (i.e., hitting, kicking, or throwing them) terminated the session. Employee's attempts at these behaviors that were foiled by the quick action of the job coach also terminated the session. The remaining types of problem behavior were tolerated to a greater degree if they occurred infrequently. These less serious problem behaviors consisted of self-injury (e.g., a single strike to the head with hand, knee, or object), destructive behavior to nonglass objects (e.g., a single hit, kick, or throw), and tantrums (e.g., screaming for 5 sec, stomping on the ground and flailing arms for 5 sec, or throwing oneself to the ground and flailing arms and legs for 5 sec). Sessions were terminated when three of these behaviors occurred in any combination [e.g., Bill's first baseline session was terminated when he: (a) slapped his face (self-injury); (b) jumped and stomped on the ground while biting one hand and flailing the other for at least 5 sec (tantrum); and (c) threw a plastic water bottle to the floor (nonglass property destruction) in rapid succession].

Functional assessment observation, a direct behavior observation strategy (O'Neill et al., 1990), took place during baseline. This assessment was used to generate hypotheses regarding the variables maintain-

ing the problem behavior. To collect the necessary information, the first author and job coach completed observation cards immediately after each baseline session. These index cards were developed previously by the authors and colleagues and consisted of a variant of the ABC (antecedents-behaviors-consequences) format focusing on the social aspects of the problem (Carr et al., 1994). Antecedents consisted of the interpersonal context for the problem behavior, and consequences referred to the social reaction to the problem behavior. In illustration, the first observation card for Bill listed the antecedent or interpersonal context as "asked to punch seed holes in soil (step 3) and physically prompted." The problem behavior was listed as "self-injury-tantrum-property destruction (plastic)." The consequence or social reaction was listed as "Terminated work. Escorted from greenhouse." The hypothesis was listed as "escape from physical prompt (negative reinforcement hypothesis)." Similar observation cards were collected for all employees and all baseline sessions. These cards were sorted by interpersonal context to establish the pattern of common antecedent conditions for each employee's problem behavior. Each grouping of cards was then stated in the general case and listed as a problem summary in Table 2. Listed problem summaries accounted minimally for 90% of the observed problem situations for each employee.

The problem summaries and hypotheses as to the variables maintaining specific problem behavior listed in Table 2 were used to develop specific corresponding intervention procedures. This approach corresponds

Table 2
Problem Summaries, Hypotheses Concerning Variables Maintaining Problem Behavior, and Interventions Based on Those Hypotheses

	Problem summary	Hypothesis	Intervention
Bill			
1.	The job coach walks to the supply area to begin the planting sequence. Bill runs from the greenhouse. If he is prevented from doing so, he screams and hits the job coach.	Escape from job coach and planting materials because they are associated with tasks (negative reinforcement).	Build rapport (establish job coach as a generalized reinforcer).
2.	Bill is given a physical prompt because he did not respond correctly to a gestural prompt to complete a planting step. He screams, jumps up and down, and knocks planting materials to the floor.	Escape from physical prompt (negative reinforcement).	Choice of alternative preferred activity. Embed demands.
3.	Bill is given the discriminative stimulus for a planting step. He shakes his head "no" and walks away from the work table. When escorted back to the work table, he screams and hits the job coach.	Escape from planting task demand (negative reinforcement).	Functional communication. Tolerance for delayed reinforcement.
Maggie			
1.	Maggie grabs and uses items not needed for the planting sequence. When prevented from taking or using the items, she hits the job coach with her head, and bites her.	Tangible reinforcement.	Choice of alternative reinforcers.
2.	Maggie is given the discriminative stimulus for a planting step. She gives an incorrect response. When given negative feedback, she hits her head with her fist several times rapidly and hits the job coach with her head.	Escape from negative feedback (negative reinforcement).	Functional communication. Tolerance for delayed reinforcement.
Michael			
1.	The job coach walks to the supply area to begin the planting sequence. Michael runs from the greenhouse. If he is prevented from doing so, he hits the job coach, pulls her hair, and hits her head with his head.	Escape from job coach and planting materials because they are associated with tasks (negative reinforcement).	Build rapport (establish job coach as a generalized reinforcer).
2.	Michael is given a physical prompt because he did not respond correctly to a gestural prompt to complete a planting step. He grabs the job coach's clothing, and hits her head with his head.	Escape from physical prompt (negative reinforcement).	Choice of alternative preferred activity. Embed demands.
3.	Michael is given the discriminative stimulus for a planting step. He runs away from the work table to an area in which there are no task materials. When escorted back to the work table, he jumps up and down, "sings" loudly, grabs the job coach's clothing, and will not let go.	Escape from planting task demand (negative reinforcement).	Functional communication. Tolerance for delayed reinforcement.

Table 3
Integration of the Five Intervention Components Across Sessions

Session number	Build rapport	Offer choices	Embed demands	Functional communication	Build tolerance for delay of rft
Bill					
1	Deliver rft noncontingently	Combine with embed demands	Offer choice prior to each step	"Break time" Prompt delay 0 sec Break 5 min	No delay of reinforcement
2	Add prompt for approach & request	same as 1	Offer choice prior to every two task steps	Prompt delay 1 sec Break 4 min	same as 1
3	same as 2	same as 1	Offer choice prior to every three task steps	Prompt delay 1 sec Break 3 min	same as 1
4	Rft on breaks only, discontinue prompts	same as 1	Offer choice prior to every four task steps	Prompt delay 2 sec then 3 sec Break 2 min	same as 1
5	same as 4	same as 1	Offer choice prior to every five task steps	Prompt delay 4 sec Break 2 min	same as 1
6	same as 4	same as 1	Offer choice prior to task step 1 only	Prompt delay 5 sec Break 2 min	same as 1
7	same as 4	same as 1	same as 6	No prompt Break 2 min	same as 1
8	same as 4	same as 1	same as 6	same as 7	Rft follow completion of one task step
9	same as 4	same as 1	same as 6	same as 7	Rft follow completion of two task steps
10–11	same as 4	same as 1	same as 6	same as 7	same as 9
Maggie					
1	not applicable	Prior to task steps 1 and 5	not applicable	"Help, please" Exaggerate cue Prompt delay 0 sec	No delay of reinforcement
2	not applicable	Continue for task step 1, fade duration for task step 5	not applicable	Whisper cue Prompt delay 0 sec	same as 1
3	not applicable	same as 2	not applicable	Shorten cue Prompt delay 0 sec	same as 1
4	not applicable	same as 2	not applicable	No cue Prompt delay 1 sec	same as 1
5	not applicable	Continue for task step 1 only	not applicable	No cue Prompt delay 2 then 3 sec	same as 1
6	not applicable	same as 5	not applicable	No cue Prompt delay 4 sec	same as 1
7	not applicable	same as 5	not applicable	No cue Prompt delay 5 sec	same as 1
8	not applicable	same as 5	not applicable	No cue No prompt	Rft follows one independent attempt
9–13	not applicable	same as 5	not applicable	same as 8	same as 8
Michael					
1	Deliver rft noncontingently	Combine with embed demands	Offer choice prior to each step	"Break time" Prompt delay 0 sec Break 5 min	No delay for reinforcement
2	Add prompt for approach & request	same as 1	Offer choice prior to every two task steps	Prompt delay 1 sec Break 4 min	same as 1
3	same as 2	same as 1	Offer choice prior to every three task steps	Prompt delay 2 then 3 sec Break 3 min	same as 1

Table 3—*Continued*

Session number	Build rapport	Offer choices	Embed demands	Functional communication	Build tolerance for delay of rft
4	Rft on breaks only, discontinue prompts	same as 1	Offer choice prior to every four task steps	Prompt delay 3 then 4 sec Break 2 min	same as 1
5	same as 4	same as 1	Offer choice prior to every five task steps	Prompt delay 5 sec Break 2 min	same as 1
6	same as 4	same as 1	Offer choice prior to task step 1 only	No prompt Break 2 min	same as 1
7	same as 4	same as 1	same as 6	same as 6	Rft follow completion of one task step
8	same as 4	same as 1	same as 6	same as 6	Rft follow completion of two task steps
9–13	same as 4	same as 1	same as 6	same as 6	same as 8

to an hypothesis-driven intervention model (Repp, Felce, & Barton, 1988; Repp & Karsh, 1990). The hypotheses may be categorized as either negative reinforcement, specifically escape from stimuli inferred to be aversive (e.g., task demands or physical prompts), or positive reinforcement, specifically tangible seeking (e.g., water hose or twine). An intervention with five basic components was derived that consisted of building rapport, offering choices, embedding demands, functional communication training, and building tolerance for delay of reinforcement.

Experimental design. The intervention was introduced in a multiple baseline design across employees with each employee receiving an increasingly greater number of baseline sessions (i.e., 28, 31, and 34 sessions).

Intervention. The job coach received an additional 8 hr of training from the first author prior to the implementation of the intervention. This training consisted of didactic instruction on the derivation and proper implementation of each intervention component. Additionally, role plays illustrating the most probable intervention scenarios for each employee were conducted. During the first five intervention sessions for each employee, the first author immediately prompted the job coach on the specific intervention component for a problem situation. In later sessions, the first author prompted the job coach only when she did not implement the proper intervention component within 5 sec of the occurrence of a problem situation. Once employees reached the criterion of 90% of planting steps completed in a session free of target problem behavior (sessions 7, 9, and 9 for Bill, Maggie, and Michael, respectively), no further prompts to the job coach were provided by the first author.

Two or three sessions were distributed across each workday. As noted previously, intervention took place in the training greenhouse only, and individuals were returned to the nearby day-service site upon comple-

tion of each session. Three criteria were used to terminate an intervention session, just as in baseline: (a) 15 min had elapsed; (b) all 10 steps of the planting sequence were completed; or (c) target problem behavior occurred.

For purposes of clarification, Table 3 presents a summary of how the five separate intervention components were integrated with one another across the various sessions of the study. We describe next the features of each intervention component.

One of our intervention components based on the hypotheses in Table 2 consisted of **rapport-building procedures.** Specifically, the first problem summaries for Bill and Michael described behaviors that occurred upon entering the greenhouse. Each individual was escorted to the worksite by familiar staff who then exited. Each entered the greenhouse and attempted to flee immediately after the job coach walked to the supply area where the work would begin. When prevented from leaving, each employee became aggressive. Although no task demands were yet presented, the environment included cues (i.e., the job coach and the task materials) that were associated with the tasks. Conceptually, these cues constituted conditioned aversive stimuli, because they had long been associated with the putatively aversive tasks. Importantly, when Bill and Michael were allowed to exit the greenhouse, they displayed no problem behavior. In sum, their pattern of aggression conformed to escape-motivated behavior in the presence of the conditioned aversive stimuli. One method for altering the conditioned aversiveness of stimuli is to pair them repeatedly with a wide variety of positive reinforcers. Pairing the job coach and task material cues with multiple positive reinforcers is operationally an example of establishing the formerly aversive conditioned stimuli as generalized reinforcers (Skinner, 1953, pp. 77–81), thereby undermining escape behavior and promoting approach behavior. Clinically, this procedure is referred to as establishing rapport. Thus, the job coach attempted to become a signal (discriminative stimulus) for the availability of multiple reinforcing events, that is, a generalized reinforcer (Carr et al., 1994). Specifically, the job coach was paired with (delivered) as great a variety of identified reinforcers as possible. A menu of reinforcers appropriate to the workplace was derived from the functional assessment interview. Reinforcers from this menu (e.g., a "high five," sharing a soda, or a joking interaction) were provided by the job coach. At first (intervention session 1), reinforcers were offered noncontingently. For Bill, whose identified reinforcers appeared more socially oriented, the job coach predominantly spent time talking about subjects of interest, joking, and making him laugh. For Michael, whose identified reinforcers appeared less socially oriented, the job coach provided food and tactile reinforcers (i.e., soda, a "high five," or a handshake). Although the specifics of rapport building (i.e., type of reinforcers used) varied across individuals according to personal preferences, the generic nature of this procedure (i.e., pairing the job coach with an array of reinforcers) was constant across the two employees. Next (intervention session 2), a contingency was added. Specifically, each employee was required to approach within an arm length of the job coach prior to receiving a reinforcer. The delivery of reinforcers was made contingent on the employee making requests using any preexisting form in his or her repertoire (i.e., leading by the hand, pointing, signing, or speech). Whenever 60 sec elapsed without a communication, the job coach prompted the employee to do so. Prompts for the preexisting communications were discontinued after session 3. Reinforcers for preexisting communication were given during breaks in activities only (see below). Maggie, unlike Bill and Michael, did not show problem behavior upon entering the greenhouse. Therefore, consistent with our strategy of deriving interventions from our assessment information, rapport building was not necessary for Maggie and, therefore, was not implemented in this context.

Choice-making was another intervention component developed from the hypotheses in Table 2. As described in her first problem summary in Table 2, Maggie often would pick up and use unneeded materials such as plant food, watering hoses, or staking twine. When prevented from doing so or when directed to stop using these items and return to planned activities, she would become self-injurious and aggressive. When allowed to continue to use these unneeded items, Maggie had no problem behavior. Her pattern of self-injury and aggression thus conformed to an hypothesis that conceptualized Maggie's problem behavior as tangibly motivated. Therefore, an intervention was needed that provided Maggie with access to the tangible reinforcers but did not interfere with task completion. We se-

lected choice making as the intervention, because it provided two advantages. First, clinicians and researchers have argued that permitting an individual to make choices of reinforcers and activities can increase desired responses while reducing disruptive problem behavior (Dunlap, Kern-Dunlap, Clarke, & Robbins, 1991; Houghton, Bronicki, & Guess, 1987; Koegel, Dyer, & Bell, 1987). Second, in the present case, choice making could be encouraged at times when it did not interfere with task performance. Thus, Maggie could not be offered the choice of which steps to perform, because all the steps of the planting sequence had to be completed. Additionally, the steps generally had to be completed in the order specified; therefore, she could not be given the choice of which step to perform next. The period between the steps of the planting sequence provided the only opportunity to offer choices. Most often in baseline, the tangible-related problem behavior took place before Maggie could complete step one. Therefore, choice making was implemented prior to gathering supplies for the planting task (step 1). Maggie was asked which items she would like first (i.e., planting sequence supplies or twine). If she failed to choose (verbally indicate) an item within 5 sec, she was offered the choice she had sought most often in the past (i.e., twine). Once Maggie had chosen (or accepted) the item, she was allowed to use it for 1 to 2 min before it was put away. Afterward, she was directed to the items not chosen (i.e., planting sequence supplies) and began the first step of the planting sequence. The same procedure was used prior to step 5 (pouring seeds and sand into holes), a time at which Maggie had the second highest frequency of tangible-related problem behavior. To increase production (percentage of planting steps completed), this second opportunity to make choices systematically was faded in subsequent sessions. Specifically, Maggie was allowed to use the chosen object for a period of time 30 sec shorter in duration than the session before (i.e., 1.5 min, 1 min, 0.5 min) until she was no longer offered the choice prior to step 5 (session 5).

The problem behavior just described for Maggie was motivated tangibly; thus, choice making related to specific tangible items sufficed as an intervention. In contrast, the second problem summaries for both Bill and Michael clearly indicated that their problem behavior, evoked by physical prompts, was likely escape motivated. The basis for this hypothesis was as follows. Bill and Michael typically ignored negative feedback and gestural prompts. (Recall that the job coach presented successive prompts after each prior prompt failed to evoke correct responding). Each individual continued incorrect responding or gave no response following negative feedback and gestural prompts. In contrast, physical prompting either stopped the incorrect responding or evoked a response if the employee was standing idle. Specifically, Bill's modal response to negative feedback and gestural prompts was to manipulate the planting materials incorrectly. No problem behavior was observed, however. In contrast, when given a physical prompt, he would pull away from the job coach, scream, jump up and down, and knock the planting materials to the floor. This pattern of behavior conformed to an escape hypothesis. Likewise, the modal response for Michael was to make an initial incorrect response and to stand still while negative feedback and gestural prompts were given. Again, no problem behavior was observed. When physically prompted, he would turn toward the job coach, grab her clothing, and attempt to hit her head with his head. Thus, for each of these employees, physical prompts were identified as stimuli controlling high rates of problem behavior in an escape paradigm.

As was the case with Maggie, we wanted to encourage Bill and Michael to make choices as well, but needed to do so using an intervention that addressed the issue of escape motivation just delineated. To accomplish this goal, we relied on research evidence demonstrating that **embedding** stimuli controlling high rates of problem behavior among stimuli controlling low (or zero) rates of problem behavior is an effective means for reducing escape motivated problem behavior (Carr, Newsom, & Binkoff, 1976; Horner, Day, Sprague, O'Brien, & Heathfield, 1991; Mace et al., 1988). Further, as described next, embedding is a procedure that easily can be combined with choice making to produce positive behavior change.

Identification of stimuli controlling low or zero rates of problem behavior was accomplished next. Among Bill's reinforcers identified on the functional assessment interview was manipulating or "sifting" soil between his hands. Further observation demonstrated that Bill would choose this activity consistently when presented with an array of identified reinforcers. Therefore, Bill was offered a choice between carrying out the task step or engaging in the preferred activity (i.e., sifting soil). He invariably chose to sift soil. His choice was then honored by his being allowed to sift soil for 1 to 2 min. At the end of this time period, the discriminative stimulus for step 1 (materials present on supply table and saying "Let's get our supplies") was given. Before beginning step 2, Bill again was provided with an opportunity to make the choice. This sequence was repeated until all steps were completed or the 15-min time allotment expired. Among Michael's reinforcers identified on the functional assessment interview were tapping pens against tables and flipping through playing cards. Direct observation showed that Michael would spend more time engaged in this activity than in any other when presented with an array of identified reinforcers. Therefore, the procedure just described for Bill was repeated for Michael with tapping pens and flipping cards as the preferred activity. To illustrate, a stack of plant labels (that Michael could

flip in the manner of playing cards) and grease pencils (that he could tap) were placed near the work table. The discriminative stimulus for step 1 was given after Michael had engaged in manipulating these objects for 1 to 2 min. Before beginning step 2, Michael again was provided with an opportunity to make the choice. This sequence was repeated until all steps were completed or the 15-min time allotment expired. To increase production, the ratio of low probability of problem behavior activities (i.e., preferred activities) to high probability of problem behavior activities (i.e., task steps) was decreased systematically in subsequent sessions. Specifically, preferred activities were presented before every two task steps (session 2), then before every three task steps (session 3), until preferred activities were presented only prior to step 1(session 6).

Although the specifics of the choice-making procedure (used in combination with embedding for Bill and Michael and alone for Maggie) varied across individuals according to personal preferences (i.e., different activities were preferred by each individual), the generic nature of this procedure (i.e., offering each employee an opportunity to choose between activities) was constant across the three employees.

Functional communication training was a fourth intervention component developed from the hypotheses in Table 2. The third problem summaries for Bill and Michael described sessions during which each employee left the work area after being given the discriminative stimulus for a planting step. This escape behavior occurred during the task rather than before the task sequence was initiated. Significantly, neither employee left the greenhouse itself. Nor did they seek out objects or activities in the greenhouse. Instead, each employee moved away from the job coach to an area of the greenhouse that had no planting materials. No problem behavior was observed. In contrast, when escorted back to the work table and again presented with the demand, each employee became aggressive. This pattern led us to hypothesize that the function of the aggressive behavior was to escape from the planting task demands per se, rather than from the conditioned aversive stimuli (i.e., job coach and task materials) identified in the first problem summaries for Bill and Michael. Bill and Michael especially were likely to become aggressive after many demands had been presented to them, raising the possibility that fatigue and/or boredom may have been a factor. Functionally, then, their aggressive behavior provided them with a break from the demands of the planting task. Therefore, one plausible intervention would be to provide them with an alternative means for securing a break, specifically, a behavior that served the same function as the aggression.

Teaching communicative behaviors that are functionally equivalent (i.e., maintained by the same reinforcers) to the problem behavior (e.g., accessing a break from activities by saying "I want a break" rather than running and aggressing) has been demonstrated to remediate the problem behavior (Bird, Dores, Moniz, & Robinson, 1989; Carr & Durand, 1985; Wacker et al., 1990). A symbol labeled "break time" that depicted a clock broken into two pieces was chosen for Bill and Michael to use to request a break. After receiving several reinforcers in the first session of the intervention (per rapport building), Bill and Michael were given "break time" picture communication symbols. These were attached to their shirts. The job coach was wearing the "break time" picture communication symbol as well. Each employee was told, "point here for a break," as the response was modeled by the job coach. As each employee completed a planting step, he was asked if he would like to take a break, and given an immediate modeling prompt to touch the "break time" picture communication symbol. The request (i.e., imitation of the modeling prompt) was honored immediately and he or she was escorted to the break area. The break area consisted of a section of the greenhouse where chairs were available and no planting materials were present. For this initial intervention session, breaks of 5 min were provided. Recall that rapport building consisted of sharing food and joking interactions with the job coach. These procedures were implemented in the break area as well. To increase production in later intervention sessions, the duration of the break provided was decreased by 1 min per session until a period of 2 min was reached (session 4 and all subsequent sessions). Similarly, modeling prompts were faded with a prompt delay procedure in which each employee's successful request (i.e., imitation of the modeled response) was followed by an increasingly longer delay of the modeling prompt on subsequent trials. Specifically, in session 1, modeling prompts were immediate. In session 2, a 1-sec prompt delay was added following three successful requests in succession. The delay was increased in this manner until a 5-sec prompt delay was reached (sessions 5 and 6 for Michael and Bill, respectively). For subsequent sessions, all prompts for break requests were discontinued (sessions 6 and 7 for Michael and Bill, respectively) and only spontaneous requests for breaks were honored.

For Maggie, functional communication consisted of slightly different procedures to address the specific circumstances described in her second problem summary. As noted in the summary, her modal problem behavior occurred after negative feedback (i.e., the initial prompt for an incorrect response). Maggie would respond reliably to this situation with self-injurious behavior. Thus, she was removed from the jobsite before any corrective instruction could take place. In contrast, when she completed the task correctly and, therefore, received no negative feedback, she did not display any problem behavior. In other

words, her problem behavior was not a response to fatigue or boredom following many demands (as presumably was the case with Bill and Michael), but rather, to negative feedback per se. This pattern conformed to an escape hypothesis; that is, problem behavior was maintained by escape from negative feedback. In this case, a plausible intervention would consist of providing Maggie with an alternative means of responding to negative feedback. A communication-based intervention model would suggest that negative feedback should be made into a discriminative stimulus for seeking assistance. Now, negative feedback would evoke requesting assistance rather than self-injurious behavior (Carr et al., 1994). Therefore, functional communication training for Maggie consisted of teaching her to request assistance. As Maggie was reported to speak in short articulate phrases, she was taught to say, "Help, please." The job coach provided a verbal cue for Maggie to imitate, because Maggie often was observed to repeat the last word spoken to her. In the first session of the intervention, Maggie was instructed, "If you make a mistake, ask for help." Immediately following each incorrect response and negative feedback, the job coach verbally prompted Maggie to ask for help. If Maggie did not make a request within 5 sec, the job coach provided the cue, "Say, 'help, please.' " Maggie's request for assistance was followed immediately by the standard sequence of prompts. The cues ("ask for help" and "say, 'help, please' ") were faded systematically in later sessions. Maggie responded consistently to the first verbal cue ("ask for help") after the first intervention session, making the second verbal cue ("say, 'help, please' ") unnecessary. The verbal cue was first faded in volume (i.e., from an exaggerated tone of voice to a whisper) and then in length (i.e., from "ask for help" to "ask . . ."). Then, a prompt delay procedure was carried out in which her successful request was followed by an increasingly longer delay of the cue on subsequent trials. Specifically, in session 1, the cue was exaggerated. In session 2, after three successful requests in succession, the cue was whispered. In session 3, after three successful requests in succession, the cue was shortened. Further, the cue was faded with a prompt delay procedure in which her successful request was followed by an increasingly longer delay of the cue on subsequent trials. In sessions 1–3, the cue was provided immediately. In session 4, a 1-sec prompt delay was added after three successful requests in succession. The delay was increased in this manner until a 5-sec prompt delay was reached (session 7). For subsequent sessions, cues were discontinued and only spontaneous requests for help were honored.

Again, as was the case for the previously described intervention components, although the specifics of functional communication training varied across employees (i.e., different types of requests were taught depending on the assessment information), the generic nature of functional communication training (i.e., teaching requests that were functionally equivalent to problem behavior) was constant across the three employees.

Building tolerance for delay of reinforcement was the final intervention component developed based on the hypotheses generated in Table 2. These procedures followed functional communication training in all cases, and were initiated after each employee was requesting spontaneously (i.e., "break" or "help"). Research has suggested that it is useful to delay contingencies and use thin schedules of reinforcement to produce generalized appropriate responding (Carr et al., 1994; Durand, 1990). Pilot observations in the present study suggested that providing immediate reinforcement for all requests for breaks would have led eventually to a session with no work accomplished and entirely composed of breaks. Similarly, providing immediate reinforcement for all requests for "help" would have led to no learning about the job, rather, a total dependence on the supervision of the job coach. These potential problem situations fostered by functional communication training were avoided by creating a delay of reinforcement. Specifically, the response to some requests was an instruction rather than a reinforcer. In the first case, the request for "break time" was met with an instruction to complete a planting step (e.g., "Sure, Michael, you can have a break as soon as you water the soil"). The delay between the request for "break time" and honoring that request (i.e., taking a break) was the time taken to complete the planting step. In the second case, involving a request for "help," a similar system was implemented. Once Maggie performed a task step without prompting for five consecutive sessions, subsequent assistance was delayed. Specifically, her request for "help" on the task steps for which she had demonstrated independence was met with an instruction to attempt that planting step again prior to receiving assistance (e.g., "Sure I'll help you, Maggie, but you try mixing the sand again"). The delay between the request for "help" and honoring that request (i.e., receiving assistance) was the time taken to attempt the planting step again. For task steps that were not yet performed independently (i.e., steps with fewer than five consecutive sessions without prompting), the standard sequence of prompts continued. These delay of reinforcement procedures were initiated in intervention sessions 8, 8, and 7 for Bill, Maggie, and Michael, respectively. Two planting steps were required in all subsequent sessions in which requests for breaks were made (i.e., starting from sessions 9 and 8 for Bill and Michael, respectively). No further attempt was made to reduce Maggie's dependence on supervision, because completion of steps rather than independence per se was the focus of this study.

Withdrawal of feedback to job coach. This phase followed the intervention. Two or three sessions were distributed across each workday as in baseline and intervention. Again, three sessions were conducted by the job coach in the generalization greenhouse for comparison. Each session was conducted using the same 10-step task analysis, discriminative stimuli, sequence of prompts, and termination criteria used in baseline. The difference from the intervention phase was that the job coach now implemented the intervention components independently. She received no prompts or feedback from the first author. All components of the intervention remained in effect.

Social validity. The social validity questionnaire shown in Table 4 was administered to the greenhouse managers to assess employers' perceptions of the outcome of the present intervention. Both managers were asked to complete ratings on this five-item seven-point Likert-type questionnaire at the end of the baseline and feedback withdrawal phases. The questions provided measures of the employers' perceptions of problem behavior severity and its impact on the social environment.

Clinical extension. Programmatic efforts continued after the outcomes of the intervention were validated by the greenhouse managers. Additional sessions were conducted by the job coach in the generalization greenhouse and were distributed across each workday as before. The job coach continued to implement the intervention components independently and all components of the intervention remained in effect. Additionally, the job coach trained the regular greenhouse employees in the implementation of the intervention. This training took place during phases 1 through 10 of the clinical extension. Shared supervision had become a practical necessity, considering the large number of hours per day that each of the three employees now worked. During phases 11 through 16 of the clinical extension, the job coach gradually reduced her supervisory time and the regular greenhouse employees gradually increased theirs so that by the 17th phase of the clinical extension and continuing to the 31st and final phase, the job coach was supervising only one third of the time and the regular employees, two thirds of the time.

Initially (first clinical phase), sessions were conducted using the same 10-step task analysis, discriminative stimuli, and sequence of prompts used throughout the study. The termination criteria were changed such that completing a single work sequence no longer ended a session. Instead, each employee was required to work for the entire 15 min. The occurrence of target problem behavior terminated sessions as before. A mastery criterion of completing five consecutive sessions without the occurrence of target problem behavior was established for each clinical phase.

Table 4
Social Validity Data for Greenhouse Mangers

	Manager	Bill Pre	Bill Post	Maggie Pre	Maggie Post	Michael Pre	Michael Post
1. I am confident that the job coach can control the employee's behavior.	1	2	6	2	6	1	6
	2	3	6	2	7	2	6
	Mean	2.5	6.0	2.0	6.5	1.5	6.0
2. I am confident that my coworkers are safe from harm.	1	3	7	4	7	2	7
	2	3	7	3	7	2	7
	Mean	3.0	7.0	3.5	7.0	2.0	7.0
3. I am confident that the greenhouse property is safe from harm.	1	2	6	3	7	4	7
	2	1	6	3	7	3	7
	Mean	1.5	6.0	3.0	7.0	3.5	7.0
4. The employee's behavior in the greenhouse is severe.	1	6	2	6	1	7	2
	2	6	1	5	1	6	1
	Mean	6.0	1.5	5.5	1.0	6.5	1.5
5. The employee could make a productive contribution to the greenhouse.	1	3	6	2	6	2	6
	2	2	5	3	6	2	5
	Mean	2.5	5.5	2.5	6.0	2.0	5.5

Note. Each question was rated on a 7-point scale. 7 = very much/always, 4 = somewhat/sometimes, and 1 = not at all/never.

For the second clinical phase, a 6-step bulb-planting sequence (i.e., task analysis) was added. Each employee worked with the original planting sequence as well as the bulb planting sequence until 15 min elapsed. For the third phase, an additional 15 min was added. Each employee worked with both planting sequences until 30 min elapsed. This pattern of alternately increasing the number of work sequences and the duration of the work session continued until each employee completed 10 4-hr work sessions that included 15 of the 18 additional work sequences listed in Table 5. The specific 15 additional work sequences chosen were not the same for each individual. Ultimately, the procedure resulted in a total of 31 clinical phases (Table 6). At a minimum of five work sessions per week, these sessions met the regulations set forth by the Developmental Disabilities Act of 1984 (P.L. 98-527) and the subsequent Rehabilitation Act Amendments of 1986 (P.L. 99-506) regarding half-time employment.

Table 5
Tasks Used for Greenhouse Work Activities During the Clinical Extension

1. Bulb planting
2. Composting
3. Flower drying
4. Flower wreath making
5. Foliar feeding
6. Foliar spray/sprayer preparation
7. Garden planting in straight rows
8. Garden preparation/sod removal
9. Hanging baskets: Wiring and planting
10. Making potpourri
11. Mulching/laying ground cover
12. Preparing multicell packs
13. Root cuttings
14. Seed planting on the surface
15. Transplanting mature plants
16. Transplanting seed packs
17. Watering: Indoors/outdoors
18. Weeding

Note: These tasks were in addition to the original seed planting task.

Response Recording and Reliability

Percentage of work steps completed and latency to target problem behavior served as the two dependent variables. Percentage of work steps completed was defined as the number of steps completed correctly prior to session termination multiplied by 100. (Recall that there were 10 steps in the planting sequence). Latency was defined as the amount of time that elapsed between the employee entering the greenhouse and (a) the first occurrence of aggression or property destruction to glass, (b) the third occurrence of self-injurious behavior, tantrums, or nonglass property destruction, or (c) the successful completion of the planting sequence in the absence of target problem behavior. Additionally, the occurrences of self-injurious behavior, tantrums, or nonglass property destruction that did not lead to session termination (i.e., two or fewer) were tallied. An index of mastery of the planting sequence was provided as an ancillary measure. Prompts (i.e., negative feedback, gestural prompt, physical prompt) were recorded for each step and were summarized as the percentage of steps prompted. Definitions of target problem behavior, termination criteria, and prompts were given earlier in the text.

The first author served as the primary observer. An undergraduate also employed in the field of developmental disabilities served as the reliability observer. Each observer was positioned between 1 m and 3 m from the employee. Each observer held a stopwatch

Table 6
Clinical Extension for Bill/Maggie/Michael, Respectively

Clinical phase	Session duration	Number of tasks	Total sessions per phase*	Sessions terminated because of problem behavior*	Average task steps completed per session*
1	15 min	1	5/5/5	0/0/0	23/29/17
2	15 min	2	5/5/5	0/0/0	29/32/25
3	30 min	2	5/5/5	0/0/0	55/77/31
4	30 min	3	5/5/5	0/0/0	57/81/33
5	45 min	3	5/5/5	0/0/0	78/122/60
6	45 min	4	5/5/5	0/0/0	92/128/64
7	60 min	4	5/5/5	0/0/0	115/149/75
8	60 min	5	5/5/5	0/0/0	121/157/77
9	75 min	5	5/5/5	0/0/0	143/159/90
10	75 min	6	5/5/5	0/0/0	144/182/92
11	90 min	6	5/7/5	0/1/0	182/166/120
12	90 min	7	5/5/5	0/0/0	189/193/123
13	105 min	7	5/5/5	0/0/0	208/234/145
14	105 min	8	5/8/5	0/1/0	212/189/153
15	120 min	8	5/5/5	0/0/0	262/221/187
16	120 min	9	5/5/5	0/0/0	277/230/198
17	135 min	9	5/5/5	0/0/0	316/278/204
18	135 min	10	9/5/5	1/0/0	225/283/227
19	150 min	10	5/5/5	0/0/0	346/326/255
20	150 min	11	5/5/5	0/0/0	356/328/268
21	165 min	11	5/5/5	0/0/0	371/356/322
22	165 min	12	5/5/5	0/0/0	374/378/349
23	180 min	12	5/5/6	0/0/1	414/421/338
24	180 min	13	5/5/5	0/0/0	428/423/378
25	195 min	13	5/5/5	0/0/0	467/464/403
26	195 min	14	5/5/5	0/0/0	485/489/420
27	210 min	14	5/5/5	0/0/0	515/532/457
28	210 min	15	5/5/5	0/0/0	527/527/476
29	225 min	15	5/5/5	0/0/0	558/562/511
30	225 min	16	5/5/5	0/0/0	569/577/526
31	240 min	16	10/10/10	0/0/0	598/626/572

Note: Number of tasks includes the original seed planting task.
*Multiple numbers refer to data for Bill, Maggie, and Michael, respectively.

and data collection sheet behind a clipboard to minimize influencing one another.

Reliability was assessed on 45%, 43%, and 43% of the sessions throughout the present study for Bill, Maggie, and Michael, respectively. Reliability was scored either as perfect agreement or no agreement on all measures. If the two observers recorded the same number of steps completed, perfect agreement was scored. If the two observers scored latencies with a difference of 5 sec or less, perfect agreement was scored. For the ancillary measure, if the two observers recorded the same prompt(s) on the same step, perfect agreement was scored. With respect to percentage of steps completed, the percentage of sessions with perfect agreement was 96% for Bill, 95% for Maggie, and 97% for Michael. With respect to latency to problem behavior, the percentage of sessions with perfect agreement was 94% for Bill, 98% for Maggie, and 96% for Michael. For the ancillary measure of prompted steps, the percentage of sessions with perfect agreement were 92% for Bill, 93% for Maggie, and 90% for Michael.

For the clinical extension, a reliability session consisted of randomly selected 15-min time periods during which the two observers took data on steps completed and the presence or absence of problem behavior. Thus, for clinical phases one and two, reliability was based on the entire session. In contrast, for phases 3 through 31 (which were longer than 15 min), reliability consisted of only a sample of the entire session. Reliability was computed on 35% of the 15-min samples cumulated across the 31 clinical phases. There were only four instances of target problem behavior terminating sessions across the 31 clinical phases (1 each for Bill and Michael; 2 for Maggie) and the reliability was 100%. Reliability for total task steps completed was 93%, 87%, and 92% for Bill, Maggie, and Michael, respectively.

Results

Figure 1 shows the latency to problem behavior requiring session termination (black histograms) or the latency to successful completion of the planting sequence (diagonal histograms) as well as the percent steps completed for the three employees during the baseline, intervention, feedback withdrawal, and generalization phases of the study (i.e., for the original

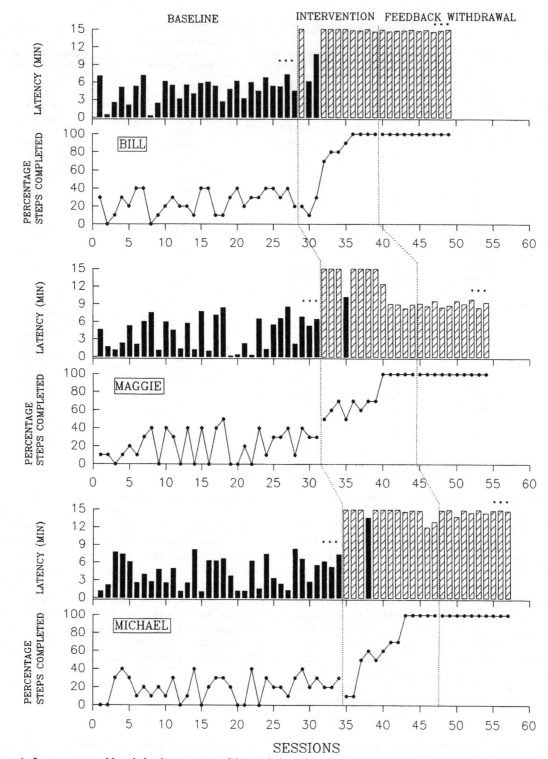

Figure 1. Latency to problem behavior or successful completion of work and percentage of steps completed for the three employees during the baseline, intervention, and feedback withdrawal phases of the study. For latency, the abscissa is recessed slightly to make brief duration sessions more visible. The black histograms denote sessions terminated because of problem behavior. The diagonal histograms denote sessions in which the planting sequence was conducted without the need to terminate because of problem behavior. The asterisks above the histograms denote sessions conducted in the generalization greenhouse.

seed planting task). The mean latency to problem behavior (black histograms) increased from the baseline level immediately after the intervention was introduced in a sequential (i.e., multiple baseline) pattern across the three employees. Target problem behavior did not occur in the feedback withdrawal phase. All baseline sessions for all employees were terminated because of problem behavior. The mean latency to problem behavior was 4 min 38 sec (range, 0 min 16 sec to 7 min 20 sec) for Bill, 4 min 8 sec (range, 0 min 11 sec to 8 min 33 sec) for Maggie, and 4 min 21 sec (range, 1 min 3 sec to 8 min 19 sec) for Michael. During the intervention, Bill had two sessions terminated due to problem behavior, one after 6 min 6 sec and the other after 10 min 47 sec. Maggie and Michael each had a single session during intervention terminated for problem behavior after 10 min 13 sec and 13 min 37 sec respectively. The data from the generalization greenhouse (asterisks) show the same pattern seen in the training greenhouse, namely, dramatic increases in latency and percent steps completed from baseline to feedback withdrawal.

The diagonal histograms represent the mean latency to completion of the planting sequence without the need to terminate for problem behavior. Completed sessions were absent in baseline for all three employees. In contrast, during intervention, completed sessions accounted for 82%, 92%, and 92% of the sessions for Bill, Maggie, and Michael, respectively. All sessions for all employees were completed in the feedback withdrawal phase. In this phase, the mean time to task completion for Bill was 14 min 47 sec for Maggie was 9 min 2 sec, and for Michael was 14 min 40 sec.

All employees also displayed an increase in the percentage of steps completed from baseline through the intervention to the feedback withdrawal phase. The criterion for ending the intervention phase of the study was 90% or more steps completed for five consecutive sessions. Bill reached criterion in 11 sessions; Maggie, in 13 sessions; and Michael, in 13 sessions. The total training time required across sessions to reach criterion was 151 min 53 sec for Bill; 162 min 52 sec for Maggie; and 188 min 30 sec for Michael. The mean percentage of steps completed by Bill increased from a baseline level of 25% (range, 0% to 40%) to a feedback withdrawal level of 100%. The mean percentage of steps completed by Maggie increased from baseline level of 21% (range, 0% to 50%) to a feedback withdrawal level of 100%. The mean percentage of steps completed by Michael increased from a baseline level of 19% (range, 0% to 40%) to a feedback withdrawal level of 100%.

Recall that the number of less serious problem behaviors in sessions that were not terminated was also tallied (i.e., self-injurious behavior, tantrums, or nonglass property destruction). The data showed that problem behavior in these sessions was extremely rare

following intervention. Specifically, in the feedback withdrawal phase, Bill displayed a mean of 0.2 problem behaviors per session; Maggie displayed a mean of 0.4 problem behaviors per session; and Michael displayed a mean of 0.1 problem behaviors per session.

The ancillary measure of task mastery was the percentage of steps in the planting sequence that had to be prompted by the job coach. The mean percentages of steps prompted in baseline, intervention, and feedback withdrawal were compared. Across the three employees, there was a consistent pattern of increasing independence from prompts as the study progressed. The percentages of prompts needed during baseline, intervention, and feedback withdrawal respectively were 97%, 85%, and 49% for Bill; 95%, 43%, and 12% for Maggie; and 98%, 76%, and 57% for Michael.

The social validity outcomes reported in Table 4 corroborate the data reported in Figure 1. The managers reported little confidence that the job coach could control the employees' behavior in baseline. They reported near total confidence at the end of the feedback withdrawal phase. Again, the managers reported little confidence that the other workers were safe from harm in baseline and reported total confidence in co-worker safety at the end of the feedback withdrawal phase. Similarly, the managers reported little confidence that the property was safe in baseline and reported near total confidence at the end of the feedback withdrawal phase. The managers reported that they found the employees' behavior to be nearly always severe in baseline and almost never severe in the feedback withdrawal phase. Finally, in baseline, the managers reported little or no production by the employees. Following intervention, the employees were reported to be able to make a productive contribution nearly always.

The clinical extension illustrated a strategy for developing initial success into half-time employment. The results of each clinical phase are listed in Table 6. At the conclusion of the clinical extension of the present study, each employee demonstrated the ability to work for 4 hr and to carry out 15 of the 18 additional greenhouse-related tasks. By the end, the employees completed an average of 598, 626, and 572 task steps per session for Bill, Maggie, and Michael, respectively. An interesting anecdotal observation was that the regular greenhouse employees began to use elements of the intervention to promote prosocial behavior among the other workers with disabilities who were employed in the greenhouse but who were not participants in this study. This observation suggests that the intervention strategies were generally acceptable to the regular greenhouse staff.

Discussion

All three employees were able to complete a planting sequence in a community greenhouse with no significant problem behavior following a multicomponent intervention. These positive results were achieved after a short period of training that varied from approximately 2½ to 3 hr across the three employees. Percentage of steps completed was demonstrated to be a sensitive measure of progress that changed predictably as a function of the intervention. Similarly, the latency measures proved to be highly responsive to intervention conditions. The positive outcomes in Figure 1 were corroborated by the social validity data in Table 4. Specifically, by the end of the study, the greenhouse managers reported considerable confidence in the job coach's ability to deal with any behavior difficulties, keeping both coworkers and property safe from harm. Additionally, the managers reported a perception that problem behavior was almost never severe following intervention, and acknowledged the employees as productive members of the greenhouse team. Importantly, the clinical extension demonstrated that the initial effects were not limited to brief sessions involving 10 steps on one task. Instead, by the end of the study, the method described enabled individuals to work for 4 hr at a time (half-time employment), a level of engagement set forth as the standard by the Development Disabilities Act of 1984 and the Rehabilitation Act Amendments of 1986. Our original plan was to have the three individuals hired by the greenhouse; however, budget cuts made that impossible. Nonetheless, because of their prior success, the individuals subsequently were hired to do other jobs in the community including landscaping and door-to-door advertising involving leaflet distribution.

This study focused on providing a desirable intervention outcome (i.e., completion of work without significant problem behavior) rather than on examining the multicomponent intervention to determine which elements were necessary. It is possible, therefore, that another combination of interventions would have produced similar if not better results. It also is possible that not every component of the package was needed for each employee. These are worthwhile research questions. At present, it has been demonstrated that the package produced the desired outcome. Further, each element of the package had an empirical and a clinical basis as reported in the published literature. Finally, each component was tied logically to hypotheses concerning the variables maintaining problem behavior delineated in Table 2.

The intervention procedures per se were not complex. As noted before, they have been reported widely in the literature and have been carried out by many service providers. At first glance, the combination of interventions may appear complex, but as Table 3 shows, it is possible to structure them in an organized format that job coaches, already trained to use the component interventions, can plausibly follow and implement, just as ours did.

A number of issues come to the fore as the logical ties between assessment and intervention are examined. First, a limited number of reasonable interventions could be derived from any given hypothesis. Thus, if a negative reinforcement hypothesis is put forth, functional communication training may focus on teaching the individual to request a break or assistance. Teaching the individual to request attention or a desired item would not be reasonable. Second strategies for intervention in the "real world" depend on (a) the specific detailed antecedent conditions (i.e., interpersonal context); (b) the constraints of the environment (i.e., a community-based jobsite including contact with customers); (c) necessary outcomes (i.e., production); and (d) identification of the variables maintaining the problem behavior (i.e., functional assessment). Selection of interventions is based on the specific details of the problem situation in question and comparisons of interventions demonstrated to be effective in the published literature. No individual study is sufficient to examine these decision rules. General guidelines are likely to emerge only after a program of research studies has been carried out.

The primary goal of this study was to have employees who had been excluded from working in the community complete a community-based job task without exhibiting the severe problem behavior that originally had led to their exclusion. This goal was met. In contrast, as noted earlier, the major goals of previous studies were cost-benefit analyses, implementation of the supported work model, conversion from sheltered employment to supported employment, increasing productivity and establishing job-related social skills. Remediation of severe problem behavior was not a focus of these previous studies; rather, reducing support was the major focus (i.e., demonstrating skills independent of support staff). In addition to eliminating severe problem behavior, this study demonstrated consistent reduction of staff support (i.e., percentage of steps requiring negative feedback, gestural prompts, and physical prompts). The relatively short training period required to reach criterion (i.e., 2½ to 3 hr) suggested that each employee already had some level of planting skills in their repertoire. Indeed, baseline observation suggested that severe problem behavior interfered with the exhibition of these skills. Relatedly, the positive support provided through the intervention enabled the employees to remain in the learning environment for longer periods of time, resulting in increased exposure to the available instruction and, consequently, improved performance.

The ultimate goal of community-based instruction is that naturally occurring stimuli will evoke correct responding rather than stimuli provided by the instructor (i.e., requests, prompts) (Snell & Browder, 1986). A key element of a supported employment program is the fading of the job coach's presence as tasks are mastered by the employee (Nisbet & Hagner, 1988). One strategy for reaching this goal is for instructor prompts initially used to cue correct responding to be faded through delay of prompting. In this study, virtually all of the planting steps were prompted in baseline (i.e., 97%, 95%, and 98%). Instructor prompts were faded, so that each employee received a substantially lesser percentage of prompts following intervention (i.e., 49%, 12%, and 57%). This outcome represents a success, because the job coach was now spending considerably less time training (i.e., providing negative feedback, gestural, and physical prompts) than was the case in baseline. Anecdotally, the consistent pattern of decreasing instructor prompts was also observed throughout the clinical extension. Thus, the progressive decrease in training time continued throughout this phase of the study. A related point comes from observations made of the co-workers with developmental disabilities who did not exhibit problem behavior. We observed, anecdotally, that the percentage of steps prompted for them was the same or greater than that for the employees of the present study. This fact, too, is a measure of success in that we reduced training time for the individuals with severe problem behavior to a level commensurate with that of their peers who did not display such behavior.

Community-based research on severe problem behavior raises the issue of the impact of that behavior on the instructor, members of the community, and community property. Baselines of severe problem behavior when measured using frequency of occurrence are typically kept as short as possible. In the present study, however, long baselines were necessary to ensure that all possible problem situations were examined. Had a measure of frequency been chosen for the 15-min work period, severe problem behavior (i.e., headbutting, slapping, and biting others; hitting one's own head; knocking pots to the floor) would have made baseline dangerous, if not impossible, to conduct. This concern was ameliorated by the choice to measure latency to problem behavior. The latency measure offered several benefits. First, the number of severe behavior crisis situations requiring the job coach to intervene physically were reduced greatly from the number anticipated using a frequency measure of problem behavior. Second, the relative reduction in severe problem behavior encountered allowed the baseline to be sustained until a consistent pattern of problem situations could be identified. Finally, because job placement may be terminated for a single occurrence of severe problem behavior, the latency measure provided an index of the duration for which an employee could work. This is a primary goal of supported employment.

Additional changes in traditional research methods appear necessary in meeting the challenges posed by community-based research. Traditional functional analyses reported in the published literature have consisted of systematic manipulations of maintaining variables to make direct observations of their effect on the behavior in question. Often environmental conditions are presented repeatedly or alternated to examine the consistency of the behavior changes that occur. The extensive effort required by this method has been an obstacle to its use in applied settings. This study would require eight separate functional analyses to produce empirical evidence on the role of the variables identified in Table 2. The practical considerations of conducting these analyses in a community greenhouse were prohibitive. Researchers have identified three strategies useful in examining behavior patterns (i.e., providing a functional assessment of behavior, Carr et al., 1994; O'Neill et al., 1990). These strategies are: (a) conduct interviews with the best informants available; (b) make direct observations of a variety of stimulus conditions; and (c) verify the behavior pattern predicted through systematic manipulations. The systematic manipulations are, in effect, a test of the predicted patterns (hypotheses). In this study, these strategies were integrated into an hypothesis-driven model. As noted above, the empirical support derived from previously published functional analyses was used in combination with the particulars of the present environment to develop the intervention. The first two strategies of functional assessment (i.e., interview and direct observation) were conducted in this study. The third strategy of testing hypotheses was conducted in a different manner, namely, intervention derived from the hypotheses was tested through implementation. As the intervention was successful in eliminating target problem behavior, the results of this test are said to be consistent with the hypotheses proposed. Intervention failure would have required further analysis. The third strategy of systematic manipulation (i.e., traditional functional analysis) would have been necessary in this case.

Identification of the causes of job termination remains a critical goal of vocational special education (Gaylord-Ross, 1990; Hanley-Maxwell et al., 1986). The present investigation demonstrates that an hypothesis-driven multicomponent intervention approach can be effective in at least one setting in which severe problem behavior leads to job termination. There remains the issue of the generality of these findings across employment settings. For example, some settings require a higher level of social interaction than would a greenhouse. Thus, stocking shelves in a supermarket not only involves the stocking task itself, but also the necessity of providing information to customers who may approach the employee to ask questions regarding item location and price. In this instance, other intervention components centering on the development of social interaction skills would be required for successful job adjustment.

The impracticality of conducting numerous functional analyses on the jobsite need not prohibit examination of severe problem behavior. An hypothesis-driven approach may provide sufficient documentation of the functional relationships between environment and behavior. As suggested by the present study, two major benefits may result from this application of applied behavior analysis in community employment settings. First, employees with developmental disabilities who have acquired jobs, then exhibit job-threatening behavior, can receive intervention on the jobsite and, thereby, retain the job. Second, employees with developmental disabilities who have been excluded from employment experiences can acquire jobs without the need to intervene on problem behavior beforehand. Rather, education relevant to job skills and intervention for problem behavior can occur simultaneously. These applications of applied behavior analysis may be crucial to the achievement of the goals of supported employment.

References

Bird, F., Dores, P. A., Moniz, D., & Robinson, J. (1989). Reducing severe aggressive and self-injurious behaviors with functional communication training. *American Journal on Mental Retardation, 94,* 37–48.

Carr, E. G., & Carlson, J. I. (1993). Reduction of severe behavior problems in the community using a multicomponent treatment approach. *Journal of Applied Behavior Analysis, 26,* 157–172.

Carr, E. G., & Durand, V. M. (1985). Reducing behavior problems through functional communication training. *Journal of Applied Behavior Analysis, 18,* 111–126.

Carr, E. G., Levin, L., McConnachie, G., Carlson, J. I., Kemp, D. C., & Smith, C. E. (1994). *Communication-based intervention for problem behavior: A user's guide for producing positive change.* Baltimore, MD: Paul H. Brookes.

Carr, E. G., Newsom, C. D., & Binkoff, J. A. (1976). Stimulus control of self-destructive behavior in a psychotic child. *Journal of Abnormal Child Psychology, 4,* 139–153.

Carr, E. G., Robinson, S., Taylor, J. C., & Carlson, J. I. (1990). Positive approaches to the treatment of severe behavior problems in persons with developmental disabilities: A review and analysis of reinforcement and stimulus-based procedures. *Monograph of The Association for Persons with Severe Handicaps, 4.*

Dunlap, G., Kern-Dunlap, L., Clarke, S., & Robbins, F. R. (1991). Functional assessment, curricular revision, and severe behavior problems. *Journal of Applied Behavior Analysis, 24,* 387–397.

Durand, V. M. (1990). *Severe behavior problems: A functional communication training approach.* New York: Guilford Press.

Durand, V. M., & Kishi, G. (1987). Reducing severe behavior problems among persons with dual sensory impairments: An evaluation of a technical assistance model. *Journal of The Association for Persons with Severe Handicaps, 12,* 2–10.

Federal Register. (1984). Developmental Disabilities Act of 1984. Report 98-527, Section 102 (11) (F).

Federal Register. (1986). Rehabilitation Act Amendments of 1986. Report 99-506, Section 103 (I).

Gaylord-Ross, R. (1990). Introduction to supported employment issues. In F. R. Rusch (Ed.), *Supported employment: Models, methods, and issues* (pp. 247–250). Sycamore, IL: Sycamore.

Hanley-Maxwell, C., Rusch, F. R., Chadsey-Rusch, J., & Renzaglia, A. (1986). Factors contributing to job termination. *Journal of The Association for Persons with Severe Handicaps, 11,* 45–52.

Haring, T. G., & Kennedy, C. H. (1988). Units of analysis in task-analytic research. *Journal of Applied Behavior Analysis, 21,* 207–215.

Haring, T. G., & Kennedy, C. H. (1990). Contextual control of problem behavior in students with severe disabilities. *Journal of Applied Behavior Analysis, 23,* 235–243.

Hill, M. L., Wehman, P. H., Kregel, J., Banks, P. D., & Metzler, H. M. D. (1987). Employment outcomes for people with moderate and severe disabilities: An eight-year longitudinal analysis of supported competitive employment. *Journal of The Association of Persons with Severe Handicaps, 3,* 182–189.

Horner, R. H., Day, H. M., Sprague, J. R., O'Brien, M., & Heathfield, L. T. (1991). Interspersed requests: A nonaversive procedure for reducing aggression and self-injury during instruction. *Journal of Applied Behavior Analysis, 24,* 265–278.

Horner, R. H., Dunlap, G., Koegel, R. L., Carr, E. G., Sailor, W., Anderson, J., Albin, R. W., & O'Neill, R. E. (1990). Toward a technology of "nonaversive" behavioral support. *Journal of The Association for Persons with Severe Handicaps, 15,* 125–32.

Houghton, J., Bronicki, G. J. B., & Guess, D. (1987). Opportunities to express preferences and make choices among students with severe disabilities in classroom settings. *Journal of The Association for Persons with Severe Handicaps, 12,* 18–27.

Hughes, C., & Rusch, F. R. (in press). People with challenging behavior in integrated work environments. In F. Brown & D. H. Lehr (Eds.), *People with disabilities who challenge the system.* Baltimore: Paul H. Brookes.

Iwata, B. A., Vollmer, T. R., & Zarcone, J. R. (1990). The experimental (functional) analysis of behavior disorders: Methodology, applications, and limitations. In A. C. Repp & N. Singh (Eds.), *Perspectives on the use of nonaversive and aversive interventions for persons with developmental disabilities* (pp. 301–330). Sycamore, IL: Sycamore.

Koegel, R. L., Dyer, K., & Bell, L. K. (1987). The influence of child-preferred activities on autistic children's social behavior. *Journal of Applied Behavior Analysis, 20,* 243–252.

Koegel, R. L., Koegel, L. K. (1988). Generalized responsivity and pivotal behaviors. In R. H. Horner, G. Dunlap, & R. L. Koegel (Eds.), *Generalization & maintenance: Lifestyle changes in applied settings* (pp. 41–66). Baltimore: Paul H. Brookes.

Mace, F. C., Hock, M. L., Lalli, J. S., West, B. J., Belfiore, P., Pinter, E., & Brown, D. K. (1988). Behavioral momentum in the treatment of noncompliance. *Journal of Applied Behavior Analysis, 21,* 123–141.

Martin, J. E., Rusch, F. R., Lagomarcino, T., & Chadsey-Rusch, J. (1986). Comparison between workers who are nonhandicapped and mentally retarded: Why they lose their jobs. *Applied Research in Mental Retardation, 7,* 467–474.

Mayer-Johnson, R. (1985). *The picture communication symbols book* (Vols. 1–3). Solana Beach, CA: Mayer-Johnson.

Nirje, B. (1969). The normalization principle and its human management implications. In R. Jugel & W. Wolfensberger (Eds.), *Changing patterns of residential services for the mentally retarded* (pp. 179–205) Washington, DC: President's Committee on Mental Retardation.

Nisbet, J., & Hagner, D. (1988). Natural supports in the

workplace: A reexamination of supported employment. *Journal of The Association for Persons with Severe Handicaps, 13,* 260–267.

O'Neill, R. E., Horner, R. H., Albin, R. W., Storey, K., & Sprague, J. R. (1990). *Functional analysis of problem behavior: A practical assessment guide.* Sycamore, IL: Sycamore.

Ponthieu, L. D., Jones, S. C., Williamson, C. & Beaird, C. L. (1994). Management response to disruptive behaviors by employees with developmental disabilities: A review and empirical study. *Journal of Vocational Rehabilitation, 4,* 37–51.

Repp, A. C., Felce, D., & Barton, L. E. (1988). Basing the treatment of stereotypic and self-injurious behaviors on hypotheses of their causes. *Journal of Applied Behavior Analysis, 21,* 281–289.

Repp, A. C., & Karsh, K. G. (1990). A taxonomic approach to the nonaversive treatment of maladaptive behavior of persons with developmental disabilities. In A. C. Repp & N. Singh (Eds.), *Perspectives on the use of nonaversive and aversive interventions for persons with developmental disabilities* (pp. 331–347). Sycamore, IL; Sycamore.

Rusch, F. R., & Hughes, C. (1989). Overview of supported employment. *Journal of Applied Behavior Analysis, 22,* 351–363.

Skinner, B. F. (1953). *Science and human behavior.* New York: Free Press.

Smith, M. D. (1990). *Autism and life in the community.* Baltimore: Paul H. Brookes.

Smith, M. D., & Coleman, D. (1986). Managing the behavior of adults with autism in the job setting. *Journal of Autism and Developmental Disorders, 16,* 145–154.

Snell, M. E., & Browder, D. M. (1986). Community-referenced instruction: Research and issues. *Journal of The Association for Persons with Severe Handicaps, 11,* 1–11.

Wacker, D. P., Steege, M. W., Northup, J., Sasso, G., Berg, W., Reimers, T., Cooper, L., Cigrand, K., & Donn, L. (1990). A component analysis of functional communication training across three topographies of severe behavior problems. *Journal of Applied Behavior Analysis, 23,* 417–429.

Wehman, P., & Kregel, J. (1985). A supported work approach to competitive employment of individuals with moderate and severe handicaps. *Journal of The Association for Persons with Severe Handicaps, 10,* 3–11.

Whitehead, C. W. (1979). Sheltered workshops in the decade ahead: Work and wages, or welfare. In G. T. Bellamy, G. O'Connor, & O. C. Karan (Eds.), *Vocational rehabilitation of severely handicapped persons* (pp. 71–84). Baltimore: University Park Press.

Wolfensberger, W. (1972). *The principle of normalization in human services.* Toronto: National Institute of Mental Retardation.

Received: February 28, 1995
Final Acceptance: September 16, 1995
Editor in Charge: James W. Halle

JASH
1998, Vol. 23, No. 2, 111–118

Reducing Aggression in Children With Autism Toward Infant or Toddler Siblings

Lynn Kern Koegel, Dara Stiebel, and Robert L. Koegel
University of California at Santa Barbara

Children with autism often lack appropriate means to communicate and may rely on aggression and other disruptive behaviors to express their needs. This may be a particularly serious problem when aggression occurs toward an infant or toddler, who could be severely injured by an older sibling. This study examined the use of functional assessment and individualized parent-implemented intervention plans in the home setting, including functional communication training with relevant ecological manipulations. Data were collected in the context of a multiple baseline design across three families. The results showed that after the intervention there were: (1) large reductions in the children's aggression toward their infant or toddler sibling, (2) increases in parent and child happiness level, and (3) increases in strangers' level of comfort with respect to interacting with the family. The results are discussed in terms of improving the overall quality of life for families of children with autism.

DESCRIPTORS: autism, functional assessment, home intervention, parent-professional relations, parents

Severe aggression, particularly directed toward a younger infant or toddler sibling, is of particular concern because of its detrimental effects on physical and emotional wellbeing. Studies of typically developing siblings continue to describe long-lasting negative consequences of sibling aggression (Gully, Dengeriak, Pepping, & Bergstrom, 1981; Steinmetz, 1978; Loeber, Weissman, & Reid, 1983). For many children with autism, aggression is a pervasive disruptive behavior. Such children often lack appropriate means to communicate their needs and instead may become aggressive (Carr & Durand, 1985).

In addition to potential sibling injury from aggres-

sion, studies document elevated stress levels in parents whose children display aggression (Moes, 1995). Similarly, concern over managing problem behaviors is one of the key factors contributing to parenting stress (Koegel et al., 1992; Moes, Koegel, Schreibman, & Loos, 1992). Furthermore, aggression and other disruptive behaviors often limit a child's inclusion into community settings (Horner, Dunlap, & Koegel, 1988; Van Bourgondien & Elgar, 1990) and are a determining factor in a child's placement in more restrictive settings (Eyman & Call, 1978).

Recent directions in the treatment of aggressive behavior have focused on identifying and teaching adaptive behaviors to replace the original disruptive behavior (Carr & Durand, 1985; Mace & Roberts, 1993). Determining the circumstances under which aggression will and will not occur is essential information necessary to develop effective interventions (Wacker et al., 1990). In addition, ecological manipulations, such as changes in the physical environment, have been used to decrease disruptive behaviors and encourage certain types of adaptive behavior (Dunlap, Kern-Dunlap, Clark, & Robbins, 1991; Nordquist, Twardosz, & McEvoy, 1991). Such procedures, often developed by using data from a functional assessment of variables related to the disruptive behavior, have been recognized as especially important in successfully producing changes in behavior. Effective programs have been implemented in various settings such as in the home (Day, Horner, & O'Neill, 1994), school (Sasso et al., 1992), and clinic (Northup et al., 1991) with many communicative partners including adults and peers.

An important extension of this work would be to apply these procedures to the problem of sibling aggression in children with autism, and to assess the effects of a parent-implemented intervention in the home setting. The specific purpose of this study was to assess whether changing antecedent stimuli associated with aggression through functional assessment and a parent-implemented intervention, including functional communication training with relevant ecological manipulations, would be effective in reducing sibling aggression in children with autism who aggress toward their infant or toddler siblings. The second goal of this study was to assess the effects of the above manipulations on child affect, parent affect, and strangers' comfort level.

This research was supported in part by Public Health Service Research Grant MH28210 from the National Institute of Mental Health, and by U. S. Department of Education Grant G0087C0234. We thank Chris Bagglio and Kimberly Mullen for their assistance with the data collection and data analysis, Mike Furlong for his helpful comments, and Kevin Glikmann and Josh Harrower for their help with the graphs.

Address all correspondence and requests for reprints to Robert L. Koegel, Counseling/Clinical/School Psychology Program, Graduate School of Education, University of California-Santa Barbara, Santa Barbara, CA 93106-9490.

Method

Participants

Three sibling dyads, who lived at home with their parents, participated in this study. Within each dyad the older sibling was diagnosed as having autism or a related developmental disability by an independent diagnostician, and the infant or toddler sibling was not diagnosed as having a disability. Additional criteria for participation in the study included complaints by parents of physical aggression directed toward the younger sibling.

Dyad 1. The first dyad consisted of a 5-year, 10-month-old girl diagnosed with autism and her 8-month-old sister. Child 1 achieved a score in the 4th percentile on the Peabody Picture Vocabulary Test—Revised. She was able to combine words to form simple sentences (although she rarely initiated verbal interactions), was toilet trained, and could perform self-help skills such as dressing herself with minimal assistance. Her parents' primary concern was her aggressive behavior directed toward her infant sibling. Aggressive behavior reported by the parents typically took the form of yelling, pinching, and hitting, which often resulted in crying by her younger sibling.

Dyad 2. The second dyad consisted of a 4-year, 3-month-old boy diagnosed with a mixed developmental disorder with autistic-like characteristics and his 7-month-old brother. The Peabody Picture Vocabulary Test–Revised and the Expressive One Word Vocabulary Test yielded scores below the 1st percentile and at the 2nd percentile, respectively. He primarily used one- and two-word utterances, was not fully toilet trained, and needed considerable assistance with most self-help skills such as dressing and bathing. In addition to concerns about general developmental delays, his parents expressed particular concern about noncompliance and aggression. Aggression toward his infant sibling was reported by his parents to be hitting, rolling over on top of his brother, pinching, shoving, and grabbing objects away from his brother.

Dyad 3. The third dyad consisted of a 4-year, 10-month-old boy diagnosed with autism and his 6-month-old brother. Although he was difficult to test because of numerous disruptive behaviors, he obtained a score at the 1st percentile on the Peabody Picture Vocabulary Test—Revised before the start of intervention. He was able to combine three to four words to form simple sentences, was toilet trained, and could complete most age-appropriate self-help skills with minimal guidance, but would typically engage in solitary self-stimulatory behavior (shaking leaves, strings, or other objects in front of his eyes) when not guided in appropriate activities. Aggressive behavior reported by his parents consisted of kicking, hitting, pinching, squeezing, head butting, poking his brother's head with his index finger, and sitting on top of his brother.

Setting and Materials

Settings and activities where aggression occurred were selected by the parents. For dyad 1, sessions took place at the kitchen table or the outside patio table during regular meal times. For dyads 2 and 3, sessions were conducted during play sessions on the living room floor. Fifty-eight percent of the sessions were videotaped and the remainder of the sessions were scored on-line. Video equipment was placed in a corner of the room; when observers scored sessions in vivo, they stood in a corner of the room and did not interact with the parents or children.

Design

Data were collected in a multiple baseline across participants (Barlow & Hersen, 1984). Sessions were conducted one to four times per week in probes throughout the experiment, with the sessions typically lasting 15 to 30 min and occurring approximately the same time each day.

Baseline

During baseline the parents were instructed to interact naturally during play sessions or meal time. The baseline period for child 1 was 10 weeks, for child 2 was 14 weeks, and for child 3 was 15 weeks. During the baseline sessions, data were recorded by a clinician using functional analysis data sheets to identify stimuli associated with the problem behavior (Frea, Koegel, & Koegel, 1993; O'Neill, Horner, Albin, Storey, & Sprague, 1990). Events preceding and following each occurrence of disruptive behavior in the home were recorded.

Intervention

The intervention plan for each of the three children was implemented through a parent consultation model, where the parents implemented the intervention plan in their own homes with prompts if necessary (see arrows in Fig. 1). This general approach consisted of three phases. First, based on information obtained during baseline, the stimuli identified as most associated with problem behavior were determined. Then, during an initial meeting, the parents and a clinician developed an intervention plan that was maximally compatible with each family's values and lifestyle. The intervention plan was designed to identify strategies for minimizing the occurrence or duration of stimuli associated with problem behavior. Second, the parent was prompted by a clinician to rearrange the environment as required and to teach appropriate replacement behaviors for the aggression that had the function of minimizing the stimuli associated with problem behaviors. Prompting initially was provided during non-crisis times, so that the appropriate behaviors would be well-established and could easily be elicited during subsequent crisis times. Third, the clinician's prompts were removed (or reduced, when necessary) as the parent and child began to exhibit the spontaneous use of their respective targeted behaviors. The details of these procedures as implemented for each of the children are described below.

Dyad 1. For child 1, four antecedent stimuli were most frequently recorded as occurring in association with aggression: (1) sibling loudly kicking the metal tray on the high chair, (2) sibling making vocal noises, (3) sibling crying, and (4) a "down time" period, when the children sat alone at the table not engaged in activities while the mother finished food preparation. A multicomponent intervention was implemented in relation to the following four stimuli. First, in relation to the baby kicking the metal try, it was hypothesized that aggression occurred to escape from aversive noise. For this function, the metal high chair tray was replaced with a plastic tray to reduce noise. Second, in response to the baby making vocal noises or crying, it was hypothesized that aggression also occurred to escape from aversive noises. Therefore, the child with autism was taught to respond to the baby's vocal noises by saying phrases to the parents such as "(baby's name) is talking" and "(baby's name) needs help." Third, as an additional intervention for this function, toys and objects (e.g., pacifier and bottle) were made accessible to child 1 so that she could respond to the infant's needs herself when the baby cried. Fourth, it was hypothesized that aggression occurred during the down time period as a way to seek attention. Therefore, the down time period was restricted by prompting the mother to prepare the bulk of the meal before sitting the children in their chairs and prompting the parents to increase family interactions through procedures 2 and 3 described above.

Specifically, at the start of intervention the parent replaced Child 1's metal tray with a plastic tray. Also, before each meal, infant toys and other objects (e.g., pacifier and bottle) were placed nearby so they would be accessible for Child 1 to give her sibling. In addition to these environmental manipulations, during the first 2 weeks (three sessions) of intervention a clinician prompted (see arrows in Figure 1) the parent to establish the functionally equivalent replacement behaviors during noncrisis times so that they could be elicited more easily during crisis times. Child 1's mother was prompted every few minutes during the first session, then just before dinner during the second and third session. The mother was prompted, when the baby was making noises, to ask Child 1 to say "(baby's name) is talking," to request the mother's assistance, and to give the sibling a toy. During these first 2 weeks the mother began spontaneously prompting the child and the child began spontaneously using the functionally equivalent replacement behavior, therefore the clinician prompts were discontinued.

Dyad 2. For Child 2, three antecedent stimuli were most frequently recorded as occurring in association with aggression: (1) Child 2's mother on the telephone or in another room, (2) Child 2's infant sibling touching or interfering with his toys, and (3) the infant approaching or being near Child 2's toys while he was playing. A multicomponent intervention was implemented in relation to these three stimuli. First, in response to his mother being on the phone or in another room, it was hypothesized that aggression occurred as a way to seek attention. Therefore, Child 2 was provided with contingent attention from his mother for gradually longer intervals of independent play. Second, in response to the infant touching or interfering with Child 2's toys, it was hypothesized that aggression occurred to maintain possession of the toys. Therefore, various infant toys were made available, and Child 2 was taught to give his brother one of the infant toys or to redirect him to play with an infant toy when he touched or interfered with Child 2's toys. Third, in relation to the infant sibling approaching or being near Child 2's toys while he was playing, it was hypothesized that aggression was used to maintain possession of the toys. Therefore, he was taught to give his brother an infant toy and/or to say to his mother, "Take (sibling's name)," as a method of soliciting the parent's assistance in reducing the infant's interference with Child 2's toys during their play activities.

Specifically, at the start of intervention, Child 2's parents placed a basket of infant toys in the play area so they would be accessible for Child 2 to give his sibling. In addition, during the first three weeks of intervention (three sessions) the clinician prompted the parent to establish the appropriate functionally equivalent response in Child 2's repertoire during noncrisis times so that it could be more easily elicited during crisis times. To do this, Child 2's mother was prompted every few minutes to ask Child 2 to give his sibling a toy or to ask his mother to remove the sibling. In addition, at the initiation of all instances of aggressive behavior, the parent was prompted to ask the child to use the functionally equivalent replacement behavior. After 3 weeks of prompting, prompts were gradually reduced (see arrows in Figure 1) over 4 weeks (four sessions) Child 2's mother began to prompt him spontaneously and Child 2 began to use the functionally equivalent response.

Dyad 3. For Child 3, three antecedent stimuli were most frequently recorded as occurring in association with aggression: (1) sibling touching or interfering with his toys, (2) sibling touching Child 3's body, and (3) sibling crying and making noises. A multi-component intervention was implemented in relation to the following stimuli. First, in relation to the infant sibling touching or interfering with Child 3's toys, it was hypothesized that aggression occurred to maintain possession of the toys. Therefore, infant toys were made accessible to Child 3 and he was taught to give his sibling one of the infant toys so that the infant would not play with Child 3's toys. The second and third interventions, in relation to the infant touching Child 3's body and/or crying and making noises, it was hypothesized that aggression was used to escape from aversive touching and to escape from noise. For these functions, Child 3's parents taught him the verbal communication "Take (sibling's name)" as a method of soliciting the mother's assistance in reducing the infant sibling's interference with Child 3's toys or to minimize the durability of the aversive noises and crying during their play activities.

The above intervention for Child 3 proceeded as follows. First, the parents placed a basket of infant toys in the play area so that it would be accessible for Child 3 to give to his younger sibling. During the first 3 weeks (six sessions) of the intervention, the clinician prompted the parent to establish appropriate functionally equivalent responses during noncrisis times so that they could be more easily elicited later during crisis times. This was accomplished by prompting the parent to ask Child 3 to give the infant a toy every few minutes, or to ask Child 3 to request the mother's assistance with respect to reducing the sibling's interference, touching, or noise level. Subsequently, at the initiation of all instances of aggressive behavior, the parent was prompted to ask the child to use the appropriate functionally equivalent response. During the first 3 weeks, the parent and Child 3 began to exhibit the spontaneous use of their respective targeted behaviors, therefore prompt fading was not necessary.

Data Collection and Response Definitions

The occurrence of aggressive behavior, as defined below for each child, was recorded in continuous 10-sec intervals (continuous 5-min intervals for Child 3 who typically interacted with his brother for longer periods of time during the sessions). The number of intervals with occurrences of aggressive behavior were then divided by the total number of intervals to yield a percentage of intervals with aggression during the session. In addition, the exact number of spontaneous (unprompted) occurrences of appropriate functionally equivalent replacement behaviors was recorded for each child. Specific definitions of aggressive behavior and appropriate replacement behaviors were as follow.

Child 1

Aggression: yelling, hitting the infant sibling with an open hand, and punching the infant sibling with a closed fist.

Spontaneous Use of Targeted Appropriate Behaviors: verbalizations such as "(baby's name) is talking" and "(baby's name) needs help" and verbal and nonverbal responses (such as handing the baby her pacifier or bottle) directed toward meeting the infant sibling's needs.

Child 2

Aggression: hitting, punching, rolling over on top of infant sibling, shoving sibling forcibly with an open hand, grabbing toys and objects forcibly from sibling, kicking sibling, and yelling at sibling.

Spontaneous Use of Targeted Appropriate Behaviors: the verbal response "take (infant's name)" to request that his parents reduce the sibling from interfering with his toys and handing the infant sibling an infant toy or redirecting his sibling to use an infant toy.

Child 3

Aggression: kicking, pinching, squeezing, grabbing, placing his foot on or sitting on his sibling, tapping the sibling's head, head butting, and attempting to strike the sibling.

Spontaneous Use of Targeted Appropriate Behaviors: the verbal response "take (infant's name)" to request that his parents reduce the sibling from interfering with his toys and handing the sibling an infant toy.

Social Validity

Social validity was assessed on three variables (Child Happiness; Parent Happiness; and Stranger Comfort with the Interactions) by using six-point Likert scales, adapted from Dunlap and Koegel (1980) and Koegel and Egel (1979) to indicate the child's level of happiness, the parents' level of happiness, and strangers' level of comfort being with the children (Table 1). A minimum of 25% of all the sessions were used to assess social validity in the three categories. This was done during baseline, treatment, and follow-up for Children 1 and 2 (who had an adequate number of videotaped sessions to represent their behavior over a period of time). The videotaped sessions were drawn randomly from each condition and then averaged separately for each social validity category to provide 12 separate scores (i.e., scores for each child for each of the three categories of social validity). The observer was an undergraduate psychology student who only recorded data for the social validation measure. The observer did not know the children, was unaware of the order of conditions, and was naive to the purpose of the experiment.

For levels of child and parent happiness, observers' ratings in the 0 to 1 range indicated unhappiness, ratings in the 2 to 3 range indicated neutral affect, and ratings in the 4 to 5 range indicated happiness. Similarly, for strangers' level of comfort if they were to be in that setting, ratings in the 0 to 1 range indicated that they would be uncomfortable, ratings in the 2 to 3 range indicated that they would feel neutral, and ratings in the 4 to 5 range indicated that they would feel comfortable.

Both of Child 1's parents were present during most of the sessions throughout the study. Therefore, an additional social validation measure was used to assess whether any changes in the parents' amount of parent-parent conversation occurred as a possible collateral result of decreases in their child's aggression. Specifi-

Table 1.
Rating Scales for Child/Parent Effect and Stranger Comfort

Child

Unhappy 0–1	Neutral 2–3	Happy 4–5
Cries, pouts, tantrums. Appears to be sad, angry, or frustrated. Child seems not to be enjoying self (score 0 or 1 depending on extent of unhappiness).	Does not appear to be decidedly happy or unhappy. May smile or frown occasionally but overall seems rather neutral in this situation (score 2 or 3 depending on extent of happiness).	Smiles and laughs appropriately and seems to be enjoying self (score 4 or 5 depending on extent of enjoyment).

Parent

Unhappy 0–1	Neutral 2–3	Happy 4–5
Parent appears frustrated. Does not seem to be or enjoying self (score 0 or 1 depending on extent of happiness).	Does not appear to be decidedly happy or particularly unhappy. May occasionally frown or smile but overall seems rather neutral in this situation (score 2 or 3 depending on extent of happiness).	Smiles and laughs appropriately. Seems to be enjoying self during meal or play period (score 4 or 5 depending on extent of happiness).

Stranger

How comfortable would you feel eating dinner or being the only adult in the setting?

Uncomfortable 0–1	Neutral 2–3	Comfortable 4–5
Not very comfortable (score 0 or 1 depending on level of comfort).	Not comfortable or uncomfortable. Appears neutral (score 2 or 3 depending on level of comfort).	Comfortable (score 4 or 5 depending on level of comfort).

cally, data were collected on the number of 10-sec intervals with parent-parent conversational interactions during each condition for this family. Parent-parent conversational interactions were defined as any verbal exchange that occurred between the parents while sitting at the dinner table.

Reliability

To measure the reliability of the dependent measures, two observers (undergraduate psychology students) independently recorded data during a minimum of 25% of the sessions for each dependent measure. For the measure of aggression (and similarly for the measure of spontaneous use of targeted appropriate behaviors), observers were considered to be in agreement when they recorded the same behavior during the same observation interval. A disagreement was defined as one observer recording a behavior and the other observer not recording the behavior or recording a different behavior. Interrater agreement was determined by dividing the number of agreements by the number of agreements plus disagreements multiplied by 100. The average percentage agreement for aggression for Child 1 was 89.6% (range 66.7–100%), for Child 2 was 90.1% (range 75–100%), and for Child 3 was 95% (range 80–100%). The average percentage agreement for spontaneous use of targeted appropriate behaviors for Child 1 was 92.6% (range 87.5–100%), for Child 2 was 96.3% (range 66.7–100%), and for Child 3 was 100%.

For the social validation ratings, agreements were defined as the two observers recording an average response for a given child in a given condition within the same range [unhappy/uncomfortable (0–1), neutral (2–3), or happy/comfortable (4–5)]. The average percent agreement was 86.7%, with never more than a one-point difference between raters. Interrater agreement also was recorded for Child 1's sessions for the parent-parent conversational interactions. The observers were considered in agreement when they both recorded a parent-parent interaction in the same 10-sec interval. A disagreement was defined as one observer recording an interaction and the other observer not recording an interaction. The average percent agreement was 87.6% (range 80–100%).

Results

Aggression

Figure 1 shows the percentage of intervals with aggressive behavior for the three participants. Aggression toward the infant or toddler sibling occurred frequently during baseline sessions, which continued for 10 to 15 weeks across the three dyads. After the initiation of the intervention, aggression decreased. Baseline data show that the mean percent of intervals with aggression was 5.76%, 18.9%, and 68.9% for Children 1, 2, and 3, respectively. After the intervention, all of the children's levels of sibling aggression decreased, with no aggression occurring during eight of the sessions for Child 1, no aggression occurring during seven of the sessions for Child 2, and no aggression occurring during the final session for Child 3.

The follow-up sessions, also shown in Figure 1, show that the effects maintained across time for two of the

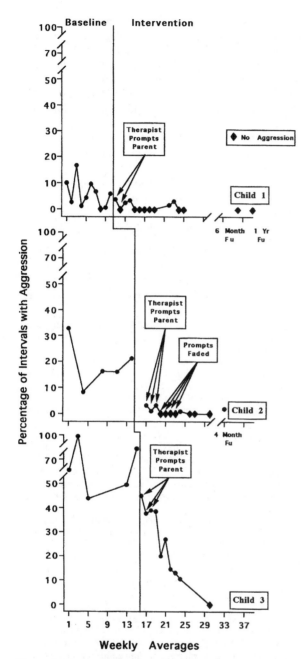

Figure 1. The percentage of intervals during which the children exhibited aggression toward their infant or toddler siblings during baseline, intervention, and follow-up. *Arrows* indicate sessions when the parents were prompted to provide the intervention. *Diamonds* indicate sessions with zero aggression.

children. That is, Child 1 demonstrated no aggression at the 6-month and 1-year follow-up periods. Similarly, aggression was near zero during a 4-month follow-up session for Child 2. Child 3 moved away and was unavailable for further data collection. In summary, all of the children's aggressive behavior decreased after intervention, and follow-up sessions suggest the effects of the intervention were durable over time.

Spontaneous Use of Targeted Appropriate Behaviors

All three children increased their spontaneous use of the relevant appropriate behaviors after intervention. For Child 1, baseline data indicate that the average number of spontaneous appropriate behaviors was 0.5 per weekly session, increasing to an average of 1.5 per session during the intervention sessions, and increased further to an average of 5.5 per session during the follow-up sessions.

For Child 2, the results indicate an average of 0.7 spontaneous appropriate behaviors per session during baseline and increased to an average of 1.3 per session during intervention. Follow-up data showed an additional increase to an average of 4 appropriate behaviors per session.

Child 3 had an average of 0.1 targeted spontaneous appropriate behaviors per session during the baseline sessions and an average of 4.9 targeted spontaneous appropriate behaviors per session during intervention. Because he moved to another state, follow-up data were not available for this child.

Social Validity

Changes in the childrens' and parents' happiness levels and strangers' comfort levels occurred. The average levels increased from the unhappy/uncomfortable level (0–1.5) or neutral level (1.6–3.5) during baseline to the happy/comfortable level (3.5–5) by the follow-up period. Specifically, Child 1's level of happiness increased from an average rating of 2.0 (low neutral) at baseline to 3.0 during the intervention and to 4.0 (happy) during follow-up. Her parents' level of happiness was rated at an average level of 2.0 (neutral) during baseline and increased to an average of 4.0 (happy) during the intervention and remained at 4.0 during the follow-up. Similarly, the stranger's comfort level increased from an average rating of 2.5 (neutral) during baseline to a rating of 4.0 (comfortable) during the intervention and remained at 4.0 during follow-up.

Child 2's level of happiness was rated at an average of 2.5 (neutral) during baseline increasing to an average of 3.5 during the intervention and 4.0 (happy) during follow-up. The parent's happiness level increased from an average of 1.5 (unhappy) during baseline to an average of 3.0 during the intervention and to 5.0 (happy) at follow-up. In addition, the stranger's comfort level increased from an average of 1.5 (uncomfortable) at baseline to an average of 3.0 during the intervention and 4.0 (comfortable) during follow-up.

The additional measure of parent-parent conversation obtained for Child 1 during dinnertime when all of the family members were present showed increases from an average of 8.9% of the intervals with conversation during the baseline, to 13.6% of the intervals with conversation during intervention, and to 22.4% of the intervals with conversation during follow-up. That is, dinnertime conversation between the mother and father occurred more frequently as the child with autism's aggression toward her sibling decreased.

Discussion

The results of this study showed that changing contextual stimuli associated with aggression through functional analysis and functional communication training with relevant ecological manipulations could be an effective treatment for children with autism who aggress toward their infant or toddler siblings. In this study the most frequent stimuli and their hypothesized function was generally clear, making the process straightforward. However, for families where there are multiple functions or less easily identified stimuli associated with aggression, the functional assessment process may need to be formalized. This study is unique in that it demonstrates the possibility of effective parent-implemented, in-home, ecobehavioral interventions to reduce severe and often dangerous levels of aggression between children with autism and their infant or toddler siblings.

Results from this study also show several interesting collateral effects. Higher levels of positive affect at follow-up suggest an overall increase in happiness for the children and their parents. Thus, targeting disharmony in the children's interactions may result in the indirect effect of improving overall harmony for the entire family. The increase in parent conversation at mealtime for Child 1 and the parents' increased level of happiness also may be an indication of increased marital satisfaction (Brody, Stoneman, & Burke, 1987) and may be an interesting area for future research.

The individual demonstrations in this study further support the conclusions of other studies, suggesting that in-home behavioral support plans can be both efficient and effective, although there are some limitations in this study (e.g., a possible decreasing trend in Child 1's baseline, and that Child 2 and Child 3's baseline were staggered by approximately the same number of weeks). The parents in this study selected the naturally occurring daily activities that were problematic for each of their children (mealtime for Child 1 and play periods for Children 2 and 3). Then, embedding the intervention into the families' naturally occurring routines (i.e., mealtime and play periods) may have been particularly important, because it provided a context in which to support and build, thereby increasing the likelihood of successful implementation (Albin, Lucyshyn, Horner, & Flannery, 1996). Intervention programs that are developed with consideration of family goals, desires, and values, and that do not require significant changes in the existing family routines, are more likely to be consistently implemented and maintained over time (Albin, Lucyshyn, Horner, & Flannery, 1996; Koegel, Koegel, Kellegrew, & Mullen, 1996).

In addition to selecting the problematic activities, the parents in this study assisted in developing alternative replacement behaviors that were manageable for both the child and the parent. The parents' active involvement in prioritizing problematic activities and in developing and implementing the treatment program may have resulted in a good contextual fit (Albin, Lucyshyn, Horner, & Flannery, 1996), and thus may have increased the likelihood of successful outcomes (Mullen & Frea, 1995; Wood, 1995). Future research studies relating to parent-professional collaboration and programs implemented in natural settings may contribute to understanding variables related to improving the overall quality of life for all family members.

References

Albin, R. W., Lucyshyn, J. M., Horner, R. H., & Flannery, K. B. (1996). Contextual fit for behavioral support plans: A model for "goodness of fit." In L. K. Koegel, R. L. Koegel, & G. Dunlap (Eds.), *Positive behavioral support including people with difficult behavior in the community* (pp. 81–98). Baltimore: Paul H. Brookes.

Barlow, D. H., & Hersen, M. (1984). Single case experimental designs: Strategies for studying behavior change. New York: Pergamon Press.

Brody, G. H., Stoneman, Z., & Burke, M. (1987). Family system and individual child correlates of sibling behavior. *American Journal Orthopsychiatry, 57,* 561–569.

Carr, E. G., & Durand, V. M. (1985). Reducing behavior problems through functional communication training. *Journal of Applied Behavior Analysis, 18,* 111–126.

Day, H. M., Horner, R. H., & O'Neill, R. E. (1994). Multiple functions of problem behaviors: Assessment and intervention. *Journal of Applied Behavior Analysis, 27,* 279–289.

Dunlap, G., Kern-Dunlap, L., Clark, S., & Robbins, F. R. (1991). Functional assessment, curricular revisions, and severe problem behavior. *Journal of Applied Behavior Analysis, 24,* 387–397.

Dunlap, G., & Koegel, R. L. (1980). Motivating autistic children through stimulus variation. *Journal of Applied Behavior Analysis, 13,* 619–627.

Eyman, R. K., & Call, T. (1978). Maladaptive behavior and community placement of mentally retarded persons. *American Journal of Mental Deficiency, 82,* 137–144.

Frea, W. D., Koegel, R. L., & Koegel, L. K. (1993). *Understanding why problem behaviors occur: A guide for assisting parents in assessing causes of behavior and designing treatment plans.* Santa Barbara: University of California.

Gully, K. J., Dengerink, H. A., Pepping, M., & Bergstrom, D. A. (1981). Research note: Sibling contribution to violent behavior. *Journal of Marriage and the Family, 43,* 333–337.

Horner, R. H., Dunlap, G., & Koegel, R. L. (1988). *Generalization and maintenance: Life-style changes in applied settings.* Baltimore: Paul H. Brookes.

Koegel, R. L., & Egel, A. L. (1979). Motivating autistic children. *Journal of Abnormal Psychology, 88,* 418–426.

Koegel, L. K., Koegel, R. L., Kellegrew, D., & Mullen, K. (1996). Parent education for prevention and reduction of severe problem behaviors. In L. K. Koegel, R. L. Koegel, & G. Dunlap (Eds.), *Positive behavioral support including people with difficult behaviors in the community* (pp. 3–30). Baltimore: Paul H. Brookes.

Koegel, R. L., Schreibman, L., Loos, L. M., Dirlich-Wilhelm, H., Dunlap, G., Robbins, F. R., & Plienis, A. J. (1992). Consistent stress profiles in mothers of children with autism.

Journal of Autism and Developmental Disorders, 22, 205–216.

Loeber, R., Weissman, W., & Reid, J. (1983). Family interactions of assaultive adolescents, stealers, and non delinquents. *Journal of Abnormal Child Psychology, 11(1),* 1–14.

Moes, D. (1995). Parent education and parenting stress. In L. K. Koegel, R. L. Koegel, & G. Dunlap (Eds.), *Positive behavioral support including people with difficult behaviors in the community* (pp. 79–93). Baltimore: Paul H. Brookes.

Moes, D., Koegel, R. L., Schreibman, L., & Loos, L. M. (1992). Stress profiles for mothers and fathers of children with autism. *Psychological Reports, 71,* 1272–1274.

Mullen, K., & Frea, W. D. (1995). A parent-professional consultation model for functional analysis. In R. L. Koegel & L. K. Koegel (Eds.), *Teaching children with autism: Strategies for initiating positive interactions and improving learning opportunities* (pp. 175–188). Baltimore: Paul H. Brookes.

Nordquist, V. M., Twardosz, S., & McEvoy, M. A. (1991). Effects of environmental reorganization in classrooms for children with autism. *Journal of Early Intervention, 15,* 135–152.

Northup, J., Wacker, D., Sasso, G., Steege, M., Cigrand, K., Cook, J., & DeRaad, A. (1991). A brief functional analysis of aggressive and alternative behavior in an outclinic setting. *Journal of Applied Behavior Analysis, 24,* 504–522.

O'Neill, R. E., Horner, R. H., Albin, R. W., Storey, K., & Sprague, A. L. (1990). *Functional analysis of problem behavior: A practical assessment guide.* Sycamore, IL: Sycamore Press.

Sasso, G. M., Reimers, T. M., Cooper, L. J., Wacker, D., Berg, W., Steege, M., Kelly, L., & Allaire, A. (1992). Use of descriptive and experimental analysis to identify the functional properties of aberrant behavior in school settings. *Journal of Applied Behavior Analysis, 25,* 809–821.

Steinmetz, S. K. (1978). Sibling violence. In J. M. Eskelaar & S. N. Katz (Eds.), *Family violence: An international and interdisciplinary study* (pp. 460–465). Toronto: Butterworth.

Van Bourgondien, M. E., & Elgar, S. (1990). The relationship between existing residential services and the needs of autistic adults. *Journal of Autism and Developmental Disorders, 20(3),* 299–305.

Wacker, F., Steege, M., Northup, J., Sasso, G., Berg, W., Reimers, T., Cooper, L., Cigrand, K., & Donn, L. (1990). A component analysis of functional communication training across three topographies of severe behavior problems. *Journal of Applied Behavior Analysis, 23,* 331–343.

Wood, M. (1995). Parent-professional collaboration in the education of children with autism: An examination of the efficacy of the IEP process. In R. L. Koegel & L. K. Koegel (Eds.), *Teaching children with autism: Strategies for initiating positive interactions and improving learning opportunities* (pp. 353–428). Baltimore: Paul H. Brookes.

Received: July 11, 1997
Final Acceptance: January 8, 1998
Editor in Charge: Mark Durand

Treating Sleep Terrors in Children with Autism

V. Mark Durand
University at Albany,
State University of New York

Abstract: Sleep terrors manifest themselves as a sudden arousal from slow wave sleep accompanied by screaming, crying, and other signs of intense fear. Children with autism spectrum disorders may be more likely to display problems with sleep, and some children experience such sleep difficulties as sleep terrors on a chronic basis. This nighttime disruption can lead to a great deal of concern, as well as disruption in sleep for other family members. In this first study of the treatment of sleep terrors among children with autism, the effectiveness of one behavioral intervention (scheduled awakenings) was evaluated. Scheduled awakenings involved arousing the child from sleep approximately 30 minutes before an expected sleep terror episode. Results through a 12-month follow-up using a multiple baseline across three children indicated that this intervention quickly and durably reduced the frequency of their nighttime difficulties. Scheduled awakenings is a potentially useful nonmedical intervention for chronic sleep terrors among children with autism.

Children with autism spectrum disorders may be among the most seriously affected when it comes to sleep problems, with some research suggesting that almost all of these individuals experience difficulty with sleep at some point in their lives (Richdale & Prior, 1995). Surveys of children with autism vary considerably but generally indicate that more than 50% of parents have reported some problem with their child's sleep, and one in four parents described the problem as severe (Hering, Epstein, Elroy, Iancu, & Zelnik, 1999; Stores & Wiggs, 1998). To make matters worse, parents also indicated that their children did not grow out of these sleep problems and that their sleeping difficulties persisted into adulthood (Durand, 1998). Problems surrounding sleep appear across the autism spectrum, with recent reports confirming increased sleep problems among individuals with Asperger syndrome (Bergeron, Godbout, Mottron, & Stip, 1997).

A number of different problems surrounding sleep are observed in children and can include bedtime tantrums, disruptive night waking, nightmares, sleep terrors, and excessive daytime sleepiness. Sleep terrors are a form of parasomnia that involve a sudden arousal from slow wave sleep and present as intense emotional upset. These episodes are often mistaken for nightmares, although unlike nightmares, sleep terrors are not manifestations of a dream and occur during the deeper stages (Stages 3 and 4) of nonrapid eye movement (NREM) sleep. Sleep terrors can be extremely upsetting, especially for an observer (Lask, 1995). The attacks usually commence with a piercing scream, the person appears to be extremely upset, and the episode is often accompanied by sweating and a rapid heartbeat. In addition, the person cannot be easily awakened and comforted, as is possible when someone has a nightmare. And in the case of sleep terror, the individual does not remember the incident, despite its often dramatic presentation (American Sleep Disorders Association, 1990).

Approximately 3% of otherwise healthy young children have sleep terrors at some point, and a small percentage of adults also display this problem (Lask, 1995). No comparable estimates currently exist for individuals with autism. Fortunately, most instances of sleep terrors decrease in frequency over time and are usually gone by the time the child is a teenager (Giles & Buysse, 1993). Relatively little is known about this sleep problem, although several theories of the cause of sleep terrors have been proposed. Psychological influences were proposed at one time, although current research seems to suggest that this may not be an important consideration (Kales, Kales, Soldatos, Caldwell, Charney, & Martin, 1980). A variety of biological theories have been proposed over the years, although little evidence supports or discounts these ideas (Karacan, 1988). Members of the same family tend to have this disorder, indicating a possible genetic component, but none has yet been found (Abe, Oda, Ikenaga, & Yamada, 1993).

Treatment for sleep terrors usually begins with the recommendation to wait and to see if they disappear on their own. When the problem is more frequent or continues to be a problem over a long period of time, sometimes medications such as antidepressants (e.g., imipramine) or benzodiazepines are recommended for treatment (Fisher, Kahn, Edwards, & Davis, 1973). These drugs tend to reduce the amount of time spent in deep (Stages 3 and 4) sleep, which in theory should reduce the number of sleep terror episodes that occur during these stages of sleep. However, the effectiveness of these drugs on chronic sleep terrors has not yet been clearly demonstrated (Mindell, 1993). In addition, their side effects—which can include daytime drowsiness—make them a less than ideal solution, especially for children. To date, little evidence supports the use of medication as an acceptable long-term solution for sleep terrors in children.

Behavioral interventions for sleep problems have been used for some time (Durand, Mindell, Mapstone, & Gernert-Dott, 1998). For example, in an early study, Williams (1959) taught parents to ignore the bedtime crying of their 4-year-old boy. The tantrums were successfully reduced until the boy's grandmother later attended to his disruptive behavior. The tantrums were subsequently eliminated after parental attention was again withdrawn. An obstacle encountered when using extinction is that parents frequently find it difficult to ignore the cries of a child for an extended period of time (Milan, Mitchell, Berger, & Pierson, 1981; Rolider & Van Houten, 1984).

An alternative to extinction that is often recommended for bedtime or middle-of-the-night disturbances is *graduated extinction* (Ferber, 1985). As with extinction, graduated extinction is appropriate when either the bedtime disturbance or night waking appears to be at least partially maintained by parental attention. In a study by Rolider and Van Houten (1984), parents were trained to use a graduated extinction procedure to decrease crying at bedtime. The procedure consisted of delaying parental attention when the child cried for a specified amount of time and then briefly attending to the child. The duration of time spent ignoring their child increased by 5 minutes in each subsequent interval, but the parents were allowed to attend to their child after waiting the specified amount of time. This graduated extinction procedure resulted in a decrease in the child's crying. Similar graduated extinction

procedures have been used to effectively reduce night waking in children (Durand, Gernert-Dott, & Mapstone, 1996; Durand & Mindell, 1990; Mindell & Durand, 1993). Other behavioral interventions that have been used to treat sleep disorders include time-out and social reinforcement (Ronen, 1991), the establishment of stable bedtime and wake-up routines (Weissbluth, 1982), relaxation training (Anderson, 1979), and an earlier bedtime schedule (Piazza & Fisher, 1991).

One difficulty in using most of these behavioral interventions for sleep terrors is that they assume that parental attention serves a role in the maintenance of these problems. Sleep terrors occur while the child is still asleep; therefore, he or she is presumably unaware of the presence or absence of others. One intervention that does not rely on the withdrawal of parental attention is *scheduled awakenings* (Durand, 1998; Durand & Mindell, 1999), which involve having the parents wake the child approximately 30 minutes before a spontaneous awakening. As the frequency of spontaneous waking decreases, scheduled awakenings are eliminated. Scheduled awakenings have been used in a number of studies to successfully reduce night waking in children (Johnson, Bradley-Johnson, & Stack, 1981; Johnson & Lerner, 1985; Rickert & Johnson, 1988) and for another slow wave sleep disturbance—sleepwalking (Frank, Spirito, Stark, & Owens-Stively, 1997). Several sleep professionals have recommended a form of scheduled awakenings as a treatment for sleep terrors, although until recently, no controlled studies existed evaluating its effectiveness (Lask, 1988; Maskey, 1993).

Durand and Mindell (1999) used scheduled awakenings to treat the chronic sleep terrors of three children who did not have developmental disabilities. Results from this study suggested that the sleep terrors displayed by these children were eliminated quickly (during the first night); these results were maintained 1 year later. The present study was designed to assess the effectiveness of scheduled awakenings on the chronic sleep terrors displayed by children with autism. It was hypothesized that waking the children approximately 30 minutes before the time they usually experienced a sleep terror would interrupt deep sleep (Stages 3 and 4 of NREM sleep) and therefore reduce the frequency of these disturbing nighttime events. Social validity data were also collected to assess parents' satisfaction with the intervention and its results.

Method

PARTICIPANTS AND SETTING

Two boys and one girl (all diagnosed with autism) were referred through their physicians to the Sleep Project at the University at Albany for evaluation and assistance with sleep problems. Their developmental pediatrician had diagnosed each child as having both autism and sleep terrors but ruled out any contributing medical problems. The parents were interviewed extensively about the sleep histories of their children. The children, ages 5, $7\frac{1}{2}$, and 3, each had a history of several years of episodes that met the criteria for severe and chronic sleep terrors (American Sleep Disorders Association, 1990). Five-year-old Tommy was reported to have been a poor sleeper almost from birth. He had difficulty falling asleep and would also awaken in the middle of the night crying. Some anecdotal evidence indicated that he had interrupted breathing during the night, primarily through observations of his loud snoring. Tommy's parents, in consultation with their pediatrician, had tried using a variety of medications (malatonin; diazapam [Valium®]; and because of suspected seizures, depakote) for his sleeping difficulties but with no success. Tommy would sleep an average of 9 hours per night, which is below the average for a child his age ($10\frac{1}{2}$ hours for children ages 5–9 years old). From about the age of 3, Tommy was described as having episodes where he would scream out but remain in bed. When his parents would try to comfort him, he would scream louder and sit up in bed, but he appeared to be asleep. He was sweaty and clearly upset, but within 10 to 15 minutes he would fall back to sleep. These episodes sometimes occurred as often as 2 to 3 times per night.

Jon, $7\frac{1}{2}$ years old, had a long history of multiple sleep problems. As a toddler he would not nap, would require almost 2 hours to fall asleep at night, and would awaken almost every night. Sleep terrors began at about the age of 3 months and continued until his participation in the study. These episodes began with a scream and sometimes followed with his walking around the house. Jon would not settle down when comforted by his parents and was eventually led back to his bed, where he would go back to sleep. At the time of this study, he slept an average of 8.5 hours per night. Jon also had a history of sleepwalking (in the absence of a sleep terror), which his parents described as occurring approximately once per month. He had no other significant health problems.

Lea was 3 years old at the start of the study. She would only occasionally nap and was sleeping only approximately 7 hours, on average, per night due to disrupted bedtime and frequent nightwaking. In addition, she frequently experienced sleep terrors. Lea's parents reported her to be quite aroused during these episodes (e.g., sweaty), but she did not seem to be negatively affected by them the next day. The sleep disruptions by all three children were causing chronic interruption of their parents' sleep as well, yet the parents felt a great deal of anxiety about helping their children with sleep terrors.

The parents were trained in the intervention techniques in their homes, with phone follow-ups two times a week for additional support and checks on the data collection. The parents served as primary intervention agents for their child's sleep terrors.

DEPENDENT MEASURES

Sleep Terror Data

The families completed sleep charts on a daily basis. Parents recorded the time the child was put to bed, how long it took the child to fall asleep, the onset and duration of sleep terrors, the time the child woke up in the morning, and the time and duration of any naps during the day. These data were collected, and the number of nights with sleep terrors was calculated weekly throughout baseline and treatment for all participants. In addition, parents completed behavior logs nightly to record their child's behavior as he or she was being put to bed and during sleep terror episodes. Parents' responses to their child's behavior during these episodes were also noted. Data on child sleep patterns were used to determine the time of the scheduled awakenings, and the behavior logs were used to evaluate parental compliance with the intervention plan. Data on sleep terrors were used to assess treatment outcome and are reported in Figure 1. Parents mailed the completed forms to the researchers weekly.

Phone calls were made to the families at least twice per week during all phases. These calls were designed to provide support to the families, to serve as checks on the data collection efforts, and—during the intervention phases—to check on the fidelity of treatment implementation. A description of the previous night's events was solicited—including frequency and duration of sleep terror episodes—and this description was later matched to the parents' written logs. These data checks were compared formally to the written logs (assessing the number of agreements and dividing by the number of agreements plus disagreements) and were 100% in agreement for the presence or absence of sleep terror episodes for all families, both in baseline and during intervention.

Social Validity Data

The parents were presented with a series of brief statements and were asked to respond with their impressions of their child's sleep terrors, the acceptability of intervention, and the effectiveness of scheduled awakenings (see Table 1). These statements were administered at three points in the study: during baseline, after a month of intervention, and at the 12-month follow-up. These data were used to assess the family's reaction to the intervention. In each case, the child's mother was the respondent because she was the parent who took primary responsibility for the child's disrupted sleep.

PROCEDURE AND DESIGN

Baseline

Parents were taught how to complete the daily sleep charts and behavior logs and were instructed to begin collecting

Table 1. Social Validity Data

Statement	Responses of Tommy's parents			Responses of Jon's parents			Responses of Lea's parents		
	Baseline	1 mo	12 mo	Baseline	1 mo	12 mo	Baseline	1 mo	12 mo
1. Scheduled awakenings are an appropriate treatment for my child's sleep problem.	N/A	4	4	N/A	4	4	N/A	3	4
2. Scheduled awakenings involve a reasonable amount of effort to help my child sleep better.	N/A	4	4	N/A	3	4	N/A	3	4
3. My child's sleep terrors are currently a serious problem.	4	0	0	4	0	0	3	0	0
4. I am satisfied with the results of the treatment on my child's sleep problem.	N/A	4	4	N/A	4	4	N/A	3	4
5. I would use scheduled awakenings again if my child's sleep problem returned.	N/A	4	4	N/A	4	4	N/A	3	4

Note. *Response scale from 0 (strongly disagree) to 4 (strongly agree).*

data on sleep terrors. Informed consent was received from the parents of each child, and a medical waiver was obtained from the child's primary physician in order to rule out any possible medical causes for the sleep disturbance. General information about the nature of the study was provided for the parents; however, no specific interventions were suggested at the initial interview. Weeks of baseline assessment (3, 6, and 9 weeks) were staggered across the participants to conform to a multiple baseline across participants (Barlow & Hersen, 1984), the design used to evaluate the effects of treatment on each child's sleep terrors.

Intervention

The intervention technique was taught to the parents of these children, and the effects of the parent-implemented procedure on the frequency of sleep terror episodes were evaluated (see Durand, 1998, for sample data sheets and a full description of the intervention procedure). Information from the sleep charts was used to determine the time that the child typically experienced a sleep terror during the night. The therapist introduced the rationale and described the steps for intervention during a 1- to 1½-hour session with the parents. The parents were provided with an explanation of how sleep progresses at night, along with a rationale for scheduled awakenings. It was explained in this way: Although we did not know precisely why this procedure helped children with nighttime sleep problems, waking them just before a sleep disruption seemed to "reboot" their deep sleep. In other words, it was as if the children had disrupted deep sleep cycles, and the awakenings

seemed to restart the cycle in a better way—almost like restarting a computer after experiencing problems of unknown origin. Each of the families had some experience with computers and appreciated the analogy.

To begin the intervention, parents were instructed to awaken their child approximately 30 minutes prior to the typical sleep terror time. Parents were told to wake the child with a light touch until the child opened his or her eyes, then allow the child to fall back to sleep. Sleep terrors were relatively predictable for each child. Tommy typically fell asleep at about 9:30 p.m., and when he had a sleep terror, it would occur at about 11:30 p.m. The initial time for his scheduled awakenings was set at 11:00 p.m. Jon was asleep at about 10:00 p.m., and his episodes would occur at about midnight. His scheduled awakenings were set at 11:30 p.m. However, Tommy seemed to wake up very easily at his scheduled time, so it was moved back 15 minutes (i.e., from 11:30 p.m. to 11:15 p.m.) during Week 1 of intervention and on all subsequent nights. Lea was asleep by about 11:30 p.m. each evening, and her sleep terrors would occur at about 12:45 a.m. Therefore, her scheduled awakenings were set at 12:15 a.m.

This plan was repeated each night until the child successfully went a full 7 nights without a sleep terror. If the child achieved this level of success, parents were told to skip 1 night (that is, no scheduled awakening) the first week and one additional night each subsequent week. If the child had a sleep terror episode, then the parents were to go back to daily night awakenings. The number of nights with scheduled awakenings was decreased until the child no longer experienced sleep terrors during the night.

Follow-up

Each family was contacted 12 months after the initial intervention for follow-up evaluation. Parents were again asked to record the number of sleep terror episodes that occurred each evening over a 2-week period. The twice-weekly phone calls were also reinstituted as observer agreement checks, and the social validity statements were readministered.

Results

The mean number of nights with sleep terror episodes per week for each child is presented in Figure 1. Tommy experienced sleep terrors every night during baseline (mean, 7.0 per week). Following the intervention, this was reduced to less than one per week (mean, .04 per week; range, 0–1), and no occurrences were observed at the 12-month follow-up. Jon had approximately three sleep terror episodes per week during baseline (mean, 3.0; range, 2–4), but this was reduced to zero immediately after the intervention and was at zero at the 12-month follow-up. The time to wake him was moved back 15 minutes after the first week because he appeared to wake up too easily. This change appeared to reduce the number of sleep terrors without fully waking him at night. Finally, Lea experienced approximately 2.5 sleep terror episodes per week in baseline (mean, 2.55; range, 1–4), which was reduced to less than one per week following treatment (mean, 0.11; range, 0–1) and was at zero at the 12-month follow-up. Figure 1 also shows the point at which the scheduled awakenings were eliminated for each child.

Total sleep time was also assessed pre- and postintervention and indicated an increase in the number of hours two of the three children slept, on average, each night. Tommy slept an average of 9 hours per night prior to intervention, and this remained stable postintervention. Jon's 8.5 hours of sleep per night increased to approximately 9 hours per night postintervention, and Lea's 7 hours of sleep per night preintervention increased to approximately 8.5 hours postintervention.

The social validity data are presented in Table 1. Parental responses indicated agreement with the appropriateness of the intervention, the amount of effort required to carry out the intervention, their satisfaction with the outcome, and their willingness to use the intervention again. Responses to the statement about the seriousness of their child's sleep terrors showed an improvement from baseline to postintervention.

Discussion

This is the first empirical study to document the successful treatment of the chronic sleep terrors of children with autism using a behavioral intervention. Scheduled awak-

enings appear to be responsible for the reduction of sleep terror episodes for these children, and the reductions were maintained 1 year following intervention. The families of these children found the intervention to be appropriate and effective, as evidenced by their ratings on the social validity measures.

The mechanism underlying the success of scheduled awakenings on the reduction of sleep terrors may have involved a change in the type of sleep experienced by these three children. The planned interrupted sleep may have changed the nature of the children's sleep patterns such that deep sleep (the stage at which sleep terrors occur) was reorganized to eliminate disruptions during this stage (i.e., sleep terrors). An additional hypothesis is that the children became conditioned to self-arousing (Frank et al., 1997). Finally, it is possible that increasing the total hours of sleep (which happened for two of the children) affected sleep terrors. Because sleep terrors occur during the deep stages of sleep (Stages 3 and 4), and sleep deprivation can result in disruption of this deep sleep, it is possible that the mechanism of change was an increase in sleep for two of the children (Durand, 1998). Unfortunately, we do not have electroencephalogram (EEG) data on the children's NREM sleep patterns to make conclusive statements about the effects of awakening. However, the present results do highlight the potential ability for a behavioral intervention (e.g., scheduled awakenings) to influence a biological (deep sleep disturbances) event. The reciprocal nature of behavioral and biological influences points to interventions that bridge both seemingly independent domains (Barlow & Durand, 1999).

The increase in total sleep time for two of the three children following intervention was encouraging. Although all three children continued to sleep less than the mean for their age—$10\frac{1}{2}$ hours—their demeanor during the day and the absence of slow wave sleep disruptions following scheduled awakenings (e.g., sleepwalking, sleep talking) suggest that they were receiving a sufficient amount of sleep. It is significant to note that one of the criteria for diagnosing a sleep disorder involves the negative influence on daytime sequelae (e.g., looking tired, irritability). Because children (and adults) have individual needs for sleep, there is a range of what is needed for each child, and these three children appeared to be getting sufficient rest for their needs.

Medical intervention with children in general is controversial, and medication for children who have chronic sleep problems is usually discouraged (Durand, 1998). The results of the present study argue against the use of medical interventions for sleep terrors as the first line of treatment, especially among children. The observed results are comparable to or better than those of previous efforts involving medication and clearly do not have the negative side effects that accompany medical approaches (Fisher et al., 1973). Although considerably more effort is required

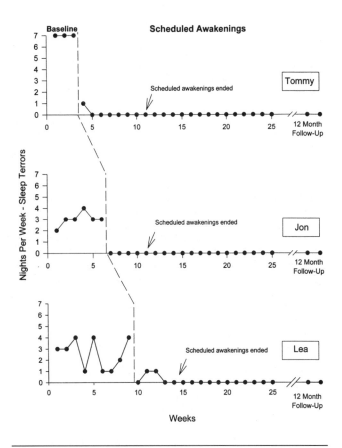

Figure 1. The number of nights per week each child experienced a sleep terror episode across both baseline and intervention.

of the parents when using scheduled awakenings, the parents in this study found the level of effort acceptable.

The social validity data suggest that the parents of these children agreed that scheduled awakenings were an appropriate treatment, that the procedure involves a reasonable amount of effort, and that they were satisfied with the results. It is important to note, however, that despite the generally positive ratings, anecdotal evidence suggests that scheduled awakenings were initially difficult to carry out. All of the parents had some difficulty staying up (or in some cases, waking up) to awaken their child. This difficulty was evidenced in how quickly each family stopped the scheduled awakenings once they appeared to be successful. Despite our instructions to gradually decrease the number of awakenings each week, each family ended their scheduled awakenings earlier than recommended. Clearly, the families were anxious to go back to a regular nighttime routine. The initial reluctance to carry out this approach seemed to be tempered by the twice-weekly phone checks that appeared to be effective as a means of supporting the families through the more difficult early times when it was not clear that their efforts would be successful. It is recommended that clinicians incorporate some type of support

mechanism for families attempting to intervene with their child's sleep difficulties. It may be asserted that because sleep terrors do not appear to negatively affect the child, simply ignoring them would be a more acceptable alternative to intervention. However, in these cases, the chronic nature of these disruptions and their negative effects on the families' sleep argued for some form of intervention.

The results of this study point to an effective, nonmedical approach to reducing the chronic sleep terrors displayed by some children with autism. Clinicians should be able to use this technique to assist families who are experiencing one more stress related to parenting their children. Additional research could help to demonstrate the generality of these findings and to help further our understanding of the mechanisms responsible for these changes in sleep patterns. We need to continue to explore intervention approaches that can help improve the lives of children with autism as well as their families.

ABOUT THE AUTHOR

V. Mark Durand, PhD, is interim dean of the College of Arts and Sciences and professor of psychology at the University at Albany, State University of New York. His research has primarily focused on the assessment and treatment of self-injurious and disruptive behavior as well as sleep disorders in persons with severe disabilities, including autism. Address: V. Mark Durand, Department of Psychology, University at Albany–SUNY, Albany, New York 12222.

AUTHOR'S NOTE

The author wishes to thank the families of these three children for their persistence and help during this study.

REFERENCES

Abe, K., Oda, N., Ikenaga, K., & Yamada, T. (1993). Twin study on night terrors, fears and some physiological and behavioural characteristics in children. *Psychiatric Genetics, 3,* 39–43.

American Sleep Disorders Association. (1990). *The international classification of sleep disorders: Diagnostic and coding manual.* Rochester, MN: Author.

Anderson, D. (1979). Treatment of insomnia in a 13-year-old boy by relaxation training and reduction of parental attention. *Journal of Behavior Therapy and Experimental Psychiatry, 10,* 263–265.

Barlow, D. H., & Durand, V. M. (1999). *Abnormal psychology: An integrative approach* (2nd ed.). Pacific Grove, CA: Wadsworth.

Bergeron, C., Godbout, R., Mottron, L., & Stip, E. (1997). Sleep and dreaming in Asperger's Syndrome. *Sleep Research, 26,* 541.

Durand, V. M. (1998). *Sleep better! A guide to improving sleep for children with special needs.* Baltimore: Brookes.

Durand, V. M., Gernert-Dott, P., & Mapstone, E. (1996). Treatment of sleep disorders in children with developmental disabilities. *Journal of the Association for Persons With Severe Handicaps, 21,* 114–122.

Durand, V. M., & Mindell, J. A. (1990). Behavioral treatment of multiple childhood sleep disorders: Effects on child and family. *Behavior Modification, 14,* 37–49.

Durand, V. M., & Mindell, J. A. (1999). Behavioral intervention for childhood sleep terrors. *Behavior Therapy, 30,* 705–715.

Durand, V. M., Mindell, J. A., Mapstone, E., & Gernert-Dott, P. (1998). Sleep problems. In T. S. Watson & F. M. Gresham (Eds.), *Handbook of child behavior therapy* (pp. 203–219). New York: Plenum Press.

Ferber, R. (1985). *Solve your child's sleep problems.* New York: Simon & Schuster.

Fisher, C., Kahn, E., Edwards, A., & Davis, D. M. (1973). A psychophysiological study of nightmares and night terrors: The suppression of Stage 4 night terrors with diazepam. *Archives of General Psychiatry, 28,* 252–259.

Frank, N. C., Spirito, A., Stark, L., & Owens-Stively, J. (1997). The use of scheduled awakenings to eliminate childhood sleepwalking. *Journal of Pediatric Psychology, 22,* 345–353.

Giles, D. E., & Buysse, D. J. (1993). *Parasomnias.* In D. L. Dunner (Ed.), *Current psychiatric therapy* (pp. 361–372). Philadelphia: W. B. Saunders.

Hering, E., Epstein, R., Elroy, S., Iancu, D. R., & Zelnik, N. (1999). Sleep patterns in autistic children. *Journal of Autism and Developmental Disorders, 29,* 143–147.

Johnson, C. M., Bradley-Johnson, S., & Stack, J. M. (1981). Decreasing the frequency of infant's nocturnal crying with the use of scheduled awakenings. *Family Practice Research Journal, 1,* 98–104.

Johnson, C. M., & Lerner, M. (1985). Amelioration of infant sleep disturbances: II. Effects of scheduled awakenings by compliant parents. *Infant Mental Health Journal, 6,* 21–30.

Kales, J. D., Kales, A., Soldatos, C. R., Caldwell, A. B., Charney, D. S., & Martin, E. D. (1980). Night terrors: Clinical characteristics and personality patterns. *Archives of General Psychiatry, 37,* 1406–1410.

Karacan, I. (1988). Parasomnias. In R. L. Williams, I. Karacan, & C. A. Moore (Eds.), *Sleep disorders: Diagnosis and treatment* (pp. 131–144). New York: Wiley.

Lask, B. (1988). Novel and non-toxic treatment for night terrors. *British Medical Journal, 297,* 592.

Lask, B. (1995). Night terrors. In C. E. Schaefer (Ed.), *Clinical handbook of sleep disorders in children* (pp. 125–134). Northvale, NJ: Jason Aronson.

Maskey, S. (1993). Simple treatment for night terrors. *British Medical Journal, 306,* 1477.

Milan, M. A., Mitchell, Z. P., Berger, M. I., & Pierson, D. F. (1981). Positive routines: A rapid alternative to extinction for elimination of bedtime tantrum behavior. *Child Behavior Therapy, 3,* 13–25.

Mindell, J. A. (1993). Sleep disorders in children. *Health Psychology, 12,* 151–162.

Mindell, J. A., & Durand, V. M. (1993). Treatment of childhood sleep disorders: Generalization across disorders and effects on family members. *Journal of Pediatric Psychology, 18,* 731–750.

Piazza, C. C., & Fisher, W. W. (1991). A faded bedtime with response cost protocol for treatment of multiple sleep problems in children. *Journal of Applied Behavior Analysis, 24,* 129–140.

Richdale, A. L., & Prior, M. R. (1995). The sleep/wake rhythm in children with autism. *European Child and Adolescent Psychiatry, 4,* 175–186.

Rickert, V. I., & Johnson, C. M. (1988). Reducing nocturnal awakenings and crying episodes in infants and children: A comparison between scheduled awakenings and systematic ignoring. *Pediatrics, 81,* 203–212.

Rolider, A., & Van Houten, R. (1984). Training parents to use extinction to eliminate nighttime crying by gradually increasing the criteria for ignoring crying. *Education and Treatment of Children, 7,* 119–124.

Ronen, T. (1991). Intervention package for treating sleep disorders in a four-year-old girl. *Journal of Behavior Therapy and Experimental Psychiatry, 22,* 141–148.

Stores, G., & Wiggs, L. (1998). Abnormal sleep patterns associated with autism. *Autism, 2,* 157–169.

Weissbluth, M. (1982). Modification of sleep schedule with reduction of night waking: A case report. *Sleep, 5,* 262–266.

Williams, C. D. (1959). The elimination of tantrum behavior by extinction procedures. *Journal of Abnormal Social Psychology, 59,* 269–273.

Action Editor: Glen Dunlap

JASH
1995, Vol. 20, No. 1, 16–30

Building an Ecology of Support: A Case Study of One Young Woman With Severe Problem Behaviors Living in the Community

Joseph M. Lucyshyn, Deborah Olson, and Robert H. Horner
University of Oregon

This case study describes 30 months in the life of a young woman with a history of life-threatening self-injurious behaviors (SIB) who moved from a large public institution to her community. Quantitative and qualitative research methods were employed to provide a nonexperimental description of her behavior and lifestyle in the community. Quantitative measurements included: (a) activity patterns, (b) social network, (c) self-injurious behaviors, (d) aggression against others, and (e) staff changes. Qualitative results emerged from semistructured interviews and participant observations conducted over a 6-month period. Together, these data revealed a young woman actively involved in a lifestyle characterized by an increase in the frequency and diversity of activities performed in the community. Problem behaviors occurred at low levels for extended periods, yet there continued to be times with major regression. Qualitative results also indicate a general reduction in the intensity of self-injurious behaviors. Results are discussed in terms of the importance of multicomponent positive interventions, the need to design environments that promote lifestyle changes, and the value of collaboratively employing quantitative and qualitative research methods.

DESCRIPTORS: autism, functional assessment, longitudinal analysis, self-injury, severe problem behavior

Adults with developmental disabilities are relocating from large institutions to local communities (Hill, Lakin, & Bruininks, 1988). Those who engage in problem behaviors, however, continue to represent a large percentage of the population of individuals who remain in institutions (Cunningham & Mueller, 1991; Lakin & Bruininks, 1985). In fact, problem behaviors are the most common reason cited for new admissions or reentry to institutions (Bromley & Blacher, 1991; Hill & Bruininks, 1984). The presumption has been that problem behaviors should be reduced before a person moves from the institution (Foxx, Bechtel, Bird, Livesay, & Bittle, 1986; Skodak-Crissey & Rosen, 1986; Zigler, Hodapp, & Edison, 1990). An alternative view that a regular lifestyle is the foundation for reducing problem behaviors is offered by proponents of (a) supported living for persons with severe disabilities (Boles, Horner, & Bellamy, 1988; Taylor, Biklen, & Knoll, 1987) and (b) positive behavioral support (Carr, Robinson, Taylor, & Carlson, 1990; Durand, 1990b; Horner et al., 1990; Meyer & Evans, 1989). Although there is some empirical evidence for supporting individuals with problem behaviors in the community (Berkman & Meyer, 1988; Horner et al., 1992), the data base remains small. In addition, the complexities and potential richness of community life suggest the value of supplementing quantitative measures of resident behavior and lifestyle with qualitative descriptions and analysis (Kaiser, 1993; Meyer & Evans, 1993a, 1993b; Nisbet, Clark, & Covert, 1991; Repp & Singh, 1990; Taylor & Bogdan, 1981).

The present case study describes the experience of one young woman with a history of life-threatening,

Preparation of this manuscript was supported in part by the U.S. Department of Education, Cooperative Agreement No. H133B20004 and by U.S. Department of Education Grant No. H133C20114. The opinions expressed herein do not necessarily reflect the position or policy of either the U.S. Department of Education of the U.S. Department of Health and Human Services, and no official endorsement by either department should be inferred.

We thank Dr. Philip M. Ferguson for his assistance with the design of the qualitative methodology, Dr. Robert E. O'Neill for his help with the summary of behavior and lifestyle data, and Dr. Richard W. Albin for his suggestions related to the clinical time series data. We also thank Jane Bell for her computer skills, Kate Werner for her early assistance with qualitative data collection and analysis, Smita Shukla, Alan Surratt, and Julie Rychards for their assistance with quantitative data collection, and Dr. Bonnie Todis for her helpful comments on the qualitative data analysis. Finally, we would like to thank family members, staff, and friends of Emma who contributed their time and effort to make this study possible.

All correspondence concerning this manuscript and requests for reprints should be sent to Robert H. Horner, Specialized Training Program, University of Oregon, Eugene, OR 97403-1235.

self-injurious behaviors who moved from a large public institution to the community. The broad purpose of this investigation is to provide a comprehensive description of the behavioral support and lifestyle outcomes experienced by one woman with severe problem behavior who returned to her community. With this broad purpose, we have three goals: (a) to provide a more in-depth picture of community-based support for a person with severe problem behaviors by describing 30 months of data and by employing both quantitative and qualitative research methods, (b) to provide an example of using lifestyle measures as well as problem behavior measures to index the outcomes of behavioral support, and (c) to illustrate the link between a functional assessment and the design and continual adaptation of multielement support plan (Carr, Robinson, & Palumbo, 1990).

Methods

Focus Participant

At the time of the study, Emma was a 26-year-old woman with the diagnosis of autism, mild to moderate mental retardation, and hyperactivity. She was physically capable and often communicated her interests and desires verbally. During the study, she was taking between 675 and 125 mg of Thorazine a day. Before moving into the community, Emma lived for 7.5 years in a residential institution for persons with developmental disabilities. Severe problem behaviors, including intense self-injury, were the primary reason for placement.

Psychologist and family reports indicated that Emma continued to engage in intense self-injurious behaviors while residing in the institution. These behaviors resulted in significant tissue damage and multiple hospitalizations. Emma would bite her hands and arms, forcefully bang her head against objects and corners, pull her hair out, or pound her face with her fist. She also engaged in aggressive behaviors toward staff. She would scratch their hands, arms, and face, pull their hair, or strike them with her protective helmet. Previously unsuccessful treatments included high dosages of psychotropic medication (e.g., 1,000 mg/day of Thorazine), contingent aversive stimulation (e.g., water mist, electric shock), and environmental enrichment (e.g., differential reinforcement of other behavior, a social "bonding" program modeled after Gentle Teaching procedures [McGee, Menousek, Hobbs & Menousek, 1987]).

Setting and Program Description

Emma lived in a small three-bedroom house in a middle class neighborhood one-third mile from the downtown district of a moderately sized city in the Pacific Northwest. She lived with one housemate, a 37-year-old woman with profound mental retardation.

Emma received 1:1 staff support during the day with an awake staff present to support Emma and her housemate at night. Emma also received assistance working at an organic foods warehouse as a produce sorter 4 hours per week. A local supported employment organization obtained this job for Emma and provided a job coach to support her during work hours.

Design of a Competent Environment

Seven months before Emma moved into the community, a series of assessment activities were conducted: (a) a functional assessment of Emma's problem behaviors was completed using procedures recommended by O'Neill, Horner, Albin, Storey, & Sprague (1990)—this assessment indicated that Emma's self-injury and aggression were multiply maintained by avoidance from aversive situations, access to preferred objects, and attention from preferred people; (b) medical support needs were identified; (c) critical features interviews were conducted with her staff and family to identify the characteristics of a community living situation that would be safe, responsive, and individually appropriate (Horner et al., 1992); and (d) a futures planning meeting was held to identify Emma's preferences, family visions for the future, and the initial members of Emma's support network (O'Brien, 1987).

Based on the assessment information, renovations were made to her new home, her housemate was identified, staff were hired and trained, and her behavior support plan was developed. During Emma's first year in the community, this support plan was revised repeatedly based on continual functional assessment information. The initial plan included a large number of features; a synthesis of the main features is provided in Table 1.

Quantitative Measurement

Quantitative measurement focused on six variables: (a) the frequency per week of self-injurious behaviors, (b) the frequency per week of aggression toward others, (c) activities performed in the community, (d) social integration (social network and socially integrated activities), (e) medication taken per week, and (f) staff changes per week. Data were collected during an 8-month period prior to her move (for some variables), and across 30 months after her move (April 1989 through September 1991).

Self-injurious behaviors. Self-injury was defined as hitting head against a surface, biting self, pulling out hair, hitting self with fist, kicking self on shins, and pinching self. Data were collected 24 hours a day by the program staff in the community using the Functional Assessment Observation Form described by O'Neill et al. (1990). Data were recorded as "events" of self-injury. An event was the occurrence of one or

Table 1
Emma's Initial Positive Behavior Support Plan

Lifestyle/Ecological Interventions

1. Provide opportunities for frequent home and community activities on a daily basis (20 community activities per week).
2. Support Emma's contact with family and/or friends at least 4 times per week.
3. Offer Emma choices for interaction, activity, possessions, foods, and snack items.
4. Give Emma control over her restraints. Emma may wear her helmet, arm guards and ankle guards at all times, but she will be given 10–20 opportunities per day to remove them. If she removes a restraint, she may get it back at any point by asking.

Antecedent Interventions

1. Increase predictability about staff schedules and activity patterns by providing Emma with a weekly staff schedule picture calendar.
2. When Emma repeats or becomes anxious about an issue write or draw a "promise" card that gives her the relevant answer or information. Place the card in her "promise book" and when she next raises the issue, refer her to the book and card.
3. Provide Emma with at least 50 positive social interactions each day.

Teaching New Behaviors

1. Teach Emma to communicate *verbally* her need for assistance, desire for attention, need for information or reassurance, and refusal to do a task or activity.
2. Teach Emma to do deep breathing as a self-control strategy to reduce her anxiety.

Reinforcement Strategies

1. Use positive contingency contracts to motivate Emma to participate in tasks and activities (e.g., getting up and dressed in the morning).
2. Praise Emma often for communicating verbally her wants and needs, remaining calm, and actively participating tasks or activities.

De-escalation Procedures

1. Block attempts at self-injury or aggression.

Emergency Procedures

1. Physically restrain Emma when she engages in intense self-injury or aggression using PART procedures.

---

more self-injurious responses. A period of at least 30 sec without self-injury was required before a new event was recorded. Data were tallied and reviewed by support staff at weekly staff meetings.

Aggression. Aggression was defined as striking others with her helmet, scratching others, hitting others with fist or objects, and/or pulling the hair of others. Measurement and review procedures for aggression were the same as for self-injurious behaviors. The results provided a weekly count of the number of events with one or more instances of aggression.

Physical integration/activities in the community. Data on the frequency of activities in the community were collected in two ways. The first was indirect measurement via the Resident Lifestyle Inventory (RLI)

(Kennedy, Horner, Newton, & Kanda, 1990). This questionnaire was completed by program staff who participated regularly in activities with Emma. The RLI provides a list of 144 activities. For each activity, staff rated (a) whether or not the activity occurred during the last 30 days, (b) the frequency of occurrence, and (c) whether it typically occurred in the community or in the home. The RLI has been demonstrated by Kennedy, Horner, Newton, and Kanda (1990) to have congruent validity of .81, test-retest reliability of .83, and social validity confirmed by more than 70% of direct service staff reporting that use of the RLI improved their effectiveness. RLI data were collected twice in the institution prior to Emma's move and one each year after her move (three total).

The second measure of activity patterns was collected through direct observation by the program staff on a 24-hr basis using the Valued Outcomes Information System (VOIS) (Newton et al., 1988). Within this system, the staff completed a small "tag" for each activity performed in the community. An event was scored as a "community activity" if it lasted at least 15 min, and was performed outside the property boundary of the home. This system produced a frequency count of the number of community activities performed per week. This count also was tallied and reviewed by support staff at weekly staff meetings.

Activity preferences. The RLI was also used to measure Emma's activity preferences. Each activity listed on the RLI that support staff had performed with Emma was rated as "preferred," "not preferred," or "unclear." Newton, Ard, and Horner (1993) recently demonstrated that staff assessment of preference using this system predicted resident choice behavior with 92% accuracy.

Social integration and activities with others. Emma's social life was measured quantitatively in two ways: through an index of her social network and through direct observation of activities performed with others. Emma's social network was measured using the Social Network Analysis Form (SNAF) (Kennedy, Horner, & Newton, 1990). This interview was completed on each administration by Emma and two staff who had worked at least 3 months with Emma, and it provided a list of the people perceived as socially important to Emma under the headings (a) family, (b) friends, (c) people paid to provide support, and (d) co-workers and housemates. The SNAF was administered twice before Emma moved from the institution and four times after she moved.

A second empirical index of Emma's social life was obtained via the VOIS direct observation system. The same activity tags used to record physical integration had space to indicate if the activity was socially integrated. To be recorded as socially integrated, the activity needed to involve a minimum of 15 min of socially reciprocated interaction with a person who was neither paid to provide support nor a housemate (Newton et al., 1988). These data were collected only after Emma moved to the community and resulted in a count of socially integrated activities that was reviewed weekly by program staff.

Staff changes. Functional assessment interviews with staff in the institution suggested that staff turnover was a significant setting event related to Emma's problem behavior. As such, staff changes in the community were monitored carefully using the personnel records of the support agency. Changes were defined as new staff starting, staff making significant changes in hours of employment (e.g., full-time to relief, relief to part-time), and staff terminating employment. The frequency of these changes was tallied and summarized as a cumulative frequency per week.

Medication. The type and amount of medication Emma took each day was recorded by medical and support staff following procedures mandated by the Oregon Administrative Rules. From these records, the weekly dosage level of Thorazine, in milligrams, was summarized.

Reliability and Validity

Because interobserver agreement scores were not gathered for weekly behavioral and lifestyle data, alternative strategies were employed to strengthen the reliability and validity of the data. The reliability and accuracy of weekly time series data (e.g., aggression, community integration) were enhanced through initial and ongoing training in data collection for all staff supporting Emma, weekly data review meetings led by a program manager, and the omission of weekly data judged to be inaccurate. The convergent validity of lifestyle data was strengthened by the use of multiple quantitative measurement strategies (e.g., time series weekly frequency data, empirically validated lifestyle assessment instruments) (Campbell & Fiske, 1959; McGrew & Bruininks, 1994; Widaman, Stacy, & Borthwick-Duffy, 1993). Finally, the convergent validity of behavioral and lifestyle data was further strengthened by the use of triangulation across research methods (Patton, 1990). Qualitative interviews and participant observations, in addition to providing an in-depth description and interpretation of Emma's life in the community, served to confirm the quantitative results.

Qualitative Measurement

Interviews and participant observations were completed over a 7-month period by the first author beginning April 1991. The social role of the researcher conducting interviews and observations was that of an insider (Jorgensen, 1989). He possessed knowledge about Emma's experiences in the community and had established a trusting relationship with staff by serving

as a volunteer behavioral consultant for the "Carol and Emma" house for 7 months prior to the initiation of the study.

Qualitative interviews. Semistructured interviews were conducted with six key informants: Emma's mother and father; a brother and sister-in-law who have been strong advocates for Emma; a staff person who had worked with Emma in the community for over 2 years; and one of Emma's closest friends, a former part-time community staff person and current relief staff person for Emma. The interviewer presented participants with open-ended questions about Emma's quality of life in the institution and/or the community, and changes in Emma's behavior since moving to the community. An interview guide ensured that each question was included in all of the interviews. Specific questions are presented in Table 2.

Interviews lasted between 2 and 5 hr and were completed across one to five sessions. A total of 17 hr of interviews were completed. All interviews were taperecorded and transcribed verbatim.

Participant observations. Participant observations were completed with Emma and her staff and/or friends as they interacted and participated in a wide

Table 2
Qualitative Interview Guide for Care Provider/Friend and Family Members

Questions for Careprovider or Friend:

1. Tell me about Emma. What is she like?
2. Tell me about Emma's life in the community. What is it like?
3. What kind of things does she do? Where does she go? Whom does she see?
4. What makes her happy? What tends to set her off?
5. Describe a good day? Describe a bad day?
6. How does Emma make her preferences known? What does she express an interest in doing or not doing?
7. How do careproviders typically respond to her preferences?
8. How happy do you believe Emma is living in the community?
9. From the time you first met her until now, how has she changed, if at all?
10. Why do you think she has changed?

Questions for Family Members:

1. Tell me about Emma. What is she like?
2. What was her life like at the institution from your perspective?
3. Describe your experience visiting Emma at the institution?
4. How often do you see Emma now?
5. What is Emma's life like in the community from your perspective?
6. Describe your experience visiting Emma in the community?
7. From the time she entered the community until now, how has she changed, if at all?
8. Why do you think she has changed?

range of activities. Experiences sampled included: (a) typical home and community activities; (b) interactions with staff and friends; and (c) different times of day and days of week. A total of nine observations were completed. Observations lasted between 1 and 5 hr with a total of 16 hr spent in the field. Immediately after an observation, detailed field notes were written describing the settings, activities, and interactions between Emma and others, including the researcher. Subjective impressions, analysis, and contextual information based on insider knowledge were written in observer comments.

Data analysis procedures. Qualitative data analysis occurred throughout data collection as new field notes and interview transcripts were analyzed for preliminary descriptive and conceptual categories (i.e., themes). After all field notes were written and all interviews were transcribed, the data were entered into the *Ethnograph* qualitative data management software program (Seidel, Kjolseth, & Seymour, 1985) in the form of individual files for each observation or interview. This resulted in 18 files consisting of 325 pages of interview data and 233 pages of participant observation data. Data were first sorted into 12 descriptive categories drawn from the interview questions (e.g., community life, changes). The basic characteristics of these categories were defined, and these definitions guided the initial coding of all files.

After the initial organization of the data, the grounded theory method of open coding described by Strauss and Corbin (1990) was used to identify 43 additional descriptive and conceptual categories (e.g., demandingness, staff relationship). Questions asked of the data included: (a) What are people doing; (b) why is the person doing this; and (c) to what class of phenomenon do these concepts relate? As each new category was identified, its characteristics were defined, and the definitions guided further coding of the data.

Axial coding (Strauss & Corbin, 1990) then was employed to organize the content of major categories (phenomenon) into a set of descriptive relationships. During this analysis, one or more of the following questions were asked for the data: (a) What are the properties and dimensions of the category (e.g., what are the properties and dimensions of the changes Emma experienced); (b) what contexts or intervening conditions promote or inhibit the phenomenon; (c) what are the interactional strategies by which the phenomenon is managed or carried out; and (d) what are the consequences of the phenomenon's promotion or inhibition? Through the process of inductive and deductive analysis, properties and relationships within each category were proposed and were checked for their further presence in the data. Theories were proposed consisting of those categories, their properties and dimensions, and statements of relationships that were grounded and verified in the actual data collected. These theories were then organized into an analytical description and interpretation of Emma and her life in the community.

Procedures to ensure data credibility and consistency. Several procedures were used to enhance the credibility and consistency of the qualitative data (Merriam, 1988; Patton, 1990). First, triangulation across research methods was employed. Quantitative behavior and lifestyle data served to validate interpretations of Emma's experience from the participant observations and interviews. Second, triangulation across qualitative sources of data was used to compare and cross-check the consistency of information derived at different times and by different means. Third, member checks were completed with interview informants and observation participants throughout the course of the study. After the analytical descriptions of Emma's life were completed, a draft was submitted to four key informants, and they were asked to evaluate the accuracy of the interpretations. Informants, for the most part, affirmed the researcher's interpretations, and suggested improvements in accuracy, emphasis, or completeness. These recommendations were then incorporated into the final interpretation.

To minimize the bias inherent in the researcher's insider role, the second author, a qualitative researcher with no association to the support program, provided guidance and feedback on the analysis and interpretation of the data, and evaluated the congruence between the emerging findings and the data. In addition, two other qualitative researchers each reviewed three randomly selected files (6 of 18 files) and assessed the degree to which the defined categories reflected what they saw in the data. Both researchers reported that the categories accurately represented the data, and were coded with a high degree of consistency.

Results

Quantitative and qualitative results were juxtaposed and merged to provide an overview of Emma's community and social integration while living in the institution and the community, her problem behavior levels, and an interpretation of the pattern and complexity of her community participation and social relationships.

Community participation. Figure 1 indicates the number of physically integrated activities performed per week from April 1989 through September 1991. During Emma's first 2 months in the community, she engaged in an average of 19.4 community activities per week. During the next year, she gradually increased her frequency of community activities to a peak of over 40 activities per week. Between August 1990 and January 1991, her rate of community activities returned to approximately 20 per week and then in-

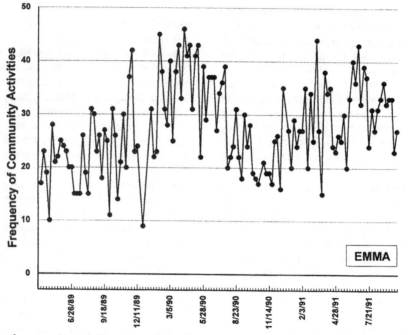

Figure 1. Frequency of community activities across 131 weeks.

creased again during 1991 to a rate of 30.6 activities per week with a range of 20 to 44. Qualitative interviews suggest that the initial growth in Emma's activity patterns was related to staff and Emma's coming to understand her preferences, and becoming more comfortable with activities and support strategies in the community. Later growth was related to staff introducing Emma to less preferred and more challenging activities and encouraging and supporting her participation. Cyclical decreases in community participation were attributed by staff to cold weather, multiple staff changes, and accompanying increases in Emma's frequency of problem behaviors.

Table 3 presents RLI data for Emma before and after her move to the community. These data confirm a high frequency of community use ($N = 171$ community activities/mo). Together these data indicate that Emma engaged in more activities in the community, more varied activities in the community, and more preferred activities in the community after her move (Table 3).

Qualitative analysis of Emma's activities reveal three major patterns: relaxing activities, lively pursuits, and challenging activities.

Relaxing activities. Many of Emma's activities in the community reflected her preference for sitting with a staff person or friend and enjoying a beverage, food, music, or an interesting view. These activities included "hanging out" at a local coffee shop, having dinner at a Thai restaurant, and watching rock climbers scale the walls of a cliff in the early evening. During these activities Emma usually expressed contentment punctuated with anxious worries or simple demands (e.g., "Melissa's coming on Tuesday?" "Fix the armguard"). When staff skillfully offered Emma reassurance, honored reasonable preferences, negotiated compromises, or communicated limits, Emma typically returned to a calm disposition.

Lively pursuits. Emma regularly participated in a smaller set of more lively activities in the community. These included going on walks, purchasing preferred items at discount stores, and dancing at a local night-

Table 3
Summary of Emma's RLI Community Participation Scores While Living in the Institution and in the Community

Measures (Number during assessed month)	Institution scores		Community scores		
	8/88	3/89	6/89	1/90	5/91
Community activities per assessed month	22	4	171	178	166
Different community activities	8	1	16	25	21
Different activities identified as "preferred" community activities	3	1	9	8	20
Mean of community activities per day	.71	.13	5.7	5.74	5.35

club. Some of these activities began as staff preferences, but over time developed into Emma's preferences as well. These activities typically generated expressions of enthusiasm, as can be seen in the following description from an interview with a staff person:

> On the way [to the coffee shop] she was skipping . . . laughing . . . I would say euphoric. It was a pretty somber band, but Emma was dancing. No one else was. Everybody just looked at her, adored her. She was making it a better experience for everybody. Her happiness was contagious. People smiled at her a lot.

Sometimes, however, anxious comments and multiple demands accompanied the activity. Staff reported, for example, a shopping trip in which Emma anxiously worried about what to buy. After finally making her purchase, she demanded to buy a different item. In situations such as this, the skillful use of support strategies (e.g., communicating limits, providing reassurance) was typically necessary to prevent escalation into problem behaviors.

Challenging activities. Emma also participated in physically demanding activities that represented the preferences of veteran staff. These staff, having successfully integrated Emma into many typical activities, attempted to further expand her experiences and interests. In some cases Emma quickly overcame some initial anxiety and developed an interest in the new activity. Examples included a Tai Chi class one year and wading in a river one summer. For other activities such as hiking, initial participation was associated with both anxiety and problem behaviors. After repeated outings and staff persistence, however, she gradually developed an interest in the activity. Field notes from a hike up a small butte near Emma's house illustrate this experience:

> As we began hiking up the steep trail on the west side of the butte, Emma demanded, "go home now." Sarah ignored her pleas and encouraged Emma to continue to hike the short distance to the top. Emma marched up the trail, punctuating her ascent with demands to "go home now." Three quarters of the way to the top she stopped, looked back at the cars driving on a highway in the distance and became transfixed. Enthusiastically she demanded, "Come back next Friday." . . . After the hike, Sarah asked, "Did you like the hike?" Emma replied, "Yes way." Sarah continued, "Do you want to do it again next week?" Emma, with much animation, replied, "Yes!"

In other cases (e.g., overnight camping trip), staff honored Emma's anxiety and protests by ending the activity and not trying to do it again. These activities appeared to represent the limits of Emma's interest in challenging, physical activities.

Social relationships. The weekly frequency of Emma's socially integrated activities is presented in Figure 2. These data indicate that Emma interacted with persons not paid to provide support an average of 6.2

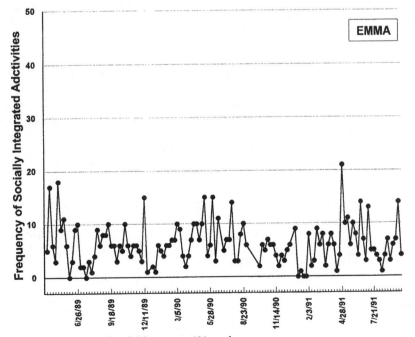

Figure 2. Frequency of socially integrated activities across 131 weeks.

times per week with high variability (*sd* = 3.9) across individual weeks. Qualitative interviews suggest that staff turnover, high levels of problem behaviors, and limited transportation funds for visits to family members contributed to the variability in Emma's social contacts.

Social network data from the SNAF are presented in Table 4 and document an increase in the size and complexity of Emma's social network after she moved to the community. Prior to her move, Emma had six to nine people actively involved in her social life. All these people were family members or people paid to provide support. While living in the community, more of her family became involved in her life, and she developed relationships with friends and co-workers without disabilities. In fact, for the first time in her adult life, Emma developed relationships with people who were typical members of her community.

A qualitative understanding of Emma's social life emerges from four descriptive or conceptual categories in the data: staff, family members, friends, and acquaintances.

Staff. In working with Emma, staff experienced both her charm and energy, as well as her anxiety, demands, and problem behaviors. Interviews and observations stressed the importance of Emma's relationships with several direct-care staff. Her sister-in-law reflected this when she commented, "I think what motivates her is people. With certain people when she's established [a positive relationship], she is fine. She'll do wonderful things." Our analysis of contextual factors and consequences observed in the data suggests that the continuity of these core relationships and the quality of these interactions often determined Emma's level of problem behavior and perceived happiness.

One pattern that emerged from the data on relationships with staff was the mutual effort of Emma and a few veteran staff to develop a friendship that went beyond the boundaries of a typical staff/client relationship. Several factors seemed to promote this process of friendship development. First, working in Emma's home created a context of informality. Second, staff and Emma had much freedom to plan their day and often engaged in enjoyable activities together. Third, the effective use of positive behavioral support strat-

egies was associated with successful experiences in the community, and with increases in Emma's positive communications and expressions of affection. These factors appeared to encourage a trust and mutual regard between Emma and some veteran staff that evolved into friendship.

Family. Emma's family included parents, three older brothers, and one older sister. Family members lived in the suburbs of a large city 120 miles to the north. Interviews with family members suggest that her relationship with them improved considerably after moving to the community. Her parents, brother, and sister-in-law reported that when she lived in the institution, they were not permitted to take her off campus, and she was not allowed to visit them at their homes because of safety and liability concerns. When they visited Emma at her cottage, she was often "out of it" because of high levels of medication and, consequently, did not engage in meaningful conversation or activity.

In contrast, informants indicated that Emma saw her family more often and developed a more active and affectionate set of relationships while living in the community. She was perceived as looking forward to seeing family members with a mixture of enthusiasm and anxiety. During family visits to Emma's home, trips by Emma to see family members, or telephone contacts, she typically engaged in animated greetings and simple conversations. When family members visited Emma, they took her shopping or out to a movie without incident. Visits with family often were associated with receiving presents, favorite foods or sweets, and outings to purchase preferred items or treats. A visit by Emma to her parents' house, as described by her mother, illustrates this finding:

She was so excited. When she came here she wanted a cold drink and then she was ready to go shopping. Glenn and Sarah were going to take her to [a shopping center]. I said, "How much money do you have?" Well, she didn't tell me so I said, "Take another ten dollars and you can really have some fun buying things" [laughter] . . . She was so happy. She took that and put it in her purse.

Table 4
Summary of Emma's Social Network Analysis (SNAF) Scores While Living in the Institution and Community

Measures (Number during assessed month)	Institution scores		Community scores			
	8/88	3/89	6/89	1/90	9/90	7/91
People paid to provide service	3	5	5	7	6	11
Friends	0	0	1	1	11[a]	3
Family members	3	4	4	4	7	5
Co-workers/roommates	0	0	0	0	2	1
Total social network size	6	9	10	12	26	20

[a] Six of the people were friends of staff members and were identified as part of Emma's social network.

Friends. Qualitative analysis suggests that the central role staff played as a source of potential friends, a resource for contacts with community members, and in the maintenance of friendships with community members. For example, two ex-staff members maintained a close relationship with Emma after leaving the agency. One of these was Teresa, who was regarded as Emma's best friend. Teresa occasionally worked relief shifts and continued to see Emma once a week during her free time, usually for dinner. Another former staff person, Melissa, continued to see Emma a few times each month.

Staff members were a resource for friends when they introduced Emma to their own friends. Heather, for example, was a close friend of a staff person named Sarah. She occasionally accompanied Emma and Sarah on day hikes, or sometimes invited them over to her country home for dinner.

The importance of staff's role in Emma's development of friends can be seen in the friendships that faltered because the community member was not a member of staff's social network. For example, Meredith was an acquaintance of Emma's sister-in-law who lived in Emma's new community. She attempted to establish a relationship with Emma during her first 2 years in the community. Eventually, however, Meredith stopped contacting Emma and the relationship faded, because Emma did not ask to see Meredith and staff did not remember to arrange contacts with her because, unlike Heather, she was not one of their friends.

Acquaintances. Interviews and observations indicated that Emma developed a large number of acquaintances while living in the community. These individuals included friends of staff, employees of small businesses, and co-workers at a supported employment job site.

Problem Behaviors

While living in the institution, the frequency and intensity of Emma's problem behaviors had placed her at major physical risk and had been perceived as a fundamental barrier to community placement. The weekly rate of problem behaviors in the institution was difficult to assess reliably given variation in measurement procedures. In the community, Emma continued to engage in problem behaviors throughout the 30 months of this analysis. Frequency counts of Emma's self-injury and aggression per week are presented in the first two panels of Figure 3. The quantitative results indicate periods with very low rates of problem behaviors punctuated by two periods of major regression. Quantitative accounts suggest changes in the topography and intensity of problem behaviors across these regressions. These perceived changes were in the direction of less intense and less physically harmful topographies.

The first 4 months of community life were associated with low levels of self-injury and aggression. There was a modest, and gradual increase in problem behaviors between September and December 1989. In the last 2 weeks of 1989, there were very high rates of very intense self-injury and aggression (biting wrists and arms, scratching others). The next 9 months were associated with sustained reductions in most problem behaviors. The final months of 1990 were associated with an increase in novel, low (knocking knuckles) and moderate (hitting self, kicking self) intensity SIB. Across 1991, there was another decrease in the frequency of problem behaviors.

These results are purely evaluative and are not part of a design that allows discussion of controlling variables. We did, however, look at the covariation of problem behaviors with (a) physical and social integration, (b) staff changes, and (c) medication levels. In addition, qualitative data about contextual factors that appeared to elevate problem behaviors contribute to the analysis.

Emma's self-injury and aggression were negatively correlated with her frequency of community activities at $r = -.21$. SIB and aggression were negatively correlated with social integration at $r = -.15$. In general, very high rates of problem behaviors were associated with reductions in integration. Emma continued to be involved in community activities and socially integrated activities during weeks when she had low to moderate elevations in problem behaviors.

Staff changes were perceived to correlate with increased levels of problem behavior. The cumulative frequency of staff changes is reported in the third panel of Figure 3. A total of 23 staff worked with Emma during the course of the study. SIB and aggression were correlated with staff changes at $r = .21$. Visual inspection suggests that multiple staff changes over a brief period were associated with an increased frequency of problem behaviors. This covariation was most apparent during the two major regressions in behavior in December 1989 and September through October 1990. Qualitative interviews confirm that Emma's intense acceleration in problem behaviors in December 1989 was associated with the departure of several staff. The acceleration in the last months of 1990 was partly attributed to a significant reduction in work hours of a favorite staff person. A second contextual factor related to these regressions was the temporary loss of program fidelity that occurred when new staff were hired and trained. A final factor, noted by staff and family, was the onset of cold and rainy weather in the fall and winter.

Emma left the institution taking 675 mg of Thorazine per day. This was decreased to 600 mg/day in September 1989 and dropped progressively to 125 mg/day by August 1990. No clear link between medication reduction and problem behavior was observed across the 30

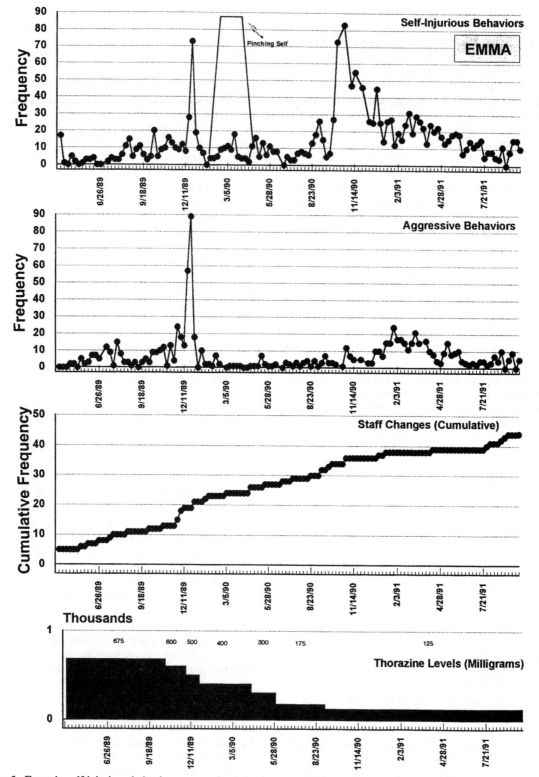

Figure 3. Emma's self-injurious behaviors, aggressive behaviors, cumulative staff changes, and Thorazine levels across 131 weeks.

months of quantitative data or reported during interviews with staff or family members.

Our analysis of the qualitative categories "problem behavior" and "dislikes" suggests several additional contextual and antecedent variables associated with problem behaviors. In addition to the perceived effect of major staff changes, other disruptions in Emma's contact with staff or friends were perceived as related to self-injury or aggression. These disruptions included staff going on vacation, unexpected schedule changes, and friends leaving after a visit. During one observation, a staff person described a particularly difficult week:

> Rebecca went on vacation and didn't tell Emma until two days before she left. On Monday, Jake got sick and had to call in a substitute staff person. Emma became very anxious Monday through Wednesday. She did a lot of anxious repeating [about staff], knocked her shins a lot, and had a major fit on Wednesday.

Problem behaviors also occurred when staff attempted to assert control over Emma. Examples included controlling Emma's access to her restraints, and demanding that she do nonpreferred tasks or activities. Other predictors included lapses in attention from staff, and failures to provide information or reassurance about anxious worries.

A final finding was the perception that Emma did not enjoy using problem behaviors to gain control over her interactions and environment. When she engaged in problem behaviors staff often perceived her as an active participant in the effort to de-escalate her behavior. As one staff described, "If she has a problem she wants you to help her . . . with Emma you go through the problem together."

Positive Changes

Concurrent with improvements in Emma's lifestyle and problem behaviors, several additional positive changes were described or observed. Qualitative analysis indicates improvements in Emma's (a) physical well-being, (b) active engagement, (c) level of security, (d) communication and social skills, (e) level of independence, (f) ability to contribute to her support, and (g) level of happiness. These changes were attributed to a number of factors occurring in Emma's life: the reduction in medication levels, her participation in community activities and social relationships, staff continuity, and the implementation of a wide array of positive behavioral support strategies.

Improvements in Emma's physical well being and activity were among the first changes noticed by family and staff. After Thorazine levels were reduced, the health of her skin and gums was noted. Although the quantitative data did not reveal a link between reduc-

tions in Thorazine levels and behavioral improvement, family members and staff viewed Emma as more alert and more responsive to attempts at interaction and support. Improvements in Emma's active participation in activities also were reported. In addition, efforts by staff to give Emma information about her day and to assuage her worries were viewed as more successful. She made eye contact more often, listened to information, and escalated less often into problem behaviors.

Emma's verbal communication and social skills also improved. She communicated a wider variety of wants, needs, and worries (e.g., "Go dancing," "Go to the bathroom," "Buy a new chin guard if this one breaks." She expressed affection more often, more successfully engaged in simple as well as abstract conversations with staff (e.g., 'When you go to heaven, can you bring your armguards?'), and began to initiate and prompt greetings with acquaintances and friends in the community.

Emma also was observed making several positive contributions to her own support. She sometimes praised herself or prompted staff to praise her (e.g., "Great hiking!" "You worked hard?"), prompted staff to use positive support strategies (e.g., "Write a promise card." "Look at the schedule."), or offered words of encouragement to staff after enjoyable activities together ("Had fun with you at Wenneker's Butte!"). During preferred activities with staff and friends, she engaged in numerous expressions that suggested contentment or happiness. As her sister-in-law observed, "If you could have seen her at [the institution] and now . . . what is obvious is that she is happy; that she is enjoying herself; and she likes it here."

Support Strategies and Continual Adaptations

Interview and participant observation data reveal several categories of support used by staff. These were: (a) increasing predictability by providing information about the daily schedule and contingencies many times during the day, and in many different forms; (b) providing many opportunities for clear choices and then honoring her choice; (c) teaching new skills that made preferred activities easier to do; (d) providing high rates of verbal praise and reassurance; (e) prompting self-directions and self-delivered praise; (f) communicating limits clearly and consistently; (g) blocking attempts at self-injury or aggression; and (h) using physical restraint when problem behaviors escalated in intensity.

When we analyzed the process by which support strategies were introduced and revised, we found a pattern of continual adaptation by staff to changes in Emma's behavior and to contextual events affecting her behavior. Adaptations included performing new functional analyses of persistent problem behaviors, improving implementation fidelity, temporarily decreasing Emma's participation in community activities during major regressions, and developing and implementing new support strategies to ameliorate recurring or new problem behaviors. Contextual factors that appeared to facilitate these adaptations included weekly staff meetings, consensual decision making, leadership by direct service staff, and flexibility in the organization of Emma's schedule.

When Emma first arrived in the community, staff implemented a set of positive support strategies based on an initial understanding of the functions of her problem behaviors and the conditions that appeared likely to promote adaptive behavior. Staff use of positive support strategies faltered, however, when several staff changes occurred and Emma's frequency and intensity of problem behaviors increased. The potential for mortal danger compelled staff to better understand the reasons for Emma's problem behaviors, and to use support strategies that would prevent or minimize these behaviors. A new functional assessment was completed with the support of a behavior specialist, and increased efforts were made to: (a) offer clear and timely information and reassurance when Emma expressed a worry; (b) teach Emma to express her wants and ask for help when she was feeling unsafe; and (c) teach Emma self-managed de-escalation tactics (e.g., deep breathing relaxation).

During Emma's second year in the community, staff's success at teaching Emma to communicate verbally her wants and needs contributed to a new set of problems that required new support strategies. Emma's assertiveness often escalated into incessant demands. Sometimes these demands were unreasonable for the time, place, or resources available, disrespectful to others, or harmful to herself. This new problem re-emphasized that Emma's aggression and SIB were used in some situations to escape nonpreferred activities and/or to obtain preferred items or activities. The support plan was revised to include strategies for negotiating compromises, communicating limits on choice, and preventing aggression and SIB from being rewarded.

The second regression in problem behaviors, although not as serious as the first, prompted staff to develop strategies to minimize problem behaviors associated with staff changes. They developed a package of interventions that included advanced notice, a going away party for terminating staff, and multiple positive experiences with new staff.

Discussion

We have combined quantitative and qualitative methods to provide a portrait of Emma and her life in the community. Together, the data reveal a young woman striving to build a lifestyle that is safe, predict-able, and filled with trusted people, favorite possessions, and preferred activities. This effort was mediated by and shared with a core staff who were committed to Emma's success, skilled in the use of a variety of support strategies, and tolerant of the stresses inherent in supporting her. This mutual endeavor was associated with substantial improvements in Emma's behavior, community participation, and social relationships compared to her life in the institution and her first year in the community. After 2½ years of support, Emma was perceived as more alert, verbally assertive, conversational, and affectionate. She was more independent, socially competent, and happy. Although problem behaviors continued to occur, the intensity of her self-injurious behavior was viewed as significantly reduced. The overall pattern of problem behaviors cautions us to view these improvements as fragile and contextually bound. Because major disruptions in staffing patterns were associated with increases in problem behaviors, we predict that problem behaviors will rise again when Emma experiences major staff changes in the future.

These data suggest that although there were long periods in which problem behaviors were of low frequency and intensity, there was no indication that Emma was "cured" of problem behaviors. It is likely that significant efforts will be needed during the remainder of her life to adjust continually her environment in response to her problem behaviors. The results also suggest, however, that these behaviors need not be viewed as a barrier to a reasonable life in the community. Her problem behaviors may require continual adjustment of the type and quality of support she receives but not elimination of her opportunity to work, play, and learn in the community.

Our qualitative analysis of the factors associated with the development of a safe, active, and valued lifestyle suggested the presence of a complex ecology of support. First, several organizational features of the residential program supported staff efforts to involve Emma in community activities, facilitate social relationships, and use positive support strategies. These features included: (a) an individualized planning process that identified community participation, social integration, behavioral support, and health and safety goals; (b) staff daily use of the VOIS lifestyle outcome monitoring system (Newton et al., 1988) and a functional assessment data collection system (O'Neill et al., 1990); (c) staff's and Emma's control over their schedule of activities, and how goals were achieved; (d) weekly meetings led by a program manager who reviewed lifestyle and behavioral data and facilitated problem-solving discussions; and (e) staff participation in the design of positive support strategies.

Second, several conditions involving staff mediated the development and effective implementation of positive behavioral support strategies. These included: (a) staff continuity; (b) staff achieving a consensus about the reasons for Emma's problem behavior; (c) leadership in the use of positive support strategies by at least one staff; (d) commitment by several staff to a relationship with Emma; and (e) mentorship by a behavioral consultant knowledgeable in positive behavioral support technology.

The support methods used in this study are responsive to the frequent call for comprehensive positive behavioral support programming (Carr et al., 1990; Durand, 1990a). This paper also addressed a need to employ multiple methodologies to reveal the complexities of current service delivery systems, and to measure meaningful outcomes of positive behavioral interventions (Kaiser, 1993; Meyer & Evans, 1993a). Emma's case study is an example of how clinical time series data, empirically validated assessment instruments, participant observations, and semistructured interviews can be combined to describe comprehensively the life of people with severe disabilities living in the community.

Despite the breadth of the results, they are limited by the methodologies employed. The nonexperimental nature of the methods does not permit any conclusions about causal relationships between contextual conditions, support strategies, and Emma's behavior or lifestyle. Qualitative interpretations presented hypotheses about relationships among categories, rather than casual associations. Quantitative results described covariation between contextual variables, interventions, and behavioral or lifestyle outcomes. Functional relationships were not identified. Also, the external validity of the results is limited because of the study's focus on one individual.

The methods also contained shortcomings that may limit the reliability or credibility of the results. The clinical data do not include reliability measures, and so the reader must view the quantitative results cautiously. Triangulation across multiple methods and multiple data sources was employed to increase the overall credibility of the data. In addition, program managers for Emma's house made efforts to maintain the accuracy of the data through staff training activities, weekly data reviews, and the omission of suspect data.

This study adds to a modest body of descriptive and experimental research that empirically examines the use of multicomponent support plans to promote behavioral and lifestyle improvement for persons with severe disabilities and severe problem behaviors (Allison, Volosov, & Axelrod, in press; Berkman & Meyer, 1988; Carr & Carlson, 1993; Dunlap, Kern-Dunlap, Clarke, & Robbins, 1991; Foxx, 1993; Malette et al., 1992). A central message these studies offer is that we must go beyond the use of single interventions and develop comprehensive, multicomponent plans of support that are responsive to the unique demands of

each person and setting and are guided continually by functional assessment data (Mace, Lalli, Lalli, & Shea, 1993). The study contributes two additional messages. First, if we are to serve people with severe disabilities and problem behaviors in the community, we need to design service environments that promote durable lifestyle change. Multicomponent positive support plans are only one feature of this larger ecology of support. Organizational structures that promote community participation, social relationships, and the use of positive support strategies are necessary elements of effective service environments (Carr, Robinson, Taylor, & Carlson, 1990; Foster-Johnson & Dunlap, 1993; Reichle & Wacker, 1993; Van Houten & Axelrod, 1993). Second, if we truly are to understand the richness, depth, and complexity of the lives of people with severe disabilities living in the community and the environments that are designed for their benefit, we will benefit from the creative use of multiple research methods (Kaiser, 1993; Meyer & Evans, 1993a, 1993b; Tharp, 1981). We believe that quantitative and qualitative researchers working together and honoring each others' unique contribution to knowledge development can enhance their capacity to influence the effectiveness and quality of community-based services for people with severe disabilities and severe problem behaviors. Emma and all people who share her history and promise deserve nothing less.

References

Allison, G. S., Volosov, P., & Axelrod, S. (in press). Moving people from more restrictive to less restrictive treatment programs. *Research in Developmental Disabilities*.

Berkman, K. A., & Meyer, L. H. (1988). Alternative strategies and multiple outcomes in the remediation of severe self-injury: Going "all out" nonaversively. *The Journal of The Association for Persons with Severe Handicaps, 13*, 76–86.

Boles, S., Horner, R. H., & Bellamy, G. T. (1988). Implementing transitions: Programs for supported living. In B. L. Ludow, A. P. Turnbull, & R. Luckason (Eds.), *Transitions to adult life for people with mental retardation: Principles and practices* (pp. 101–118). Baltimore: Paul H. Brookes.

Bromley, B. E., & Blacher, J. (1991). Parental reasons for out-of-home placement of children with severe handicaps, *Mental Retardation, 29*, 275–280.

Campbell, D. T., & Fiske, D. W. (1959). Convergent and discriminant validation by the multitrait-multimethod matrix. *Psychological Bulletin, 56*, 81–105.

Carr, E. G., & Carlson, J. J. (1993). Reduction of severe behavior problems in the community using a multicomponent treatment approach. *Journal of Applied Behavior Analysis, 26*, 157–172.

Carr, E. G., Robinson, S., & Palumbo, L. W. (1990). The wrong issue: Aversive vs. nonaversive treatment. The right issue: Functional vs. nonfunctional treatment. In A. C. Repp & N. N. Singh (Eds.), *Perspectives on the use of nonaversive and aversive interventions for persons with developmental disabilities*, (pp. 361–379). DeKalb, IL: Sycamore Press.

Carr, E. G., Robinson, S., Taylor, J. C., & Carlson, J. I.

(1990). Positive approaches to the treatment of severe behavior problems in persons with developmental disabilities: A review and analysis of reinforcement and stimulus-based procedures. *The Association for Persons with Severe Handicaps, Monograph 4.*

Cunningham, P. J., & Mueller, C. D. (1991). Individuals with mental retardation in residential facilities: Findings from the 1987 national medical expenditure survey. *American Journal of Mental Retardation, 96,* 109–117.

Dunlap, G., Kern-Dunlap, L., Clarke, S., & Robbins, F. R. (1991). Functional assessment, curricular revision, and severe behavior problems. *Journal of Applied Behavior Analysis, 24,* 387–397.

Durand, V. M. (1990a). Reader response: The "Aversives" debate is over: And now the work begins. *The Journal of The Association for Persons with Severe Handicaps, 15,* 140–141.

Durand, V. M. (1990b). *Severe behavior problems: A functional communication training approach.* New York: Guilford Press.

Foster-Johnson, L., & Dunlap G. (1993). Using functional assessment to develop effective, individualized interventions for challenging behaviors. *Teaching Exceptional Children, 25,* 44–57.

Foxx, R. M. (1993). *Confluence therapy for highly dangerous aggressive and self-injurious behavior: Producing lasting effectiveness.* Paper presented at the 19th annual meeting of the Association for Behavior Analysis, Chicago.

Foxx, R. M., Bechtel, D. R., Bird, J. R., Livesay, J. R., & Bittle, R. G. (1986). A comprehensive institutional treatment program for aggressive-disruptive high functioning mentally retarded persons. *Behavior Residential Treatment, 1,* 39–56.

Hill, B. K., & Bruininks, R. H. (1984). Maladaptive behavior or mentally retarded individuals in residential facilities. *American Journal of Mental Deficiency, 88,* 380–387.

Hill, B. K., Lakin, K. C., & Bruininks, R. H. (1988). Characteristics of residential facilities. In L. W. Heal, J. I. Haney, & A. R. Novak Amado (Eds.), *Integration of developmentally disabled individuals into the community* (2nd ed.) (pp. 283–297). Baltimore: Paul H. Brookes.

Horner, R. H., Close, D. W., Fredericks, H. D., O'Neill, R. E., Albin, R. W., Sprague, J. R., Kennedy, C., Flannery, K. B., Tuesday-Heathfield, L. (1992). *Oregon Community Support: Providing support for people with severe problem behaviors.* Paper presented at the 18th annual meeting of the Association for Behavior Analysis, San Francisco.

Horner, R. H., Dunlap, G., Koegel, R. L., Carr, E. G., Sailor, W., Anderson, J., Albin, R. W., & O'Neill, R. E. (1990). Toward a technology of "nonaversive" behavioral support. *Journal of The Association for Persons with Severe Handicaps, 15,* 125–132.

Jorgensen, D. L. (1989). *Participant observation: A methodology for human studies.* Newbury Park, CA: Sage Publications.

Kaiser, A. P. (1993). Understanding human behavior: Problems of science and practice. *Journal of The Association for Persons with Severe Handicaps, 18,* 240–242.

Kennedy, C. H., Horner, R. H., & Newton, J. S. (1990). The social networks and activity patterns of adults with severe disabilities: A correlational analysis. *Journal of The Association for Persons with Severe Handicaps, 15,* 86–90.

Kennedy, C. H., Horner, R. H., Newton, J. S., & Kanda, E. (1990). Measuring the activity patterns of adults with severe disabilities using the resident lifestyle inventory. *Journal of The Association for Persons with Severe Handicaps, 15,* 79–85.

Lakin, K. C., & Bruininks, R. H. (1985). Contemporary ser-

vices for handicapped children and youth. In R. H. Bruininks & K. C. Lakin (Eds.), *Living and learning in the least restrictive environment* (pp. 3–22). Baltimore: Paul H. Brookes.

Mace, F. C., Lalli, J. S., Lalli, E. P., & Shea, M. C. (1993). Functional analysis and treatment of aberrant behavior. In R. Van Houten & S. Axelrod (Eds.), *Behavior analysis and treatment* (pp. 75–99). New York: Plenum Press.

Malette, P., Mirenda, P., Kandborg, T., Jones, P., Bunz, T., & Rogow, S. (1992). Application of a lifestyle development process for persons with severe intellectual disabilities: A case study report. *Journal of The Association for Persons with Severe Handicaps, 17,* 179–191.

McGee, J. J., Menousek, F. J., Hobbs, D. C., & Menousek, P. E. (1987). *Gentle teaching: A non-aversive approach to helping persons with mental retardation.* New York: Human Sciences Press.

McGrew, K. S., & Bruininks, R. H. (1994). A multidimensional approach to the measurement of community adjustment. In M. F. Hayden & B. H. Abery (Eds.), *Challenges for a service system in transition: Ensuring quality community experiences for persons with developmental disabilities* (pp. 65–79). Baltimore: Paul H. Brookes.

Merriam, S. B. (1988). *Case study research in education: A qualitative approach.* San Francisco: Jossey-Bass.

Meyer, L. H., & Evans, I. M. (1989). *Nonaversive interventions for behavior problems: A manual for home and community.* Baltimore: Paul H. Brookes.

Meyer, L. H., & Evans, I. M. (1993a). Meaningful outcomes in behavioral intervention: Evaluating positive approaches to the remediation of challenging behavior. In J. Reichle & D. Wacker (Eds.), *Communicative alternatives to challenging behavior* (pp. 407–428). Baltimore: Paul H. Brookes.

Meyer, L. H., & Evans, I. M. (1993b). Science and practice in behavioral intervention: Meaningful outcomes, research validity, and usable knowledge. *Journal of The Association for Persons with Severe Handicaps, 18,* 224–234.

Newton, J. S., Ard, W. R., & Horner, R. J. (1993). Validating predicted activity preferences of individuals with severe disabilities. *Journal of Applied Behavior Analysis, 26,* 239–245.

Newton, J. S., Stoner, S. K., Bellamy, G. T., Boles, S. M., Horner, R. H., LeBaron, N., Moskowitz, D., Romer, L., Romer, M., & Schlesinger, D. (1988). *Valued outcomes information system (VOIS) operations manual.* Eugene: University of Oregon, Center on Human Development.

Nisbet, J., Clark, M., & Covert, S. (1991). Living it up! An analysis of research on community living. In L. H. Meyer, C. A. Peck, & L. Brown (Eds.), *Critical issues in the lives of people with severe disabilities* (pp. 115–144). Baltimore: Paul H. Brookes.

O'Brien, J. (1987). A guide to lifestyle planning: Using *The Activities Catalog* to integrate services and natural support systems. In B. Wilcox & G. T. Bellamy (Eds.), *A comprehensive guide to The Activities Catalog: An alternative curriculum for youth and adults with severe disabilities* (pp. 175–189). Baltimore: Paul H. Brookes.

O'Neill, R. E., Horner, R. H., Albin, R. W., Storey, K., & Sprague, J. R. (1990). *Functional analysis of problem behavior: A practical assessment guide.* Sycamore, IL: Sycamore Publishing Co.

Patton, M. Q. (1990). *Qualitative evaluation and research methods* (2nd ed.). Newbury Park, CA: Sage Publications.

Reichle, J., & Wacker, D. P. (1993). *Communicative alternatives to challenging behavior: Integrating functional assessment and intervention strategies.* Baltimore: Paul H. Brookes.

Repp, A. C., & Singh, N. N. (1990). *Perspectives on the use of nonaversive and aversive interventions for persons with developmental disabilities.* Sycamore, IL: Sycamore Publishing Co.

Seidel, J., Kjolseth, R., & Seymour, E. (1985). *The ethnograph.* Littleton, CO: Qualis Research Associates.

Skodak-Crissey, M., & Rosen, M. (1986). *Institutions for the mentally retarded: A changing role in changing times.* Austin, TX: PRO-ED.

Strauss, A., & Corbin, J. (1990). *Basics of qualitative research: Grounded theory procedures and techniques.* Newbury Park, CA: Sage Publications.

Taylor, S. J., Biklen, D., & Knoll, J. (1987). *Community integration for people with severe disabilities.* New York: Teachers College Press.

Taylor, S. J., & Bogdan, R. (1981). Qualitative methods and cultural perspectives in the study of community adjustment. In R. H. Bruininks, C. E. Meyers, B. B. Sigford, & K. C. Lakin (Eds.), *Deinstitutionalization and community adjustment of mentally retarded people* (pp. 133–144).

Washington, D.C.: American Association on Mental Deficiency.

Tharp, R. G. (1981). The metamethodology of research and development. *Educational Perspectives, 20,* 42–48.

Van Houten, R., & Axelrod, S. (1993). *Behavior analysis and treatment.* New York: Plenum Press.

Widaman, K. F., Stacy, A. W., & Borthwick-Duffy, S. A. (1983). Construct validity of dimensions of adaptive behavior: A multitrait-multimethod evaluation. *American Journal of Mental Retardation, 98,* 219–234.

Zigler, E., Hodapp, R. M., & Edison, M. R. (1990). From theory to practice in the care and education of mentally retarded individuals. *American Journal of Mental Retardation, 95,* 1–12.

Received: November 22, 1993
Final Acceptance: July 5, 1994
Editor in Charge: James W. Halle

A Demonstration of Behavioral Support for Young Children with Autism

Glen Dunlap
University of South Florida

Lise Fox
University of South Florida

Abstract: Young children with autism sometimes display severe behavior problems that can cause great disruptions in family life and interfere with attempts to provide needed services. Strategies are needed to resolve these behavior problems in a manner that is effective, durable, and consistent with current approaches to positive, comprehensive, and inclusionary practice in early childhood intervention. This article provides a description of behavioral support as applied in the context of a family-centered early intervention program for young children with autism. Demonstration data are presented to illustrate the effects of the approach in reducing the problem behaviors of six children. The practices and data are discussed in the context of changing perspectives toward early intervention and the prospects of developing effective preventive strategies and functional deterrents to the emergence and occurrence of serious problem behaviors.

The occurrence of serious problem behaviors in the repertoires of young children with autism can represent substantial problems for the children's development, access to appropriate services, and the functioning of the children's families. Although not all children with autism display serious disruptive or destructive behaviors, a large number exhibit behaviors such as self-injury, aggression, property destruction, and violent, protracted tantrums. Such behavior patterns are sources of great concern because they can

1. Compete with the development of desirable interactions and conventional communication skills;
2. Present risk of injury to the child or to others in proximity;
3. Interfere with placements in least restrictive (e.g., inclusive) childcare and preschool services;
4. Produce high levels of parenting stress; and
5. Portend the presence of undesirable behavioral characteristics that deleteriously affect the child's opportunities and social development throughout the later years of childhood and beyond.

There is a clear need for intervention strategies to reduce, eliminate, and prevent serious problem behaviors and their associated repercussions.

Recent approaches to problem behaviors have expanded from a concentration on contingency management to broad tactics that incorporate a variety of assessment-based intervention strategies, including instruction on functional alternatives (e.g., Durand, 1990; Meyer & Evans, 1989), antecedent manipulations (Dunlap & Kern, 1993; Luiselli & Cameron, 1998), self-control procedures (e.g., Koegel & Koegel, 1990), and other options that are designed, on an individualized basis, to enrich the person's environment and build competencies that make the performance of problem behaviors unnecessary and irrelevant. *Positive behavioral support* (Horner et al., 1990; Koegel, Koegel, & Dunlap, 1996) is the term that has been invoked to designate the process in which functional assessment information (Repp & Horner, in press) is used to build a multicomponent support plan (Horner & Carr, 1997; Koegel, Koegel, Kellegrew, & Mullen, 1996). Over the past decade, a large number of experimental studies and empirical case studies have demonstrated the efficacy of positive behavioral support for resolving problem behaviors, establishing more adaptive repertoires, and facilitating improved lifestyles for people with disabilities (Koegel, Koegel, & Dunlap, 1996). However, few data have focused on the problem behaviors of children who are still in early childhood.

The work that has described positive behavioral support approaches for the problem behavior of young children with significant disabilities (e.g., autism) has been largely in the form of model descriptions (e.g., Dunlap & Fox, 1996; Fox, Dunlap, & Philbrick, 1997; Wacker, Peck, Derby, Berg, & Harding, 1996), although some case study and experimental data have begun to appear (e.g., Arndorfer, Miltenberger, Woster, Rortvedt, & Gaffaney, 1994; Derby et al., 1997; Reeve, 1996). An important focus of much of this work has been on the generalization and maintenance of the decelerative effects on problem behavior. For example, Dunlap, Johnson, and Robbins (1990) provided some summary data on the destructive and highly disruptive behaviors of 12 children who participated in a family-focused model of early intervention for children with autism in a rural region of Appalachia. The individualized interventions in this program were based on comprehensive child and family assessments and emphasized a skill-building approach for managing problem behaviors (e.g., Carr et al., 1994; Meyer & Evans, 1989). Data from sessions when the children were alone with their mothers showed substantial reductions after an initial 3-month period of relatively intensive family training and consultation. Importantly, the data showed even lower levels of problem behavior when the assessments were repeated after one year, despite the fact that professional contact with the children and families had been sharply curtailed during this follow-up period. Reeve (1996) provided data showing that functional communication (i.e., skill building) training could produce relatively greater reductions and prevention of problem behaviors than a more traditional communication intervention, suggesting that the development of functionally equivalent communication, as part of a behavioral support program, could be a vital ingredient in the longitudinal remediation of problem behaviors in children with disabilities. These data support the notion that an early intervention model that includes a systematic emphasis on the development of functional communication skills has the potential for remediation and prevention of serious problem behaviors that can afflict the lives and development of children with autism (Dunlap et al., 1990).

The purpose of the present article is to describe a programmatic model known as the Individualized Support Project (ISP) that has been designed to help families address the serious problem behaviors of their young children with autism. The basic foundations and components of the ISP model have been described elsewhere (e.g., Dunlap & Fox, 1996; Fox et al., 1997); however, there has not been an explicit delineation of the procedures used to address the children's problem behaviors, nor have recent data been supplied to support the model's expectations. Therefore, in this article we focus on the aspects of the approach that are concerned most directly with problem behaviors, and we provide some data to demonstrate the effects of the process with the first six children who participated in the current version of the program.

The ISP has been developed over the past dozen years in West Virginia and surrounding states (e.g., Dunlap, Robbins, Dollman, & Plienis, 1988; Dunlap, Robbins, Morelli, & Dollman, 1988) and, more recently, in the Tampa Bay area of west-central Florida (Dunlap & Fox, 1996; Fox et al., 1997). The model is designed to be implemented in home and community contexts via a relatively short period of intensive assistance and capacity building, followed by longitudinal follow up, evaluation, and consultation. The supports provided through ISP are adjunctive, in that they are not intended to constitute nor replace ongoing, daily services delivered by childcare, preschool, homebound, or clinical providers. ISP is oriented toward helping families gain the knowledge and practical skills needed to resolve immediate problems and the competence and confidence needed to continue effective intervention and advocacy over the course of their child's development (Fox et al., 1997; Risley, 1997).

The ISP model addresses problem behaviors within a framework of positive behavioral support. As applied to the behavioral challenges of young children in a family context, this framework includes a three-fold emphasis on

1. The provision of comprehensive and individualized family support;
2. Developing the child's social competence and comfortable participation in typical childcare (and preschool) and community environments; and
3. Developing functional skills for the child to use in communication and other aspects of social engagement.

This three-fold emphasis is organized into a support effort that includes an initial period of assessment and relationship building (approximately 2 weeks), a process of person-centered planning and development of a comprehensive plan for individualized child and family support (approximately 1 week), implementation of the plan's components in home, childcare (or preschool), and community contexts (approximately 3–6 months), and transition to an ongoing period of follow up, evaluation, and consultation. The objective is to have the family—by the end of the relatively intensive implementation phase—achieve a level of competence and confidence that will enable continued progress and problem solving without the immediate assistance of ISP personnel.

In the remainder of this article, we describe the ISP approach used for addressing the serious problem behaviors exhibited by the first six children who participated in the program in the Tampa Bay area of Florida. The descriptions and most of the data displays are focused on the methods and outcomes that pertain specifically to the occurrence of the children's problem behaviors. Additional descriptions that encompass the other aspects of the ISP model are presented in other publications (e.g., Dunlap & Fox, 1996; Fox et al., 1997).

Participants

The children who participated in ISP were referred to the program through private physicians and early intervention providers. All the children had diagnoses of pervasive developmental disorder (e.g., autistic disorder, pervasive developmental disorder-not otherwise specified [PDD-NOS]). One child was diagnosed as autistic, secondarily to having tuberous sclerosis. As described in Table 1, the children ranged in ages from 29 to 44 months and had developmental equivalent scores of 10–20 months, as measured by the Battelle Developmental Inventory (BDI; Newborg, Stock, & Wnek, 1984). All the children showed evidence of behaviors that are characteristic of autism, with scores on the Autism Behavior Checklist (ABC; Krug, Arick, & Almond, 1980) that ranged from 64 to 90 (in the standardization sample, the mean score for children who have later diagnoses of autism is 77 and the mean score for typically developing children is 3.9). None of the children were verbal at the beginning of intervention, although one child (Noah) used two or three echoic phrases with low frequency. Five of the children engaged in frequent (more than six times per day) and prolonged (more than 20 minutes) tantrums that caused extreme disruption to their families. One child (Michele) engaged in stereotypy the majority of her waking hours.

The children and families who participated represented diversity in race and socioeconomic status. The majority of the children were White, with one Hispanic American and one Asian American child. Two of the families had low incomes and parental educational levels of some high school and a high school diploma. The other four families had middle-class to upper-middle-class incomes.

An Approach to Problem Behavior

The ISP model provides a family-centered application of the process of positive behavioral support (Lucyshyn, Dunlap, & Albin, in press). Thus, the six participating children and their families engaged in a process that included a functional assessment of problem behaviors and the development and implementation of a multicomponent support plan. Although we do not describe other elements of the ISP program in this article, it is important to acknowledge that substantial efforts were undertaken to help all the participating families gain competence and strength in other aspects of their childrearing responsibilities (Dunlap & Fox, 1996; Fox et al., 1997).

The behavioral support process began with a functional assessment to determine the nature of the problem behavior, the contexts in which problem behavior was and was not occurring, the antecedents and consequences related to the problem behavior, and the communicative behavior of the child (Foster-Johnson & Dunlap, 1993). Functional assessment involved the parents completing a modified version of the Functional Assessment Interview (FAI; O'Neill et al., 1997) form. An interview was also conducted with teachers if children were in childcare, early intervention, or school programs. In addition to the interviews, observations of each child occurred within the contexts identified by families as particularly problematic.

Table 1. Participant Descriptions

Child	Age at entry (months)	BDI age equivalent (months)	ABC	Communication level	Problem behavior description
Michele	29	10	68	Nonverbal	Hand gazing, hyperventilating, wandering
Mario	32	17	71	Nonverbal	Frequent and prolonged tantrums that included screaming, dropping to the floor, and throwing toys
Larry	37	15	64	Nonverbal	Frequent and prolonged tantrums that included screaming, dropping to the floor, and kicking
Noah	44	20	79	Echolalic	Frequent and prolonged tantrums that included screaming and pushing on adults, destroying objects, dumping shelves, and biting
Tom	29	15	90	Nonverbal	Frequent and prolonged tantrums that included screaming and pulling away from adults
Anthony	33	14	75	Nonverbal	Frequent and prolonged tantrums that included body extension, head banging, dropping to the floor, and screaming

Note. BDI = Battelle Developmental Inventory (Newborg, Stock, & Wnek, 1984); ABC = Autism Behavior Checklist (Krug, Arick, & Almond, 1980).

These contexts included play time, meal time, community outings and activities, bed times, time spent riding in the car, and classroom time. Direct observation was used to identify the social context of problem behavior, the intensity and topography of problem behavior, and the responses to behavior (Carr et al., 1994).

The FAI and direct observations were used to develop hypotheses about the antecedents, purpose(s), and maintenance of consequences of the problem behavior. Behavioral hypotheses were developed by ISP staff members working as a team and then discussed with the family. The discussion of the behavioral hypotheses with the family was the first of many occasions on which the theory and process of positive behavioral support was explained to the family. Family members were taught to view their child's problem behavior as being functional or purposeful and that appropriate intervention included changing the environment, interactions with the child, and teaching the child new skills.

When behavioral hypotheses were identified, the ISP team and the family developed a comprehensive plan of behavioral support that addressed four major areas: long-term supports, prevention strategies, replacement skills, and consequences. *Long-term supports* included strategies and supports that assist the child and family in supporting the child's development and achieving meaningful outcomes. Long-term supports included plans for teaching new skill repertoires and shaping extended periods of social interaction and communication. *Prevention strategies* included antecedent manipulations and strategies that supported the child to engage in interactions and activities without using problem behavior. Prevention strategies typically involved the use of stimulus control techniques, especially the addition of cues that had been identified as being associated with desirable rather than problem behavior. *Replacement skills* included communication skills that served as adaptive alternatives to the problem behavior and other skills needed by the child to negotiate social contexts without using problem behavior. Replacement skills were targeted for each child and were identified as being functionally equivalent to the problem behaviors (Carr et al., 1994; Durand, 1990). Specific instructions were included in the *consequences* section of the plan that provided ways to respond to problem behavior so that the behavior was ineffective for the child.

The plan included strategies and supports that the ISP team and the family felt were functionally related to the problem behavior; were feasible for use within a variety of natural contexts, positive in nature, developmentally and contextually appropriate; and would result in skill development by the child. The strategies and supports included in the plan were designed to be implemented by a variety of providers in all of the child's routines and activities. The support plan was not specific to an isolated context (e.g., instructional session) or designed to address an isolated behavior (e.g., biting). The plan represents comprehensive supports that are designed to be implemented throughout the day and in all environments (sample plans are available from the authors upon request). Table 2 provides an abbreviated summary of the components that were included in the behavioral support plans for each of the participating children.

The strategies and supports included in the support plans were demonstrated by the ISP early interventionist within the contexts and routines that families had described as problematic. Families and teachers were encouraged to implement the support plans in all environments but were not asked to demonstrate implementation of the plan until (a) the ISP early interventionist had provided several days of demonstration of the supports and strategies and (b) data had been collected that supported the effectiveness of the plan. At that point, the family and child's teacher were encouraged to implement the support plan while being coached by the ISP early interventionist. Coaching occurred in all the contexts and routines identified by the family as difficult and within the typical activities of the child. Coaching included a review of the support plan, feedback to the parent or teacher when interacting with the child, and a review of the child's progress and the comfort of the adult in implementing the support plan. In addition, parents and teachers watched the ISP early interventionist demonstrate the use of the support plan within play sessions or classroom activities with the child.

Measurement

The ISP provides for the collection of data on a variety of child and family variables. All data are collected with the participation and agreement of the children's parents and other family members. The primary purposes of data collection in the operation of ISP have been to monitor child and family progress and share evidence with the child's parents. Data have been obtained through a battery of standardized instruments, project-developed interviews, staff notes, and direct observations. Included among the standardized instruments are the BDI and the ABC.

Most pertinent to the occurrence of serious problem behavior are systematic probes that have been collected frequently during the intervention phases. These probes were conducted in the context of developmentally appropriate play sessions in which a staff member interacted with the child in a manner that maintained a consistent level of demands and reinforcers across sessions. Probes were conducted in the child's home with at least one parent present (in addition, data were collected in Tom's childcare setting, as explained below). No more than one probe session was conducted per day. On the average, sessions were conducted once or twice per week. Session length was constant for each child; generally the length was 15 or 20 minutes.

Table 2. Summary of Components in Individualized Behavior Support Plans

	Long-term supports	Prevention strategies	Replacement skills	Consequences
Michele	Teach family communication and social skill development strategies; provide predictable activity schedule; teach family strategies to support active participation in daily routines; teach caregivers to respond to nonverbal communication signals.	Provide accessible toys; increase choices; increase toy play and social interaction opportunities	Use nonverbal signals to request social interaction, "more," "want," and "no"	Redirect to use replacement skill
Mario	Teach family communication and social skill development strategies; provide predictable activity schedule; assess nutritional status	Provide transition warnings; simplify language when making requests; pair verbal directions with gestures or visuals; increase choices; provide wait time following request; provide visual activity schedule	Request "help," "want"; state "no"; make choices using visual menu	Redirect to use replacement skill; follow through if escape (escape extinction)
Larry	Teach family communication and social skill development strategies; teach family how to build routines for participation; teach family how to promote play	Provide transition warnings; pair verbal directions with gestures or visuals; increase choices; provide visual activity schedule; provide visual prompt sequences; simplify language for requests	Request "more"; state "no"; request social game	Redirect to use replacement skill; follow through if escape (escape extinction)
Noah	Provide predictable activity schedule; facilitate peer social interaction; increase play skill repertoire	Provide transition warnings, increase choices; provide visual activity schedule; increase social attention; provide hobby boxes; build routines around daily activities	State "no"; state "want"; state "up" (for hug)	Redirect to use replacement skill; block access if aggressive or destructive
Tom	Change environment to increase predictability (e.g., desired items in same place); develop consistent expectations across care providers; facilitate peer friendship development	Provide transition warnings, increase choices; provide wait time following request; provide visual activity schedule; follow difficult activity with preferred activity	Request activity choice using visual schedule; state "no"	Redirect to use replacement skill; follow through if escape (escape extinction)
Anthony	Teach family communication and social skill development strategies; provide predictable activity schedule; develop consistent expectations across care providers	Provide transition warnings; increase choices; provide wait time following request; provide visual activity schedule; simplify language when making requests; provide warning before physically assisting	Request activity choice using visual schedule; state "no"	Redirect to use replacement skill; follow through if escape (escape extinction)

Data were collected in vivo or from videotapes. Observers were staff members who were familiar with the behaviors of young children with autism and were well trained in the definitions of problem behavior and the data collection procedures. The data collection procedures varied across children and depended on the characteristics (e.g., topography, rate) of the dependent variables. For many children, a partial-interval recording procedure was used, in which the presence or absence of defined problem behavior was recorded during consecutive 10-second intervals with observers scoring the entire videotaped probe. For two children (Tom and Noah), the number of discrete tantrums per session was observed and recorded in vivo.

Interobserver agreement was assessed during 30% of the total sessions across conditions and children. To assess interobserver agreement, two recorders observed the same sessions independently and then compared their recordings. Reliability quotients were obtained through conventional calculations (McReynolds & Kearns, 1983). Occurrence reliability was calculated for probes, using interval recording by dividing the number of agreements that a behavior occurred by the number of agreements plus disagreements and multiplying by 100%. Reliability for frequency counts (number of tantrums) was calculated by dividing the smaller total by the larger and multiplying by 100%. Reliability calculations for all sessions produced agreements of greater than 80%, with the vast majority (90%) of the sessions producing agreements greater than 90%.

Additional observations used in this report were derived from field notes recorded on a regular basis by the program staff and from interviews conducted with the parent participants. These notes and interviews were reviewed to obtain observations relevant to the behavioral support outcomes.

Evaluation Procedures

Probe data were collected before intervention was introduced (i.e., during baseline) on a minimum of 3 days over a period of 2 to 4 weeks. Probe sessions during baseline were conducted by using the strategies described by parents (and confirmed by observation) as being used with their children within a developmentally appropriate play context. The procedures for addressing the children's problem behaviors during the intervention phases followed the assessment-based behavioral support strategies developed by the child's support team (e.g., program staff, parents). Probe sessions were continued until rates of problem behaviors stabilized, with the duration of the final (intervention) phase ranging from 2 to 6 months.

For one participant, Tom, the evaluation included a design involving multiple baseline across settings. The first baseline and intervention conditions were conducted in Tom's childcare setting. After the intervention phase was associated with a detectable change in the number of tantrums at childcare, intervention was introduced against the second baseline at home. As with the other children, all data were collected during probe sessions.

Results

Figure 1 presents the results of the probe sessions within the multiple baseline analysis for Tom. Tom's support plan was implemented first in his childcare setting and subsequently at home. The ordinate depicts the number of tantrums, and the abscissa shows 20-minute sessions

aligned by the days on which they occurred. The data indicate clear decelerative effects in both environments, with the concluding points all showing zero tantrums for several consecutive observations.

Figures 2 and 3 portray the probe results for the other five participating children. Figure 2 shows the data for Anthony, Michele, and Larry. Each of these graphs shows the percentage of intervals with occurrences of problem behavior. Baselines were all collected within 1 month, and the duration of interventions covered periods of 6, 3, and 6 months, respectively. Although the data have some variability, they all show decreasing trends and result in extended periods with very low levels of problem behaviors.

Figure 3 presents the results for Mario and Noah. Here, dependent variables were measured with different systems—percentage of intervals with tantrums for Mario, and number of tantrums for Noah. Again, baselines were completed within 1 month; the intervention data span periods of 4 and 2 months, respectively. The data show functions that are analogous to the preceding graphs; that is they all show decreasing trends and numerous data points with minimal or no evidence of problem behaviors during the later stages of data collection.

Table 3 shows the data from the ABC in the third and fouth columns, and the BDI in the fifth and sixth columns. The second column shows the time the child spent in intervention before the posttesting was conducted (note that this time could exceed the total time over which probe data were collected). In addition, the proportional change index (PCI; Wolery, 1983), in column seven, depicts the rate of change that occurred at the time of intervention. The PCI provides a mechanism to compare a child's rate of development during intervention with his or her rate of development prior to intervention. Progress equivalent to the developmental rate prior to intervention would produce a PCI of 1.00, and increased rates of development would be represented by a PCI greater than 1.00. Table 3 shows that all the ABC data show clear reductions, whereas the BDI shows some gains. The PCI reflects changes in the BDI, all of which were greater than 1.00.

Table 4 offers excerpts from observations and parent interviews that provide more global information about the children's progress related to their behavioral support plans. These excerpts reflect the children's performance in areas that were addressed by the program's behavioral support strategies.

Discussion

The results from the six participants described in this article attest to the efficacy of the assessment-based, individualized support plans that were developed for each child. The direct observation data indicate that the interventions were successful in reducing serious problem behaviors.

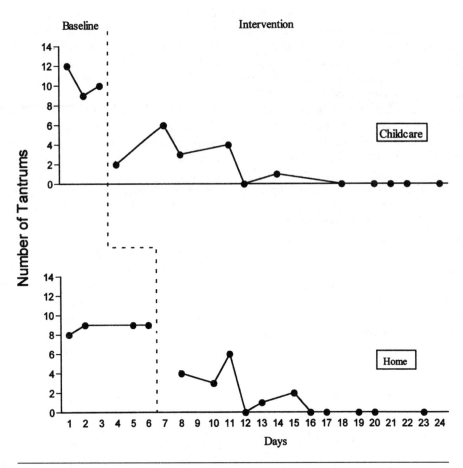

Figure 1. Number of tantrums displayed by Tom in childcare and home settings.

Furthermore, the excerpts from parent interviews and observations suggest that the children were making developmental gains and learning new ways to control their environments through conventional and socially desirable behaviors.

The demonstrations reported herein are consistent with a growing literature on comprehensive behavioral support (Dunlap, Vaughn, & O'Neill, 1998; Horner & Carr, 1997). For example, the behavioral support plans were based on functional assessment protocols (Repp & Horner, in press). Also, they were highly individualized and incorporated communication-based strategies (e.g., Carr et al., 1994) as well as contextual manipulations designed to enhance the environment and thus prevent excessive problems (Dunlap & Kern, 1996; Kern & Dunlap, 1998). Importantly, the plans were developed in collaboration with the children's family members and other caregivers (Fox et al., 1997) and thereby were assured of some degree of contextual fit. As several authors have argued (e.g., Albin, Lucyshyn, Horner, & Flannery, 1996), support plans have little chance of long-term effectiveness if they are not designed to be used in the real context of values, habits, preferences, and routines that

characterize all social environments. Collaboration with families and other pertinent caregivers is a chief feature of the ISP and may be an important explanation for the favorable outcomes reported to date.

The data described in this article are demonstration data and, therefore, need to be qualified in some important respects. First, for the most part, the data were not collected in the context of experimental designs and, thus, it may be risky to attribute the reductions in problem behavior solely to the interventions. Although this limitation is justified, the presence of the multiple baseline for Tom (Figure 1) and the clarity of the remaining data functions can be viewed as encouraging evidence in support of the interventions. Second, because the interventions involved multiple components, and because each of the children's interventions was different, it is not possible to attribute the effects to any particular variable or intervention element. The interventions in the present demonstration were not identifiable techniques or procedures, but rather a process of assessment and comprehensive support. Increasingly, as the field of behavioral support seeks real-life applications and ecological validity, this focus on process is

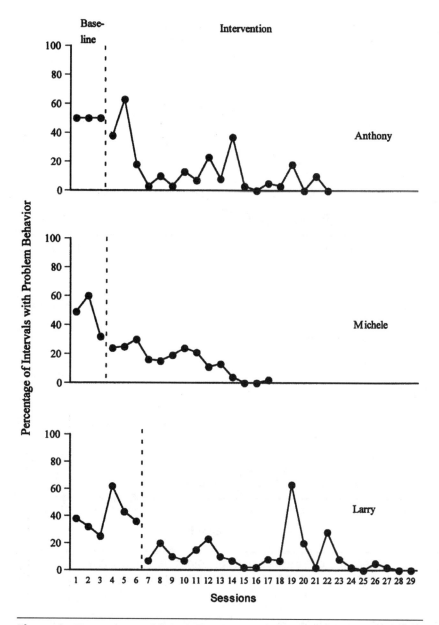

Figure 2. Percentage of intervals with problem behavior during home observations for Anthony, Michele, and Larry.

achieving some recognition as a legitimate and important pursuit, at least in applied research and practice (Dunlap, Fox, Vaughn, Bucy, & Clarke, 1997; Horner & Carr, 1997; Vaughn, Clarke, & Dunlap, 1997).

Another limitation is that the principal data were collected as planned probes. Although the probes (i.e., play sessions) were always collected in the natural environment, a member of our staff conducted the sessions in order to maintain administration of a consistent rate of demands and reinforcers. Ideally, the probe data would have been supplemented with direct observations of problem behavior over extended periods in natural contexts as the children interacted with the parents, teachers, and peers. In

this case, the collection of such data was not feasible to engineer due to the preferences of family members and teachers, as well as limitations in resources.

Still, there is considerable evidence that the favorable changes displayed during the probe sessions reflected generalized improvements in the children's behavior. Table 2 provides some observations that were derived from field notes and parent interviews. These observations indicate that the children's repertoires were improving and that rates and intensities of problem behavior were declining. Such improvements are consistent with changes detected in previous analyses of similarly constructed intervention plans (e.g., Dunlap et al., 1990) and from other data sources.

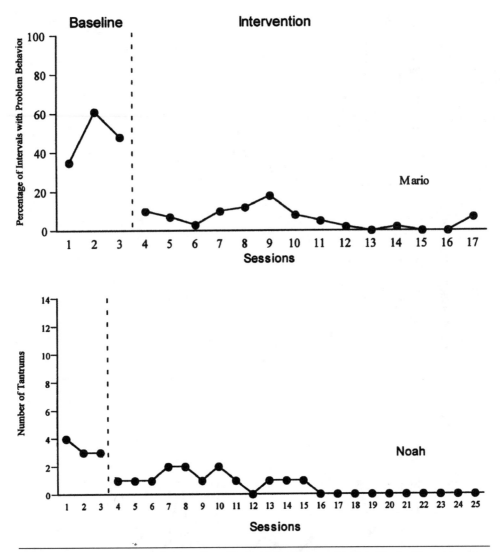

Figure 3. Percentage of intervals with problem behavior for Mario (top graph) and number of tantrums for Noah (bottom graph) during home observations.

Table 3. Assessment Outcomes of Child Participants

| Child | Time in intervention (months) | ABC | | BDI | | PCI |
		pre	post	pre (age in months)	post (age in moths)	
Michele	5	68	41	10 at 29	13 at 34	1.74
Mario	7	71	36	17 at 32	22 at 39	1.34
Larry	6	64	40	15 at 37	18 at 43	1.23
Noah	7	79	52	20 at 44	N/A[a]	N/A[a]
Tom	7	90	47	15 at 29	19 at 36	1.10
Anthony	6	75	33	14 at 32	19 at 38	1.90

Note. ABC = Autism Behavior Checklist (Krug, Arick, & Almond, 1980). Mean score for autism is 77, with a mean score of 4 for typically developing children; BDI = Battelle Developmental Inventory (Newborg, Stock, & Wnek, 1984) age equivalent score; PCI = Proportional change index (Wolery, 1983). Calculation of a child's rate of development compared to the rate of development prior to intervention.
[a]Child moved before posttesting completed.

Table 4. Intervention Outcomes

Child	Postintervention outcomes
Michele	Michele's family was able to engage her in toy play with no evidence of her stereotypy. She was able to select toys from a toy box and play by herself and with her siblings. She began to communicate by pulling adults to items that she desired and shifting her eye gaze from the item to the adult.
Mario	Mario's reduction of problem behavior allowed him to access a wider array of community environments, including entering preschool. He would actively participate in self-care and family routines with no tantrumming. Mario began to use single words (70-word vocabulary) paired with pictures to make requests for objects, activities, and social routines.
Larry	Larry learned to play with toys with peers and family members. He was enrolled in an inclusive community preschool program where he needed minimal supports (i.e., visual schedule and prompting) to maintain engagement within play and classroom routines. He became independent in toileting and eating with utensils. He began to communicate by using simple gestures paired with vocalizations.
Noah	Noah learned to cope within a variety of community contexts (restaurants, stores, parks, Sunday school) without tantrums, property destruction, or biting. He began to use spontaneous one-word utterances to make requests. He was able to engage in a variety of play activities with adults and peers, including simple social play (e.g., tea party, feeding the baby).
Tom	Tom was able to maintain engagement in his inclusive community preschool classroom with minimal supports and no problem behavior. He began to communicate his needs and requests by pointing to pictures. Tom stopped carrying the cloth diaper that he liked to hold and chew. He learned to sit at the table for meals and was able to accompany his family to new environments without tantrum behavior.
Anthony	Anthony learned to make transitions and respond to requests without tantrum behavior. His reduction in problem behavior occurred at home, in the community, and within his inclusive community childcare program. He began to use gestures and vocalizations to make requests and choices.

A purpose of the ISP is to establish a functional foundation for longitudinal progress. For children with autism and histories of serious problem behaviors, longitudinal progress is likely dependent on effective and durable amelioration of the destructive and highly disruptive behaviors that typically exclude children from opportunities for participation and social development. The data from this demonstration may be seen as encouraging progress toward this end; however, they represent only one step. Future work must examine outcomes over a more extended period of time and in greater depth. The path toward significant lifestyle enhancements for children and families affected by autism and problem behaviors will continue to require comprehensive and collaborative support programs and the contributions of data from multiple sources and multiple perspectives.

ABOUT THE AUTHORS

*Glen Dunlap, PhD, is a professor of child and family studies and special education and serves as director of the Division of Applied Research and Educational Support (DARES) at the University of South Florida. **Lise Fox,** PhD, is an associate professor, associate director of DARES, and project director of the Individualized Support Project at the University of South Florida. Address: Glen Dunlap, Department of Child and Family Studies, Florida Mental Health Institute, University of South Florida, 13301 Bruce B. Downs Blvd., Tampa, FL 33612.*

AUTHORS' NOTE

The project described in this article and the article preparation were supported by EEPCD Model Demonstration Grant from the U.S. Department of Education No. H133G60119. The opinions are those of the authors and no official endorsement should be inferred.

REFERENCES

Albin, R. W., Lucyshyn, J. M., Horner, R. H., & Flannery, K. B. (1996). Contextual fit for behavioral support plans: A model for "goodness of fit." In L. K. Koegel, R. L. Koegel, & G. Dunlap (Eds.), *Positive behavioral support: Including people with difficult behavior in the community* (pp. 81–98). Baltimore: Brookes.

Arndorfer, R. A., Miltenberger, R. G., Woster, S. H., Rortvedt, A. K., & Gaffaney, T. (1994). Home-based descriptive and experimental analysis of problem behaviors in children. *Topics in Early Childhood Special Education, 14,* 64–87.

Carr, E. G., Levin, L., McConnachie, G., Carlson, J. I., Kemp, D. C., & Smith, C. E. (1994). *Communication-based interventions for problem behavior: A user's guide for producing behavior change.* Baltimore: Brookes.

Derby, K. M., Wacker, D. P., Berg, W., DeRaad, A., Ulrich, S., Asmus, J., Harding, J., Prouty, A., Laffey, P., & Stoner, E. A. (1997). The long-term effects of functional communication training in home settings. *Journal of Applied Behavior Analysis, 30,* 507–531.

Dunlap, G., & Fox, L. (1996). Early intervention and serious problem behaviors: A comprehensive approach. In L. K. Koegel, R. L. Koegel, & G. Dunlap (Eds.), *Positive behavioral support* (pp. 31–50). Baltimore: Brookes.

Dunlap, G., Fox, L., Vaughn, B. J., Bucy, M., & Clarke, S. (1997). In quest of meaningful perspectives and outcomes: A response to five commentaries. *Journal of the Association for Persons with Severe Handicaps, 22,* 221–223.

Dunlap, G., Johnson, L. F., & Robbins, F. R. (1990). Preventing serious behavior problems through skill development and early intervention. In A. C.

Repp & N. N. Singh (Eds.), *Current perspectives in the use of non-aversive and aversive interventions with developmentally disabled persons* (pp. 273–286). Sycamore, IL: Sycamore Press.

Dunlap, G., & Kern, L. (1993). Assessment and intervention for children with the instructional curriculum. In J. Reichle & D. Wacker (Eds.), *Communicative approaches to the management of challenging behavior* (pp. 177–203). Baltimore: Brookes.

Dunlap, G., Robbins, F. R., Dollman, C., & Plienis, A. J. (1988). *Early intervention for young children with autism: A regional training approach.* Huntington, WV: Marshall University.

Dunlap, G., Robbins, F. R., Morelli, M. A., & Dollman, C. (1988). Team training for young children with autism: A regional model for service delivery. *Journal of the Division for Early Childhood, 12,* 147–160.

Dunlap, G., Vaughn, B. J., & O'Neill, R. (1998). Comprehensive behavioral support: Application and intervention. In A. M. Wetherby, S. F. Warren, & J. Reichle (Eds.), *Transitions in prelinguistic communication* (pp. 343–364). Baltimore: Brookes.

Durand, V. M. (1990). *Functional communication training: An intervention program for severe behavior problems.* New York: Guilford Press.

Foster-Johnson, L., & Dunlap, G. (1993). Using functional assessment to develop effective, individualized interventions. *Teaching Exceptional Children, 25,* 44–50.

Fox, L., Dunlap, G., & Philbrick, L.A. (1997). Providing individualized supports to young children with autism and their families. *Journal of Early Intervention, 21,* 1–14.

Horner, R. H., Dunlap, G., Koegel, R. L., Carr, E. G., Sailor, W., Anderson, J., Albin, R. W., & O'Neill, R. E. (1990). Toward a technology of "nonaversive" behavioral support. *Journal of The Association for Persons with Severe Handicaps, 15,* 125–132.

Horner, R. H., & Carr, E. G. (1997). Behavioral support for students with severe disabilities: Functional assessment and comprehensive intervention. *The Journal of Special Education, 31,* 84–104.

Kern, L., & Dunlap, G. (1998). Curricular modifications to promote desirable classroom behavior. In J. K. Luiselli & M. J. Cameron (Eds.), *Antecedent control: Innovative approaches to behavioral support* (pp. 289–307). Baltimore: Brookes.

Koegel, L. K., Koegel, R. L., & Dunlap, G. (1996). *Positive behavioral support: Including people with difficult behavior in the community.* Baltimore: Brookes.

Koegel, L. K., Koegel, R. L., Kellegrew, D., & Mullen, K. (1996). Parent education for prevention and reduction of severe problem behaviors. In L. K. Koegel, R. L. Koegel, & G. Dunlap (Eds.), *Positive behavioral support: In-*

cluding people with difficult behavior in the community (pp. 3–30). Baltimore: Brookes.

Koegel, R. L., & Koegel, L. K. (1990). Extended reductions in stereotypic behavior of students with autism through a self-management treatment package. *Journal of Applied Behavior Analysis, 23,* 119–127.

Krug, D. A., Arick, J. R., & Almond, P. J. (1980). *Autism behavior checklist.* Austin, TX: PRO-ED.

Lucyshyn, J., Dunlap, G., & Albin, R. W. (Eds.). (in press). *Families, family life, and positive behavioral support: Addressing the challenge of problem behaviors in family contexts.* Baltimore: Brookes.

Luiselli, J. K., & Cameron, M. J. (Eds.). (1998). *Antecedent control: Innovative approaches to behavioral support.* Baltimore: Brookes.

McReynolds, L. V., & Kearns, K. P. (1983). *Single-subject experimental designs in communicative disorders.* Austin, TX: PRO-ED.

Meyer, L. H., & Evans, I. M. (1989). *Nonaversive intervention for behavior problems: A manual for home and community.* Baltimore: Brookes.

Newborg, J., Stock, J. R., & Wnek, L. (1984). *Battelle developmental inventory.* Allen, TX: DLM Teaching Resources.

O'Neill, R. E., Horner, R. H., Albin, R. W., Sprague, J. R., Storey, K., & Newton, J. S. (1997). *Functional assessment and program development for problem behavior.* Pacific Grove, CA: Brookes/Cole.

Reeve, C. E. (1996). *Prevention of severe behavior problems in children with developmental disabilities.* Unpublished doctoral dissertation, State University of New York at Stony Brook.

Repp, A. C., & Horner, R. H. (in press). *Functional analysis of problem: From effective assessment to effective support.* Pacific Grove, CA: Brooks/Cole.

Risley, T. R. (1997). Family preservation for children with autism. *Journal of Early Intervention, 21,* 15–16.

Vaughn, B. J., Clarke, S., & Dunlap, G. (1997). Assessment-based intervention for severe behavior problems in a natural family context. *Journal of Applied Behavior Analysis, 30,* 713–716.

Wacker, D.P., Peck, S., Derby, K.M., Berg, W., & Harding, J. (1996). Developing long-term reciprocal interactions between parents and their young children with problem behavior. In L. K. Koegel, R. L. Koegel, & G. Dunlap (Eds.), *Positive behavioral support: Including people with difficult behavior in the community* (pp. 51–80). Baltimore: Brookes.

Wolery, M. (1983). Proportional change index: An alternative for comparing child change data. *Exceptional Children, 50,* 167–170.

Action Editor: Robert L. Koegel

Comprehensive Multisituational Intervention for Problem Behavior in the Community:

Long-Term Maintenance and Social Validation

Edward G. Carr,
Len Levin,
Gene McConnachie,
Jane I. Carlson,
Duane C. Kemp,
Christopher E. Smith, and
Darlene Magito McLaughlin

*State University of New York
at Stony Brook and Developmental
Disabilities Institute*

Abstract: Assessment and intervention approaches for dealing with problem behavior need to be extended so that they can be effectively and comprehensively applied within the community. To meet assessment needs, the authors developed a three-component strategy: description (interview followed by direct observation), categorization (aggregating multiple instances of problem behavior into thematic groups, each characterized by a specific function), and verification (manipulating situational parameters to test the accuracy of the assessment data). To meet intervention needs, the authors employed a five-component, assessment-based, hypothesis-driven strategy consisting of rapport building, functional communication training, tolerance for delay of reinforcement, choice, and embedding. Following intervention, improvements in participants' lifestyle, communication, and problem behavior were noted. The intervention was practical in that parents, teachers, job coaches, and group home staff were able to efficiently implement it without compromising high levels of task engagement. Long-term maintenance of intervention effects (ranging from 1.5 to 2.5 years in duration) was also observed. Finally, 100 group home staff judged the effects to be socially valid in that problem behavior was rated as less severe and less dangerous, and as requiring less restraint following intervention. In light of these results, the authors discuss how future community-based intervention will require additional changes in assessment practices and intervention strategies and a redefinition of successful outcomes to include lifestyle change and life-span perspectives.

Over the past 30 years, behavior analysts have made great strides in the assessment of and intervention for severe problem behavior (Didden, Duker, & Korzilius, 1997; Scotti, Ujcich, Weigle, Holland, & Kirk, 1996). Much of this research has focused on highly controlled experimentation designed to identify and assess the variables controlling the behavior in question (Carr, Robinson, Taylor, & Carlson, 1990). This assessment information has then been used in the design of specific interventions (Carr et al., 1994; Gardner & Sovner, 1994; Koegel, Koegel, & Dunlap, 1996). Generally, research has focused on internal validity concerns that relate to making unambiguous causal statements about problem behavior and its remedi-

ation. Data generated from this approach have provided valuable assessment and intervention guidelines, and the field has now evolved to the point of being able to determine how broadly applicable these guidelines are in the natural environment. Specifically, how can we best extend present technology to address external validity concerns?

Three aspects of external validity are of particular interest to stakeholders (including parents, teachers, and job coaches). First, stakeholders want interventions that produce comprehensive lifestyle changes (Risley, 1996; Turnbull & Ruef, 1997). Problem behavior reduction per se thus is no longer seen as a sufficient criterion for defining a successful outcome, which instead is now seen as one wherein an individual is able to participate meaningfully in a variety of home, school, community, and work settings from which he or she was previously excluded due to the problem behavior. For example, reduction in aggressive behavior would need to be accompanied by an increase in the frequency with which the individual was able to demonstrate self-care skills, go shopping, have a meal at a restaurant, and hold a job.

Second, stakeholders want interventions that are practical and relevant (Carnine, 1997; Turnbull & Ruef, 1996). With respect to practicality, it means that any competent adult should be able to carry out the intervention. Traditionally, much problem behavior remediation has involved experts and/or researchers as the main intervention agents. What is needed, however, are concrete examples of parents, group home staff, teachers, and job coaches—among others—successfully implementing the kind of multicomponent interventions that are frequently needed to deal with problem behavior in community settings. With respect to relevance, the main issue is whether intervention packages can be implemented across all the contexts in which it is important for the person to function successfully on a daily basis. Much previous research has focused on settings that represent simulations or analogs of the natural environment (Carr et al., 1997). Although this research has helped identify important functional relationships, it does not answer the question of whether information derived from experimental analysis is applicable to all relevant contexts (Wahler & Fox, 1981).

Third, stakeholders want long-term behavior change (Nickels, 1996). A reduction in problem behavior that maintains for a few weeks or even a few months is seen as inadequate. Unfortunately, the published literature to date has provided only a handful of studies where behavior change lasted even 6 months (Carr et al., 1997). Long-term behavior change requires long-term implementation of intervention strategies (Turnbull & Turnbull, 1996; Vandercook, York, & Forest, 1989); therefore, intervention packages that are applicable over a period of years need to be developed.

Some aspects of the external validity criteria we have just noted have been explored in the literature (Carr & Carlson, 1993; R. H. Horner et al., 1996; Kemp & Carr, 1995; Lucyshyn, Olson, & Horner, 1995; Lutzker & Campbell, 1994; Northup et al., 1994; Singer & Irvin, 1989). For example, Carr and Carlson (1993) showed that a multicomponent intervention could successfully ameliorate problem behavior displayed by children in a supermarket shopping situation and, further, could be implemented by group home staff. This research thus met the criteria of lifestyle change and practicality. Similarly, Kemp and Carr (1995) demonstrated that a multicomponent intervention could remediate problem behavior displayed by adults in a greenhouse work situation and also could be implemented by job coaches. This research also met the lifestyle change

and practicality criteria previously noted. Typically, most research, including the studies just described, does not comprehensively address the three external validity criteria described previously. Carr and Carlson—and Kemp and Carr—did not demonstrate implementation of interventions across all the contexts relevant for the individuals studied (i.e., the supermarket situation and the greenhouse situation represented only one set of circumstances in which the individuals involved displayed problem behavior). Nor did these studies examine whether the beneficial behavior changes were maintained over a period of years.

In view of what we have just outlined, there is a clear need for a controlled research study that (a) addresses the issue of remediating problem behavior while producing lifestyle change and (b) uses procedures that are practical, relevant, and capable of generating long-term maintenance. The purpose of the present study was to address each of these goals.

Method

PARTICIPANTS

Participants were selected on the basis of interviews conducted with group home staff, parents, and classroom teachers working in an agency serving persons with developmental disabilities. Included in the study were the first three people who met the following criteria:

1. The individual was reported to display severe problem behavior in the home, community, and/or school;
2. The individual was currently excluded from participating in community activities because of past displays of problem behavior in the community;
3. The individual's problem behavior included any combination of aggression, self-injury, property destruction, and/or tantrums;
4. The individual's problem behavior was severe, as demonstrated by the need for physical restraint and/or medical attention;
5. The individual was documented to have some communicative abilities in the form of speech, sign language, gestures, or use of picture communication symbols.

The selected participants—Val, Gary, and Juan—were 14, 17, and 38 years old, respectively. Val was diagnosed as having cerebral palsy with ataxia and dyskinesia, as well as mental retardation. Gary and Juan were diagnosed as having mental retardation with autistic features. On the Stanford-Binet (Form L-M), Val, Gary, and Juan received IQ scores of 30, 28, and 12, respectively. With respect to communication skills, Val spoke in short phrases that were poorly articulated, Gary generally spoke in short phrases but occasionally used full sentences, and Juan had a repertoire of 10 poorly articulated spoken words that necessitated his use of picture symbols for effective communication.

Val's problem behavior was characterized by tantrums, property destruction, and aggression (e.g., pulling hair, tearing clothes, kicking, spitting, and slapping). Gary's problem behavior included aggression (punching, spitting, tearing clothing), property destruction, tantrums, and self-injurious behavior (hand biting). Juan's problem behavior consisted of aggression (kicking, slapping, hitting, throwing objects at people), self-injurious behavior (face slapping), property destruction, and tantrums.

Val and Gary lived at home with their parents. Juan had lived in the Willowbrook Developmental Center for 30 years and had just been placed in a group home with three other men.

PROCEDURE

A detailed manual describing the assessment and intervention procedures that we used in the present study has been published (Carr et al., 1994). This manual can be consulted for details; therefore, we will present only an overview of the procedures here. We will mostly use Gary as an example of how procedures were implemented.

Assessment

Assessment consisted of three phases: *describe, categorize,* and *verify.*

Describe. This phase involved an initial interview followed by a period of direct observation. During a 2- to 3-week period, the authors interviewed all relevant informants (e.g., parents, teachers, job coaches, and community residence staff), using a variant of an A-B-C (Antecedent-Behavior-Consequence) assessment format. The published literature has demonstrated the critical role of social variables in most episodes of problem behavior (Carr & Durand, 1985); therefore, our A-B-C assessment emphasized both interpersonal context (as antecedents) and the social reactions of others to the problem behavior (as consequences). For example, one of the authors interviewed Gary's mother and asked her to list the situations in which Gary displayed problem behavior. Initially, the interviewer asked her to describe the behavior (B) in specific, concrete terms (e.g., "Could you give me some specific examples of Gary's problem behavior?"). Then the interviewer asked Gary's mother to describe an example of the social context (A) that preceded such behavior (e.g., "In what situations does Gary act this way with you?"). Finally, the interviewer asked her to describe her reaction (C) to such behavior (e.g., "When Gary is aggressive, what do you do?").

The interview information was then used to select situations for direct observations, which were subsequently made (i.e., where, when, and with whom). Because the interview process identified so many problem situations, direct observations had to be carried out during significant portions of each participant's normal day. Specifically, observations were made 2 to 4 hours per day (mean = 3 hours), 3 to 5 days per week, including weekends (mean = 4 days), over 2 to 4 weeks (mean = 3 weeks). For example, one of the problem situations identified during the interview with Gary's mother involved lunch preparation; therefore, the assessor visited Gary's home during lunchtime in order to confirm the interview information through observation. Each instance of problem behavior that occurred during the observation period was recorded on an index card using the A-B-C narrative approach illustrated in the top section of Figure 1. This process was repeated for all of the situations identified during the interview, resulting in a large number of index cards for each of the participants.

In the example just given, the results of the direct observation confirmed those obtained from the interview. There also were instances in which direct observation failed to confirm the interview information. For example, during the interview Val's teacher reported that when Val became aggressive during an independent work activity, she (the teacher) would never attend to such behavior. However, during several direct observations, the assessor reported that Val's teacher consistently gave protracted reprimands (i.e., negative attention) in response to problem behavior in that situation. When the results of direct observation contradicted those derived from the interview, only the direct observation results (summarized on an index card) were considered in planning subsequent interventions.

It is important to note that several instances occurred in which direct observation yielded information not mentioned in the interview. For example, no group home staff member ever stated in an interview that Juan became aggressive when someone turned the TV off while he was watching his favorite program. (The experienced staff knew not to do this.) During one direct observation, a newly hired staff member did turn the TV off during Juan's program, precipitating an episode of aggression by Juan. That staff member reacted to this behavior by immediately turning the TV on again, thereby calming Juan. When new information was first obtained via direct observation rather than interview, such information was noted on an index card and was also considered in planning subsequent interventions.

This assessment was an ongoing process that took place throughout the 6 years of the study (baseline, intervention, and maintenance), as needed. The following events triggered additional descriptive assessment carried out in the manner just outlined:

1. Any significant change in the person's life situation (i.e., with respect to work, educational ac-

NAME: Gary	OBSERVER: Gene	DATE: 04/10
GENERAL CONTEXT: Home chore (making sandwich)		TIME: 12:30 P.M.

(A) INTERPERSONAL CONTEXT: Gary had been making a peanut butter sandwich for the past 5 minutes. His mother was standing nearby. She said, "Gary, you need to clean up the mess you made."

(B) BEHAVIOR PROBLEM: Gary threw the silverware on the floor and bit himself. Then, he screamed "No!" and ran out of the kitchen.

(C) SOCIAL REACTION: His mother jumped out of his way. Three minutes later, she cleaned up the mess herself.

PANEL MEMBERS: Gary's mother, the consulting psychologist, and a doctoral student who worked with Gary's family.

HYPOTHESIS (Purpose): Gary engages in property destruction (throwing silverware) and self-injury (biting himself) to avoid having to clean up the kitchen area (ESCAPE).

Figure 1. Index card format used in the functional assessment of Gary's problem behavior. In addition to A-B-C information, the card shows the composition of the panel used to formulate an hypothesis concerning the function (purpose) of the behavior.

tivities, staff, living situations, or social relationships);

2. Residual problem behavior that was observed after an otherwise successful intervention had been implemented;

3. Problem behavior that had been under control following intervention but unexpectedly reappeared.

Categorize. The describe phase generated more than 100 index cards per individual. Because this number of problem situations would have made intervention planning cumbersome, we had to develop a method for reducing the array of problem situations to a limited number of functional categories. Our method consisted of three steps: formulate hypotheses about function, group by functional categories, and find common themes within a functional category. These steps were carried out by a panel of three people (example shown in Figure 1, bottom section), two of whom had conducted the earlier describe phase and one of whom was a caregiver (e.g., parent, teacher, job coach).

With respect to the first step (formulate hypotheses), panel members were asked to examine each card independently and formulate an hypothesis about the function (purpose) of the behavior in each situation described (shown in Figure 1, bottom section). All panel members had received information from the authors about the variety of functions served by problem behavior. Hypothesis categories were *Attention, Escape, Tangible,* or *Other.* Specifically, each panel member was told to pay particular attention to the social reaction to the problem behavior (listed on the card), because the research literature has documented that this variable provides the clearest indication of the purpose the problem behavior actually serves (Carr et al., 1990; Reichle & Wacker, 1993). In the three examples described earlier, the social reaction to Gary, Val and Juan's problem behavior was *task removal, contingent lengthy reprimands,* and *reinstitution of TV time,* respectively, leading to hypothesis formulation of *Escape, Attention,* and *Tangible/Activity,* respectively. If two out of three panel members formulated the same hypothesis (e.g., Escape) and one member formulated a different hypothesis (e.g., Attention), the hypothesis chosen for subsequent intervention planning was the one put forth by the majority (i.e., Escape). If the majority hypothesis was Other or if there was no agreement among any of the panel members, the information on the specific index card involved was not used to plan subsequent interventions; instead, the problem behavior was dealt with via crisis management procedures described later. (This situation occurred for less than 1% of the cards.)

In the second step of the categorization method, the index cards were grouped together into the three functional categories (Attention, Escape, Tangibles) based on the majority judgment of the panel. In the third step (find common themes within a category), panel members examined the interpersonal context described on each card and, through discussion, grouped the cards into common themes within each functional category. In other words, themes were stimulus situations that had a defined set of shared features. This step was taken because it is generally not possible to design specific intervention strategies applicable to a wide variety of naturalistic situations based simply on generic hypotheses about functional categories (Carr, 1994; R. H. Horner, 1994). Instead, within a functional category (e.g., Escape), more specific information about the antecedent variables that control problem behavior is needed for intervention planning. This information comes from a detailed examination of interpersonal context. Various interpersonal contexts can be grouped together according to whether they share related stimulus features, giving rise to the concept of a theme. Thus, in the case of Gary, the primary generic functional category was Escape. Within that category, many index cards included information on the interpersonal context in which Gary was performing a task incorrectly and received negative feedback. For example, in a flower-potting task, he put the seeds in too deeply; in making his bed, he put the sheet on top of the blanket; in sweeping the sidewalk, he got dirt on the clean areas. In each case, the negative feedback that he received for poor task performance subsequently evoked aggression and self-injurious behavior. Despite the differences in tasks, people who were present, setting, and type of negative feedback received, the three interpersonal contexts just described for Gary all shared the same critical feature: presence of negative feedback following poor task performance. Therefore, these three cards—and all others that shared the same critical feature—constituted the theme "negative feedback for poor task performance" within the generic functional category of Escape. The same categorization procedure applied to the remaining index cards for Gary produced the themes of "prompted completion of an ongoing series of tasks" (i.e., Gary failed to complete a task in which he was involved and was subsequently prompted to finish up) and "presentation of nonpreferred tasks." Both were associated with self-injury and aggression. The procedure just described was applied across all functional categories for all participants. Space limitations do not permit listing the specific themes associated with each participant or the number of index cards related to each theme; interested readers are referred to Carr et al. (1994).

Verify. The third assessment phase (verify) was carried out as the baseline. Its purpose was to confirm that the situations represented by the identified themes did indeed evoke problem behavior, thereby corroborating the validity of the data collected and organized during the describe and categorize phases of assessment. Specifically, in this phase the interpersonal context and social reaction were manipulated (rather than passively observed). For example, we used the descriptive data represented in Figure 1 to set up a similar general context, interpersonal context, and social reaction to verify that aggressive and self-injurious behavior did indeed occur for Gary within the situation identified in the descriptive phase. On a given day, we maintained the situation represented in Figure 1 for 15 minutes, during which time, data were collected. Thus, one example (i.e., home chore: sandwich making) drawn from one theme (i.e., prompted completion of an ongoing series of tasks) was used to verify information from the describe and categorize phases. On the same day, the process was repeated two more times: Two more themes from the pool were examined using one specific example of each. Therefore, on a given day, there were three 15-minute theme sessions. Data collected from these sessions were pooled to produce a single baseline probe point of 45 minutes, On the next probe day, three more themes that had not yet been sampled were selected, and one specific example from each was used in the verification process. This process (i.e., sampling without replacement) was continued across probes until all the themes had been sampled. At this point, the themes were recycled with one restriction—the specific example representing a theme could not have been used in any prior probe.

Intervention

The format used in conducting baseline sessions (just described) was repeated during intervention, which was a comprehensive multicomponent approach consisting of building rapport, providing functional communication training (FCT), building tolerance for reinforcement delay, providing choices, and using embedding. All of these approaches were applied continuously throughout the 5 years of the intervention portion of the study, as needed.

Building Rapport. The purpose of this component was to increase positive social interaction between the person with disabilities (the participant) and his or her caregivers because this type of interaction had been infrequent. Increased social interaction was seen as an important initial step in eventually enhancing a communication-based intervention.

First, caregivers provided a wide variety of individualized reinforcers (e.g., foods, games, conversation) to the participant. They thus acted as discriminative stimuli for approach behavior by the person with disabilities. After approach behavior became reliable, caregivers withheld reinforcers until the participant requested them spontaneously or after prompting. Requests made through speech, sign, or gestures were acceptable. As general approach and requesting were being established, steps were taken to enhance the participant's physical appearance (personal hygiene, grooming, clothing) to reduce the possibility of social rejection by caregivers and others. In addition, interests shared between the caregivers and the participant were identified (e.g., jogging, going out for pizza). To further facilitate social interaction, we used these shared interests as one of the bases for programming community-based routines (e.g., daily jogging or weekly visits to the pizzeria). The procedures for building rapport were implemented each time that a new caregiver or support person became involved with the participant.

Functional Communication Training. The increased social interaction that followed successful rapport building provided a useful context for building communicative skills that were directly focused on ameliorating problem behavior. The purpose of the FCT component was to teach the participant a variety of communicative responses that were functionally equivalent to various classes of problem behavior, thereby making further display of such behavior unnecessary. We used the standard FCT procedure reported in the literature (Carr & Durand, 1985). Briefly, this procedure involved matching the function of the communicative response to the function of the problem behavior as identified through the previously described generic categories of behavioral function: Escape, Attention, and Tangibles/Activities.

The category associated with the greatest number of index cards was addressed first (e.g., for Gary, Escape). Further, the theme associated with the greatest number of index cards within that category (e.g., for Gary, "prompted completion of an ongoing series of tasks") became the initial focus of intervention. For example, Figure 1 shows that the function of Gary's self-injury and property destruction during sandwich making was escape from the prompted task. Therefore, a communicative response that served the same function as the problem behavior (escape) was taught (after a few minutes of sandwich making, Gary was prompted to say, "I need a break," and his request was honored). Over time, the prompts were faded, and Gary's spontaneous communicative acts were honored with a short break prior to his returning to the task.

Because the problem behavior function varied for each participant, many different communicative forms had to be taught. The specific form was determined by the theme that it addressed. In the illustration just given, Gary's self-injury and property destruction were, putatively, escape-motivated behaviors related to the theme of "prompted completion of an ongoing series of tasks." Each index card pertaining to that theme identified an opportunity for teaching Gary to request a break. When Gary had mastered the break request in the situation identified by the first index card (i.e., sandwich making), the FCT procedure was repeated for a second index card for the same theme (home chore: vacuuming). Repetitions of the procedure continued for all the index cards related to that particular theme until spontaneous generalization occurred for three additional cards (e.g., Gary spontaneously requested a break from washing the family car, planting a flowerbed, or making a salad). At this point, a new theme from the Escape category ("negative feedback for poor task performance") was examined in order to create opportunities for teaching the next communicative response ("Help me"). This theme was selected because it was associated with the second greatest number of cards within the generic Escape category. The FCT procedure that had been used to address the first Escape theme was now implemented for the second Escape theme and each succeeding Escape theme. In cases in which there were only a few index cards in a theme, spontaneous generalization sometimes did not occur; therefore, the FCT procedure was applied to all of the situations represented by these cards.

Once training had been completed with respect to the Escape category, the entire FCT procedure just described was repeated for the generic category containing the second greatest number of index cards (in the case of Gary, Tangibles) and then the third greatest (Attention, for Gary).

As noted earlier, if the majority hypothesis of the panel was that problem behavior was a function of variables other than those specifically listed or if a consensus regarding function could not be achieved, no intervention specific to the hypothesis was possible. In these cases, problem behavior was dealt with through the use of crisis management procedures (Carr et al., 1994). We employed five such procedures: *ignore, momentary restraint, protect, remove,* and *introduce cues* (Carr & Carlson, 1993). (For reasons of safety and ethics, these procedures were also employed during the baseline [verify] phase of the study.)

We used the ignore strategy to handle minor problem behavior (e.g., screaming) that had a history of leading to more serious problems if not stopped. For example, when Gary screamed, his mother would sometimes reprimand him, and Gary's screaming would accelerate to self-injury. To avoid this outcome, we taught his mother to simply ignore the screaming; the behavior typically subsided. We used the momentary restraint and introduce cues procedures to handle self-injury. When Gary bit his hand, his mother was taught to hold his hand away from his mouth for a few seconds (momentary restraint) and to present discriminative stimuli (introduce cues) for a highly preferred activity (e.g., putting on a music tape that Gary liked to sing to). These cues typically evoked competing, nonproblem behavior. We used the protect and remove procedures to deal with aggression. If Gary hit his brother, his mother was taught to step between Gary and his brother (protect) and have the brother move to a different room in the house (remove). Often, these procedures were supplemented with introduce cues (e.g., Gary's mother might turn on music following protect and remove, a procedure that resulted in Gary's becoming engaged in singing rather than hitting). Because the hypothesis of "Other" involved only a small number of situations—as was the case for a lack of consensus regarding function— use of crisis management procedures was very rare once intervention had begun. In contrast, during baseline, when problem behaviors were frequent, these procedures had to be used more often. Even after intervention had begun, occasional episodes of problem behavior occurred. These also were dealt with by employing crisis management procedures.

Building Tolerance for Reinforcement Delay.
Following successful FCT, there was a strong tendency for each participant to use the newly acquired communicative responses at a very high rate, and caregivers found such responding problematic. Specifically, an individual might (a) ask for so many breaks that little work would be completed, (b) ask for so much attention that the teacher was unable to attend to other students, and (c) ask for tangibles at an inopportune moment or that could not be provided. To address these issues, we built in tolerance for reinforcement delay.

When a participant requested a particular reinforcer, the parent or teacher (for example) acknowledged the request and told the individual that he or she could have the desired item after a specific activity (e.g., chores, independent leisure activity) had been completed. If necessary, the participant was prompted to carry out the activity; these prompts were faded over time. For example, after receiving FCT, Gary made so many requests for breaks that he seldom finished making his sandwich (see Figure 1). A procedure was implemented such that when Gary asked for a break, his mother acknowledged his request ("Sure, Gary, you can have a break") but told him that he could only have a break after he had completed more of the task ("First, you need to spread the peanut butter and jelly on the bread, and then you can take a little break."). Initially, Gary's mother had to help him by physically prompting the extra required work, but over time she was able to fade out these prompts. Now when Gary was told to do the extra work, he readily did so prior to repeating his request for a break. Over many weeks, Gary's mother recycled this procedure so as to gradually increase the duration of the work required prior to having break requests honored. Gary eventually was required to gather all the lunch supplies, make the entire sandwich, pack his drink and snacks, and clean up the food preparation area prior to having his break request honored. At the end of this training, his mother's acknowledgment ("Sure, Gary, you can have a

break but first . . .") became a natural cue for him to complete the entire lunch-making sequence, and the completion of that sequence became a natural cue for him to reiterate his break request. The procedure just described was repeated in all situations in which the too frequent use of communicative responses interfered with task completion and/or a caregiver's need to attend to others. The procedure was also used to deal with excessively high rates of requests for activities and tangibles. If, however, the individual requested an item or activity that could not be provided, a fourth procedure—choice—was used.

Providing Choices.
We used a choice strategy to deal with requests that could not be honored and thus might result in problem behavior. Research has demonstrated that providing choices to an individual can be an effective way to reduce problem behavior (Dyer, Dunlap, & Winterling, 1990). For example, Gary once asked to go for a walk during a violent rainstorm. His mother was taught to respond to such requests by encouraging him to choose among several alternative options. Specifically, she began by acknowledging the request (e.g., "Yes, Gary, it would be fun to go for a walk, but it's too dangerous to go outside now."). Then, she offered Gary at least two alternative exercise options (e.g., "Gary, you could use the treadmill in the recreation room, or you could work out with the exercise videotape in the den. Which would you like to do?"). When Gary indicated a preference, his mother honored his request. This procedure was repeated in all situations in which requests for certain tangibles could not be honored for safety reasons or because caregivers were otherwise occupied. The choice procedure just described was also used for attention-seeking problem behavior. For example, Gary might ask to talk with his mother while she was on the phone. If this happened, his mother would respond as follows: "Gary, I know you want to talk, but I'm on the phone. Your brother (Pete) and father are not busy now. Do you want to talk to Dad or Pete?" Depending on the choice made, Gary's mother motioned for the relevant person to approach Gary and speak with him.

Gary sometimes refused the choices. In this case, the caregiver repeated the options; if Gary still refused to state a preference, the caregiver went about his or her business and made no further comments to Gary. If problem behavior arose (this was rare), the appropriate crisis management procedures were carried out.

The choice procedure was also used for escape-motivated problem behavior. Consistent with the literature (Dunlap et al., 1994), we had Gary's family members and teachers offer him choices when appropriate. For example, on various days Gary might prefer one task to another (e.g., vacuuming versus washing the car versus sweeping the floor). We taught Gary's parents to offer him task choices because it was not necessary for him to do all of the tasks each day. Thus, after school and before Gary began his chores, his mother asked him, "Gary, what would you like to do today—vacuum, wash the car, or sweep the floor?" When Gary indicated his preference, his mother allowed him to do the task indicated. Occasionally, Gary refused to choose any option. In this case, a fifth procedure, embedding, was used.

Using Embedding. We used this procedure to deal with escape-motivated behavior in situations in which a participant refused to choose a task option. In the embedding procedure, stimuli that are discriminative for problem behavior (e.g., task demands) are interspersed among stimuli that are discriminative for socially appropriate behavior (e.g., music could be discriminative for singing, dancing, humming, and smiling). Research has demonstrated that embedding (also referred to as interspersal training and behavioral momentum) can be effective in reducing problem behavior (Carr, Newsom, & Binkoff, 1976; Dunlap & Koegel, 1980; Mace et al., 1988).

For example, Gary's mother might have asked him to choose one of three task options (e.g., "Gary, do you want to vacuum, wash the car, or sweep the floor first?"). If Gary refused to choose, his mother repeated the options. If he still refused to choose, his mother initiated the embedding procedure. Specifically, Gary had a history of responding to his favorite music tapes by humming and singing (socially appropriate behavior). Therefore, after Gary twice refused to make a choice, his mother turned on one of his favorite music tapes. Gary responded by humming and singing. After 2 minutes, his mother turned the music off. Gary immediately requested more music. His mother responded by saying, "Sure, Gary, you can have more music, but first let's do some work. Do you want to vacuum, wash the car, or sweep the floor first?" Typically, Gary then chose one of the options. As he began to work, his mother turned the music on again. In this manner, the demands associated with work were embedded in the music-listening context. If Gary refused to choose one of the options, the procedure was repeated. Following subsequent termination of the music, the stimuli associated with the music were made more salient (e.g., the tape recorder was placed within Gary's field of vision and his mother talked about what a great tune they had just heard and how much she enjoyed singing along with him). This was done in order to help focus Gary's attention on the music stimulus so that it would be more likely to evoke a request for continuation that, in turn, would allow Gary's mother to reintroduce the work options. If at any time Gary responded to the termination of the music by engaging in problem behavior, his mother would initiate the relevant crisis management procedures.

Generalization

We were also concerned with the transfer of intervention success from one specific situation to other situations

(generalization). The scope of generalization in terms of the intervention agents, settings, and tasks involved is illustrated in Table 1. Two strategies were employed to enhance generalization: programming generalization and conducting additional descriptive assessments and interventions in situations in which a problem behavior continued or reemerged.

Programming Generalization. Programming generalization involved identifying a successful intervention in one situation and then systematically introducing it into various functionally related situations. There is evidence in the literature that successful programming of generalization across a number of situations will evoke spontaneous generalization in other situations (Stokes & Baer, 1977). For example, we previously mentioned that during FCT, Gary's mother had programmed the "I want a break" response for tasks such as sandwich making and vacuuming. After she programmed several more tasks (washing hands and face, making the bed, drying dishes), Gary spontaneously generalized his requests for breaks to several new tasks (washing the car, planting a flowerbed, and making a salad) that were functionally related to the original tasks (i.e., the problem behavior in all situations was escape motivated).

Conducting Descriptive Assessments and Interventions in New Situations. After Gary's mother had produced spontaneous generalization across tasks at home, she decided that Gary was ready to participate in new activities in the community. One situation involved shopping at the supermarket. The first few expeditions were associated with high levels of aggressive behavior; therefore, the descriptive assessment procedure described earlier was repeated in the supermarket. The assessment revealed that Gary's problem behavior in the new situation was motivated not by Escape, but by Tangibles; specifically, when certain favorite snacks (e.g., cookies) were inaccessible (out of reach or prohibited by Gary's mother), Gary became aggressive. Gary's mother used the new assessment information to design a variant of FCT relevant to the function identified for the aggressive behavior: she prompted and reinforced verbal requests for snacks (e.g., "I want the cookies"), combining this strategy with building tolerance for reinforcement delay, as described earlier. Following this intervention, Gary's aggressive behavior decreased.

Maintenance

The procedural distinction between the intervention and maintenance phases was as follows: During intervention, we were present several days a week in the home, school, employment, and community situations to coach and provide feedback to caregivers regarding the design and implementation of intervention strategies. During main-

Table 1. Multisituational Intervention Implementation: Agents, Settings, and Tasks

Intervention agent	Setting	Task
Parents	Home	Laundry (sort, wash, dry, fold)
Siblings	Parents' home	Exercises/physical education
Group home staff	Group home	Put on makeup
Classroom teachers	School	Wash hands and face
Gym teachers	Class	Brush teeth
Speech therapists	Gym	Shave
Bus drivers	Speech room	Set table
Job coaches	Bus/van	Make sandwiches
Undergraduate clinical assistants	Field trips	Perform academic tasks
	Community	Pack lunch
	Supermarket	Clear and wipe table
	Park	Dry dishes
	Restaurant	Load and empty dishwasher
	Fast-food restaurant	Put dishes/silverware away
	Swimming pool	Sweep floor
	Church	Mop floor
	Hotels	Vacuum
	Trains	Brush hair
	Work	Clean bathroom
	Greenhouse	Clean kitchen
		Wash windows
		Wash car/van
		Ride exercycle
		Make bed

tenance, we visited relevant sites 1 day per month and made phone contact once per month. In addition, we invited caregivers to phone us as needed if questions arose.

Occasionally, problem behavior reemerged during the maintenance phase, typically at low frequencies. When this happened, we repeated the descriptive assessment in the same manner as that just described for generalization, and we built relevant interventions based on the new assessment data.

Social Validity

During this phase, we obtained judgments from direct service providers as to the efficacy of the intervention.

Choice of Judges. A total of 100 group home staff, representing approximately 90% of the total direct care staff in three service agencies on Long Island, were selected as judges based on their availability at the time of validity testing. We selected these individuals as judges because all three study participants were currently in or about to enter group homes; therefore, it was important to know how primary caregivers perceived the seriousness of the problem behavior being addressed.

Choice of Video Segments. We randomly selected one 15-min session from the last day of baseline (pre-intervention segment) and one 15-min session from the last day of intervention (postintervention segment) from the videotapes of each of the three participants (i.e., two for each participant or six segments in all). The viewings were administered to groups of 5 to 10 judges at a time, with the pre- and posttapes randomly selected from across the participants (e.g., the first group of judges saw a 15-min pre-intervention tape for Val, a 15-min postintervention tape for Gary, and a 15-min postintervention tape for Juan). The type of tape shown was counterbalanced across groups of judges (e.g., the second group saw a 15-min postintervention tape for Val, 15-min pre-intervention tape for Gary, and a 15-min pre-intervention tape for Juan). The randomization and counterbalancing procedures were repeated for judging groups until all 100 judges had been tested. We thus avoided having a single judge view the pre- and posttapes for the same participant, which eliminated the potential for biased ratings based on prior exposure. Each of the three pre-intervention tapes was viewed by 50 judges from the pool; each of the three postintervention tapes was viewed by the other 50 judges.

Judges' Ratings. Prior to viewing a 15-min segment, the top paragraph in Figure 2 was read to the judges. After the viewing was completed, the second paragraph in Figure 2 was read, and the judges filled out each of the three 7-point rating scale (7 = *strong agreement with a statement,* and 1 = *strong disagreement*) statements regarding severity, danger, and physical restraint. The latter procedure was repeated for each of the remaining two 15-min segments.

You will be viewing a videotaped session approximately 15 minutes in length. Please watch the session carefully. Afterward you will be asked to respond to the questions below, which will be read aloud for your convenience. Please consider each session separately and answer the questions based solely on the session you have just viewed.

Imagine that the videotaped session you have just seen represents this person's typical daily behavior. To what extent do you agree or disagree with the following statements? Please circle the number that most clearly reflects your response.

1.   This person's problem behavior is severe.

     Agree   Disagree
     Strongly   7   6   5   4   3   2   1   Strongly

2.   This person is a danger to him- or herself or others.

     Agree   Disagree
     Strongly   7   6   5   4   3   2   1   Strongly

3.   This person is likely to require physical restraint at least occasionally.

     Agree   Disagree
     Strongly   7   6   5   4   3   2   1   Strongly

Figure 2. Instructions given to judges who made social validity ratings, and the scales used to make those ratings.

RESPONSE DEFINITIONS, RECORDING, AND RELIABILITY

Response Definitions

One independent variable was recorded as a measure of intervention integrity. This was defined as the response of the intervention agent to the communicative act displayed by the participant (henceforth referred to as responsivity). Three dependent variables—task engagement, communicative acts, and problem behavior—were recorded for each participant.

Responsivity (intervention integrity) was defined as any of the following three variables: no response, acknowledged, and reinforced. *No response* meant that the intervention agent failed to provide the reinforcer specified in the participant's request and, in addition, failed to comment in any way on the request (e.g., the person with disabilities said, "I want a break," but the intervention agent remained silent or made an unrelated comment such as "You are wearing a nice shirt today"). *Acknowledged* meant that the intervention agent failed to provide the reinforcer but did recognize that a request had been made (e.g., the person with disabilities said, "I want a break," and the intervention agent responded by saying, "Sure, you can have a break, but why don't we finish washing the table

first?"). *Reinforced* meant that the intervention agent provided the specified reinforcer (e.g., the person with disabilities said, "I want a break," and the intervention agent responded, "Okay, why don't you sit down on the couch for a few minutes and relax?").

Problem behavior was defined as the occurrence of any of the following:

1. Aggression toward a person
   - hitting, punching, kicking, biting, or shoving another person;
   - grabbing the clothes, skin, or hair of another person;
   - spitting;
   - taking or attempting to take a tangible reinforcer from another person without permission;
   - hitting another person with an object; and
   - attempting to do any of the preceding behaviors but missing the victim because he or she moved out of the way.
2. Aggression toward an object
   - hitting, punching, or kicking an object;
   - hitting, punching, or kicking the floor, a wall, or a door.
3. Destroying property

4. Injuring one's self (hitting the head with a hand or biting a hand, for example).

A *communicative act* was defined as the occurrence of a spontaneous verbal request (e.g., requesting a tangible item, asking for help when working on a difficult task, requesting a break, calling out a person's name) or nonverbal request (e.g., tapping another person on the shoulder, pointing to a desired object, leading another person by the hand towards a desired object, presenting a picture symbol with the word "break" written on it). To be considered spontaneous, the request could not occur within 5 seconds of a verbal prompt. In addition, at least 3 seconds had to have elapsed between two communicative responses that were not acknowledged or reinforced for each to be scored as a separate response. Thus, if an individual said, "orange" 5 times within a 3-second period, the 5 responses were scored as a single communicative act.

Task engagement was defined as actively participating in an ongoing work, academic, or home chore activity either independently or with prompting from a support person or caregiver. For example, when Gary was washing the family car and he held the hose and sprayed the car with water, his behavior was scored as task engagement. If his brother had had to guide Gary's hands to the hose and help him direct the spray, that activity also would have been scored as task engagement. However, if Gary simply had stood next to the car while his brother filled a bucket with soap and water, Gary's behavior would not have been scored as task engagement.

Response Recording

As noted previously, each baseline, intervention, and maintenance session consisted of three 15-min observation periods conducted on a given day. Each of these periods was videotaped for subsequent reliability analysis. Typically, data were recorded during 3 consecutive or near consecutive days in a row, depending on participant availability. Generally, a set of 3 days was defined as a probe, but this number could vary from 2 to 4 days. During intervention, probes were separated from one another by an average of 3 to 4 months. This interprobe interval was gradually extended so that, by the end of the study, it was as long as 1 year.

Reliability

A psychology doctoral student served as the primary reliability observer. This student viewed each of the videotapes and scored all the variables using the response definitions noted earlier. Responsivity, communicative acts, and problem behavior were all scored as frequency counts summed across the three 15-min observation periods that constituted a session. Task engagement was scored using a time-sampling procedure consisting of continuous 10-sec intervals.

An undergraduate with extensive employment experience in the field of developmental disabilities served as the reliability observer. For frequency data, the reliability index was the percentage of agreement between the two observers, calculated for each probe by dividing the smaller total frequency by the larger. For interval data, observer records were compared on an interval-by-interval basis. Agreement scores were computed as the number of agreements divided by the number of agreements plus disagreements. The percentage of sessions for which reliability was assessed for each class of variable, the mean percentage of interobserver agreement, and the range of agreement for all three participants are given in Table 2. The mean percentage of agreement varied from 82% to 96% across the three participants.

EXPERIMENTAL DESIGN

A multiple-baseline probe analysis was carried out within a multiple-baseline-across-participants design (R. D. Horner & Baer, 1978). Ethical considerations prohibited the use of a standard multiple-baseline design across participants (i.e., continuous data collection) because such a design would have required large numbers of baseline sessions in which participants could have harmed themselves or others due to the severity of their problem behaviors. Because intervention was focused on changing problem behavior and communication per se, the multiple baseline was used to demonstrate experimental control with respect to these two variables. Other variables (e.g., task engagement) were not explicit intervention targets. Data on these variables were not the subject of the controlled experimentation and represent ancillary measures only.

Results

INDEPENDENT VARIABLE

The data on responsivity are provided in Figure 3. (As noted earlier, intervention agents had three response options: no response, acknowledged, or reinforced.) The data shown in Figure 3 were pooled across each phase of the intervention; thus, the baseline data represent the responses of the intervention agents pooled across all the baseline sessions for a given participant. Likewise, the intervention data represent the responses of the intervention agents pooled across all the sessions for each of the probes that constituted the intervention data set. The total frequency of the three types of intervention agent responses was summed, and the percentage of that total for each type was computed.

No response and acknowledged together constituted the vast majority of responses during baseline, whereas the reinforced response rarely occurred. The type of responses

Table 2. Reliability Data for Each Class of Behavior

Behavior	Participant	% Sessions with reliability	Mean % agreement	Range (%)
Responsivity	Val	40	87	70–100
	Gary	40	89	70–100
	Juan	40	82	64–100
Communicative acts	Val	23	84	70–96
	Gary	19	87	69–98
	Juan	20	83	64–100
Problem behavior	Val	23	96	80–100
	Gary	19	82	60–100
	Juan	20	92	72–100
Task engagement	Val	21	87	75–99
	Gary	26	92	83–96
	Juan	25	95	91–97

that occurred varied across intervention agents in that Val primarily received no response, but Gary and Juan primarily received acknowledged. The percentage of the total responses representing the reinforced option was 0%, 22%, and 13%, respectively, for Val, Gary, and Juan.

With respect to the intervention data, all three intervention agents showed an immediate and substantial increase in the percentage of their reinforcing responses during the first probe. However, in successive probes the reinforced category diminished from its initially high levels, and the acknowledged category generally increased from initially low levels so that by the final probe, the percentage of the two types of responses were more comparable. Nonetheless, across all the probes, the level of the reinforced category was substantially higher than that observed during baseline for all three participants and, by the final probe, was 55%, 70%, and 45% for Val, Gary, and Juan, respectively. Additionally, the level of the no response category generally remained low throughout all the intervention probes.

DEPENDENT VARIABLES

The percentages of intervals of task engagement across baseline, intervention, and maintenance probes are shown in Figure 4. As noted previously, task engagement was not directly manipulated in a controlled experimental fashion. For all participants, task engagement occurred at low levels during baseline, increased during intervention, and continued to increase or remained stable during maintenance. Specifically, for Val, task engagement occurred at a mean level as follows:

- 6% of the intervals in baseline (range: 1%–18%),
- 41% in intervention (range: 24%–59%), and
- 69% during maintenance (range: 50%–85%).

For Gary, task engagement occurred as follows:

- baseline level of 36% (range: 23%–49%),
- intervention level of 54% (range: 18%–78%), and
- maintenance level of 70% (range: 52%–80%).

Finally, for Juan, mean levels of task engagement occurred as follows:

- 25% in baseline (range: 1%–52%),
- 35% in intervention (range: 4%–57%), and
- 39% during maintenance (range: 36%–51%).

The frequency of spontaneous (unprompted) communication and problem behavior across baseline, intervention, and maintenance probes is shown in Figure 5. Across all three participants, baseline levels of communication were low and stable across time. In contrast, following intervention, frequency of communication increased in multiple-baseline fashion. During maintenance, there was some diminution in the level of communication for Val and Gary, but none for Juan. Mean frequencies of communication for each participant follow.

1. Val
   - baseline was 23 (range: 20–30),
   - intervention was 61.8 (range: 48–89), and
   - maintenance was 45.4 (range: 25–95).
2. Gary
   - baseline was 9.3 (range: 2–22),
   - intervention was 54.1 (range: 29–64), and
   - maintenance was 25.1 (range: 14–42).
3. Juan
   - baseline was 7.6 (range: 0–17),
   - intervention was 52.5 (range: 32–95), and
   - maintenance was 59.2 (range: 38–92).

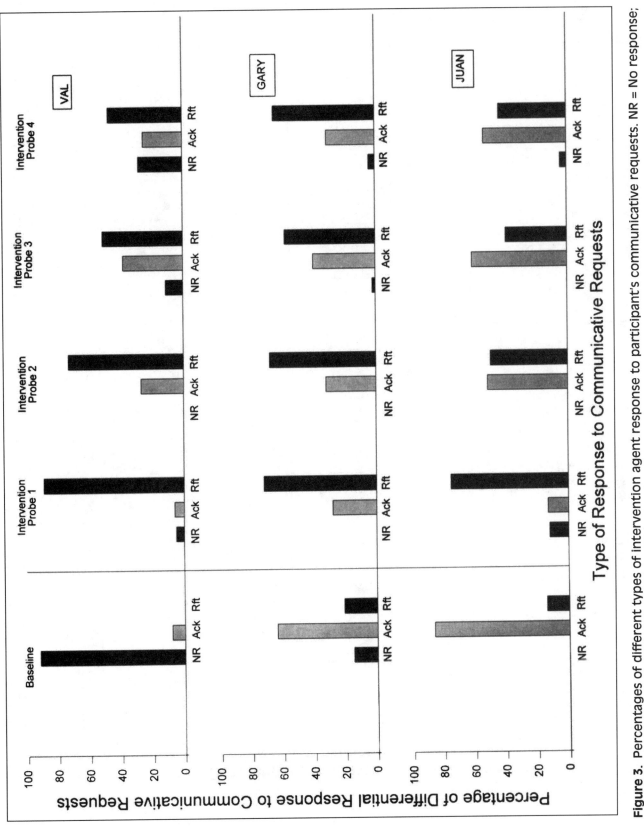

Figure 3. Percentages of different types of intervention agent response to participant's communicative requests. NR = No response; Ack = Acknowledged request; Rft = Reinforced request.

230

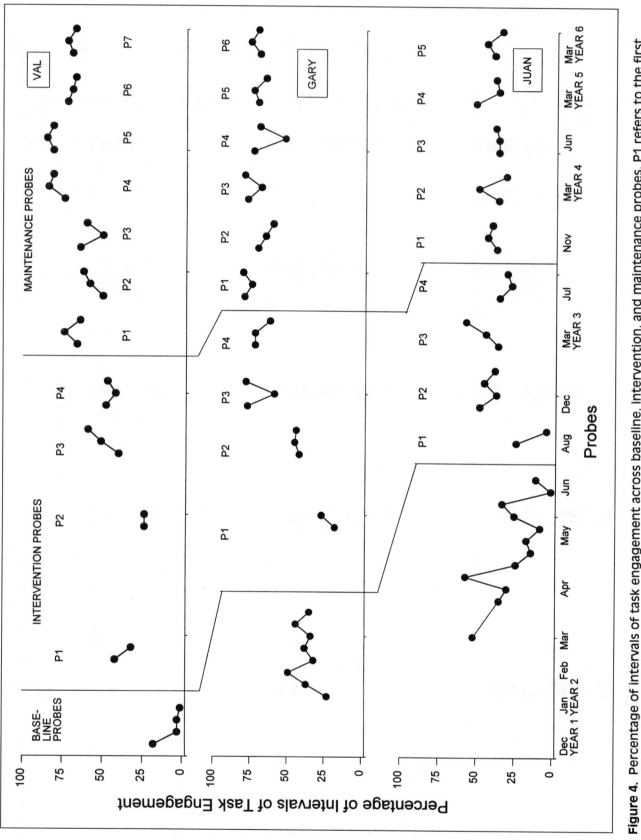

Figure 4. Percentage of intervals of task engagement across baseline, intervention, and maintenance probes. P1 refers to the first probe in a phase, P2 to the second probe, and so on.

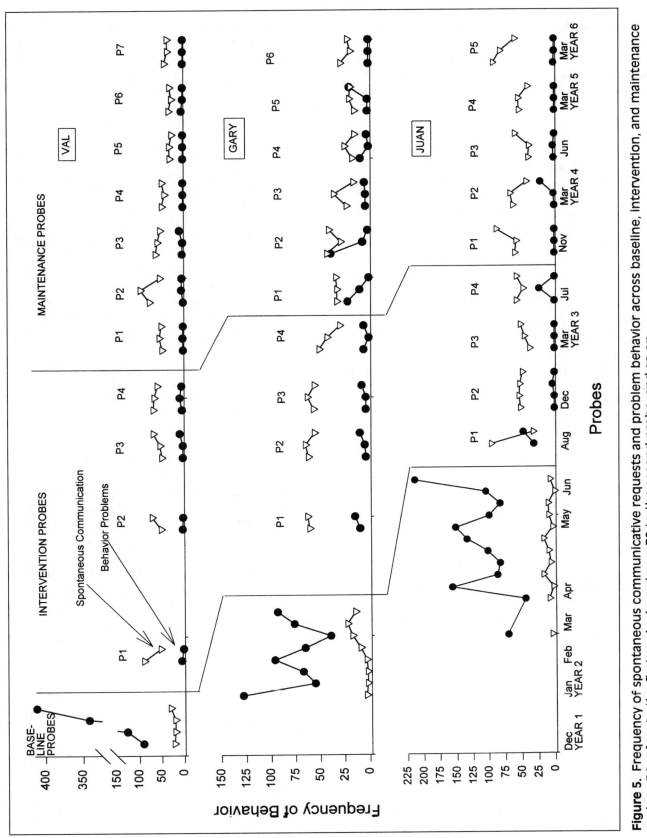

Figure 5. Frequency of spontaneous communicative requests and problem behavior across baseline, intervention, and maintenance probes. P1 refers to the first probe in a phase, P2 to the second probe, and so on.

Figure 5 also shows a high baseline frequency of problem behavior for all three participants, followed by a dramatic decrease in frequency at the beginning of intervention. This decrease lasted throughout the intervention and maintenance phases. The mean frequencies of problem behavior for each participant follow.

1. Val
   - baseline was 243 (range: 91–412),
   - intervention was 3.4 (range: 1–8), and
   - maintenance was 1.0 (range: 0–8).
2. Gary
   - baseline was 77.4 (range: 39–128)
   - intervention was 5.5 (range: 0–14),
   - maintenance was 6.4 (range: 0–38).
3. Juan
   - baseline was 110 (range: 44–213),
   - intervention was 9.5 (range 0–23), and
   - maintenance was 1.7 (range: 0–21).

The data on social validity are provided in Table 3. The ratings obtained from judges who viewed pre-intervention segments were significantly different (t test, $p < .005$) than the ratings obtained from judges who viewed postintervention segments; that is, following intervention, problem behavior was judged to be significantly less severe, less dangerous, and requiring less restraint than problem behavior displayed prior to intervention.

Discussion

INTERVENTION

Our study showed the intervention package to be effective and feasible. The five-component intervention package was successful in reducing severe problem behavior in three individuals across many different community-based contexts over a protracted maintenance period (1.5 to 2.5 years). As was the case in previous studies (Bird, Dores, Moniz, & Robinson, 1989; Carr & Durand, 1985; R. H.

Horner & Day, 1991), there was a strong inverse relationship between communicative responding and severe problem behavior. Although the data are consistent with the notion that increased communicative competence has an ameliorative effect on problem behavior, the presence of several other intervention components in this study bars the conclusion that the positive outcomes were due solely to FCT. Indeed, the critical aspect of the present study was its scope: The daily application of multiple intervention procedures across multiple situations over very long periods of time. The data on social validity corroborate the direct observation data pertaining to effectiveness displayed in Figure 5. Specifically, key stakeholders (i.e., group home staff) judged problem behavior to be significantly less severe, less dangerous, and requiring less restraint following intervention. In sum, the intervention package produced long-term maintenance and positive lifestyle changes.

With respect to feasibility, our multicomponent intervention addressed several issues raised in the literature (Carr & Carlson, 1993; Kemp & Carr, 1995). First, given the centrality of communication, there is a legitimate concern that individuals may make increasingly more requests as their communication pays off, thereby dominating the time of their caretakers and relatives. The data shown in Figure 5 contradict this possibility. Specifically, instead of an upward trend in communicative requests, Val and Gary displayed a downward trend and Juan remained stable. Second, the data on responsivity also relate to the issue of feasibility. Specifically, requests were not honored 100% of the time for any of the participants. Indeed, with respect to requests honored, Val and Juan's data showed a downward trend over probes and Gary's data were stable. Third, the data on task engagement (see Figure 4) also relate to the feasibility issue. Specifically, even though parents and teachers honored requests throughout the study, such behavior on their part did not limit active engagement in a variety of academic, work, and household tasks by each of the three participants. The dramatic increase in task engagement from that observed during baseline per-

Table 3. Social Validity Ratings for Pre- and Postintervention Videotaped Segments

Behavior characteristic	Intervention for Val		Intervention for Gary		Intervention for Juan	
	Pre-	Post-	Pre-	Post-	Pre-	Post-
Severity	4.06	1.72	4.76	0.56	5.02	1.90
	$t = 5.71$		$t = 17.50$		$t = 9.45$	
Danger	3.66	1.12	4.76	0.52	5.16	1.04
	$t = 7.70$		$t = 17.67$		$t = 15.85$	
Restraint	3.94	1.42	4.40	0.54	4.88	1.40
	$t = 6.81$		$t = 11.70$		$t = 9.94$	

Note. A 7-point rating scale was used (1 = desirable, 7 = undesirable). All pre–post scores were significant at the $p < .0005$ level.

sisted throughout the intervention period and increased during maintenance. Indeed, one reason for the decrease in frequency of communicative requests noted earlier may be related to the sharp increase in level of task engagement; that is, the participants may have simply been too busy to make requests. Finally, as problem behavior decreased to negligible levels in maintenance, intensive intervention became less and less necessary. Thus, caregivers had fewer intervention demands over time, a factor that also contributed to the long-term feasibility of the approach.

ASSESSMENT

As noted earlier, the total assessment took approximately 36 hours per participant. The research literature, on the other hand, reported the use of formal functional analyses that often averaged only 10 to 15 min per session over a small number of sessions (Carr et al., 1997). At first glance, the present assessment may seem overly time consuming. However, functional analyses have typically been carried out in restricted contexts, often as simulations or analogs of natural contexts. Our assessment was multidimensional and involved a large number of problem situations across many intervention agents, settings, and tasks. (Our assessment produced over 100 index cards per participant.) Conducting a formal functional analysis for this many situations is neither feasible nor practical. There are rarely enough people who are trained to do functional analysis, and, in the present case, the need to do multiple analyses in many different situations further exacerbated the problems associated with insufficient expert personnel. Also, the amount of time required to conduct this many functional analyses would be prohibitive. With respect to feasibility, functional analysis requires that problem behavior be evoked repeatedly in order to identify functions unequivocally. Repeated evocation of problem behavior in community settings such as restaurants, supermarkets, and churches is unacceptable because it would provoke other community members to respond strongly and negatively due to fear and/or safety concerns.

We attempted to avoid the problems associated with doing formal functional analysis in the community by using the describe and categorize components of our assessment. Specifically, our assessment method did not involve the repeated evocation of problem behavior and, therefore, was socially acceptable to parents, teachers, and other caregivers. Further, the narrative method associated with the use of index cards could be used by typical members of the community because they did not need the special training required for functional analysis. In other words, the describe and categorize procedures are potentially feasible and practical.

The subjective and qualitative aspects of our assessment method pose some concerns for behavior analysts. Both the interview process and the judgments of the panel members during categorization were clearly subjective in nature. Although not subjective, the direct observation component substituted narrative accounts for quantifiable units and thus was qualitative in nature. Most important, however, subsequent analyses of quantitative data validated and supported the use of our assessment procedures. First, the baseline (verification) procedure generated high rates of problem behavior. As noted previously, the baseline situations were derived exclusively from the describe and categorize assessment information; therefore the high rates of baseline problem behaviors confirm the accuracy and utility of this information. Second, most of the intervention components (e.g., FCT, choice, embedding) were based on hypotheses about function derived from our assessment. The fact that the intervention was successful suggests that the hypotheses were useful, and it further validates the utility of our assessment method.

Finally, it should be emphasized that the intensive nature of the initial assessment may reflect the fact that—in general—researchers have less experience investigating comprehensive community-based interventions than analog-style interventions. It is plausible that subsequent research may produce less time-consuming strategies. For example, the systematic assessment packages developed by O'Neill, Horner, Albin, Storey, and Sprague (1997) include several strategies for reducing time demands and enhancing the feasibility of community-based assessment. We should also note that the severity and ubiquitousness of problem behavior for the three participants in the present study may have necessitated a more intensive approach to assessment and intervention. Future research may establish that less effort is needed in the assessment and intervention of individuals exhibiting milder and/or more circumscribed problem behavior. In any case, in clinical practice, where experimental design is not an issue, it may be possible to assess the most problematic situations first and quickly initiate interventions in those situations. Once problem behavior has been reduced to acceptable levels, one may repeat the assessment and intervention protocol for less serious problem situations. In this manner, the demands of assessment would be spread out over a protracted period of time, thereby enhancing feasibility.

Future Directions

Carrying out an intervention across multiple community settings that involves natural support persons for protracted periods of time represents the ultimate challenge for current technology. The present study was conceived as a step in the direction of extending our technology to deal with this challenge. Our data raise issues in several different areas relevant for future research: assessment, intervention, outcomes, and measurement related to each of these.

ASSESSMENT PRACTICES

Traditionally, the first step in remediating problem behavior involves a functional assessment of such behavior (Carr, 1994; Desrochers, Hile, & Williams-Moseley, 1997). Although this proved useful in the present study, the multicomponent intervention that was built upon it suggested that other assessment foci might also be worth pursuing as we extend applied research efforts into the community. Specifically, the use of rapport building, FCT, choice, and embedding draws attention to the importance of assessing the integrity of living environments and skill repertoires in addition to problem behavior per se. With respect to living environments, because an absence of social relationships or the presence of poor relationships can influence problem behavior, it would be useful to develop instruments that assess rapport. Similarly, low levels of choice are correlated with problem behavior; thus, global assessment instruments that measure the degree of choice and the number of options available in a living situation would likewise be useful. Finally, embedding is only one example of a shift in instructional strategies. More generally, because the quality of instruction can be an important determinant of problem behavior, a variety of assessment instruments that measure different dimensions of instruction (e.g., functionality of the curriculum; facets of instructional presentation such as prompting, pacing, variety, and motivation) would be useful. With respect to skill repertoires, low levels of communicative competence, social skills, and self-management abilities can be correlated with problem behavior; hence, assessment of these types of skills could be useful in subsequent intervention planning.

Clearly, the kinds of assessment we have described for living environments and skill repertoires require measurement practices that are different from those typically used at present. Rapport might be measured sociometrically (e.g., documentation of social preference hierarchies), which is a type of measurement that differs from traditional frequency or time sampling. Even problem behavior requires different types of assessment and measurement in the community. The narrative approach that we carried out was feasible because it did not rely on counting frequencies or time samples of dangerous behavior in public situations. Other forms of naturalistic assessment need to be developed to deal with the various situations that constitute community living.

In sum, because the types of interventions used in the present study were oriented toward changing aspects of living environments and enhancing skill repertoires, future work in assessment could profit from developing new instruments that from the outset measure the living environment quality and the skills that the person with disabilities has for coping with environmental challenges. This shift in assessment practices (from a focus on problem behavior to a focus on living environments and skill repertoires) would in turn produce a shift in intervention practices.

INTERVENTION PRACTICES

Traditionally, intervention has focused on problem behavior reduction per se. A central message of our study is that the scope of intervention needs to be expanded when working in the community. The ultimate goal is not to remediate problem behavior but to remediate problem contexts. Although extensive, Table 1 represents only a sample of all relevant problem contexts because as a person's life circumstances change over time, so will the array of relevant problem contexts. Best practice would demand intervention strategies that address all relevant contexts (Lutzker & Campbell, 1994; Singer & Irvin, 1989). This strategy contrasts with much traditional research in which the goal is to demonstrate definitive causal relationships within a restricted laboratory or analog situation.

The central issue for future research concerns the difference between *static* versus *dynamic* intervention plans. Presently, clinicians will sometimes put in place an intervention plan and modify it only when problem behavior recurs (static plan; Carr et al., 1997). Our research suggests the wisdom of constantly changing intervention plans, even in the absence of problem behavior, as new problem contexts are identified and old ones drop out (dynamic plan). What is needed is a set of guidelines for building dynamic intervention plans that reflect changing assessment information for relevant problem contexts. Clearly, one aspect of these guidelines would be to stress that intervention will almost always be multicomponent in nature. As noted, the unresolved question for the field pertains to how to identify and integrate the constituent elements of a multicomponent intervention.

A second implication of our study is that intervention would have no end point. Circumstances continually arise that produce new problem contexts. These in turn would require modification of the plan. Inevitably significant changes will occur in a person's living situation, and these changes will need to be addressed. In this sense, maintenance is programmed rather than hoped for. Thus, traditional issues related to the maintenance of intervention effects following intervention termination do not apply to our model because there is no termination point. With this perspective in mind, it becomes critical for researchers to develop a set of generic guidelines for building interventions that are sensitive to changes in living circumstances over long periods of time.

A third implication of our study is that problem behavior is best dealt with proactively. All of our interventions took place when problem behavior was not occurring (i.e., both the environmental reorganization and skill-building aspects of our intervention package were oriented toward making positive behaviors more probable, thereby undermining the need for future displays of problem behavior). Therefore, an important research priority for the future concerns the proactive assessment of environmental deficiencies (goodness-of-fit) and deficiencies in coping behaviors (skills) with a view to using this information to build strategies that effectively prevent the display of problem behavior (Albin, Lucyshyn, Horner, & Flannery, 1996).

A fourth study implication relates to the observation that the three individuals with whom we worked still required extensive support from others, even at the end of the study. For example, both FCT and embedding made time demands on parents and group home staff that might not be sustainable indefinitely. This issue pertains to autonomy and independence: We need to structure long-term interventions that permit the individual to achieve his or her goals and satisfy his or her needs without excessive dependence on others. This theme becomes especially important as individuals spend more time in the community, where close supervision and moment-to-moment programming are neither feasible nor normative.

Finally, the future research agenda that we have been outlining calls for the development of new methods of measurement. Frequency and time sampling, so prominent a feature of past research on problem behavior, are often not relevant for dealing with variables such as the ones we have described (Wahler & Fox, 1981). Documenting the salutary effects of environmental reorganization (e.g., changing schedules, matching roommates, building social relationships) may require measurement methods related to sociometrics, consumer satisfaction, and the like that do not lend themselves to traditional microanalytic measurement procedures.

OUTCOMES

The longitudinal nature of our data suggests two issues related to intervention outcomes that need to be considered: lifestyle change and life-span perspectives.

Lifestyle Change

As noted, traditionally, the main focus of intervention has been on the elimination or management of problem behavior per se. Many advocates and stakeholders have criticized this approach as being too narrow and have pointed out that reduction of problem behavior is only meaningful if it is accompanied by positive changes in the person's lifestyle (Risley, 1996; Turnbull & Ruef, 1997). These changes involve greater inclusion in the community and an improved ability to deal with difficult situations in home, school, and work settings. Our intervention approach documents the necessity of dealing with problem behavior in many different settings, across intervention agents, and across tasks. As a result, the individual's quality of life improves because he or she is now able to take advantage of many community activities. As it becomes clear that successful intervention requires the use of strategies that promote adaptation and integration in various integrated settings, future work will need to focus at the outset on the assessment of barriers to integration with a view to promoting those behaviors that lead to greater inclusion. The identification and measurement of these broader outcomes is one important future research priority. For example, direct and systematic measurement of the outcomes associated with Table 1 would be one important way of extending the research protocol described in the present study. Recent discussions in the literature (Turnbull, Friesen, & Ramirez, in press) pointed to (a) the importance of researchers and stakeholders collaborating in the identification of outcomes and (b) the centrality of stakeholder satisfaction ratings as a key outcome measure.

Life-Span Perspectives

During the 1.5- to 2.5-year maintenance period of the present study, it became clear that many changes occurred in each participant's life situation (e.g., residence, employment status, recreational opportunities). These changes necessitated additional assessments and modification of intervention strategies. Problems associated with transition over the life span (e.g., school to work, living with one's parents versus independent living) are a major concern of stakeholders (e.g., families, teachers) and have become a discussion focus in the literature (Turnbull & Turnbull, 1996). Ultimately, maintenance does not refer even to the time period of our study but, rather, to periods measured in decades as the individual progresses from childhood through adolescence and adulthood. This life-span perspective has become the new measure of maintenance and will require research into methods for identifying and achieving meaningful change over protracted periods of time. In support of this position, we should note that personal futures planning (Vandercook et al., 1989) is one innovation having to do with the identification of life-span goals. This type of identification method will need to drive the construction of systematic approaches for producing intervention strategies that are sensitive to an individual's needs at different stages of development.

ABOUT THE AUTHORS

Edward G. Carr, PhD, is a professor in the Department of Psychology at SUNY–Stony Brook and director of research and continuing education at the Developmental Disabilities Institute in Long Island, New York. His research interests include community integration, systems change, and problem behavior. **Len Levin, PhD,** *is the director of support services at Alpine Learning Group (ALG), a center-based education program for students with autism. Dr. Levin coordinates*

ALG's supported inclusion program and family consultation services. He has also done extensive work in the area of food selectivity with children with autism. **Gene McConnachie, PhD,** *works as a positive behavior support consultant and trainer for the State of Washington Division of Developmental Disabilities in the Seattle area. He also holds an adjunct faculty position in the Department of Psychiatry and Behavioral Sciences at the University of Washington's medical school.* **Jane I. Carlson, MA,** *is the inclusion coordinator at the Developmental Disabilities Institute in Smithtown, New York, and a research associate and doctoral candidate at SUNY–Stony Brook.* **Duane C. Kemp, PhD,** *is a coordinator of the Young Autism Program at the Developmental Disabilities Institute and is responsible for curriculum and staff development for preschool students with autism who are subsequently included in general education kindergarten programs.* **Christopher E. Smith, PhD,** *is the program coordinator for clinical services in the Children's Residential Program at the Developmental Disabilities Institute.* **Darlene Magito McLaughlin, MA,** *is the director of clinical services in the Adult Residential Division at the Developmental Disabilities Institute and is currently a research associate and doctoral candidate at SUNY–Stony Brook. Address: Edward G. Carr, Department of Psychology, State University of New York, Stony Brook, NY 11794-2500.*

AUTHORS' NOTES

1. *Preparation of this manuscript was supported in part by Grant Nos. G0087C0234 and H133B20004 from the National Institute on Disability and Rehabilitation Research.*
2. *We thank Joe Pancari, Denise Berotti, Karen Pierce, Julie Soriano, Tracey Vaiano, Sandi Diamond, Lisa Storey, and the members of "Gary's" family for helping to carry out the interventions and for collecting the data.*

REFERENCES

Albin, R. W., Lucyshyn, J. M., Horner, R. H., & Flannery, K. B. (1996). Contextual fit for behavior support plans. In L. K. Koegel, R. L. Koegel, & G. Dunlap (Eds.), *Positive behavioral support: Including people with difficult behavior in the community* (pp. 81–98). Baltimore: Brookes.

Bird, F., Dores, P. A., Moniz, D., & Robinson, J. (1989). Reducing severe aggressive and self-injurious behaviors with functional communication training. *American Journal on Mental Retardation, 94,* 37–48.

Carnine, D. (1997). Bridging the research-to-practice gap. *Exceptional Children, 63,* 513–521.

Carr, E. G. (1994). Emerging themes in the functional analysis of problem behavior. *Journal of Applied Behavior Analysis, 27,* 393–399.

Carr, E. G., & Carlson, J. I. (1993). Reduction of severe behavior problems in the community using a multicomponent treatment approach. *Journal of Applied Behavior Analysis, 26,* 157–172.

Carr, E. G., & Durand, V. M. (1985). Reducing behavior problems through functional communication training. *Journal of Applied Behavior Analysis, 18,* 111–126.

Carr, E. G., Horner, R. H., Turnbull, A. P., Marquis, J., Magito McLaughlin, D.,

McAtee, M. L., Smith, C. E., Anderson Ryan, K., Ruef, M. B., & Doolabh, A. (1997). *Positive behavior support as an approach for dealing with problem behavior in people with developmental disabilities: A research synthesis.* Manuscript submitted for publication.

Carr, E. G., Levin, L., McConnachie, G., Carlson, J. I., Kemp, D. C., & Smith, C. E. (1994). *Communication-based intervention for problem behavior. A user's guide for producing positive change.* Baltimore: Brookes.

Carr, E. G., Newsom, C. D., & Binkoff, J. A. (1976). Stimulus control of self-destructive behavior in a psychotic child. *Journal of Abnormal Child Psychology, 4,* 139–153.

Carr, E. G., Robinson, S., Taylor, J. C., & Carlson, J. I. (Eds.). (1990). Positive approaches to the treatment of severe behavior problems in persons with developmental disabilities: A review and analysis of reinforcement and stimulus-based procedures. *Monograph of The Association for Persons with Severe Handicaps, 4.*

Desrochers, M. N., Hile, M. G., & Williams-Moseley, T. L. (1997). Survey of functional assessment procedures used with individuals who display mental retardation and severe problem behaviors. *American Journal on Mental Retardation, 101,* 535–546.

Didden, R., Duker, P. C., & Korzilius, H. (1997). Meta-analytic study on treatment effectiveness for problem behaviors with individuals who have mental retardation. *American Journal on Mental Retardation, 101,* 387–399.

Dunlap, G., dePerczel, M., Clarke, S., Wilson, D., Wright, S., White, R., & Gomez, A. (1994). Choice making and proactive behavioral support for students with emotional and behavioral challenges. *Journal of Applied Behavior Analysis, 27,* 505–518.

Dunlap, G., & Koegel, R. L. (1980). Motivating autistic children through stimulus variation. *Journal of Applied Behavior Analysis, 13,* 619–627.

Dyer, K., Dunlap, G., & Winterling, V. (1990). Effects of choice making on the serious problem behaviors of students with severe handicaps. *Journal of Applied Behavior Analysis, 23,* 515–524.

Gardner, W. I., & Sovner, R. (1994). *Self-injurious behavior.* Willow Street, PA: VIDA.

Horner, R. D., & Baer, D. M. (1978). Multiple-probe technique: A variation on the multiple baseline. *Journal of Applied Behavior Analysis, 11,* 189–196.

Horner, R. H. (1994). Functional assessment: Contribution and future directions. *Journal of Applied Behavior Analysis, 27,* 401–404.

Horner, R. H., Close, D. W., Fredericks, H. D. B., O'Neill, R. E., Albin, R. W., Sprague, J. R., Kennedy, C. H., Flannery, K. B., & Heathfield, L. T. (1996). Supported living for people with profound disabilities and severe problem behaviors. In D. H. Lehr & F. Brown (Eds.), *People with disabilities who challenge the system* (pp. 209–240). Baltimore: Brookes.

Horner, R. H., & Day, H. M. (1991). The effects of response efficiency on functionally equivalent competing behaviors. *Journal of Applied Behavior Analysis, 24,* 719–732.

Kemp, D. C., & Carr, E. G. (1995). Reduction of severe problem behavior in community employment using an hypothesis-driven multicomponent intervention approach. *Journal of The Association for Persons with Severe Handicaps, 20,* 229–247.

Koegel, L. K., Koegel, R. L., & Dunlap, G.(Eds.). (1996). *Positive behavioral support: Including people with difficult behavior in the community.* Baltimore: Brookes.

Lucyshyn, J. M., Olson, D., & Horner, R. H. (1995). Building an ecology of support: A case study of one woman with severe problem behaviors living in the community. *Journal of The Association for Persons with Severe Handicaps, 20,* 16–30.

Lutzker, J. R., & Campbell, R. V. (1994). *Ecobehavioral family interventions in developmental disabilities.* Pacific Grove, CA: Brooks/Cole.

Mace, F. C., Hock, M. L., Lalli, J. S., West, B. J., Belfiore, P., Pinter, E., & Brown, D. K. (1988). Behavioral momentum in the treatment of noncompliance. *Journal of Applied Behavior Analysis, 21,* 123–141.

Nickels, C. (1996). A gift from Alex—The art of belonging: Strategies for academic and social inclusion. In L. K. Koegel, R. L. Koegel, & G. Dunlap (Eds.), *Positive behavioral support: Including people with difficult behavior in the community* (pp. 123–144). Baltimore: Brookes.

Northup, J., Wacker, D. P., Berg, W. K., Kelly, L., Sasso, G., & DeRaad, A.

(1994). The treatment of severe behavior problems in school settings using a technical assistance model. *Journal of Applied Behavior Analysis, 27,* 33–47.

O'Neill, R. E., Horner, R. H., Albin, R. W., Storey, K., & Sprague, J. R. (1997). *Functional assessment and program development for problem behavior.* Pacific Grove, CA: Brooks/Cole.

Reichle, J., & Wacker, D. P. (1993). *Communicative alternatives to challenging behavior.* Baltimore: Brookes.

Risley, T. (1996). Get a life! In L. K. Koegel, R. L. Koegel, & G. Dunlap (Eds.), *Positive behavioral support: Including people with difficult behavior in the community* (pp. 425–437). Baltimore: Brookes.

Scotti, J. R., Ujcich, K. J., Weigle, K. L., Holland, C. M., & Kirk, K. S. (1996). Interventions with challenging behavior of persons with developmental disabilities: A review of current research practices. *Journal of The Association for Persons with Severe Handicaps, 21,* 123–134.

Singer, G. H. S., & Irvin, L. K. (Eds.) (1989). *Support for caregiving families.* Baltimore: Brookes.

Stokes, T. F., & Baer, D. M. (1977). An implicit technology of generalization. *Journal of Applied Behavior Analysis, 10,* 349–367.

Turnbull, A. P., Friesen, B. J., & Ramirez, C. (in press). Participatory Action Research as a model of conducting family research. *Journal of The Association for Persons with Severe Handicaps.*

Turnbull, A. P., & Ruef, M. (1996). Family perspectives on problem behavior. *Mental Retardation, 34,* 280–293.

Turnbull, A. P., & Ruef, M. (1997). Family perspectives on inclusive lifestyle issues for people with problem behavior. *Exceptional Children, 63,* 211–227.

Turnbull, A. P., & Turnbull, H. R. (1996). Group action planning as a strategy for providing comprehensive family support. In L. K. Koegel, R. L. Koegel, & G. Dunlap (Eds.) *Positive behavior support: Including people with difficult behavior in the community* (pp. 99–114). Baltimore: Brookes.

Vandercook, T., York, J., & Forest, M. (1989). The McGill action planning systems (MAPS): A strategy for building the vision. *Journal of The Association for Persons with Severe Handicaps, 14,* 205–215.

Wahler, R. G., & Fox, J. J. (1981). Setting events in applied behavior analysis: Toward a conceptual and methodological expansion. *Journal of Applied Behavior Analysis, 14,* 327–338.

Action Editor: Robert L. Koegel

Using Multiple Measures to Evaluate Positive Behavior Support:

A Case Example

Shelley Clarke
Jonathan Worcester
Glen Dunlap
University of South Florida

Marcey Murray
Hillsborough County Public Schools

Kathy Bradley-Klug
University of South Florida

Abstract: In recent years, calls to expand the criteria by which behavior support efforts are evaluated have increased. Success is now said to depend on outcomes that transcend a reduction in the occurrence of problem behaviors and include the achievement of new competencies and improvements in one's quality of life. This single-case investigation was conducted as an effort to evaluate the effects of a positive behavior support intervention with multiple measures that included experimental analyses of the participant's problem behavior, engagement, happiness, and efficiency in completing transitions, as well as adult and peer perceptions of aspects of the participant's quality of life. Multiple baseline analyses indicated that the assessment-based intervention was effective in producing durable improvements in all of the measured variables and that the procedures were socially valid. The results are discussed in the context of the growing number of empirical case studies in positive behavior support, and the need to develop more efficient strategies for evaluating the essential outcomes of intervention.

Positive behavior support (PBS) is a rapidly evolving approach for meeting the needs of people who experience challenges associated with behavioral adaptation. PBS began in the 1980s as a set of nonaversive strategies designed primarily to reduce serious problem behaviors (Horner et al., 1990) and has developed in the past decade to become a comprehensive discipline that incorporates individualized and systems interventions to enhance participants' behavioral repertoires. Whereas the primary emphasis was initially on problem behavior, the focus has shifted to lifestyle change and an enhanced quality of life, with reductions in problem behavior becoming an important but secondary or intermediate goal (Carr et al., 2002). This vital development in the conceptualization of PBS has implications for research and for the evaluation of PBS interventions.

This major tenet of PBS, that lifestyle improvements represent the overarching goal of intervention, suggests that outcomes must be measured not simply in terms of levels of problem behavior but also in terms of the participants' social relationships, productivity, opportunity, affect, and personal satisfaction (Carr et al., 2002; Risley, 1996; Turnbull & Ruef, 1997). Quality of life is a notion that fits well with the goals of PBS, and there have been a number of laudatory efforts to define and even quantify the construct (Hughes, Hwang, Kim, Eisenman, & Killian, 1995; Knoster, 1999a; Schalock, Keith, Hoffman, & Karan, 1989). However, a single measure that can efficiently and reliably be used to assess with sensitivity the lifestyle changes that might be sought or anticipated as a function of individualized PBS programs has not yet been developed. This is not surprising given the highly idiosyncratic nature of behavior support efforts, the circumstances in which they are applied, and the diversity of individual, family, and setting factors that must be conspicuous ingredients in evaluation plans.

Traditionally, analyses of behavioral interventions in the research literature have been limited to direct observations of problem behavior and, perhaps, one targeted alternative, such as on-task responding or a specific communicative response. This focus was understandable given the constraints on applied research (i.e., collecting valid and reliable data in natural settings) and the research emphasis on internal validity and the delineation of functional variables. However, the new emphasis of PBS to produce broad, lifestyle benefits has led authors to advocate that more flexible methodologies and, in particular, broader measurement strategies are needed if research and evaluation are to match the proclaimed mandate of PBS (e.g., Carr et al., 2002; Dunlap, Fox, Vaughn, Bucy, & Clarke, 1997). Indeed, researchers have increasingly been including multiple measures in order to provide broader validation of their interventions with participants in school, home, and community settings (e.g., Lucyshyn, Olson, & Horner, 1995; Stiebel, 1999; Todd, Horner, & Sugai, 1999; Vaughn, Dunlap, Fox, Clarke, & Bucy, 1997). For instance, investigations of PBS in the past few years have included a variety of social validation assessments (e.g., Carr, Horner, et al., 1999; Jensen, McConnachie, & Pierson, 2001; Lucyshyn, Albin, & Nixon, 1997; McConnachie & Carr, 1997), as well as measures of child affect (e.g., Moes, 1998), activity patterns and social integration (e.g., Lucyshyn et al., 1995; Luchyshyn et al., 1997), cooperation (e.g., Vaughn, Dunlap, et al., 1997), contextual fit (e.g., Lucyshyn et al., 1997; Moes & Frea, 2000), and task performance and task completion (Todd et al., 1999; Vaughn, Clarke, & Dunlap, 1997).

The current study was intended to further the trend toward an expanded evaluation of PBS interventions. By collecting numerous measures pertinent to the lifestyle of the participant, the purpose was to assemble a broader picture of relevant outcomes than could be managed by more limited data collection. In this case, a female middle school student with very serious problem behaviors was supported by a team that adopted an assessment-based, PBS approach to intervention. Measures were collected using time series and pre–post schedules to assess levels of problem behavior, engagement, efficiency in completing routines, and the participant's affect, as well as the perceptions of adults and peers regarding the participant's quality of life and the social validity of the intervention process.

Method

PARTICIPANT, SETTING, AND FOCUS ACTIVITIES

Mindy, a 12-year-old student, served as the participant in the investigation. Mindy was a slender girl who liked to laugh, listen to music, play on the computer, and interact with others. Mindy lived at home with her teenage brother and parents. The family had moved to the area from a different state at the beginning of the school year. Mindy's family was close-knit, and the primary language spoken in the home was Polish. She was enrolled in a classroom for students with severe and profound mental retardation within a regular public school campus. Mindy's classroom included four other female classmates, her teacher, and a paraprofessional. Mindy had been diagnosed with autism spectrum disorder and several medical/developmental conditions, including hyperthyroidism, dysmorphic syndrome, hypotonia, asthma, temporomandibular joint syndrome, and a visual impairment. Mindy communicated with a few one-word vocalizations, gestures, and a variety

of problem behaviors. Mindy often displayed problem behavior when she was given requests or demands to complete an activity and during transitions from one activity to another. At such times, she often engaged in self-injurious behavior (biting), physical resistance, aggression, property destruction, and screaming. Mindy also had difficulty staying on task during preacademic activities.

Mindy's classroom teacher (the fourth author) requested consultative assistance from our university-based research group in PBS. A first step in the consultation was to establish a collaborative team to conduct assessments, develop a behavior support plan, and provide the intervention (Hieneman & Dunlap, 1999). The team included all members of Mindy's family as well as her classroom teacher and paraprofessional, her speech teacher, the adaptive physical education coach, and two behavioral consultants (the first and second authors). The team was responsible for developing all steps of the assessment and intervention process.

The study was conducted on Mindy's middle school campus in her special education classroom and in the context of transitions from one school location to another. The team identified specific activities and routines that were especially problematical. Four of the routines were daily school preacademic activities that took place in the classroom in a one-to-one instructional context. These activities included putting a puzzle together, a match-to-sample task, an assembly task, and a sorting activity. All activities occurred consecutively each morning at Mindy's desk located in the corner of the classroom. Three transition activities, in which Mindy was required to physically move from one area to another, were also selected for intervention. The transition activities selected for intervention included transition to the cafeteria, transition to preacademics, and transition to physical education. All of these activities were selected for intervention by the team because of their association with significant problem behavior and disruptions to the entire classroom.

GENERAL PROCEDURES AND EXPERIMENTAL DESIGN

The study was conducted as a detailed, experimental case study with multiple measures. The procedures followed the general PBS protocol (Hieneman et al., 1999) including team formation, functional assessment of problem behaviors, development of a support plan, and assessment-based intervention. Intervention was conducted by the classroom teacher and paraprofessional, with consultation from the behavioral consultants.

Two multiple baseline across activities designs were implemented to demonstrate the efficacy of the independent variable, which was defined as the individualized, assessment-based intervention plan constructed for each activity. One multiple baseline design was conducted across the four preacademic activities, and a second multiple baseline design was conducted across the three transition routines. The two multiple baselines were run concurrently. Follow-up measures were obtained following the implementation of the multiple baseline protocols. Maintenance was also assessed by conducting probes one year following intervention, in the subsequent school year. Dependent variables included levels of problem behavior, student engagement, affect, and duration of transitions. Additional measures sampled the interaction behaviors of classroom personnel, perceptions of student quality of life, and adults' satisfaction with the PBS strategies. All measures are described in a subsequent Measurement section of the methodology.

FUNCTIONAL ASSESSMENT

Following the establishment of the collaborative team, a functional assessment was conducted in order to produce a full description of Mindy's problem behavior, a precise description of the contexts in which the behaviors occurred, a statement of the presumed operant functions of the behaviors in each context, and a delineation of Mindy's preferences for stimuli and activities that might be utilized in her school curriculum (O'Neill, Vaughn, & Dunlap, 1998). The functional assessment was conducted over a period of approximately 4 weeks and included interviews, direct observations, and a review of archival records (Foster-Johnson & Dunlap, 1993; O'Neill et al., 1997). Interviews were conducted with Mindy's parents and all school staff involved in the team. Direct observations were conducted by the consultants during all routines throughout the entire school day. The interviews and observations were valuable, but the information available from Mindy's previous school records was scant, and none of it was judged ultimately to be pertinent to the functional assessment objectives.

The assessment process confirmed that Mindy's problem behavior was very serious and that it was displayed primarily during daily school preacademic activities and transitions. School staff stated that Mindy's problem behaviors impeded her ability to be successful, disrupted the classroom daily schedule, and had begun to affect her classmates in a negative way, primarily by throwing them off their schedules and frightening them. It was also observed that Mindy's behavior would quickly escalate, which resulted in staff restraining Mindy to prevent self-injury. This often led to Mindy becoming more agitated, falling to the ground, and exhibiting physical aggression toward staff or property. These incidents also occurred during transitions, such as at the end of the school day when staff were in the process of escorting students from the classroom to the bus. Problem behaviors (including a refusal to walk) during transitions were so severe and disruptive that Mindy was placed by staff in a wheelchair and transported or physically carried by school staff to the

school bus. Mindy's parents were very concerned about the use of the wheelchair, and removing the need for the chair became a high priority for intervention.

The interviews and direct observations led the team to suspect that Mindy's problem behaviors were motivated primarily by escape. It appeared to team members that the preacademic activities were difficult for Mindy and generated frustration. In particular, some of the activities required manipulation of small objects (e.g., puzzle pieces), which seemed to be especially challenging for Mindy given her physical and visual limitations. The repetitive nature of some of the task requirements may also have been unpleasant and may have contributed to escape motivation. Escape also appeared to be the function of Mindy's problems during transitions. Mindy was typically instructed to transition from something that she enjoyed (e.g., eating breakfast, playing on the computer) to an activity that involved increased demands. Team members also suspected that walking was difficult for Mindy, and that she might have been confused about the purpose or objectives of some transitions.

Preferences identified during the functional assessment included a number of activities and objects that could be incorporated in the support plan. For instance, Mindy demonstrated positive affect and approach behaviors when she interacted with "P.E. buddies," who were typical seventh and eighth graders who assisted the coach during physical education class. Mindy also appeared to enjoy listening to music and often engaged others in singing or dancing with her. In addition, school staff reported that Mindy was attracted to cartoon characters with large facial features, objects that were colored yellow, clear plastic, and logos and characters associated with McDonald's restaurants.

The results of the functional assessment were summarized as hypothesis statements for each activity routine. The hypotheses suggested a variety of simple modifications that could constitute an intervention plan. Before developing and implementing the plan, Mindy's classroom teacher, assisted by the consultants, tested the efficacy of some of the suggested modifications by implementing brief intervention probes. Data recorded during these brief probes indicated that the modifications produced favorable changes in Mindy's behavior.

INTERVENTION

Prior to the collection of baseline data, the consultants and data collectors were present in the school and classroom for several days to allow the teachers and students to habituate to their presence. Baseline data were then collected simultaneously in each of the targeted routines throughout the process of functional assessment. All personnel involved with Mindy were asked to continue their ongoing practices and interactions throughout baseline. At the conclusion of the assessment process, the team used the summary and hypothesis statements to develop multicomponent intervention strategies for each of the targeted routines. The strategies were based on the assessment information related to the function and context that appeared to govern the occurrence of problem behavior, as well as the information regarding Mindy's preferences. Table 1 summarizes the hypotheses and the intervention components (strategies) developed by the team for each activity and transition.

All interventions were conducted by Mindy's classroom teacher, except for the transition to P.E., when a peer buddy provided the majority of assistance. Immediately prior to the first intervention sessions, the consultants reviewed the intervention components with the teacher, rehearsed the procedures, and answered questions raised by the teacher and other team members. The consultants also discussed Mindy's progress and reviewed the intervention plan with the team throughout the intervention phase, but never during the actual implementation of the intervention strategies.

In accordance with the multiple baseline protocol, intervention was implemented in one activity (puzzle), while the other three activities remained in baseline. When change was evident in the first activity, intervention was introduced to the second activity (match-to-sample), and so on until intervention was implemented in all four activities. The same multiple baseline sequence was followed for the three transitions, beginning with the transition to the bus and ending with the transition to P.E.

After intervention was implemented in all activities and transition, a follow-up phase was introduced for 6 weeks. Follow-up was identical to intervention except that the consultants were present and data were collected only one day per week instead of every day as during intervention.

MEASUREMENT

A variety of direct and indirect measures were obtained to evaluate the impact of the intervention plan on a number of dimensions of Mindy's behavior. Direct observations were collected on Mindy's problem behavior, engagement, happiness, time required to complete transitions (duration), and affect. These data were scored from video recordings that were obtained for every session of every targeted activity and routine. Videotapes were recorded with a handheld camcorder and scored at a later time using a 10-s continuous interval system. Videotaping and data collection were initiated when Mindy was instructed to start an activity or begin a transition, and continued until all steps of the routine were completed, either independently or with assistance, or until the activity was terminated because of an escalation in problem behavior (this occurred only once, during the baseline of transition to bus).

Problem behavior was defined as any occurrence of self-injurious behavior (wrist biting), collapsing on the floor, physically turning away or resistance, aggression, property destruction (throwing objects or mouthing or kicking objects), screaming, crying, elopement (walking or running out of assigned area), or masturbation. An interval was scored as an occurrence if any instance of problem behavior was displayed. *Engagement* was defined as being on task and following the sequence of the task appropriately. Engagement was scored if Mindy was engaged for at least 70% of an interval, as determined by observer judgement (i.e., Vaughn, Clarke, & Dunlap, 1997). *Happiness* was scored if the interval included any instance of smiling, laughing, dancing, or clapping.

The same 10-s interval system was used to record positive and negative adult interactions with Mindy. *Positive adult interactions* included any occurrence of praise statements, physical affection, or positive gestures (i.e., thumbs up, smiling at Mindy) within the interval. *Negative adult interactions* included corrections, reprimands, or physical redirection/guidance used by the instructor.

Two other types of systematic measurement data collection procedures were implemented during the investigation. *Child affect ratings* (Dunlap, 1984; Dunlap & Koegel, 1980) were recorded following every minute for all targeted school activities, and following each session of targeted transitions. Observations of Mindy's facial expression reflecting enthusiasm, happiness, and interest were rated using a 6-point Likert-type scale that ranged from a score of 0 = *extremely negative affect* to 5 = *extremely positive affect*. Guidelines and scoring anchors were taken from Dunlap (1984). Previous studies using the affect ratings have shown adequate interobserver agreement, and the ratings have been demonstrated to distinguish between different treatment conditions (Dunlap, 1984; Dunlap & Koegel, 1980; Koegel & Egel, 1979; Moes, 1998).

The videotapes were also used to obtain data on the duration of each transition routine. This measure was obtained because duration was a concern to school personnel, and it was hoped that intervention would increase the efficiency and timeliness of the transitions. Duration was determined by calculating the total number of 10-s intervals that passed from the time that the initial instruction was given until the routine was completed.

In addition to direct observation measures, two pre–post supplemental measures were completed with school team and family members serving as respondents. These measures were obtained prior to baseline data collection, and then repeated once the intervention packages had been implemented across all activities. The *Quality of Life Survey* (Knoster, 1999c) was distributed in an effort to assess Mindy's quality of life before and after the implementation of intervention. The survey uses a 5-point Likert scale (1 = *much worse* to 5 = *much better*) to assess an individual's relationship with family, peers, and others in

Table 1. School Activities, Problem Summaries, Hypotheses, and Component Descriptions

Academic activity	Problem summary	Hypotheses	Multicomponent intervention description
Puzzle activity *Baseline:* Puzzle Cardboard puzzle, 12–14 small pieces, small cartoon characters, muted colors *Intervention:* Modified puzzle activity, included preference and choice	Problem behavior exhibited when instructed to put puzzle together during work activity following transition from breakfast.	M engaged in problem behavior to escape from nonpreferred activity that was difficult due to visual impairment and poor motor skills.	Provide an activity with an operationally similar task requirement. Rotate materials to prevent satiation. Modify materials (using preferred characters, wood material, larger images to facilitate visual accommodation and fine motor skills) in order to promote engagement and pleasurable interactions with teacher. Provide animated praise and attention when M successfully completes the activity.
Matching *Baseline:* Matching cardboard letters representing formal name and applying to letters with velcro *Intervention:* Identifying and matching body parts to cutout figure of boy and girl	Problem behavior exhibited when instructed to complete matching task.	M engaged in problem behavior to escape from nonpreferred activity that was difficult due to a lack of prerequisite skills and visual impairment.	Provide an activity with an operationally similar task requirement. Introduce a work activity that is more functionally relevant and meaningful to M. Modify materials using colorful, realistic pictures, in order to accommodate visual impairment. Rotate materials (boy and girl) to prevent satiation. Provide activity that could be bridged into more functional and educational activities. Provide animated praise and attention when M successfully completes the activity.
Assembly activity *Baseline:* Pegboard Place four color-coded foam forms onto matching colored pegs and assemble all pieces by color *Intervention:* McDonald's® Happy Meal Assembly Match plastic chicken nuggets with two nugget containers, french fries with containers, and pies with boxes, place corresponding pieces into containers, and assemble Happy Meal by placing all containers into Happy Meal box	Problem behavior exhibited when instructed to complete pegboard activity.	M engaged in problem behavior to escape from nonpreferred task that lacked a functionally relevant outcome.	Provide an activity with an operationally similar task requirement. Introduce an activity that is more functionally relevant and meaningful to M. Provide an activity that could be bridged into more functional and educational activities. Provide animated praise and attention when M completes activity.
Sorting activity *Baseline:* Shape sorter, plastic box with specifically shaped openings that correspond to plastic shapes that are to be matched to the holes and pushed through *Intervention:* Sorting utensils into drawer holder, stacking dishes	Problem behavior exhibited when instructed to complete shape sorter activity.	M engaged in problem behavior to escape from nonpreferred task that lacked a functionally relevant outcome and did not accommodate visual impairment and poor motor skills.	Provide an activity with an operationally similar task requirement. Introduce an activity that was more functionally relevant and meaningful to M. Modify materials in order to accommodate her visual impairment. Provide an activity that could be bridged into more functional and educational activities. Provide animated praise and attention when M successfully completes the activity.
Transition to work *Baseline:* M placed in Ritfon chair, then instruction was given, "It's time to work." M was then pushed in chair to the work table from breakfast area.	Problem behavior exhibited when instructed to transition to work area.	M engaged in problem behavior to escape nonpreferred activity that was difficult and lacked predictability.	Same operational requirements. Minimize distractions (audio, visual) for 5 minutes prior to transition. Give clear instructions prior to transitions. Provide animated praise and attention when M successfully transitions to the work area.

(table continues)

(Table 1 continued)

Academic activity	Problem summary	Hypotheses	Multicomponent intervention description
Intervention: Modified environment and presentation of instruction			
Transition to P.E. activity *Baseline:* M placed in Rifton chair at computer area and instructed, "It's time for P.E." She was then pushed in her chair to the P.E. area. *Intervention:* Modified environment and presentation of instruction	Problem behavior exhibited when instructed to transition to the P.E. area.	M engaged in problem behavior to escape a non-preferred activity that was difficult and lacked predictability.	Same operational requirements. Minimize distractions (audio, visual) for 5 minutes prior to transition. Invite a preferred peer (a P.E. buddy) to assist M with transition. Use a preferred object to promote positive social interaction during the transition. Give clear instructions prior to transition. Once M transitions successfully to the P.E. area, provide her with the preferred object, praise, and attention.
Transition to cafeteria *Baseline:* M instructed, "Put on your backpack, and then it's time to go to the cafeteria." *Intervention:* Modified environment and presentation of instruction	Problem behavior exhibited when instructed to transition to the cafeteria.	M engaged in problem behavior to escape nonpreferred activity that was difficult and lacked predictability.	Same operational requirements. Minimize distractions (audio, visual) for 5 minutes prior to transition. Invite a preferred peer to assist M with transition. Introduce a preferred activity (tape player) for M to enjoy during the transition. Give clear instructions prior to transition. Provide M with a preferred item (e.g., plastic lid) to hold while walking to the cafeteria. Rotate materials to prevent satiation. If M drops to the ground, provide a clear redirection, turn off music, and wait before physically assisting M. Provide music, praise, and attention when M stops resisting and starts walking. Provide praise and attention when M successfully transitions to the cafeteria.

the community, as well as participation and involvement in daily activities. The survey was completed jointly by Mindy's parents and independently by Mindy's teacher, classroom paraprofessional, speech teacher, and the school's special education coordinator. In addition, a modified quality of life survey was developed for the four typical peer buddies who interacted with Mindy during physical education class. The focus of this survey had similar themes relating to peer perceptions of Mindy's friendships, interactions, and progress and happiness at school and also used a 5-point Likert scale (1 = *very poor or strongly disagree* to 5 = *very good or strongly agree*).

A separate measure of social validation was obtained following intervention. The *Positive Behavioral Support Satisfaction Survey* (Knoster, 1999b) was distributed to all school and family team members in an effort to assess satisfaction with intervention outcomes as well as to evaluate the effectiveness of the team process. All 15 questions were presented to raters with responses encompassing a 4-point Likert scale (1 = *disagree* to 4 = *strongly agree*) to assess the extent to which a member of the team was satisfied with

the course of intervention and the positive behavior support process.

OBSERVERS AND RELIABILITY

Observers were graduate students who had received extensive training in recording data from videotapes. All observers were experienced with developmental disabilities and school settings. Prior to recording data for the study, observers practiced with the operational definitions for all dependent variables and achieved a minimum of 80% agreement on each measure.

Interobserver agreement was assessed for 63% of sessions for all school and transition activities across all conditions. School activities averaged 95% agreement (range = 79–100%) for occurrence of problem behavior, and 95% (range = 75–100%) for intervals with engagement. Transition activities had an average of 96% (range = 50–100%) interobserver agreement for problem behavior and a mean total agreement of 96% (range = 50–100%) for engagement. Total agreement reliability for happiness averaged

92% (range = 67–100%) for school activities and 97% (range = 67–100%) for transitions. Adult behavior reliability averages for total agreement during school activities were 84% (range = 73–100%) and 87% (range = 72–100%) for positive and negative interactions, respectively. Transitions yielded a mean total agreement for positive interactions of 95% (range = 63–100%) and negative interaction total agreement of 90% (range = 67–100%). Reliability for the duration of each routine was calculated by comparing the number of 10-s intervals that were independently marked for each session by the data collectors. Interobserver agreement was assessed for 63% of sessions with 100% agreement. Ratings for child affect were considered an agreement if ratings for each interval or session were within 1 point of each other. Interobserver agreement on child affect had a total agreement that always exceeded 92% with 57% of the sessions scored for reliability for all activities.

SECOND YEAR FOLLOW UP

One year after the study was initiated, a series of probe sessions was conducted to evaluate maintenance of behavior change in six of the seven activities (the transition to P.E. routine was no longer pertinent). In addition, data were collected during seven sessions of a new domestic living activity that was added to Mindy's curriculum. A "laundry activity" consisted of Mindy walking to the washer with a basket of clothes and towels collected from the classroom, loading the washer, adding soap, and, once the cycle was completed, removing the clothes and towels from the washer and loading them into the dryer. She then walked back to the classroom with the basket. The same direct observation measures that had been collected during the initial analyses were obtained during these sessions. Interobserver agreement was assessed during 61% of the probe sessions, with quotients exceeding 85% for all measures collected during these second year follow-up activities.

Results

The data depicting Mindy's problem behavior and engagement during the four school activities are shown in Figure 1. Percentage of intervals in which the behaviors occurred is plotted on the ordinate and consecutive days are plotted on the abscissa during the baseline and intervention phases. Follow-up data are plotted by weeks. The data indicate that problem behavior was lower during all intervention conditions for each of the school activities, and engagement was higher. Problem behavior occurred during a mean of 44% of intervals across all activities during baseline, and was reduced to a mean of 11% during intervention. Engagement during baseline averaged 60%, and then increased to a mean of 95% for intervention. Although there were a few exceptions, follow-up data were generally

consistent with the levels achieved during intervention.

The data for problem behavior and engagement during the targeted transitions are presented as mean percentage of intervals during baseline, intervention, and follow up (Figure 2). Although conducted within a multiple baseline protocol, these data are displayed as histograms because the varied, and occasionally very brief, duration of the transitions led to a spurious appearance of instability when plotted as session-by-session line graphs. Nevertheless, the means demonstrate a clear and consistent difference between the two phases, with problem behavior decreasing from an average of 75% during baseline to 31% during intervention, and 29% in follow up. Engagement increased from 12% during baseline to 80% during intervention and 85% in follow up.

Duration of transition sessions was also recorded for both the baseline and intervention phases. For transition to bus the average length of duration was reduced from 5 min 17 s during baseline to 3 min 10 s during intervention and 4 min 2 s in follow up. Transitions to work yielded a mean of 1 min 9 s during baseline and decreased to an average of 15 s during both intervention and follow up. For transition to P.E., the duration was lowered from a mean of 2 min 14 s during baseline to 34 s in intervention and 27 s during follow up.

The percentage of intervals during which Mindy displayed behaviors defined as happiness also showed improvements from baseline to intervention. The mean percentage of intervals with happiness for all four school activities increased from a mean percentage of 26% to an average of 42% during intervention and 33% in follow up. Data obtained for happiness during the transitions showed a mean of 24% for the three transitions during baseline and 29% and 32% in intervention and follow up, respectively.

Table 2 displays the mean percentage of days with child affect rated as positive (i.e., an average rating of 4 or 5) for the four activities and transitions. The percentage of days with positive ratings increased from a mean 62% for all school activities during baseline to 100% of the sessions during intervention and 96% during follow up. Transition data for positive ratings demonstrate a similar effect: Positive affect ratings for all transitions averaged 29% of the baseline days, with an increase to a mean of 78% of the days recorded as positive affect during intervention and a further increase to 94% for follow up.

The collateral data collected on adult interactive behavior are presented in Figure 3 for each school and transition routine. The mean percentage of positive adult interactions across the four school activities rose from 42% during baseline to an average of 48% and 58% during intervention and follow up, respectively. Negative adult interactions declined from a mean of 46% to 7% for intervention and 10% for follow up. Transition data for adult interactions demonstrate similar trends with positive in-

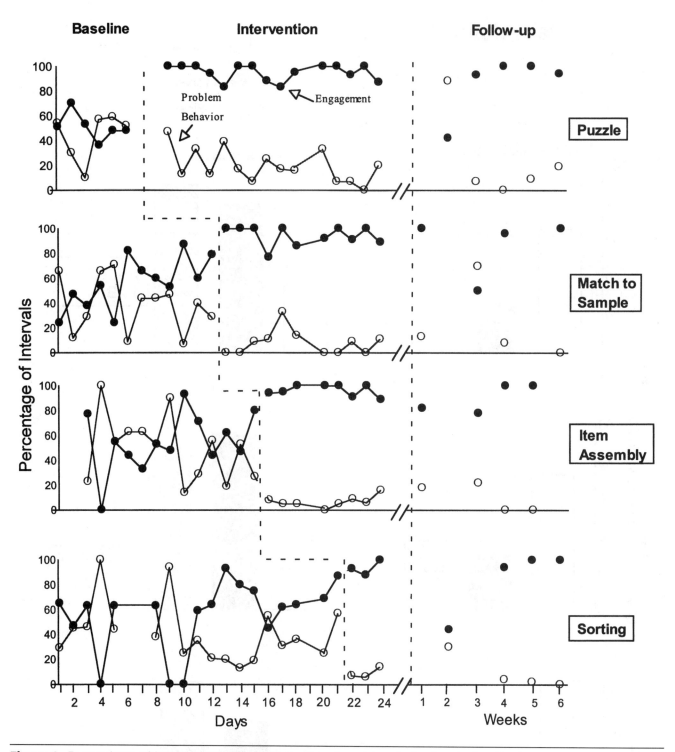

Figure 1. Percentage of intervals with engagement and problem behavior during the four classroom activities across baseline, intervention, and follow-up phases.

teractions increasing from a mean of 24% to a mean of 40% and 45% across the three phases, and negative interactions declining from an average of 50% intervals to14% and 1%. An exception is evident in the positive interaction data for transition to bus: Rates were essentially equal across baseline and intervention, although this is likely related to a substantial decrease in the number of social interaction opportunities in intervention because typically developing peers served as the primary intervention agents during this transition routine.

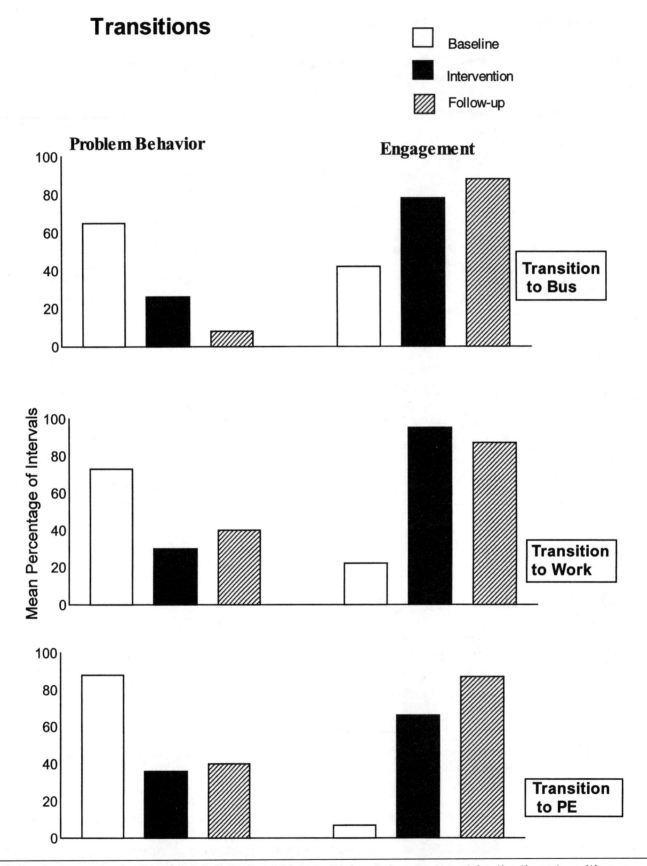

Figure 2. Mean percentage of intervals with problem behavior and engagement for the three transition routines across baseline, intervention, and follow-up phases.

Table 2. Percentage of Days with Child Affect Rated as Positive

Activity	Baseline (%)	Intervention (%)	Follow up (%)
School activity			
Puzzle	57	100	83
Match to sample	55	100	100
Item assembly	58	100	100
Sorting	76	100	100
Transition activity			
Transition to bus	62	69	100
Transition to work	25	80	83
Transition to P.E.	0	75	100

Results for the quality of life survey completed by school staff are displayed in Table 3. This table shows the survey's questions and the average ratings computed before and after intervention. The assessments indicate that important aspects of quality of life domains (e.g., interpersonal, self-determination, social inclusion, personal development, emotional well-being) were perceived as improved by teachers and parents alike.

The modified quality of life evaluations completed by the P.E. buddies reflect similar trends as the ratings of the school staff. The means for all of the P.E. buddies are displayed in Table 4 for pre and post measures. All questions presented were rated higher following intervention.

In addition to the pre–post measures, team members were asked to rate their level of satisfaction with the interventions using the PBS survey table. The responses are shown in Table 5. These data indicate a strong positive consensus across school and family raters for satisfaction ratings.

Results for the probe data collected during the 2nd year for the school activities showed that levels of engagement and happiness data remained high, and problem behavior remained low. A minimum of four probe sessions were conducted for the four preacademic activities and one each for transitions. Problem behavior never exceeded 20% for any probe session conducted. Engagement data were always above 89% for all probe sessions scored. Happiness averaged 34% across all probe sessions for all school activities. The affect data collected during the 2nd-year probes were also similar to the 1st-year intervention and follow up, with all 2nd-year probe sessions rated as positive. Collateral measures of adult positive interactions averaged 47% for all 2nd-year data collected and 1% for negative adult interactions.

The new laundry activity yielded similar results to the probe data for the seven sessions in which measures were recorded. Problem behavior averaged 14% for all sessions, with mean engagement totaling 90%. Happiness averaged 30% of intervals, and all sessions received positive affect ratings. Positive adult interactions for the laundry activity were consistent with follow-up data for 2nd-year probes with a mean of 40%, while negative adult interactions remained low in this new activity, averaging 2% across all sessions.

Discussion

The primary purpose of this experimental case study was to demonstrate the use of multiple measures to evaluate outcomes associated with a school-based PBS intervention. The data showed that the PBS strategies produced the following effects: (a) Mindy's levels of problem behavior were reduced substantially in four classroom activities and three school transitions; (b) engagement was increased across each of the activity and transition routines; (c) the time required to complete each of the three transitions was reduced appreciably; (d) the percentage of intervals that contained happiness behaviors was increased across all routines; (e) ratings of positive affect were higher across all routines; (f) adults' interactions with Mindy were more positive during intervention than baseline; (g) adults' and peers' perceptions of Mindy's quality of life improved over the course of the study; (h) team members were generally satisfied with the PBS procedures and process; and (i) follow-up data provided some assurance that the gains demonstrated in intervention could be maintained, even across school years. In short, the data offer a relatively broad and consistent picture of important improvements in Mindy's behavior and in the way she engaged within the classroom and school environments.

It is useful to add some depth to this summary description. First, it is important to recall that prior to intervention, Mindy's problem behavior had become so severe that two staff members were required to provide physical guidance during transitions. As her behavior deteriorated, a wheelchair was eventually used to ensure safety. Following intervention, Mindy's problem behavior was reduced markedly in all contexts, and neither a wheelchair nor physical guidance were needed to effect transitions. Instead, Mindy began to walk with her same-age peers, and transitions became enjoyable interactions with peers and staff. This quality of improvement is manifested also in the

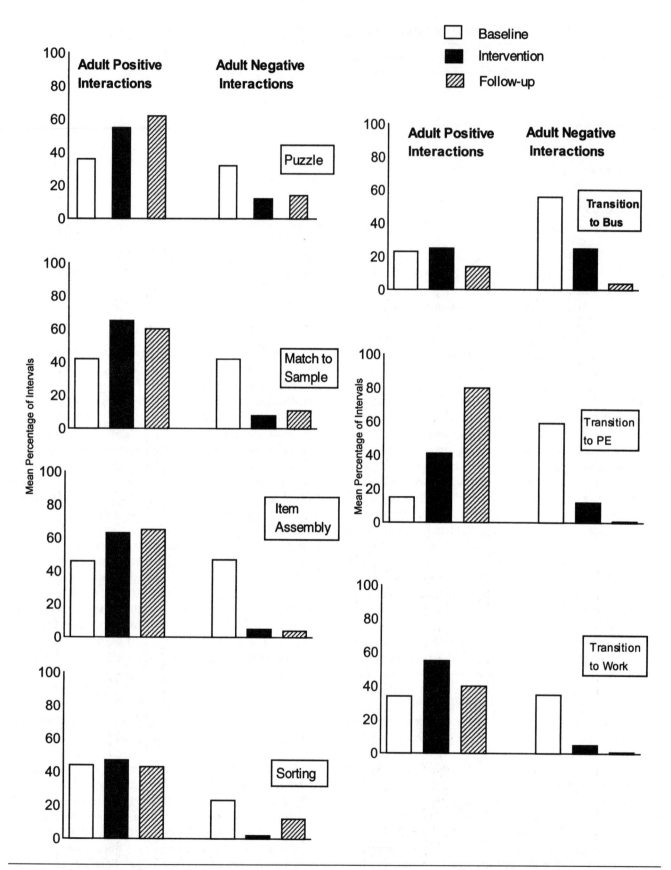

Figure 3. Mean percentage of intervals with positive and negative adult interactions for the four classroom activities and the three transition routines across baseline, intervention, and follow-up phases.

Table 3. Quality of Life Survey, Pre- and Post-Teacher and Parent Ratings

Question	Preintervention teacher mean rating	Postintervention teacher mean rating	Preintervention parent rating	Postintervention parent rating
The relationships with peers the child now has are . . .	2.3	4.0	2	3
The child's participation in school and/or community activities of her choice is . . .	3.0	4.0	3	4
The child's ability to express personal preferences is . . .	3.3	3.5	3	4
The response (friendly or not friendly) the child receives from peers is . . .	2.5	3.5	2	4
The child's ability to engage in leisure activities with peers is . . .	2.3	3.7	n/a	5
The child's access to activities that are personally stimulating is . . .	3.0	4.3	2	4
The child's ability to learn new skills is . . .	3.3	4.0	3	4
The child's general happiness is . . .	3.0	4.3	3	4
As a result of PBS, I feel the child's quality of life is . . .	n/a	3.8	n/a	4
The child's general health and well-being is . . .	3.0	3.8	3	3

Note. *1* = much worse, *2* = worse, *3* = slightly better, *4* = better, *5* = much better, *and n/a* = not applicable.

Table 4. Quality of Life Survey, Pre- and Post-Typical Peer Ratings

Question	Preintervention mean ratings	Postintervention mean ratings
Friendships with her peers now are . . .	2	4.2
Ability to express personal preferences is . . .	2.8	4.4
Amount of time spent interacting with peers . . .	2	3.8
The response (friendly or not friendly) Mindy receives from her peers is . . .	2.3	4
Mindy's relationships with her teachers are . . .	2.3	4.4
Mindy's progress in school (i.e., completing tasks, learning new skills) is . . .	2.3	4.4
The child's ability to learn new skills is . . .	3.3	4.0
General happiness is . . .	2.3	3.8
Behavior is appropriate.	1.5	3
I enjoy spending time with Mindy.	2.8	4.2
I would be comfortable being with Mindy on a field trip.	3.3	3.6
I could picture Mindy in a less restrictive environment.	1.8	2.8

Note. *1* = much worse/strongly disagree, *2* = worse/disagree, *3* = slightly better/neutral, *4* = better/agree, *and 5* = much better/strongly agree.

observational data on happiness and the observer ratings of positive affect. These measures indicate that Mindy appeared to enjoy her life in school to a much greater degree following intervention than she did during baseline.

The data presented constitute a more comprehensive evaluation of a student's behavioral progress than exists in comparable case studies in the literature. Nevertheless, it is apparent that there are still aspects of Mindy's behavior that were not assessed and that could be viewed as very reasonable priorities for evaluation. For instance, data were not obtained on specific interactions with peers or on progress toward the acquisition of particular (e.g., communicative) skills. The decisions regarding what to measure were made by Mindy's support team (e.g., teacher, parents, consultants) in terms of perceived priorities, but the priorities could easily change over time, in the same

Table 5. Positive Behavioral Support Satisfaction Survey Ratings

Question	Respondents					
	Parents	Teacher	Paraprofessional	Speech teacher	ESE coordinator	M
1. The team is able to agree on strategies for the focus individual.	5	5	5	5	5	5
2. The team works together to address the focus person's needs.	5	5	5	5	5	5
3. Team members are meeting identified timelines consistently.	4	5	5	5	5	4.8
4. The team is able to agree on a plan that reflects the focus person's desires.	4	5	5	5	5	4.8
5. The team is able to collectively problem solve.	4	5	5	5	5	4.8
6. Team facilitation is effective.	4	5	5	5	5	4.8
7. This team is able to address the focus person's desires as written in the plan.	4	5	5	5	5	4.8
8. The agencies that agreed to work with the team to meet the focus person's needs continue to be involved.	4	5	4	5	5	4.6
9. There has been an increase in the number of agencies that support the individual.	4	3	4	4	5	4
10. The interactions between agencies, support providers, and family members is productive.	5	4	4	4	5	4.4
11. There has been an increase in the number of nonpaid support staff that support the individual.	4	5	5	4	5	4.5
12. My vision for a positive future for this child has improved.	4	3	5	3	5	4
13. The number of environmental changes that support the child at home has increased.	4	5	5	3	5	3.5
14. The number of environmental changes that support the child at school has increased.	5	4	5	4	5	4.6
15. The number of environmental changes that support the child in the community has increased	4	5	5	5	5	4

Note. ESE = *exceptional special education.* *1* = strongly disagree, *2* = disagree, *3* = slightly agree, *4* = strongly agree, *5* = not applicable.

way that educational objectives are reconsidered on a regular basis.

An issue that authors often raise in discussing goals of PBS is quality of life (e.g., Carr et al., 2002; Koegel, Koegel, & Dunlap, 1996; Turnbull & Ruef, 1997). At present, there is no parsimonious way to measure changes in quality of life associated with behavior support efforts. It is possible, however, to view a combination of pertinent measures as constituting an aggregate estimate of quality of life, at least to some extent. While the current array of indices would not meet all of the criteria referred to by authorities in the conceptualization of quality of life (e.g., Goode, 1994; Schalock et al., 1989), the data may be seen as a meaningful approximation. An important area of research development will be to integrate the conceptual and practical work on quality of life assessment with the exigencies of individual program evaluation.

This study contains some noteworthy limitations. Most obvious, there was only one participant, so it is im-

possible to extrapolate from the current data to the behavior of other children. External validity will be established by conducting other multiple-measure analyses with additional participants. As noted earlier, another limitation pertains to the limited measurement of Mindy's school performance. Because engagement was the only positive outcome measured during the four classroom activities, it is not possible to draw inferences regarding Mindy's accuracy and work productivity. A more robust indicator of academic performance might have strengthened the results and implications of the study. In this case, Mindy's team did not identify activity performance measures as a high priority compared with other data elements, although they would certainly be regarded more highly for many students and, in particular, for those students experiencing academic challenges. Related to the activities is a question about the relevance of the curricular content. It may be argued that the scheduled activities did not constitute a functionally oriented curriculum, as one would expect for a middle school student with severe disabilities, and that this may possibly have contributed to Mindy's problem behavior. This question was eventually addressed by the team, and subsequent to the completion of data collection, some curricular revisions were introduced so that Mindy spent increasing amounts of her school schedule engaged in more functional activities, including domestic living and self-care routines.

While the current investigation contributes to the PBS literature in terms of providing a demonstration of multiple-measurement evaluation, it is also important to note that the study offers a systematic replication of assessment-based behavior support in a school environment. Reports of detailed PBS case studies have been conducted in community (e.g., Vaughn, Dunlap, et al., 1997) and home (e.g., Clarke, Dunlap, & Vaughn, 1999; Lucyshyn et al., 1997) settings, but few have been carried out in schools (e.g., Dunlap, Kern-Dunlap, Clarke, & Robbins, 1991). The current data may be seen to enhance the literature by contributing another exemplar of individualized PBS that included functional assessment (O'Neill et al., 1997), curricular modifications (Dunlap & Kern, 1996), and an infusion of preferred stimuli and activities (Foster-Johnson, Ferro, & Dunlap, 1994). In this respect, the data add to the growing evidence in support of PBS as an effective approach to the challenge of problem behavior and behavioral adaptation (Carr, Horner, et al., 1999).

ABOUT THE AUTHORS

Shelley Clarke, MA, is a state-certified behavior analyst, and the assistant director of research within the Division of Applied Research and Educational Support at the Louis de la Parte Florida Mental Health Institute located at the University of South Florida. **Jonathan Worcester,** MA, is a doctoral candidate in school psychology at the University of South Florida. He is currently involved in applied research with an emphasis on positive behavior support at the Florida Mental Health Institute. **Glen Dunlap,** PhD, is director of the Division of Applied Research and Educational Support and a professor of child and family studies at the Louis de la Parte Florida Mental Health Institute at the University of South Florida. Dr. Dunlap also serves as principal investigator for the Rehabilitation Research and Training Center on Positive Behavioral Support. **Marcey Murray,** MA, has been a special education teacher of students with severe/profound mental handicaps in a public school setting for the past 6 years. **Kathy Bradley-Klug,** PhD, is an assistant professor of school psychology at the University of South Florida. Her research interests include the use of curriculum-based assessment in reading, and assessment and intervention strategies for children and adolescents with pediatric health disorders. Address: Glen Dunlap, Department of Child and Family Studies, Florida Mental Health Institute, MHC 2113A-DARES,

University of South Florida, 13301 Bruce B. Downs Blvd., Tampa, FL 33612.

AUTHORS' NOTES

1. The project described in this article and the article preparation were supported by the Research and Rehabilitation Training Center on Positive Behavior Support (RRTC-PBS), funded by the U.S. Department of Education (NIDRR, Grant No. H133B980005), and the Center for Autism and Related Disabilities, funded by the Florida legislature. The opinions are those of the authors, and no official endorsement should be inferred.

2. The authors would like to acknowledge the input of the RRTC-PBS research group at the University of South Florida throughout the investigation and, in particular, the following research assistants who contributed to the collection, summary, and analysis of the data: Kathryn Bolen, Terri C-Garves, Amy L. Collins, Michelle Duda, Lisa Grant, and Stephanie Strobeck. In addition, we express our thanks and appreciation to Dr. Dwight Rains and the entire staff of Mindy's middle school campus in the Hillsborough County Public Schools system. We also wish to acknowledge and extend our gratitude to Mindy and all members of her family.

REFERENCES

Carr, E. G., Dunlap, G., Horner, R. H., Koegel, R. L., Turnbull, A. P., Sailor, W., et al. (2002). Positive behavior support: Evolution of an applied science. *Journal of Positive Behavior Interventions, 4,* 4–16.

Carr, E. G., Horner, R. H., Turnbull, A. P., Marquis, J. G., McLaughlin, D. M., McAtee, M., et al. (1999). *Positive behavior support for people with developmental disabilities: A research synthesis.* Washington, DC: American Association on Mental Retardation.

Carr, E. G., Levin, L., McConnachie, G., Carlson, J. I., Kemp, D. C., Smith, C. E., & Magito-McLaughlin, D. (1999). Comprehensive multisituational intervention for problem behavior in the community: Long-term maintenance and social validation. *Journal of Positive Behavior Interventions, 1,* 5–25.

Clarke, S., Dunlap, G., & Vaughn, B. (1999). Family-centered, assessment-based intervention to improve behavior during an early morning routine. *Journal of Positive Behavior Interventions, 1,* 235–241.

Dunlap, G. (1984). The influence of task variation and maintenance tasks on the learning and affect of autistic children. *Journal of Experimental Child Psychology, 37,* 41–64.

Dunlap, G., Fox, L., Vaughn, B. J., Bucy, M., & Clarke, S. (1997). In quest of meaningful perspectives and outcomes: A response to five commentaries. *Journal of the Association for Persons with Severe Handicaps, 22,* 221–223.

Dunlap, G., & Kern, L. (1996). Modifying instructional activities to promote desirable behavior: A conceptual and practical framework. *School Psychology Quarterly, 11,* 297–312.

Dunlap, G., Kern-Dunlap, L., Clarke, S., & Robbins, F. (1991). Functional assessment, curricular revision, and severe behavior problems. *Journal of Applied Behavior Analysis, 24,* 387–397.

Dunlap, G., & Koegel, R. L. (1980). Motivating autistic children through stimulus variation. *Journal of Applied Behavior Analysis, 13,* 619–627.

Foster-Johnson, L., & Dunlap, G. (1993). Using functional assessment to develop effective, individualized interventions for challenging behaviors. *Teaching Exceptional Children, 25,* 44–50.

Foster-Johnson, L., Ferro, J., & Dunlap, G. (1994). Preferred curricular activities and reduced problem behaviors in students with intellectual disabilities. *Journal of Applied Behavior Analysis, 27,* 493–504.

Goode, D. (1994). The national quality of life for persons with disabilities project: A quality of life agenda for the United States. In D. Goode (Ed.), *Quality of life for persons with disabilities* (pp. 139–161). Cambridge, MA: Brookline Books.

Hieneman, M., & Dunlap, G. (1999). Issues and challenges in implementing community-based behavioral support for two boys with severe behavioral difficulties. In J. Scotti and L. Meyer (Eds.), *Behavioral interventions, principles, models and practices* (pp. 363–384). Baltimore: Brookes.

Hieneman, M., Presley, J., Gayler, W., Nolan, M., DeTuro, L., & Dunlap, G. (1999). *Facilitator's guide: Positive behavioral support.* Tallahassee, FL: State of Florida, Department of State.

Horner, R. N., Dunlap, G., Koegel, R. L., Carr, E. G., Sailor, W., Anderson, J. A., Albin, R. W., & O'Neill, R. E. (1990). Toward a technology of "non-aversive" behavioral support. *Journal of the Association for Persons with Severe Handicaps, 15,* 125–132.

Hughes, C., Hwang, B., Kim, J. H., Eisenman, L. T., & Killian, D. J. (1995). Quality of life in applied research: A review and analysis of empirical measures. *American Journal on Mental Retardation, 99,* 623–641.

Jensen, C. C., McConnachie, G., & Pierson, T. (2001). Long-term multicomponent intervention to reduce severe problem behavior: A 63-month evaluation. *Journal of Positive Behavior Interventions, 3,* 225–236.

Knoster, T. (1999a). *Behavioral outcomes survey.* Unpublished manuscript, Tri-State Consortium on Positive Behavior Support, Central Susquehanna Intermediate Unit, Lewisburg, PA.

Knoster, T. (1999b). *Positive behavioral support satisfaction survey.* Unpublished manuscript, Tri-State Consortium on Positive Behavior Support, Central Susquehanna Intermediate Unit, Lewisburg, PA.

Knoster, T. (1999c). *Quality of life survey.* Unpublished manuscript, Tri-State Consortium on Positive Behavior Support, Central Susquehanna Intermediate Unit, Lewisburg, PA.

Koegel, R. L., & Egel, A. L. (1979). Motivating autistic children. *Journal of Abnormal Psychology, 88,* 418–426.

Koegel, L. K., Koegel, R. L., & Dunlap, G. (1996). *Positive behavioral support: Including people with difficult behavior in the community.* Baltimore: Brookes.

Lee, Y., Sugai, G., & Horner, R. H. (1999). Using an instructional intervention to reduce problem and off-task behaviors. *Journal of Positive Behavior Interventions, 1,* 195–204.

Lucyshyn, J. M., Albin, R. W., & Nixon, C. D. (1997). Embedding comprehensive behavioral support in family ecology: An experimental, single-case analysis. *Journal of Consulting and Clinical Psychology, 65,* 241–251.

Lucyshyn, J. M., Blumberg, E. R., & Kayser, A. T. (2000). Improving the quality of support to families of children with severe behavior problems in the first decade of the new millennium. *Journal of Positive Behavior Interventions, 2,* 113–114.

Lucyshyn, J. M., Olson, D., & Horner, R. H. (1995). Building an ecology of support: A case study of one young woman with severe problem behaviors living in the community. *Journal of the Association for Persons with Severe Handicaps, 20,* 16–30.

McConnachie, G., & Carr, E. G. (1997). The effects of child behavior problems on the maintenance of intervention fidelity. *Behavior Modification, 21,* 123–158.

Moes, D. R. (1998). Integrating choice-making opportunities within teacher-assigned academic tasks to facilitate the performance of children with autism. *Journal of the Association for Persons with Severe Handicaps, 23,* 319–328.

Moes, D. R., & Frea, W. D. (2000). Using family context to inform intervention planning for the treatment of a child with autism. *Journal of Positive Behavior Interventions, 2,* 40–46.

O'Neill, R. E., Horner, R. H., Albin, R. W., Sprague, J. R., Storey, K., & Newton, J. (1997). *Functional assessment and program development for problem behavior.* Pacific Grove, CA: Brooks/Cole.

O'Neill, R. E., Vaughn, B. J., & Dunlap, G. (1998). Comprehensive behavioral support assessment issues and strategies. In A. M. Wetherby, S. F. Warren, & J. Reichle (Eds.), *Transitions in prelinguistic communication* (pp. 313–341). Baltimore: Brookes.

Risley, T. (1996). Get a life! In L. K. Koegel, R. L. Koegel, & G. Dunlap (Eds.), *Positive behavioral support* (pp. 425–437). Baltimore: Brookes.

Schalock, R. L., Keith, K. D., Hoffman, K., & Karan, O. C. (1989). Quality of life: Its measurement and use. *Mental Retardation, 27,* 25–31.

Shukla, S., Kennedy, C. H., & Sharon-Cushing, L. (1999). Intermediate school students with severe disabilities: Supporting their social participation in general education classrooms. *Journal of Positive Behavior Interventions, 1,* 130–140.

Stiebel, D. (1999). Promoting augmentive communication during daily routines: A parent problem-solving intervention. *Journal of Positive Behavior Interventions, 1,* 159–169.

Todd, A. W., Horner, R. H., & Sugai, G. (1999). Effects of self-recruited praise on problem behavior, academic engagement, and work completion in a typical classroom. *Journal of Positive Behavior Interventions, 1,* 66–76.

Turnbull, A. P., & Ruef, M. (1997). Family perspectives on inclusive lifestyle issues for people with problem behavior. *Exceptional Children, 63,* 211–227.

Vaughn, B. J., Clarke, S., & Dunlap, G. (1997). Assessment-based intervention for severe behavior problems in a natural family context. *Journal of Applied Behavior Analysis, 30,* 713–716.

Vaughn, B. J., Dunlap, G., Fox, L., Clarke, S., & Bucy, M. (1997). Parent-professional partnership in behavioral support: A case study of community-based intervention. *Journal of the Association for Persons with Severe Handicaps, 22,* 186–197.

Action Editor: Robert Koegel

PART IV
Families and Family Support

〜

It has long been recognized that serious problem behaviors affect not only the individual who is actually engaging in the behaviors but also those persons who care for and are close to the individual and whose lives are intermingled with his or her life. There has also been an appreciation that an individual's life and behaviors are inextricably influenced by the social context in which they occur. For many people, particularly during childhood and adolescence, the family context is among the most prominent and influential of social contexts. Positive behavior support (PBS) has sought to broaden its impact beyond that of the individual so as to involve and benefit families and family systems (see Lucyshyn, Dunlap, & Albin, 2002; Turnbull & Turnbull, 1996).

The collection of articles in this section offers data and discussion relevant to this pursuit. Moes and Frea (2002) described procedures in which an explicit appreciation of and accounting for the family context was employed to help design and implement intervention support for a child with autism. Santarelli and her associates (2001) offered an enlightening and useful discussion about the same theme, but with the added consideration of providing support for culturally diverse families. The examples provided by these authors represent the collaborative, respectful, and family-centered strategies that are characteristic of PBS for families.

The remainder of the section is composed of two companion articles about a parent–professional partnership (Vaughn et al., 1987; Fox et al., 1987) and the commentaries that were published in response to the articles. The companion articles presented two perspectives on a 10-month process of community-based support for a family that in-cluded a boy with Cornelia de Lange syndrome and severe challenging behavior and his mother, who was a coauthor of both articles. In the first article, a traditional, quantitative time series design was described, while an analysis of qualitative data from family interviews and the mother's audio journal was presented in the second article. These articles were published in tandem and received the inaugural Thomas G. Haring Award for Research from TASH in 1998. The articles are considered heuristic in that they serve mainly to raise issues and questions relevant to PBS with families. Recognizing this, the JASH editor at the time of the articles' publication, Lori Goetz, invited five authors—Carr (1997), Horner (1997), Schwartz (1997), Singer (1997), and Snell (1997)—to respond with brief commentaries. Because we believe that these commentaries contributed in important ways to a discussion and appreciation of family-centered PBS, we have included them in this section. The final selection is a response to these commentaries by the authors of the companion articles (Dunlap et al., 1997) that was also included in the original JASH issue.

—Glen Dunlap

REFERENCES

Lucyshyn, J., Dunlap, G., & Albin, R. W. (2002). *Families and positive behavior support: Addressing problem behaviors in family contexts.* Baltimore: Brookes.

Turnbull, A. P., & Turnbull III, H. R. (1996). Group action planning as a strategy for providing comprehensive family support. In L. K. Koegel, R. L., Koegel, & G. Dunlap (Eds.), *Positive behavioral support: Including people with difficult behavior in the community* (pp. 99–114). Baltimore: Brookes.

Using Family Context to Inform Intervention Planning for the Treatment of a Child with Autism

Doug R. Moes
University of California–Los Angeles

William D. Frea
California State University–Los Angeles

Abstract: Children with autism often engage in problem behavior that can be highly disruptive to ongoing family practices and routines. This case study demonstrated child and family outcomes related to two distinct treatment approaches for challenging behavior (prescriptive vs. contextualized) in a family raising a child with autism. The processes of behavior change directed either solely by the interventionist (prescriptive) and in collaboration with the family (contextualized) were compared. The family-directed intervention involved an assessment of family context (i.e., via discussion of daily routines) to inform the design of a behavioral support plan. Information gathered from the assessment of family routines was used to (a) help select specific behavioral strategies that were compatible with family characteristics and preferences, and (b) construct teaching methods that fit with the family's ongoing practices, routines, and interaction goals. More favorable results (i.e., reductions in challenging behavior, an increase in on-task behavior) were observed within the contextualized treatment-planning phase than were observed within the prescriptive treatment-planning phase. The procedures and results are discussed in relation to the emerging literature documenting the importance of contextualizing behavioral supports applied within family settings.

The number of empirically validated behavioral intervention strategies addressing challenging behavior has steadily grown over the past 2 decades (Cipani & Spooner, 1997). Procedures such as differential reinforcement of alternative behavior (DRA), functional communication training (FCT), extinction, and demand fading are examples of the behavioral technologies currently available for developing treatment packages targeting problem behaviors (Durand & Carr, 1991; Lalli, Casey, & Kates, 1995; Piazza, Moes, & Fisher, 1996). More recently, systematic application of these behavioral technologies in family settings has begun to emerge (Arndorfer, Miltenberger, Woster, Rortvedt, & Gaffaney, 1994; Derby et al., 1997; Frea & Hepburn, 1999; Lucyshyn, Albin, & Nixon, 1997; Vaughn, Clarke, & Dunlap, 1997). This growing literature has raised important issues for both service providers and researchers to consider when facilitating behavioral change in natural family contexts (Griest & Forehand, 1982; Lucyshyn & Albin, 1993).

A central issue raised when working in family settings relates to the role of caregivers as treatment providers. Caregivers are assuming increasing levels of responsibility for implementing behavioral supports, and have clearly demonstrated the capacity to acquire the skills necessary to implement specific intervention plans (Frea & Hepburn, 1999; Koegel, Koegel, & Dunlap, 1996; Moes, 1995). There is an underlying expectation that caregivers assuming this role will implement intervention strategies consistently over time and across important family settings when direct support from service providers is no longer available. A second, and equally significant, issue is how well behavioral interventions fit within family settings (Dunlap & Fox, 1996). If behavioral interventions are not compatible with ongoing family practices and routines, they are unlikely to be sustained over time and will likely fail to produce their intended benefits (Bernheimer & Keogh, 1995). Clearly, these issues have major implications for the design and success (i.e., generalization and maintenance) of behavioral support plans applied in family settings (Robbins, Dunlap, & Pleinis, 1991; Singer & Irvin, 1991).

Several recent studies examining the application of behavioral interventions in family settings have utilized prescriptive treatment approaches (Arndorfer et al., 1994; Derby et al., 1997). Prescriptive treatment approaches are characterized by standardized protocols and highly structured teaching formats that are designed to direct intervention efforts. The use of prescribed treatments to address challenging behavior has obvious appeal given their success in more controlled settings (e.g., inpatient units, outpatient clinics). One potential drawback to a prescriptive approach, however, is that the intervention strategies and teaching format selected may not fit within the family context (Albin, Lucyshyn, Horner, & Flannery, 1996). In addition, prescribed treatments may produce undesirable outcomes (e.g., increased behavioral challenges, rigid patterns of family interaction; Dennis, Williams, Giangreco, & Cloniger, 1993; McConnachie & Carr, 1997).

To overcome the potential limitations of prescriptive treatment planning, researchers have begun exploring methods of contextualizing behavioral supports applied in family settings. The process of contextualizing behavioral interventions involves assessment beyond maintaining variables of problematic behavior. For example, assessment of settings, values, and beliefs are conducted to inform the intervention planning process and increase the compatibility between behavioral intervention and ongoing family routines and practices. Several investigators have focused on the assessment of family ecology to guide the intervention planning process when contextualizing behavioral supports it (Albin et al., 1996; Simeonsson, Bailey, Huntington, & Comfort, 1986). These efforts have demonstrated the importance of ongoing parent–professional collaboration and the need to use information about family context in developing behavioral support plans.

Daily routines have become an increasingly important unit of analysis in the assessment of family context (Lucyshyn et al., 1997; Vaughn et al., 1997). Family routines represent the specific contexts in which challenging behaviors occur and intervention is to be embedded. Assessment of daily routines can help identify important parameters of the contexts in which challenging behavior occurs that can directly inform intervention planning (O'Donnell, Tharp, & Wilson, 1993). Daily routines also represent a desirable unit of analysis because they are familiar to families and readily discussed (Nihira, Weisner, & Bernheimer, 1994). Through consideration of family routines, it may be possible to make behavioral interventions highly compatible with ongoing family practices and values so that they are more likely to be sustained over time,

produce their intended benefit, and remain meaningful for families (Albin et al., 1996; Bernheimer & Keogh, 1995).

The purpose of the present case study was to demonstrate child and family outcomes related to two distinct treatment approaches for challenging behavior (prescriptive vs. contextualized) in a family raising a child with autism. The processes of behavior change directed either solely by the interventionist (prescriptive) or in collaboration with the family (contextualized) were compared. The family-directed intervention planning involved an assessment of family context (i.e., daily routines) to inform the design of a behavioral support plan. Information gathered from the assessment of family routines was used (a) to help select specific behavioral strategies that were compatible with family characteristics and preferences, and (b) to construct teaching methods that fit with the family's ongoing practices, routines, and interaction goals.

Method

PARTICIPANT AND SETTING

Matthew was a 3-year-old boy diagnosed with autism and a mood disorder. He showed age-appropriate cognitive abilities. Despite mild delays in his receptive and expressive language abilities and the presence of delayed echolalia, Matthew could communicate with others verbally. Matthew had several interests and activities that he engaged in at home, yet he typically carried them out in a highly rigid manner with little tolerance for failure, direction from others, or changes in his routine. This rigidity made it difficulty for Matthew to interact socially with peers and adults. He lived at home with his parents and 4-year-old brother. Both parents worked outside the home during the day and were present in the late afternoon and evenings to supervise their children and attend to ongoing family activities.

All assessment and intervention sessions took place in Matthew's home and were implemented by his family members (i.e., parents and sibling). Training and generalization probes were conducted within the context of specific routines that Matthew's parents identified as problematic because of his challenging behaviors. Matthew's parents selected routines that took place in the living room and bedroom, places he was expected to clean up after himself (i.e., put toys away, pick up clothes). Training sessions were conducted in the bedroom routine only. Generalization probes occurred in the living room routine to monitor the transfer of treatment gains achieved during the bedroom routine. All observation sessions were videotaped with an 8mm camcorder, and scored in continuous 10-second intervals. Matthew's family was seen once a week throughout baseline, prescriptive, and contextualized treatment planning phases.

PROCEDURES

Dependent Variables

Dependent variables included disruptive and on-task behavior, functional communication, and parent ratings for the degree of sustainability of the support plans. Disruptive behavior consisted of hitting, pushing, crying, screaming, throwing, banging and grabbing for objects, and dropping to the ground. On-task behavior was defined as all responses following a parental request that were consistent with demand specifications and facilitated progress toward task completion (e.g., picking up clothes and putting them in the closet, putting toys on the shelf, throwing away trash). In the prescriptive treatment-planning phase, a functional communication response was defined as Matthew's independent use of the phrase "can I have a break please?" following a parental request. In the contextualized treatment-planning phase a functional communication response was defined as Matthew's independent use of the phrase "can I have help please?" following a parental request.

Interobserver Agreement

Interobserver agreement was determined for 33% of all sessions. Exact agreement averaged 98% (range, 90% to 100%) for disruptive behavior, 94% (range, 87% to 100%) for functional communication, and 92% (range, 77% to 100%) for on-task behavior.

Sustainability

Sustainability of the support plan was assessed by parent evaluations of how well the treatment package fit with the family context, using a 20-item self-report questionnaire. Questions focused on the compatibility between the treatment package and family (a) resources and constraints; (b) beliefs, values, and goals; and (c) abilities and needs. Family members rated each item on a 5-point scale (1 = not at all to 5 = very much). The questionnaire was completed at the end of each intervention phase to compare how parents rated the sustainability of the prescriptive and contextualized support plans. Sustainability scores represent an average across the 20 items, separately for each parent. The following ranges were used to characterize average sustainability scores: 1 to 1.5 = not at all, 1.5 to 2.5 = not much, 2.5 to 3.5 = can't tell, 3.5 to 4.5 = much, and 4.5 to 5 = very much.

BASELINE

Baseline data were collected during two initial home visits in which the authors wanted to observe the specific routines that Matthew's parents were most concerned about due to the presence of his challenging behavior. Observation probes in the bedroom (training) and living room (generalization) routines measured preintervention levels of disruptive and on-task behavior, and functional communication.

INTERVENTION PLANNING

Both support plans employed were based on the results of a functional assessment that generated and confirmed specific hypotheses about what maintained Matthew's problem behavior. Functional assessment results indicated that his behavior was maintained primarily by negative reinforcement. More specifically, Matthew utilized his challenging behavior to avoid the requests that his parents placed on him.

Prescriptive Treatment Planning

For the prescriptive treatment approach to address Matthew's challenging behavior, the authors selected a treatment package combining functional communication training, extinction, and demand fading that was implemented in two stages. The support plan and teaching format were outlined in a protocol derived from previous literature (Derby et al., 1997; Lalli et al., 1995). Matthew's parents were then trained to implement the prescribed treatment package (i.e., FCT, extinction, demand fading). Training began with a brief discussion of the functional assessment results and a rationale for using the selected treatment package. During this discussion a functional communication response (i.e., "can I have a break please?") was identified. In Stage 1, Matthew's parents were then given a protocol outlining functional communication training and extinction, and the procedures were modeled for them during a preliminary training session (see Table 1). In Stage 2, demand fading procedures were added to the protocol, and Matthew's parents were given the opportunity to practice during additional training sessions. Matthew's parents were given feedback on their use of the intervention strategies during training sessions conducted during the bedroom routine.

Contextualized Treatment Planning

The contextualized treatment-planning approach incorporated an assessment of family context and parent–professional collaboration to develop a support plan addressing Matthew's challenging behavior. The assessment consisted of an interview asking Matthew's parents to describe their daily routines in significant detail. During the interview process, the first author used open-ended questions to gather information about daily routine features and organization. Routines in which Matthew's parents experienced success and difficulties were discussed. The specific parameters used to guide the evaluation of family routines were (a) abilities and needs of family members, (b) activities taking place, (c) competing demands and responsibilities, (d) available resources and support, and (e) current and desired patterns of social interaction (Albin et al., 1996; Bernheimer & Keogh, 1995; Dunlap & Fox, 1996; Nihira et al., 1994). These parameters were selected to provide operational specificity of family routines that could

Table 1. Summary of Components in Prescriptive and Contextualized Treatments

Component	Prescriptive treatment planning	Contextualized treatment planning
Intervention strategies	FCT ("break please") Escape extinction demand fading (FR = 1)	FCT ("help please") DRA (reinforce compliance; FI = 5 min.)
Participants	Mother, Matthew	Mother, father, Matthew, sibling
Prompting sequence	Verbal (request), Gestural (request & modeling), Physical (request & physical guidance)	Verbal (request, remind of contingencies, three count)
Contingencies		
Problem behavior	Prompt (verbal, gestural, physical)	Prompt (verbal), Deliver consequence (privilege removal)
Noncompliance	Prompt (verbal, gestural, physical)	Prompt (verbal), Deliver consequence (privilege removal)
Functional communication	1-minute break before request reintroduced	Parent assistance with request until task completed
Compliance	Verbal praise given by parent	Verbal praise and given access to preselected item/activity when finished working on specified task (FI = 5 min.)

Note. *FR & FI correspond with fixed ratio and fixed interval schedules of reinforcement.*

directly inform the selection of compatible behavioral strategies and teaching methods. The information gained during this interview was used during parent–professional collaboration in developing a new protocol that would direct subsequent training sessions with the bedroom routine.

The protocol developed for the contextualized treatment-planning phase involved adaptations based on family preferences and characteristics gathered during the assessment of family context (see Table 1). Both of Matthew's parents indicated that they were primarily interested in rewarding him for following through with their requests. Consequently, a DRA procedure was selected in order to reward Matthew's compliance. In implementing the DRA procedure within the contextualized treatment-planning phase, Matthew was expected to spend approximately 5 minutes cleaning up after himself before he could gain access to a preselected item or activity of his choice. Although both parents valued teaching Matthew functional communication, they agreed that having Matthew ask for "help" rather then "a break" more accurately reflected their expectations of him and desired patterns of interaction. It was particularly important for his mother to offer him assistance to reduce his frustration in these situations. As a result, functional communication training within the contextualized treatment-planning phase involved teaching Matthew to ask for help in order to facilitate his completion of parental requests. Matthew's parents indicated that the three-step prompting sequence (i.e., verbal, gestural, physical) used to make requests in the prescriptive treatment-planning phase was not consistent

with their current practices and preferences. Specifically, they expressed concern with the confrontations that were generated from physically guiding Matthew through the tasks. As an alternative, Matthew's father wanted to build on his typical approach to making requests, which included using a three-count procedure before delivering consequences for noncompliance (e.g., privilege removal). In addition, Matthew's mother wanted to clarify what he could earn for complying with requests they placed on him. Therefore, requests were made using a sequence of verbal prompts in the contextualized treatment phase. For example, first a verbal prompt issuing a request, such as "pick up your shirt please," was used. Then a reminder of the contingencies was provided (e.g., "if you finish cleaning up you will get a chance to play with _____"). If needed, a three-count procedure ("1, 2, 3 . . .") would follow. Finally, it was important for both parents that Matthew's older brother participate in the teaching sessions. They wanted him to follow the same contingencies as Matthew, and were concerned about demonstrating any preferential treatment to either child. They also valued the older brother's role as a model for Matthew.

Results

Behavioral outcomes across baseline, prescriptive, and contextualized treatment-planning phases are depicted in Figure 1. Baseline results indicated that Matthew engaged in high levels of disruptive behavior and did not exhibit the use of functional communication during the training (i.e., bedroom) or generalization (i.e., living room) rou-

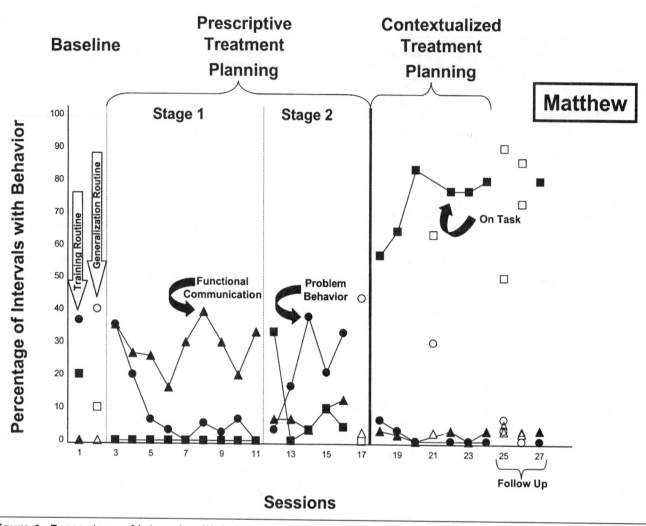

Figure 1. Percentage of intervals with behavior across baseline, prescriptive, and contextualized treatment-planning phases.

tines. In addition, relatively low levels of on-task behavior were observed during the baseline phase (see Figure 1).

The support plan generated from the prescriptive treatment-planning approach was implemented in two stages. Initially, emphasis was placed on the use of FCT and extinction procedures to teach Matthew a response that could replace disruptive behavior associated with parental requests. As shown in Figure 1, disruptive behavior decreased significantly when Matthew successfully acquired the new communication response. However, during this initial stage Matthew did not engage in on-task behavior, instead using his communication response at a high rate to escape parent requests. When disruptive behavior was significantly reduced, parental concerns with Matthew's lack of compliance was addressed through implementation of the demand fading procedure in Stage 2. In order to promote success, Matthew was expected to complete one request (e.g., pick up your shirt) before being given the opportunity to take a break. Although Matthew appeared

to have initial success when the demand fading procedure was introduced, subsequent sessions reveal a return in disruptive behavior to baseline rates. Following the second session of Stage 2, Matthew's parents indicated that they continued to be concerned about disruptive behavior and lack of compliance. The generalization probe in the living room routine corroborated the lack of progress in reducing disruptive behavior and increasing compliance in non-training settings. Parent feedback (e.g., "It feels as if we are going backwards," "I used to be able to get him to follow through with some things," "He won't even do one thing I ask") reflected their frustration with the prescribed support plan. Average mother and father ratings of support plan sustainability within the prescriptive treatment-planning phase were 3.1 and 3.3, respectively. These ratings indicated that both parents were uncertain (i.e., scores between 2.5 and 3.5 = *can't tell*) about how well the support plan fit their resources, constraints, beliefs, values, goals, abilities, and needs.

Following implementation of the contextualized treatment-planning phase, increases in Matthew's level of on-task behavior and decreases in disruptive behavior in the training routine were immediately observed (see Figure 1). Matthew also consistently used his functional communication response (e.g., "help please") when he wanted assistance in completing the requests placed on him. Generalization probes conducted during the contextualized treatment phase also revealed a dramatic improvement in Matthew's performance. Moreover, these improvements in behavioral outcomes corresponded with an increase in parent ratings on the sustainability of the contextualized support plan. Specifically, average mother and father ratings improved to 3.9 and 3.8, respectively. These average ratings suggest that both parents found the contextualized support plan to be sustainable, or highly compatible with their resources, constraints, beliefs, values, goals, abilities, and needs (i.e., scores between 3.5 and 4.5 = *much*). Follow-up data, collected approximately 3 months later, showed that positive behavioral changes achieved through the contextualized support plan were maintained within the training and generalization routines.

Discussion

The current case study compared the process of behavior change, using prescriptive and contextualized treatment-planning approaches. Both the prescribed and contextualized support plans were based on the results of functional assessment procedures and represented technically sound treatment packages. Despite these similarities, the outcomes achieved through each approach were very different. More specifically, significant reductions in challenging behavior and an increase in compliance during important family routines were observed within the contextualized treatment-planning phase. Similar benefits were not obtained during the prescriptive treatment-planning phase. These differences suggest that Matthew and his family may have benefited from the process of contextualizing behavioral supports.

This case study contributes to a growing literature that has begun to delineate important parameters for assessing family context in order to individualize positive behavioral supports (Albin et al., 1996; Bernheimer & Keogh, 1995; Fox et al., 1997; Nihira et al., 1994; Trivette, Dunst, Deal, Hamer, & Propst, 1990). As with previous case studies, daily routines appeared to be a particularly useful unit of analysis in conducting an assessment of family context (Lucyshyn et al., 1997; Vaughn et al., 1997). Taking inventory of routine features and organization may help interventionists clearly define specific family contexts, allowing for finer discriminations about what behavioral strategies are best suited for a particular family and how teaching opportunities can be incorporated into ongoing routines.

Results also suggest that sustainability may be an important measure to evaluate behavioral support plans (Bernhiemer & Keogh, 1995). The current data suggest that behavioral support plans that are sustainable (e.g., compatible with family resources, constraints, beliefs, value, goals, abilities, and needs) may contribute to the generalization and maintenance of treatment gains. One would suspect that improved family perception and increased family involvement in treatment would result in better generalization. Interestingly, positive behavioral changes were also achieved in the living room routine (i.e., nontraining), suggesting that the process of contextualizing behavioral supports to fit within family routines may actually facilitate the process of generalization. This suggests that consideration of daily routine features and organization may be pivotal to the generalization of training goals across important family settings. Future research needs to systematically investigate the functional relationships between behavior change, the degree of sustainability of behavioral support plans, generalization, and maintenance. Additional research in this area may be fruitful in addressing limitations in generalization and maintenance, which continue to be significant issues when applying behavioral technologies in natural settings (Dunlap, Fox, Vaughn, Bucy, & Clarke, 1997).

There are several limitations with the current case study. In the absence of an experimental design, conclusions on the functional relationship between behavioral outcomes and components that distinguish the prescriptive and contextualized treatment-planning approaches remain inconclusive. In addition, the application of these two treatment-planning approaches to a single family limits the ability to generalize findings to other children and families. Despite these limitations, conducting an assessment of family ecology and working within the context of established daily routines may represent best practices for addressing the larger relationship and systems issues that are often overlooked in behavioral research (Carr, Carlson, Langdon, Magito-McLaughlin, & Yarbrough, 1998; Carr, Reeve, & Magito-McLaughlin, 1996). Behavioral interventions should not be selected arbitrarily or solely on the basis of their technical merit (Albin et al., 1996). Clearly, family participation in the decision-making process is critical to avoid developing support plans that families may perceive as incompatible with their values, ongoing practices, and daily routines (Bernheimer & Keogh, 1995). The assessment and intervention strategies that characterized the contextualized treatment-planning phase are consistent with a growing literature on the use of positive behavioral support in community settings (Dunlap, Vaughn, & O'Neill, 1998; Horner & Carr, 1997; Koegel et al., 1996). By recognizing the role of families as both experts and collaborators in the assessment and intervention-planning process, practitioners can effectively respond to the individual needs and challenges of the families they serve. In doing so, practitioners may optimize the benefits of behavioral technologies applied in family settings.

ABOUT THE AUTHORS

Doug R. Moes, PhD, is clinical director of Devereux–Santa Barbara and an assistant research psychologist at the Neuropsychiatric Institute, University of California–Los Angeles. His research interests include the application of behavioral assessment and intervention strategies in community settings, working with children with special needs and their families from diverse backgrounds. **William D. Frea, PhD, is the director of autism programs at California State University–Los Angeles, where he is an assistant professor in the Charter School of Education. His research interests include comprehensive interventions for children with autism. Address: Doug R. Moes, PO Box 1079, Santa Barbara, CA 93102.**

REFERENCES

Albin, R. W., Lucyshyn, J. M., Horner, R. H., & Flannery, K. B. (1996). Contextual fit for behavioral support plans: A model for "goodness of fit." In R. L. Koegel, L. K. Koegel, & G. Dunlap (Eds.), *Positive behavioral support: Including people with difficult behavior in the community* (pp. 81–98). Baltimore: Brookes.

Arndorfer, R., Mitlenberger, R., Woster, S., Rortvedt, A., & Gaffaney, T. (1994). Home-based descriptive and experimental analysis of problem behaviors in children. *Topics in Early Childhood Special Education, 14,* 64–87.

Bernheimer, L. P., & Keogh, B. K. (1995). Weaving interventions into the fabric of everyday life: An approach to family assessment. *Topics in Early Childhood Special Education, 15,* 415–433.

Carr, E. G., Carlson, J. I., Langdon, N. A., Magito-McLaughlin, D., & Yarbrough, S. C. (1998). Two perspectives on antecedent control. In J. K. Luiselli & M. J. Cameron (Eds.), *Antecedent control* (pp. 3–28). Baltimore: Brookes.

Carr, E. G., Reeve, C. E., & Magito-McLaughlin, D. (1996). Contextual influences on problem behavior in people with developmental disabilities. In L. K. Koegel, R. L. Koegel, & G. Dunlap (Eds.), *Positive behavioral support: Including people with difficult behavior in the community* (pp. 403–423). Baltimore: Brookes.

Cipani, E., & Spooner, F. (1997). Treating problem behaviors maintained by negative reinforcement. *Research in Developmental Disabilities, 18,* 329–342.

Dennis, R. E., Williams, W., Giangreco, M. F., & Cloniger, C. J. (1993). Quality of life as context for planning and evaluation of services for people with disabilities. *Exceptional Children, 59,* 499–512.

Derby, K. M., Wacher, D. P., Berg, W., DeRaad, A., Ulrich, S., Asmus, J., Harding, J. Prouty, A., Laffey, P., & Stoner, E. A. (1997). The long-term effects of functional communication training in home settings. *Journal of Applied Behavior Analysis, 30,* 507–531.

Dunlap, G., & Fox, L. (1996). Early intervention and serious problem behavior: A comprehensive approach. In L. K. Koegel, R. L. Koegel, & G. Dunlap (Eds.), *Positive behavioral support: Including people with difficult behavior in the community* (pp. 31–50). Baltimore: Brookes.

Dunlap, G., Fox, L., Vaughn, B. J., Bucy, M., & Clarke (1997). In quest of meaningful perspectives on outcomes: A response to five commentaries. *Journal of the Association for Persons with Severe Handicaps, 22,* 221–223.

Dunlap, G., Vaughn, B. J., & O'Neill, R. (1998). Comprehensive behavioral support: Application and intervention. In A. M. Wetherby, S. F. Warren, & J. Reichle (Eds.), *Transition in pre-linguistic communication* (pp. 343–364).

Durand, V. M., & Carr, E. G. (1991). Functional communication training to reduce challenging behavior: Maintenance and application in new settings. *Journal of Applied Behavior Analysis, 24,* 251–264.

Fox, L., Dunlap, G., & Philbrick, L. A. (1997). Providing individualized supports to young children with autism and their families. *Journal of Early Intervention, 21,* 1–14.

Frea, W. D., & Hepburn, S. L. (1999). Teaching parents of children with autism to perform functional assessments to plan interventions for extremely disruptive behaviors. *Journal of Positive Behavioral Interventions, 1,* 112–116.

Griest, D. L., & Forehand, R. (1982). How can I get any parent training done with all these other problems going on? The role of family variables in child behavior therapy. *Child and Family Behavior Therapy, 4,* 73–80.

Horner, R. H., & Carr, E. G. (1997). Behavior support for students with severe disabilities: Functional assessment and comprehensive intervention. *The Journal of Special Education, 31,* 84–104.

Koegel, R. L, Koegel, L. K., & Dunlap, G. (1996). *Positive behavioral support: Including people with difficult behavior in the community.* Baltimore: Brookes.

Lalli, J. S., Casey, S., & Kates, K. (1995). Reducing escape behavior and increasing task completion with functional communication training, extinction, and response chaining. *Journal of Applied Behavior Analysis, 28,* 261–268.

Lucyshyn, J. M., & Albin, R. W. (1993). Comprehensive support to families of children with disabilities and behavior problems: Keeping it friendly. In G. H. S. Singer & L. E. Powers (Eds.), *Families, disability, and empowerment: Active coping skills and strategies for family interventions* (pp. 365–407).

Lucyshyn, J. M., Albin, R. W., & Nixon, C. D. (1997). Embedding comprehensive behavioral support in family ecology: An experimental, single-case analysis. *Journal of Consulting and Clinical Psychology, 65,* 241–251.

McConnachie, G., & Carr, E. G. (1997). The effects of child behavior problems on the maintenance of intervention fidelity. *Behavior Modification, 21,* 123–158.

Moes, D. (1995). Parenting stress and parent education. In R. Koegel & L. Koegel (Eds.), *Teaching children with autism* (pp. 79–94). Baltimore: Brookes.

Nihira, K., Weisner, T. S., Bernheimer, & L. P. (1994). Ecocultural assessment in families of children with developmental delays: Construct and concurrent validities. *American Journal on Mental Retardation, 98,* 551–566.

O'Donnell, C. R., Tharp, R. G., & Wilson, K. (1993). Activity settings as the unit of analysis: A theoretical basis for community intervention and development. *American Journal of Community Psychology, 21,* 501–520.

Piazza, C. C., Moes, D. R., & Fisher, W. W. (1996). Differential reinforcement of alternative behavior and demand fading in the treatment of escaped-maintained destructive behavior. *Journal of Applied Behavior Analysis, 29,* 569–572.

Robbins, F. R., Dunlap, G., & Plienis, A. J. (1991). Family characteristics, family training, and the progress of young children with autism. *Journal of Early Intervention, 15,* 173–184.

Simeonsson, R. J., Bailey, D. B., Huntington, G. S., & Comfort, M. (1986). Testing the concept of goodness of fit in early intervention. *Infant Mental Health Journal, 7,* 81–94.

Singer, G. H. S, & Irvin, L. K. (1991). Supporting families of persons with severe disabilities: Emerging findings, practices, and questions. In L. H. Meyer, C. A. Peck, & L. Brown (Eds.), *Critical issues in the lives of persons with severe disabilities* (pp. 271–312). Baltimore: Brookes.

Trivette, C. M., Dunst, C. J., Deal, A. G., Hamer, A. W., & Propst, S. (1990). Assessing family strengths and family functioning style. *Topics in Early Childhood Special Education, 10,* 16–35.

Vaughn, B. J., Clarke, S., & Dunlap, G. (1997). Assessment-based intervention for severe behavior problems in a natural family context. *Journal of Applied Behavior Analysis, 30,* 713–716.

Action Editor: Robert L. Koegel

EDITOR'S NOTE: *The Forum section of the* Journal of Positive Behavior Interventions *provides for an exchange of opinions, perspectives, ideas, and informative personal accounts. We welcome brief articles from family members, professionals, friends, advocates, administrators, researchers, and other individuals who are concerned with behavioral support issues. The purpose of the Forum is to facilitate a constructive dialog among our many stakeholders regarding important issues in practice, research, training, program development and policy.*

In this issue, the Forum section contains a description of a parent education program authored by Santarelli, Koegel, Casas, and Koegel. The discussion focuses on cultural diversity and raises extremely important issues regarding cultural sensitivity and cultural competence. We believe that our field needs greater attention to these issues, and we encourage additional submissions that will help us ensure that our efforts in the realm of positive behavior support are responsive to all of the children and families comprising our increasingly diverse society.

Culturally Diverse Families Participating in Behavior Therapy Parent Education Programs for Children with Developmental Disabilities

Grace Santarelli,
Robert L. Koegel,
J. Manuel Casas, and
Lynn Kern Koegel
University of California, Santa Barbara

This article discusses the importance of considering cultural and socioeconomic variables in the development of parent education programs for culturally diverse families. Specifically, the development of behavior intervention techniques, ecocultural theory (Gallimore, Weisner, Bernheimer, Guthrie, & Nihira, 1993), and the concepts of "goodness of fit" (Bailey et al., 1990) and "contextual fit" (Albin, Lucyshyn, Horner, & Flannery, 1996) will be discussed in terms of developing culturally and linguistically sensitive treatment plans for children and families.

The importance of understanding the "ecology" of the family when developing support programs for families of children with disabilities is not a new idea in the literature. Ecocultural theory, a concept discussed in Gallimore et al. (1993), suggests that an analysis of a family's activities and

daily routines provides a window into the family's ecology, which is an essential component in the development of a behavioral support program. Bailey et al. (1990) used the "goodness of fit" framework to describe the match between early intervention support and the individual characteristics of the children and their families. Lucyshyn and Albin (1993) highlighted the importance of "keeping it friendly" when providing comprehensive support to families of children with disabilities and behavior problems: "The family-friendly features of the process, such as honoring the family's perspective and collaboratively agreeing on goals, interventions, and support strategies, make it easier for families to adopt positive behavioral support in the home and local community" (p. 404). Albin et al. (1996) extended the idea of a good "contextual" fit to include not only work with families, but behavioral support in the schools, home, work, and other community contexts. Lucyshyn, Nixon, Glang, and Cooley, (1996) emphasized the importance of understanding ecocultural influences on the family when providing support services and ensuring the "goodness of fit between the support plan and family ecology" (p. 105). Albin et al. (1996) suggested a support plan with good contextual fit: (a) is responsive to the values and goals of plan implementers, (b) uses the experience, knowledge and skills these people bring to the implementation environment, and (c) is compatible with the typical routines and daily activities that characterize implementation environments and contribute to their uniqueness.

Forehand and Kotchick (1996), however, asserted that "the influence of cultural values on parenting behavior has been ignored in behavior therapy research" (p. 187). Although the effect of "contextual variables," such as maternal depression and divorce, on the ecology of the family have been documented (Forehand & Wierson 1993; Patterson, Capaldi, & Bank 1991), Forehand and Kotchick (1996) suggested that "behavior therapists have traditionally stopped short of culture and ethnicity in their conceptualization of parenting behavior" (p. 189). Additionally, Forehand and Kotchick proposed that "parent training programs have been developed and evaluated primarily with children from European American backgrounds" (p. 190). The values of children and families from European American backgrounds may differ significantly from the values of culturally diverse children and families, potentially rendering such parent education programs less effective.

It is our contention that considering cultural and socioeconomic variables within a family's ecology is a logical additional criterion for creating a behavioral intervention parent education program with "good contextual fit". Some preliminary work in our center suggests that there may be a number of cultural variables that influence, for example, Latino families' perceptions of the availability of services. One concern regarded language barriers. Although many services are provided in Spanish, many Latino families felt that they would have to access these services through a variety of agencies that may not speak Spanish. Also, many of the Latino families had strong social support networks (often extended families) and did not feel the need for specialized services that may address these issues. Others have suggested that some cultures may not perceive the presence of a "disability" in a negative light and therefore may experience less of a need or urgency for intervention. In addition, many agencies and insurance companies may not willingly provide services. Some families may not question a perceived "authoritarian figure," which may be necessary in some cases to access services.

It is also important to consider potential barriers to service related to a family's socioeconomic status. For example, some families in our clinic did not own or have access to a car and the location of clinical services were often some distance from their residence. Although bus services were available, families often had to transfer from one bus to another at least once, which may be quite burdensome with a child with a disability.

Another significant area to explore when working with families from diverse cultural backgrounds relates to our own cultural identities. As researchers and practitioners in this country, we have perhaps grown accustomed to the European American norms established in our society. When the culture of the client and practitioner do not match, cultural dissonance can occur, creating yet another barrier to appropriate and effective interventions. For effective intervention plans and positive outcomes, it is important to analyze the effect our own biases and the assumptions our own culturally bound norms can have on our work (Harry, 1992).

In light of these and other variables, the Autism Research and Training Center at the University of California, Santa Barbara, began a clinical outreach program to culturally diverse families who have children with autism who were eligible for state-funded services for severe disabilities, but were not receiving these services. Below is a typical case history.

José, a 6-year-old Latino boy with a diagnosis of autism, was referred for a parent education program through a state agency. José displayed language delays and severe problem behaviors, including noncompliance, aggressiveness towards his 2-year-old sister and other members of the family, and a lack of social skills. When the initial contact was made with the child's mother, she expressed a number of concerns about beginning services with our center. First, she discussed the fact that both parents spoke very limited English and that Spanish was the primary language spoken in the home. While she wanted José to learn as much English as possible, she expressed concerns regarding her ability to work with him given her limited English. Second, the family was concerned regarding their ability to participate in our Center's program given factors related to their lower socioeconomic status. For example, the family did not own or have access to a car, and they could not afford to take the bus very often. They generally walked everywhere. Our clinic, however, is located about 8 miles from the family home. In addition, while José's mother did not work outside the home, financial necessity required José's father to work in construction from 6:00 a.m. to 6:00 p.m. José's mother requested that the father, as the head of the household, be present during most if not all parent education sessions.

In keeping with contextual fit theory, a program was created that would break down the potential barriers to the provision of services by our clinic (including barriers related to culture and socioeconomic status). First, the family was contacted by a Spanish-speaking clinician and was assured that the services would be provided in the native language of the family. This is consistent with findings in the literature that point to the importance of shared language between clinician and client (Altarriba & Santiago-Rivera, 1994). Second, the parent education sessions were provided in the family home. These sessions were videotaped for later supervision. In addition to solving the logistical problems for this family, intervention in the home setting is often recommended in the literature as an "ideal setting" for family-based intervention services for culturally diverse families (Wayman, Lynch & Hanson, 1991). Finally, to ensure participation of both parents, we scheduled our parent education sessions in the early evening when both parents were present and available. After intervention began, it became clear that in addition to a younger sibling, José shared his home with an extended family including two aunts and one uncle. Because these individuals interacted with him frequently, they were incorporated into the intervention sessions as well. This is consistent with the literature that emphasizes the importance of understanding the role of the family as well as the extended family (McDermott, 2001; Casas, 1976). In addition, this increased the likelihood that the procedures would be implemented consistently across all individuals in the home setting.

During intervention, other issues arose that were not directly addressed by the family, but related to individual family ecology and needs. For example, the family, originally from Mexico, had been living in the United States for a short time. Each parent had received only a few years of grammar school instruction in Mexico, and read and wrote at a grammar school level. Although our parent education manuals have been translated into Spanish (Koegel et al., 1989), the family was unable to read them. This situation was discussed with the family with great sensitivity, and the family provided input as to what they felt would work best with them in terms of written material. In order to provide this information to the family, the main points of the parent education manuals were rewritten in very basic terms in Spanish and described in detail verbally, rather than orthographically. Interestingly, the family chose to hang these points on their refrigerator.

Related to the above point, another method currently being investigated in the literature is the dissemination of intervention practices through the *fotonovela*. A fotonovela is print form of a drama told in captioned black and white photographs. The characters and storied depicted in the fotonovela provide symbols that can educate and instruct in a simple, easy-to-follow format. Fotonovelas are used throughout Central and South America to educate Spanish-speaking individuals on many different health issues, including alcohol abuse prevention, HIV/AIDS, domestic violence, diabetes, prenatal and early intervention, and aging. In fact, at our university, researchers in the Graduate School of Education developed a fotonovela entitled *Sí Se Puede!* ("You Can Do It!") which successfully encouraged parental participation in the schools (Casas & Furlong, 1991). José's family did, in fact, complete our clinic's parent education program. A few months after the completion of the program, this article's first author bumped into José, his parents, and younger sister at a local shopping mall. José approached the author, and without prompting, stated "*¡Hola Graciela! ¡Mira mi juguete nuevo! ¡Mamá me lo compró porque fui bueno esta semana!*" ("Hi Graciela! Look at my new toy! Mom bought it for me because I was good this week!"). The author was pleased not only with José's socially appropriate greeting but with the joy on his mother's face as she described how the number of José's inappropriate behaviors had remained low during the few months after the conclusion of the parent education program.

Summary

This representative example of a parent education program suggests important points to consider when working with families of children with disabilities from diverse cultures. First, there appears to be an important need to become familiar with the cultural values and unique circumstances of each family prior to planning an intervention program. Second, as suggested by Albin et al. (1996), there is an important need to involve families in every step of the process, during both planning and implementation. By actively involving the family members, the likelihood that culturally sensitive intervention plans are developed will increase. In addition, when intervention plans are developed that consider the families' values, priorities and unique individual characteristics, there is a much greater likelihood that goals will be implemented on an on-going basis and maintained over time. Finally, whenever possible, "member checking," or verifying the appropriateness of the treatment methodology with informed members of the same cultural group, is likely to allow interventionists to become familiar with the specific culture of the families with whom we work. This may include conducting a literature review, interviewing individuals who represent the particular cultural group on current practices, or whenever possible, selecting interventionists who are familiar with the culture.

ABOUT THE AUTHORS

Grace Santarelli, MA, is a doctoral student in special education, disabilities, and risk studies at the University of California, Santa Barbara and a school psychologist-intern with the Santa Barbara City Schools District. Her major interests include bilingual special education, parent education programs for culturally and linguistically diverse children and their families, and culturally sensitive assessment practices for children in the schools. *Robert L. Koegel*, PhD, is director of Autism Research Center and a professor in the Counseling/

Clinical/School Psychology Program and Special Education, Disability and Risk Studies Emphasis at the Graduate School of Education, University of California at Santa Barbara. **J. Manuel Casas,** *PhD, is a professor in the Counseling, Clinical, and School Psychology at the University of California, Santa Barbara. He has published widely in professional journals in the area of cross-cultural counseling and education. His most recent research and publication endeavors have focused on Hispanic families and children who are at risk for experiencing educational and psychosocial problems.* **Lynn Kern Koegel,** *PhD, is clinic director of the Autism Research Center at the Graduate School of Education, University of California at Santa Barbara. Address: Robert L. Koegel, Counseling/Clinical/School Psychology Program, University of California, Santa Barbara, CA 93106-9490.*

REFERENCES

Albin, R. W., Lucyshyn, J. M., Horner, R. H., & Flannery, K. B. (1996). Contextual fit for behavioral support plans: A model for "Goodness of Fit." In L. K. Koegel, R. L. Koegel, & G. Dunlap (Eds.), *Positive behavioral support: Including people with difficult behaviors in the community* (pp. 81–98). Baltimore: Brookes.

Altarriba, J., & Santiago-Rivera, A. L. (1994). Current perspectives on using linguistic and cultural factors in counseling the Hispanic client. *Professional Psychology, 25*(4), 388–397.

Bailey, D. B., Simeonsson, R. J., Winton, P. J., Huntington, G. S., Comfort, M., Isbell, P., O'Donnell, K. J., & Helm, J. M. (1990). Family-focused interventions: A functional model for planning, implementing and evaluating individualized family services in early intervention. *Journal of the Division for Early childhood, 10,* 156–171.

Casas, J. M., & Furlong, M. J. (1991). *Sí se puede! La serie de padres y escuela unidos.* [You can do it! Parents and schools unite series]. Santa Barbara: University of California.

Casas, Jesus M. (1976). Applicability of a behavioral model in serving the mental health needs of the Mexican American. *Spanish Speaking Mental Health Research Center Monograph Series, 3,* 61–65.

Forehand, R., & Kotchick, B. A. (1996). Cultural diversity: A wake-up call for parent training. *Behavior Therapy, 27,* 187–206.

Forehand, R., & Wierson, M. (1993). The role of developmental factors in planning behavioral interventions for children: Disruptive behavior as an example. *Behavior Therapy, 24,* 117–141.

Gallimore, R., Weisner, T. S., Bernheimer, L. P., Guthrie, D., & Nihira, K. (1993). Family responses to young children with developmental delays: Accomodation activity in ecological and cultural context. *American Journal on Mental Retardation, 98*(2), 185–206.

Harry, B. (1992). Developing cultural self-awareness: The first step in values clarification for early interventionists. *Topics in Early Childhood Special Education, 12*(3), 333–350.

Koegel, R. L., Schreibman, L., Good, A., Cerniglia, L., Murphy, C., & Koegel, L. K. (1989). *Cómo enseñar conductas pivotales a niños con autismo: Manual de entrenamiento.* [How to teach pivotal behaviors to children with autism: A training manual]. Santa Barbara: University of California.

Lucyshyn, J. M., Nixon, C., Glang, A., & Cooley, E. (1996). Comprehensive family support for behavior change in children with ABI. In G. H. S. Singer, A. Glang, & J. M. Williams (Eds.), *Children with aquired brain injury: Educating and supporting families* (pp. 99–136). Baltimore: Brookes.

Lucyshyn, J.M., & Albin, R.W. (1993). Comprehensive support to families of children with disabilities and behavior problems: Keeping it friendly. In G. H. S. Singer & L. E. Powers (Eds.), *Families, disabilities and empowerment: Active coping skills for family interventions* (pp. 365–407). Baltimore: Brookes.

McDermott, D. (2001). Parenting and ethnicity. In M. J. Fine & S. W. Lee (Eds.), *Handbook of diversity in parent education: The changing faces of parenting and parent education* (pp. 73–96). San Diego, CA: Academic Press.

Patterson, G. R., Capaldi, D., & Bank, L. (1991). An early starter model for predicting delinquency. In D. J. Pepler & K. H. Rubin (Eds.), *The development and treatment of childhood aggression* (pp. 139–168). Hillsdale, NJ: Erlbaum.

Wayman, K. I., Lynch, E. W., & Hanson, M. J. (1991). Home-based early childhood services: Cultural sensitivity in a family systems approach. *Topics in Early Childhood Special Education, 10*(4), 56–75.

Action Editor: Glen Dunlap

JASH
1997, Vol. 22, No. 4, 186–197

Parent-Professional Partnership in Behavioral Support: A Case Study of Community-Based Intervention

Bobbie J. Vaughn, Glen Dunlap, Lise Fox, Shelley Clarke, and Millie Bucy
University of South Florida

In this study and a companion article (Fox et al., 1997), we present an investigation that uses multiple research perspectives to study community-based, family-centered behavioral support. This study describes the intervention strategies and quantitative analyses that were used to address the challenging behaviors of a boy with severe disabilities. A collaborative team that included the boy's mother designed and implemented functional assessments and hypothesis-based interventions in three settings: a drive-through bank, a large grocery store, and a fast food restaurant. Data showed that the interventions reduced problem behaviors in all three settings and that concomitant increases were observed in desirable mother-child interactions. Specific tantrums associated with transitions through doorways were decreased substantially. Social validation data supported the efficacy and feasibility of the support strategies. This quantitative analysis provides further testimony for the use of positive behavioral support in complex, public environments.

DESCRIPTORS: community-based situations, developmental disabilities, functional assessment, methodology, parents

Positive behavioral support is a maturing enterprise based on person-centered values and comprised of assessment and intervention strategies that are designed to reduce challenging behaviors while promoting adaptive and socially desirable alternatives (Horner et al., 1990; Koegel, Koegel, & Dunlap, 1996; Meyer & Evans, 1989). Although research and practice in positive behavioral support have produced substantial gains over the past decade, there is still a great need for empirical

This research was supported by Cooperative Agreement H133B2004 and by Field-Initiated Research grant H133G60119 from the U.S. Department of Education.

We thank the Bucy family for their participation throughout this research and Arcadia Vera for assistance with data collection. The opinions expressed are those of the authors and no official endorsement should be inferred.

Address all correspondence and requests for reprints to Glen Dunlap, Division of Applied Research and Educational Support, Department of Child and Family Studies, FMHI, University of South Florida, 13301 Bruce B. Downs Boulevard, Tampa, FL 33612.

analyses and demonstrations of behavioral support practices being implemented in community settings by typical caregivers and support personnel. Currently, the overwhelming majority of published research in the area of behavioral support has been conducted in contained and structured settings (e.g., classrooms), with procedures being implemented by researchers or highly trained professionals. However, if the procedures of positive behavioral support are to be widely used by family members and community-based support providers, it is necessary for studies to describe their implementation under typical circumstances (e.g., Kemp & Carr, 1995). In particular, if the approaches are to benefit children with severe behavioral challenges, it is important that they be examined when they are used in the usual kind of circumstances that present the most significant and common difficulties, such as in public settings during the completion of routine errands in the community (e.g., Carr & Carlson, 1993).

In response to this need for enhanced ecological validity, several authors have advocated for a partnership approach in which professionals collaborate with families and/or support providers to design and implement behavioral support plans (e.g., Eno-Heineman & Dunlap, in press; Lucyshyn, Albin, & Nixon, 1997). This may be especially important in family-based behavioral support because family members have singular expertise regarding the behavior of their family members and the ecologies in which their family interacts (Dunlap & Fox, 1996; Powell, Hecimovic, & Christensen, 1993; Turnbull & Turnbull, 1990). Furthermore, families are the essential judges regarding the fit between various support options and the families' values, tolerances, and routines (Albin, Lucyshyn, Horner, & Flannery, 1996). Therefore, the active involvement of family members in the identification of problems and the design of behavioral support strategies may be a determining variable in the likelihood that an intervention will be effective and implemented with fidelity and durability.

In addition to consumer (e.g., family) involvement in the development of support plans, perspectives on research in disabilities have been affected by a movement toward consumer participation in the design and implementation of applied research projects (Whyte, 1991). In particular, there has been a charge to involve family members in research that focuses on family issues and interventions that affect family members (e.g., Turnbull, Friesen, & Ramirez, 1996; Turnbull & Turnbull, 1993). This recommendation is based on a desire to increase the responsivity of research activities and research findings to the real needs and concerns of those that the research is ostensibly intended to benefit. The ramifications of such a participatory approach are significant, suggesting that multiple methodologies will need to be invoked to detect and synthesize the various perspectives of family members, professionals, researchers, and others who are invested in building support programs that result in outcomes that have meaningful lifestyle benefits (Dunlap, Vaughn, Fox, & Foster-Johnson, 1996).

This investigation was undertaken as an initial effort in a larger research project designed to provide community-based behavioral support in partnership with family members and to learn from the participating families their perspectives as the support was being developed and implemented. In this study a collaboration was established between a team of professionals and a family that included a 9-year-old boy with severe developmental and behavioral disabilities. The assessment and support process focused on the boy's behavior in three community settings that had been identified by the family as especially problematic: a drive-through bank, a fast food restaurant, and a large grocery store. Assessment data were collected, hypotheses were developed, and a multicomponent behavioral support plan was implemented in all three settings. Data were collected on the boy's disruptive behavior and cooperative responding and on his mother's interactions. Additional data served to analyze an especially difficult transition period and to assess the social validity of the interventions. In a companion article (Fox, Vaughn, Dunlap, Bucy, 1997), we describe qualitative data provided by the family regarding their views of the support process and outcomes.

Method

Participants

The principal participant in this investigation was Jeffrey, a 9-year-old boy with Cornelia DeLange Syndrome, severe intellectual disabilities, chronic medical challenges (especially gastrointestinal problems), and significant disruptive and destructive behaviors that had been a concern for most of his life. Jeffrey was nonverbal and communicated through gestures, objects, vocalizations, and challenging behaviors such as whining, scratching, yelling, biting, hitting, throwing objects, and head banging. Although Jeffrey had significant problem behaviors, he was a fun-loving child with an infectious laugh and smile. He liked to watch tele-

vision, play in the yard with his dogs, throw a ball, and swim. He attended a special education class on a public elementary school campus in his community.

Jeffrey lived at home with his parents and 11-year-old brother in a small town adjacent to a major metropolitan area. Jeffrey's mother, Millie, worked part time as a family support provider at a university-based early intervention project and as a parent advisor at a diagnostic clinic for children with disabilities. Millie was active in school activities for both of her sons. Jeffrey's father was a truck driver and spent most of his time on the road, returning home on weekends.

The investigation was conducted in a participatory manner. Millie (the fifth author) served as a member of the research team. Other members of the team were university-based faculty and staff (the other authors) who joined Millie in the design and implementation of the behavioral support and research strategies.

Settings

The settings were three community locales in which Jeffrey exhibited frequent and intense problem behaviors. Millie and other family members selected these locations because they frequented them on a regular basis, the settings were located within their local community, and they had been associated with substantial behavior problems for many years. The settings were a drive-through bank, a large grocery store, and a fast food restaurant. Jeffrey's problem behavior in the store and the restaurant was intense throughout the routines, but especially problematic when entering and exiting through doorways. Therefore, special analyses were conducted for these transitions. In the car, Jeffrey exhibited problem behaviors until Millie pulled away from the drive-through facility.

General Procedures

The investigation was conducted as a collaborative process in which the research team (the authors) met regularly to plan and review the intervention and research components. The process involved the following components: (1) functional assessment of Jeffrey's problem behavior within each setting; (2) collection of baseline data; (3) development of hypotheses regarding environmental influences on problem behavior; (4) development and validation of multicomponent interventions based on the assessment data; (5) implementation of interventions; and (6) collection of follow-up and social validation data. In general, the procedural steps were those that have been recommended by numerous authors in the area of positive behavioral support (e.g., Carr et al., 1994; Dunlap & Kern, 1993; Horner, Sprague, & Flannery, 1993).

The design of the investigation included brief, in-context analyses of key intervention components and a quasiexperimental time series analysis of assessment-based intervention in three community settings. We decided in favor of a quasiexperimental design over an experimental multiple baseline design because Millie indicated that the continuation of baseline conditions in some settings while intervention was occurring in others could have placed an awkward and artifical constraint on her interactions with Jeffrey and her desire to resolve the disruptive behavior, and because the potential threats to internal validity (e.g., maturation and history) that could be controlled by the multiple baseline across settings were considered in this case to be negligible, especially given the lengthy status of the problems (Kazdin, 1982).

Measurement

Dependent Variables

Three categories of measures were obtained to document Jeffrey's behavior. These included disruptive behavior, cooperative responding, and transitions through doorways.

Disruptive behavior. Disruptive behavior included self-injurious behavior, such as headbanging; pushing palms to face or mouth with vocalizations; crying, screaming, and whining; attempting to leave (escape) the activity; refusal to proceed with the activity (dropping to the ground); and aggression such as scratching, hitting, or biting.

Cooperative responding. Cooperative behavior was scored whenever Jeffrey exhibited gestural, visual, or physical movement in response to a question or instruction related to the task or activity (e.g., looked at and interacted with picture schedule or shook head "no" when presented with a toy). To be scored as cooperative, the response needed to be appropriate to the context and initiated within 3 sec of the request or question.

Transitional behaviors. Jeffrey displayed extremely intense behaviors (e.g., screaming and aggression) on entering and exiting doorways. This was particularly dangerous when exiting the store because he dropped to the street or parking lot, often in the path of automobiles and shoppers trying to enter the store. To gauge the degree to which transitions caused salient problems for Jeffrey and Millie, transitions were scored from videotape by naive observers as constituting "no problems," "minor problems," or "significant problems." A score of "no problems" was used to describe Jeffrey entering or exiting the setting willingly with no vocalizations, resistance, or aggression. A score of "minor problems" described entering or exiting where Jeffrey displayed slight resistance and slight or short vocalizations. A rating of "significant problems" was used when Jeffrey dropped to the ground, exhibited long persistent vocalizations, and attempted to scratch and/or extended his body to resist being placed in the grocery cart.

Parent Behavioral Measures

Data were obtained on Millie's behavior as she participated with Jeffrey in the three settings.

Instructions related to task included any statement, instruction, or question that related directly to the activity.

Praise related to task was any praise statement, acknowledgment, or physical affection displayed in response to Jeffrey's appropriate task-related behavior (e.g., "You're eating by yourself!").

Praise unrelated to task was scored when there was an occurrence of any praise statements, acknowledgments, or affections that were unrelated to Jeffrey's task-related responding, including praise that was issued during tantrums or the exhibition of problem behavior (e.g., "You look so cute in that outfit!," displaying physical affection in response to a temper tantrum).

Instructions unrelated to task involved statements, comments, or instructions that had a persuading, calming, sing-song tone to them (e.g., "Come on Jeffrey, be good for mama," "It's all right Jeffrey, we are almost done").

Reprimands included any directive that was stated exclusively to terminate Jeffrey's behavior (e.g., "No!" "Don't!" "Stop!").

Measurement Procedures

Direct observation data collection. All data were obtained from tapes that were recorded on a small handheld video recorder. Data on the direct observation measures were collected from the tapes by two research staff members who each had more than 5 years experience recording research data in the area of behavioral and developmental disabilities. Before the start of the investigation, each observer practiced with the behavioral definitions during nonexperimental videotaped observations until an 80% criterion level was reached on each of the behavioral definitions. Frequency and duration data on Jeffrey and Millie's behavior were coded on a computer by using observation software developed by Repp, Harman, Felce, VanAcker, and Karsh (1987). Frequency data were reported as either frequency or rate and duration data were reported as percentage of session.

Transitional behavior. To capture the overall degree to which transitions were a problem for Jeffrey and Millie, observers who were unfamiliar with the participants were asked to score videotaped segments of each session's entrance and exit from the restaurant and store across all phases of the study. A special videotape was prepared by using standard starting and stopping points (based on physical landmarks in each setting). The length of the 44 segments varied, depending on the speed and efficiency of the transition, with the average being 2 min. The segments were randomly sequenced on the videotape. The observers were two employees of the university who had previous coding experience and were familiar with children who have developmental disabilities. The observers scored each segment independently.

Social Validation

To obtain data on the social validity of the procedures and the results, four parents of children with developmental disabilities and problem behavior were asked to observe videotaped segments and rate the acceptability, success, and ease of implementation of the interventions. These ratings were obtained subsequent to the follow-up phase of intervention. The first videotape was 3 min in length and consisted of two, 30-sec sequences randomly selected from all baseline and intervention sessions in the bank, store, and restaurant settings. In the bank and store settings, baseline appeared first and intervention second in the video segment. For the restaurant, the order was reversed to control for observer bias. After observing the segments, the parents were asked to independently compare the second video segment to the first. Parents were asked to rate the differences in child behavior, parent management of behavior, and child participation in the routine. A three-point scale was used for the ratings: 1, worse; 2, same; and 3, better.

The parents then viewed a second videotape that consisted of four, 1-min segments illustrating the components implemented during intervention. The use of a different component or components was demonstrated in each setting. Each rater viewed the 1-min segment that represented a particular strategy and was then asked to indicate agreement with the following two statements: (1) The strategies used to support this child were appropriate and (2) The strategies used to support this child could easily be used by other parents.

Interobserver Agreement

Interobserver agreement was assessed in 30% of the sessions for all of the direct observation variables in each of the community settings across all conditions. The data collectors coded the tapes simultaneously but independently on computers separated by 3 meters. Agreement percentages for Jeffrey's and Millie's behavior were calculated within a 3-sec window with software developed by Repp et al. (1987). The calculation divided the agreements by the sum of the agreements plus disagreements and reported a percentage for each code.

The mean agreement measure was calculated across all conditions for both Jeffrey's and Millie's event and duration behaviors. Interobserver agreement for Jeffrey's cooperative responding was 93% (range 80–100%). Interobserver agreement scores for Millie's instructions related to task was 97% (range 82–100%) and for instructions unrelated to task 97% (range 88–100%). Interobserver agreement was 100% for praise related to task and 99% (range 88–100%) for praise

unrelated to task. Interobserver agreement for reprimands was 97% (range 71–100%). Interobserver agreement for Jeffrey's disruptive behavior was 95% (range 61–98%).

Interobserver agreement for the ratings of transition segments was obtained for 30% of the sessions across both the restaurant and store settings and under baseline, intervention, and follow-up conditions. Reliability calculations required reliability raters to match exactly on segments containing significant problems. The agreement for all restaurant and store transitions was 95% (range 83–100%).

Procedures

The procedures of this study included an initial phase of functional assessment in which information was gathered and hypotheses were developed. The hypotheses were used as the basis for the multicomponent interventions designed for use in the three targeted settings. The specific components involving the addition of materials unique to the natural setting were analyzed to confirm their positive impact on the behavior. After the collection of baseline data, intervention was implemented in each of the three settings. During the first three sessions of intervention in each setting, the first author offered prompts and feedback for Millie to assist in the implementation of the intervention strategies. After those three sessions, the intervention was implemented by Millie without external feedback or support. The final phase was a series of follow-up probe observations obtained approximately 6 months after intervention. Throughout the study Millie was actively involved in all aspects of the design and implementation of the assessment and intervention strategies.

Functional Assessment and Hypothesis Development

A functional assessment of Jeffrey's problem behavior was conducted in each setting according to procedures that have been described in various sources (e.g., Dunlap & Kern, 1993; O'Neill, Vaughn, & Dunlap, 1998). The first step of the assessment process was a structured interview (O'Neill, Horner, Albin, Storey, Sprague, 1990) with Millie that was administered to identify variables that set the occasion for and maintained the problem behavior. Then observations were conducted in Jeffrey's home and school and, in particular, the three community settings that were targeted for intervention. These observations were intended to obtain information relevant to the circumstances (i.e., antecedents, consequences, and ecological variables) surrounding desirable and undesirable behavior and to confirm and/or embellish on the interview information. After 2 weeks of information gathering, the team assembled to develop hypotheses regarding the problem behaviors in the three settings. In addition, intervention components were formulated that would be: (1) logi-

Table 1
Problem Summaries, Principal Hypotheses, and Intervention Components for Each Setting

Setting	Problem summary	Hypotheses	Intervention components
Bank	Tantrums and aggression while waiting in car during banking transactions	Waiting in stationary vehicle was aversive because of absence of reinforcing stimulation	Provide preferred toys one at a time in order of preference to produce engagement with reinforcing activity and promote pleasurable and manageable interactions while waiting for banking transactions to be completed
Restaurant	Severe tantrums during transitions through doorways	Doors were highly reinforcing stimuli; tantrums postponed removal from doors.	Provide a competing reinforcer, present picture of preferred toy before transition, and provide toy (reinforcer) when leaving restaurant to compete with reinforcement of the doors
	Screaming and aggression while waiting in restaurant	Waiting was aversive because of absence of reinforcing stimulation	Provide a picture book as a reinforcing and contextually appropriate way for Jeffrey to occupy himself
Store	Severe tantrums during transitions through doorways	Doors were highly reinforcing stimuli; tantrums postponed removal from doors.	Provide a competing reinforcer, present picture of preferred toy before transition, and provide toy (reinforcer) when leaving store to compete with reinforcement of the doors
	Tantrums (screaming and aggression) while completing store routine	The process of shopping was aversive because it was without reinforcers and a means for Jeffrey to participate	Provide a picture schedule to depict the routine and offer a means for participation and provide a picture book for Jeffrey to occupy himself during periods when active participation was unlikely (e.g., during the checkout process)

cally connected and responsive to the hypotheses, (2) appropriate to the context, and (3) considered by Millie to be suitable and comfortable for use in the context of her ongoing routines. The principal hypotheses and intervention components are summarized in Table 1.

The first hypothesis that applied to all three settings was that problem behavior was likely to occur when Jeffrey was obliged to wait without access to preferred (reinforcing) activities. This was evident in the car when Millie was waiting for service in the drive-through facility, in the restaurant during the period when Millie was ordering and waiting to obtain the food, and in the store when Millie was engaged in locating and selecting grocery items. The interview and observations indicated that these periods were especially problematic and they appeared to lack reinforcers for Jeffrey's participation or desirable behavior. The intervention components that were devised to address this hypothesis included the provision of favored toys (bank), a picture book (restaurant and store), and a picture schedule (depicting steps in the shopping routine in the store).

The second hypothesis stated that the doorways were highly reinforcing and the severe tantrums exhibited during transitions served to postpone their disappearance. The intervention component was to present Jeffrey before the transition with a picture of a powerful, competing reinforcer (e.g., a particularly favored noise-making toy) and to provide that reinforcer (toy) on reaching the destination (e.g., the car). This component was used during transitions in the store and restaurant.

In addition to the two principal hypotheses, the assessment process suggested some other strategies that could contribute to more positive participation in the three settings. These strategies included the use of appropriate praise, redirecting Jeffrey when he engaged in challenging behavior, using clear and concise instructions, and by using an adapted bowl and spoon that he used at home in the restaurant.

Component Validation

To acquire some validation of the components that addressed the principal hypotheses, brief tests were conducted in each of the three community settings. For each, two sessions were conducted by the first author and videotaped for scoring at a later time. The sessions consisted of a 2-min condition without the component followed by a brief interval and the presentation of the component for another 2 min. Component testing occurred in the store from the checkout line to the car, in the restaurant while Jeffrey waited for the food, and as Jeffrey waited in the back seat of the car at the drive-through bank. The validation demonstrated the effects of the intervention component on the percentage of time Jeffrey exhibited disruptive behavior in each setting. The use of the toy during the banking routine decreased disruptive behavior from 69% to 0%. A decrease from 94% to 6% in disruptive behavior was noted with use of the picture book in the fast food restaurant. The picture schedule in the store setting decreased disruptive behavior from 82% to 46%. Although these manipulations did not include reversals and did not control for a number of potential confounds (e.g., novelty), they provided some evidence that the components might be effective in helping to overcome Jeffrey's disruptive behavior.

Baseline

Across all settings and conditions, community trips originated from the family's home. Each of the settings was approximately 15 min from home. The family vehicle was used for all of the outings and Jeffrey rode in the back seat. Other than Millie, two individuals (the first and fourth authors) were present. One individual recorded the sessions (with a hand-held videocamera) and the other served as back up in the event of excessive disruptions. During each session in the store and the restaurant, team members remained at least 3 to 5 meters from Millie and Jeffrey. Starting and stopping points for video recordings were predetermined for each setting and remained constant across all conditions throughout the study.

Millie conducted all sessions in all settings across all conditions. The sessions varied in duration; however, to maintain some consistency across the settings, measurement of the dependent variables (except for the transitions) was obtained only for the first 11 min of each session, which was the approximate duration of the typical bank sessions. No more than one session occurred per day. Banking trips occurred on the usual banking day for Millie, Fridays between 4:00 and 5:00 p.m. The restaurant trips occurred on various days of the week, always at a typical eating time for Jeffrey (e.g., 5 p.m.). The store trips usually occurred on Mondays after Jeffrey returned from school (around 4 p.m.).

During baseline, Millie performed her activities in the same manner as usual. The team did not develop interventions, nor were there any specific suggestions offered. Table 2 provides a detailed description of the course of activities in each setting for baseline, intervention, and follow-up phases.

Intervention

In preparation for the use of the multicomponent intervention strategies, the strategies were discussed and videotapes were reviewed to demonstrate the use of the major intervention components (e.g., toy, picture book, and picture schedule). During the first 3 days of intervention in each setting, Millie was provided with prompts and feedback on the use of the intervention strategies. Subsequent sessions were conducted by Millie without assistance. Intervention was conducted as described in Table 2. Before each session, Millie was encouraged to use the intervention procedures but no within-session assistance was provided.

Follow-up. Follow-up data were collected 6 months after the last intervention session. The same procedures were maintained for the community trips as in all other phases of the investigation. However, as indicated in Table 2, a notable change in the procedures occurred in the store setting where Jeffrey walked into the store with Millie rather than being placed in the cart as he had been previously.

Results

Figure 1 shows the percentage of time that Jeffrey engaged in seriously disruptive behavior during baseline, intervention, and follow-up in each of the three community settings. These data indicate that the intervention procedures were associated with improvements in Jeffrey's behavior. In the drive-through bank, disruptive behavior declined from a mean of 68.5% of intervals during baseline to less than 1% of intervals during intervention and 0% at follow-up. The data in the restaurant revealed similar results. The data in the store were less clear, although the trends were favorable. Baseline in this setting showed relatively low levels of disruptive behavior (22%) and a reduction in intervention to 10%. Follow-up observations in the store showed a mean of 2% with disruptive behavior.

Table 3 shows the results of Jeffrey's cooperative responding to Millie's requests and questions (statements) that were related to the activities of banking, dining in a fast food restaurant, and shopping, respectively. The first data column in this table shows the mean number of activity-related statements that were issued by Millie during the session, the second column shows the mean number of statements that were followed by a cooperative response from Jeffrey, and the third column shows the percentage of statements with cooperative responses. The pattern is consistent across settings. Baseline sessions included very low levels of activity-related statements and almost no cooperative responses. Intervention produced substantial gains in statements and responses. The gains achieved during the intervention were maintained at the 6-month follow-up period.

As a part of Jeffrey's repertoire of problem behavior, he presented an intense preoccupation with doors, which was associated with intense tantrums during many transitions into and out of places of commerce. To evaluate the extent to which such transitions were problematic during the various phases of this investigation, observers who were unfamiliar with Jeffrey and his circumstances judged from videotapes whether each transition for the store and restaurant constituted "no problem," "some problem," or a "significant problem." Table 4 shows the percentage of transitions that were considered to be a significant problem (i.e., a major disruptive episode). These data show that most transitions in each setting were evaluated as significantly disruptive during baseline, that intervention reduced this percentage dramatically in both settings, and that this improvement was maintained at follow-up. Although one of the two store exits was judged to be a significant problem at follow-up, there were no significant problems during the entrances or at the restaurant.

The measurement of Millie's behavior demonstrated changes in how Millie interacted with her son before and after intervention (Table 5). As indicated previ-

Table 2
Description of Activities in Each Setting

Bank Activity Summary	Bank Intervention Process
Jeffrey sat in the back seat of car during drive to bank	During wait time at the bank, Millie gave Jeffrey three to four toys sequentially in the order of least to most preferred.
Millie pulled up to drive-through window to conduct banking transaction while Jeffrey was expected to sit appropriately in the back seat of car.	Millie intermittently interacted with Jeffrey until banking was completed.
Millie completed banking and exited bank while Jeffrey continued to sit in back seat until they arrived home	Jeffrey continued playing with the last toy during the ride home.
	Follow-up: sessions took place 6 months after the last intervention session with all intervention strategies remaining the same.

Restaurant Activity Summary

Jeffrey entered restaurant holding Millie's hand and walked with Jeffrey to booth

Millie instructed Jeffrey to sit in the booth and sat next to him.

Chris then took Millie's place in booth while she ordered food at counter.

Once Millie returned with food, she took Chris's spot in the booth and Chris sat across from Millie and Jeffrey.

Millie prepared plate of mashed potatoes and prompted Jeffrey to eat.

Millie fed Jeffrey first bite and instructed him to take spoon and feed himself.

Once everyone was finished eating, Millie stated "It's time to go."

Millie assisted Jeffrey out of booth.

Jeffrey held Millie's hand and walked through doors to the car.

Restaurant Intervention Process

After Jeffrey was seated at restaurant booth, Millie took out picture book and looked at it with Jeffrey.

Once Jeffrey was engaged, Chris took his mother's place of looking at picture book with Jeffrey; this continued until Millie returned with food.

Millie prepared a serving of mashed potatoes into an adaptive bowl brought from home and asked Jeffrey to eat.

Millie assisted hand over hand if Jeffrey did not pick up spoon to start eating.

If Jeffrey requested more food, Millie refilled his bowl and praised him for requesting.

If Jeffrey finished his meal first, he was presented with picture book and Millie looked at book with him.

When everyone finished eating, Chris cleared the table and Millie verbally cued Jeffrey that it was time to put the book away.

Millie then showed Jeffrey a picture of a preferred toy and stated, "Let's go get the toy, it's in the car."

At the car, Millie placed Jeffrey in the back seat and provided him with the toy.

Follow-up: sessions took place 6 months after the last intervention session with all intervention strategies remaining the same.

Store Activity Summary

Jeffrey entered the store holding Millie's hand.

Jeffrey was placed in grocery cart by Millie.

Millie pushed the cart down each aisle.

Millie selected four to eight food items for purchase while Jeffrey remained in cart.

After items were selected, Millie pushed the cart to checkout line and stood in line.

Millie placed items onto the counter while Jeffrey remained seated in the cart.

Millie paid bill after grocery items were totaled.

Millie removed Jeffrey from cart.

Bagged groceries were placed in the cart and store employee pushed cart through doors to car.

Millie held Jeffrey's hand walking through doors and parking lot.

Store Intervention Process

Once inside the store, Millie placed Jeffrey in shopping cart and showed Jeffrey the shopping schedule.

Millie showed first item on shopping schedule (yogurt) then pointed to picture and said, "Let's go get the yogurt."

Cart was pushed to yogurt section and Millie asked Jeffrey to help put yogurt in basket, but if he resisted, she guided him hand over hand.

At a specific location in the second aisle Jeffrey was helped out of the cart to walk for the remainder of the shopping trip.

At the same spot, Jeffrey was given an opportunity to select another item as part of the transition.

As Jeffrey walked down the aisles holding his mother's hand, he continued to be given the opportunity to select items on the shopping schedule. In between stops Millie used the schedule to remind him of next stop.

After the last item was selected, Millie showed Jeffrey the schedule, removed the picture of the item, and stated, "Jeffrey, we are done shopping now."

After walking to the checkout line, Millie offered the picture book to Jeffrey while in line.

Jeffrey looked at the picture book while Millie unloaded the groceries for checkout.

After the groceries were purchased and bagged, Millie put the picture book away and showed Jeffrey a picture of a preferred toy and stated, "Let's get the toy, it's in the car."

At the car, Millie placed Jeffrey in the back seat and handed him the toy to play with.

Follow-up: sessions took place 6 months after the last intervention session, with all intervention strategies remaining the same except that Jeffrey was no longer seated in a grocery cart but walked along side Millie for entire store routine.

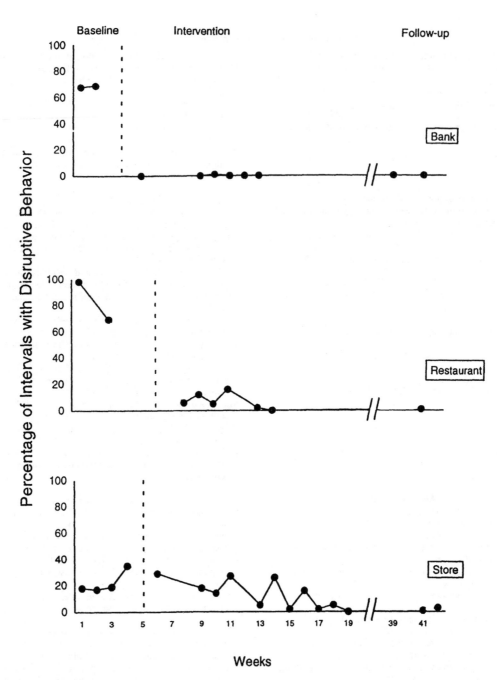

Figure 1. Intervals with disruptive behavior during all phases of the behavioral support process in each of the three community settings.

ously, the data showed substantial increases in the number of instructions related to task from baseline through intervention and follow-up. In addition, unrelated statements (e.g., "Shhh, you'll be alright") were frequent during baselines but were virtually eliminated thereafter. The frequency of praise statements that were related as opposed to unrelated to task showed a dramatic switch. Before intervention, most praise statements were not pertinent to the activity and were ap-

parent efforts to keep Jeffrey in a good mood; subsequent to intervention, the praise was related to Jeffrey's cooperative and engaged responding. Another consistent trend was the absence of reprimands after intervention was initiated.

Four parents viewed baseline and intervention videotaped segments to validate the impact of the intervention on Jeffrey's behavior, participation in the routine, and Millie's management of Jeffrey's behavior. All

Table 3
Mean Number of Instructions and Cooperative Responses per Session

	Instructions related to tasks	Cooperative responses	Percentage of instructions with cooperative responses
Bank sessions			
Baseline	2	0	0
Intervention	17	15	89
Follow-up	11	10	96
Restaurant sessions			
Baseline	17	7	53
Intervention	25	19	75
Follow-up	4	4	100
Store sessions			
Baseline	6	3	55
Intervention	24	19	82
Follow-up	23	15	64

Table 4
Percentage of Entering and Exiting Transitions Rated with Significant Problems

	Entering	Exiting	Total
Baseline			
Restaurant	50	100	75
Store	100	33	67
Intervention			
Restaurant	0	0	0
Store	13	0	7
Follow-up			
Restaurant	0	0	0
Store	0	50	25

parents rated Jeffrey's behavior and participation in the routine as being worse during baseline when compared with intervention in the bank and the restaurant. When provided with videotaped segments of the store in the reverse sequence, all parents rated Jeffrey's behavior and participation as being better in intervention when compared with the baseline. All parents felt Millie's management of Jeffrey was worse during baseline in the bank and restaurant. In the store three parents thought Millie's management of Jeffrey was better during intervention, whereas one parent believed it remained the same.

The parents were asked two other questions regarding the appropriateness and feasibility of the intervention components. All of the parents agreed or strongly agreed with the statements about the appropriateness of the strategies used to support the child and the ease with which they could be used by other parents for all intervention components (schedule indicating toy, grocery store schedule, and picture book) except for the toy. One parent disagreed with the appropriateness of using a toy. All parents agreed that the toy could be easily used by other parents. Thus, the social validity data provide further evidence that Jeffrey's behavior improved and that the components were appropriate and generally easy to use.

Discussion

The methods and results of this study can be seen as providing several contributions to the literature on community-based behavioral support for families and children affected by severe disabilities. First, the findings add an empirical demonstration to the relatively sparse database regarding the application of positive behavioral support in public community settings. Second, the procedures were conducted by a parent who was also explicitly involved in the assessment process as well as the design and evaluation of the intervention program. Third, the study presents some methodological features that diverge somewhat from typical intervention research strategies and which may represent a step toward a more widespread and vigorous documentation of effective behavioral support in common community settings. Finally, along with a set of companion data (Fox et al., 1997) this study provides multiple perspectives on the process and outcome of community-based, family-centered behavioral support.

Positive behavioral support has become a well-researched approach to problem behaviors and it is intended to provide broad lifestyle benefits for participating consumers in typical community settings and circumstances (Horner et al., 1990; Koegel et al., 1996; Meyer & Evans, 1989). However, the vast majority of relevant research has been conducted by professionals in relatively controlled settings such as classrooms and clinics. This investigation demonstrated the process of functional assessment and intervention packages that produced important reductions of problem behaviors in a large grocery store, fast food restaurant, and drive-through bank. Special analysis was devoted to problem behaviors that occurred during transitions through public doorways. The reductions in significant problem behavior in all of these circumstances contributed to meaningful differences in the family's approach to problem behaviors and community outings (Fox et al., 1997). Furthermore, the changes were documented in

Table 5
Mean Frequency of Adult Interactive Behavior

	Instructions related to task	Statements unrelated to task	Praise related to task	Praise unrelated to task	Reprimands
Bank sessions					
Baseline	2	65	0	13	8
Intervention	17	0	4	0	0
Follow-up	11	0	4	0	0
Restaurant sessions					
Baseline	17	7	1	3	0
Intervention	25	0	2.7	0	.2
Follow-up	4	0	2	0	0
Store sessions					
Baseline	6	16	1	15	1
Intervention	24	1	5.5	1.2	.1
Follow-up	23	0	6	0	0

follow-up probes to be durable and were judged by other family members to be important and feasible.

An important aspect of this research is that it was conducted in partnership with a family in order to benefit a family's ability to participate in their community. Many families who have children with serious problem behaviors experience social isolation because interventions are not designed for use in public settings or to meet the preferences and routines of the individual family (Albin et al., 1996). Throughout this research endeavor the mother, Millie, was actively and purposefully involved in every aspect of the assessment and intervention process, including the identification of the problems and settings, the assessment and hypothesis development, the formulation of appropriate intervention plans, intervention, and the selection of measures and designs. Millie contributed her perspective and her family's perspective on how each step of the research and intervention fit with the family construction (Lucyshyn et al., 1997). It is likely that this active partnership contributed to the effectiveness and durability of the program. In addition, it provides one of the few examples of participatory research in the enterprise of behavioral support (Lucyshyn et al., 1997).

The methodology that was used in this study carries some limitations and, perhaps, some implications for future empirical analyses of behavioral support in natural contexts. This research was designed to demonstrate and evaluate a behavioral support process in three public settings, as well as describe the process from multiple perspectives (Fox et al., 1997). The interventions were packages that included various assessment-based components that were incorporated because they were expected to be effective and because they were compatible with characteristics of the participants and ecology. Because the interventions were individually constructed packages, we cannot determine the specific impact of any single component. Indeed, the independent variable in this type of research (e.g., Dunlap, Kern-Dunlap, Clarke, & Robbins, 1991; Kern, Childs, Dun-

lap, Clarke, & Falk, 1994; Umbreit, 1995) is probably described best as a process of functional assessment and assessment-based intervention.

A question may be raised about the ecological validity of the demonstration because of the presence of two additional persons and a videocamera. Typically, however, these individuals did not interact with Millie or Jeffrey during sessions, except for the initial intervention sessions during which the first author provided coaching. The other person did not interact and always attempted to be as inconspicuous as possible with the hand-held camera. Still, these individuals were available to provide backup assistance if Jeffrey displayed dangerous or excessively disruptive behavior. Such precautions were part of Millie's routine. Because of the long history of severe disruptions, Millie typically brought assistance (e.g., Jeffrey's brother, Chris) when she and Jeffrey engaged in community errands.

It is important to note that the design of this study was quasiexperimental (Campbell & Stanley, 1963). Although we considered using a multiple baseline across settings design (Hersen & Barlow, 1976; Kazdin, 1982), we determined that such a design in this case would control for minimal threats to internal validity. Furthermore, we were concerned that the imposition of ongoing baselines in some settings after demonstrable improvements in others would have altered the natural implementation of the multicomponent intervention. Although a multiple baseline could have been engineered, a choice was made in this circumstance to proceed with the approach that would yield the more natural demonstration and still provide empirical evidence of effectiveness. It may be argued that the quasiexperimental approach that we adopted can still render confidence in the internal validity of the demonstration, especially given the long history of Jeffrey's behavior problems in the three targeted settings (Kazdin, 1982).

The challenges involved in the use of traditional experimental designs in natural contexts, although surmountable, may be substantial enough to dissuade applied researchers from working in contexts that are the most meaningful from the perspective of community participation and lifestyle significance. Within-case experimental designs are well suited to the precise delineation of functional variables but it is possible that they are not the most appropriate vehicle for demonstrating or analyzing community interventions, at least in some situations. It may behoove professionals in this field to encourage additional approaches to community-based research by placing an emphasis on case study analyses and a focus on social validity, ecological fit of the design and intervention, generalization and maintenance, and the use of multiple measures and methodologies.

To promote the value of behavioral support practices for families, research must continue to investigate the use of assessment and intervention procedures in those circumstances that are identified by families as the most distressing or consequential. Researchers must examine behavioral support with families from diverse backgrounds and cultural and economic circumstances, and researchers should initiate procedures that will be optimal for learning about priorities and experiences directly from families. Within the context of this investigation we conducted a qualitative inquiry of the family's perceptions and experiences as they proceeded through the process of behavioral support. As we report in a companion article (Fox et al., 1997), the qualitative methods of data collection yielded various conceptual themes, all of which should inform and guide our future efforts to develop optimal support programs.

References

Albin, R. W., Lucyshyn, J. M., Horner, R. H., & Flannery, K. B. (1996). Contextual fit for behavioral support plans: A model for "goodness of fit." In L. K. Koegel, R. L. Koegel, & G. Dunlap (Eds.), *Positive behavioral support: Including people with difficult behavior in the community* (pp. 81–98). Baltimore: Paul H. Brookes.

Campbell, D. T., & Stanley, J. C. (1963). *Experimental and quasiexperimental designs for research.* Chicago: Rand McNally College Publishing Company.

Carr, E. G., & Carlson, J. I. (1993). Reduction of severe behavior problems in the community using a multicomponent treatment approach. *Journal of Applied Behavior Analysis, 26,* 157–172.

Carr, E. G., Levin, L., McConnachie, G., Carlson, J. I., Kemp, D. C., & Smith, C. E. (1994). *Communication-based intervention for problem behavior: A user's guide for producing positive change.* Baltimore: Paul H. Brookes.

Dunlap, G., & Fox, L. (1996). Early intervention and serious problem behaviors: A comprehensive approach. In L. K. Koegel, R. L. Koegel, & G. Dunlap (Eds.), *Positive Behavioral Support* (pp. 31–50). Baltimore: Paul H. Brookes.

Dunlap, G., & Kern, L. (1993). Assessment and intervention for children within the instructional curriculum. In J. Reichle & D. Wacker (Eds.), *Communicative approaches to the management of challenging behavior* (pp. 177–203). Baltimore: Paul H. Brookes.

Dunlap, G., Kern-Dunlap, L., Clarke, S., & Robbins, F. R. (1991). Functional assessment, curriculum revision, and severe behavior problems. *Journal of Applied Behavior Analysis, 24,* 387–397.

Dunlap, G., Vaughn, B. J., Fox, L., & Foster-Johnson, L. (1996). Developing and evaluating family networks in positive behavioral support (Field-Initiated Research grant H133G60119). Washington, DC: U.S. Department of Education, National Institute on Disability and Rehabilitation Research.

Eno-Heineman, M., & Dunlap, G. (in press). Some issues and challenges in implementing community-based behavioral support: Two illustrative case studies. In J. R. Scotti & L. H. Meyer (Eds.), *New directions for behavioral intervention: Principles, models, and practices.* Baltimore: Paul H. Brookes.

Fox, L., Vaughn, B. J., Dunlap, G., & Bucy, M. (1997). *Parent-professional partnership in behavioral support: A qualitative analysis of one family's experience.* Manuscript submitted for publication.

Hersen, M., & Barlow, D. H. (1976). *Single-case experimental designs: Strategies for studying behavior change.* New York: Pergamon Press.

Horner, R. H., Dunlap, G., Koegel, R. L., Carr, E. G., Sailor, W., Anderson, J., Albin, R. W., & O'Neill, R. E. (1990). Toward a technology of "nonaversive" behavioral support. *The Journal of The Association for Persons with Severe Handicaps, 15,* 125–132.

Horner, R. H., Sprague, J. R., & Flannery, K. B. (1993). Building functional curricula for students with severe intellectual disabilities and severe problem behaviors. In R. VanHouten, & S. Axelrod (Eds.), *Behavior analysis and treatment* (pp. 47–71). New York: Plenum.

Kazdin, A. E. (1982). *Single case research designs.* New York: Oxford University Press.

Kemp, D. C., & Carr, E. G. (1995). Reduction of severe problem behavior in community employment using an hypothesis-driven multicomponent intervention approach. *The Journal of The Association for Persons with Severe Handicaps, 20,* 229–247.

Kern, L., Childs, K. E., Dunlap, G., Clarke, S., & Falk, G. D. (1994). Using assessment-based curricular intervention to improve the classroom behavior of a student with emotional and behavioral challenges. *Journal of Applied Behavior Analysis, 27,* 7–19.

Koegel, L. K., Koegel, R. L., & Dunlap, G. (1996). *Positive behavioral support: Including people with difficult behavior in the community.* Baltimore: Paul H. Brookes.

Lucyshyn, J. M., Albin, R. W., & Nixon, C. D. (1997). Embedding comprehensive behavioral support in family ecology: An experimental, single-case analysis. *Journal of Counseling and Clinical Psychology, 65,* 241–251.

Meyer, L. H., & Evans, I. M. (1989). *Nonaversive intervention for behavior problems: A manual for home and community.* Baltimore: Paul H. Brookes.

O'Neill, R. E., Horner, R. H., Albin, R. W., Storey, K., & Sprague, J. R. (1990). *Functional analysis of problem behavior: A practical assessment guide.* Pacific Grove, CA: Brooks/Cole Publishing.

O'Neill, R. E., Dunlap, G., & Vaughn, B. (1998). Comprehensive behavioral support: Assessment issues and strategies. In A. M. Wetherby, S. F. Warren, & J. Reichle (Eds.), *Transitions in prelinguistic communication: Preintentional to intentional and presymbolic to symbolic.* (pp. 313–341). Baltimore: Paul H. Brookes.

Powell, T. H., Hecimovic, A., & Christensen, L. (1993). Meeting the unique needs of families. In D. E. Berkell (Ed.), *Autism: Identification, education and treatment* (pp. 187–224). Hillsdale, NJ: Lawrence Earlbaum Associates.

Repp, A. C., Harman, M. L., Felce, D., VanAcker, R., & Karsh, K. L. (1987). *A real time, parallel entry portable com-*

puter system for observational research. Unpublished manuscript. DeKalb, IL: Northern Illinois University.

Turnbull, A. P., Friesen, B. J., & Ramirez, C. (1996). *Participatory action research: Forging collaborative partnerships with families in the study of disability.* Manuscript submitted for publication.

Turnbull, A. P., & Turnbull, H. R., III. (1990). *Families, professionals, and exceptionality: A special partnership.* New York: Merrill.

Turnbull, A. P., & Turnbull, H. R., III. (1993). Participatory research on cognitive coping from concepts to research planning. In A. P. Turnbull, J. M. Patterson, S. K. Behr, D. L. Murphy, J. G. Marquis, & M. J. Blue-Banning (Eds.), *Cognitive coping, families, and disability* (pp. 1–14). Baltimore: Paul H. Brookes.

Umbreit, J. (1995). Functional assessment and intervention in a regular classroom setting for the disruptive behavior of a student with attention deficit hyperactivity disorder. *Behavioral Disorders, 20,* 267–278.

Whyte, W. F. (Ed.) (1991). *Participatory action research.* Newbury Park, CA: Sage Publications.

Received: October 26, 1996
Final Acceptance: October 10, 1997
Editor in Charge: Lori Goetz

JASH
1997, Vol. 22, No. 4, 198–207

Parent-Professional Partnership in Behavioral Support: A Qualitative Analysis of One Family's Experience

Lise Fox, Bobbie J. Vaughn, Glen Dunlap, and Millie Bucy
University of South Florida

Behavioral support with families is a multifaceted endeavor that should be studied from the various perspectives that affect its feasibility, efficacy, and potential to produce outcomes that are durable and meaningful to people's lives. This study describes a qualitative analysis of one family's experience during a 10-month process of assessment and intervention for the behavioral challenges of a boy with multiple and severe disabilities. Data collection included an audiojournal recorded by the boy's mother and a series of semistructured interviews with both parents and the boy's older brother. The data were synthesized to chronicle the impressions of the family relating to the phases of the positive behavioral support process. The data yielded two pervasive themes that describe the impact of the problem behavior on the family and the effects of the behavioral support process on the child and his family. Together, with a companion article that presents the procedures and quantitative analyses (Vaughn et al., 1997), the methods and findings from this study offer a broader view of behavioral support than has been evident in the literature thus far. The findings are presented as a heuristic for researchers to engage in participatory investigations that can illuminate important features of support processes with the intention of increasing responsiveness to consumers (e.g., families) and enhancing the benefits of community-based support efforts.

DESCRIPTORS: behavior modification, ecology, families, measurement, parent-professional relations

In the past decade there has been an important shift in how professionals view the role of the family in the development of intervention and support programs for individuals with disabilities. Researchers, policy makers, educators, and other support providers have recognized that the family is central to the well-being of the individual with disabilities and that support providers must consider family support within their programs.

Adress correspondence and requests for reprints to Glen Dunlap, Department of Child and Family Studies, Louis de la Parte Florida Mental Health Institute, University of South Florida, 13301 Bruce B. Downs Boulevard, Tampa, FL 33612.

The emphasis within the field of developmental disabilities on family support is part of a larger national and international family support movement (Dunst & Trivette, 1994; Singer & Powers, 1993; Weissbourd & Kagan, 1989). This movement is aimed at strengthening the capacity of adults as parents, nurturers, and providers in early intervention, health care, mental health, and child welfare (Singer & Powers, 1993). The family support perspective moves beyond an emphasis on parent involvement and collaboration in securing and developing education and support programs, to a focus on the importance of developing interventions driven by family needs that assist families in strengthening their capacities and mobilizing family resources (Turnbull & Ruef, 1996). One salient area in which effective intervention and support are needed by families involves the occurrence of challenging behaviors.

Positive behavioral support is the application of a comprehensive set of procedures and strategies aimed at providing the individual with problem behavior with an improved lifestyle that includes a reduction of problem behavior, changes in social relationships, an expansion of skills, and an increase in community inclusion (Horner et al., 1990; Koegel, Koegel, & Dunlap, 1996; Meyer & Evans, 1989). A foundational tenet of the positive behavioral support process is that one must understand the individual within an ecological context and aim the intervention at influencing the ecology of the individual with problem behavior (Anderson, Albin, Mesaros, Dunlap, & Morelli-Robbins, 1993; Dunlap & Fox, 1996). Important advances have been made in the practice of positive behavioral support and there is a growing body of research that provides testimony to the power and effectiveness of this approach (Koegel, et al., 1996). Despite these advances and the ecological perspective, little of the research has been conducted within the family context and in a manner that fully reflects family-centered perspectives.

There are several reasons why researchers who are interested in meaningful and optimally effective behavioral support within the family contexts should focus their attention on issues relating to the family. First, the family has a singular expertise regarding the behavior of their family members and the ecologies in which their family interacts (Dunlap & Fox, 1996; Turnbull and Summers, 1987). Second, only the family can judge the fit between a support option and the family values that may be an important contributor to both the usefulness and maintenance of an intervention (Albin, Lucyshyn, Horner, & Flannery, 1996). Third, the family is the most important and often the sole source of information regarding the effects of an intervention and its impact on the child and the family system. Finally, the family may search for a provider of positive behavioral support when they are in crisis and struggling with their child's problem behavior (The Family Connection Staff, DiVault, Krug, & Fake, 1996). Thus, it is particularly important to develop behavioral support partnerships with families who are focused on building the family's capacity to support their child with minimal reliance on an expert.

We believe that it is vital to gain an enhanced understanding of the positive behavioral support process with families by incorporating and studying multiple perspectives through a research partnership where the family participates actively with the researcher(s) from the initial design of a study through to the presentation of results and discussion of the implications (Turnbull, Friesen, & Ramirez, 1996; Turnbull & Ruef, 1996; Turnbull & Turnbull, 1990). Conducting research in partnership with families offers an opportunity for both the researcher and the family to engage in a problem-solving process that can lead to more relevant questions, more acceptable interventions, and results that are interpreted with meaning and application to relevant contexts (Graves, 1991; Turnbull & Ruef, 1996; Turnbull & Turnbull, 1993).

We believe that there is a gap in our knowledge about the application of positive behavioral support within the family. Thus far, it has been primarily the knowledge and values of the researcher that have driven research efforts. The knowledge and values of the family or other participants are rarely examined or included, although there have been recent efforts at promoting the importance of this perspective (Albin et al., 1996; Dunlap, Robbins, & Darrow, 1994; Lucyshyn, Albin, & Nixon, 1997; Turnbull & Ruef, 1996). The research described in this study was conducted because we believe that the process can increase an understanding of the impact of positive behavioral support on the family and result in the development of strategies that will be optimally supportive of the individual with disability within the family and community system.

The specific purpose of this study is to describe the use of qualitative methods that chronicled the impressions and reflections of one family as they experienced the process of positive behavioral support. The procedures and quantitative analyses of this process, representing a complementary perspective, are detailed in a companion article (Vaughn, Dunlap, Fox, Clarke, & Bucy, 1997). These impressions and reflections of the family were captured through the use of interviews and an audiojournal that was recorded by the mother. This study offers a description of the family's experiences during the process of positive behavioral support and a description of two themes that pervaded the impressions and experiences of the family. The overriding goal of this study is to offer an initial effort toward understanding the process of positive behavioral support from a family perspective (Dunlap, Vaughn, Fox, & Foster-Johnson, 1996; Albin et al., 1996). In presenting the voices of one family we have not made the assumption that they represent all families. Rather, we want to initiate a dialogue within our field about family perspectives on positive behavioral support and provide the interpretation of those experiences as a mechanism to begin this important endeavor.

Method

Participants and Context

Millie, the mother of a 9-year-old boy with Cornelia DeLange Syndrome, participated in this research project to provide an insider's perspective on the process of positive behavioral support with families. As a parent consultant for an early intervention project, whose primary emphasis was working with families of children with problem behavior, she approached us seeking help for her son Jeffrey's disruptive behavior. Jeffrey frequently engaged in self-injurious and aggressive behavior including screaming, hitting, biting, head banging, scratching, and pinching. Millie described his problem behavior as an issue for the family since Jeffrey was 2.5 years old. In the last several years his behavior had become so problematic that the family was unable to participate in social and domestic activities in the community. Jeffrey was enrolled in a special education class for students with moderate and severe disabilities in an elementary school. He was a nonverbal child who communicated through the use of vocalizations and gestures. Jeffrey's problem behavior made even the simplest of community outings difficult, if not impossible. As a result, the family had abandoned many typical family outings and avoided taking Jeffrey on routine community outings by trying to accomplish these while he was in school or when someone could stay home with Jeffrey.

With the dire family situation as a starting point, we formed a collaborative team that included Millie. Through weekly meetings over a 10-month period, the team designed the framework, assessment and measurement process, research procedures, and intervention components. Millie requested that the intervention focus on changing Jeffrey's problem behavior at the drive-through bank, restaurant, and grocery store. These were settings the family frequented and where Jeffrey had extreme difficulties. Millie conducted all sessions of her son's intervention, kept an audiojournal of her experiences with the project, and provided additional perspectives of the positive behavioral support process through interviews.

Jeffrey's father, Bob, worked as a self-employed truck driver and traveled extensively during the week and often on the weekends. He had limited involvement in the support process but offered his perceptions of changes in Jeffrey and their family life through interviews. Chris, Jeffrey's 11-year-old brother, offered his perspective through interviews and actively participated in supporting Jeffrey in one of the three settings.

Data Collection

The qualitative measurement occurred over a 10-month period (November-August) by the first two authors and Millie, Jeffrey's mother. This process of data collection coincided with the research phases in the quantitative companion article by Vaughn et al. (1997). The specific measurement procedures included semistructured interviews and an audiojournal. The first two authors conducted five of the six semistructured interviews with Millie, Bob, and Chris. Millie conducted the final interview with her husband, Bob. All of the interviews were audiotaped and transcribed for later review and analysis.

Initial interviews with family members were scheduled before intervention and second interviews were conducted at the end of the intervention phase. Interview length varied from 30 to 90 min. In general, the semistructured questions asked about the experience of raising a child with developmental disabilities, family experiences and perceptions of participating in positive behavioral support, the effects of Jeffrey's problem behavior on the family in various settings and situations, and how problem behavior was seen to affect Jeffrey's future and the future of the family. Initial interviews with family members focused primarily on what the family's life was like before and at the time of the study and how it felt to begin the process of positive behavioral support. The second interviews centered on family perceptions of positive behavioral support and its effect on Jeffrey's behavior and the family members, how the support process felt from beginning to the end of intervention, and how positive behavioral support changed their lifestyle.

Millie maintained an audiojournal where she recorded her feelings and perceptions of the support process and subsequent changes in Jeffrey's behavior and family functioning. The taped journal contained approximately 8 hr of journal entries over the course of the project. Every 2 months the tapes were gathered from Millie and transcribed for coding purposes.

Data Interpretation/Analysis

All interviews and audiojournal entries were transcribed and coded as the study proceeded. An open coding approach to data analysis determined the major coding categories and axial coding served to organize and merge those categories, thereby creating logical connections (Strauss & Corbin, 1990). As a part of this analysis, questions were asked of the data regarding the properties of the categories, how events occurred along a continuum how events changed over time, and what events intervened to inhibit or promote a situation (Strauss & Corbin, 1990). Through an inductive process, conditions and phenomenon were connected in a sequential and relational fashion to arrive at a final analysis.

The first and second authors initially coded all transcriptions independently as they occurred, beginning with the first journal entry by Millie (November–December) and the initial interviews with the family members. Each author established, through the use of the analysis structure discussed above, preliminary relational coding categories across all initial data sets. At each coding session the authors then discussed and merged the preliminary categories to arrive at an agreed on array of coding categories. Memos were written with features of these categories and substantiating quotes. These were shared with Millie and other members of the research team. As coding proceeded, the constant comparative method (Strauss & Corbin, 1990) was used to develop new subcategories and merge existing categories. Sequential coding occurred as a means of establishing family experiences and perspectives along the continuum of the positive behavioral support process. The analysis occurred by extracting from the relational categories data representative of the unfolding process with Millie and her family.

Methodological Credibility

Credibility was established through several methods (Lincoln & Guba, 1985; Miles & Huberman, 1994). First, there was prolonged engagement (approximately 10 months) with the family within their home and community that promoted the development of trust and intimacy. For instance, the second author visited weekly for 2 months (November–December) with Millie, Jeffrey, and other family members, thereby establishing rapport and trust. The visits included lengthy discussions with Millie about her thoughts on Jeffrey's problems and capacities and the strengths and needs of the family. The prolonged engagement also provided opportunities to detect distortions in perceptions both on the part of the researchers and the family.

A second method of establishing credibility occurred with member checks, a method of confirming data analysis with the original sources (Lincoln & Guba, 1985; Miles & Huberman, 1994). As the data analysis progressed, the authors were periodically summarizing the data through research memos and offering Millie the opportunity to respond to the accuracy of the data and whether quotes depicting the coding category matched the descriptions. At each juncture, Millie agreed and provided feedback as to the accuracy of the data interpretation.

The third confirmation of credibility occurred with the use of triangulation (Denzin, 1978; Huberman & Miles, 1994; Janesick, 1994). Denzin (1978) and Janesick (1994) suggest the use of several types of triangulation such as multiple and different sources, methods, investigators, and theories. The interviews with family members other than Millie offered different data sources. Although Chris and Bob participated in less active roles in the intervention and research development, they offered perspectives that supported Millie's perceptions of life with Jeffrey before and during the project. The gathering of the family's perspective through interviews and Millie's audiojournal entries generated different methods of data collection. The data were analyzed independently by the first two authors with identical sets of transcriptions. The applications of the coding categories were shared with other team members to ensure accurate application of the codes, the refinement of category descriptions, inclusion of new categories or development subcategories, and the development of similar themes throughout the analysis. In addition, the investigators were informed and influenced by their active participation in the implementation of the behavioral support process and the collection of quantitative data (Vaughn et al., 1997).

Findings

The findings presented in this section are gleaned from Millie's audiojournal and the family interviews. These findings provide a chronicle of events, family reactions, and reflections during the process of positive behavioral support and are presented in this study as they occurred over time. In addition to providing insight about reactions to the phases of the support process, Millie's audiojournal and the interviews with family members provided reflections that clustered within two themes revealed through the data analysis process.

Support Process

Positive behavioral support includes at least two phases. The first phase, functional assessment, is focused on gaining an understanding of the behavior. In the second phase, interventions and supports are applied and outcomes are monitored. The process used in this study, as depicted in Table 1, also included a relationship development phase in which the interventionist developed an understanding of the family structure, routines, needs, and capacities. During the functional assessment phase, observational and interview assessments were used to determine the hypotheses of problem behavior, and a personal futures planning process (Mount & Zwernick, 1988) was used to develop an understanding of the participants' lifestyle, capacities, and needs. The last phase, behavioral support, included the

Table 1
Process of Collaborative Behavioral Support

Relationship development with family
   Develop an understanding of family structure
   Develop an understanding of family routines
   Identification of family capacities and needs
Functional assessment of problem behavior
   Observation and assessment of child's capacities, preferences, and routines
   Observation of problem behavior
   Interview with caregivers
   Person-centered planning
   Collaborative identification of target settings, routines, and problem behavior
   Hypotheses development
   Collaborative development of support components
   Validation of support components
   Baseline observations of behavior in routines
Behavioral support
   Collaborative development of support strategies
   Coaching of caregiver in target settings
   Implementation of support plan
   Person-centered planning to expand use of support strategies
   Maintenance of support strategies

development of support strategies, coaching the parent in the use of the support strategies, and the use of strategies in community settings.

Relationship development with the family. The initial activities of the support process were focused on developing an understanding of Jeffrey and the family. The second author spent many hours with the family watching family routines, going in the community with the family, and building rapport with Jeffrey and his brother. Millie also attended several meetings at the university to discuss the launching of the positive behavioral support process.

Millie began her audiojournal entries as the project began. Her initial entries moved quickly from expressing excitement about the prospect of family support and solutions for the problem behavior to discussing the difficulties the problem behavior presented and its impact on the family. She described her family's interest in trying to resolve Jeffrey's problem behavior and meeting family needs in the following statement: ". . . we are all pretty tired of the scratching and biting and not being able to successfully take Jeffrey to places that we would normally go."

Millie described the impact of Jeffrey's problem behavior on others by stating ". . . it scares them. People don't like to be scratched. They don't like to be bitten. And I can understand that. I don't like it either. And we had sort of gotten to the point that this was the way life was, but it was getting old real fast." Millie described Jeffrey's behavior as whining, yelling, scratching, biting others, biting himself, banging his head, kicking, and sleep difficulties. She indicated that during a particular incident she perceived the behavior as an attempt of Jeffrey's to communicate as she stated in her journal

"... scratching, kicking, biting, and whining and any other thing he could think of to get his point across that he didn't like it there."

As the interventionist began building a relationship with the family and probed more deeply into understanding Jeffrey's problem behavior, the family began to express emotions that had been hidden. Millie described how Jeffrey's brother had expressed his frustration and anger at the problem behavior and the difficulties that were faced as a consequence. She described this expression of emotion by Jeffrey's brother in her journal: "... he really started telling me how he was very disturbed at Jeffrey's behavior and he was really tired of it and really wished we could just fix him somehow." Millie also shared that beginning the process of positive behavioral support caused her to reflect on her own anger about Jeffrey's disability and her perception that they could not be a normal family. She stated in her journal, "I thought, I don't like this. This is not fair. I don't know why we can't be a normal typical family. I'm really tired of dealing with this. And all of these ugly emotions started coming out and it kind of surprised me."

Functional assessment of the problem behavior. The functional assessment process involved observing Jeffrey within the intervention settings selected by the family (i.e., the bank, restaurant, and grocery store) to determine the antecedents, consequences, and functions of the problem behavior. In addition, the interventionist spent time with Jeffrey within community settings and at home to assess his capacities and interests. During this period, Millie's journal reflections indicated that she was also engaged in thinking more deeply about Jeffrey's problem behavior and its impact on the family.

The family had developed many unique strategies for accommodating Jeffrey's problem behavior. For example, the family went into the community when they were sure that the location would not be crowded or sang to him throughout a shopping trip to keep him entertained and distracted. Millie described singing to Jeffrey in her journal:

... on this particular visit he did pretty well going in but then immediately got really upset when he realized he'd gotten through those doors without stopping to look at them. And he began his little whining, yelling noise that he does and also trying to bite me, bite himself, and scratch me. We managed to get through the store by my singing to him "Old MacDonald" throughout the trip.

When the interventionist began spending time with the family, Millie was very concerned that Jeffrey engage in the problem behavior so that the interventionist witnessed the behavior and validate her involvement in Jeffrey's intervention. She reflected on her anxiety

about wanting the interventionist to witness his problem behavior in her journal by stating:

I found myself thinking, oh no, she's going to think maybe I exaggerated this, you know, he's being too good. Maybe she feels like I wasted her time and yes, I know, this is not what she is thinking, but the parent side of me.... This attitude, I think, has been cultivated over many years in dealing with medical professionals ... you need to go in and get business done and don't waste our time.

During this phase, Christmas and Jeffrey's birthday occurred. These were events that caused Millie to feel angry and sad. She reflected on a holiday gathering with relatives where she felt as if they viewed her with pity and described her anger at them because "I don't want to be pitied because I have this child with a disability." When Jeffrey's birthday occurred, she reflected on how this birthday brings her back to his difficult beginnings and how she was "plunged into the disability world."

In the functional assessment phase of the support process, the interventionist tried new strategies and assessed Jeffrey's strengths. Millie was excited to see that the interventionist had a good rapport with Jeffrey and could tap his abilities. She stated that "... he seemed to connect right away.... I think part of it was that you had a way to let him know that you understood him and gave him ... a means of relating to you."

A person-centered planning meeting was held to bring together family members and Jeffrey's teacher to develop a vision for Jeffrey and establish a shared commitment to supporting Jeffrey in achieving that vision. The personal futures plan meeting was attended by Jeffrey's paternal grandparents, his brother, and his teacher. Millie was pleased with the results of the meeting and how the process brought together the family and the teacher to work on the same vision. She was especially pleased that Chris contributed to the meeting and she expressed surprise at Chris's insight when he stated that Jeffrey didn't have any peer friends and that a goal should be to help him have more friends and do more fun activities. Bob was unable to attend the meeting and Millie reflected in her journal that they had discussed his regret about not attending especially when Bob's parents were "... bubbling over with what had happened and how it was different from anything else they had attended."

An interview was conducted with Bob and Chris before the implementation of the intervention. It was interesting to hear Millie's husband reflect on many of the same issues that Millie had been discussing in her audiojournal. Bob described the family's frustration at not finding support in the community and the impact of the problem behavior on the family. He also discussed how the roles were divided in their family with Millie providing the children's day-to-day care and support and he worrying about finances. He described how he tries to help Millie when he can by offering this example: "Sometimes I'll go in and sleep with him so that she can at least get one full night's sleep." Bob also expressed his worries about Jeffrey's problem behavior and his frustrations with Jeffrey's persistent aggression. He told the interviewer:

I come home and see Millie with battle scars, I say "you know we gotta do something," we bought some gloves . . . and I said "you know you either have to put these gloves on him . . . I can't come home and see you with scratches all up and down your arms and on your face and everything else."

Bob described himself as eager to learn strategies that may work with Jeffrey, he shared with the interviewer that ". . . you know I have a lot of time to think about things, I rack my brains for doing things that will help protect him." Bob summarized the impact Jeffrey has on the family in this statement, "Well on a good day, you know it's real good. You know when Jeffrey feels good, you know it makes life a lot easier on the family."

Chris, Jeffrey's brother, was not a talkative child in general and was reticent (in a typical preadolescent manner) in his interview. He did share that he found Jeffrey's behavior annoying and that he would like it better if family members did not have to sing to Jeffrey at the grocery store or if he could sit in a restaurant. When asked about what would be good for Jeffrey to learn, Chris identified that Jeffrey needed a better way to communicate, to "eat better," and be able to go more places.

The assessment phase moved slowly and Millie became anxious for the intervention to begin. Millie "dreaded" the baseline period where Jeffrey would go through his community routines without support. His problem behaviors were so extreme that Millie did not want to have to expose Jeffrey to the public or the public to him unless necessary.

Behavioral support. Through the functional assessment process, it was determined that Jeffrey was engaging in problem behavior at the bank, restaurant, and grocery store for specific reasons (Vaughn et al., 1997). An intervention plan was developed to assist Jeffrey in completing the community routines without problem behavior, which included the use of specific strategies and procedures by Millie. Millie was taught to offer Jeffrey a toy to play with as he waited at the bank. In the restaurant, Millie used a picture of a desired toy to prompt Jeffrey to move through the doors so that he could play with the toy in the car after exiting. She also gave Jeffrey a picture book of favorite photographs to look at while he waited for his food. In the grocery store, Millie was taught to use the picture book and toy strategies in addition to providing Jeffrey with a picture schedule and shopping list to support his participation in the shopping routine.

When Millie began using the support strategies she initially felt awkward, but quickly became more fluent and proficient in their use. Millie was delighted to see that the strategies would work and that in addition to not having problem behavior Jeffrey was smiling, laughing, and enjoying himself. She described the changes in Jeffrey as "wonderful", "remarkable", and "dramatic". She stated that "the more he goes, the better it gets." There were a few occasions where the power of the strategies was tested and Millie expressed her surprise that Jeffrey could cope with a situation that in the past would have evoked problem behavior. Millie describes Jeffrey's behavior during a restaurant trip in her journal: "Jeffrey wasn't hungry, so he didn't want to eat too much. He just ate a few bites and just couldn't really get him interested in that. But, he sat at the table appropriately, sat quietly, waited for Chris to finish eating and we had no problems."

Millie continued her audiojournal during this phase and one interview was conducted with her at the time intervention began. In her journal, Millie reflected on how important it was that she understood the process because it had altered her life to a great extent. Although she stated that the intervention had been designed in a way to "fit" with her family, it was also an imposition into her daily routines and family life. For example, she said in her interview: "There might be a day that you just think, oh I would just as soon not do this . . . I would just as soon chill out for the afternoon." As intervention progressed, Millie's journal provided a barometer of Jeffrey's successes and difficulties and the family's reactions to those events. When Jeffrey had appropriate behavior and was able to participate in a community routine, all was well with the world. When Jeffrey had difficulty, Millie felt worried and depressed.

Millie came to view the interventionist as a source of social support for herself and Jeffrey. She noted that Jeffrey looked forward to the arrival of the interventionist and she worried that when the intervention ended that he would miss seeing these new people in his life. Over time, Jeffrey became quite proficient in his ability to participate and cope with the routines. But Millie still entered situations with a measure of apprehension as she described in this journal entry, ". . . . we decided to stop in the grocery store on the way home because it would be very convenient for us . . . so I thought that this is going to be the test. It was amazing how well he did."

The process of positive behavioral support resulted in important changes for Jeffrey and his family. Millie reflected in her journal that "I'm seeing differences every day in Jeffrey, little things that he is learning to do. This has just had a powerful impact on him and on us too." During the course of the support process, Millie had many reflections in her journal that indicated she was viewing her son in a new perspective. She became aware of Jeffrey's capacities to communicate and understand others that was not evident before intervention.

The outcomes of the positive behavioral support process extended far beyond the reduction of problem behavior. The family was very excited to see Jeffrey handle community routines that were in the past a disaster for him. Moreover, they were most excited about Jeffrey's generalized use of new skills and their feeling that he could be part of the community and build new social relationships.

Another person-centered planning was held in the home with the immediate and extended family members and Jeffrey's teacher to explain how positive behavioral support was used to assist Jeffrey in the community and to enlist family support in thinking about additional ways to support Jeffrey. Millie expressed her apprehension about describing the importance of positive behavioral support to her extended family members in the meeting in her journal: "I have a little fear inside that when they see what this really means, that they are going to think 'Gosh, I don't know if I can do this.'" Millie was pleased that the meeting went very well as she stated, "It was nice to see how family members just clicked right in and were offering good suggestions and really understood it much better than I gave them credit for."

The monitoring of Jeffrey's progress in community settings ended with the expectation that the intervention would continue. Millie continued her journal and offered her reflections as she continued to implement the intervention stategies. It was unfortunate that the end of the project activities occurred simultaneously with the end of summer school for Jeffrey. Millie felt this loss of social support and talked about feeling depressed at this very difficult time of year with the demands of child care and work.

In September, 2 months after the last community trip monitored by the project, Millie reflected back on the process of the study. She remembered that the pace of the project was hectic and that it was frustrating to try to complete all of the activities and stay on schedule. Yet she felt like it was a good experience for Jeffrey and the family. She was pleased that Jeffrey continued to be successful in the community and commented on how amazed his father was at Jeffrey's behavior during an impromptu trip to the grocery store. Millie described his continued use of the picture schedule: "Even if you don't do it again for a month, he still has it and remembers and he can generalize things. It just reinforces my feeling that I knew he had a lot more inside than he could ever show people."

Millie noted that Jeffrey was more communicative and seemed to be more confident in his interactions with other people. She was pleased that people in the grocery store recognized him and greeted him and stated that he is more able to connect with peers. She described the impact of the project on Jeffrey's inclusion in her statement, "I could tell that they recognized him and said 'Hi' to him . . . I think that helps me and hopefully helps him to feel like he's part of the community and that was one of our major goals."

Final interviews were conducted with each family member to glean their reflections about the process and Jeffrey's growth. Millie's comments reflected much of what she had discussed in her audiojournal as she described the impact of the project on Jeffrey and the family. Jeffrey's father noted that Jeffrey had "definitely improved in his communication, he seems to be understanding a lot more, as far as communicating with him." Jeffrey's brother described the picture schedule as helping Jeffrey see what he was doing. He said that Jeffrey was better in the restaurant and that it was good for the family because "then we could eat and not worry about these things with his yelling and stuff."

Themes

These data fall into two pervasive themes, as highlighted by this chronicle of a family's experience with positive behavioral support. The first theme was the impact of the problem behavior on the family that we titled "*You End Up Jumping Through Hoops,*" a quotation from Millie that summarized her family's perspective. The second theme, "*A Powerful Impact,*" described the impact of positive behavioral support on Jeffrey and his family. A summary of the data supporting each of those themes is described in the following sections.

You end up jumping through hoops. Jeffrey's problem behavior effected the family in a dramatic and pervasive manner. In the family interviews and Millie's audiojournal there were many vivid descriptions of the intensity of the problem behavior and the social, emotional, and physical impact of those behaviors on the family and their lifestyle. Millie described the behaviors as being mostly self-injurious when he was young and becoming mostly aggressive as he became older. Bob described Millie as having "battle scars" from her interactions with Jeffrey. Chris discussed how he was awakened in the night when Jeffrey screamed or banged his head on the adjoining bedroom wall.

Millie described the family's accommodation to the problem behavior by saying, "So you end up jumping through hoops to try to get it to stop and even when it doesn't work, you still do it." In essence, the family had developed survival strategies (i.e., jumping through hoops) that ranged from singing to him in the grocery store to taking turns sleeping with him. Each family member described their role in accommodating Jeffrey and minimizing the impact of the problem behavior. Bob described the way Jeffrey's problem behavior impacted on the climate of the family by stating that ". . . on a good day, you know it's real good. You know when Jeffrey feels good, you know it makes life easier on the whole family."

The problem behavior also resulted in the social isolation of Jeffrey and his family as Millie stated, "... any place in public is pretty hard for him and pretty hard for our family, so we tend to either leave him at home or avoid these places." This family described living a life that was often dominated by their fears of the problem behavior and worries about Jeffrey's future. Millie reflected in her journal "... the biggest fear for me is what's going to happen because I've been his window on the world since he's been born. I've been his facilitator, his guardian angel, and everything rolled into one." The problem behavior affected family roles, relationships, and lifestyle as family members did all they could to try to minimize the impact of the behavior, often with minimal success. Millie described her life as being saturated with activities related to supporting Jeffrey (e.g., doctors, therapies, and special education) with little time left for typical family activities. She stated in her journal that "... there's still that problem of us not feeling like we fit into the regular world a lot of times." In her journal and interviews Millie repeatedly described her efforts to make sure that Chris was able to enjoy the typical experiences of a 10 year old but shared with us that Chris thought it was unfair that family life was restricted by Jeffrey's difficulties. In short, it was evident from all of the data that Jeffrey's problem behaviors were a dominant and pervasive influence on family functioning and that the influence was manifested in many ways that are not always apparent to support providers.

A powerful impact. In describing how the process of positive behavorial support effected Jeffrey and the family, Millie stated in her journal, "This has had a really powerful impact on him ... and on our lives." The impact she described in her journal and interviews not only included outcomes for Jeffrey and the family, but also the efforts of the family in working to achieve those outcomes. The process of positive behavorial support was emotionally and physically challenging for the family. The outcomes for Jeffrey were significant, but not effortlessly achieved.

The process involved a deeper examination of the problem behavior that resulted in confronting emotions about the problem behavior that had been buried for a long time. Millie poignantly described how the sharpened focus on Jeffrey's problem behavior precipitated the expression of feelings about Jeffrey's behavior and its impact on family life by both Chris and herself. She described telling Chris about the project and her surprise when Chris revealed to her his anger at Jeffrey's behavior and his desire to "fix him somehow." She stated in her journal that "until something like this comes along, it sort of hits you that 'Gee this has been pretty hard.'" Millie described herself as feeling angry after a very difficult day at the store and expressed

surprise at all of the "ugly emotions" that were coming out.

When the intervention was developed, it required a significant effort by Millie to learn the strategies used to support Jeffrey's appropriate behavior. Millie described practicing the strategies and becoming more fluent in their use over time. She also described that sometimes she did not feel like putting forth the effort that was required to take Jeffrey into the community.

The process precipitated changes in Millie's perspectives about Jeffrey's abilities and needs. She discussed the need to view him as a 9 year old, rather than the preschooler he physically resembled. She purchased age-appropriate toys for him and began to focus on thinking of ways to support him to develop peer relationships. Millie discussed her realization that Jeffrey needed to be pushed to learn new skills and reflected that in the past she may have maintained his dependence on her by doing things for him.

The family attributed the success of the support to the intervention components and the relationship that developed between the interventionist and the family. Millie described an emotional connection to the interventionist that began with the first home visit by saying "... you showed me the first night that there were things he could do. So I knew we were on the right track." The rapport established between the interventionist and Jeffrey led Millie to have high expectations for the behavioral support process as described in this statement: "I can remember telling people the next day, 'This is going to be important. This is going to be big. This is going to work.'" Millie's reflections about the relationship between the interventionist and the family suggested that there was an emotional bond that was an important component of the support process.

The impact of the support process extended beyond affecting only Jeffrey's problem behavior to also affecting his ability to communicate, his social inclusion, and the family's lifestyle. Millie described Jeffrey's growth by stating, "I'm seeing differences every day in Jeffrey, little things that he is learning to do." She described Jeffrey as being more open with people and more confident and remarked that people outside of the family also noticed the difference. She said that the growth in his communication skills has been significant and that "... now with the picture schedule he is requesting things." She also noted that Jeffrey became better at connecting with his peers and was being included more often in the community. Millie described Jeffrey as a "happier child, he's happier in school, and everywhere we go he enjoys places a lot more. Overall, I think its helped him tremendously and had a good impact on our family."

Because problem behavior was firmly linked to family roles and lifestyle, changes in problem behavior precipitated changes for the entire family. Bob reflected on Jeffrey's growth and what the family had experienced with the process of positive behavioral support and summarized his thoughts to Millie by saying that "the change was worth the process."

Summary and Implications

This collaborative endeavor chronicled the experiences of one family as they were involved in positive behavioral support. In this study, the rhythm of the emotions, issues, and perceptions of Millie and her family are described to provide the voice of the family to professionals and researchers in the field of severe disabilities (Ferguson, Ferguson, and Taylor, 1992). Although many advances have been made in the provision of positive behavioral support (Koegel et al., 1996; Meyer & Evans, 1989; Scotti & Meyer, in press), an emphasis has not been placed on understanding family perspectives as they experience and participate in the endeavor. The methods and findings of this study may offer a starting point for additional work in this area.

The findings and the intention of this research extend beyond an examination of social validity. Rather, the quest is for approaches that can help support providers understand how problem behaviors and interventions affect families. Appreciation of the complexity of this issue and all of its ramifications should increase a professional's capacity for designing interventions that result in lifestyle changes. The story of Jeffrey's family indicates that support providers should realize that problem behavior has a pervasive and critical impact on each family member and the family as a system. The family offered vivid descriptions of their emotions, worries, and concerns and the importance of the relationship developed with their support provider. Being family centered implies a level of trust, openness, and reciprocity that is discussed in the literature but not operationalized. In the effort of positive behavioral support to influence an individual's lifestyle and the lifestyle of the family, it is important to understand the related social and emotional aspects (Turnbull & Ruef, 1996). By doing so, we may more closely approximate the goals of durable behavior change and the achievement of meaningful lifestyle enhancements for children and families.

The process of this endeavor raises issues about practices within research and behavioral support that have not been discussed adequately (Meyer & Evans, 1993). One major concern involves the manner with which research is developed and implemented. Perhaps there should be more dialogue with families to identify strategies with which to conduct investigations that are respectful and nonintrusive and that deliver valid information about the multifaceted impact of behavioral support. Families may have much to offer regarding potential impositions of the experimental process, research design, measurement tools, nature of the intervention, and the definition of appropriate, meaningful

outcomes. Answers to these and other questions may have important implications for the design of optimal support processes but it is likely that the full implications will not be evident without more intensive, comprehensive, and multimethod investigations, including systematic longitudinal studies that include families representing numerous cultures and demographic and economic characteristics.

With regard to this study, it is important to acknowledge the presence of several methodological limitations. First, certain biases are indigenous to qualitative research, including the subjective impressions and interactions of the researcher. As the researcher becomes immersed in a project or culture he/she may tend to identify with one particular person or aspect of the project. In this project, the second author spent many hours with Jeffrey and Millie in their home and with their family. Furthermore, the relationship that Millie developed with the second author undoubtedly influenced her experiences and may have affected the way that she provided data in the audiojournal and interviews. The development of those relationships, although beneficial in important programmatic respects, may have contributed to the presence of bias. As discussed earlier, the use of member checks and triangulation were used to minimize or neutralize researcher bias.

A second limitation has to do with the use of a single case. Although case study methodology is considered adequate for examining phenomena within a real-life context and with multiple data sources (Yin, 1989), it is also considered to be a restriction from the perspective of external validity. In this study there are several sources of data collected over a lengthy period of time, however, it is limited to one family. Therefore, the findings should be judiciously and cautiously applied to other families and their experiences in caring for a child with developmental disabilities and problem behavior.

Although the methodology of this study was limited, and the findings must be accepted within that context, the process of the undertaking may have messages for future applied research in complex home and community contexts. This analysis was accompanied by a companion study of the same behavioral support process that focused on the procedures and quantitative data that are more commonly associated with research in the area of positive behavioral support (Vaughn et al., 1997). Thus, the research project brought multiple methodologies and multiple perspectives to bear on a particular problem and set of issues that are increasingly salient in community-based support for people with severe disabilities. It is our contention that progress will be most evident when researchers adopt innovative approaches for acquiring the kinds of knowledge that may be difficult to obtain with traditional research (e.g., experimental) criteria. By using various quantitative, qualitative, and case study methodologies, we may be able to ask questions that are broader in scope, transcend the restrictions of artificial circumstances, and are more directly pertinent to the lives of people with disabilities and their families.

References

Albin, R. W., Lucyshyn, J. M., Horner, R. H., & Flannery, K. B. (1996). Contextual fit for behavioral support plans: A model for "goodness of fit." In L. K. Koegel, R. L. Koegel, & G. Dunlap (Eds.), *Positive behavioral support: Including people with difficult behavior in the community* (pp. 81–98). Baltimore: Paul H. Brookes.

Anderson, J. L., Albin, R. W., Mesaros, R. A., Dunlap, G., & Morelli-Robbins, M. (1993). Issues in providing training to achieve comprehensive behavioral support. In J. Reichle & D. P. Wacker (Eds.), *Communicative alternatives to challenging behavior: Integrating functional assessment and intervention strategies* (pp. 363–406). Baltimore: Paul H. Brookes.

Denzin, N. K. (1978). *Sociological methods.* New York: McGraw-Hill.

Dunlap, G., & Fox, L. (1996). Early intervention and serious problem behaviors: A comprehensive approach. In L. K. Koegel, R. L. Koegel, & G. Dunlap (Eds.), *Positive behavioral support* (pp. 31–50). Baltimore: Paul H. Brookes.

Dunlap, G., Robbins, F. R., & Darrow, M. A. (1994). Parents' reports of their children's challenging behaviors: Results of a statewide survey. *Mental Retardation, 32,* 206–212.

Dunlap, G., Vaughn, B. J., Fox, L., & Foster-Johnson, L. (1996). *Developing and evaluating family networks in positive behavioral support.* (Field-Initiated Research grant H133G60119). Washington, DC: U.S. Department of Education, National Institute on Disability and Rehabilitation Research.

Dunst, C. J., & Trivette, C. M. (1994). What is effective helping? In C. J. Dunst, C. M. Trivette, & A. G. Deal (Eds.), *Supporting and strengthening families: Methods, strategies and practice* (volume 1, pp. 162–170). Cambridge, MA: Brookline Books.

The Family Connection Staff, DeVault, G., Krug, C., Fake, S. (1996). Why does Samantha act that way? *Exceptional Parent, 9,* 43–47.

Ferguson, P. M., Ferguson, D. L., & Taylor, S. J. (1992). The future of interpretivism in disability studies. In P. M. Ferguson, D. L. Ferguson, & S. J. Taylor (Eds.), *Interpreting disability: A qualitative reader* (pp. 295–302). New York: Teachers College Press.

Graves, W. H. (1991). *Participatory action research: A new paradigm for disability and rehabilitation research.* Paper presented at the annual conference of the National Association of Rehabilitation Research and Training Centers, Washington, DC.

Horner, R. H., Dunlap, G., Koegel, R. L., Carr, E. G., Sailor, W., Anderson, J., Albin, R. W., & O'Neill, R. E. (1990). Toward a technology of "non-aversive" behavioral support. *Journal of The Association for Persons with Severe Handicaps, 15,* 125–132.

Huberman, A. M., & Miles, M. B. (1994). Data management and data analysis. In N. K. Denzin & Y. S. Lincoln (Eds.), *Handbook of qualitative research* (pp. 428–444). Newbury Park, CA: Sage Publications.

Janesick, V. J. (1994). The dance of qualitative research: Metaphor, methodolatry, and meaning. in N. K. Denzin & Y. S. Lincoln (Eds.), *Handbook of qualitative research* (pp. 209–219). Newbury Park, CA: Sage Publications.

Koegel, L. K., Koegel, R. L., & Dunlap, G. (1996). *Positive behavioral support: Including people with difficult behavior in the community.* Baltimore: Paul H. Brookes.

Lincoln, Y. S., & Guba, E. G. (1985). *Naturalistic inquiry.* Newbury Park, CA: Sage Publications.

Lucyshyn, J. M., Albin, R. W., & Nixon, C. D. (1997). Embedding comprehensive behavioral support in family ecology: an experimental, single-case analysis. *Journal of Counseling and Clinical Psychology, 65,* 241–251.

Meyer, L. H., & Evans, I. M. (1989). *Nonaversive intervention for behavior problems: A manual for home and community.* Baltimore: Paul H. Brookes.

Meyer, L. H., & Evans, I. M. (1993). Science and practice in behavioral intervention: Meaningful outcomes, research validity, and usable knowledge. *The Journal of The Association for Persons with Severe Handicaps, 18,* 224–234.

Miles, M. B., & Huberman, A. M. (1994). *Qualitative data analysis: A source book of new methods.* Beverly Hill, CA: Sage Publications.

Mount, B., & Zwernik, K. (1988). It's never too early, it's never too late (publication 421-88-109). St. Paul, MN: Metropolitan Council.

Scotti, J. R., & Meyer, L. H. (in press). *New directions for behavioral intervention: Principles, models, and practices.* Baltimore: Paul H. Brookes.

Singer, G. H. S., & Powers, L. E. (1993). Contributing to resilience in families. In G. H. S. Singer & L. E. Powers (Eds.), *Families, disability, and empowerment : Active coping skills and strategies for family interventions* (pp. 1–25). Baltimore: Paul H. Brookes.

Strauss, A., & Corbin, J. (1990). *Basics of qualitative research: Grounded theory procedures and techniques.* Newbury Park, CA: Sage Publications.

Turnbull, A. P., Friesen, B. J., & Ramirez, C. (1996). *Participatory action research: Forging collaborative partnerships with families in the study of disability.* Manuscript submitted for publication.

Turnbull, A. P., & Ruef, M. (1996). Family perspectives on problem behavior. *Mental Retardation, 34,* 280–293.

Turnbull, A. P., & Summers, J. A. (1987). From parent involvement to family support: Evolution to revolution. In S. M. Pueschel, C. Tingey, J. W. Rynders, A. C. Crocher, & D. M. Crutcher (Eds.), *New perspectives on Down's syndrome: Proceedings on the state-of-the-art conference* (pp. 289–306). Baltimore: Paul H. Brookes.

Turnbull, A. P., & Turnbull, H. R., III (1990). *Families, professionals, and exceptionality: A special partnership.* New York: Merrill.

Turnbull, A. P., & Turnbull, H. R., III (1993). Participatory research on cognitive coping from concepts to research planning. In A. P. Turnbull, J. M. Patterson, S. K. Behr, D. L. Murphy, J. G. Marquis, & M. J. Blue-Banning (Eds.), *Cognitive coping, families, and disability* (pp. 1–14). Baltimore: Paul H. Brookes.

Weissbourd, B., & Kagan, S. L. (1989). Family support programs: Catalysts for change. *American Journal of Orthopsychiatry, 59,* 20–31.

Vaughn, B. J., Dunlap, G., Fox, L., Clarke, S., & Bucy, M. (1997). Parent-professional partnership in behavioral support: A case study of community-based intervention. Manuscript submitted for publication.

Yin, R. K. (1989). *Case study research: Design and methods.* Newbury Park, CA: Sage Publications.

Received: May 15, 1997
Final Acceptance: October 10, 1997
Editor in Charge: Lori Goetz

JASH
1997, Vol. 22, No. 4, 208–209

Invited Commentary

The Evolution of Applied Behavior Analysis into Positive Behavior Support

Edward G. Carr
State University of New York at Stony Brook

The field of applied behavior analysis is in the process of bifurcating. One branch of the field maintains the traditional focus on internal validity concerns, emphasizing elegance, experimental control, microanalysis of cause and effect, and conceptual purity. A second and newer branch focuses on external validity concerns, emphasizing ecological relevance, meaningful outcomes in the form of lifestyle change, macroanalysis of systems, and practicality defined by nonresearcher consumers. The first branch continues to be referred to as applied behavior analysis but the second branch has now evolved to the point of meriting a new name, positive behavior support (Koegel, Koegel, & Dunlap, 1996). Positive behavior support could not have come into existence without the previous 30 years of research in applied behavior analysis, research that has provided important contributions with respect to assessment methods, guidelines for intervention, and a conceptual framework. However, it is also true that positive behavior support has both incorporated and moved beyond the parent discipline of applied behavior analysis to assume its own identity, an identity shaped by the realities of conducting research and intervention in natural community settings and embracing changes in assessment methods, intervention strategy, and the definition of what constitutes a successful outcome. The research of the University of South Florida group (Fox, Vaughn, Dunlap, & Bucy, 1997; Vaughn, Dunlap, Fox, Clarke, & Bucy, 1997) crystallizes the essential features of this evolutionary process and helps define and clarify a major turning point in our field, one that can be described along several dimensions.

Consumers as Collaborators, Not Helpers

Traditionally, behavior analysts have for the most part functioned as experts, defining the issues, selecting and designing interventions, and soliciting the assistance of consumers (e.g., families and teachers) in implementing strategies. In contrast, the approach taken by Fox et al. (1997) and Vaughn et al. (1997) involved a Participatory Action Research model (Turnbull, Friesen, & Ramirez, in press) that views families,

Address correspondence and requests for reprints to Edward G. Carr, Department of Psychology, SUNY—Stony Brook, Stony Brook, NY 11794-2500.

in this case, as collaborators rather than helpers. Through weekly meetings over a 10-month period, the family and the researcher worked together to design the assessment and measurement methods, select goals, and structure the intervention. The process was one of mutual education and not one of experts instructing helpers. Because the family was instrumental in developing the approach used and was not the mere recipient of an externally imposed approach, one might therefore expect a high level of cooperation as well as long-term integrity with respect to implementation and, indeed, this was the case.

Ecological Validity

Within traditional applied behavior analysis, internal validity concerns are of the highest priority. Practices are therefore designed to enhance experimental control. Frequently, these practices include the involvement of atypical (nonnormative) intervention agents (e.g., researchers and psychologists), atypical intervention settings (e.g., clinics and laboratory situations), brief intervention sessions (e.g., 10–15 min in duration), and highly circumscribed venues for intervention (e.g., only one situation out of the many that may be associated with problem behavior) (Carr et al., 1997). In contrast, the Florida group demonstrated the priority given by positive behavior support to issues of external validity. Practices were designed to enhance ecological validity. These practices included the involvement of typical intervention agents (e.g., a mother), typical intervention settings (i.e., bank, restaurant, and store), and intervention applied for the entire duration of the community-based activity as well as across all venues designated by the consumer as pertinent.

Lifestyle Change

Most research in traditional applied behavior analysis has focused on the reduction of problem behavior per se. Although this outcome is also valued within the context of positive behavior support, it is not by itself viewed as a successful outcome. Instead, outcome success is defined in terms of changes in lifestyle that permit an individual to be included in community-based activities from which he/she was formerly excluded (Risley, 1996; Turnbull and Ruef, 1997). Again, the research of the Florida group demonstrates this change in emphasis by focusing intervention planning to reflect the family's desire to take their child into the community without anxiety and embarrassment, and by documenting qualitatively and quantitatively subsequent successful inclusion.

Systems Orientation

The microanalytic approach of traditional applied behavior analysis often leads to intervention strategies that stress changing the individual with disabilities (i.e., the person with the identified problem). In contrast, the macroanalytic approach of positive behavior support is systems oriented and views the individual with disabilities as only one participant in a complex, interactive system (Carr et al., in press). The approach developed by the Florida group represents a systems orientation because of its focus on relationship development with the family to understand family structure, routines, capacities, and needs; support for family members and the person with the disability; and long-term, person-centered planning to address multiple elements of community inclusion.

Although positive behavior support differs from past approaches in many other ways as well (Carr et al., 1997), the four dimensions just discussed are among the most critical. Fox et al. (1997) and Vaughn et al. (1997) demonstrate that incorporating these critical dimensions produces meaningful behavior change in the community. In so doing, they provide encouragement to

other researchers and service providers to continue the development of positive behavior support as an emerging applied science.

References

Carr, E. G., Carlson, J. I., Langdon, N. A., Magito-McLaughlin, D., & Yarbrough, S. C. (in press). Two perspectives on antecedent control: Molecular and molar. In J. K. Luiselli & M. J. Cameron (Eds.), *Antecedent control procedures for the behavioral support of persons with developmental disabilities.* Baltimore: Paul H. Brookes.

Carr, E. G., Horner, R. H., Turnbull, A. P., Marquis, J., Magito-McLaughlin, D., McAtee, M. L., Smith, C. E., Ryan, K. A., Ruef, M. B., & Doolabh, A. (1977). Positive behavior support as an approach for dealing with problem behavior in people with developmental disabilities: A research synthesis. Unpublished manuscript, State University of New York at Stony Brook.

Fox, L., Vaughn, B. J., Dunlap, G., & Bucy, M. (1997). Parent-professional partnership in behavioral support: A qualitative analysis of one family's experience. *The Journal of The Association for Persons with Severe Handicaps, 22,* 186–195.

Koegel, R. L., Koegel, L. K., & Dunlap, G. (1996). *Positive behavioral support.* Baltimore: Paul H. Brookes.

Risley, T. (1996). Get a life! In L. K. Koegel, R. L. Koegel, & G. Dunlap (Eds.), *Positive behavioral support* (pp. 425–437). Baltimore: Paul H. Brookes.

Turnbull, A. P., Friesen, B., & Ramirez, C. (in press). Participatory Action Research as a model of conducting family research. *The Journal of The Association for Persons with Severe Handicaps.*

Turnbull, A. P., & Ruef, M. (1997). Family perspectives on inclusive lifestyle issues for people with problem behavior. *Exceptional Children, 63,* 211–227.

Vaughn, B. J., Dunlap, G., Fox, L., Clarke, S., & Bucy, M. (1997). Parent-professional partnership in behavioral support: A case study of community-based intervention. *The Journal of The Association for Persons with Severe Handicaps, 22,* 196–206.

JASH
1997, Vol. 22, No. 4, 210–212

Invited Commentary

Encouraging a New Applied Science: A Commentary on Two Papers Addressing Parent-Professional Partnerships in Behavioral Support

Robert H. Horner
University of Oregon

Carr (1997) recently reviewed research on positive behavioral support and concluded that if we are to achieve current behavioral goals, a new applied science will be needed. The two articles by Fox, Vaughn, Dunlap, and Bucy, (1997) and Vaughn, Dunlap, Fox, Clarke, and Bucy, (1997) may provide a window toward that new applied science. The gist of this commentary is that we are facing new challenges that are reshaping both how behavior support is designed and how applied research is conducted.

Behavior analysis had its beginning in the careful definition and measurement of the operant (Skinner, 1938). The ability to define and measure individual responses (and features of individual responses) was a tremendous advance (Gilbert, 1958). From the ability to define and measure behavior came attention to the environmental variables that resulted in change in behavior. The mechanisms by which behaviors are learned and maintained became more clear, and as they were understood, researchers demonstrated that use of these mechanisms (interventions) could produce important changes in both the acquisition of desired behaviors and the reduction of problem behaviors (Browning & Stover, 1971; Kazdin, 1989; Rachlin, 1976). The advent (Bijou & Baer, 1961; Bijou, Peterson, & Ault, 1968; Carr, 1977) and application (Carr et al., 1994; Durand, 1990; Iwata, Dorsey, Slifer, Bauman, & Richman, 1982 and 1994) of functional assessment technology improved the match between interventions and problem behavior situations. Today, however, this technology is stretching the methods and assumptions that have guided development. Three major factors are reshaping the field of behavioral support, and each of these factors is exemplified in the two articles by Fox et al. (1997) and Vaughn et al. (1997). The three factors are (a) change in the **outcomes** of research/intervention, (b) change in the **comprehensive nature of interventions,** and (c) change in the **contexts** in which research is conducted.

A fruitful and productive history of behavioral research has resulted from intense efforts to understand fundamental mechanisms of behavior. Behavioral re-search procedures have served as a powerful microscope, allowing observation of elementary functions of behavior, but often at the expense of observing their interactions and ultimate impact. We have learned a tremendous amount from this approach to science, and current trends suggest that a tremendous amount of valuable information is yet to be delivered. Now is not the time to cast off careful rigorous detailed analysis of behavior. However, now is the time to add companion approaches to knowledge development that focuses on broader **outcomes, comprehensive** (interacting) support, and multimethod analysis of behavior in **real contexts.** These themes apply both to the way we conduct clinical efforts and the way we use research to guide improvement in our understanding of behavioral support.

Outcomes of Behavioral Support

Among the most important variables effecting both clinical support and research efforts in positive behavioral support is the shift in the expected outcomes of support. As always, one key outcome is the substantive reduction in problem behavior. However, now it is recognized that reduction in head hitting, self-biting, or aggression is a necessary but insufficient accomplishment. The impact of behavioral support should be reflected not only in reduced tissue damage, but in improved social contacts, enriched patterns of activity, access to real learning, and the construction of a pattern of life that reflects the personal preferences of the individual (Turnbull & Ruef, 1997). Behavior support needs to produce a substantive, durable change in behavior that results in new opportunities and an enriched pattern of living. Fox et al. (1997) and Vaughn et al. (1997) provide the reader with an empirical demonstration that the behavioral support applied to Jeffrey was associated with the functional change in disruptive behavior in the bank, restaurant, and store. They then provide a qualitative analysis suggesting that the changes in Jeffrey's behavior were more than reductions in aversive behaviors. The behavior changes provided Jeffrey with the opportunity to be both a member of his community and a contributing member within his family. The discussion of how Jeffrey's behaviors effected family life will be very recognizable to JASH readers who live with a person with severe problem

Address correspondence and requests for reprints to Robert H. Horner, Specialized Training Program, 1235 University of Oregon, Eugene, OR 97405-1235.

behaviors. The complex impact of the successful reduction of these behaviors hopefully will be familiar. Children live in a complex ecology of family, friends, teachers, and (in some cases) staff. An important message from the two articles is that if behavioral support is to result in lifestyle change, attention must be given to the range of behavioral options available to the child and the complex interactions the child's behavior has with others in his/her life. Reducing problem behaviors is a necessary but insufficient focus of behavioral support.

Comprehensive Support

Comprehensive behavioral support (a) addresses all problem behaviors performed by an individual, (b) is driven by a functional assessment, (c) is applied throughout the day (or relevant portions of the day), (d) blends multiple procedures, and (e) incorporates procedures that are consistent with the values, skills, and resources of the people doing the implementation (Horner & Carr, 1997). If the goal of behavioral support is to produce substantive durable effects, our experience suggests that more than one intervention procedure will be needed. When our research has focused on defining fundamental mechanisms, we needed to minimize the breadth of the analysis. This continues to be appropriate for a clear understanding of isolated mechanisms. Of equal importance, however, is study of the interacting effects achieved when we combine procedures such as curriculum revision, schedule redesign, altering the physical environment, changing the pacing and format of instruction, teaching new communication skills, reducing the reward for inappropriate behavior, maximizing the predictability of the activity, providing choice, and ensuring that appropriate behaviors are followed contingently by functional, personalized reinforcers. It is necessary to conduct research documenting the independent effects of specific procedures and analysis of the basic mechanisms that make procedures effective. It also is necessary to begin the difficult process of understanding how these procedures interact when used in concert. It is particularly interesting to note how Fox et al. (1997) and Vaughn et al. (1997) used multiple functional assessment methods to define the mechanisms maintaining problem behavior in the parent-selected routines. Their decisions to teach Jeffrey new skills, to introduce powerful competing reinforcers, and to increase (rather than decrease) his exposure to difficult situations are all well supported by behavioral research. However, what we seldom see are research examples of these procedures used together.

Real Contexts

Fox et al. (1997) and Vaughn et al. (1997) provide two studies that describe both research and clinical intervention conducted in Jeffrey's natural contexts by the people who must live with the effects of the inter-

vention. Most *JASH* readers live, work, and/or play with children, youth, and adults with severe disabilities. Contrasting the contextual control described in some research reports against the managed chaos of real life is something we all experience with varying levels of frustration. One of the elements of a new applied science will be an effort to understand how principles of behavior apply to the real environments where children live, learn, and play. The physical and behavioral ecologies of our homes, schools, and workplaces will alter how we use our existing science and will guide how new knowledge is developed. Fox et al. (1997) and Vaughn et al. (1997) provide two descriptions of a real family struggling to make changes in real settings. The routines under analysis in these studies were selected by Millie (Jeffrey's mother). The interventions were developed to fit the skills, resources, and values of Millie. Even the research design was adjusted in response to needs defined by Millie and her family. These are exactly the kinds of conditions that result in exasperating experimental confounds, yet they also are the conditions that make research results relevant for families. Fox et al. (1997) and Vaughn et al. (1997) are candid in acknowledging how their efforts to conduct research in natural contexts affected not only changes in the way that behavioral interventions were designed, but the ways the research was conducted. The attempt to present two different visions of this study (quantitative and qualitative) is worthy of reflection. It is to the credit of the *JASH* editorial staff that these articles are offered as a pair. Each paper holds gems, but also suffers from limitations. Together they form a picture that is more believable than either study can present alone. The empirical analysis offers excellent measurement features documenting the change in Jeffrey's and Millie's behavior, but the experimental design is far too compromised to attribute these changes to any procedures described in the study. However, the qualitative report adds substantive depth to our understanding of how the behavior changes were perceived by the family. Small changes in frequency could be of real importance for family routines. Changes in behavior intensity could alter social approaches from family members, willingness to engage in outings, and a dramatic sense that "this might work." This is in part because of the decision to focus on important behaviors in real contexts, and because the authors clearly worked in true collaboration with Millie and her family.

My only reservations with these two studies stem from concerns that would be common to any case study. This is a fairly unique analysis. As a professional, Millie clearly brought a great deal to this process that would be hard for other families to provide. In addition, although I enjoyed reading how the authors used functional assessment methods to construct their intervention, the study served more as a description of a complex process than as a model of an intervention that could be applied by others. The articles do not offer any new suggestions regarding how and why problem behaviors occur. They do, however, offer important messages for how collaborative research and collaborative behavioral support can be conducted. If we are to extrapolate from this study to future work, I would encourage efforts to achieve experimental control even within natural designs. Good research will not only describe events under analysis, but help us understand why those events occurred. I continue to find experimental control an important element for this level of understanding.

Fox et al. (1997) and Vaughn et al. (1997) offer a fascinating description not only of important behavior change, but the collaborative exploration that resulted in the observed change. Their work suggests important challenges for how behavior support should be developed and how we learn from that process. In a very direct way they recommend that any new applied science should be characterized by practical, family-driven research as much as by rigorous, research-driven interventions.

References

Bijou, S., & Baer, D. M. (1961). *Child development: A systematic and empirical theory* (Volume 1). New York: Appleton-Century-Crofts.

Bijou, S. W., Peterson, R. F., & Ault, M. H. (1968). A method to integrate descriptive and experimental field studies at the level of data and empirical concepts. *Journal of Applied Behavior Analysis, 1,* 175–191.

Browning, R. M., & Stover, D. O. (1971). *Behavior modification in child treatment: An experimental and clinical approach.* Chicago: Aldine/Atherton, Inc.

Carr, E. G. (1997). *Positive behavior support: What researchers know and what consumers want.* Presentation at the 1997 NIDRR Positive Behavior Support Conference, Santa Barbara, CA.

Carr, E. G., Levin, L., McConnachie, G., Carlson, J. I., Kemp, D. C., & Smith, C. E. (1994). *Communication-based intervention for problem behavior. A user's guide for producing positive change.* Baltimore: Paul H. Brookes.

Carr, E. G. (1977). The motivation of self-injurious behavior: A review of some hypotheses. *Psychological Bulletin, 84*(4), 800–816.

Durand, V. M. (1990). *Severe behavior problems: A functional communication training approach.* New York: Guilford Press.

Gilbert, T. F. (1958). Fundamental dimensional properties of the operant. *Psychological Review, 65*(5), 272–282.

Fox, L., Vaughn, B. J., Dunlap, G., & Buch, M. (1997). Parent-professional partnership in behavioral support: A qualitative analysis of one family's experience. *The Journal of The Association for Persons with Severe Handicaps, 22,* 186–195.

Horner, R. H., & Carr, E. G. (1997). Behavioral support for students with severe disabilities: Functional assessment and comprehensive intervention. *Journal of Special Education, 31*(1), 84–104.

Iwata, B. A., Dorsey, M. F., Slifer, K. J., Bauman, K. E., & Richman, G. S. (1982). Toward a functional analysis of self-injury. *Analysis and Intervention in Developmental Disabilities, 2,* 3–20.

Iwata, B. A., Dorsey, M. F., Slifer, K. J., Bauman, K. E., & Richman, G. S. (1994). Toward a functional analysis of self-injury. *Journal of Applied Behavior Analysis, 27,* 197–209.

Kazdin, A. E. (1989). *Behavior modification in applied settings.* Pacific Grove, CA: Brooks/Cole Publishing Company.

Rachlin, H. (1976). *Introduction to modern behaviorism.* San Francisco: W. H. Freeman and Company.

Skinner, B. F. (1938). *The behavior of organisms.* New York: Appleton-Century-Crofts.

Turnbull, A. P., & Ruef, M. (1997). Family perspectives on inclusive lifestyle issues for individuals with problem behavior. *Exceptional Children, 63*(2), 211–227.

Vaughn, B. J., Dunlap, G., Fox, L., Clarke, S., & Bucy, M. (1997). Parent-professional partnership in behavioral support: A case study of community-based intervention. *The Journal of The Association for Persons with Severe Handicaps, 22,* 196–206.

JASH
1997, Vol. 22, No. 4, 213–214

Invited Commentary
It Is Just a Matter of Priorities:
A Response to Vaughn et al. and Fox et al.

Ilene S. Schwartz
University of Washington

It was a pleasure to read and review the two articles by Fox et al. (1997) and Vaughn et al. (1997). There is much to note in these two articles about the direction that the field of special education needs to move. I was impressed by the thoughtfulness of the intervention and the care taken to develop an intervention that was effective and sustainable. I was also impressed by the active participation of Jeffrey's mother in all stages (e.g., initiation, design, implementation, evaluation, and dissemination) of the research process. The thoughtful manner in which quantitative and qualitative methods were used to explore multiple dimensions of this issue, to document different outcomes of the same intervention, and to provide information by using multiple voices and hopefully appealing to multiple audiences was impressive. Finally, I was pleased with the change that this intervention made in the lives of Jeffrey and his family, and I am reminded that we have the technology to make these kinds of lifestyle changes in the lives of many children with significant disabilities if we just had the skills and the will to use them.

The intervention, as described, sounds deceivingly simple. Anyone who has conducted functional analyses of challenging behavior knows the difficulty of matching effective interventions to specific behaviors and contexts. When the emphasis is in on doable and sustainable interventions, this level of difficulty increases. When I read about the process that this research team conducted, I can begin to imagine how many hours went into this project and I am confident that I am underestimating the effort. Then I think about how many children like Jeffrey I (and my colleagues) know and when I do the math, the number of human hours and other resources we are talking about is overwhelming. These concerns do not take away at all from the importance of the intervention described in these studies, rather the elegance of the design, effectiveness of the intervention, and the poignance of Millie's comments make me think about why this type of intervention is so unusual and what we need to do to make these practices commonplace.

What do we need to do so that the report of a family receiving appropriate levels of family support to deal with challenging behaviors in a socially valid manner in real-life community settings is not so unusual that it results in two journal articles and a number of invited commentaries? Do we have the will to really answer that question?

One way to attempt to answer that question is to look at how we are preparing special education teachers and support staff and the roles that these staff play in the lives of children with disabilities and their families. It is interesting that in the study Jeffrey's teachers were not involved. Did they know that behavior in the community was a priority for the family? Had they tried to provide support in this area? Did they have similar problems at school? I wonder how many special education teachers or behavior specialists in the public school have the skills necessary to conduct the type of intervention described in these articles. Although I work with some extremely talented teachers, I imagine that most of those teachers do not have the skills necessary or the resources available to implement this type of intervention. In an attempt to prepare special educators to be good collaborators with general education and to be more knowledgeable about the general education curriculum, have we eliminated components of the special education curriculum that prepare teachers to work with challenging behaviors in a systematic manner in the classroom and community? Where does training—explicit, practical, and sustained training—in behavioral support fit into the preservice curriculum of special education teachers?

The challenge of turning this type of intervention into a more common practice can also be addressed by looking at how we define appropriate educational services and how family support is provided within public school programs. There is a strong family support movement in this country that has largely ignored and been ignored by people in the disability community. This movement is dedicated to strengthening families through systemic and institutional reform. Central to the mission of family support is its stance as a prevention strategy whose purpose is to optimize the development of children in all domains of their lives. The goal is building healthy families that will raise healthy children, rather than using resources to repair damage once it has occurred (Bowman, 1994). One aspect of family support is reinventing the way that schools and

---

Address correspondence and requests for reprints to Ilene S. Schwartz, University of Washington, Experimental Education Unit, Box 357925, Seattle, WA 98195.

other institutions interact with families, including collaborations across systems so that families can access comprehensive services through a single system. This study is an excellent example of a type of family support that could be extremely beneficial to many families, yet provided to few. Advocates, researchers, and practitioners who work with people with disabilities and their families need to enter into the family support dialogue and be sure that the unique supports needed by families of children with disabilities are put on the table. We need to be active in this process so that when people in the family support movement talk about supporting America's families, they are talking about all of America's families.

These articles present another clear demonstration of some of the unique challenges faced by families with children with disabilities. As with Jeffrey and his family, the challenges faced by many occur outside of school. As we work toward truly including people with disabilities as full members of our society, we must look outside of schools for support, activities, and membership. What occurs within school is important but is a limited part of a child's life. Full inclusion cannot be achieved until children with disabilities can participate in all the services and activities available in their community. When we talk about support and inclusion we must broaden the discussion to include discussions of community and systems beyond school.

So, when are we going to do that? When are we going to provide more specialized training in behavior support for special educators and work with the family support movement to ensure that the needs of families with children with disabilities are considered in the dialogue? How can we add more demands when the curricula are already packed and our professional plates are full? As a close friend and mentor often said to me, "It is not a matter of time, it is a matter of priorities." The issues raised by these studies force us to take a hard look at the priorities that are embodied in the systems we are creating to provide services to children with disabilities and their families, how we are training special educators, and the types of services these systems and professionals can offer. It is essential that we look outside of schools to the broader community to plan for full inclusion and the entire array of supports necessary to facilitate the true participation and membership of all people with disabilities.

References

Bowman, B. T. (1994). Home and school: The unresolved relationship. In S. L. Kagan & B. Weissbourd (Eds.), *Putting families first: America's family support movement and the challenge of change* (pp. 51–73). San Francisco: Jossey-Bass, Inc.

Fox, L., Vaughn, B. J., Dunlap, G., & Bucy, M. (1997). Parent-professional partnership in behavioral support: A qualitative analysis of one family's experience. *The Journal of The Association for Persons with Severe Handicaps, 22,* 186–195.

Vaughn, B. J., Dunlap, G., Fox, L., Clarke, S., & Bucy, M. (1997). Parent-professional partnership in behavioral support: A case study of community-based intervention. *The Journal of The Association for Persons with Severe Handicaps, 22,* 196–206.

JASH
1997, Vol. 22, No. 4, 215–217

Invited Commentary

Participatory Action Research Meets the Emic, the Etic, and Program Evaluation: A Response to Vaughn et al. and Fox et al.

George H. S. Singer
University of California at Santa Barbara

There are three issues that arise from the joint publication of the articles by Vaughn, Dunlap, Fox, Clarke, and Bucy (1997) and Fox, Vaughn, Dunlap, and Bucy (1997): (a) the Participatory Action Research method, (b) use of an AB single subject design across different settings, and (c) use of qualitative data including parental self-report as a way to describe and partly evaluate the intervention. I begin with a cautionary tale.

In a book on the history of lobotomy, *Great and Desperate Cures* (Valenstein, 1986), there is a photo of Dr. Walter Freeman, an early and evangelical promoter of lobotomy. It shows him hammering a sharp tool through the eye socket and into the brain of a mental patient who had been knocked unconscious with electric shock. The caption under the photo reads in part: "Dr. Walter Freeman demonstrating transorbital lobotomy at the Green Gables Sanatorium, Lincoln, Nebraska, August 6, 1951; *note his dispassionate manner.*" (italics added) Prefrontal lobotomy was all the rage in the postwar U. S. Dr. Freeman drove from state hospital to state hospital, often performing a dozen or more psychosurgeries in a day and eventually chalking up 400 or more between 1949 and 1951. Several of the recipients of his tender mercies were people with mental retardation and challenging behaviors. For several years proponents of the procedure, which consisted of little more than hammering an ice pick through the eye socket and wiggling it around to root out the offending tissue, carried the torch for the most "modern" treatment of people with mental illness, including people with mental retardation. Dozens of studies attested to the efficacy of the procedure. Unfortunately, most of the studies were reported by proponents of lobotomy who used personal observations to attest to the benefits. Proponents also ignored data from both animal research and observations of post lobotomy patients that presented evidence of deterioration after surgery. The favorable studies were short term and mostly noted how people stopped misbehaving. Gradually long-term studies by more independent observers using both quantitative and qualitative reports began to show that many people suffered devastating losses of memory and executive functions and that they deteriorated over time. By the mid-1950s the bloom was off the procedure and lobotomy was discredited. Unfortunately, it left behind hundreds of people who got worse over time and who were not able to be treated effectively with new medications when they became available because of the destruction of brain cells wrought by this much ballyhooed modern scientific treatment.

There were at least three forces that led to such a tragic outcome. The first was bad science. Observations of animals and then humans who were lobotomized were presented by fervent proponents of the procedure using mostly qualitative methods without anything that we would now call evidence for reliability, validity, or triangulation. The second was an almost total lack of legal protection for institutionalized patients and the absence of effective alternatives. Although it must be said that when informed consent from relatives was sought, it was often granted by desperate families who believed in the promise of this seemingly scientific intervention. The third, I believe was the dispassionate clinical stance that Valenstien (1986) notes in his captioned photo. Foucault (1975) describes this stance as "the gaze," a position of seeming objectivity that emerged in the early 1800s in France, England, and Germany as a result of the growing science of medicine and the enlightenment commitment to see things anew. On the one hand, it was this stance that allowed Itard to systematically test a series of instructional procedures for teaching communication and home living skills to the feral child, Victor. Many of these techniques appear virtually identical to those developed and evaluated by behavior analysts 150 years later. So the stance and the faith in empirical testing, holding most variables constant and varying one at a time, allowed for progress. On the other hand, this dispassionate stance allowed Itard to try his experiments, which involved hanging Victor by his heels over a stairwell to punish him, locking him in a dark closet to teach him to feel guilt, and finally to abandon him when Victor failed to develop speech, Itard's goal (Hardin, 1976).

One way to break down "the gaze" is to change the stance of the researcher from dispassionate observer to that of friend, ally, and colleague of the people who are listed as "subjects" in our methods section. Participa-

Address correspondence and requests for reprints to George H. S. Singer, Graduate School of Education, Phelps Hall, University of California at Santa Barbara, Santa Barbara, CA 93106.

tory Action Research (PAR) makes this mutual relationship central to the research enterprise. I applaud the authors for including Mrs. Bucy as an author, developing a working alliance with her as a conscious part of the treatment, designing the treatment around her priorities, and regarding her as an ally in developing and implementing a successful intervention. This kind of alliance has long been held to be essential in the field of counseling psychology but is only belatedly being introduced to our field. Because the authors also used the methods and attitude inherent in positive behavioral support, I think it reasonable to describe Jeffrey, the child with troubling behavior, as an ally.

In terms of the, by now, overworked debate over qualitative versus quantitative research, I adopt the stand of a pragmatist who asks simply, "Does this research method advance the goals of our science and does it work in this specific case?" Successful working is the criterion for deciding on its usefulness (Pepper, 1942). From this viewpoint both quantitative (etic) and qualitative (emic) methods have their place. In this case the goal was to reduce suffering in a family by successfully teaching a parent how to modify her child's problematic behavior. Do the mother's and other family members' accounts help us in doing other such important work? It seems clear to me that the answer is yes. For example, is it not strange that it should be new to our literature that there is an emotional side of introducing behavioral interventions into a family? Might it not help us be better at what we do if we also attended to the thoughts and feelings of parents and siblings, as well as the child with problematic behavior? Would such attention perhaps help reduce the high rate of drop outs in our studies? If we also want to help parents and siblings with other problems such as marital discord and depression, it is necessary to attend to family members thoughts and feelings (Singer & Powers, 1993).

Another question about successful working concerns whether or not these papers together represent good science. In particular there is a question of whether an AB design without the controls established by staggering the intervention across settings, adding a reversal design, or alternating treatments is convincing evidence that this combination of PAR and positive behavioral support was effective in this case. In general, I think that we disregard tests of causality and experimental control at great peril. Such disregard helped fuel the lobotomy craze and other untested fads in the guise of treatments. The established cannons of what constitutes reliable evidence have, I believe, generally evolved in response to the problems of evangelic claims of poor science. We happen to work in a field that is routinely plagued by periodic movements in support of new treatments that make extravagant claims for efficacy. Whether the claims are that repeating motor movements over thousands of hours repatterns the brain, mega vitamins alter genetic conditions, dolphins help people with autism, or that autism can be cured with a communication facilitator, we are subject to the outrageous that is often supported with passionate intensity. And so good science matters, strict science with experimental controls and its hard-nosed demand that we rule out other factors before we claim causality.

I find Habermas's (1988) analysis of three kinds of knowledge to be very useful. He writes about technical knowledge that grows out of the human struggle to control nature and that involves the use of quantitative methods and careful controls as one kind of modern knowledge (Habermas, 1988). Unlike many postmodernists, he recognizes the tremendous power of this methodology to reveal nature and especially to demonstrate causality. The various designs that are commonly required in applied behavior analysis and other experimental traditions are prime examples of rules and methods designed to isolate and demonstrate causality. The AB design is a rather weak form. If the authors were introducing a new treatment, I would not be convinced by this design. If, for example, they were presenting a new technique to treat people with mental retardation I would need to see more and tighter quantitative evidence and would not place much faith in qualitative studies alone that cannot deal effectively with the issues of causality and experimental control. However, I believe that this article is not so much about new methods as a new attitude. What is new here is not the functional analysis or the use of preferred activities to replace challenging behavior, but the tone and nature of the working relationship with the parent. What is also relatively new is the focus on family routines, including community activities. As such, I do not mind the weaker design. These problem behaviors were long established and treatment spillover effects are uncommon with problem behaviors across such diverse settings. But I hope the publication of this article does not herald a general loosening of research standards. Another way to view this study is as a kind of program evaluation.

It has long been recognized by researchers who focus on program evaluation that evaluation often cannot be conducted under ideal conditions of control (Cronbach, 1982) . Instead they accept compromises in design, aim for the strictest control possible under the real world conditions of program implementation, and then try to build up layers of evidence by including multiple perspectives. They often combine qualitative and quantitative data. I see these studies primarily as an effort to test a program made up of several components, including PAR and the provision of positive behavioral support.

Habermas (1988), like many others, has also supported the great value of research that accepts accounts of private events and personal perspectives. He argues that human life is interpreted life and that research that does not account for the meanings people assign to events simply does not do justice to that which is being studied, human beings. I think the value of Mrs. Bucy's account is self-evident. Valuing such accounts may take us at least part of the way toward turning Foucault's (1975) gaze into a demeanor of friendship and concern and an attitude of mutual alliance. Habermas (1988) sees a place for both kinds of research. However, he has one more concern, that there is a third kind of knowledge that he refers to as liberating. It is rooted in a humanistic critique of the values and practices present in market-driven societies. Although one may not agree with his critique, the idea that we also need to take a stance that takes us beyond self-report and quantitative accounts and asks about our values is an essential one. Ultimately, the pragmatist is forced to account for what she means by successful working; here careful listening to people is essential but perhaps not sufficient. In this case, if we want to know why positive behavioral supports are needed, we can turn to Mrs. Bucy's account of how her son's behavior had limited options and constrained daily routines for the entire family, and we can look at the baseline data. These both help root us in a reason for proceeding and a definition of what matters here. Her account of how it felt to learn positive behavioral methods also tells us that successful working is not simply a matter of good outcomes. The way it feels, the kinds of support and concern provided by the interventionists also matter. But to make a modest effort to attain more liberating knowledge, we need to question this multiple perspective, multiple method study from a societal perspective.

For example, why had Mrs. Bucy and her family been left alone with this problem for such a long time? Why was she not taught these methods much earlier? I believe that home visiting for families of children with severe disabilities ends much too early. Home-based early intervention ends right around the time that problem behaviors related to instruction following and ex-

pressive communication begin to emerge. Where were the schools? Why isn't the teacher in the picture? Again, I believe that in practice we only give lip service to schools as a source of family support. In my experience, parents do not see the school as a place to talk about problems at home and teachers do not concern themselves with the family life of their students. Is this separation necessary? Furthermore, why aren't positive behavioral support programs more widely available? Most of this technology has been known for years. Perhaps the use of PAR, so elegantly presented in these two studies, will help researchers, parents, and advocates fight for the kind of community-based family support that would ultimately reduce a great deal of suffering for many families. My thanks to the authors for their work.

References

Cronbach, L. J. (1982). *Designing evaluations of educational and social programs.* San Francisco: Jossey-Bass, Inc.

Foucault, M. (1975). *The birth of the clinic: An archeology of human perception.* In A. M. S. Smith (Ed.). New York: Vintage/Random House.

Fox, L., Vaughn, B. J., Dunlap, G., & Bucy, M. (1997). Parent-professional partnership in behavioral support: A qualitative analysis of on family's experience. *The Journal of The Association for Persons with Severe Handicaps, 22,* 186–195.

Habermas, J. (1988). *On the logic of the social sciences.* In S. W. Nicholsen & Jerry A. Stark (Eds.). Cambridge, MA: MIT Press.

Hardin, L. (1976) *The wild boy of Aveyron.* Cambridge, MA: Harvard University Press.

Pepper, S. C. (1942). *World hypotheses: A study in evidence.* Berkeley: University of California Press.

Singer, G. H. S., & Powers, L. (1993). *Families, disability, and empowerment.* Baltimore: Paul H. Brookes Publishing.

Valenstein, E. S. (1986). *Great and desperate cures: The rise and decline of psychosurgery and other radical treatments for mental illness.* New York: Basic Books.

Vaughn, B. J., Dunlap, G., Fox, L., Clarke, S., & Bucy, M. (1997). Parent-professional partnership in behavioral support: A case study of community-based intervention. *The Journal of The Association for Persons with Severe Handicaps, 22,* 196–206.

JASH
1997, Vol. 22, No. 4, 218–220

Invited Commentary

Parent-Professional Partnerships, the Critical Ingredient: A Response to Vaughn et al. and Fox et al.

Martha E. Snell
University of Virginia

Imagine a need for change that is so intense that most of your days revolve around hoping for its arrival. Couple these hopes for change with the despair that comes from repeated failure to achieve a resolution: living for years with a child having a serious behavior problem that has defied all efforts at remediation. The companion articles in this issue of *The Journal of the Association for Persons with Severe Handicaps* describe one such family where the parents (Millie and Bob) and older brother (Chris) were at a loss on how to remediate the destructive behavior of the youngest member, 9-year-old Jeffrey. Jeffrey's behavior problems included tantrums, crying, screaming, scratching others, head banging, and aggressive refusals to continue with an activity and attempts to leave an activity. He engaged in these behaviors in public places like the grocery store, restaurants, and in the car at the drive-through bank, places where typical families must go once or several times a week.

Families in this predicament are unusual but hardly rare. When there is little change in the child's behavior problem over the years, the support systems that these families have erode. Grandparents and friends run out of suggestions and neighbors turn away. Siblings' dreams are characterized both by the discovery of magic solutions and a total escape from the situation. Parents together or separately move in and out of self-blame, child blame, and other blame. It is not unusual for mothers to become very isolated, enmeshed with the "problem," while other family members carry on the family's essential functions (earning an income and education of siblings) and try to achieve some semblance of normalcy in their lives by distancing themselves from the child with the problem. Many "nonessential" family functions (recreation, affection, and socialization) often go neglected.

Schools may also have given up or simply have failed to achieve meaningful change with their intervention programs that characteristically are noncollaborative, episodic, and school limited: programs that stop abruptly at the school boundaries and the end of the

school day. We do not know about Jeffrey's school day, nor about his successes or failures in school or his teachers' interactions with his family. Although the school was not mentioned as a source of information or a location for intervention, we clearly understand that Jeffrey's behavior problems were intense within the family's regular routines. This omission of the school is perhaps the sole weakness in these studies. Not knowing makes most of us who are concerned with the school environment and the home-school partnership worry.

Despite this omission, these companion articles, which detail two complementary analyses of a family-centered behavior support program, are significant in several ways. First, these two studies present what is necessary to document behavior change and to describe the change process: (a) meaningful reductions were shown in Jeffrey's behavior problems across three community locations, (b) increases in desirable mother-child interactions were evident, (c) other parents socially validated that Jeffrey and his mother's behavior changes constituted meaningful change and that the strategies Millie used were generally appropriate and feasible for families, and (d) a study of the family's perspectives (via interview, field observations, and mother's diary comments) reveal the poignant effects of Jeffrey's behavior and its change during each phase of the support process and before and after intervention. Researchers applied this novel combination of two research methodologies to a single 10-month period of baseline, intervention, and follow-up. A single-case analysis allowed behavior change in both Jeffrey and Millie to be quantified and stated in numbers, and a qualitative analysis of the words of family members over time brought into focus the viewpoints of Jeffrey's parents and his brother, thereby revealing the pictures that had been familiar only to family members. What each research methodology lacked, the other in part supplied. Numbers with pictures make a powerful combination.

Second, and perhaps more importantly, these combined studies demonstrate the potent effects that can result from a partnership between families who understand the context where change is needed and professionals who understand the procedures that produce change. A family-centered orientation meant that the researchers and the family members worked together collaboratively, intentionally establishing "trust, open-

Address correspondence and requests for reprints to Martha E. Snell, Curriculum, Instruction, and Special Education, Curry School of Education, Ruffner Hall, Charlottesville, VA 22903-2495.

ness, and reciprocity" (Fox, Vaughn, Dunlap, & Bucy 1997). Getting to this point was not easy; it required the deliberate synchronization of family information and viewpoints with each phase of the behavior support process: relationship building, functional assessment, design of the support plan, and use of the support intervention. Starting with a family who both needed and wanted assistance with behavior change, the partnership evolved through these four successive phases with the help of reciprocal information sharing, creative problem solving, and shared decision making:

1. Building a relationship between the family and the researchers
   - Researchers learned about the family's structure, routines, capacities, and needs.
   - Senior researcher (Vaughn) established rapport with Jeffrey.
   - Family members learned about the process of functional assessment and behavioral support.
   - Both developed respect for each other's knowledge and viewpoint.
2. Collaboration during the functional assessment: Defining Jeffrey's skills, preferences, and routines, the problem behaviors, and their predictive antecedents and maintaining consequences; developing hypotheses; conducting observations.
3. Collaboration during the development of a behavior support plan: Building support strategies for family members to use and discussing their "fit" with family routines.
4. Collaboration during the implementation and expansion of the support plan: Coaching Millie on the use of support strategies in the community and additional person-centered planning to expand use of support strategies and to maintain their effects.

None of these four phases could proceed without a partnership that worked. One of the initial activities to build this partnership was a person-centered planning session during which family members, grandparents, Jeffrey's teacher, and researchers developed a vision of Jeffrey's future and established "a shared commitment to supporting Jeffrey in achieving that vision" (Fox et al., 1997). The goals of the partnership were to achieve both durable behavior change for Jeffrey and meaningful lifestyle enhancements for the family. The functional assessment, on which program design depended, required information from the family that was captured through the interview process, reflection with trust, and observation of their routines. Later in the assessment phase, Millie expressed her fears about the effects of baseline on Jeffrey: she "dreaded" the thoughts of Jeffrey being exposed to the public without support. In response to Millie's concerns, the research team modified both the design and the baseline and intervention

conditions to ensure safety. The quasi-experimental design used in Vaughn, Dunlap, Fox, Clarke, and Bucy, (1997) was intentionally chose to avoid lengthy baselines and to allow for more natural implementation of behavior support procedures in the three community settings; researchers added social validation procedures to strengthen the design. To ensure safety, two members of the research team always rode in the van with Millie, although they stayed 3 to 5 meters away in the store and restaurant to promote her independence. Millie was coached through the support procedures by using prompts and feedback on the first 3 days of intervention, after which she only needed encouragement but still had support present. Members of the partnership were open with each other, listened, and responded.

The collaborative partnership described in these companion articles illustrates beautifully the concept of contextual fit (Albin, Luchshyn, Horner, & Flannery, 1996) and goodness-of-fit (Bailey et al., 1990). Both concepts pertain to the compatibility between educational plans and the family and child for whom they are meant. Compatibility or good contextual fit can only result from collaboration between the key players involved. Behavior support plans that have good contextual fit mean that:

1. Key players are comfortable with the plan's goals and strategies, feel they have the skills or resources to implement the plan, and believe it will be successful.
2. Family members are active collaborators on an ongoing basis.
3. Key players reach agreement at each phase of planning (conditions and functions of behavior problems, support plan design, support strategies, and modifications in plan).
4. Plans are technically sound and reflect "best practices."
5. Plans are consistent with the strongly held values and living patterns of the people involved.
6. Plans address sources of stress in a family.
   Plans are designed to fit into existing routines and daily living patterns as much as possible.
7. Plans are designed to build on the focus person's strengths and capabilities.
8. Plans tap into existing resources so that the required time, effort, and dollars are not prohibitive (Albin et al., 1996).

From this work we learn once again that schools need to extend their view beyond the school yard, seek invitation into the family's circle, nurture a partnership, and apply the concept of contextual fit. Learning that does not generalize past school boundaries is typically short lived and school-designed behavior support programs that reflect only school assessment and thinking cannot hold the same promise of meaningful, durable behavior change.

References

Albin, R. W., Luchshyn, J. M., Horner, R. H., & Flannery, K. B. (1996). Contextual fit for behavioral support plans. In L. K. Koegel, R. L. Koegel, & G. Dunlap (Eds.), *Positive behavioral support* (pp. 81–98).

Bailey, B. D., Simeonsson, R. J., Winton, P. J., Huntington, G. S., Comfort, M., Isbell, P., O'Connell, K. J., & Helm, J. M. (1990). Family-focused intervention: A functional model of planning, implementing, and evaluating individualized family services in early intervention. *Journal of the Division for Early Childhood, 10,* 156–171.

Fox, L., Vaughn, B. J., Dunlap, G., & Bucy, M. (1997). Parent-professional partnership in behavioral support: A qualitative analysis on one family's experience. *The Journal of The Association for Persons with Severe Handicaps, 22,* 186–195.

Vaughn, B. J., Dunlap, G., Fox, L., Clarke, S., & Bucy, M. (1997). Parent-professional partnership in behavioral support: A case study of community-based intervention. *The Journal of The Association for Persons with Severe Handicaps, 22,* 196–206.

JASH
1997, Vol. 22, No. 4, 221–223

In Quest of Meaningful Perspectives and Outcomes: A Response to Five Commentaries

Glen Dunlap, Lise Fox, Bobbie J. Vaughn, Millie Bucy, and Shelley Clarke
University of South Florida

The primary focus underlying the production of our two articles was to induce a discussion within the field about the processes and analyses of family-centered and community-based behavioral support. We have been concerned that the strictures of methodological tradition may be impeding the development of a more complete understanding of behavioral support with families (Meyer & Evans, 1993), and that hierarchical service strategies may be inconsistent with the kinds of help-giving interactions that are (or may be) prerequisites for optimal outcomes (Dunst, Trivette, & Deal, 1994; Powell, Batsche, Ferro, Fox, & Dunlap 1997). Although great progress has occurred (e.g., Lucyshyn, Albin, & Nixon, 1997), we believe that gaps continue to separate the professional expectations of behavioral support from the actual outcomes experienced by the recipients. We also believe that it is crucial for researchers and support providers to gain an enhanced understanding and appreciation of the myriad ways that behavioral support processes can affect participating individuals and families. The careful consideration of multiple perspectives is arguably a requisite step in our efforts to elevate the enterprise of behavioral support.

We undertook this multifaceted effort primarily to help Jeffrey adopt more congenial patterns of responding in troublesome situations and to support Jeffrey's family in their desire to understand and alleviate Jeffrey's behavioral problems while improving the tenor of familial and community interactions. We also sought to explicitly value the integrity of the family unit, develop a collaborative partnership, and explore mechanisms for examining the vicissitudes of the behavioral support process from the family's perspective. Our prominent aspiration from the vantage point of research was to learn from our participants. Our expectations and hopes have been that multiple perspectives and multidimensional data will serve to enrich our understanding and, possibly, help us create support options that are increasingly effective because of their heightened sensitivity to the individual exigencies of complex family systems. The overriding goal was to produce a juxtaposition of data and methodologies that would heuristically illuminate some essential issues pertaining to research and practice in family-centered behavioral support.

We appreciate the reflections and insights that are shared so eloquently in the preceding commentaries by Edward Carr, Robert Horner, Ilene Schwartz, George Singer, and Martha Snell. We believe that, together, the authors of these responses have done a wonderful job of elucidating the key issues that characterize the process and findings of our investigation. They have produced a discussion and thereby realized our ambition. Their commentaries offer much to ponder but, from our outlook, there is little with which to quibble. Therefore, in our limited space our priority will not be to reply directly to the individual responses but, instead, will be to amplify and elaborate on a few of the themes that seem to us the most germane.

The Importance of Multiple Perspectives and Multiple Research Methodologies

The enormous majority of research examines phenomena from a single perspective and it typically does so with a limited set of focused measures. This strategy has been useful for obtaining specific kinds of information and, in the case of behavioral support, it has led to an array of intervention options, many of which have been demonstrated to be effective and replicable, at least in many circumstances (Horner et al., 1990; Scotti & Meyer, in press). However, a major assumption of our position is that substantial progress beyond the description of an intervention technology will depend on our ability to adopt additional lenses in our analyses and evaluations of behavioral support. This is the case for at least two reasons. The first reason is that the efficacy of support strategies in producing outcomes that are durable and meaningful to the people involved is utterly dependent on the degree with which such procedures fit the ecological and familial contexts in which they are implemented (Albin et al., 1996). Such congruence cannot be accomplished without access to the

Address correspondence and requests for reprints to Glen Dunlap, Department of Child and Family Studies, Louis de la Parte Florida Mental Health Institute, University of South Florida, 13301 Bruce B. Downs Boulevard, Tampa, FL 33612.

distinctive preferences, beliefs, habits, and world views of the participants. The specific elements that define relevant contextual information and the means by which this information can be obtained are just beginning to be understood, but it is clear that the information must be obtained from the various viewpoints of participants and key consumers.

A second basis for multiple perspectives is that behavioral support of any type produces a multiplicity of outcomes that affect in one way or another everyone involved. For example, family members, especially parents, experience behavioral support procedures that are developed for their children, yet we have virtually no information on how this transpires, what the effects are, and what implications should be considered. We agree with George Singer's observation that it seems strange that we are just now appreciating the emotional side of behavioral interventions, and that it is logical that knowledge of family members' thoughts and feelings could help us arrange more effective behavioral support. However, beyond this we need to be aware of the possibility that certain behavioral prescriptions might have unanticipated iatrogenic effects, particularly when they affect established patterns of family interactions. At this point in our field's evolution, we are just beginning to appreciate the ramifications of our actions and the social and emotional interconnections that define family systems. Our studies do not provide answers, but we hope they lead to useful questions and broader issues and that they help inspire more holistic investigations.

In terms of research methodology, two respondents (Robert Horner and George Singer) noted the absence of experimental control in our direct observation data and expressed some concern that the publication of nonexperimental data be construed as a precedent for reduced standards. We certainly concur that experimental designs are crucial for isolating cause and effect (functional) relations and demonstrating the replicability of specific interventions. We believe that their use will continue to be instrumental in developing the basis for family-centered behavioral support (e.g., Lucyshyn et al., 1997; Vaughn, Clarke, & Dunlap, 1997), and we would join in protest of diminished criteria. Still, it is not necessary or appropriate for all research to be considered from an experimental orientation. In our study, we easily could have engineered a multiple baseline across settings of experimental design by simply adding a few baseline sessions in the restaurant and store, however, we deliberately avoided this codified temptation because the central purpose of our investigation was not experimental and the extension of baseline phases would have been an unwelcomed and potentially deleterious intrusion on the partnership we were seeking to achieve. As we explained in our article (Vaughn et al., 1997), it is unclear what potential confounds might have been controlled in this case by a multiple baseline protocol, or what such a protocol might have contrib-

uted. We believe that the crucial issue for evaluating natural case study data such as ours is whether the data are credible and the effects convincing (Baer, Wolf, & Risley, 1988; Hayes, 1985).

The challenge of behavioral support in family and community contexts presents an immense array of questions and conditions that are not necessarily amenable to the rules of experimentation. Experimental designs require some arbitrariness in the application of an independent variable, but this requirement can be contradictory to the distinctively nonarbitrary process of collaborative and family-centered support. In addition, experimental designs (especially single-case designs) may have reduced usefulness as behavioral support efforts are defined increasingly as multicomponent and longitudinal processes. Manipulating discriminable independent variables so that they produce temporally distinguishable effects on specified dependent variables within an experimental framework is an endeavor that will remain vital for many fundamental research objectives, but it may be less apropos for addressing complex issues of support strategies in typical home and community settings (Evans & Meyer, 1993). Fortunately, various quantitative and qualitative methodologies are available. In particular, we believe that an accumulation of rich, multidimensional case study data (Yin, 1994) can be extremely valuable for informing the field about effective practices. As long as research methods conform to pertinent standards of credibility and believability, and as long as data are presented in an appropriate and judicious context, the field will benefit from a pragmatic selection of research approaches.

Benefit and Challenge of Partnerships

Every respondent discussed the value of collaborative partnerships, with Martha Snell issuing perhaps the most emphatic voice on their behalf. Respectful and constructive relationships between professionals and family members have been talked about a great deal but they have been rarely practiced. In this project, we enjoyed an especially close and trusting partnership and we submit that meaningful benefits ensued. However, we acknowledge Robert Horner's message that the circumstances that facilitated the collaboration were atypical. A foundation of familiarity and trust had already been established by the time that the behavioral support process began.

We believe strongly that a collaborative (rather than hierarchical) model is integral to meaningful support, but we recognize that the process can be challenging and sometimes insurmountable. The development of rapport and trust between families and professionals does not happen automatically or easily. This is an area that merits research attention. In addition, we urge that particular emphasis be paid to underserved and underrepresented segments of our society, thereby encompassing the range of our cultural and economic diversity. The extent to which behavioral support providers (and researchers) collaborate with diverse families in diverse circumstances will ultimately determine the usable scope of our processes and strategies.

Issues Related to Practice and Research in Behavioral Support

The respondents raised several issues regarding the evolution and practice of behavioral support. We accept the views of Edward Carr and Robert Horner that our field is broaching a new kind of applied science mandated, perhaps, by the broadening perspectives and guidelines of practice. Although applied behavior analysis has provided an indispensable lineage of procedural and methodological resources, the expanded demands for meaningful outcomes have obliged researchers to embrace additional means of acquiring knowledge and assembling supports. Although the process of behavioral support that was implemented in the three community settings was derived directly from applied behavior analysis, the goals and results of our qualitative data clearly were not.

Ilene Schwartz identified a crucial dilemma that must be addressed if this type of research is to lead to palpable benefits in the implementation of behavioral support. We have illustrated a complex and time-consuming process that involved relationship development, functional assessment, and graduated intervention in multiple environments. The process required knowledge of appropriate practice, some degree of skill and experience, and appreciable time and commitment. As we seek meaningful outcomes for children and families affected by significant behavioral challenges, we must ask about the resources and the will that must be mobilized to achieve these goals. We doubt that schools can assume responsibility for substantial in-home and in-community support, unless they are reformed (and refunded) substantially to truly realize a full-service accountability. We agree that supports should come from the broader community and be coordinated with school-based collaborators, but equally important is that it becomes a priority. Comprehensive support for families that include children with significant behavioral challenges needs to be regarded as a complex, multifaceted and longitudinal endeavor. But it is a worthwhile endeavor; one that merits our creative and spirited dedication.

Behavioral support has been established as a person-centered (and family-centered) enterprise that attempts to reduce problem behaviors and achieve other meaningful outcomes that are defined from the perspectives of all participants. Behavioral support requires that we listen to and learn from these multiple perspectives. To do this means that a new applied science needs to incorporate not only the important features identified by Edward Carr and Robert Horner, but that it also include expanded ways for acquiring, analyzing, and synthesizing knowledge. We are thankful for the opportunity to engage in this important and encouraging dialogue and we hope that our studies have provided a small addition to the process.

References

Albin, R. W., Lucyshyn, J. M., Horner, R. H., & Flannery, K. B. (1996). Contextual fit for behavioral support plans: A model for "goodness of fit." In L. K. Koegel, R. L. Koegel, & G. Dunlap (Eds.). *Positive behavioral support: Including people with difficult behavior in the community* (pp. 81–98). Baltimore: Paul H. Brookes.

Baer, D. M., Wolf, M. M., and Risley, T. R. (1987). Some still current dimensions of applied behavior analysis. *Journal of Applied Behavior Analysis, 20,* 313–327.

Dunst, C. J., Trivette, C. M., & Deal, A. G. (Eds.) (1994). *Supporting & strengthening families: Methods, strategies, and practices.* Cambridge, MA: Brookline Books.

Evans, I. M., & Meyer, L. H. (1993). Once more with feeling: On the importance of moving forward. *The Journal of the Association for Persons with Severe Handicaps, 18,* 304–311.

Hayes, S. C. (1985). Natural baselines across persons: A reply to Harris and Jenson. *Behavioral Assessment, 7,* 129–132.

Horner, R. H., Dunlap, G., Koegel, R. L., Carr. E. G., Sailor, W., Anderson, J., Albin, R. W., & O'Neill, R. E. (1990). Toward a technology of "nonaversive" behavioral support. *The Journal of the Association for Persons with Severe Handicaps, 15,* 125–132.

Lucyshyn, J. M., Albin, R. W., & Nixon, C. D. (1997). Embedding comprehensive behavioral support in family ecology: An experimental, single case analysis. *Journal of Consulting and Clinical Psychology, 65,* 241–251.

Meyer, L. H., & Evans, I. M. (1993). Science and practice in behavioral intervention: Meaningful outcomes, research validity, and usable knowledge. *The Journal of the Association for Persons with Severe Handicaps, 18,* 224–234.

Powell, D., Batsche, C. J., Ferro, J., Fox, L., & Dunlap, G. (1997). A strength-based approach in support of multi-risk families: Principles and issues. *Topics in Early Childhood Special Education, 17,* 1–26.

Scotti, J. R., & Meyer, L. H. (Eds.). (in press). *New directions for behavioral intervention: Principles, models, and practices.* Baltimore: Paul H. Brookes.

Vaughn, B. J., Clarke, S., & Dunlap, G. (1997). Assessment-based intervention for severe behavior problems in a natural family context. *Journal of Applied Behavior Analysis, 30,* 713–716.

Vaughn, B. J., Dunlap, G., Fox, L., Clarke, S., & Bucy, M. (1997). Parent-professional partnership in behavioral support: A case study of community-based intervention. *The Journal of The Association for Persons with Severe Handicaps, 22,* 196–206.

Yin, R. K. (1994). *Case study research: Design and methods* (2nd Edition). Thousand Oaks, CA: Sage Publications, Inc.

PART V
Capacity Building

~

How does a practice go from a research study to essential supports for people with severe disabilities? That transformation happens through planning, hard work, capacity-building, provision of training for the many people who will implement the intervention, and involvement of consumers in the process. The adoption of educational innovation is of great interest to people with disabilities, their families, advocates, practitioners, and researchers. Developing and validating procedures are important, but a major challenge lies in getting these procedures implemented in schools and communities on a regular basis. Part of this challenge lies in developing an intervention or collection of practices that can be described, outlining the procedures, implementing the procedures with high fidelity across many providers, and still producing robust outcomes. Helping an educational innovation make the move from state-of-the-art to state-of-the-practice takes more than a well-developed training package. It requires consideration of the social and ecological validities of the intervention, inclusion of the perceptions of consumers, and careful study of the elements of the practice that must be present to facilitate positive outcomes. The articles in this section describe how people have worked to make quality PBS programs standard practice for all people with disabilities who demonstrate challenging behaviors.

The article in this section by Weigle (1997), provided a context for thinking about training and capacity-building in schools. It described problems encountered when practitioners attempted to implement PBS, discussed the support in federal law for this approach, and provided a model for thinking about how inclusive education is supported and promoted through the use of PBS. Hieneman and Dunlap (2000) interviewed various stakeholders to understand essential elements needed for the successful implementation of PBS. They described issues for training and research that will be useful to consumers (family members, practitioners, advocates, researchers) across all levels.

The article by Dunlap, Hieneman, Knoster, Fox, Anderson, and Albin (2000) proposed a set of core components that should be included in all training related to PBS. The identification of essential elements assists trainers in providing comprehensive and comparable information about PBS across geographical settings, university programs, in-service training providers, and others. This type of information will help improve the quality of PBS plans developed and implemented for people with disabilities, wherever they live.

Finally, the article by Bambara, Gomez, Koger, Lohrmann-O'Rourke, and Xin (2001) examined issues of training from the perspective of the trainees—that is, the people receiving the training and providing the supports. PBS as an approach depends on a well-functioning team—and in this article, individuals shared their experiences while working on teams implementing PBS. This article reminds us that the most comprehensive list of essential elements for training will be rendered useless if the culture of the team and the relationships among team members are not considered when providing training and attempting to build capacity for the use of PBS.

—Ilene S. Schwartz

JASH
2001, Vol. 26, No. 4, 213–228

More Than Techniques: Team Members' Perspectives on Implementing Positive Supports for Adults With Severe Challenging Behaviors

Linda M. Bambara, Ophelia Gomez, Freya Koger, Sharon Lohrmann-O'Rourke,
and Yan Ping Xin
Lehigh University

How teams implement and understand the process of positive behavior support provides an important source of information for improving supports for adults with developmental disabilities who engage in severe challenging behaviors in community settings. The purpose of the present study was to describe how positive behavior support was experienced and understood by team members from four residential, community-based teams who achieved positive outcomes for adults with severe challenging behaviors. In-depth, semistructured interviewing was the primary data source involving 19 participants. Data were analyzed within and across teams revealing team members' perceptions on their guiding values, struggles and barriers to implementing positive approaches, ways to support team members, the importance of staff relationships, and key elements of their direct support. Moving beyond techniques, the findings depict an overall culture of support consisting of interrelated layers of social context. Implications for practice and future research directions are discussed.

DESCRIPTORS: positive behavior support, team process, residential supports, adults with developmental disabilities, challenging behaviors

Positive approaches[1] or positive behavior support refers to a comprehensive, value-based approach toward the support of individuals with developmental disabili-

ties who engage in severe challenging behaviors. With roots both in applied behavior analysis and person-centered planning, positive behavior support has emerged over the last 15 years into a comprehensive support ecology consisting of multiple interventions derived from diverse theoretical and philosophical perspectives (Carr et al., in press; Koegel, Koegel, & Dunlap, 1996). Early examples of positive approaches focused on the application of single nonaversive interventions (e.g., differential reinforcement interventions) to reduce problem behaviors (e.g., Donnellan, LaVigna, Negri-Shoultz, & Fassbender, 1988). However, more recently, increasingly less emphasis is being placed on selecting specific behavior reducing interventions per se, and more emphasis is being placed on changing deficit or problematic environments, teaching alternative skills, and improving the quality of life for people with developmental disabilities and their families (Carr et al., in press; Carr et al., 1999; Koegel et al., 1996; Meyer & Evans, 1989). Consequently, the ultimate goal of positive approaches is not just the simple reduction of problem behaviors, but rather the achievement of broad-based outcomes and lifestyle changes that are meaningful to consumers, particularly the person with disabilities and his or her family (Meyer & Evans, 1993; Turnbull & Turnbull, 2000).

Positive behavior support is grounded in a thorough understanding of the individual within his or her social context (Bambara & Knoster, 1998). This feature includes ongoing assessments to identify environmental explanations for problem behaviors (e.g., Demchak & Bossert, 1996; Foster-Johnson & Dunlap, 1993) as well as a focus on the individual's, and where appropriate

The authors are forever grateful for the generosity of the four teams who contributed their time and shared their invaluable experiences and insights with us. Thanks also to the state-level trainers and consultants who guided us to find exemplary teams.

Address all correspondence and requests for reprints to Linda M. Bambara, Department of Education and Human Services, Lehigh University, 111 Research Drive, Iacocca Hall, Bethlehem, PA 18015. E-mail: lmb1@Lehigh.edu

[1] At its inception, the terms *positive approaches* and *positive behavior support* were used interchangeably to describe an emerging, nonaversive, comprehensive system of support (e.g., see Bambara, Mitchell-Kvacky, & Gill, 1994; Horner et al., 1990). Currently, reference to positive approaches is still

sometimes made (e.g., TASH Committee on Positive Approaches), however nationally, positive behavior support is the most widely used term. In the current article, we elected to use both terms interchangeably to refer to the same system of support. In doing so, our intent was to communicate to a broad national audience, while respecting Pennsylvania's (the state in which the study was conducted) use of the term *positive approaches* in the community mental health and mental retardation service system.

the family's, preferences and goals throughout the planning process (e.g., Turnbull & Turnbull, 1996).

Strongly influenced by person-centered planning, another essential feature of positive behavior support is the development and implementation of support strategies by collaborative problem-solving teams consisting of members most relevant to the support and well being of the individual (e.g., service providers, family members, friends) (Albin, Lucyshyn, Horner, & Flannery, 1996; Anderson, Russo, Dunlap, & Albin, 1996; Turnbull & Turnbull, 1996). According to the concept of contextual fit (Albin et al., 1996), the long-term success of any support plan is dependent on the degree of fit between the support strategies and the characteristics of the daily environments in which the plan is implemented, as well as the fit with the values, beliefs, and goals of the team members who carry out the plan. Thus, teaming may be conceptualized as serving both an intervention planning and social process (Dunlap, Hieneman, Knoster, Fox, Anderson, & Albin, 2000; O'Brien, O'Brien, & Mount, 1997). The planning process ensures that interventions are tailored to an individual's needs and matched to the resources and demands of everyday environments, whereas the social process focuses on building the capacity and commitment of team members to carry out the plan consistent with their values and beliefs.

This study is concerned with the positive support of adults with developmental disabilities who engage in severe challenging behaviors in community settings. Despite the relatively large number of controlled investigations that have evaluated the effectiveness of single interventions or isolated components of positive behavior support, little is known about how the approach, resulting in broad lifestyle changes, is actually carried out by community-based teams (Carr et al., 1999). Such information is vital to the field's understanding if positive behavior support is to produce strategies and outcomes that are practical and meaningful to consumers. To date, only a few published case studies exist that illustrate how behavior support plans are implemented for adults in community settings (e.g., Berkman & Meyer, 1988; Lucyshyn, Olson, & Horner, 1995). Furthermore, despite the emphasis on teaming, little is known about the process that teams take to design supports, or the perspectives of team members in terms of their values, adoption of positive practices, struggles with implementation, and their beliefs about key elements needed for success. Recently, using focus group interviewing, two qualitative investigations explored the perspectives of various stakeholder groups (e.g., direct service providers, administrators/policy makers, family members) that supported children (Hieneman & Dunlap, 2000), and children and adults (Ruef, Turnbull, Turnbull, & Poston, 1999) with challenging behaviors.

Although these studies provide a starting point for understanding some of the issues experienced by various constituency groups, the experience of teams and team members in implementing positive behavior support remains essentially unexplored.

The present study was designed to describe the experiences and perspectives of team members from four residential community-based teams that successfully supported an adult identified as having developmental disabilities and a history of engaging in severe challenging behaviors. Believing that the field could benefit from the experiences of good community exemplars (Bogdan & Taylor, 1990), we defined "successful teams" as those that were both committed to implementing positive approaches and had achieved broad-based outcomes or lifestyle changes for the adult with disabilities. Using semistructured interviews as the primary source of data gathering, our analysis was guided by the overarching question: How do team members describe their team's approach to supporting an adult with severe challenging behaviors? More specifically, we were interested in describing and understanding the underlying values that guided the teams' support activities; the struggles or barriers experienced by team members in implementing positive approaches, and the strategies employed to address these struggles; and team members' perspectives on the essential elements of positive behavior support that contributed to their success.

METHODS AND PROCEDURES

Drawing primarily upon interprevist interview methods (McCracken, 1988; Patton, 1990; Seidman, 1991), we employed a multisite design (Bogdan & Biklen, 1992) to collect data across teams from different residential agencies. Using a constant comparative method of analysis (Glaser & Strauss, 1967), data were collected and analyzed concurrently and recursively throughout the study by all authors who formed the research team. Data were analyzed successively first within and then across teams, enabling us to clarify and confirm information, modify coding categories, and shape subsequent interviews and data collection according to the information obtained. To ensure consistency among researchers, the research team met regularly with each member participating in decision-making throughout all phases of the study. The research team consisted of a university professor (first author) and doctoral students in special education, each with five or more years of direct and/or administrative service in residential agencies for adults with developmental disabilities.

Team Selection

Four teams were selected purposively from community residential agencies in Pennsylvania. We sought successful teams that provided ongoing positive behavior support (2 or more years) to an adult with a primary diagnosis of mental retardation and a history (5 or more years) of engaging in severe challenging behaviors that had significantly interfered with community inclusion (e.g., history of institutionalization, hospitalization, placement in residential schools, frequent placement change). Successful teams were defined in terms of key positive behavior support characteristics described in the literature (e.g., Bambara & Knoster, 1998; Carr et al., 1999; Dunlap et al., 2000) and positive outcomes achieved for the adult with disabilities. Specifically, we looked for evidence (later verified through interviews and documents) that teams (a) articulated a positive, person-centered philosophy, (b) formulated environmental hypotheses for problem behavior based on team observations and assessments, (c) used multiple support strategies designed to teach alternative skills or modify the environment, and (d) achieved broad-based outcomes including reductions in problem behavior and improvements in the person's quality of life.

Teams were selected by seeking nominations from state-level trainers with expertise in positive approaches and first-hand knowledge about good examples of community-based teams and/or agencies using positive approaches in the state. Nominated teams were invited to participate in a telephone-screening interview to explore their potential match with our selection criteria and their willingness to participate in the study. Screening interviews, approximately 1 hour each, were conducted with one team representative, typically a team leader, who had the broadest understanding of the team's history and practices. In addition to meeting our selection criteria, final selection depended on se-curing team members' and the focus person's informed consent.

Teams and Participants

Because community-based teams can be large and include people who are only peripherally involved in planning, we asked a team leader from each of the four teams to identify four to six core team members for interviewing (we later verified these nominations through subsequent discussions with other team members). Core team members were those who were regularly involved with developing and implementing supports for the focus person (i.e., adult with disabilities) and, to insure that varied perspectives were represented, consisted of at least one team leader who organized the team's activities, and one direct support staff who worked regularly with the focus person. This definition resulted in a total of 19 participants across the four teams representing a range of positions including agency directors, behavior/program specialists, program supervisors, direct support staff, and outside consultants who were hired by the host agencies to work with the team to develop positive supports (see Table 1 for participant demographic information). Although it was not our intention to exclude families, only one family member, George's mother (Team 3), was included as a participant. Close family members from other teams were deceased, estranged, or participated minimally in the teams' planning efforts.

Table 2 provides descriptive information for each focus person including age, diagnoses, challenging behaviors, and positive outcomes reported by the teams. Because of the severity of the individuals' challenging behaviors and support needs, all teams provided 24-hour

Table 1
Participant Demographic Information

Team	Members[a]	Position	Race	Age (years)
1	Robert	Consultant/Team Leader	Caucasian	30–39
	Kathy	Program Specialist	Caucasian	20–29
	Simon	Supervisor/Direct Support Staff	African American	30–39
	Alex	Direct Support Staff	African American	20–29
2	Sally	Program Specialist/Team Leader	Caucasian	30–39
	Keith	Assistant Director	Caucasian	40–49
	Helen	Consultant	Caucasian	50–59
	Cecelia	Roommate/Director Support Staff	African American	50–59
	Joan	Direct Support Staff	African American	40–49
3	Phillip	Consultant/Team Leader	Caucasian	30–39
	Marcie	Program Specialist/Team Leader	Caucasian	30–39
	Jason	Supervisor/Direct Support Staff	Caucasian	20–29
	Barbara	Direct Support Staff	Caucasian	20–29
	Jennifer	Mother	Caucasian	50–59
4	Ann	Program Specialist/Team Leader	Caucasian	20–29
	Rick	Behavior Specialist/Team Leader	Caucasian	30–39
	Roseann	Direct Support Staff	Caucasian	40–49
	Frank	Direct Support Staff	Caucasian	40–49
	Terri	Direct Support Staff	African American	30–39

[a] Pseudonyms.

Table 2
Focus Person Information

Team	Name[a]	Age (years)	Diagnosis	Challenging behavior(s)	Outcomes[b]
Team 1	Lawrence	30	Mental retardation Bipolar disorder	Inappropriate sexual behavior in public (stripping, masturbation, touching others) Elopement Aggression	Near zero rates of problem behaviors Works part-time at McDonald's Participates in a wide range of community activities (e.g., works out at a gym, attends sporting events) Improved relationship with mother; visits regularly Increased autonomy/decision making
Team 2	Sara	40	Mental retardation Bipolar disorder	Severe property destruction/tantrums Severe aggression	Near zero rates of problem behaviors No psychiatric hospitalization within 2 years Shares home with a non-disabled roommate Holds full-time job, volunteers at a nursing home Established community friendships (e.g., neighbors)
Team 3	George	21	Mental retardation Autism Legal blindness	Severe aggression Property destruction	Reduced severest forms of aggression and use of mechanical restraints Attends a public school Lives in an apartment close to family; visits regularly Better able to express concerns and preferences
Team 4	Salvator	50	Mental retardation (severe/profound) Anxiety disorder	Self injury Severe tantrums	Near zero rates of severe self-injury Improved health (e.g., better sleeping patterns, less gastrointestinal problems) Participates regularly in community activities More communicative and affectionate

[a] Pseudonyms.
[b] Data sources include support plans, data summaries, and interviews.

support. We introduce each team and focus person by providing a brief historical overview.

Team 1. Team 1 supported Lawrence, a 30-year-old man diagnosed with mental retardation and bipolar disorder, for 2 years. The team formed to help transition Lawrence from a locked ward in a state developmental disability center to a home in the community. Lawrence was placed in the center in his early 20's because of sexually inappropriate behaviors (stripping, public masturbation, inappropriate sexual initiations), incidents or threats of physical assault, and frequent elopement from service providers. At the time of the study, Lawrence lived in an apartment with another roommate with disabilities, maintained a part-time position at McDonald's (via supported employment), and was an active participant in his community (e.g., worked out at a gym, attended sport events, enjoyed shopping for clothes). Problem behaviors were reduced to near zero levels.

Team 2. Team 2 supported Sara, a 40-year-old woman diagnosed with mental retardation and atypical bipolar affect disorder. Because of severe aggression and property destruction (e.g., starting fires, smashing cars, threatening staff with knives), Sara spent most of her adult life in and out of psychiatric hospitals and group homes until the current residential agency, agreeing to support Sara, found her living an "unhealthy lifestyle" in a boarding house with inadequate staff support. Team 2 formed when Cecelia, a staff person assigned to work with Sara, offered to live with Sara as a paid roommate. At the time of the interviews, Sara and Cecelia had shared an apartment together for 3 years (additional part-time staff provided day-time assistance on weekdays and weekends). Sara had just secured a full-time job, had not engaged in severe acts of aggression, and had no psychiatric hospitalizations for over a year.

Team 3. Team 3 supported George, a young 21-year-old man diagnosed with autism, mental retardation, and legal blindness. Because of the severity and frequency of his physical aggression, his family was unable to care for him at home. They placed him in two out-of-state residential schools during his elementary school and teen years. At the time of the study, Team 3 had supported George for 3 years. After years of living far away from his family, he lived in a three-person group home in his hometown. Because George's physical aggression often led to staff injury, physical restraint was a part of the team's crisis management plan. His parents, fearing further injury during physical contact, obtained a state waiver for the staff to use mechanical restraints (leather arm and leg shackles) to interrupt his aggression. However, after noting that George spent 72 hours in mechanical restraints one month with no signs of improvement, the team sought the guidance of an outside consultant trained in positive approaches to help them change their intervention strategies. At the time of the interviews, the team had followed a positive behavior support plan for 2 years. Although aggression still occurred, the frequency and intensity decreased substantially, and use of mechanical restraints was reduced dramatically (90 minutes over 3 months). During the last 2 years, George attended a special education classroom in his local public school.

Team 4. Team 4 supported Salvator, a 50-year-old nonverbal man diagnosed with severe/profound mental retardation and a seizure disorder. When Salvator's severe tantrums (sometimes lasting hours) and head banging (resulting in facial disfigurement) became unmanageable at home, he was placed in a large state institution at age 26 years, which was later closed because of neglect and abuse of the residents. Team 4 supported Salvator for 6 years, beginning 2 years after he was released from the institution. Neither his previous group home nor the institution was able to effectively address the frequency and intensity of his challenging behaviors. At the time of the study, Salvator lived in his own apartment with individualized staff supports and had become an active participant in community activities. Although he still hits his face lightly on occasion, which staff interpret as communicative gestures, severe tantrums and self-injury were virtually eliminated.

Data Sources and Collection

In-depth, semistructured interviews served as the primary data source. Using an interview guide (Patton, 1990), each team member was interviewed individually in a quiet location at the team's host agency. Interviews were conducted flexibly, allowing us to explore, adapt questions, and probe as participants set the direction of the conversation; however, the guide ensured that the same key topics were covered across participants. Interview questions focused on (a) the focus person's and team's history (e.g., Tell me how the team formed? What was it like in the early days?); (b) team process (e.g., How does your team work to achieve goals? Overcome barriers?); (c) supports for the focus person (e.g., What approach did your team take to support George? Describe the strategies used.); and (d) team member's personal experiences and meaning of their work (e.g., What does positive approaches mean to you? What aspects of support are most essential for success?).

Interviews ranged from 90 to 150 minutes and were completed within a 3-week period involving two to four site visits for each team. Participants were interviewed once, however, nine participants, from Teams 1, 2, and 3, were interviewed a second time within 4 months of the initial interview to clarify issues and to verify our initial data interpretations. Interviews were audiotaped and transcribed verbatim, resulting in approximately 1,000 pages of single-spaced text.

Two secondary data sources were used to contextualize, broaden, and verify the information obtained from the team interviews. Written documents including recent (within 2 years) behavior support plans, individualized habilitation plans, and historical intervention/program summaries provided information on the teams' and the adults' history, programmatic outcomes, and current/past behavioral supports. In addition, a single, formal observation, ranging from 90 to 150 minutes, was conducted of the focus person with at least one support staff from each team during a typical home or community activity. Our focus during the observation was to describe focus person/staff interactions and how supports were implemented.

Data Analysis

Adapting procedures for consensual agreement and data reduction within research teams (Hill, Thompson, & Williams, 1997), data analysis progressed in five stages. In stage 1, two researchers developed preliminary coding categories based on the emerging themes from the first set of interviews obtained from Team 1. In stage 2, after the entire research team met to refine the codes, each transcript was coded successively across teams by pairs of researchers who coded independently, and then met to compare their categorization and resolve differences by coming to a consensual agreement. Code definitions were continually modified as they were applied across transcripts to accommodate new ideas. Previously coded transcripts were recoded as codes were redefined. Agreed upon coded text units were entered into the QSR NUD*IST (1985) computer software program for data management and retrieval.

In stage 3, participant summaries were prepared for each transcript by pairs of researchers who met to write abstracts of the core ideas expressed by participants in each coded category. This was done to reduce the data for subsequent cross analyses in stages 4 and 5.

In stage 4, a team profile summarizing themes across participants within the same team was prepared. To develop a team profile, the entire research team met after reading the participant summaries to identify patterns within categories across team participants. Pairs of researchers then wrote a summary of the themes (team profile), checking the adequacy of their summarizations against the raw data and with one another. A third researcher audited the team profiles by again checking the summaries against the raw data and, looking for confirming or disconfirming evidence, against the written documents and observation field notes which were also coded with the final codes. Any modification to team profiles or discrepancies between the auditor and pair were resolved in the larger team.

In stage 5, team profiles were compared to conduct a cross-team analysis. After the entire research team met

to identify potential themes, the first author prepared a written analysis linking various categories from the team profiles into larger themes and sub-themes, noting particular patterns across team leaders and direct support staff. The entire research team then evaluated the internal consistency and accuracy of the final report by checking it against the team profiles, individual summaries, and raw data.

To validate our interpretations against the participants' view, participants were mailed a report organized in three sections: (a) overall themes found across teams, (b) key themes found within the participant's team, and (c) excerpts from the participant's interview that contributed to the development of the team's themes. For each section, participants were asked to judge the adequacy and accuracy of the findings and respond either in writing, using an open-ended response form, or over the telephone. Sixteen participants responded; three participants, each from a different team, could not be reached. With the exception of some suggested word changes, all respondents affirmed the findings and our interpretations of their experiences.

FINDINGS

Our analysis revealed the emergence of interrelated themes pertaining to the teams' experiences while supporting the adults with severe challenging behaviors. These themes are grouped into three areas: guiding values, support for team, and direct supports for the focus person.

Guiding Values

It wasn't about this technique [and] then you have success. It was about the context that we were going to look at him in.

Shared among all team leaders was the belief that positive approaches are more than a set of techniques, but rather the approach is a context, world view, or philosophy for understanding the person, identifying reasons for problem behavior, and providing appropriate and respectful supports that address the person's needs. Two themes captured the overarching guiding values of the teams. The first was *seeing the person as a person*. A strong sentiment expressed by participants across teams was above all, despite the person's difficult or unusual behaviors, he/she was a person with characteristics, needs, desires, and interests no different from themselves. As expressed by most team members, this view guided them to develop supports in the manner that they would want to be treated or have others treat their loved ones. Some suggested that only when the focus person could be seen as having similar characteristics to them, could the person's actions and true needs be understood.

The second guiding value, *following the person's lead,* is exemplified by the words of one direct support staff, "We are here for him." This commitment required that team members discover what the person wanted and ultimately what made the person happy, so that they could adapt, make changes, and make things happen accordingly. Following the person's lead required a willingness to take direction from the person and a measure of self-restraint against imposing their own ideas about what is best. Said Barbara (Team 3), "What we think George needs, and what he truly needs are probably two different things."

Support for the Team

Much of the teams' positive approach was devoted to supporting team members. Across all teams, leaders stressed that in order to support the focus person, team members, particularly direct support staff, must first be supported, because, in the words of one team leader, "Nothing happens without them." Specifically, Team 2 leaders viewed their central mission as "supporting Cecelia" to enable her to maintain her relationship and commitment to Sara her roommate. In contrast, leaders from the other three teams viewed support for the team as a matter of "cultivating" or "investing" staff in the team's values and practices. Before we describe how teams supported their members, we introduce team struggle as a rationale for team support.

Struggles

Teams often struggled with issues that threatened their commitment or ability to carry out supports consistent with their values. Left unresolved, these issues created temporary or long-term barriers to effective team functioning, and ultimately, the teams' ability to provide quality supports for the focus person. Three major categories of team struggle emerged from the data.

The challenge of challenging behaviors: "Feelings of complete dread." The emotional and physical stress caused by challenging behaviors was one struggle reported by participants from all four teams. Participants expressed that their darkest days were during their team's initial months of support when the frequency and intensity of challenging behaviors were the highest. Using the words "grueling," "chaotic," and "feelings of complete dread," team members described a period that was filled with anxiety, fear of getting hurt, and uncertainty about what to do to support the focus person. It was also a period of constant staff turnover, placing additional burdens on core team members who attempted to stand by the focus person during this difficult transition.

During these initial months, several team members questioned their ability to ever provide effective supports or to understand reasons for problem behaviors, especially after their early attempts at interventions repeatedly failed. Others, who tried to live out their commitment, questioned their endurance to "stick it out." Said Jason (Team 3) about George's most aggressive days, "It made me question why I was even coming to work."

Several Team 3 members and Cecilia from Team 2 discussed their struggle with taking challenging behaviors personally when problem behaviors were directed toward them. Said Barbara, "It is hard not to take it personally when you are his target . . . the worst [time] he ever hit me I was angry, truly angry." As illustrated, when team members perceived challenging behaviors as personal attacks, they expressed feelings of both anger and intolerance. Moreover, explained the leaders from Team 3, when team members took challenging behaviors personally they were blinded to seeking alternative, environmental explanations for problem behaviors and could not look beyond seeing George as "just a mean guy."

Team arguments: "Being right." Interpersonal conflicts and arguments among team members was a second major struggle experienced by two teams. Members from Teams 3 and 4 discussed that particularly when challenging behaviors intensified and things were not going right, efforts to communicate their concerns were often viewed as being harshly critical, sarcastic, and blaming of one another. In short, team members either felt blamed or blamed others for their failures. As a result, rather than working collaboratively to solve problems, team members reported spending more time defending their positions and feeling hurt, angry, and under-appreciated by their teammates. However, even when increases in challenging behaviors were not an issue, team members sometimes argued uncompromisingly about the best or right way of providing support to the focus person. Said Frank (Team 4), "We all have Salvator's best interest at heart, we just have different opinions about what his best interests are." Several team members believed that the crux of the problem was not that team members had different opinions, but that arguments about what was "right" were often based on team members' preferences and needs and not the focus person's. Explained Phillip (Team 3 consultant), "It is not about being right; it's about being helpful [by addressing the person's needs]. As we argue about what is right, George is the one left suffering."

Conflicts with "upper administration" and "outside professionals." A third struggle experienced by all teams was dealing with the conflicting actions of the "upper administration" of their agency or other professionals (e.g., physicians, mental health workers, school personnel, workshop administrators) outside of their team. Team members believed that when others outside their core team did not share their values, or acted in ways that were inconsistent with their values, their efforts to provide positive, person-centered supports were undermined or thwarted, resulting not only in poor services for the focus person, but feelings of frustration and distress by team members.

For example, although Team 1 and 4 participants viewed their agency's administration as generally supportive of their person-centered approach, they expressed disillusionment when administrative decisions appeared driven by fiscal or regulatory priorities rather than the needs of the person. Terri (Team 4) angrily expressed that she could not understand why it took her agency over a year to reduce Salvator's day program hours to half days when it was clear to her, and the rest of the team, that he banged his head because he was unhappy going full time. Team 1 members told a story in which Lawrence's roommate was suddenly replaced with another without consulting Lawrence, the team, or the prospective roommate, creating "tremendous upheaval" for Lawrence. Said Robert (Team 1 leader), "This great person-centered approach crumbles real quick under an administrative decision to put another person [Lawrence's roommate] in here."

In a somewhat different situation, Phillip (Team 3 consultant) believed that the host agency had not yet developed the overall administrative culture to sustain the team's person-centered activities. Failing to build in sufficient time for team meetings, failing to hire staff who could drive, and overloading team leaders with other agency responsibilities, were viewed as unsupportive actions that had a negative rippling effect on George, resulting in increases in challenging behaviors. Eventually, argued Phillip, George gets blamed for the failure to provide sufficient resources to the team.

Finally, all teams expressed that a major impediment to their positive support efforts was dealing with other outside professionals who did not share in their team's beliefs and values. Participants from all teams described difficulties with advocating on the focus person's behalf and acquiring good services when other professionals dismissed their perspectives about the focus person and strategies for support.

Ways to Support Team Members

From the teams' discussion of their struggles, it was clear that developing or maintaining a positive, person-centered approach was not an automatic process, but one that demanded continuous nurturing and development. Participants identified several ways in which their teams were supported.

Creating an atmosphere "where all are listened to and heard." According to leaders from Teams 1, 3, and 4, team support began by establishing a culture where all team members felt free to express their ideas and concerns, and where all ideas would be listened to and respected by other team members. Robert (Team 1) recalled that one of the first things he did in building his team was to "create an atmosphere where no idea was too trivial, stupid, or outlandish, and that all ideas would be appreciated; all efforts appreciated." Accord-

ing to team leaders, such a culture served as a critical foundation for team planning and for understanding the beliefs, concerns, and support needs of its members. It was also viewed by some as a chief strategy for investing all team members into the process and values of the team, and empowering individual members to seek solutions to problems. Several direct support staff commented that having a voice and being listened to made them feel valued and important. Said Barbara (Team 3), "You are not somebody who doesn't have a brain." In describing her experience on Team 1, Kathy commented: "Titles are nothing; everyone is equal. Just because you are a behavior specialist doesn't mean that your opinion is worth more than mine."

Creating opportunities for team members to freely express their view was also seen as a way to diffuse negative tensions among team members, according to several team leaders. However, during times of interpersonal conflict where team members may be unable to listen to one another, Team 3 leaders stressed that team members had to be actively guided to carefully listen to both the "what" and the "whys" (i.e., underlying reasons) of their team members concerns, similar to the way they tried to understand reasons for focus person's problem behaviors. As explained by Marcie, when team members made a concerted effort to truly understand and acknowledge others' perspectives, defensiveness was eliminated.

Addressing the personal/emotional needs of staff: "We're there for one another." Another way that team support was offered was to directly address the personal/emotional needs of team members when they felt tired, frustrated, scared, or simply "bad" about themselves after experiencing failure. An important source of support, particularly for direct support staff, was knowing that despite their worst experiences, team leaders and other team members were always available, any time of day or night, to offer assistance. Across all teams, most direct support staff reported feeling free to call team leaders, or one another, to brainstorm solutions to problems, seek reassurance for taking the right course of action, ask for additional staff support, or simply to "vent" their frustrations, fears, or concerns. For some, having the opportunity to vent their feelings to team leaders, without experiencing criticism or ridicule, provided an immediate stress relief and the acknowledgement that their difficult experiences were real and recognized.

To reduce fatigue, three teams built in frequent opportunities for staff to take short breaks during their shifts. Respite for Cecilia, Sara's roommate, was conceptualized much like that provided to families by scheduling daily time away from home and several short vacations during the year.

Leaders from Teams 1, 2, and 3 discussed strategies for overcoming team members' lack of confidence, hesitation, or fear of trying new intervention approaches, many of which were untested and were viewed as potentially placing the staff or the focus person in jeopardy, particularly in community settings. Team 2 instituted frequent "circle meetings" where team members, along with friends of Sara and Cecelia, celebrated both Sara's and Cecelia's accomplishments. Leaders from Teams 1 and 3 emphasized the importance of encouraging staff to take risks. To encourage risk taking, Team 3 leaders lavishly praised staff member's "acts of courage" and novel solutions to problems "no matter how small." Said Barbara, Team 3 direct care staff, "It got to the point where we were willing to try anything, no matter how [seemingly] bizarre or off-the-wall the approach was." In addition to praise, Robert (Team 1) stressed team consensus making as a way to encourage risk taking by his team. He argued that as long as staff tried the approaches agreed upon by the team, no one person would feel blamed if things went wrong. Once the fear of blame was eliminated, Robert believed that his team felt encouraged to explore and try new options.

Staying person-centered: "Getting on the same page." A third approach to team support was to ensure that all team members were unified in their beliefs and values, and kept the focus person's needs at the "center" of their work. To facilitate a common understanding of the focus person's needs and reasons for challenging behaviors, participants spoke of first untangling preconceived notions or negative impressions about the person. A common approach used by all teams was perspective taking, or opening themselves up to considering alternative explanations for problem behaviors. Leaders from Teams 1 and 3 guided team members to relate aspects of the focus person's experiences to their own lives, thinking about how they might feel in similar situations. Sara's team used illustrated wall charts chronicling Sara's life to help team members relate to her difficult life experiences. Teams 3 and 4 brought in neurologists, nutritionists, and psychologists, to help team members understand how the person's disability, medical condition, or life experiences could have affected the person's actions and view of the world. Ann (Team 4) explained that a major turning point for her team was understanding that much of Salvator's challenging behaviors stemmed from the trauma of experiencing many years of abuse and neglect in the institution. Most participants expressed that by trying to understand the focus person's experiences in relation to their own helped them to consider alternative explanations and support options that they ignored in the past.

To promote a shared understanding of the specific reasons for problem behaviors and successful support strategies, participants from all teams described sharing and analyzing their observations and insights with one another during team meetings. Specifically, team members spoke of "picking apart" or "processing events" so that *all* might understand what was working and why,

and what factors appeared to provoke problem behaviors. For example, Robert reported using reflective questioning with his team as they processed events: "What kinds of positive things did you find out about Lawrence? What interests of his can we use to meet his needs? What problems arose; why did it happen? What were the factors involved . . . could it be . . .?" From the perspective of several participants, this group processing of events not only helped them to problem solve and identify successful intervention approaches, but it was also a way of reframing teammates' beliefs, particularly when they were locked into one way of seeing things (e.g., taking challenging behaviors personally). For example, Barbara (Team 3) explained how this process reversed her thinking and feelings about George. When George hit Barbara in the face, she recalled saying furiously, "If my nose is broken, I'm going to press charges. I don't care." However, after "walking through" the day's events with Marcie, Barbara realized that George was not out to get her, but that George was reacting to a series of five difficult events that day, each one of which could be prevented in the future.

To break down conflicts regarding team member's differences about what was "right," all teams emphasized coming to a group consensus, even if the consensus was to not fully agree, but to try a particular approach. However, several participants urged that the key to group consensus making was to stay focused on the person's needs and preferences and not on their own. To facilitate this process, participants from Teams 1, 3, and 4 spoke about gently challenging one another's ideas about what strategies or supports should be employed. They were asked to consider: "In what way is this helpful?" "How does this address *his* needs?" "How does this contribute to *his* happiness?" To keep the focus person's preferences ever present during team discussions, Teams 1 and 2 encouraged Lawrence and Sara to attend and, at times, lead team meetings by telling everyone what they wanted. As expressed by one Team 1 member, while everyone expresses his or her own opinion about what to do or how to do it, the ultimate decision has to rest with Lawrence. "In fact, he must agree to it."

Direct Supports

Direct supports refer to the strategies used by the teams to directly address the focus person's needs. Although all teams reported using a variety of intervention strategies, the following describes the participants' views on the essential elements of their support.

The Context for Direct Supports: Staff–Focus Person Relationships

Uniformly across all teams, participants emphasized that the relationships formed between support staff and the focus person was the most essential element of their support.

The nature of relationships: "We have a bond." Across teams, participants spoke of the special relationships formed between certain direct support staff and the focus person. Consistently, these relationships were described in terms of close emotional attachments. Using words such as "deep bond relationship," "love," and "caring" to describe their feelings, most direct support staff characterized their relationship with the focus person as a deep friendship that was likely to continue after their employment has ended. Some drew analogies to family relationships. "I love him like a brother," said Alex. "We have a mother-daughter relationship," said Cecilia. "He is half-way between a family member and a friend," said Roseann. Most team members expressed that the focus person mutually shared their feelings of attachment. Said Ann about her team (Team 4), "I think all the staff that work with Salvator now— he is close to. They all care about him."

Although several noted that their relationship was initially propelled by their desire to help, most direct care staff indicated that the deepening of their relationship occurred by spending time with the person. More than putting in time, spending time was described as sharing in daily activities, going through both good times and bad, "hanging out together" and taking the time to really listen and get to know the person. Most direct support staff spoke of the focus person becoming an integral part of their personal lives. These team members described doing things together after work and inviting the focus person into their homes and family life. In many ways, staff extended their personal relationships with their families and friends to the focus person. Said Cecilia (Team 2) in an illustrative quote:

> When I brought Sara into my life, I made her a part of my family also. I mean, Sara is truly a part of my life and family. . . . She goes to Baltimore to spend time with my son and his family. She's at my mother's house a lot, involved with the staff person who is my sister-in-law actually. So, she's over to her house with grandkids and my brother. She is loaded down with friends.

Although most direct care staff viewed themselves as a friend, each clarified that they also had a "working relationship" with the focus person. They acknowledged that it was their job to attend to the person's needs, promote his or her independence, and when necessary, intervene upon problem behavior by guiding the person to act in more socially acceptable ways.

All teams encouraged close staff relationships. When hiring, teams sought out staff who expressed special interests in the focus person, and subsequently built supports around the relationships and mutual interests that were naturally formed. Alternatively, teams elimi-

nated staff who did not get along with the focus person, or whom the focus person did not like. However, although close relationships were encouraged, there was no expectation that all team members should have the same relationship, act in the same way, or do the same things in exactly the same way with the focus person. Relationships were viewed as unique bonds, determined by the individuals' unique personalities. For Team 4, this recognition dissolved team arguments about staff members' different style of interaction: Roseann, the motherly-type, who liked to stay at home and cook for Salvator; and Terri, the outgoing friend-type who liked to do things with Sal in the community. Said Terri, "He [Salvator] just does things differently with everybody. We all have Sal's interest in mind that we try to meet, but we may do it differently . . . what is important, is that Sal is happy."

The importance of relationships. Three themes explain why teams viewed relationships as a critical foundation for their support. First, *relationships fostered staff commitment and motivation.* Consistently across all four teams, participants stressed that their relationship with the focus person fostered their commitment and motivation to persist and not back away during difficult times. Said Jason (Team 3), "I think it comes down to commitment level. You know if you don't have it, you're not gonna stay put . . . It's easy to see that the people who are not personally involved in the situation typically back away when times are rough."

More specifically, some noted that it was the "caring" in the relationship that motivated staff to persist and define the extent to which they were willing to give. As explained by Marcie (Team 3), "George is very reliant on us to provide what he needs. So depending on the person, and what that person is willing and able to do, depends on the depth of the relationship."

Second, *relationships facilitated understanding and empathy.* Participants across all teams stressed that a deep understanding of the focus person required an intimate knowledge that could only be achieved through personal relationships. Several made a distinction between knowing the person, achieved through relationships, and knowing about the person, nonpersonal knowledge achieved through written reports and assessments. Only knowing the person can lead to an understanding. Expressed Alex (Team 1), "You can't gain insight [into Lawrence] unless you are there experiencing him."

By knowing the person, several team members explained that they are able to accurately interpret actions and behaviors that are otherwise incomprehensible to those who do not know the focus person well, and as a result, are able to respond to the person's needs and avoid problem situations that can lead to challenging behaviors. Rick (Team 4) stressed that relationships must come first, before understanding Salvator's nonverbal communication. Said Terri in the same team, "It's impossible to figure out what Sal is trying to tell you if you don't know him." Taking it a step further, several Team 3 members explained that their relationships helped them to better empathize with George, step inside "his world" of autism and "see through his eyes." Said Jason, "I think I'm pretty in tune to what he is thinking about."

Third, *relationships facilitated a sense of security and trust for the focus person.* As described by several participants from all teams, trust is imparted when the focus person feels safe and cared for; it is knowing that staff will "be there for him [her]" during times of need. Although some speculated that it was the consistency and predictability of their actions that contributed to trust, most emphasized the caring aspects of their relationship as key. That is, trust was facilitated through respect, a genuine concern for the focus person's needs, and not backing away during times of difficulty.

Given the focus persons' histories of broken relationships, restrictive interventions, and abuse, several team members believed that there was little reason for the focus person to trust them initially. In fact, several perceived a direct link between the absence of trust and problem behavior, particularly during their early days of support. Said Terri (Team 4) about Salvator:

> I guess he felt that he could trust me. He felt that I was there for him. But when he first met me, he didn't know me. So he acted up banging his head on the sidewalk, the walls; [he] tried to hit me, to hit anybody in his way—yelling, screaming, trying to pinch because he didn't know me. He didn't know whether I was going to hurt him, or whether he could trust me or not.

As exemplified by this quote, trust is about the focus person knowing about his or her caretakers. From the view of several team members, trust served to reduce individuals' fear about how they would be treated or whether staff would leave them because they were bad. Moreover, once established, team members' perceived that trust facilitated an openness and receptivity to staff guidance and feedback. Consistently across teams, participants noted that the focus person was more accepting of staff guidance and more willing to communicate and share their concerns with those who had the closest, trusting relationship.

Specific Support Strategies: Key Elements

Supportive listening: "Tell me what's wrong." One of the most pervasive elements of the teams' direct support was *listening,* a term used by participants across teams to describe an ongoing, interpretive, and responsive dialogue between support staff and the focus person. Although all teams reported interpreting problem behaviors during team meetings where participants formulated hypotheses based on data, observations, and

insights, all stressed that understanding reasons for challenging behaviors must also occur as part of the staff's daily interactions with the focus person. A chief assumption held by all teams was that instances of challenging behaviors signaled that some event, either internal (e.g., illness) or external (e.g., change of routine), was troublesome to the individual and needed to be addressed. Because a myriad of unanticipated day-to-day factors could cause problems, participants emphasized making immediate on-the-spot interpretations and flexible modifications in response to the focus person's changing actions. Explained Marcie (Team 3), successful supports for George required that staff "keep a fluid idea of what George seems to be like on a particular day—how he responds, defines how you will respond, you've got to keep it open."

Listening involved open receptiveness to understanding reasons for problem behavior from the focus person's perspective. Participants from Teams 2 and 3 described sitting down and talking with George and Sara, sometimes for hours, to figure out what might be causing problem behaviors from their point of view. Referring to an incident in which Sara angrily chopped-off her hair, Cecelia (Team 2) described:

> We talk about why. I want to find out where this is coming from. Where is she coming from at the moment? Why, when she gets angry she doesn't feel the trust to come to me? I say Sara, let's sit down and discuss what it is that made you do it. Why are you upset? Did something happen at work? Was it something I did? Was it something I said? We need to talk about it so it does not happen again.

For participants in Teams 3 and 4, listening also involved paying close attention and responding to all forms of behavior, spoken and nonspoken, as communicative acts. They asserted that by following the person's subtle cues (e.g., clenched fist, repetitive verbalizations, light face slaps) problems could be prevented. However, listening involved an element of trust that following the focus person's requests was indeed the appropriate course of action. Several participants described overcoming their hesitation to listen when requests clashed with their own ideas about what was best (e.g., trusting that George's request for a car ride would indeed lessen his anxiety rather than result in aggression).

Elements of listening were written directly into George and Salvator's behavior support plan. Staff were expected to provide frequent opportunities for communication (e.g., asking questions, waiting for initiations) and to honor all requests unless dangerous or otherwise inappropriate. Furthermore, at the first sign of challenging behavior, they were expected to explore reasons by asking questions like "What's wrong?" or

"What's bothering you?" and to test their interpretations by changing aspects of the setting or their own behavior and then observing changes in the focus person's behavior. Several participants from these two teams commented that their interactive approach radically departed from the inflexible prescriptions contained in traditional behavior management plans. Marcie (Team 3) surmised that when her team adhered to prescribed intervention hierarchies (e.g., "If this happens, do this."), they were insensitive to George's communication, and in effect, contributed to his problem behaviors. Said Marcie, " [problem behaviors] changed because we weren't just observing and reacting; we were listening and responding, you know, in a more supportive way."

"Building a quality life." Emphasis on creating a quality life was another essential element of the teams' direct support. Across all teams, participants stressed that their focus was not on reducing challenging behaviors per se, but on taking a broad, comprehensive approach toward addressing "all aspects of a person's life" (e.g., health, employment, leisure, relationships). Their goal was to enrich the person's life, increase his or her happiness, and thereby eliminate the need for challenging behaviors.

Teams described three approaches taken toward creating a quality life. The first approach was to attend to the focus person's basic, most human needs. Participants from Teams 1, 2, and 4 reported that their first order of business was to establish a safe and secure home in the community surrounded by friends, family, and staff whom the focus person could trust. Teams 2 and 4 also prioritized major health concerns—finding the right balance of medications to address Sara's psychiatric issues, and understanding and addressing Salvator's complex illness and medical disorders (e.g., gastrointestinal problems, allergies, sleep disturbances).

A second approach was to build in lifestyle changes based on the person's preferences. This included making relatively simple modifications in daily routines for George and Salvator (e.g., "a cup of hot chocolate in the morning, a walk in the afternoon") and more comprehensive changes such as a job at McDonald's for Lawrence, vacations for Sara, and one-on-one individualized day supports for Sal. Several participants commented that understanding what changes to make was largely trial and error and involved a process of constantly exposing the person to new things that were once previously denied or restricted (e.g., community activities, foods, recreational activities).

A third approach toward creating a quality life was to "one by one" eliminate or modify factors that contributed to problem behaviors. For Sara and Lawrence, this included reversing the lack of opportunity for control by providing frequent opportunities for choice, decision-making, and staff direction. For example, Simon (Team 1) explained that they addressed Lawrence's elopement by giving him "freedom and more freedom" to participate in the community activities that he wanted. Simon stated that his team tried to impress upon Lawrence that "there is no need to run." For George and Salvator, small, but multiple adaptations, such as reducing waiting time, increasing the predictability of events, and adhering to sequences in routines, were built into the men's daily activities to eliminate events that caused stress and anxiety.

"Honesty" and "limit setting." Despite the teams' emphasis on preventing problem behaviors through listening and establishing a quality life, participants described times when the focus persons' requests could not or should not be honored and when instances of problem behaviors needed to be curtailed. In such situations, participants from all teams stressed honesty and limit setting as other important elements of their support.

As described by several team members, honesty involved a sincere expression of their feelings and explanations for why certain requests could not be fulfilled—either because the request could not be reasonably met or because it infringed on their rights or rights of others. By being honest, team members believed that they were extending a common courtesy that should be given to all people. Some participants saw the absence of honesty as not only jeopardizing their relationship with the focus person, but also contributing to problem behaviors once the person learned that their responses were not truthful.

Limit setting involved making the boundaries of acceptable social behaviors explicit by stating clear expectations for appropriate behavior, providing social feedback, and introducing "natural consequences" should problem behaviors occur (e.g., terminating a community activity if Lawrence insisted on public masturbation). Participants from all teams viewed limit setting not as staff "control," but as a way of introducing social rules and providing feedback for acceptable behavior expected from all people in society; rules that are often not applied to people with disabilities because of years of segregation and artificial interventions.

Despite the importance of these elements of support, several participants acknowledged that honesty and limit setting may be difficult for some, and worked best with those who had established close relationships with the focus person. They explained that those who did not have a close relationship often backed away from setting limits in fear of upsetting the focus person or they found the focus person unresponsive to their feedback.

DISCUSSION

With roots in applied behavior analysis and person-centered planning, positive behavior support is both technological (focused on strategies for assessment and intervention) and process oriented (focused on building teams and staff/organizational capacity for implementing positive supports). In this study, team members stressed the social process of their work, an aspect of positive behavior support that remains largely unaddressed among its predominately technological descriptions (e.g., Horner, 2000). This is not to say that the participants found the techniques of positive behavior support unimportant. All teams implemented a variety of assessment and intervention strategies that could be technologically described. But rather, through discussion of their personal experiences, participants emphasized broader social contexts that apparently gave meaning to their work and set the stage for making the techniques of positive approaches successful. At least three interrelated layers of social context were emphasized in the teams' discussions, each contributing to an overall culture of support. Discussing each social context, we raise implications for future practice and research.

Support for team was the first social context highlighted by the findings. All four teams stressed that direct support staff and their collective membership created the mechanism for change; therefore, their primary focus was on developing and sustaining the capacities, beliefs, and commitment of team members in order to provide support to the focus person. Although the need for team support has gained increased recognition (e.g., Dunlap et al., 2000; Knoster, Villa, & Thousand, 2000; Ruef, Turnbull, Turnbull, & Taylor, 1999), support is often conceptualized as providing increased technical assistance (skill training) or resources to teams. In contrast, in the present study, support for the team meant keeping team members focused on their person-centered values and addressing the social/emotional conflicts that arose during times of struggle.

Team members depicted their struggle as ongoing tension between establishing and living out their positive, person-centered values (e.g., seeing the person as a person, following the person's lead) with barriers that threatened their values or ability to carry out their person-centered plans. Many of their difficulties were linked directly to challenging behaviors. Specifically, participants spoke of taking challenging behaviors personally, their own or others' fear of getting hurt and taking risks, and they questioned their ability to understand challenging behaviors or to persist during times of intense behavioral challenges. However, their struggle may be attributed also to the conflicts inherent in implementing person-centered practices in a systems-oriented culture. According to Holburn and Vietze (1999), infusing person-centered practices in a culture that has traditionally emphasized programs "erodes organizational uniformity and predictability, creates tension and uncertainty, and destabilizes the system" (p. 118). As described by these authors, team members are asked to think and act differently using an ambiguous process (i.e., no explicit formula exists on how to achieve highly individualized person-centered goals) in a system that often conflicts with their ideas of best practice. Adding this conflict to the stress inherent in supporting adults who engage in severe challenging behaviors (Mitchell & Hastings, 2001), it is no wonder that the team members experienced ongoing tension and interpersonal conflicts with one another.

The primary implication for practice to be derived from this finding, and one that is consistent with the views of contemporary organizational change leaders (e.g., Hagner, 2000; Holburn & Vietze, 1999; O'Brien, O'Brien, & Mount, 1997), is that foremost, team conflict and tension are inherent in positive, person-centered planning efforts and should be acknowledged. Conflicts are unavoidable as team members wrestle with new ideas about how to provide the best support under highly unpredictable circumstances. Second, given these challenges, support for the team should be conceptualized as an ongoing nurturing process that fosters and renews commitment among team members, especially during times of crisis. As evident in this study, team support requires strong facilitators who can assist team members in learning the tools and strategies of positive approaches, and address the social/emotional barriers, such as frustration, fear, and interpersonal conflicts, that can undermine team work Interestingly, many of the same strategies used by the participating teams to generate support plans for the focus person (e.g., group processing of events, consensus making) were viewed as helpful for fostering team values and reframing team members' perceptions about the focus person and causes of problem behaviors. A critical direction for future research is to better understand team support as a social process, paying close attention to the support needs of teams and the social/emotional factors that can enhance or impede their work.

Close, personal relationships formed between certain direct support staff and the focus person was the second social context highlighted by the findings. All teams stressed that the emotional bonds formed between support staff and the focus person created an essential foundation for their direct support. Despite years of viewing support staff as merely functionaries, such as behavioral skill trainers (e.g., Parsons & Reid, 1995) or more recently, social connectors for facilitating community relationships (e.g., Amado, 1993; Racino, 1995), the present study underscores a small, but growing literature acknowledging that staff–focus person relationships are important to the overall quality of supports and should not be overlooked (e.g., Evans, 2000; O'Brien & O'Brien, 1994; Racino, Walker, O'Connor, & Taylor, 1993). Similar to other qualitative investigations involving innovative, person-centered residential agencies (e.g., Olney, Frantangelo, Lehr, 2000; Racino et al., 1993), the participants described their relationships in terms of personal attachments that transcended the boundaries of traditional staff roles. In this study, as in others, staff viewed themselves as both social guides and friends, standing in sharp contrast to the professional distancing encouraged by traditional practice.

An important contribution of the present study is the participants' perspectives on the importance of their relationships in their work. Participants saw their relationships, and the deepening of their relationships, as providing the motivation to make a difference, to "hang in there" despite adversity and their own personal struggles. They persevered because, as friends, they truly cared for the individual. They also saw their relationships as essential for developing empathy and understanding, facilitating perhaps a *local* understanding (Kliewer & Landis, 1999) about who the person is and how he or she communicates, that others, who do not know the person well, fail to see. According to the concept of accepting relationships (Bogdan & Taylor, 1987), the participants' relationships with the focus person may have facilitated their seeing "the person as a person" and not just a collection of challenging behaviors. Finally, the participants viewed their relationships as essential for creating a safe, trusting atmosphere in which the adults felt comfortable enough to accept feedback and guidance

Staff participants' views on the meaning of their relationships go beyond "rapport" building sometimes discussed in the behavioral literature as precursor or warm-up strategy for establishing effective interventions (e.g., Carr et al., 1994). Rather, the descriptions are more synonymous with the developmental (e.g., Greenspan & Weider, 1999) and the counseling psychology (e.g., Bordin, 1983) literatures in which close personal bonds between teachers/therapists and students/clients are consistently acknowledged as an essential element of the helping process, either serving to mediate the efficacy of interventions or providing direct therapeutic benefits. For example, after reviewing research in counseling interventions, Bordin (1983) concluded that techniques alone do not matter. Rather, effective interventions are wholly dependent on the relationship, or the feelings of liking, caring, and trusting, that the participants (therapist and client) share.

These findings on relationships raise numerous questions for researchers and practitioners, calling for further exploration into the nature and importance of staff relationships in the support of people who engage in challenging behaviors. First, what impact or role do relationships play in enhancing the motivation of support staff and for creating positive learning environments for the person with disabilities? Second, what roles should support staff fulfill in establishing these relationships? What bonds or elements of interpersonal relationships are necessary for quality support? Are friendships necessary or are the elements of caring and empathy key? Third, if close relationships are indeed important, then

how may teams support or enhance them? In the current study, teams seemed to take advantage of the relationships that were formed naturally, but must teams wait for a match? Perhaps, part of the answer for fostering relationships may be found in the current teams' support strategies for its members (e.g., perspective taking) and direct supports for the focus person (e.g., listening and participating in meaningful social activities).

The third layer of social context to emerge from the findings is evidenced in the teams' key elements or strategies for direct support. All teams operated from the assumption that challenging behaviors signaled that certain aspects of the environment needed to be changed. As such, rather than focusing on reducing problem behaviors per se, they emphasized creating meaningful and responsive contexts through listening and building a better life. Again, this is not to say that teams did not use multiple intervention strategies that could be categorized as antecedent, consequence, or teaching interventions, but that their focus was on the big picture of creating motivating contexts for growth and learning.

Elements of the teams' direct support may be viewed as an extension or manifestation of the close relationships formed between support staff and the individual. Listening and honesty are known strategies for facilitating trust and respect in a relationship (e.g., O'Brien & O'Brien, 1994; Racino, 1995). In addition, limit setting, used by the teams when environmental adaptations failed to prevent challenging behaviors, was perceived as successful when implemented by those who established a close trusting relationship with the person. Although the reasons are unclear, it is plausible that the adults with disabilities were more accepting of social boundaries once a climate of responsiveness and trust was established. It is also possible that only the support staff, who knew the person well, felt comfortable enough in their relationship to take the risk of saying "no" without fear of negative consequences.

The participants described listening as a means for deepening their understanding of the focus person's perspective and interpreting ongoing interactions between the person and themselves or others. Identifying factors that precipitate challenging behaviors is the hallmark of positive behavior support. However, unlike the formalized functional assessment practices prevalent in the literature, the participants in the current study stressed that interpretation must occur at the interpersonal level, as part of their daily interactions, if they are to be immediately responsive to the person's changing needs. This interactive process of reading and interpreting behaviors and making flexible adaptations in response to the person's actions is rarely discussed as a feature of positive behavior support. It is, however, consistent with responsive partnering emphasized in the communication literature (e.g., Prizant & Rubin,

1999) and is considered by some as essential to establishing supportive relationships (e.g., Lovett, 1996).

These findings suggest a need to more fully understand behavior support as an interactive process. Understanding reasons for problem behavior can occur simultaneously at the formal (i.e., functional behavioral assessment), and informal, interpersonal level with perhaps each serving a different role in creating responsive contexts. For example, formal functional assessments may be helpful for establishing initial hypotheses, but ongoing interpersonal interpretations may be necessary for refining hypotheses and translating supports into daily practice. Furthermore, as suggested by several participants, viewing support as an interactive process may require a reconceptualization of written support plans and staff training. Emphasis may be placed on teaching staff to read and interpret social cues, use good judgment, and respond flexibly, rather than rigidly adhering to prescribed intervention sequences.

This study provides rich information about the perspectives of team members, however, readers are cautioned to interpret the findings with several methodological limitations in mind. First, the relatively short episodic nature of data collection and the emphasis on cross-team analysis allow us only to make broad generalizations about teams. Information on the unique qualities of teams and the specific factors that may have contributed to each team's success was lost in our analysis. Second, our primary reliance on interview data obscures the connection between how participants talk about their work and on how their work was actually carried out. Third, given that family participation is crucial in teaming, the inadequate representation of families in the current study presents a severe limitation. Different themes might have emerged with more active family participation. Researchers are urged to address these limitations in future studies.

In summary, this study provides an in-depth look at the experiences of four community-based teams in their positive support of an adult with severe challenging behaviors. The findings presented here are not intended as conclusions about all community-based teams, but are raised as issues to broaden our discussions about implications for practice and future research. Moving beyond techniques, this study calls for a greater understanding of social contexts in which positive behavior support is implemented.

References

Albin, R. W., Lucyshyn, J. M., Horner, R. H., & Flannery, B. K. (1996). Contextual fit for behavioral support plans: A model for "goodness of fit." In L. K. Koegel, R. L. Koegel, & G. Dunlap (Eds.), *Positive behavioral support: Including people with difficult behavior in the community* (pp. 81–98). Baltimore: Paul H. Brookes.

Amado, A. N. (1993). Steps for supporting community connections. In A. N. Amado (Ed.), *Friendships and community connections between people with and without disabilities* (pp. 299–326). Baltimore: Paul H. Brookes.

Anderson, J. L., Russo, A., Dunlap, G., & Albin, R. W. (1996). A team training model for building the capacity to provide positive behavioral supports in inclusive settings. In L. K. Koegel, R. L. Koegel, & G. Dunlap (Eds.), *Positive behavioral support: Including people with difficult behavior in the community* (pp. 467–490). Baltimore: Paul H. Brookes.

Bambara, L. M., & Knoster, T. P. (1998). Designing positive behavior support plans. *Innovations* (No. 13). Washington, DC: American Association on Mental Retardation.

Bambara, L. M., Mitchell-Kvacky, N., & Gill, S. (1994). Positive behavioral support for students with severe disabilities: An emerging multicomponent approach for addressing challenging behaviors. *School Psychology Review, 23,* 263–278.

Berkman, K. A., & Meyer, L. H. (1988). Alternative strategies and multiple outcomes in the remediation of severe self-injury: Going "all out" nonaversively. *Journal of The Association for Persons with Severe Handicaps, 13,* 76–86.

Bogdan, R. C., & Biklen, S. K. (1992). *Qualitative research for education: An introduction to theory and methods* (2nd ed.). Boston: Allyn and Bacon.

Bogdan, R., & Taylor, S. J. (1987). Toward a sociology of acceptance: The other side of the study of deviance. *Social Policy, 18*(2), 34–39.

Bogdan, R., & Taylor, S. J. (1990). Looking at the bright side: A positive approach to qualitative policy and evaluation research. *Qualitative Sociology, 13,* 183–192.

Bordin, E. S. (1983). A working alliance based model of supervision. *The Counseling Psychologist, 11,* 35–41.

Carr, E. G., Dunlap, G., Horner, R. H., Koegel, R. L., Turnbull, A. P., Sailor, W., Anderson, J., Albin, R. W., Koegel, L., & Fox, L. (in press). Positive behavior support: Evolution of an applied science. *Journal of Positive Behavior Interventions.*

Carr, E. G., Horner, R. H., Turnbull, A., Marquis, J. G., McLaughlin, D. M., McAtee, M. L., Smith, C. E., Ryan, K. A., Ruef, M. B., & Doolabh, A. (1999). *Positive behavior support for people with developmental disabilities: A research synthesis.* Washington, DC: American Association on Mental Retardation.

Carr, E. G., Levin, I., McConnachie, G., Carlson, J. I., Kemp, D. C., & Smith, C. E. (1994). *Communication-based intervention for problem behavior: A user's guide for producing positive change.* Baltimore: Paul. H. Brookes.

Demchak, M. A., & Bossert, K. W. (1996). Assessing problem behaviors. *Innovations* (No. 4). Washington, DC: American Association on Mental Retardation.

Donnellan, A. M., LaVigna, G. W., Negri-Shoultz, N., & Fassbender, L. L. (1988). *Progress without punishment: Effective approaches for learners with severe behavior problems.* New York: Teachers College Press.

Dunlap, G., Hieneman, M., Knoster, T., Fox, L., Anderson, J., & Albin, R. W. (2000). Essential elements of inservice training in positive behavior support. *Journal of Positive Behavior Interventions, 2,* 22–32.

Evans, I. M. (2000). Staff development, caring, and community. In J. R. Scotti & L. H. Meyer (Eds.), *Behavioral intervention: Principles, models, and practices* (pp. 413–431). Baltimore: Paul H. Brookes.

Foster-Johnson, L., & Dunlap, G. (1993). Using functional assessment to develop effective individualized interventions for challenging behaviors. *Teaching Exceptional Children, 25,* 44–50.

Glaser, B., & Strauss, A. L. (1967). *The discovery of grounded theory: Strategies for qualitative research.* Chicago: Aldine.

Greenspan, S. I., & Weider, S. (1999). A functional developmental approach to autism spectrum disorders. *Journal of*

The Association for Persons with Severe Handicaps, 24, 147–361.

Hagner, D. (2000). Supporting people as part of the community. In J. Nisbet & D. Hagner (Eds.), *Part of the community: Strategies for including everyone* (pp. 15–42). Baltimore: Paul H. Brookes.

Hieneman, M., & Dunlap, G. (2000). Factors affecting the outcomes of community-based support: I. Identification and description of factor categories. *Journal of Positive Behavior Intervention, 2,* 161–169.

Hill, C. E., Thompson, B. J., & Williams, E. N. (1997). A guide to conducting consensual qualitative research. *The Counseling Psychologist, 25,* 517–572.

Holburn, S., & Vietze, P. (1999). Acknowledging the barriers in adopting person-centered planning. *Mental Retardation, 37,* 117–124.

Horner, R. H. (2000). Positive behavior supports. *Focus on Autism and Other Developmental Disabilities, 15,* 97–105.

Horner, R. H., Dunlap, G., Koegel, R. L., Carr, E. G., Sailor, W., Anderson, J., Albin, R. W., & O'Neill, R. E. (1990). Toward a technology of "nonaversive" behavioral support. *Journal of The Association for Persons with Severe Handicaps, 15,* 125–132.

Kliewer, C., & Landis, D. (1999). Individualizing literacy instruction for young children with moderate to severe disabilities. *Exceptional Children, 66,* 85–100.

Knoster, T. P., Villa, R. A., & Thousand, J. S. (2000). A framework for thinking about systems change. In R. A. Villa & J. S. Thousand (Eds.), *Restructuring for caring and effective education: Piecing the puzzle together* (pp. 93–131). Baltimore: Paul H. Brookes.

Koegel, L. K., Koegel, R. L., & Dunlap, G. (1996). *Positive behavior support: Including people with difficult behaviors in the community.* Baltimore: Paul H. Brookes.

Lovett, H. (1996). *Learning to listen: Positive approaches and people with difficult behaviors.* Baltimore: Paul H. Brookes.

Lucyshyn, J. M., Olson, D., & Horner, R. H. (1995). Building an ecology of support: A case study of one young woman with severe problem behaviors living in the community. *Journal of The Association for Persons with Severe Handicaps, 20,* 16–30.

Meyer, L. H., & Evans, I. M. (1989). *Nonaversive interventions for behavior problems: A manual for home and community.* Baltimore: Paul H. Brookes.

Meyer, L. H., & Evans, I. M. (1993). Meaningful outcomes in behavioral intervention: Evaluating positive approaches to the remediation of challenging behavior. In J. Reichle & D. Wacker (Eds.), *Communication alternatives to challenging behavior* (pp.407–428). Baltimore: Paul H. Brookes.

McCracken, G. (1988). *The long interview.* Newbury Park, CA: Sage.

Mitchell, G., & Hastings, R. P. (2001). Coping, burnout, and emotion in staff working in community services for people with challenging behaviors. *American Journal on Mental Retardation, 106,* 448–449.

O'Brien, J., & O'Brien, C. L. (1994). More than just an address: Images of organizations for supported living agencies. In V. J. Bradley, J. W. Ashbaugh, & B. C. Blaney (Eds.), *Creating individualized supports for people with developmental disabilities: A mandate for change at many levels* (pp. 109–140). Baltimore: Paul H. Brookes.

O'Brien, C. L., O'Brien, J., & Mount, B. (1997). Person-centered planning has arrived . . . or has it? *Mental Retardation, 35,* 480–484.

Olney, M. F., Frantangelo, P., & Lehr, S. (2000). Anatomy of commitment: An in vivo study. *Mental Retardation, 38,* 234–243.

Parsons, M. B., & Reid, D. H. (1995). Training residential supervisors to provide feedback for maintaining staff teaching skills with people who have severe disabilities. *Journal of Applied Behavior Analysis, 28,* 317–322.

Patton, M. Q. (1990). *Qualitative evaluation and research methods.* Newbury Park, CA: Sage.

Prizant, B., & Rubin, E. (1999). Contemporary issues for interventions for autism spectrum disorders: A commentary. *Journal of The Association for Persons with Severe Handicaps, 24,* 199–208.

QSR NUD*IST (Revision 3) [Computer software]. (1985). Victoria, Australia: Qualitative Solutions and Research.

Racino, J. A. (1995). Community living for adults with developmental disabilities: A housing and support approach. *Journal of The Association for Persons with Severe Handicaps, 20,* 300–310.

Racino, J. A., Walker, P., O'Connor, S., & Taylor, S. J. (1993). *Housing, support, and community: Choices and strategies for adults with disabilities.* Baltimore: Paul H. Brookes.

Ruef, M. B., Turnbull, A. P., Turnbull, H. R., & Poston, D. (1999). Perspectives of five stakeholder groups: Challenging behavior of individuals with mental retardation and/or autism. *Journal of Positive Behavior Interventions, 1,* 43–58.

Seidman, J. E. (1991). *Interviewing as qualitative research.* New York: Columbia University, Teachers College Press.

Turnbull, A. P., & Turnbull, R. H. (1996). Group action planning as a strategy for providing comprehensive family support. In L. K. Koegel, R. L. Koegel, & G. Dunlap (Eds.), *Positive behavioral support: Including people with difficult behavior in the community* (pp. 99–114). Baltimore: Paul H. Brookes.

Turnbull, A., & Turnbull, R. (2000). Achieving "rich" lifestyles. *Journal of Positive Behavior Interventions, 2,* 190–192.

Article received: February 6, 2001
Final acceptance: June 5, 2001
Editor in charge: Charles Peck

Essential Elements of Inservice Training in Positive Behavior Support

~

Glen Dunlap
University of South Florida

Meme Hieneman
University of South Florida

Tim Knoster
Instructional Support System of Pennsylvania

Lise Fox
University of South Florida

Jacki Anderson
California State University, Hayward

Richard W. Albin
University of Oregon

Abstract: Positive behavior support is an effective and proactive approach for resolving serious problem behaviors that has been recommended by a growing number of professionals, advocates, policies, and laws. Building the capacity of educators and other professionals to provide positive behavior support is a vital concern as schools and community agencies serve increasingly diverse populations that include children and youth with disabilities and problem behaviors. This article describes issues and essential elements for building such capacity through inservice training. A core curriculum is outlined, and a national exemplar of comprehensive inservice training is described. Essential features of training that are needed for the development of practical skills are discussed.

Positive behavior support is a broad process of intervention that is becoming accepted as a proactive and effective way to support individuals who exhibit disruptive and/or dangerous behaviors. The approach has emerged over the past decade as an outgrowth of applied behavior analysis (Alberto & Troutman, 1990; Cooper, Heron, & Heward, 1987) in which validated behavior change procedures are guided by a person-centered philosophy. It contrasts with traditional behavior management strategies that have often depended extensively on the manipulation of consequences and, in some cases, the use of aversive punishment procedures, particularly for people with severe developmental disabilities (Guess, Helmstetter, Turnbull, & Knowlton, 1987; Repp & Singh, 1990; Singer, Gert, & Koegel, 1999). The efforts of advocates, family members, and concerned professionals have produced increasing prohibitions against the use of aversive interventions, as well as the promotion of research and training in positive, nonaversive approaches for addressing the challenges of severe problem behavior. *Positive behavior support* is a term that

has come to describe a set of assessment and intervention strategies, based on person-centered values, that is intended to produce reductions in problem behavior along with increases in desirable behavior and access to richer and more satisfying lifestyles (Horner, Dunlap, et al., 1990; Koegel, Koegel, & Dunlap, 1996).

Positive behavior support has been described in a variety of ways (Horner, Dunlap, et al., 1990), but there is general agreement that it has a number of central features: (a) it is founded on a philosophy of respect for the individual and a desire to help achieve more agreeable lifestyles; (b) the interventions are based on an understanding of the individual's interactions with the environment, acquired through an individualized process of functional assessment (Foster-Johnson & Dunlap, 1993; Repp & Horner, 1999); (c) the interventions are focused on teaching new skills and improving patterns of adaptation, rather than simply suppressing unwanted behavior (Carr et al., 1994; Evans & Meyer, 1985); (d) the approach acknowledges the influence of the social, curricular, and ecological context, and incorporates such variables into the support plan (e.g., Dunlap & Kern, 1993, 1996; Munk & Repp, 1994); and (e) the support plans typically include multiple components, including antecedent, consequence, and contextual manipulations, all of which are identified on an individual basis (Horner & Carr, 1997).

At this point, a great deal of research has been conducted on positive behavior support processes, and many demonstrations have documented the effectiveness of the approach in home, community, and school settings (Koegel et al., 1996). In addition, a number of states have passed legislation or enacted educational policies that require positive behavior support practices to be implemented in school programs, and the 1997 amendments to the Individuals with Disabilities Education Act further mandate the use of positive behavior interventions and functional behavioral assessment under appropriate conditions (Tilly et al., 1998). Thus, the concepts and procedures of positive behavior support are being increasingly incorporated into the expected daily practice of educators and other professionals.

In order to carry out the mandate of such directives and to implement positive behavior support in a comprehensive and effective manner, concerted efforts are needed to provide training and build the capacity of educators, community support providers, and collaborative teams. This article describes a process of inservice training in positive behavior support and highlights features that are considered necessary for comprehensive skill acquisition that results in effective support for individuals with disabilities and histories of problem behaviors. The article begins with a description of a core curriculum and competencies that comprise comprehensive training in positive behavior support. It continues with a brief description of a team training model that has been developed over the past decade and implemented in more than 20 states. The article also presents a discussion of the essential elements of the inservice training model.

Curriculum Content

A comprehensive training curriculum on positive behavior support is designed to promote the development of a range of technical skills and competencies focused on creating individualized, assessment-based interventions that not only improve behavior, but also enhance overall quality of life. The curriculum presented here builds on previous work of researchers and practitioners associated with positive behavior support (Anderson, Albin, Mesaros, Dunlap, & Morelli-Robbins, 1993; Anderson, Russo, Dunlap, & Albin, 1996; Meyer & Evans, 1989), wherein direct benefits to students, educators, families, and other support providers have been demonstrated. The core content focuses on teaching teams to work within the context of immediate settings, as well as the larger social milieu. The

organizational framework for the curriculum is based on units of instruction (rather than specific procedures) that parallel the process of positive behavior support.

The curriculum is based on learning objectives that provide practical knowledge and a generalizable process for intervention. The content incorporates a variety of interdependent topic areas, including

1. Establishing a collective vision and goals for intervention
2. Collaborating and building teams among families and professionals
3. Conducting functional assessments (i.e., gathering information and identifying behavior–environment relations)
4. Designing hypothesis-driven, multicomponent support plans
5. Implementing intervention strategies that include environmental adjustments, replacement skills, appropriate consequences, and lifestyle enhancements
6. Monitoring and evaluating intervention outcomes
7. Infusing positive behavior support into broader systems.

Each of these elements is summarized in Table 1 and described in the following sections.

1. Establishing a Collective Vision and Goals for Intervention. An essential foundation of the curriculum is that participants understand the basic tenets of positive behavior support and establish mutually agreed on goals for intervention. The central theme is that interventions designed to address challenging behavior must be based on a comprehensive understanding of contexts and functions affecting a person's behavior, the nature of the environments in which they participate, and the people who support the individual. These principles, coupled with a person-centered perspective and an emphasis on inclusion in typical school and community settings, serve as cornerstones in the training curriculum. In this initial content area, participants are taught to establish intervention goals by identifying specific behaviors of concern and determining the larger, quality-of-life outcomes desired. The latter objective is often facilitated through person-centered planning (e.g., Kincaid, 1996; Mount & Zwernik, 1988), a collaborative process that focuses on the capacities of an individual and the development of a positive, long-term vision. With this broad perspective, teams emphasize how individualized support is localized within larger contexts and systems.

2. Collaborating and Building Teams Among Families and Professionals. A team orientation is another key feature of the training program, as well as a primary focus of instruction. During the training, participants are taught how

Table 1. Core Competencies and Curriculum Content

Content area	Selected references
1. Establishing a collective vision and goals for intervention. A. Basic tenets and assumptions of positive behavioral support.	Horner & Carr, 1997; Horner, Dunlap, et al., 1990; Koegel, Koegel, & Dunlap, 1996; Meyer & Evans, 1989

B. *Establishing goals:*
       Person-centered planning to identify lifestyle outcomes
       Defining behaviors of concern (and establishing baseline)
	Alberto & Troutman, 1990; Kincaid, 1996; O'Brien, Mount, & O'Brien, 1991; Sulzer-Azaroff & Mayer, 1991; Turnbull & Turnbull, 1996

2. Collaborating and building teams among families and professionals	Dunst, Trivette, & Johanson, 1994; Givner & Haager, 1995; Mullen & Frea, 1995; Rainforth, York, & MacDonald, 1992; Walker & Singer, 1993

3. Conducting functional assessment of behavior
    A. Gathering information
      1. Interviews and checklists (e.g., structured interviews, rating scales)
      2. Direct observation
      3. Ecological/curricular assessments
	Bailey & Pyles, 1989; Demchak & Bossert, 1996; Foster-Johnson & Dunlap, 1993; Lohrmann-O'Rourke, Knoster, & Llewellyn, 1999; O'Neill et al., 1997

B. Developing hypotheses
      1. Identifying patterns in data
      2. Developing hypotheses statements related to contexts, functions, and broader ecological variables affecting behavior
      3. Testing hypotheses via systematic manipulations (when necessary and possible)
	Bambara & Knoster, 1998; Carr et al., 1994; Iwata, Vollmer, & Zarcone, 1990; Repp & Horner, 1999

4. Designing hypothesis-driven, individualized, comprehensive behavioral support plans
    A. Competing behavior model (functional equivalence)
    B. Selecting interventions that have contextual fit
    C. Crisis management
	Albin et al., 1996; Bambara, Mitchell-Kvacky, & Iacobelli, 1994; Bishop & Jubala, 1995; Horner, O'Neill, & Flannery, 1993; O'Neill et al., 1997

5. Implementing intervention strategies A. Adjusting the environment	Albin, Horner, & O'Neill, 1993; Carr et al., 1994; Dunlap & Kern, 1996; Fox & Conroy, 1995; Horner, Vaughn, Day, & Ard, 1996
B. Teaching replacement skills and general competencies C. Managing consequences	Carr & Durand, 1985; Lewis & Sugai, 1993; Reichle & Wacker, 1993 Carr, Robinson, & Palumbo, 1990; Iwata, Vollmer, Zarones, & Rodgers, 1993; Wacker, Wendy, Harding, & Asmus, 1996
D. Promoting lifestyle changes	Bellamy, Newton, LeBaron, & Horner, 1990; Hughes, Hwang, Kim, Eisenmayer, & Killian, 1995; Meyer & Evans, 1993
6. Monitoring and evaluating outcomes	Meyer & Evans, 1993
7. Infusing positive behavioral support into broader systems	Bambara & Knoster, 1995; Colvin, Kameenui, & Sugai, 1993; Flannery, Sprague, & Todd, 1996; Hedeen, Ayres, Meyer, & Waite, 1996; McEvoy, Davis, & Reichle, 1993; O'Neill, Williams, Sprague, Horner, & Albin, 1993; Tilly et al., 1998; Taylor et al., 1997; Topper, Williams, Leo, Hamilton, & Fox, 1994

Note. Adapted from Anderson, J. L., Albin, R. W., Mesaros, R. A., Dunlap, G., & Morelli-Robbins, M. (1993). Issues in providing training to achieve comprehensive behavioral support, pp. 377–378. In J. Reichle & D. P. Wacker (Eds.), Communication and language intervention strategies (pp. 63–406). Baltimore: Brookes.

to improve functioning within existing team structures (e.g., Individual Education Program teams) and/or to recruit team participation in situations where there is no collaborative process in place. Trainers guide and assist participants to develop operating principles (i.e., ground rules, agendas), determine roles and responsibilities of team members, and operate from a cooperative approach characterized by positive, productive, and respectful interaction.

3. *Conducting Functional Assessment (Gathering Information and Developing Hypotheses).* The primary emphasis of this curriculum content area is to enable participants to engage in a process of information-gathering and synthesis in order to identify the contexts, functions, and broader ecological variables affecting an individual's behavior. The information-gathering process involves interviews and direct observations to identify variables

surrounding occurrences of a specified problem behavior, as well as to collect information about a child's history, preferences, and life circumstances. Participants are taught to obtain information through interviews, review of other data sources (e.g., curricular assessments), and observations during relevant periods during the day. Based on the data, participants learn to generate specific and global hypotheses that summarize the assessment results, specify the conditions in which the behavior is most and least likely to occur, and identify the outcomes achieved through the behavior. These hypotheses become a foundation from which interventions can be designed.

4. *Designing Comprehensive Behavior Support Plans.* This content area focuses on teaching participants to build multicomponent behavioral support plans that are logically linked to the hypotheses derived through functional assessment. The emphasis is on designing support plans that are proactive, educative, and functional in nature. Although short-term prevention and crisis management may be important elements of a plan, the overall focus is on promoting broad, durable changes through environmental manipulation, skill development, and lifestyle enhancement. Participants are instructed to design plans that have technical integrity and to ensure the presence of "contextual fit," meaning that they incorporate a good match with respect to the focus individual, team members, and relevant environmental factors (e.g., resources, needs, routines in the environment).

5. *Implementing Intervention Strategies.* Training participants may need to develop specific skills to implement the support plan strategies, including systematic instruction and mechanisms to promote broader lifestyle enhancements. Essential competencies are associated with manipulating aspects of the physical or social environment (e.g., the curriculum, physical setting, routines), teaching alternative skills to replace problem behavior and improve general competence, and delivering effective reinforcers. Participants learn how to focus strategies on promoting significant, meaningful improvements in the behavior of individuals. The goal is not only to effect changes in observable behaviors, but also to promote quality-of-life improvements (e.g., facilitating friendships, embedding instruction in integrated activities and experiences) and include other elements that may help facilitate generalization and maintenance. Often, participants must learn ways to support the team members implementing the interventions, as well as the person for whom the plan is designed.

6. *Monitoring and Evaluating Outcomes.* Positive behavior support is not a static approach. Rather, it involves an ongoing process of assessment, planning, intervention, and evaluation. This content area of the curriculum provides participants with the skills necessary to monitor progress as a result of implementing the behavioral support plan in tandem with making adjustments to the plan, when warranted. The data collection procedures presented

build on those associated with functional assessment, and include methods for objectively evaluating changes in behavior and quality of life. These data are paired with a set of decision-making rules related to plan modification. In addition, this content area includes methods to ensure that families and direct service providers are adequately supported and have opportunities for maintaining their team communications.

7. *Infusing Positive Behavior Support into Broader Systems.* Implementation of individual behavioral support plans occurs within the context of the broader classroom, school, family, and community ecology. It is important that training participants be sensitized to particular factors that may affect intervention within and across systems (e.g., policies, procedures, organization, discipline codes, staff development priorities). Accommodating for these factors may increase the likelihood that new skills learned by staff members will translate into changes in practice that will benefit not only the specific child in need, but also other children in future applications. This content area represents a logical expansion of previous work as it specifically highlights (a) the generalization of behavioral support practices across individuals; (b) self-assessment, using the setting or program as a unit of analysis; and (c) policy and legal issues in providing positive behavior support.

The seven elements in Table 1 represent the breadth of content that should be addressed within an inservice training program on positive behavior support. References are provided that offer resources for training lectures and participant readings. The content and structure of inservice training and the methods used to deliver training should be crafted specifically to meet the factors affecting the participating individuals and agencies. In the following section, we provide an example of an effective inservice training model by highlighting key features that should be considered as inservice training is designed.

Key Features of a National Inservice Training Model

The Rehabilitation Research and Training Center on Positive Behavior Support (RRTC-PBS; NIDRR Cooperative Agreement H133B2004 and Grant No. H133B980005) has implemented a national inservice training model that may serve as an exemplar of in-service training in positive behavior support. Since its inception in 1987 the RRTC-PBS has contributed to the development of 20 state-level training teams that provide comprehensive inservice training for providers, professionals, and family members who provide support for individuals with disabilities and histories of problem behaviors (Anderson et al., 1993; Anderson et al., 1996). The state training teams were developed to provide an expert resource for participating states and an explicit effort to develop improved local capacities for supporting people with disabilities in the context of their school, home, and community participation.

The model was designed with the goal of optimizing the probability that the training would build an enduring capacity to provide effective support resulting in lifestyle benefits for a range of individuals with behavioral support needs. Therefore, the model emphasizes a process in which participants work together over several months to develop practical competencies in assessment, problem solving, and broad-based intervention. The training process utilizes a case study format that results in the development of a comprehensive behavioral support plan for an individual with disabilities and problem behavior. By working together over an extended training period to develop outcomes for the focus individuals, training participants learn improved approaches to interdisciplinary and interagency collaboration.

In the 10-year period during which the initial state training teams were developed, the combined efforts of the RRTC-PBS and state-level trainers have resulted in more than 200 rounds of comprehensive inservice training for more than 4,500 family members, teachers, and other direct support providers. In addition, the network's training personnel have provided abbreviated skill-building workshops, presentations, and technical assistance that have benefited more than 33,500 participants in the 20 states. These latter data reflect efforts undertaken by state-level trainers who have used elements of the RRTC-PBS's training model to establish positive behavior support competencies (e.g., functional assessment, functional communication training) in the repertoires of professional and nonprofessional community members within their own states (Anderson et al., 1996; Eno-Hieneman, Dunlap, & Fox, 1995).

The national inservice training model described by Anderson and colleagues (1993, 1996) was developed in accordance with the existing literature on inservice training and systems change. Our experience over the past decade has supplemented that knowledge and emphasized the importance of its key features (Eno-Hieneman, Dunlap, & Fox, 1995). In essence, the nature of positive behavior support (i.e., an individualized, contextually based approach utilized by natural support providers in typical environments) has dictated an integrated, focused approach to inservice training that allows participants to develop capacities in practical and nonintrusive methods to support individuals with severe challenging behavior in their community. The approach is dynamic and interactive, providing for the delivery of information over an extended period of time, integrating opportunities for typical support providers to apply the skills obtained, and creating communities or teams that support ongoing use of positive behavior support.

The national inservice training model has five key features, which can be considered essential in the provision of comprehensive inservice training in positive behavior support:

1. The training targets a *multidisciplinary* audience and is delivered in a manner that promotes *collaboration* among the participants. It uses a case study format so that the participants are able to apply information to benefit an individual in the community.
2. It uses a *case study format* so that the participants are able to apply informatin to benefit an individual in the community.
3. It incorporates a *dynamic training process* that engages the participants in practical activities and assists them in developing generalizable skills.
4. It is *comprehensive* in nature, addressing a broad range of topics associated with positive behavior support.
5. It involves elements specifically focused on promoting *community building* so that systems can be enhanced to promote ongoing support for participants and extend positive behavior support efforts.

These five features are described in greater detail below.

MULTIDISCIPLINARY TEAMS/COLLABORATION

The team training model is multidisciplinary and collaborative in nature. The model is specifically designed to disseminate information and build capacities among teams of people representing multiple agencies, disciplines, and constituencies. It incorporates mechanisms to facilitate collaborative interactions among the training participants and within the community.

Recent literature supports designing and implementing interventions for individuals with disabilities from an interdisciplinary and collaborative perspective (Briggs, 1991; Gutkin, 1993; Orelove & Sobsey, 1991; Rainforth, York, & MacDonald, 1992; Thousand & Villa, 1994) and via family–professional partnerships (Dunst, Trivette, & Johanson, 1994; Fox, Vaughn, Dunlap, & Bucy, 1997; Vaughn, Dunlap, Fox, Clarke, & Bucy, 1997). Working collaboratively may result in more comprehensive and integrated interventions and improved coordination among service delivery systems. Sharing a consistent knowledge base and working together toward common goals may be particularly important when attempting to promote broad, durable changes in an individual's behavior (Hieneman & Dunlap, in press; Mullen & Frea, 1995).

Inservice training has typically been provided to particular agencies or programs and has usually targeted participants representing a single orientation or discipline. This approach to training may help agencies meet specific obligations for service delivery, but it does not focus on individualization or comprehensive support for people with disabilities, nor does it prepare professionals to work together (Racino, 1990). In contrast, providing training to all team members simultaneously may facilitate the use of positive approaches to behavioral support in community settings (Dunlap, Robbins, Morelli, & Dollman, 1988; Meyer & Evans, 1989).

The inservice training model encourages using transdisciplinary teams in a number of ways. Both trainers and participants include representatives from various agencies and constituencies, interacting as integrated teams. The training is provided by interagency and multidisciplinary state training teams that include representatives from each major human services agency in the state (e.g., education, developmental services, family groups), thereby promoting an integrated curriculum and ongoing collaboration among constituents. The training participants include teams of people involved in supporting individuals with disabilities and behavioral challenges in their home, school, and community settings. For example, a team for a school-age child might include the child, parent(s), teacher, behavior specialist, speech–language pathologist, developmental services case worker, general education teacher, administrator, and others. People from each of these different roles learn and work together, and support one another throughout the training.

Establishing and maintaining collaborative interactions is an essential emphasis of the team training curriculum and program design. Each team member or training participant is likely to have different goals for his or her involvement, ranging from designing effective interventions for particular individuals to enhancing the ability to provide training and technical assistance in his or her own programs or agencies. The training is designed to appeal to heterogeneous groups and to promote teams' competencies. Participants proceed through the training together, assisting one another in acquiring skills and actively supporting and learning from one another. They are taught to function as a unit (i.e., to collaborate) to meet the objectives of the training and to design effective interventions.

CASE STUDY FORMAT

The team training approach is provided using a case study format. The participants are brought together to address the needs of specific focus individuals in the natural contexts of their lives. Through the case study format, participants have the opportunity to apply skills and knowledge to an actual person and to design support strategies based on the unique circumstances.

Traditional approaches to behavior management training have usually focused on the application of a set of practices and procedures (e.g., rewards, prompts, timeout). Progressively, the fields of applied behavior analysis

and positive behavior support are shifting away from standard technique-oriented approaches in favor of more assessment-based, individualized, and contextually relevant approaches (Albin, Lucyshyn, Horner, & Flannery, 1996; Foster-Johnson & Dunlap, 1993; Horner, Dunlap, et al., 1990; Meyer & Evans, 1989). In addition, there is a growing appreciation for person-centered approaches that provide a holistic view of the needs, strengths, and preferences of individuals and keep these personal characteristics in the forefront of consideration when designing supports and services (Kincaid, 1996; Mount & Zwernik, 1988; Vandercook & York, 1990).

Training in positive behavior support is facilitated by the direct application of the training content to people with disabilities and behavioral challenges in typical settings. The case study format helps the training maintain an emphasis on three vital objectives. First, there is ongoing emphasis on individualizing interventions based on the focus person's characteristics and lifestyle. Second, support plans are created to fit within the settings in which they will be used, and are designed to be feasible and acceptable to those implementing them (Albin et al., 1996). Third, applying strategies directly allows the participants to see the outcomes and benefits of the training while in process.

In the inservice training model, individuals with challenging behavior and disabilities are the focus of the assessment and intervention efforts associated with the training. Case study groups, which include family members and service providers, become the core recipients of the training. Through the training, teams of participants work collaboratively to establish goals for intervention, conduct assessments, and design and implement behavioral support plans specifically for the individual. The result is individualized, comprehensive behavior support plans that address the unique circumstances and confluence of resources available in the person's settings. As case study groups move through the process of developing and providing positive behavior support, they inform the larger training audience by sharing their observations and experiences.

DYNAMIC TRAINING PROCESS

The team training process is dynamic, with presentations of curriculum content interspersed with opportunities for supported application of the concepts and skills. Participants gain direct experience with the content through activities, examples, practice, and feedback. In addition, the training includes mechanisms to ensure mastery of skills and to promote the transfer of knowledge to relevant examples in typical settings. Transfer of skills to target contexts has been a formidable challenge in behavioral support (Smith, Parker, Taubman, & Lovaas, 1992). The literature suggests that learning may be enhanced by giving participants opportunities to apply their skills and receive coaching and feedback (Joyce & Showers, 1980). The case study format is the basis for a framework for practical application, collaborative coaching relationships, and feedback from others facing similar challenges or who have more extensive experience.

The inservice training model is designed to be informative and to promote active involvement of participants. The training typically extends over a 4- to 6-month period. Between sessions, the teams complete extension activities associated with team building, ecological and functional assessment, and design and implementation of interventions in the community settings. The teams are assigned readings to assist in understanding the concepts and to facilitate completion of the extension activities.

During the training sessions, the presenters use a variety of formats, including lecture and guided discussion, presentation of case examples (e.g., videotapes), group activities, and role playing. For example, participants may be asked to record data from videotaped vignettes and role play instructional sequences. Teams are also given opportunities in their case study groups to generate plans and complete preliminary work associated with completing the extension activities. Teams provide updates on their progress and share their behavioral support plans so that the participants can benefit from each others' experiences and unique applications of the concepts. During these large and small group activities, the trainers are available to provide feedback and modified coaching.

COMPREHENSIVENESS OF TRAINING

As described previously, the curriculum addressed within the team training model is comprehensive in nature, addressing both the conceptual and philosophical foundations of positive behavior support and processes associated with assessment and intervention. Key themes that recur throughout the training include individualization through assessment, using proactive and educative strategies, working collaboratively, and promoting broad and durable lifestyle change.

Positive behavior support represents a broadening in perspectives regarding effective intervention perspectives. This implicates the need for an extensive and diverse array of skills and knowledge to adequately support people with disabilities and challenging behavior in school, home, and community settings (Anderson et al., 1996; Horner, Dunlap, et al., 1990). These skills include the ability to analyze and integrate information from a variety of sources in order to design and implement effective behavior support plans for individuals in the community. In addition, each element of comprehensive behavior support (e.g., teaching replacement skills) requires the development of unique competencies.

The team training curriculum is a complex, multitopic training sequence that addresses a breadth of interwoven elements. The training sequence is provided within 10 to 12 days, scheduled across several months; however, the actual number of training days can be adjusted according to the context and existing community resources. The curriculum addresses all aspects of positive behavior support while participants design interventions that are multi-element in nature and promote positive lifestyle changes for the focus individual. The topics are presented in modules focused on the philosophy, values, and fundamental themes underlying positive behavior support; collaboration and longitudinal planning; ecological and functional assessment; development and evaluation of behavioral support plans; and systems issues that promote durability of change. Typical elements of behavioral support plans (e.g., communication, skills instruction, contextual modifications, utilization of effective consequences) are individually presented and practiced, promoting a breadth of capacities among the participants. Additionally, the training curriculum is continually updated to reflect extensions in the current knowledge base.

NETWORKING, SYSTEMS CHANGE, AND COMMUNITY BUILDING

In addition to focusing on the development of practical competencies for participants, the team training model also addresses broader systems issues that may affect the support for individuals with disabilities and challenging behavior in the community settings. This entails working with representatives from the local sites to establish, enhance, and maintain support systems that promote positive behavior support. Through these mechanisms, it may be possible to extend the application of the training throughout the community.

The degree to which organizational and cultural features of systems and communities promote positive behavior support may be a critical factor in the effectiveness and longevity of behavioral support efforts. A range of systems characteristics have been identified as important issues in behavioral intervention. These include existing structures, policies, and general philosophical milieu, allocation of resources, and mechanisms for ongoing monitoring and support of interventions (Durand & Kishi, 1987; Janney & Meyer, 1990; Meyer & Evans, 1989; Strain, McConnell, Carta, & Fowler, 1992). Some specific considerations for enhancing the impact of community-based training may include the following:

- adequacy of administrative support
- availability of staff development opportunities
- rules governing interaction with families
- interagency and interdisciplinary collaboration
- intervention policies and procedures
- funding mechanisms and available resources
- mission and philosophies articulated
- consultation, monitoring, and technical assistance

Training efforts that are self-perpetuating are essential given the number and variety of individuals in need of training (e.g., educators, family members, direct service providers) and the propensity for transition and turnover in human services professions (Buckley, Albin, & Mank, 1988). The training-of-trainers model used to establish state training teams promotes the spread of effect from the initial training (Demchak & Browder, 1990; Peck, Killen, & Baumgart, 1989) and provides a forum for ongoing communication and coordination among representatives of the constituent agencies.

The team training model addresses these considerations by engaging the community in interagency planning and system-development activities before, during, and after the training. Specific methods are used to enhance participant networking, systems change, and community building. Mechanisms are established for continued communication and support among the training team members and participants. For example, in one community in Florida, the training led to the school district reevaluating the role of its intervention assistance teams, supplementing its inservice training program, and establishing a mentoring system among participants.

Through team training, individuals from multiple levels within agencies and systems, as well as from a variety of settings, are functionally united to address the problem behaviors of the focus individuals. Identification of key individuals who may be in positions to facilitate change (e.g., administrators, politicians, community members), and engaging them as partners in the training process, can be important to facilitate creative problem solving. As teams identify long-term goals for the individuals, they may also identify system barriers that must be overcome to support the person. Brainstorming potential solutions may lead to broader systemic changes that will benefit all the consumers of their services.

The national inservice training model offers a comprehensive, interactive approach to competency development in positive behavior support. A description of the content and foundational elements of the model has been provided to systems as an example of how to design inservice efforts in positive behavior support. The body of experience in team training has offered repeated validations that thorough and thoughtful training efforts of this nature will result in successful translation of research-based knowledge into practice.

Conclusion

Standards for providing behavioral support in communities and schools are changing rapidly in directions described under the auspices of positive behavior support. To comply with these standards, and to support people with behavioral challenges in appropriate and effective ways, communities must identify improved strategies for building their capacity to offer collaborative, comprehensive behavioral support. Inservice training is an accepted and necessary means for building such capacity, yet it is crucial that such inservice training be conducted in a way that is most likely to achieve the desired outcomes.

In this article, we have described some curricular features and design elements that have been shown to be useful in equipping communities with the perspectives and competencies of positive behavior support. To effectively implement inservice training in school and community settings, it is also important to consider logistical challenges such as time, resources, personnel, and administrative issues associated with the delivery of comprehensive training. Flexibility and creativity are necessary to respond to these concerns in a way that matches the changing circumstances and needs of typical school, home, and community settings. Although there are essential features of effective training in positive behavior support, there will always be a need for well-considered adaptations that ensure optimal acceptance and adoption of the training content by community participants.

ABOUT THE AUTHORS

Glen Dunlap, PhD, is a professor of child and family studies at the University of South Florida. He serves as director of the Division of Applied Research and Educational Support and principal investigator for the Research and Training Center on Positive Behavioral Support. Meme Hieneman, PhD, is an assistant professor in the Department of Child and Family Studies, Louis de la Parte Florida Mental Health Institute, University of South Florida. Her interests focus on behavioral support in school, home, and community settings. She is project director for a statewide training and technical assistance program and co-training coordinator for the Research and Training Center on Positive Behavior Support. Tim Knoster, EdD, is a program director of the Interagency Support Project of the Instructional Support System of Pennsylvania. He is also the principal investigator of the Tri-State Consortium on Positive Behavioral Support, a federally funded outreach project through the U.S. Department of Education's Office of Special Education. Lise Fox, PhD, currently directs programs and conducts research in autism, early intervention, and positive behavioral support. Jacki L. Anderson, PhD, is a professor of special education in the Department of Educational Psychology at California State University–Hayward and coordinator of credential and master's degree programs in the area of moderate/severe disabilities. She is also co-training coordinator of the Research and Teaining Center on Positive Behavioral Support. Her interests include inclusion, positive behavioral supports, and effective instruction for individuals with severe disabilities. Richard W. Albin, PhD, is a senior research associate/associate professor in the Department of Special Education and Community Resources at the University of Oregon. His research and training interests include positive behavioral support procedures and strategies for effective personnel training and development. Address: Glen Dunlap, University of South Florida, Louis de la Parte Florida Mental Health Institute, Department of Child and Family Studies/DARES, 13301 Bruce B. Downs Blvd., Tampa, FL 33612.

AUTHORS' NOTES

1. *The authors express appreciation to all individuals who have participated in the development and delivery of the RRTC inservice training curriculum and to all the members of the training teams around the country who have provided positive behavior support for people with behavioral challenges.*

2. *Preparation of this article was supported by Rehabilitation Research and Training Center Grant No. H133B980005 from the National Institute on Disability and Rehabilitation Research, U.S. Department of Education. Additional support was provided by a grant from the Office of Special Education Programs, U.S. Department of Education (Grant No. H326S980003).*

3. *For further information about the RRTC-PBS inservice training approach, please contact the authors care of RRTC-PBS, Division of Applied Research and Educational Support, Department of Child and Family Studies, FMHI, University of South Florida, 13301 Bruce B. Downs Blvd., Tampa, FL 33612.*

REFERENCES

Alberto, P. A., & Troutman, A. C. (1990). *Applied behavior analysis for teachers* (3rd ed.). New York: Macmillan.

Albin, R. W., Horner, R. H., & O'Neill, R. E. (1993). *Proactive behavioral support: Structuring and assessing environments.* Unpublished manuscript, University of Oregon, Specialized Training Program, Eugene.

Albin, R. W., Lucyshyn, J. M., Horner, R. H., & Flannery, B. K. (1996). Contextual fit for behavioral support plans: A model for "goodness of fit." In L. Koegel, R. Koegel, & G. Dunlap (Eds.), *Positive behavioral support: Including people with difficult behavior in the community* (pp. 81–98). Baltimore: Brookes.

Anderson, J. L., Albin, R. W., Mesaros, R. A., Dunlap, G., & Morelli-Robbins, M. (1993). Issues in providing training to achieve comprehensive behavioral support. In J. Reichle & D. Wacher (Eds.), *Communicative alternatives to challenging behavior: Integrating functional assessment and intervention strategies* (pp. 363–406). Baltimore: Brookes.

Anderson, J. L., Russo, A., Dunlap, G., & Albin, R. W. (1996). A team training model for building the capacity to provide positive behavioral supports in inclusive settings. In L. Koegel, R. Koegel, & G. Dunlap (Eds.), *Positive behavioral support: Including people with difficult behavior in the community* (pp. 467–490). Baltimore: Brookes.

Bailey, J., & Pyles, D. A. M. (1989). Behavioral diagnostics. In E. Cipani (Ed.), The treatment of severe behavior disorders [Monograph]. *AAMR Monographs, 12,* 85–107.

Bambara, L. M., & Knoster, T. P. (1998). Designing positive behavior support plans. *Innovations* (No. 13). Washington, DC: American Association on Mental Retardation.

Bambara, L. M., & Knoster, T. P. (1995). *Guidelines: Effective behavioral support.* Harrisburg: Pennsylvania Department of Education, Bureau of Special Education.

Bambara, L. M., Mitchell-Kvacky, A. A., & Iacobelli, S. (1994). Positive behavioral support for students with severe disabilities: An emerging multicomponent approach for addressing challenging behavior. *School Psychology Review, 23,* 263–278.

Bellamy, G. T., Newton, J. S., LeBaron, N., & Horner, R. H. (1990). Quality of life and lifestyle outcomes: A challenge for residential programs. In R. Schalock (Ed.), *Quality of life: Perspectives and issues* (pp. 127–137). Washington, DC: American Association on Mental Retardation.

Bishop, K. D., & Jubala, K. D. (1995). Positive behavioral support strategies. In M. A. Falvey (Ed.), *Inclusive and heterogeneous schooling: Assessment, curriculum, and instruction* (pp. 159–186). Baltimore: Brookes.

Briggs, M. H. (1991). Team development: Decision-making for early intervention. *The Transdisciplinary Journal, 1,* 1–9.

Buckley, J., Albin, J. M., & Mank, D. (1988). Competency-based staff training for supported employment. In G. T. Bellamy, L. E. Rhodes, D. M. Mank, & J. M. Albin (Eds.), *Supported employment: A community implementation guide* (pp. 229–245). Baltimore: Brookes.

Carr, E. G., & Durand, V. M. (1985). Reducing behavior problems through functional communication training. *Journal of Applied Behavior Analysis, 18,* 111–126.

Carr, E. G., Levin, L., McConnachie, G., Carlson, J. I., Kemp, D. C., & Smith, C. E. (1994). *Communication-based intervention for problem behavior: A user's guide for producing positive change.* Baltimore: Brookes.

Carr, E. G., Robinson, S., & Palumbo, L. W. (1990). The wrong issue: Aversive versus nonaversive treatment. The right issue: Functional versus nonfunctional treatment. In A. Repp & N. Singh (Eds.), *Perspectives on the use of nonaversive and aversive interventions for persons with developmental disabilities* (pp. 361–379). Sycamore, IL: Sycamore.

Cline, D. (1984). Achieving quality and relevance in inservice teacher education: Where are we? *Teacher Education and Special Education, 7,* 199–208.

Colvin, G., Kameenui, E. J., & Sugai, G. (1993). Reconceptualizing behavior management and school-wide discipline in general education. *Education and Treatment of Children, 16,* 361–381.

Cooper, J. O., Heron, T. E., & Heward, W. L. (1987). *Applied behavior analysis.* Columbus, OH: Merrill.

Demchak, M. A., & Bossert, K. W. (1996). Assessing problem behaviors. *Innovations* (No. 4). Washington, DC: American Association on Mental Retardation.

Demchak, M. A., & Browder, D. M. (1990). An evaluation of the pyramid model of staff training in group homes for adults with severe handicaps. *Education and Training in Mental Retardation, 25,* 150–163.

Dunlap, G., & Kern, L. (1993). Assessment and intervention for children within the instructional curriculum. In J. Reichle & D. Wacker (Eds.), *Communicative alternatives to challenging behavior* (pp. 177–203). Baltimore: Brookes.

Dunlap, G., & Kern, L. (1996). Modifying instructional activities to promote desirable behavior: A conceptual and practical framework. *School Psychology Quarterly, 11,* 297–312.

Dunlap, G., Robbins, F. R., Morelli, M. A., & Dollman, C. (1988). Team training for young children with autism: A regional model for service delivery. *Journal of the Division for Early Childhood, 12,* 147–160.

Dunst, C. J., Trivette, C. M., & Johanson, C. (1994). Parent–professional collaboration and partnerships. In C. J. Dunst, C. M. Trivette, & A. Deal (Eds.), *Supporting and strengthening families, Volume 1: Methods, strategies, and practices* (pp. 197–211). Cambridge, MA: Brookline Books.

Durand, V. M., & Kishi, G. (1987). Reducing severe behavior problems among persons with dual sensory impairments: An evaluation of a technical assistance model. *Journal of the Association for Persons with Severe Handicaps, 12,* 2–10.

Eno-Hieneman, M., Dunlap, G., & Fox, L. (1995). *[Research and Training Center on Positive Behavior Support: State training team needs assessment].* Unpublished raw data.

Evans, I. M., & Meyer, L. H. (1985). *An educative approach to behavior problems: A practical decision making model for interventions with severely handicapped learners.* Baltimore: Brookes.

Flannery, B. K., Sprague, J. R., & Todd, A. (1996). Including students with behavioral challenges: Blending school-wide discipline and individual supports. In L. Power-deFur & F. P. Orelove (Eds.), *Inclusive schools: A comprehensive guide to successful implementation* (pp. 227–244). Gaithersburg, MD: Aspen.

Foster-Johnson, L., & Dunlap, G. (1993). Using functional assessment to develop effective individualized interventions for challenging behaviors. *Teaching Exceptional Children, 25,* 44–50.

Fox, J., & Conroy, M. (1995). Setting events and behavioral disorders of children and youth: An interbehavioral field analysis for research and practice. *Journal of Emotional and Behavioral Disorders, 3,* 130–140.

Fox, L., Vaughn B. J., Dunlap, G., & Bucy, M. (1997). Parent–professional partnership in behavioral support: A quantitative analysis of one family's experience. *Journal of the Association for Persons with Severe Handicaps, 22,* 198–207.

Givner, C. C., & Haager, D. (1995). Strategies for effective collaboration. In M. A. Falvey (Ed.), *Inclusive and heterogeneous schooling: Assessment, curriculum, and instruction.* Baltimore: Brookes.

Guess, D., Helmstetter, E., Turnbull, H. R., III, & Knowlton, S. (1987). Use of aversive procedures with persons who are disabled: An historical review and critical analysis. *Monograph of the Association for Persons with Severe Handicaps, 2*(1).

Gutkin, T. B. (1993). Demonstrating the efficacy of collaborative consultation services: Theoretical and practical perspectives. *Topics in Language Disorders, 14,* 81–90.

Hedeen, D. L., Ayres, B. J., Meyer, L. H., & Waite, J. (1996). Quality inclusive schooling for students with severe behavioral challenges. In D. Lehr & F. Brown (Eds.), *People with disabilities who challenge the system* (pp. 127–171). Baltimore: Brookes.

Hieneman, M., & Dunlap, G. (in press). Some issues and challenges in implementing community-based behavioral support: Two illustrative case studies. In J. Scotti & L. Meyer (Eds.), *New directions for behavioral intervention: Principles, models, and practices.* Baltimore: Brookes.

Horner, R. H., & Carr, E. G. (1997). Behavioral support for students with severe disabilities: Functional assessment and comprehensive intervention. *The Journal of Special Education, 31,* 84–104.

Horner, R. H., Dunlap, G., Koegel, R. L., Carr, E. G., Sailor, W., Anderson, J., Albin, R. W., & O'Neill, R. E. (1990). Toward a technology of "nonaversive" behavioral support. *Journal of the Association for Persons with Severe Handicaps, 15,* 125–132.

Horner, R. H., O'Neill, R. E., & Flannery, K. B. (1993). Building effective behavior support plans from functional assessment information. In M. E. Snell (Ed.), *Systematic instruction for persons with severe handicaps* (4th ed., pp. 184–214). Columbus, OH: Merrill.

Horner, R. H., Vaughn, B. J., Day, H. M., & Ard, W. R. (1996). The relationship between setting events and problem behavior: Expanding our understanding of behavioral support. In L. Koegel, R. Koegel, & G. Dunlap (Eds.), *Positive behavioral support: Including people with difficult behavior in the community* (pp. 381–402). Baltimore: Brookes.

Hughes, C., Hwang, B., Kim, J. H., Eisenman, L. T., & Killian, D. J. (1995). Quality of life in applied research: A review and analysis of empirical measures. *American Journal on Mental Retardation, 99,* 623–641.

Iwata, B. A., Vollmer, T. R., Zarcone, J. R., & Rodgers, T. A. (1993). Treatment classification and selection based on behavioral function. In R. Van Houton & S. Axelrod (Eds.), *Behavior analysis and treatment* (pp. 101–125). New York: Plenum.

Iwata, B. A., Vollmer, T. R., & Zarcone, J. R. (1990). The experimental (functional) analysis of behavior disorders: Methodology, applications, and limitations. In A. Repp & N. Singh (Eds.), *Perspectives on the use of nonaversive and aversive interventions for persons with severe disabilities* (pp. 301–330). Sycamore, IL: Sycamore.

Janney, R. E., & Meyer, L. H. (1990). A consultation model to support integrated educational services for students with severe disabilities and challenging behaviors. *Journal of the Association for Persons with Severe Handicaps, 15,* 186–199.

Joyce, B., & Showers, B. (1980). Improving inservice training: The age of research. *Educational Leadership, 37,* 379–385.

Kincaid, D. (1996). Person-centered planning. In L. Koegel, R. Koegel, & G. Dunlap (Eds.), *Positive behavioral support: Including people with difficult behavior in the community* (pp. 439–465). Baltimore: Brookes.

Koegel, L. K., Koegel, R. L., & Dunlap, G. (1996). *Positive behavioral support: Including people with difficult behavior in the community.* Baltimore: Brookes.

Lewis, T. J., & Sugai, G. (1993). Teaching communicative alternatives to socially withdrawn learners: An investigation on maintaining treatment effects. *Journal of Behavioral Education, 3,* 61–75.

Lohrmann-O'Rourke, S., Knoster, T., & Llewellyn, G. (1999). Screening for understanding: An initial line of inquiry for school-based settings. *Journal of Positive Behavioral Interventions, 1,* 35–42.

McEvoy, M., Davis, C., & Reichle, J. (1993). District-wide technical assistance teams: Designing intervention strategies for young children with challenging behaviors. *Behavioral Disorders, 19,* 27–34.

Meyer, L. H., & Evans, I. M. (1989). *Nonaversive intervention for behavior problems: A manual for home and community.* Baltimore: Brookes.

Meyer, L. H., & Evans, I. M. (1993). Science and practice in behavioral intervention: Meaningful outcomes, research validity, and usable knowledge. *Journal of the Association for Persons with Severe Handicaps, 18,* 224–234.

Mount, B., & Zwernik, K. (1988). *It's never too early, it's never too late: A booklet about personal futures planning.* St. Paul, MN: Metropolitan Council.

Mullen, K. B., & Frea, W. D. (1995). A parent–professional consultation model for functional analysis. In R. Koegel & L. Koegel (Eds.), *Teaching children with autism: Strategies for initiating positive interactions and learning opportunities* (pp. 175–188). Baltimore: Brookes.

Munk, D. D., & Repp, A. C. (1994). The relationship between instructional variables and problem behavior: A review. *Exceptional Children, 60,* 390–401.

O'Brien, J., Mount, B., & O'Brien, C. (1991). *Framework for accomplishment: Personal profile.* Decatur, GA: Responsive Systems Associates.

O'Neill, R. E., Horner, R. H., Albin, R. W., Sprague, J. R., Storey, K., & Newton, J. S. (1997). *Functional assessment and program development for problem behavior: A practical handbook.* Pacific Grove, CA: Brooks/Cole.

O'Neill, R. E., Williams, R., Sprague, J. R., Horner, R. H., & Albin, R. W. (1993). Providing support for teachers working with students with severe problem behaviors: A model for providing consultation support within school districts. *Education and Treatment of Children, 16,* 66–89.

Orelove, F. P., & Sobsey, D. (1991). *Educating children with multiple disabilities: A transdisciplinary approach* (2nd ed.). Baltimore: Brookes.

Peck, C. A., Killen, C. C., & Baumgart, D. (1989). Increasing implementation of special education instruction in mainstream preschools. Direct and generalized effects of nondirective consultation. *Journal of Applied Behavior Analysis, 22,* 197–210.

Racino, J. A. (1990). Preparing personnel to work in community support services. In A. P. Kaiser & S. M. McWhorter (Eds.), *Preparing personnel to work with persons with severe disabilities* (pp. 203–226). Baltimore: Brookes.

Rainforth, B., York, J., & MacDonald, C. (1992). *Collaborative teams for students with severe disabilities: Integrating therapy and educational services.* Baltimore: Brookes.

Reichle, J. E., & Wacker, D. P. (1993). *Communicative alternatives to challenging behavior: Integrating functional assessment and intervention strategies.* Baltimore: Brookes.

Repp, A. C., & Horner, R. H. (1999). *Functional analysis of problem behavior: From effective assessment to effective support.* Belmont, CA: Wadsworth.

Repp, A. C., & Singh, N. N. (1990). *Perspectives on the use of nonaversive and aversive interventions for persons with developmental disabilities.* Sycamore, IL: Sycamore.

Singer, G. H. S., Gert, B., & Koegel, R. L. (1999). A moral framework for analyzing the controversy over aversive behavioral interventions for people with severe mental retardation. *Journal of Positive Behavioral Interventions, 1,* 88–100.

Smith, T., Parker, T., Taubman, M., & Lovaas, O. I. (1992). Transfer of staff training from workshops to group homes: A failure to generalize across settings. *Research in Developmental Disabilities, 13,* 57–71.

Strain, P. S., McConnell, S. R., Carta, J. J. & Fowler, S. A. (1992). Behaviorism in early intervention. *Topics in Early Childhood Special Education, 12,* 121–141.

Sulzer-Azaroff, B., & Mayer, G. R. (1991). *Behavior analysis for lasting change.* Chicago: Holt, Rinehart & Winston.

Taylor-Greene, S., Brown, D., Nelson, L., Longton, J., Gassman, T., Cohen, J., Schwartz, J., Horner, R. H., Sugai, G., & Hall, S. (1997). School-wide behavioral support: Starting the year off right. *Journal of Behavioral Education, 7,* 99–112.

Thousand, J. S., & Villa, R. A. (1994). Collaborative teams: A powerful tool in school restructuring. In R. Villa, J. Thousand, W. Stainback, & S. Stainback (Eds.), *Restructuring for a caring and effective education: An administrative guide to creating heterogeneous schools* (pp. 73–108). Baltimore: Brookes.

Tilly, W. D., Knoster, T. K., Kovaleski, J., Bambara, L., Dunlap, G., & Kincaid, D. (1998). *Functional behavioral assessment: Policy development in light of emerging research and practice.* Alexandria, VA: National Association of State Directors of Special Education.

Topper, K., Williams, W., Leo, K., Hamilton, R. W., & Fox, T. A. (1994). *Positive approach to understanding and addressing challenging behaviors.* Burlington: University Affiliated Program of Vermont.

Turnbull, A. P., & Turnbull, H. R. (1996). Group action planning as a strategy for providing comprehensive family support. In L. K. Koegel, R. L. Koegel, & G. Dunlap (Eds.), *Positive behavioral support: including people with difficult behavior in the community* (pp. 99–114). Baltimore: Brookes.

Vandercook, T., & York, J. (1990). A team approach to program development and support. In W. C. Stainback & S. B. Stainback (Eds.), *Support networks for inclusive schooling: Interdependent integrated education* (pp. 95–122). Baltimore: Brookes.

Vaughn B. J., Dunlap, G., Fox, L., Clarke, S., & Bucy, M. (1997). Parent–professional partnership in behavioral support: A case study of community-based intervention. *Journal of the Association for Persons with Severe Handicaps, 22,* 185–197.

Wacker, E., Wendy, K., Harding, J., & Asmus, J. (1996). A functional approach to dealing with severe challenging behavior. In S. B. Stainback & W. C. Stainback (Eds.), *Inclusion: A guide for educators* (pp. 327–342). Baltimore: Brookes.

Walker, B., & Singer, G. H. S. (1993). Improving collaborative communication between professionals and parents. In G. H. S. Singer & L. E. Powers (Eds.), *Families, disability, and empowerment: Active coping skills and strategies for family interventions.* Baltimore: Brookes.

Action Editor: Robert L. Koegel

Factors Affecting the Outcomes of Community-Based Behavioral Support:

I. Identification and Description of Factor Categories

∽

Meme Hieneman
University of South Florida

Glen Dunlap
University of South Florida

Abstract: This study was the first of a two-phase investigation of factors affecting the outcomes of behavioral support for individuals with severe disabilities in community settings. It involved an initial literature review and semistructured interviews to obtain the perspectives of informed participants from three constituent groups: family members, direct service providers, and trainers/consultants. The descriptive data from these interviews were synthesized via content analysis procedures, resulting in the identification of 12 factor categories. The categories ranged from individual, setting, and plan-specific variables to broader considerations such as support provider interactions and systemic issues (e.g., agency/program-wide procedures, prevailing philosophies). The results of this study offer implications for practice and new directions for investigation.

Positive behavior support (PBS) is an approach to supporting individuals with problem behaviors that is based on person-centered values and designed to assist individuals to experience improved lifestyles in the context of their everyday home and community functioning (Koegel, Koegel, & Dunlap, 1996). PBS is based on the technical and methodological foundations of applied behavior analysis, but has expanded its parent discipline to incorporate increased focus on ecological validity (i.e., a commitment to implementation in natural contexts) and accountability defined in terms of meaningful, socially valid outcomes (Carr, 1997; Dunlap, Fox, Vaughn, Bucy, & Clarke, 1997). Defining outcomes in terms of broad, durable changes in a person's lifestyle has led to the adoption of individualized, multicomponent intervention packages (Horner & Carr, 1997) and broader systemwide applications of positive behavioral support (Sugai et al., 1999; Turnbull & Turnbull, 1990). Over the past decade, the PBS approach has gained acceptance and credibility; however, its continued impact will depend on a growing, empirical record of efficacy.

Although it is expanding, the research foundation of PBS is still largely dependent on studies conducted in segregated, controlled contexts. The majority of relevant intervention research is limited by artificial, analog settings,

reliance on atypical, specialized intervention agents, and very brief periods of systematic observation (Dunlap, Clarke, & Steiner, 1999). For example, Scotti, Evans, Meyer, and Walker (1991) found that less than 10% of studies between 1976 and 1987 occurred in home or community environments. In a more recent comprehensive analysis of the PBS literature, Carr, Horner, and Turnbull (in press) reported similar limitations in dimensions of ecological validity. These authors also noted that relatively few investigations include measures of maintenance or lifestyle outcomes.

It is likely that the tendency to conduct intervention research in controlled settings (e.g., clinics, special education classrooms) has also limited the types of intervention variables, or factors, that have been studied. It is one thing to produce behavior change in a restricted setting over a brief period of time; it may be quite a different challenge to produce equivalent amplitudes of change, in a range of natural settings, over an extended time frame, and in a way that affects multiple dimensions of an individual's functioning and lifestyle. It is probable that the achievement of these PBS goals necessarily involves the contribution of a number of factors that extend well beyond the existing technology of behavior management or applied behavior analysis.

In recent years, some authors have begun to examine and speculate about the range of factors that are instrumental in achieving successful, community-based behavioral support. In addition to the technical integrity of the interventions, several authors have considered the "acceptability" of an intervention to the people charged with implementation (e.g., Gutkin, 1993; Miltenberger, Suda, Lennox, & Lindeman, 1991; O'Brien & Karsh, 1990; Reimers, Wacker, Derby, & Cooper, 1995; Schwartz & Baer, 1991), the degree to which interventions "fit" with the resources and routines of the context (e.g., Albin, Lucyshyn, Horner, & Flannery, 1996, Berg & Sasso, 1993; Meyer & Evans, 1993), and the degree to which individuals and agencies collaborate as partners in the behavioral support enterprise (e.g., Hieneman & Dunlap, 1999). These factors, and others, have begun to be appreciated as potentially influential variables and, thus, as worthy targets for future applied research. However, other factors undoubtedly exist, and to date there have been no systematic efforts to identify the full range of variables that may be instrumental in the success of community-based behavioral support.

The purpose of the current study was to establish an initial itemization and categorization of factors that may affect the success of community-based behavioral support for children with severe disabilities. The study was the first of a two-phase project, in which the second phase (to be published subsequently) sought to prioritize and rank-order the identified factors. To identify factors in the current study, we first conducted a preliminary survey of the relevant literature to establish an initial list. Then, we conducted in-depth interviews with knowledgeable and experienced representatives of three stakeholder groups (parents/guardians, trainers/consultants, and direct service providers). The data from the interviews were analyzed and synthesized in order to produce a set of factor categories.

Method

The methods for this investigation involved a review of literature followed by semistructured interviews conducted with three groups of informed participants: trainer/consultants, parents or guardians, and direct service providers. The results were obtained from an analysis of descriptive information obtained through the literature review and interviews.

LITERATURE REVIEW

A literature review was conducted to identify potential factors contributing to the effectiveness of community-based behavioral support. The sources included discussion articles, chapters, and research articles focused on community-based intervention. The chapters or articles had to focus on intervention with people with severe disabilities in home, school, or community environments. A search was conducted through a number of databases (e.g., PsychLit, PsychInfo, ERIC) using the following keywords: positive behavioral support, functional assessment, behavioral intervention, severe disabilities, and community environments. In addition, experts were asked to nominate additional materials (e.g., unpublished and prepublication documents) that might not emerge through the database search. Through this process, 153 sources were identified, including 56 research articles, 40 discussion articles, 36 chapters, and 20 books and manuals (see Note 1). The majority of the items (97) focused on behavioral intervention, and the remainder addressed related topics such as treatment acceptability, instructional practices, program implementation, and issues associated with the consultative process.

Once the articles and chapters were located, the first author reviewed their content and identified factors described as being relevant to effective outcomes. To be identified as a factor, the variable had to be described in at least two sources as a consideration or explanation of success or failure in behavioral support. A list was made of all factors identified, and this list was then reduced to a set of mutually exclusive categories.

INTERVIEWS

Semistructured phone interviews were conducted with participants of three constituent groups. This was done to elaborate and expand on the factor categories identified in the literature review.

Participants

The interview participants were selected using purposive sampling in order to obtain perspectives of informants who were knowledgeable about community-based behavioral support. Criteria for participation included that individuals were required to have a minimum of 3 years experience in behavioral support for school-age (i.e., ages 5–21) children with severe developmental disabilities (e.g., severe mental retardation, autism) and significant behavior problems, such as self-injury, aggression, and destruction of property. Professionals were required to have had involvement in supporting a minimum of 10 individuals with these characteristics during their careers. Behavioral support efforts provided by participants had to have occurred in multiple community settings (i.e., not restricted to residential placements). Participants were also required to have participated in one or more training activities in behavioral support and to have used functional assessment procedures to design behavioral interventions.

The sample was obtained via nominations provided by members of the state training team network established by the Research and Training Center on Positive Behavioral Support, a federally funded project that promotes practical, nonaversive methods to support individuals with challenging behavior in the community (Dunlap, Hieneman, Knoster, Fox, Anderson, & Albin, 2000). Participant selection was based on the strength of the nomination (e.g., the individual was described as particularly knowledgeable), the recency and extensiveness of his or her pertinent experience, and with an effort to produce geographic diversity and a balance of professional affiliations (e.g., education, residential support).

Fifteen participants were selected, five from each constituent group: parents/guardians, trainer/consultants, and direct service providers. The participants were from 15 different states across the country and represented a range of characteristics. They included four mothers and a mother and father of adolescents and young adults with autism and moderate to severe mental retardation ranging in age from 13 to 29 years old; direct service providers from a variety of educational and residential programs; and researchers, administrators, and others in consultation and training roles. The direct service providers and trainers/consultants included six men and four women. The extent of their experience ranged from 7 years to more than 20 years. Professional participants had supported numerous individuals (from 40 to well over 100) ranging in age from birth to old age with autism, severe mental retardation, and other disabilities who experienced severe aggression, disruption, and other behavioral concerns. There was also a degree of overlap in the roles of participants (e.g., family members who were involved in training, direct service providers who provided consultation).

Data Collection

This study employed semistructured phone interviews because they allowed for a breadth of responses and creative exploration of the phenomenon, while maintaining a degree of consistency in the questions and interviewing procedures (Bernard, 1994; Fowler, 1988). The questions and procedures were refined through expert review and pilot testing. Eight individuals representing the three constituent groups (i.e., three trainers/consultants, two parents, and three direct service providers) were asked to evaluate the questions and probing techniques and to provide input regarding conducting interviews prior to implementation. Pilot interviews were then conducted by phone with three people.

The interview guide was designed to obtain three types of information: demographic characteristics, definitions of "effectiveness," and information regarding factors affecting behavioral support. Questions regarding the backgrounds and characteristics of the participants were included to ensure that they met the criteria for involvement in the study. Questions related to the participants'

1. In your experience, what factors contribute to the effectiveness of behavioral support in home, school, and community environments?

2. Of the factors you have just mentioned, which ones do you feel are most important? Please name the top three.

3. Please think about circumstances or periods of time in which you experienced your greatest successes and challenges in providing behavioral support in community settings for (your child/individuals you were working with). Could you share a story of a successful experience/a challenging experience?

4. What do you believe contributed to the successes? What contributed to the challenges or failures?

5. I'm going to describe three areas that could have an impact on behavioral support in the community and ask you to describe the factors in those specific areas that could influence the outcomes of behavioral support. You may identify factors that we have discussed earlier; that is fine.

6. What factors related to the _____ affect behavioral support efforts?
   . . . *conditions/settings* in which support plans are used
   . . . *attitudes and beliefs* of the individuals involved
   . . . *specific behaviors* or *activities* of those involved

7. What obstacles to effective behavioral support in the community have you experienced?

Figure 1. Main interview questions.

definitions of goals and outcomes of behavioral support efforts helped ensure some degree of consistency in interpretations of effectiveness. The main questions were related to specific issues that may facilitate or impede behavioral support in community settings; these are provided in Figure 1.

The phone interviews were conducted by presenting the open-ended questions verbatim. Additional probes were delivered to clarify the information provided or to obtain more depth from the respondent. Interviews were conducted over a 3-week period. With the exception of one 3-hour interview, they lasted between 45 minutes and an hour. Procedural integrity was evaluated during the pilot tests and actual interviews to ensure consistency in the procedures. In addition, a second researcher reviewed 25% of the transcripts to identify any discrepancies.

DATA ANALYSIS

Initial categories derived from the literature review (technical soundness, ecological relevance, social validity, systemic issues, and collaborative teamwork) led to the development of an initial organizational scheme focused on the characteristics of the procedures, settings, people, and systems involved in behavioral support, as well as the collaboration or interactions among providers. These categories were revised and expanded in order to encapsulate the data obtained during the interviews.

The analysis involved multiple steps, including developing factor categories, coding and sorting the data by category, unitizing and labeling factors, synthesizing the factors into a content summary, and conducting member checks. Definitions and decision rules to assign the data segments to categories (e.g., when described as an interaction between two categories) were developed to improve the consistency in this process. These steps enabled the organization and reduction of the raw data, generation of meaningful categories of factors, and interpretation of patterns or themes in the data (Tesch, 1990; Wolcott, 1994).

To develop the factor categories, the first author cycled through the transcripts, noting segments that corresponded to the initial framework, those that did not, and extraneous comments (e.g., interruptions). Only the participants' responses, not the interviewer's questions or comments, were coded. The data were segmented based on topics described and then coded using three-letter labels corresponding to predetermined categories. Information that did not readily fit into a category was singled out for further analysis, generating additional categories until all of the data were accounted for. After codes were assigned, the data were sorted by category within the individual transcripts, combined by group, and merged into one data file. This process was facilitated by using Ethnograph, a computer program for analyzing qualitative data.

Once the data segments were divided into the broad categories, factors were unitized and labeled within categories. This involved assigning descriptive labels to each data segment and then generating a complete list of factors under each. Concepts from the literature were used to guide the establishment of categories where natural distinctions between the factors were not apparent. The information contained within each of the broad categories was then used to create a narrative content summary that included two- to three-paragraph descriptions of the categories with examples from the transcripts and lists of factors. The content summary was sent to the interview participants to provide an additional opportunity for review and feedback (i.e., member checks).

To enhance the consistency of the data analysis procedures and the degree to which the summary adequately reflected the information shared by the participants, a number of measures were taken. First, the researcher drew from multiple sources of information. Five respondents per constituency group were interviewed, providing a variety of perspectives. The literature provided an additional source for identifying potential factors and was used to refine theoretical constructs identified by the participants. Second, the process of coding and reviewing the data was

articulated clearly, defining each stage of the analysis. And third, more than one person was responsible for checking accuracy and analyzing the data.

Findings

The interviews produced 12,951 lines of text, with totals of 3,874, 4,472, and 6,605 from each participant group (parent/guardian, direct service, and trainer/consultant), respectively. Review of the data resulted in the identification of issues related to providing supports in natural, dynamic environments; components of and process for designing behavioral support plans; social, political, and economic realities one has to face; and a wide variety of support provider issues believed to influence intervention.

IDENTIFIED FACTOR CATEGORIES

Twelve factor categories emerged from the data; the analysis aligned with an ecological framework in which factors are organized at microlevels (individual, settings) and macrolevels (systemic and sociocultural issues). Some categories were directly related to the design and implementation of the plan, whereas others were related to contextual variables and resources that are inclined to affect outcomes. Quotes that illustrate the categories are provided in Table 1.

1. *Characteristics of the focus individual.* A category of factors that was not addressed in the literature review, but was articulated clearly in the interviews, involves characteristics of the person who is the focus of behavioral support. The participants described physiological, behavioral, and motivational characteristics of the individuals that would affect the person's ability to respond to intervention efforts. Physiological issues related to the person's disability, other conditions or illnesses (e.g., seizure disorders, allergies), utilization of medication, developmental changes that occur as a person matures, and a person's sensitivity to characteristics of his or her surroundings (e.g., tolerance for temperature, light, noise). Behavioral and motivational issues included the person's skills for communicating his or her needs, independence in performing typical daily activities, and existing repertoires that allow the person to express preferences and control the environment. In addition, the person's preferences and goals regarding personal lifestyle and satisfaction or comfort with current circumstances were mentioned.

2. *Nature and history of the behavior.* A second area was the nature and history of the focus individual's behavior, including the type, frequency, intensity, and variability of problem behavior. This included the degree to which the person's behaviors endangered that person and others, disrupted the environment, or created social stigma. Participants relayed incidents of problem behavior and their impact on other people and surroundings, and the chal-

Table 1. Quotes Illustrating Categories of Factors

Category	Illustrative quotes
Characteristics of the focus individual	"I think you have to take it into account where you take the person and where the person is functioning, you know. If they're a person who needs peace and quiet, it makes no sense to take them into a really noisy environment filled with people. If they're kind of a big person who kind of blusters around, it's probably a good idea to look for an environment where other people aren't real fragile or timid." *(parent/guardian)*
Nature and history of the behavior	"The more dangerous the behavior, the more physically challenging, the more visually provocative it is, the harder it is to get people not to react to it." *(trainer/consultant)*
	"Well, I think clearly there's some history there. That used to be something he did all the time. That was his way to respond to every situation, probably 10 years ago. And I don't know if that's why he's choosing that or if he's choosing it. I don't know, but it makes him feel terrible afterwards." *(direct service provider)*
Behavioral support plan design	"Well what we have tried to do is first of all, collect a lot of data, you know. We're zeroing in on something that is really a major issue that we're going to work on. We're going to figure out how often it occurs and in what circumstances it occurs, what's going on at the time. And get a lot of concrete stuff down before we even come up with some ideas on what we're going to do next." *(parent/guardian)*
Integrity of implementation	"I believe there is always going to be a drift in every environment back to what people are used to doing unless the things that you tell them to do are easy and have an immediate impact that reinforces them for continuing to try it. Otherwise, they'll simply go back to what has worked in the past." *(trainer/consultant)*
Nature of the physical environment	"How much light, how much noise does the rain make falling on the roof? All of these things are going to affect our efforts." *(parent/guardian)*
	"Another primary piece would be typical settings that would have relevance to the kid's routine. So that these are not artificially contrived settings or simulated settings. But that you're dealing with the real child and real people and real situations that have relevance to the child and family, as well as the staff, but most particularly the child and the family." *(trainer/consultant)*
Buy-in with the intervention	"I think that if people buy into the notion of functional assessment and really understand what we are trying to do; and they buy into the answers the assessment . . . that come out of the process; and they really truly see themselves as part of the environment in which the behaviors occur, that's the best thing that you can have to at least assure some early success."
Capacity of support providers	"Another thing that's gonna really affect acquisition has to do with parental health and disability issues . . . And if one isn't aware of these contextual issues that impact the parent, then you're not gonna be real good at supporting that parent as they strive to implement a rather rigorous plan." *(trainer/consultant)*
	"But when I look at families with children with disabilities, they're doing everything that they possibly can. But there's only so much that they can do given the nature of their situation." *(parent/guardian)*
Relationships with the individual	"I would say the biggest is the relationships. That we, as providers and staff, can create a trusting relationship with the individual and then, acting as a bridge for that person, to really open up the world or open up the doors for them. And that's really, in my opinion anyway, the actual relationship between the staff and the individual has really been the key." *(direct service provider)*
Match with prevailing philosophy	"So even if you didn't have the belief system, if you have authority, if you have supervision, if you have a higher level of support, then you could probably get other things to happen that may be contrary to beliefs." *(trainer/consultant)*
	"Often there are relatives, or friends, who drift in and out of people's lives. It's kind of maintaining a certain decorum and order with these transient members who often have a very important impact on the plan you're trying to implement with some consistency." *(parent/guardian)*
Responsiveness of the system	"Failures usually end up due to the system either not having enough money, not having enough time, or not having enough environmental change to meet the needs of the individual." *(direct service provider)*
	"Obstacles are sometimes the rules that people have for how things should be done. If the rules can't be changed, then that becomes a huge obstacle. I think, you know, people who are supporting folks that we love really need to get good at convincing people that they can change the rules. That's OK to do." *(parent/guardian)*

(table continues)

(Table 1 continued)

Category	Illustrative quotes
Collaboration among providers	"The reality is that no teacher by themselves, no parent by themselves . . . if we're talking about kids with really significant problem behavior . . . are going to be able to go this alone, even though many families get stuck in that mode, unfortunately." *(trainer/consultant)*
	"We think parents communicating with other parents is a real big factor because parents who have children with behavioral problems are immediately put at ease when we talk about our sons. They just feel they are in good company and they don't have to be embarrassed or afraid to talk about what they are going through. That's a really big factor." *(parent/guardian)*
Community acceptance	"So the fact that the attitude that's out in the community makes it very, very difficult, even when we know what needs to happen, because we have a twofold mission. Not only do we have to change the behavior of the person with the disability, we have to change the behavior of people in society. It's no small task." *(parent/guardian)*

lenge associated with changing ingrained patterns of behavior. An individual's prior exposure to particular settings and intervention approaches was also implicated as a factor influencing behavioral support efforts.

3. *Behavioral support plan design.* A factor category related to the design of behavioral support plans included characteristics of the assessment process, planning an preparation methods, and elements of the behavioral support plan. One consistent theme was the importance of using a process of ecological and functional assessment that includes objectively defining the target behaviors, data collection procedures, data analysis, and hypothesis development to design comprehensive interventions. Other factors were the degree to which the support plan is based on proactive planning (e.g., person-centered planning), full consideration of the conditions in which it will be used, and consideration of the degree of alignment with the individual's goals, needs, and preferences.

4. *Integrity of implementation.* Participants identified issues related to the integrity of support plan implementation and the need for consistency, ongoing data-based monitoring, careful decision making, and evaluation. Participants described issues related to the introduction of plan elements within natural contexts, the degree to which the plan could be implemented across people and settings, and the extent to which outcomes were inclined to generalize. In addition, participants noted the importance of the immediacy and visibility of outcomes (e.g., clear changes in target behaviors, lifestyle changes, and benefits for support providers).

5. *Nature of the physical environment.* Characteristics of the physical settings within which individuals participate were described as potential resources or barriers to successful implementation of behavioral support plans. This category of factors emerged in discussions of variables that needed to be assessed in the design of effective plans. Issues that were prevalent in the transcripts were the availability of material resources and organization of environments, including the facilities, equipment, and space

available; locations in which supports were provided (e.g., integrated v. segregated contexts); availability of reinforcers in the setting; and specific sensory characteristics (lighting, noise, temperature) that may affect the person's behavior. Another area related to the characteristics of physical settings was the variety and schedule of activities and typical routines within the settings (e.g., clarity of rules, predictability of events, time constraints). Potential dangers posed by the settings (e.g., traffic, sharp objects) were also included as variables affecting behavioral support efforts.

6. *Buy-in with the intervention.* Considerable discussion among interview participants was associated with the support provider's commitment to participate in the implementation of support plans. They described a variety of issues that may influence "buy-in," including their satisfaction with plan elements and beliefs regarding its anticipated effectiveness. Specific issues in this area related to their perceived responsibility for creating behavior change and willingness to consider alternative perspectives, try new approaches, and take risks. These attitudes were affected by the degree to which plans addressed support providers' priorities and needs, the perceived urgency for addressing the problem behavior, and the empowerment of the support providers to advocate for services. Perseverance in plan implementation (rather than returning to "old habits") and support providers' ability to appreciate small gains were also described as factors in this area.

7. *Capacity of support providers.* Another category of factors emerged from discussions of circumstances in which support providers "wanted to follow through with the plan, but were incapable of doing so." These factors included knowledge regarding the principles and practices of behavioral support (e.g., view that behavior is functional, communicative, and focused on long-term quality of life improvements) and the specific plan for the individual. In addition, capacities were associated with the support providers' energy reserve for putting interventions in place, as well as their emotional well-being (e.g., stressors, burnout), physical health, and confidence in their ability to

safely support persons with challenging behavior. These issues were also articulated in relation to the need for training and support for families and professionals.

8. *Relationships with the individual.* A considerable amount of text from the interviews was dedicated to descriptions of characteristics of support providers that are essential to effectively support individuals with problem behavior and to enhance relationships. In relation to these positive relationships, participants identified the importance of acceptance and respect for the individual; understanding and appreciating their strengths and limitations; and valuing their dignity, privacy, and autonomy. The term *connectedness* was used to describe the nature of relationships that are likely to promote successful interactions. This referred to the support provider's ability to read an individual's (nonverbal) cues, to acknowledge the individual's needs, and to adapt accordingly (e.g., by adjusting pacing). This category related to the sensitivity and trust in the relationship and the degree to which it is based on shared interests and mutual appreciation.

9. *Match with prevailing philosophy.* In addition to the influence of contextual variables that are proximal to behavioral support efforts, participants also acknowledged the impact of larger system variables. Often, factors in this category were described in discussions of obstacles to effective behavioral support (e.g., traditional, expert models; layers of bureaucratic structure; and competing priorities within systems). Prevailing philosophies of systems and the degree to which support plans match their traditions, standards, policies, and procedures for addressing behavioral challenges were identified as key issues influencing the allocation of resources and support for plan implementation. Specifically, factors in this category included the degree to which systems embrace individualized support and collaborative decision making, and their eligibility and exclusion criteria that affect the accessibility of services.

10. *Responsiveness of the system.* A counterpart to the previous category of factors (match with prevailing philosophy) identified by participants was the flexibility of systems in responding to the needs of an individual with behavioral challenges and ensuring support plan implementation. Participants described incidents in which modifications were made to typical structures and rules, making behavioral support plan implementation more feasible. The degree of local control over settings and resources, and the flexibility of the system with regard to policy implementation, were mentioned as important factors. Participants described several characteristics of systems they believed to influence its responsiveness: the availability of administrative support (i.e., supervision, leadership), mechanisms to monitor plan implementation and promote accountability, consistency in the people and resources present, frequency of reorganization within the system, and the variability of policies and procedures of the system.

11. *Collaboration among providers.* Participants addressed the importance of support providers working together to support an individual with challenging behavior in a variety of ways. Collaboration was described as involving open communication among all support providers and agencies, coordination of intervention across settings, and support for the people implementing behavioral support plans. One issue in this category was the degree to which family members, educators, and other direct support providers are involved in the design and implementation of interventions. Establishment of a shared vision and goals (rather than conflicting agendas) was described as an important factor in behavioral support efforts. Immediacy and consistency of support (especially during times of risk taking and crisis) and the mutual celebration of successes were elements associated with this factor.

12. *Community acceptance.* Sociocultural values associated with disability and diversity were described by participants as broader ecological variables affecting access to appropriate behavioral supports and inclusion of people in society. Participants suggested that perceptions regarding the rights of individuals with disabilities and behavioral challenges to equal treatment can mediate the availability of resources and services. Community acceptance was demonstrated through public reactions to problem behavior (e.g., disgusted reactions to a child having a tantrum in the mall) and tolerance, rather than ridicule or exclusion, for behavioral differences. These attitudes were seen as being related to the interpretations of the causes of problem behavior and to social norms rather than as differences.

SIMILARITIES AND DIFFERENCES ACROSS GROUPS

All three of the stakeholder groups described issues and elements within each of the factor categories; however, their descriptions sometimes reflected distinctive views on the same issues. Informal comparisons indicated similarities and some differences among the perspectives. Overall, the greatest consistency appeared to be the discussion of the process and elements of positive behavioral support. Every participant mentioned the importance of assessment as the foundation for intervention and multicomponent, contextually relevant plans. In addition, most participants addressed the need to understand the preferences of the individual and his or her unique characteristics in designing effective plans. The only apparent differences across the groups were the amount of emphasis each group placed on the different factors related to the support providers (the most extensively discussed categories) and how community acceptance was defined by each group. Whereas the direct service providers and trainers/consultants talked more about the need for buy-in, parent/guardians were more descriptive about the characteristics of support providers that may contribute to their commitment or capacity and their relationships with the individual.

Descriptions of sociocultural factors also reflected certain idiosyncratic perspectives among the three groups (e.g., parents focused on community acceptance of people, direct service providers spoke more of public reactions to problem behavior, and trainers/consultants described sociopolitical issues affecting behavioral support). Interestingly, the variability in participants' responses seemed to be related more to their unique perspectives and values (e.g., regarding inclusion, collaborative processes) than to constituency group membership.

Discussion

This study employed semistructured interviews with informed participants to identify 12 categories of factors that may affect the outcomes of community-based behavioral support for individuals with severe disabilities. The factors identified encompassed issues related to various aspects of behavioral support situated at multiple levels, including individual support, procedural issues, the social and physical environment, and systemic concerns. Whereas some factor categories appeared to be relatively discrete (e.g., procedural elements of interventions), others focused on issues of greater complexity and breadth pertaining to the ecology of behavioral support (e.g., characteristics of change agents).

Prior to discussing implications of this study, we must acknowledge particular limitations. This study was a preliminary investigation of an extremely complex issue. As such, there are limitations associated with the methods employed and, therefore, the data obtained. Limitations relate to the participant sample and the subjectivity inherent in qualitative analysis procedures. The participants were selected based on nominations from the Rehabilitation Research and Training Center state training network, resulting in a somewhat homogeneous sample and a degree of overlap in roles among the three stakeholder groups. In addition, although mechanisms were used to enhance the accuracy of the information distilled from the interview transcripts, considerable interpretation was associated with the development of factor categories. The groupings of factors and the labels used to define categories were subjective and, therefore, it is quite possible that different labels could be adopted to describe the data.

Despite these limitations, the data provide some useful information and indicate future directions. Probably the most important contribution this study makes to existing knowledge is the enumeration of a broad range of factors that may have an impact on support efforts. The participants described numerous factors, in extensive detail, attesting to the complexity of supporting children with behavioral challenges in community settings (Albin et al.,

1996). Of particular emphasis was the role of support providers' commitment and capacity as they relate to the success or failure of intervention efforts. Only a few of these factors, such as the features of effective behavioral intervention (Blakeslee, Sugai, & Gruba, 1994; Carr et al., in press; Scotti et al., 1991) and treatment acceptability (Miltenberger et al., 1991; O'Brien & Karsh, 1990; Reimers, Wacker, & Koeppl, 1987), have been the focus of empirical research, and those that have been investigated have not been addressed in any great depth.

Another important finding is that, although factors were delineated as discriminable categories, participants typically described factors in relation to one another rather than as separate issues. This "interconnectedness" among factors was illustrated in the participants' discussions of the settings and support plans matching the needs and preferences of individuals and their support providers. The following quote from a trainer/consultant offers a case in point for this perceived interplay: "I look at the implementation of behavior change programs for an individual and the establishment of those plans in environments as the same process. They both involve a good assessment of the environment. They both involve full and systemic introduction. And they both involve the need for good reinforcement of effort."

A third interesting finding was the degree of consistency in the factors identified across participant groups. Although there were minor variations in how factor categories were described, members from each group described the full range of factors represented in the categories. This suggests general agreement regarding the scope and complexity of factors among families, trainers/consultants, and direct service providers.

Positive behavioral support has expanded in the past decade to focus on the development of assessment-based and comprehensive interventions that address the specific contexts and functions of behavior in typical home, school, and community environments (Horner & Carr, 1997; Horner et al., 1990). The complexity of this endeavor has required the expansion of perspectives on behavioral support to account for a broader array of variables. The recent focus on goodness of fit of behavioral support plans, the influence of setting events on behavior, and emphasis on durable lifestyle changes reflect a trend toward acknowledging a broader range of considerations. It has become increasingly apparent that the multitude of factors that can affect behavioral support in complex community settings cannot be captured adequately in a narrowly defined framework.

The results of the current study reiterate the value of designing contextually relevant, person-centered plans that are based on the resources available in natural settings and the preferences of support providers. The variety of factors related to the broader social and physical ecology identified within this study support the need for an expanded framework. In particular, the data reflect the need to view behavioral support from an ecological framework, to attend more specifically to the role of support providers in the process, and to continue to refine and elaborate on the concept of contextual fit (Albin et al., 1996).

ABOUT THE AUTHORS

Meme Hieneman, PhD, is an assistant professor in the Department of Child and Family Studies at the University of South Florida. She is the project director for a state-funded training and technical assistance program on positive behavioral support and co-training coordinator for the Rehabilitation Research and Training Center on Positive Behavioral Support. **Glen Dunlap,** *PhD, is director of the Division of Applied Research and Educational Support and a professor of child and family studies at the Louis de la Parte Florida Mental Health Institute. He also serves as principal investigator for the Rehabilitation Research and Training Center on Positive Behavioral Support. Address: Glen Dunlap, University of South Florida, Department of Child and Family Studies, Division of Applied Research and Educational Support (MHC 2-113a), 13301 Bruce B. Downs Blvd., Tampa, FL 33612; e-mail: eno@fmhi.usf.edu*

AUTHORS' NOTES

1. *This research was supported by Grant No. H133B980005, the NIDRR Rehabilitative Research and Training Center on Positive Behavioral Support, funded by the U.S. Department of Education, and by the Positive Behavioral Support Project, a special project funded by the Florida Department of Education. However, the opinions expressed are those of the authors and no official endorsement from any supporting agency should be inferred.*

2. *The authors are grateful to Rob Horner, Ann Cranston-Gingras, and Neal Berger for their input and guidance during the preparation of the first author's dissertation research, from which the content of this manuscript is drawn. The authors also extend appreciation to the participants for their willingness to share their knowledge and experience.*

NOTE

A list of sources identified through the literature review is available from the authors upon request.

REFERENCES

Albin, R. W., Lucyshyn, J. M., Horner, R. H., & Flannery, B. K. (1996). Contextual fit for behavioral support plans: A model for "goodness of fit." In L. Koegel, R. Koegel, & G. Dunlap, (Eds.), *Positive behavioral support: In-*

cluding people with difficult behavior in the community (pp. 81–98). Baltimore: Brookes.

Berg, W. K., & Sasso, G. M. (1993). Transferring implementation of functional assessment procedures from the clinic to natural settings. In J. Reichle & D. Wacker (Eds.), *Communicative alternatives for challenging behavior: Integrating functional assessment and intervention strategies* (pp. 343–362). Baltimore: Brookes.

Bernard, H. R., (1994). *Research methods in anthropology: Qualitative and quantitative approaches.* Thousand Oaks, CA: Sage

Blakeslee, T., Sugai, G., & Gruba, J. (1994). A review of functional assessment in data-based intervention studies. *Journal of Behavioral Education, 4,* 397–413.

Carr, E. G. (1997). Invited commentary: The evolution of behavior analysis into positive behavior support. *Journal of the Association for Persons with Severe Handicaps, 22,* 208–209.

Carr, E. G., Horner, R. H., & Turnbull, A. P. (in press). Positive behavior support for people with developmental disabilities: A research synthesis. *American Association on Mental Retardation Monograph.*

Carr, E. G., Horner, R. H., Turnbull, A. P., McLaughlin, D. M., McAtee, M. L., Smith, C. E., Ryan, K. A., Ruef, M. B., & Doolabh, A (1999). *Positive behavior support for people with developmental disabilities: A research synthesis.* Washington, DC: American Association on Mental Retardation.

Dunlap, G., Clarke, S., & Steiner, M. (1999). Intervention research in behavioral and developmental disabilities: 1980–1997. *Journal of Positive Behavior Interventions, 1,* 170–180.

Dunlap, G., Fox, L., Vaughn, B. J., Bucy, M., & Clarke, S. (1997). In quest of meaningful perspectives and outcomes: A response to five commentaries. *Journal of the Association for Persons with Severe Handicaps, 22,* 221–223.

Dunlap, G., Hieneman, M., Knoster, T., Fox, L., Anderson, J., & Albin, R. W. (2000). Essential elements of inservice training in positive behavior support. *Journal of Positive Behavior Interventions, 2,* 22–32.

Fowler, F. J. (1988). *Applied social reasearch: Vol. 1. Survey research methods.* Newbury Park, CA: Sage.

Gutkin, T. B. (1993). Demonstrating the efficacy of collaborative consultation services: Theoretical and practical perspectives. *Topics in Language Disorders, 14,* 81–90.

Hieneman, M., & Dunlap, G. (1999). Issues and challenges in implementing community-based behavioral support for two boys with severe behavioral difficulties. In J. R. Scotti & L. H. Meyer (Eds.), *Behavioral intervention: Principles, models, and practices* (pp. 363–384). Baltimore: Brookes.

Horner, R. H., & Carr, E. G. (1997). Behavioral support for students with severe disabilities: Functional assessment and comprehensive intervention. *The Journal of Special Education, 31,* 84–104.

Horner, R. H., Dunlap, G., Koegel, R. L., Carr, E. G., Sailor, W., Anderson, J. A., Albin, R. W., & O'Neill, R. E. (1990). Toward a technology of "non-aversive" behavioral support. *Journal of the Association for Persons with Severe Handicaps, 15,* 125–132.

Koegel, L. K., Koegel, R. L., & Dunlap, G. (1996). *Positive behavioral support: Including people with difficult behavior in the community.* Baltimore: Brookes.

Meyer, L. H., & Evans, I. M. (1993). Science and practice in behavioral intervention: Meaningful outcomes, research validity, and usable knowledge. *Journal of the Association for Persons with Severe Handicaps, 18,* 224–234.

Miltenberger, R. G., Suda, K. T., Lennox, D. B., & Lindeman, D. P. (1991). Assessing the acceptability of behavioral treatments to persons with mental retardation. *American Journal on Mental Retardation, 96,* 291–298.

O'Brien, S., & Karsh, K. G. (1990). Treatment acceptability: Consumer, therapist, and society. In A. Repp & N. Singh (Eds.), *Perspectives on the use of nonaversive and aversive interventions for persons with developmental disabilities* (pp. 503–516). Pacific Grove, CA: Brooks/Cole.

Reimers, T. M., Wacker, D. P., Derby, K. M., & Cooper, L. J. (1995). Relation between parents' attributions and the acceptability of behavioral treatments for their child's behavior problems. *Behavioral Disorders, 20,* 171–178.

Reimers, T., Wacker, D. P., & Koeppl, G. (1987). Acceptability of behavioral interventions: A review of the literature. *School Psychology Review, 16,* 212–227.

Schwartz, S., & Baer, D. M. (1991). Social validity assessments: Is current practice state of the art? *Journal of Applied Behavior Analysis, 24,* 189–204.

Scotti, J. R., Evans, I. M., Meyer, L. H., & Walker, P. (1991). A meta-analysis of intervention research with problem behavior: Treatment validity and standards of practice. *American Journal on Mental Retardation, 96,* 233–256.

Sugai, G., Horner, R. H., Dunlap, G., Hieneman, M., Lewis, T. J., Nelson, C. M., Scott, T. S., Liaupsin, C., Sailor, W., Turnbull, H. R., Wickham, D., Ruef, M., & Wilcox, B. (1999). *Applying positive behavior support and functional behavioral assessment in schools.* Washington, DC: Office of Special Education Programs, Center on Positive Behavioral Interventions and Support.

Tesch, R. (1990). *Qualitative research: Analysis types and software tools.* New York: Falmer.

Turnbull, A. P., & Turnbull, H. R. (1990). A tale about lifestyle changes: Comments on Toward a Technology of "Nonaversive" Behavioral Support. *Journal of the Association for Persons with Severe Handicaps, 15,* 142–144.

Wolcott, H. F. (1994). *Transforming qualitative data: Description, analysis, and interpretation.* Thousand Oaks, CA: Sage.

Action Editor: Robert L. Koegel

JASH
1997, Vol. 22, No. 1, 36–48

Positive Behavior Support as a Model for Promoting Educational Inclusion

Karen L. Weigle
West Virginia University

Positive behavior support (PBS) has been advanced as a model for effectively managing behavior in school settings and facilitating inclusive education. Numerous systems adaptations and administrative supports, however, are necessary for the successful application of PBS in the schools. This article identifies difficulties in the application of best practices within current school systems, and considers federal and state laws, school system organization, the roles of teachers and administrators, and other factors that are relevant for inclusive education. Issues pertinent to the application of PBS are discussed, and practical steps for achieving progress are recommended.

DESCRIPTORS: applied behavior analysis, behavioral excesses, best practices, challenging behavior, developmental disabilities, inclusion, positive behavior support, systems changes

Over the past few decades, inclusive environments have become more available to people with disabilities and behavioral challenges (e.g., Kubicek, 1994; Orelove, 1991; Slavin, 1990). The current school reform movement, which purports to provide inclusive education to all students (Sugai & Horner, 1994), actually has its roots in the passage of a series of laws beginning in the 1970s (i.e., Education of the Handicapped Act of 1975 [EHA], 1977; PL 98-199, 1985; PL 99-457, 1989; Americans with Disabilities Act [ADA], 1991; Individuals with Disabilities Education Act [IDEA], 1992). Further impetus was added to the current movement in the mid-1980s with the Regular Education Initiative (Will, 1986).

Concurrent with the passage of the aforementioned laws, societal and philosophical changes occurred. Normalization is a principle asserting that the attainment of socially valued outcomes by socially valued means be available for all persons, with special focus on people with disabilities (Wolfensberger, 1972). As normalization has become more of a reality through the ADA, community inclusion for people with challenging behaviors and disabilities has become more accepted and demanded.

In particular, over the past 2 decades, educational issues have changed focus from that of determining appropriate individual student placements in their least restrictive environment to implementing some level of inclusion for *all* students (Kubicek, 1994; Sailor, 1996). With the ensuing inclusion movement, numerous concerns have arisen: (a) How will teachers be able to teach students performing at such a variety of levels?, (b) What roles will special and regular educators play in inclusion?, (c) What effect will inclusion have on students with physical and intellectual disabilities and behavioral challenges?, (d) What effect will inclusion have on regular education students?, and (e) How will teachers be able to manage student behavior in integrated classrooms? This final question is one of great concern for teachers, parents, administrators, and psychologists. Controlling student behavior currently is considered by teachers to be both one of their greatest challenges and the greatest deficits in their training (Arick, Falco, & Brazeau, 1989; Coates, 1989; Horner, Diemer, & Brazeau, 1992; Kampwirth, 1988; Merrett & Wheldall, 1993; Munk & Repp, 1994).

Undoubtedly, inclusion will lead to increased behavioral and cognitive challenges in the classroom. In the past, teachers have been able to refer children with behavioral and cognitive challenges to special, segregated classrooms (Reichle et al., 1996). With inclusion, this no longer will be an option. Within the current school systems, teachers likely will have difficulty controlling student behavior while continuing to provide learning opportunities to students with various abilities (Ayres, Meyer, Erevelles, & Park-Lee, 1994; Fuchs & Fuchs, 1994; Slavin, 1990). In fact, many have suggested that entire school reform will be necessary to implement inclusion successfully (e.g., Horner et al., 1992; Loucks-Horsley & Roody, 1990; McDonnell, McDonnell, Hardman, & McCune, 1991; Miller, 1990; Sailor, 1996; Slavin, 1990).

The present paper focuses on a plan for the successful inclusion of students with severely challenging be-

Correspondence and requests for reprints may be addressed to Karen L. Weigle, Department of Psychology, P. O. Box 6040, West Virginia University, Morgantown, WV 26506-6040.

haviors and severe intellectual disabilities into regular education settings. First is a review of behavior management techniques currently used by regular and special educators and a discussion of the effectiveness of those techniques. Second, positive behavior support (PBS) is discussed as an alternative model for effectively managing behavior in school settings. Third, system adaptations and administrative supports required for the successful application of PBS are discussed.

Current Behavior Management in the Classroom

Teacher Reports of Behavior Management Techniques

Both regular and special education teachers consistently have reported that student behavior is the number one difficulty and biggest disruption in their classrooms (e.g., Coates, 1989; Kampwirth, 1988; Merrett & Wheldall, 1993; Munk & Repp, 1994). Numerous reports (Fueyo, 1991; Gleason & Hall, 1991; Merrett & Wheldall, 1993) have indicated that most teacher training programs (for both regular and special educators) provide little or no training on classroom control and discipline techniques. The discipline techniques teachers typically use are those learned from anecdotal stories shared among teachers (Kampwirth, 1988; Merrett & Wheldall, 1993).

Although special educators are typically thought to have more knowledge of behavioral principles and strategies than regular educators, the literature does not necessarily support this assumption. In a study by Weigle (1995), special educators reported using treatments for excess behavior in a blanket form for all students and all excess behaviors, rather than tailoring interventions individually according to the function of the excess behavior. When presented with functional analysis information (i.e., a description of the function of the behavior and antecedents and consequences maintaining the behavior) about a particular behavior in a scenario, the teachers were unable to identify which interventions would be effective and which would exacerbate the excess behavior (Weigle, 1995).

However, the self-report of special educators in a study by Ayres and colleagues (1994) indicated that other factors impeded the application of best practices, regardless of the level of knowledge and skills the teachers possessed. Lack of time for planning and development of interventions, high student-to-staff ratio, and a lack of administrative support for efforts to include students with severe disabilities were all identified as deterring the use of best practices.

In a national survey of regular and special educators, it was revealed that regular educators most frequently used parent-teacher conferences and reinforcement procedures to intervene with student excess behavior (Ringer, Doerr, Hollenshead, & Wills, 1993). The special educators were most likely to use aversive procedures, followed by parent-teacher conferences and reinforcement procedures (Ringer et al., 1993). Considering the results of these studies, it seems that two conclusions can be made: (a) both special and regular educators use reinforcement procedures at a fairly high rate (but for what behaviors, we do not know); and (b) neither group has the skills or supports to effectively assess excess behaviors and delineate interventions that match the function of the excess behaviors, which would likely increase the effectiveness of the intervention (Wacker et al., 1990).

In general, the literature indicates that teachers use isolated procedures for any array of excess behaviors (Kampwirth, 1988; Trovato, Harris, Pryor, & Wilkinson, 1992; Weigle, 1995). They typically do not use functional analyses and usually have no data-based means of determining intervention strategies (Snell, 1988). More often, teachers use a hierarchy of treatments determined anecdotally from their own and other teachers' experiences (Hall, Panyan, Rabon, & Broden, 1968; Kampwirth, 1988; Merrett & Wheldall, 1993). Considering this lack of demonstration of effective behavior management techniques by educators, it is necessary to evaluate the effects of typical behavior management strategies in classroom settings.

Effects of Current Behavior Management

The occurrence of excess behaviors in the classroom has many effects on students and teachers. First, student excess behaviors have the potential to distract both teachers from the lessons they are presenting and students from the task at hand (Leach & Dolan, 1985). Reports indicate that teachers spend only half the school day on academic instruction; much of the remaining time is spent "managing" behavior (Karweit, 1984). Thus, disruptive behavior in the classroom may lead to lower rates of student learning because of a decrease in information and tasks provided and more difficulty attending to those tasks.

Second, student behavior is affected by teachers' lack of knowledge of the most effective behavioral procedures to manage excess behaviors. Research has shown that most behavior management techniques used by teachers are rarely effective, particularly in managing behavior over time (Merrett & Wheldall, 1993). As described above, teachers often use interventions in a trial-and-error fashion and use interventions that are immediately effective but may increase excess behavior over time (also called "quick fix" interventions; Anderson, Albin, Mesaros, Dunlap, & Morelli-Robbins, 1993; Kampwirth, 1988). For example, a student may regularly scream when presented a reading task. The teacher responds by placing the student in time-out and notices that, over time, the behavior increases and the student falls further behind in reading. Although time-out is immediately effective for this situation (i.e., it stops the student's screaming and removes the distraction from the classroom), over time the behavior occurs more frequently and the child's skills do not improve. The child has learned that if he screams, he will be allowed to escape the reading task. For this particular child, time-out is not effective for decreasing screaming, rather it negatively reinforces screaming. If teachers use such "quick fix" interventions on a regular basis, excess behaviors could occur more frequently, increasing, rather than decreasing, disruption in classrooms.

Third, teachers themselves are affected by not using best practices. In the case described above, not only would the excess behaviors of the student increase with "quick fix" interventions, but the teacher would become less effective in his/her job. When students are removed from an activity because of their excess behaviors, they are not receiving education on the skills being targeted. Thus, teachers are not teaching all students the skills that are part of their curricula. This decrease in the quality of teaching, because of the increase in time and effort teachers spend on ineffective behavior management (i.e., no improvement in student behavior), contributes to "teacher burn-out" and job dissatisfaction (Lee, Dedrick, & Smith, 1991; Merrett & Wheldall, 1993).

Fourth, teachers' use of ineffective behavior management techniques will affect the future behavior of students. People can learn behavior through observation of others' behavior (e.g., Bandura, 1977; Masia & Chase, in press). Considering that teachers often model discipline techniques to children, teachers who use randomly determined, punitive, or otherwise ineffective interventions in response to challenging behaviors are teaching poor discipline techniques to their students. This may perpetuate poor behavior management in schools, as well as in homes, as students will become the teachers and parents of the future.

Finally, teachers' lack of effective modification of the excess behaviors of students will also greatly affect the success of inclusion. Currently, students typically are not placed in regular education classrooms until their behavior is considered "under control" or minimally disruptive—the "eliminative" approach (Anderson et al., 1993; Meyer & Evans, 1989). Students with challenging behaviors will be included in typical classrooms, perhaps for the first time, and regular education

teachers will be responsible for managing their excess behavior and ensuring that they learn (Arick et al., 1989). If teachers are unable to effectively control and modify the challenging behaviors of these students, inclusion will only exacerbate the current problems in classrooms. Thus, during this time of transition to a model of inclusion, a more widespread school reform seems essential. This reform must focus not only on changes in administrative policies and procedures, but on changes in the performance of all school personnel (e.g., Arick et al., 1989; Horner et al., 1992; Miller, 1990).

A PBS model provides one framework from which to begin to address some of these current barriers to successful inclusion. The application of the PBS model also increases the likelihood of positive "side effects" of inclusion, as discussed below.

An Alternative Model of Classroom Control: Positive Behavior Support as a School-Wide Approach

Basic Tenets of Positive Behavior Support

Positive behavior support[1] is an approach designed to address challenging behaviors of individuals within a broad, lifestyle context using the most current, empirically-validated technologies. It is not only a set of procedures and processes for decreasing challenging behaviors, but a set of values and information regarding what constitutes quality of life and the rights of persons with disabilities (Anderson et al., 1993; Horner et al., 1990). This values-based approach follows directly from the principle of normalization (Wolfensberger, 1972) and the standards of the ADA (PL 101-336, 1991). Table 1 depicts the basic tenets of PBS and provides a brief description of each.

PBS has a broad emphasis in approaching treatment for challenging behaviors and considers long-term goals and outcomes in developing behavior support plans. The focus of intervention is long-term lifestyle changes that will ultimately decrease excess behaviors. The interventions typically involve multiple components to address the wide array of behavioral and lifestyle issues targeted for change (e.g., Carr & Carlson, 1993; Kemp & Carr, 1995).

---

[1]The basic tenets of positive behavior support and their descriptions are taken from the *Training in Positive Behavior Support Trainer's Guide*, developed by staff at the West Virginia University Affiliated Center for Developmental Disabilities (unpublished manuscript, 1994), and are similar to those outlined by Anderson et al. (1993). The practices and principles are based on experimental research findings (for a brief review see Anderson et al., 1993).

Table 1
Overview of the Basic Tenets of PBS

Tenet	Description
Broad emphasis	Focuses on lifestyle concerns (e.g., happiness with amount of friends, social outings, independence), not just excess behavior
Long-term goals	Considers long-term goals and outcomes over the span of years rather than on short-term behavioral outcomes
Functional analysis	Determines function of behavior rather than determining a behavior program based on topography of behavior
Individuality and effectiveness	Interventions are based on individual needs and effectiveness rather than hierarchies of intervention strategies
Teach functional skills	Teaches useful, functionally equivalent skills to replace excess behaviors
Positive (reinforcing)	Utilizes reinforcement procedures whenever possible
Antecedents	Focuses on antecedent procedures to prevent the occurrence of excess behaviors (rather than consequence procedures to punish the behavior), including curricular adaptations
Multicomponent intervention	Interventions may include antecedent intervention procedures, consequence procedures, social skills training, etc.

PBS emphasizes the use of functional analyses of behavior. A functional analysis of behavior can be defined as determining the antecedent and consequence variables that maintain or change a particular behavior (Baer, Wolf, & Risley, 1968; Carr et al., 1994; Carr, Robinson, & Palumbo, 1990; Durand, 1987; Snell, 1988). After a thorough functional analysis is completed, interventions are determined based on the function of the excess behavior rather than the form. That is, a function-treatment matching approach (Eifert, Evans, & McKendrick, 1990; Wacker et al., 1990) is applied and functional replacement skills are taught utilizing an "educative approach" (Meyer & Evans, 1989). Using this approach inherently involves determining interventions individually, rather than determining interventions based on an established hierarchy (Scotti, Evans, Meyer, & Walker, 1991).

As discussed previously, many teachers focus on decreasing excess behaviors by presenting a negative consequence (e.g., Merrett & Wheldall, 1993; Ringer et al., 1993; Weigle, 1995). Whenever possible, however, PBS integrates antecedent manipulations as a part of interventions addressing challenging behaviors. This approach helps prevent excess behaviors from occurring and can decrease the need for future intervention planning (Munk & Repp, 1994).

The tenets of PBS are met through various team-based activities (see Baumgart & Ferguson, 1991, for a review of the efficacy of team approaches). Table 2 outlines the sequence of the processes involved in PBS (for more detailed descriptions of the steps in the proc-

ess, see Anderson et al., 1993; Kincaid, 1996). Teams are formed with the focus person and consist of all the relevant people in his or her life. The activities typically begin with the personal profiles activity in which the team meets and completes poster-sized forms regarding the focus person's lifestyle, strengths, health, and numerous other topics, as they apply. Based on the information gathered in the personal profiles, the team establishes a future plan that delineates the future goals for the focus person. Throughout the PBS process the team creates work plans, which determine who will be responsible for what activities to move the focus person toward the goals outlined in the future plan.

A functional analysis is completed by team members for each challenging behavior. This is followed by the development of a behavior support plan. The behavior support plan includes multiple components, as described previously and outlined in Table 2. All team members are responsible for the implementation of the behavior support plan across settings.

The team meets regularly to work on accomplishing the goals of the focus person. The process is continual and relies on data-based evaluation to guide progress and modification. As the goals are met, the future plan is reassessed and new goals are set. As is appropriate, the team makes modifications to the work plan, functional analysis, and behavior support plan. Obviously, team members may change over time, but the work already completed should be shared with new members and plans should be passed along so that the process continues uninterrupted.

Table 2
The Processes Involved in Applying the PBS Approach*

Processes and Sequence**

1. Describe the student and the contexts in which the student spends his or her time
   –Begin personal profiles and futures plan process
2. Identify and operationally define the behavior(s) or behavior class(es) of concern
   –Collect baseline data
3. Implement behavioral supports as needed while conducting assessments
   A. Lifestyle issues begin to be addressed
   B. Begin implementing general positive procedures
   C. Crisis prevention and emergency intervention procedures as necessary
4. Conduct assessments
   A. Quality of life, person-centered assessments, needs analysis
   B. Ecological environmental systems, interaction observation form, curriculum activity profile, service delivery assessments
   C. Functional assessment of target behavior(s)
   D. Communication repertoire assessment
   E. Learning characteristics assessment
5. Analyze results of assessments
   A. Generate hypotheses regarding function(s) of behavior(s)
   B. Construct a replacement behavior analysis
   C. Conduct functional analysis manipulations to test hypotheses if necessary
6. Articulate new and ongoing questions and strategies for continued assessment
7. Design hypotheses-driven comprehensive Behavior Support Plan
   A. Lifestyle enhancement specific to assessment and hypotheses
   B. Setting and immediate antecedent modifications
   C. Changes in curriculum and instruction strategies
   D. Functional equivalence training/instructional programs
   E. Communication, social skills instruction
   F. Positive procedures such as DRO and stimulus control
   G. Self-regulatory strategies
   H. Emergency management procedures
8. Outcomes of support plan implementation and evaluation criteria
   A. Improvements in quality of life
   B. Effectiveness of instruction
   C. Basic health and safety improved
   D. Target behavior(s) reduced or eliminated (and replaced)
9. Establish process and schedule for ongoing positive behavioral support
   A. Team of friends, coworkers, family members, and service providers
   B. Long-term goals/personal future plans
   C. Evaluation of effects of intervention and subsequent adjustments
   D. Evaluation of lifestyle, social networks, personal preferences, and process for facilitating changes over time
   E. Mechanism for cycling back through the functional assessment intervention process as new behavior, needs, and/or situations arise

Positive Behavior Support Applied to the School

Sugai and Horner (1994) have proposed a model for applying PBS for both students and teachers within schools. Sugai and Horner expanded the tenets of PBS to incorporate best teaching practices and inclusion in schools and suggested the following empirically vali- dated techniques be utilized in the behavioral support practices within schools: (a) applied behavior analysis; (b) direct instruction; (c) formative, outcome-based assessment and evaluation; (d) proactive prevention; (e) supportive behavioral programming; (f) school-wide

Table 3
Description of Operations of Effective Behavioral Support Systems*

System	Description of operations
School-wide support systems	
1.	Expectations are clearly defined
2.	Students and staff know the expectations/consequences
3.	Appropriate social behavior is TAUGHT
4.	Discipline procedures are implemented consistently
5.	Student positive behaviors are acknowledged
6.	Rapid response to dangerous situations
7.	Behavior is monitored and feedback given to staff
Specific setting systems	
1.	Appropriate behaviors are defined
2.	Consequences for inappropriate behaviors are defined
3.	Student positive behavior is acknowledged
4.	Teachers have a clear, simple system to report problem settings
5.	A behavior support team is in place to address problems
6.	Practical solutions are developed within 20 working days
7.	Behavior is monitored and feedback is given to staff
Individual student system	
1.	Two people available who can give suggestions
2.	Supervisors who can observe and offer suggestions
3.	Collaboration among teachers is encouraged
4.	A behavior support team exists for referrals
5.	The referral process is simple and efficient
6.	The behavior support team is competent
7.	Referrals result in assistance within 10 working days
8.	Staff time is allocated to behavioral support
9.	Action teams can be established
10.	All relevant staff, family, community support contacted by action team
11.	Behavior is monitored and feedback is given to staff

*Taken from Sugai and Horner, 1994

general/regular education environments; and (g) team-based staff development.

Sugai and Horner's (1994) model outlines a systems approach to changing behavior at the school-wide, classroom, and individual levels. Table 3 presents an overview of these systems and a description of their operations. Those individuals who should take responsibility in the system of behavioral support include most school personnel, as well as parents of students with challenging behaviors. The key players in PBS form teacher-based behavior support teams (BST; Sugai & Horner, 1994) that provide (a) ongoing assistance to individual teachers who have a student with severe behavioral challenges, (b) school-wide behavioral support, and (c) training and staff development in behavior support.

According to Sugai and Horner (1994), assistance from the BST is prompted by a request from a single teacher or from groups of school personnel who have difficulty modifying a particular behavior. The BST collaborates with the teacher(s) to apply PBS as described in the section above (Sugai & Horner, 1994). Teams are formed around the focus student and PBS activities are conducted on an individual, as needed basis. A member of the BST leads the team and provides training and technical assistance. The BST also continually evaluates outcomes, modifying interventions and training techniques as necessary (Sugai & Horner, 1994). Evaluation of outcomes may involve direct observation, ongoing data collection methods, or interviews regarding target behavior change. If target behaviors are not changing in the desired direction, the intervention may be fine tuned until desired changes are observed. If it is observed that the teachers implementing the plan are not doing so accurately or consistently, further training may be provided to teachers by the BST.

Having the BST train other teachers and school personnel is based on the trainer-of-trainer model, in which a core group of individuals receives intensive training on PBS and trains others in their school and community (e.g., Anderson et al., 1993; Anderson, Russo, Dunlap, & Albin, 1996; Langone, Koorland, & Oseroff, 1987). Training should include evaluation and feedback to individuals and groups regarding their performance of the skills learned. Evaluation measure could include: (a) direct observation of the application of skills, (b) measures of knowledge of PBS tenets and behavioral principles, and (c) measures of attitudes related to PBS philosophy. This evaluation and feedback process within the natural environment (e.g., classrooms, hallways, cafeterias) should improve the performance of teachers (Ford, 1984). Typically, the application of skills that are trained is not monitored (Colvin, Kameenui, & Sugai, 1993; Sloat, Tharp, & Gallimore, 1977; Sugai & Horner, 1994); however, research indicates that without monitoring and follow-up consultation, knowledge-based training does not typically result in application of learned skills to the natural environment (Anderson et al., 1993; Colvin et al., 1993; Demchak, 1987; Langone et al., 1987; Reichle et al., 1996; Sloat et al., 1977). Training activities should begin with educating all school personnel on the best practices of effective behavioral support. After staff have mastered those skills, other training topics may be addressed as needed. Such training and monitoring of application of skills should be organized, planned, and continuous as part of the school's routine functioning.

In a summary statement, Sugai and Horner (1994) indicated that effective behavioral support in the schools should:

1. Focus on all students, but especially those with severe behavior [and intellectual] challenges;
2. Attend to the needs of general and special educators;
3. Emphasize system level issues, problems and strategies;
4. Emphasize proactive, positive, and effective behavioral support systems and technologies;
5. Include follow-up activities for teacher skills maintenance and generalization;
6. Use a peer-based model of staff development; and
7. Rely on research validated academic and social behavior instruction and management strategies. (p. 114)

Thus, through the application of this model, PBS is provided to both students and teachers. Student social and academic behavior is supported through the implementation of skills training, reinforcement, curricular adaptations, and direct instruction techniques directed by school personnel. Teachers' effective teaching and implementation of behavior support is supported by the BST through training, consultation, and on-going monitoring and evaluation of teacher behavior with corrective and positive feedback.

Consideration of Adaptations and Administrative Supports Necessary for Positive Behavior Support in the School

When reading about the PBS model applied to schools, one might be pessimistic about this model working in the "real world." This pessimistic view holds some truth (Ayres et al., 1994; Fuchs & Fuchs, 1994; Miller, 1990; Sailor, 1996). As schools and our entire education system are managed currently, this model likely would not be effective. Perhaps this is why the term "school reform movement" (Sugai & Horner, 1994) was chosen to describe the changes that will need to take place in our education system to implement inclusion effectively. The entire system within which schools currently function must be adapted. Nevertheless, we must be aware that such changes do not occur quickly, if at all. Research indicates that experimental models of innovation are not readily accepted by typical schools, as important supports are often overlooked (Ayres et al., 1994; Miller, 1990). However, with the appropriate supports, complete systems changes may be more likely to occur (Arick et al., 1989; Ayres et al., 1994), but it may take years to achieve a complete system change, with teachers and administrators making successively closer approximations toward the end goal (Loucks-Horsley & Roody, 1990).

The change process itself is difficult for most teachers and administrators, as they are in a position in which they are asked to be independent and "professional," as well as to follow many constraining mandates set forth by government and local boards of education (Loucks-Horsley & Roody, 1990). Again, teachers and administrators will require many supports to successfully integrate a new system of operation. Such supports will need to be addressed at federal, state, and local governmental levels (Mansell, 1994). The basic missions of schools will need to be adapted to include a focus on the inclusion of all students in all activities possible and the teaching not only of academic skills, but also of social and other appropriate behaviors (Merrett & Wheldall, 1993; Sugai & Horner, 1994). Along with this change in school missions, utilization of the revenues allotted for particular student groups will need to be coordinated so that the needs of all students are met (Biklen, 1991; Sailor, 1991). Federal and state laws requiring some form of inclusion would provide the needed impetus for school system change. State laws and regulations regarding teacher certification, as well as state-wide reward systems for exemplary school performance toward meeting inclusion objectives could also provide motivation for change. The allocation of state funds could be contingent on school and teacher performance toward successfully implementing PBS practices; that is, schools performing the best could receive the most nonessential or "extra" funds. Within the schools, that money could be used to reward teachers demonstrating exemplary skills or could be used in ways that teachers and administrators determine as a group. Loucks-Horsley and Roody (1990) explained that although mandates often are necessary to initiate change in schools, supports at the school level are required to ensure successful change.

To modify the current organization of the school to that of PBS, the active support of school administrators, particularly school principals, will be necessary to keep staff and educators involved and motivated (Ayres et al., 1994; Bickel & Bickel, 1986; Colvin et al., 1993; Littrell, Billingsley, & Cross, 1994; Miller, 1990; Williams, Fox, Thousand, & Fox, 1990). As Kiracofe (1993) explained, administrative support is necessary to begin a system change process, as well as to maintain the change once it occurs. Kiracofe has outlined a number of steps for initiating system change that may be helpful in implementing the PBS approach in schools. The steps, applied to PBS, include: (a) establishing commitment from the administrators, teachers, and staff to follow the process; (b) building ownership of key stakeholders by enlisting those who are most enthusiastic to be the first to be actively involved in PBS; (c) having the key stakeholders begin the PBS activities; (d) having the key stakeholders reflect on and share their experiences with PBS in an ongoing manner; (e) providing follow-up training and consultation to the key stakeholders and the remaining personnel to begin the process; (f) analyzing outcomes of both targeted students and personnel in training, and analyzing the efficacy of current school-wide discipline programs; and (g) developing action plans to remediate areas of concern.

In addition to enlisting administrative support and motivating key stakeholders, the roles of both special and regular educators must be addressed. In an inclusive school, the roles of special and regular educators will likely change drastically, for educators will need to share their expertise with one another to adequately address the needs of all students in one classroom setting (Miller, 1990). This may be accomplished in any number of ways, including: (a) regular and special educators being paired and sharing classrooms (e.g., Fuchs & Fuchs, 1994); (b) special educators serving as consultants to regular educators (e.g., McDonnell et al., 1991); or (c) each teacher being responsible for teaching both regular and special education students, and consulting with other teachers (Stainback, Stainback, & Jackson, 1992). This will likely vary state-by-state, and perhaps even by county or school, and may best be an individual district decision based on the expertise and consultation skills of current staff.

At the university level, standards for degrees in education should also reflect the integration of regular and special education (Blackhurst, Cross, Nelson, & Tawney, 1973). Perhaps teachers in training will be taught the most effective, empirically validated teaching and behavior support techniques that work with all populations (Arick et al., 1989; Baumgart & Ferguson, 1991; Gleason & Hall, 1991), rather than receiving education specific to a particular population. A model teacher training curriculum that fits this perspective is that of the University of Kentucky (see Schuster, Collins, Nelson, Gast, & Wolery, 1991). Such a curriculum would best serve teachers in the coming millennium, allowing them to be effective with all populations and across situations (Blackhurst et al., 1973). State-level teacher certification guidelines must change to parallel changes in teacher education and specialization (Sailor, 1991).

Additionally, teachers' schedules must be modified to allow for team work, data collection, implementation of individual and classroom behavior plans, and intervention planning and evaluation. Lack of time and resources have been identified as leading causes of unsuccessful change processes within schools (Ayres et al., 1994; Miller, 1990; Williams et al., 1990). Therefore, the typical school day may be altered, with more shared teaching among teachers, professionals, and paraprofessionals (Sailor, 1996). For instance, if a classroom has students who require speech services, perhaps the speech therapist could work with the entire class on an activity that would incorporate the speech goals of the target children while presenting educational material applicable to all the children (Stainback et al., 1992). This would allow the classroom teacher more planning or meeting time, or the chance to observe his/her class and gather data.

To accommodate the changes in teaching, administrative supports will be needed so that teachers can handle the extra work load allocated by the PBS approach (Ayres et al., 1994; Staub & Peck, 1995). Administrators might be responsible for arranging teachers' schedules and obtaining coverage for all classrooms and common areas (e.g., lunchroom, playground, halls). If there are insufficient staff to cover such activities, administrators themselves may need to stand in for teachers on occasion (Littrell et al., 1994).

Further, administrators (including principals and other members of boards of education) will have the obstacle of maintaining the PBS system within budget restraints and other state-guided limitations. Thus, administrators' jobs will become more difficult until the PBS systems are in place and functioning semi-independently. However, this work likely will pay off in the long run, as placements outside of the public school system will decrease, teacher satisfaction and performance will increase, and student performance and behavior will improve (Mansell, 1994).

Teacher unions may play an important role in facilitating systems changes. In many states and school districts, teacher unions and boards of education are in opposition regarding the extent of union power over educational reform issues (Black, 1992). For example, teacher unions are becoming more involved in determining curricula, use of textbooks, and sizes of classes; administrators are threatened, believing that such power will ultimately reduce their responsibilities and governance (Black, 1992; Gaziel & Taub, 1992). Administrators will need to accept and facilitate teacher union input to ensure that teachers will become invested in the implementation of PBS. Without the support of teacher unions for PBS, teachers may: (a) be able to avert PBS activities, as unions may direct that teacher contracts exclude the changes necessary for PBS; or (b) be oppositional to the changes imposed. In recent years, the two national teacher unions have supported school reform and have aided in promoting change in at least a few states (Porter & Osthoff, 1993).

As stated previously, change occurs slowly in most cases. Although many believe that attitude change (i.e., self-report of change in thoughts) is necessary for behavior change, this has not been supported in the literature. Loucks-Horsley and Roody (1990) explained that often behavior change can lead to attitude change by virtue of experience with and observation of positive outcomes related to behavior. PBS assumes such a process of change: teach teachers skills for effective behavior support and help them to carry out the procedures, and teachers' use of the approach will be reinforced by the positive outcomes they observe with PBS applications.

Conclusion

According to Loucks-Horsley and Roody (1990), innovations must have several characteristics to succeed. First, innovations must be well defined (Loucks-Horsley & Roody, 1990). The PBS approach as applied to schools is defined in behavioral terms, rather than in idealistic terms. The behaviors and procedures involved in using this approach are clearly defined and easily transferred into action. The second quality of successful innovations is that they be shown effective in practice, without relying solely on anecdotal data (Loucks-Horsley & Roody, 1990). The components of

PBS, which are based on applied behavior analysis, are backed by applied research indicating their efficacy with numerous populations (e.g., Anderson et al., 1993; Bickel & Bickel, 1986; Dickie et al., 1991; Ford, 1984; Kemp & Carr, 1995; Meyer & Evans, 1989; White, 1988). The use of PBS in model schools is being investigated by Horner and his colleagues, and preliminary findings indicate positive outcomes (Positive Behavior Support Conference, 1995). The third characteristic defining successful innovations is that they be "classroom friendly" (Loucks-Horsley & Roody, 1990). PBS is designed in such a way that it is immediately useful and ready to apply in any situation. It is a base knowledge of a set of principles that can be applied to modify any behavior or environment. Once teachers and administrators have the tools PBS offers, they will be armed to successfully intervene with any situation that arises.

In considering how challenging behaviors are treated using PBS as opposed to traditional behavior management, there is a definite advantage with PBS. Whether the presenting behavior be a deficit or excess, using PBS it is considered a lack of a more appropriate skill in the child's repertoire or a lack of reinforcement for the use of the more appropriate skill. A complete functional analysis will reveal the maintaining factors of the excess behavior and a replacement skill that can serve the same function. This often precludes direct intervention with the challenging behavior, other than the use of extinction, or not allowing the student to obtain the desired consequence for engaging in that behavior. PBS also is appropriate for students without behavioral challenges, in that PBS strives to enhance one's lifestyle. That is, anyone exhibiting a behavioral deficit (which could include everyone) can be taught new skills using this approach.

Also, the contingencies for receiving reinforcement for teachers differ between schools implementing PBS and traditional school systems (Loucks-Horsley & Roody, 1990). By using effective behavior change techniques with their students, they are rewarded by a decrease in challenging behaviors and an increase in student abilities. In turn, they can experience self-reinforcement for being more effective in their jobs and finding their jobs less difficult (Lee et al., 1991). Teachers also are rewarded externally for their application of new skills and for increasing their efficacy in the classroom. By making pay and seniority raises and certification contingent on teacher performance, entire school systems will become more effective in teaching our children academic and social behaviors.

Once teachers are adequately trained in the best practices in behavior support and are performing at a mastery level, much of student aberrant behavior will decrease while social skills and other appropriate behaviors will increase. Teachers will have more time in class to actually teach academic subjects and will be more effective in teaching appropriate social and self-management skills, which are equally important in education and future success (Merrett & Wheldall, 1993; Sugai & Horner, 1994). Although teachers may initially have more work to do, they will be far more effective in their jobs and perhaps more satisfied. Also, less time and energy will be spent by administrators directly dealing with student referrals to the office, as effective interventions will take place in the classrooms and other school areas.

Although theoretically the application of PBS to schools is sound and the individual components of PBS have been shown effective through empirical means, the application of PBS at a systems level needs further research. Empirical evidence of the systems level effects of PBS would provide additional rationale for its widespread use. Although the supports necessary for the successful implementation of PBS have been outlined, empirical investigations of those supports are necessary. Among the questions that remain unanswered are: (a) What policies must change to support PBS and how can they best be changed?; (b) What best motivates teachers and administrators to change and remain committed to the change process?; (c) What types of teaching techniques will be best for heterogeneous groups of students, and for what subject matters?; (d) What are the criteria and measures of student learning and achievement?; and (e) What extent of inclusion is best for which students?

It is not being suggested, however, that the application of PBS as a model of inclusion be postponed until the data come in. On the contrary, it is being suggested that schools undertake the application of PBS and conduct program evaluation on a continual basis to expand the literature regarding the fundamental procedures for effecting successful systems changes. Such comprehensive research will require both quantitative and qualitative data to portray the full range of issues and outcomes involved in complete systems changes.

We do not need more publications demonstrating the abilities of disabled students to learn both social and academic skills, or the efficacy of teacher training in PBS components and similar procedures; rather, it is time to begin making systems changes and empirically investigating them to fill the gaps in the literature (Meyer, 1991). By implementing systems changes in natural settings and investigating the processes and outcomes on numerous levels, the problem many teachers and administrators have of applying lab-based findings to the "real world" will be avoided.

Overall, with the implementation of more effective behavior support techniques, schools will be better equipped to execute inclusion plans effectively. Evi-

dence suggests that students benefit both socially and academically from the experience of interacting with peers who are different from themselves (Evans, Salisbury, Palombaro, Berryman, & Hollowood, 1992; Fuchs & Fuchs, 1994; McDonnell et al., 1991; Meyer, 1991; Snell, 1988; Stainback et al., 1992; Staub & Peck, 1995). Teachers and other personnel may benefit from interacting with students with disabilities and behavioral challenges, and may become more accepting of differences (Snell, 1988). This is an admirable goal for all society to embrace. By successfully including and accepting persons with disabilities and behavioral challenges into schools entirely, the adults of the future will be learning to interact with and value such individuals (McDonnell et al., 1991). Hopefully, in this way we will be building a better future for all citizens.

References

Americans with Disabilities Act of 1990, Pub. L. No. 101-336, 104 Stat. 327 (1991).

Anderson, J. L., Albin, R. W., Mesaros, R. A., Dunlap, G., & Morelli-Robbins, M. (1993). Issues in providing training to achieve comprehensive behavioral support. In J. Reichle & D. P. Wacker (Eds.), *Communicative alternatives to challenging behavior: Integrating functional assessment and intervention strategies*, volume 3 (pp. 363–406). Baltimore: Paul H. Brookes.

Anderson, J. L., Russo, A., Dunlap, G., & Albin, R. W. (1996). A team training model for building the capacity to provide positive behavioral supports in inclusive settings. In L. K. Koegel, R. L. Koegel, & G. Dunlap (Eds.), *Positive behavior support: Including people with difficult behavior in the community* (pp. 467–189). Baltimore: Paul H. Brookes.

Arick, J., Falco, R., & Brazeau, K. (1989). Prioritizing in-service needs for educators of students with severe handicaps in heterogeneous integrated settings. *Education and Training in Mental Retardation, 24*, 371–380.

Ayres, B. J., Meyer, L. H., Erevelles, N., & Park-Lee, S. (1994). Easy for you to say: Teacher perspectives on implementing most promising practices. *Journal of the Association for Persons with Severe Handicaps, 19*, 84–93.

Baer, D. M., Wolf, M. M., & Risley, T. R. (1968). Some current dimensions of applied behavior analysis. *Journal of Applied Behavior Analysis, 1*, 91–97.

Bandura, A. (1977). *Social learning theory*. Englewood Cliffs, NJ: Prentice-Hall.

Baumgart, D., & Ferguson, D. L. (1991). Personnel preparation: Directions for the next decade. In L. H. Meyer, C. A. Peck, & L. Brown (Eds.), *Critical issues in the lives of people with severe disabilities* (pp. 313–352). Baltimore: Paul H. Brookes.

Bickel, W. E., & Bickel, D. D. (1986). Effective schools, classrooms, and instruction: Implications for special education. *Exceptional Children, 52*, 489–500.

Biklen, D. P. (1991). Social policy, social systems, and educational practices. In L. H. Meyer, C. A. Peck, & L.

Brown (Eds.), *Critical issues in the lives of people with severe disabilities*. Baltimore: Paul H. Brookes.

Black, S. (1992). Is curriculum on your bargaining table? *American School Board Journal, 179,* 30–32.

Blackhurst, A. E., Cross, D. P., Nelson, C. M., & Tawney, J. W. (1973). Approximating noncategorical teacher education. *Exceptional Children, 39,* 284–288.

Carr, E. G., & Carlson, J. I. (1993). Reduction of severe behavior problems in the community using a multicomponent treatment approach. *Journal of Applied Behavior Analysis, 26,* 157–172.

Carr, E. G., Levin, L., McConnachie, G., Carlson, J. I., Kemp, D. C., & Smith, C. E. (1994). *Communication-based intervention for problem behavior: A user's guide for producing positive change.* Baltimore: Paul H. Brookes.

Carr, E. G., Robinson, S., & Palumbo, L. W. (1990). The wrong issue: Aversive versus nonaversive treatment. The right issue: Functional versus nonfunctional treatment. In A. C. Repp & N. N. Singh (Eds.), *Perspectives on the use of nonaversive and aversive interventions for persons with developmental disabilities* (pp. 361–379). Sycamore, IL: Sycamore Press.

Coates, R. D. (1989). The regular education initiative and opinions of regular classroom teachers. *Journal of Learning Disabilities, 22,* 532–536.

Colvin, G., Kameenui, E. J., & Sugai, G. (1993). Reconceptualizing behavior management and school-wide discipline in general education. *Education and Treatment of Children, 16,* 361–381.

Demchak, M. (1987). A review of behavioral staff training in special education settings. *Education and Training in Mental Retardation, 22,* 205–217.

Dickie, R. F., Bauman, R. A., Belch, P. J., Lancaster, P. L., Lazor, R., Mule, B., & Seman, M. (1991). Special education teacher training: A noncategorical approach. *Education and Treatment of Children, 14,* 299–315.

Durand, V. M. (1987). "Look Homeward Angel" A call to return to our (functional) roots. *The Behavior Analyst, 10,* 299–302.

Education of the Handicapped Act of 1975, Pub. L. No. 94-142, 89 Stat. 773 (1977).

Education of the Handicapped Act Revisions of 1983, Pub. L. No. 98-199, 97 Stat. 1357 (1985).

Education of the Handicapped Act Amendment of 1986, Pub. L. No. 99-457, 100 Stat. 1145 (1989).

Eifert, G. H., Evans, I. M., & McKendrick, V. G. (1990). Matching treatments to client problems no diagnostic labels: A case for paradigmatic behavior therapy. *Journal of Behaviour Therapy and Experimental Psychiatry, 21,* 163–172.

Evans, I. M., Salisbury, C. L., Palombaro, M. M., Berryman, J., & Hollowood, T. M. (1992). Peer interactions and social acceptance of elementary-age children with severe disabilities in an inclusive school. *Journal of the Association for Persons with Severe Handicaps, 17,* 205–212.

Ford, J. E. (1984). A comparison the three feedback procedures for improving teaching skills. *Journal of Organizational Behavior Management, 6,* 65–77.

Fuchs, D., & Fuchs, L. S. (1994). Inclusive schools movement and the radicalization of special education reform. *Exceptional Children, 60,* 294–309.

Fueyo, V. (1991). Implementing a field-based elementary teacher training program. *Education and Treatment of Children, 14,* 280–298.

Gaziel, H. H., & Taub, D. (1992). Teachers unions and educational reform—A comparative perspective: The cases of France and Israel. *Educational Policy, 6,* 72–86.

Gleason, M. M., & Hall, T. E. (1991). Focusing on instructional design to implement a performance-based teacher training program: The University of Oregon Model. *Education and Treatment of Children, 14,* 316–332.

Hall, R. V., Panyan, M., Rabon, D., & Broden M. (1968). Instructing beginning teachers in reinforcement procedures which improve classroom control. *Journal of Applied Behavior Analysis, 1,* 315–322.

Horner, R. H., Diemer, S. M., & Brazeau, K. C. (1992). Educational support for students with severe problem behaviors in Oregon: A descriptive analysis from the 1987-1988 school year. *Journal of The Association for Persons with Severe Handicaps, 17,* 154–169.

Horner, R. H., Dunlap, G., Koegel, R. L., Carr, E. G., Sailor, W., Anderson, J., Albin, R. W., & O'Neill, R. E. (1990). Toward a technology of "nonaversive" behavioral support. *Journal of The Association for Persons with Severe Handicaps, 15,* 125–132.

Individuals with Disabilities Education Act of 1991, Pub. L. No. 102-119, 105 Stat. 587 (1992).

Kampwirth, T. J. (1988). Behavior management in the classroom: A self-assessment guide for teachers. *Education and Treatment of Children, 11,* 286–293.

Karweit, N. (1984). Time-on-task reconsidered: Synthesis of research on time and learning. *Educational Leadership, 41,* 32–35.

Kemp, D. C., & Carr, E. G. (1995). Reduction of severe problem behavior in community employment using an hypothesis-driven multicomponent intervention approach. *Journal of The Association for Persons with Severe Handicaps, 20,* 229–247.

Kincaid, D. (1996). Person-centered planning. In L. K. Koegel, R. L. Koegel, & G. Dunlap (Eds.), *Positive behavior support: Including people with difficult behavior in the community* (pp. 439–465). Baltimore: Paul H. Brookes.

Kiracofe, J. (1993). Strategies to help agencies shift from services to supports. In V. J. Bradley, J. W. Ashbaugh, & B. C. Blaney (Eds.), *Creating individual supports for people with developmental disabilities: A mandate for change at many levels* (pp. 281–298). Baltimore: Paul H. Brookes.

Kubicek, F. C. (1994). Special education reform in light of select state and federal court decisions. *Journal of Special Education, 28,* 27–42.

Langone, J., Koorland, M., & Oseroff, A. (1987). Producing changes in the instructional behavior of teachers of the mentally handicapped through inservice education. *Education and Treatment of Children, 10,* 146–164.

Leach, D. J., & Dolan, N. K. (1985). Helping teachers increase student academic engagement rate: The evaluation of a minimal feedback procedure. *Behavior Modification, 9,* 55–71.

Lee, V. E., Dedrick, R. F., & Smith, J. B. (1991). The effect of the social organization of schools on teachers' efficacy and satisfaction. *Sociology of Education, 64,* 190–208.

Littrell, P. C., Billingsley, B. S., & Cross, L. H. (1994). The effects of principal support on special and general educators' stress, job satisfaction, school commitment, health, and intent to stay in teaching. *Remedial and Special Education, 15,* 297–310.

Loucks-Horsley, S., & Roody, D. S. (1990). Using what is known about change to inform the Regular Education Initiative. *Remedial and Special Education, 11,* 51–56.

Mansell, J. (1994). Policy and policy implications. In E. Emerson, P. McGill, & J. Mansell (Eds.), *Severe learning disabilities and challenging behaviours: Designing high quality services* (pp. 297–313). London: Chapman and Hall.

Masia, C. L., & Chase, P. N. (in press). Vicarious learning revisited: A contemporary behavior analytic interpretation. *Journal of Behaviour Therapy and Experimental Psychiatry, 27.*

McDonnell, A., McDonnell, J., Hardman, M., & McCune, G. (1991). Educating students with severe disabilities in their neighborhood school: The Utah elementary integration model. *Remedial and Special Education, 12,* 34–45.

Merrett, F., & Wheldall, K. (1993). How do teachers learn to manage classroom behaviour? A study of teachers' opinions about their initial training with special reference to classroom behaviour management. *Educational Studies, 19,* 91–105.

Meyer, L. H. (1991). Advocacy, research, and typical practices: A call for the reduction of discrepancies between what is and what ought to be, and how to get there. In L. H. Meyer, C. A. Peck, & L. Brown (Eds.), *Critical issues in the lives of people with severe disabilities* (pp. 629–649). Baltimore: Paul H. Brookes.

Meyer, L. H., & Evans, I. M. (1989). *Nonaversive intervention for behavior problems.* Baltimore: Paul H. Brookes.

Miller, L. (1990). The regular education initiative and school reform: Lessons from the mainstream. *Remedial and Special Education, 11,* 17–22.

Munk, D. D., & Repp, A. C. (1994). The relationship between instructional variables and problem behavior: A review. *Exceptional Children, 60,* 390–401.

Orelove, F. P. (1991). Educating all students: The future is now. In L. H. Meyer, C. A. Peck, & L. Brown (Eds.), *Critical issues in the lives of people with severe disabilities* (pp. 67–87). Baltimore: Paul H. Brookes.

Porter, A., & Osthoff, E. (1993). *External strategies for stimulating and supporting school restructuring.* Madison, WI: Center on Organization and Restructuring of Schools. (ERIC Document Reproduction Service No. ED 363 959)

Reichle, J., McEvoy, M., Davis, C., Rogers, E., Feeley, K., Johnston, S., & Wolff, K. (1996). Coordinating preservice and in-service training of early interventionists to serve preschoolers who engage in challenging behavior.

In L. K. Koegel, R. L. Koegel, & G. Dunlap (Eds.), *Positive behavior support: Including people with difficult behavior in the community* (pp. 227–264). Baltimore: Paul H. Brookes.

Ringer, M. M., Doerr, P. F., Hollenshead, J. H., & Wills, G. D. (1993). Behavior problems in the classroom: A national survey of interventions used by classroom teachers. *Psychology in the Schools, 30,* 168–175.

Sailor, W. (1991). Community school: An essay. In L. H. Meyer, C. A. Peck, & L. Brown (Eds.), *Critical issues in the lives of people with severe disabilities* (pp. 379–385). Baltimore: Paul H. Brookes.

Sailor, W. (1996). New structures and systems change for comprehensive positive behavioral support. In L. K. Koegel, R. W. Koegel, & G. Dunlap (Eds.), *Positive behavior support: Including people with difficult behavior in the community* (pp. 163–206). Baltimore: Paul H. Brookes.

Schuster, J. W., Collins, B., Nelson, C. M., Gast, D. L., & Wolery, M. (1991). The University of Kentucky program in developmental and behavioral disorders. *Education and Treatment of Children, 14,* 333–348.

Scotti, J. R., Evans, I. M., Meyer, L. H., & Walker, P. (1991). A meta-analysis of intervention research with problem behavior: Treatment validity and standards of practice. *American Journal on Mental Retardation, 96,* 233–256.

Slavin, R. E. (1990). General education under the regular education initiative: How must it change? *Remedial and Special Education, 11,* 40–50.

Sloat, K. C. M., Tharp, R. G., & Gallimore, R. (1977). The incremental effectiveness of classroom-based teacher-training techniques. *Behavior Therapy, 8,* 810–818.

Snell, M. E. (1988). Curriculum and methodology for individuals with severe disabilities. *Education and Training in Mental Retardation,* 302–314.

Stainback, S., Stainback, W., & Jackson, H. J. (1992). Toward inclusive classrooms. In S. Stainback & W. Stainback (Eds.) *Curriculum considerations in inclusive classrooms: Facilitating learning for all students* (pp. 3–17). Baltimore: Paul H. Brookes.

Staub, D., & Peck, C. A. (1995). What are the outcomes for nondisabled students? *Educational Leadership, 52,* 36–40.

Sugai, G., & Horner, R. (1994). Including students with severe behavior problems in general education settings: Assumptions, challenges, and solutions. In J. Marr, G. Sugai, & G. Tindal (Eds.), *The Oregon Conference Monograph, volume 6* (pp. 109–120). Eugene, OR: University of Oregon.

Trovato, J., Harris, J., Pryor, C. W., & Wilkinson, S. C. (1992). Teachers in regular classrooms: An applied setting for successful behavior programming. *Psychology in the Schools, 29,* 52–61.

Wacker, D., Steege, M., Northup, J., Reimers, T., Berg, W., & Sasso, G. (1990). Use of functional analysis and acceptability to assess and treat severe behavior problems: An outpatient clinic model. In A. C. Repp & N. N. Singh (Eds.) *Perspectives on the use of nonaversive and aversive interventions for persons with developmental disabilities* (pp. 349–360). Sycamore, IL: Sycamore Publishing Company.

Weigle, K. (1995). *The effects of functional analysis information on ratings of treatment acceptability and effectiveness.* Unpublished master's thesis, West Virginia University, Morgantown.

West Virginia University Affiliated Center for Developmental Disabilities. (1994). *Training in positive behavior support trainer's guide.* Unpublished manuscript

White, W. A. T. (1988). A meta-analysis of the effects of direct instruction in special education. *Education and Treatment of Children, 11,* 364–374.

Will, M. C. (1986). *Educating children with learning problems. A shared responsibility. A report to the secretary.* Washington, DC: U.S. Department of Education.

Williams, W., Fox, T. J., Thousand, J., & Fox, W. (1990). Level of acceptance and implementation of best practices in the education of students with severe handicaps in Vermont. *Education and Training in Mental Retardation, 25,* 120–131.

Wolfensberger, W. (1972). *The principle of normalization in human services.* Toronto: National Institute on Mental Retardation.

Article received: May 8, 1996
Final acceptance: December 14, 1996
Editor in charge: Glen Dunlap

PART VI
Extended Applications:

Focus on Systems Change

This section extends the basic precepts of individualized positive behavior supports (PBS) to broad systems change and to youth with or at risk for developing disabilities. A central idea of the articles in the section is that individualized behavior support cannot be optimally effective without supportive school, home, and community systems. Furthermore, the authors of these articles have acknowledged the fact that problem behavior is environmentally determined and the first line of defense against the development of problem behavior thus is *prevention*—creating responsive and proactive contexts where fewer individuals will require the individualized supports described in this book. Imagine the possibilities. The articles in this section capture some of the exciting developments in wide-scale, system-oriented prevention.

In the first article, Sugai and his co-authors (2000) offered a model of school-wide PBS and made the case for it. The authors stressed that school-wide efforts are needed to enhance a positive school culture, reduce the number of students exposed to disciplinary action (e.g., suspension and expulsion), and create a framework that will sustain individualized supports when needed. Building on this model, Scott (2001) illustrated the process and positive outcomes of school-wide supports through a case example in an inner-city elementary school.

As school-wide supports are tested in urban settings where issues of poverty, violence, crime, and drugs are familiar, lessons about the daily challenges faced by children, teachers, and their families are learned. Reflecting on their personal experiences with implementing school-wide supports in urban school settings, Warren and colleagues (2003) offered recommendations for addressing family and community systems that may help set the stage for the successful implementation of school-wide supports. Utley, Kozleski, Smith, and Draper (2002) added another piece to the school prevention puzzle by arguing that success for all students also requires an understanding of culturally influenced social behaviors to avoid the misattribution of "problem behavior" and to build multicultural elements into PBS. Finally, continuing the theme of urban settings, but focusing on preschool-age children, Fox, Dunlap, and Powell (2002) discussed prevention of problem behavior through the design of family-centered behavior supports.

Taken together, the articles in this section create a sense of excitement about how far we have come in understanding and preventing problem behaviors and how far we can go to address the complex systems that can contribute to effective, proactive solutions. From individualized supports for people with severe disabilities to systems-wide supports that affect much larger populations, the articles in this section signal our emergence into a new age for PBS.

—Linda M. Bambara

Applying Positive Behavior Support and Functional Behavioral Assessment in Schools

OSEP Center on Positive Behavioral Interventions and Supports:

George Sugai and Robert H. Horner
University of Oregon

Glen Dunlap and Meme Hieneman
University of South Florida

Timothy J. Lewis
University of Missouri

C. Michael Nelson, Terrance Scott, and Carl Liaupsin
University of Kentucky

Wayne Sailor, Ann P. Turnbull, H. Rutherford Turnbull III, Donna Wickham, and Brennan Wilcox
University of Kansas

Michael Ruef
Cal Poly University

Abstract: Positive behavior support (PBS) and functional behavioral assessment (FBA) are two significant concepts of the 1997 amendments to the Individuals with Disabilities Education Act. These two concepts are not new, but they are important for improving the quality of efforts to educate children and youth with disabilities. The purposes of this article are to describe (a) the context in which PBS and FBA are needed and (b) definitions and features of PBS and FBA. An important message is that positive behavioral interventions and supports involve the whole school, and successful implementation emphasizes the identification, adoption, and sustained use of effective policies, systems, data-based decision making, and practices. Systems-level challenges are also discussed.

On June 4, 1997, amendments to the Individuals with Disabilities Education Act (IDEA) became law (P.L. 105-17). These amendments introduced several new concepts, two of which are particularly important to the education of children whose behaviors violate school codes of conduct or are outside personal or interpersonal norms of accept-

able social behavior: (a) positive behavior support (PBS) and (b) functional behavioral assessment (FBA). Section 614 (d)(3)(B)(i) of P.L. 105-17 states that "in the case of a child whose behavior impedes his or her learning or that of others, the child's IEP [Individualized Education Program] team must consider, when appropriate, strategies, including positive behavioral intervention strategies and supports, to address that behavior." Section 615 (k)(1)(B)(i) of the law states, "If the local educational agency did not conduct a functional behavioral assessment and implement a behavioral intervention plan for such child before the behavior that resulted in the suspension described in subparagraph (A), the agency shall convene an IEP meeting to develop an assessment plan to address that behavior." In addition, "If the child already has a behavioral intervention plan, the IEP Team shall review the plan and modify it, as necessary, to address the behavior" (Section 615(k) (1)(B)(ii)).

PBS and FBA are not new. However, in the context of IDEA, they represent an important effort to improve the quality of behavioral interventions and behavior support planning. As schools organize to meet these requirements and to build their capacity to meet the behavioral needs of all students, especially students with disabilities, attention must be given to the definitions, features, and uses of PBS and FBA. The purpose of this article is to describe what is meant by *positive behavior support* and *functional behavioral assessment*.

Context

Schools are important environments in which children, families, educators, and community members have opportunities to learn, teach, and grow. For nearly 180 days each year and 6 hours each day, educators strive to provide students with learning environments that are stable, positive, and predictable. These environments have the potential to provide positive adult and peer role models, multiple and regular opportunities to experience academic and social success, and social exchanges that foster enduring peer and adult relationships.

Despite these positive attributes, teachers, students, families, and community members face significant contemporary challenges (see Figure 1). Every year schools are being asked to do more with fewer resources. New initiatives to improve literacy, enhance character, accommodate rapidly advancing technologies, and facilitate school-to-work transitions are added to the educator's workday. Schools are being asked to achieve new and more results, yet seldom are allowed to cease work on the growing list of initiatives.

Educators also are being asked to educate an increasingly heterogeneous population of students. A growing number of students in our schools have English as a second language; limited family supports; significant learning and/or behavioral problems; families who face financial barriers; and a great need for mental health, social welfare, medical, and vocational assistance (Knitzer, 1993; Knitzer, Steinberg, & Fleisch, 1990; Stevens & Price, 1992). Although most attention has focused on students with externalizing problem behavior (e.g., aggressive, antisocial, or destructive conduct), students with internalizing problem behavior (e.g., social withdrawal, depression) also represent an important concern of families, schools, and communities (Kauffman, 1997).

In addition, the challenges associated with educating students with severe problem behavior are increasing (Biglan, 1995; Kauffman, 1997; Sprague, Sugai, & Walker, 1998;

Sugai & Horner, 1994; Walker, Colvin, & Ramsey, 1995). Although these students represent only 1% to 5% of a school enrollment, they can often account for more than 50% of the behavioral incidents handled by office personnel and consume significant amounts of educator and administrator time (Sugai, Sprague, Horner, & Walker, 2000; Taylor-Greene et al., 1997). Many of these students require comprehensive behavioral supports that involve family, school, and community participation (Eber, 1996; Eber & Nelson, 1997; Epstein et al., 1993; Walker et al., 1995; Walker et al., 1996).

Many schools lack the capacity to identify, adopt, and sustain policies, practices, and systems that effectively and efficiently meet the needs of all students (Mayer, 1995;

- A suburban high school with 1,400 students reported more than 2,000 office referrals from September to February of one school year.

- An urban middle school with 600 students reported more than 2,000 discipline referrals to the office from September to May.

- A rural middle school with 530 students reported more than 2,600 office referrals. A total of 304 students had at least one referral, 136 students had at least 5 referrals, 34 students had more than 20 referrals, and 1 student had 87 office referrals (Taylor-Greene et al., 1997).

- In one state, expulsions increased from 426 to 2,088, and suspensions increased from 53,374 to 66,914 over a 4-year period (Juvenile Justice Fact Sheet).

- In another state, expulsions increased from 855 to 1,180 between the 1994–1995 and 1995–1996 school year (a 200% increase from 1991–1992 school year; Juvenile Justice Fact Sheet).

- Being suspended or expelled from school is reported by students as one of the top three school-related reasons for leaving school (National Association of Child Advocates, 1998).

- In one state, 11% of students who had been suspended or expelled also were found in the state's Department of Juvenile Justice Database; 5% of suspended students were arrested while on suspension; and 19% were arrested while on expulsion (National Association of Child Advocates, 1998).

- Thirty-six percent of general public school parents fear for the physical safety of their oldest child at school, and 31% fear for the physical safety of their oldest child while playing in their neighborhood (Rose & Gallup, 1998).

- The general public rated fighting/violence/gangs, lack of discipline, lack of funding, and use of drugs as the top four biggest problems facing local schools. These same four have been in the top four for over 15 years (Gallup, Elam, & Rose, 1998).

Figure 1. Examples of contemporary challenges for schools, families, and communities.

Sugai & Horner, 1994, 1999; Taylor-Greene et al., 1997; Walker et al., 1996). Schools often rely on outside behavioral expertise because local personnel lack specialized skills to educate students with significant problem behaviors. School morale is often low because ongoing staff support is limited. Although many students have significant social skills needs, social skills instruction is not a conspicuous and systemic component of the schoolwide curriculum. Behavioral interventions are not based on information obtained from assessments. In general, systems for the identification, adoption, and sustained use of research-validated practices are lacking.

In sum, the challenges facing educators are significant and persistent. If not addressed, their impact on students, school personnel, families, and community members can be dramatic. However, the problem is not that schools lack procedures and practices to address these challenges. Procedures and practices have been defined and have been growing over the past 30 years (Mayer, 1995; Peacock Hill Working Group, 1992; Sugai, 1998; Walker et al., 1995; Walker et al., 1998). The greater problem has been that we have been unable to create and sustain the "contextual fit" between our procedures and practices and the features of the environments (e.g., classroom, workplace, home, neighborhood, playground) in which the student displays problem behavior (Albin, Lucyshyn, Horner, & Flannery, 1996). The systemic solution is to create effective "host environments" that support the use of preferred and effective practices (Sugai & Horner, 1994, 1999; Zins & Ponti, 1990). Effective host environments have policies (e.g., proactive discipline handbooks, procedural handbooks), structures (e.g., behavioral support teams), and routines (e.g., opportunities for students to learn expected behavior, staff development, data-based decision making) that promote the identification, adoption, implementation, and monitoring of research-validated practices.

As a society, we are looking to schools to be or become settings where our children learn the skills for successful adulthood (e.g., IDEA, Goals 2000, Improving America's Schools Act) in the context of an increasingly heterogeneous general student body, some of whom exhibit intense patterns of chronic problem behavior. The growing expectation is that schools will deliver socially acceptable, effective, and efficient interventions to ensure safe, productive environments where norm-violating behavior is minimized and prosocial behavior is promoted. PBS and FBA represent important efforts toward achieving these goals.

Increasingly, efforts to establish school-linked service arrangements for children and families are appearing around the country (Sailor, 1996). These models have been tested and described in numerous schools (Adelman & Taylor, 1997; Dryfoos, 1997; Kagan, Goffin, Golub, & Pritchard, 1995; Schorr, 1997). In Kentucky, for example, efforts have been made to establish school-linked services in the context of statewide school reform (Illback, Nelson,

& Sanders, 1998). More recently, these school, family, and community partnerships have been described under the "community schools" rubric (Benson & Harkavy, 1997; Lawson & Briar-Lawson, 1997).

These comprehensive systems-change initiatives are designed (a) to create a seamless web of supports and services that "wrap around" children and families and (b) to bring an end to the current fragmentation and categorical separation of school agency–directed programs. These systems-change efforts create opportunities to integrate PBS methods into the culture of the school and to extend effective and coordinated participation in the behavior support plan to family members and community agency personnel (Sailor, 1996, in press).

What Is PBS?

Optimizing the capacity of schools to address schoolwide, classroom, and individual problem behavior is possible in the face of current challenges but only if working policies, structures, and routines emphasize the identification, adoption, and sustained use of research-validated practices. In recent years, PBS has been emerging as an approach to enable schools to define and operationalize these structures and procedures. New journals (e.g., this journal), technical assistance centers (e.g., Beach Center, Center on Positive Behavioral Interventions and Supports), and personnel preparation programs have established PBS as the focus of their purpose and activities.

DEFINITION

Positive behavior support is a general term that refers to the application of positive behavioral interventions and systems to achieve socially important behavior change. PBS was developed initially as an alternative to aversive interventions used with students with significant disabilities who engaged in extreme forms of self-injury and aggression (Durand & Carr, 1985; Meyer & Evans, 1989). More recently, the technology has been applied successfully with a wide range of students, in a wide range of contexts (Carr et al., 1999; Horner, Albin, Sprague, & Todd, 1999), and extended from an intervention approach for individual students to an intervention approach for entire schools (Colvin, Kame'enui, & Sugai, 1993; Colvin, Sugai, Good, & Lee, 1997; Lewis, Colvin, & Sugai, in press; Lewis, Sugai, & Colvin, 1998; Taylor-Greene et al., 1997; Todd, Horner, Sugai, & Sprague, 1999).

PBS is not a new intervention package or a new theory of behavior, but an application of a behaviorally based systems approach to enhance the capacity of schools, families, and communities to design effective environments that improve the fit or link between research-validated practices and the environments in which teaching and learning occur. Attention is focused on creating and sustaining school environments that improve lifestyle results (personal, health, social, family, work, recreation, etc.) for all children and youth by making problem behavior less effective, efficient, and relevant and making desired behavior more functional.

The use of culturally appropriate interventions also is emphasized in the PBS approach. *Culturally appropriate* describes interventions that consider the unique and individualized learning histories (social, community, historical, familial, racial, gender, etc.) of all individuals (children with problem behaviors, families, teachers, community agents, etc.) who participate in the PBS process and approach. Data-based problem solving and individualized planning processes can help to establish culturally appropriate interventions; however, individual learning histories ultimately can affect how data are summarized, analyzed, and used.

Haring and De Vault (1996) have indicated that PBS is composed of (a) "interventions that consider the contexts within which the behavior occurs," (b) "interventions that address the functionality of the problem behavior," (c) "interventions that can be justified by the outcomes," and (d) "outcomes that are acceptable to the individual, the family, and the supportive community" (p. 116).

FEATURES

At the core, PBS is the integration of (a) behavioral science, (b) practical interventions, (c) social values, and (d) a systems perspective (see Table 1).

Behavioral Science

An existing science of human behavior links the behavioral, cognitive, biophysical, developmental, and physical/environmental factors that influence how a person behaves (Baer, Wolf, & Risley, 1968; Bijou & Baer, 1978; Schwartz, 1989; Wolery, Bailey, & Sugai, 1988). Of particular interest are factors that affect the development and durability of disruptive and dangerous behaviors (Biglan, 1995; Kauffman, 1997; Mayer, 1995; Patterson, Reid, & Dishion, 1992; Walker et al., 1995). To a great extent, when these behaviors are observed in our schools, they can be traced to unintentional behavioral student, peer, and/or teacher exchanges (Gunter, Denny, Jack, Shores, & Nelson, 1993; Sasso, Peck, Garrison-Harrell, 1998; Shores, Gunter, & Jack, 1993; Shores, Jack, et al., 1993).

Although learning and teaching processes are complex and continuous and some behavior initially is not learned (e.g., biobehavioral), key messages from this science are that much of human behavior *is* learned, comes under the

Table 1. Foundations and Features of Positive Behavior Support

Behavioral science	Practical interventions	Lifestyle outcomes	Systems perspective
• Human behavior is affected by behavioral, biobehavioral, social, and physical/environment factors.	• Functional behavioral assessments are used to develop behavior support plans.	• Behavior change must be socially significant, comprehensive, durable, and relevant.	• The quality and durability of supports are related directly to the level of support provided by the host environment.
• Much of human behavior is associated with unintentional learning opportunities.	• Interventions emphasize environmental redesign, curriculum redesign, and removing rewards that inadvertently maintain problem behavior.	• The goal of PBS is enhancement of living and learning options.	• The implementation of practices and decisions is policy driven.
• Human behavior is learned and can be changed.	• Teaching is a central behavior change tool.	• PBS procedures are socially and culturally appropriate. Applications occur in least restrictive natural settings.	• Emphasis is placed on prevention and the sustained use of effective practices.
	• Research-validated practices are emphasized.	• The fit between procedures and values of students, families, and educators must be contextually appropriate.	• A team-based approach to problem solving is used.
	• Intervention decisions are data based.	• Nonaversive interventions (no pain, tissue damage, or humiliation) are used.	• Active administrative involvement is emphasized.
			• Multisystems (district, schoolwide, nonclassroom, classroom, individual student, family, community) are considered.
			• A continuum of behavior supports is emphasized.

Note. *PBS = positive behavior support.*

control of environmental factors, and can be changed. The strength of the science is that problem behaviors become more understandable, and as our understanding grows, so does our ability to teach more socially appropriate and functional behavior. The PBS approach is founded on this science of human behavior. Different procedures and strategies are applied at different levels, but the fundamental principles of behavior are the same.

Practical Interventions

The science of human behavior has led to the development of practical strategies for preventing and reducing problem behavior (e.g., Alberto & Troutman, 1999; Cooper, Heron, & Heward, 1987; Kerr & Nelson, 1998; Koegel, Koegel, & Dunlap, 1996; Reichle & Wacker, 1993; Wolery, Bailey, & Sugai, 1988). *Practical* describes strategies that emphasize the contextual fit among problem behaviors, environments in which problem behaviors are occurring, and interventions that are developed and implemented (Albin, Lucyshyn, Horner, & Flannery, 1996). Priority is given to interventions that improve implementation efficiency, intervention effectiveness, and relevance of outcomes by (a) involving recipients of PBS in the design of behavior support plans, (b) considering the values of recipients and implementers of PBS, (c) considering the skills of implementers of PBS, (d) securing the approvals and endorsements of recipients and implementers of PBS, (e) considering the resources and administrative supports needed to implement strategies, and (f) providing the supports needed to sustain the use of effective strategies over time.

Although implementation details vary across age groups, contexts, and behavior, PBS interventions have common features. Foremost among these features is the application of FBA, but equally important are emphases on environmental redesign (changing aspects of the setting), curriculum redesign (teaching new skills), modification of behavior (teaching and changing student and adult behavior), and removing rewards that maintain problem behaviors (Carr, Levin, et al., 1994; Luiselli & Cameron, 1998; O'Neill et al., 1997).

PBS procedures emphasize assessment prior to intervention, manipulation of antecedent conditions to reduce or prevent the likelihood that a problem behavior will occur, development of new social and communication skills that make problem behaviors irrelevant, and careful redesign of consequences to eliminate factors that maintain problem behaviors and to encourage more acceptable replacement social skills and behaviors. PBS is an approach that emphasizes teaching as a central behavior change tool and focuses on replacing coercion with environmental redesign to achieve durable and meaningful change in the behavior of students. As such, attention is focused on adjusting adult behavior (e.g., routines, responses, instruc-

tional routines) and improving learning environments (e.g., curricular accommodations, social networks).

Educators, parents, and community agents must "work smarter" (Kame'enui & Carnine, 1998) by using time more efficiently and strategically selecting instructional and behavioral strategies for which clear evidence of their effectiveness exists. Working smarter means using what works for all students, not just those with learning and behavioral difficulties (Delpit, 1995). The PBS approach emphasizes the identification, adoption, and sustained use of practices that have been research validated. For students with serious antisocial behaviors, several recent meta-analyses and descriptive literature reviews support the use of strategies that can be applied by educators in school environments, especially (a) contextually targeted social skills instruction, (b) academic and curricular restructuring, and (c) behaviorally based interventions (Gottfredson & Gottfredson, 1996; Lipsey, 1991, 1992; Lipsey & Wilson, 1993; Tolan & Guerra, 1994). Other, more specific research-validated practices include FBAs, direct instruction, and other applied behavior analytic strategies (Carr et al., 1999).

Finally, the PBS approach emphasizes the use of data collection and analysis (e.g., direct behavioral observations, curriculum-based measurement) to inform decision making. A variety of data sources (e.g., office discipline referrals, attendance and tardy reports, and academic progress) are collected through a range of methods (e.g., archival review, interviews, direct observations) and from multiple sources (e.g., students, family members, educators, community members). In addition to behavioral factors, assessments consider cognitive, biophysical, developmental, and physical/environmental factors to assist in understanding problem behavior and in guiding the development of comprehensive behavior support plans. Collectively, these data can be used to determine the student's current level of functioning, the impact of the intervention on problem behavior, and improvements in other lifestyle elements (e.g., family, work, recreation). With ongoing data collection, intervention and instructional modifications can be made in a timely manner.

Social Values

PBS emphasizes consideration of social values in both the results expected from behavioral interventions and the strategies employed in delivering the interventions. A central PBS tenet is that behavior change needs to be socially significant. Behavior change should be (a) *comprehensive,* in that all relevant parts of a student's day (before, during, and after school) and important social contexts (home, school, neighborhood, and community) are affected, (b) *durable,* in that the change lasts for long time periods, and (c) *relevant,* in that the reduction of problem behaviors and increases in prosocial behaviors affect living and learning opportunities (academic, family, social, work).

The goal of PBS is more than the control of problem behavior; it also includes the enhancement of the living and learning options available to the student and to his or her peers and family (Risley, 1996; Turnbull & Turnbull, 1996).

Social values are also important in defining acceptable types of intervention procedures. PBS emphasizes the importance of procedures that are socially and culturally appropriate. The contextual fit between intervention strategies and the values of families, teachers, schools, support personnel, and community agency personnel may affect the quality and durability of support efforts (Albin & Sandler, 1998; Sailor, 1996). No intervention should cause pain, tissue damage, or humiliation to children and their families. Finally, careful consideration is given to lifestyle outcomes that go beyond simple behavior reduction and enhancement. The development of behavior support plans and the evaluation of their effects consider the student's current and future quality of life in all settings and circumstances. Koegel et al.(1996, p. xiv) added that "interventions should strive to enhance a person's competencies and access to desirable environments, social circumstances, and activities" and "all people should be treated with respect and dignity and that interventions must therefore refrain from interactions that are degrading, humiliating, or pain inducing."

Systems Perspective

PBS is of particular importance for schools, given the emphasis on behavioral "systems" in addition to the emphasis on individual children. A systems perspective provides support for the adoption and sustained use of effective school practices (Sugai & Horner, 1994, 1999). Without a systems approach, identification of practices is limited, adoptions are incomplete, and attention to school initiatives to address discipline is episodic and short term (e.g., 18–24 months; Sugai & Horner, 1999; Zins & Ponti, 1990).

PBS implementations consider multiple contexts: community, family, district, school, classroom, nonclassroom (e.g., cafeteria, hallways, bus, playground, parking lot), and individual. Efforts are policy driven to ensure accountability, maximum positive results, participation in and progress through the general curriculum, and effective and efficient communications. In addition, a proactive perspective (positive and preventative) perspective is maintained along three levels:

1. *Primary*—reduces the number of new cases of problem behavior,
2. *Secondary*—reduces the number of current cases of problem behavior, and
3. *Tertiary*—reduces the intensity and complexity of current cases (Walker et al., 1996).

A team-based approach is applied to program assessment, development, and problem solving (Adelman & Taylor,

1997; Lawson & Briar-Lawson, 1997). This approach enables input from multiple sources, a broader expert knowledge base, and improved sustainability over time.

At all levels in the system, active administrator support and participation are required. Without strong leadership from school administrators, program efforts often are inefficient, incomplete, and ineffective (Colvin & Sprick, 1999). Similarly, when problem behavior is chronic and intense, comprehensive linkages with other human service agencies (e.g., juvenile justice and corrections, mental/public health, child and family services) are considered (Eber, 1996; Eber & Nelson, 1997; Epstein et al., 1993; Walker et al., 1995; Walker et al., 1996).

Taken as a whole, a systems perspective to PBS provides a continuum of behavior support (see Figure 2) in which prevention is emphasized and intensity of problem behavior and context are considered. As a continuum, the following four change elements characterize PBS: (a) change of systems (policies, structures, routines), (b) change of environments, (c) change of student and adult (parent, teacher, staff) behavior, and (d) change in appreciation of appropriate behavior in all involved individuals (student, staff, family, etc.).

Behavior Support Planning Based on FBA

Among the most important changes in applied behavioral analysis in the past 20 years has been the development of FBA (special issue, *Journal of Applied Behavior Analysis*, 1994). The development of positive behavioral interven-

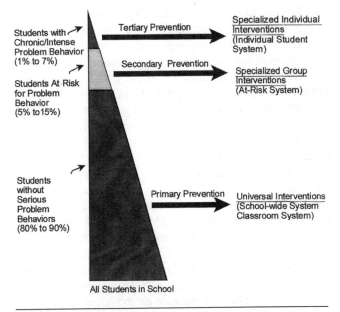

Figure 2. Continuum of positive behavior support that emphasizes a systems approach, preventive perspective, and specialized interventions.

tions and plans that are guided by FBA is the foundation of the PBS approach. A central message from this advancement is that the design of successful behavior change interventions requires identification of the events that reliably predict and maintain problem behaviors (Carr, 1994; Horner, 1994; O'Neill et al., 1997; Repp, 1994; Sugai, Lewis-Palmer, & Hagan, 1998). Historically, problem behaviors have been viewed as residing within a child, and the diagnostic emphasis has been on the type of problem behavior or the link with disability type (i.e., within the individual). Although all types of information may be useful in the design of effective support, the current emphasis is on careful documentation of the predicting and maintaining events associated with problem behaviors.

Although useful in guiding decision making at all levels, the FBA approach is the cornerstone of systems that address the educational programming of students who display the most significant and challenging problem behavior. These students require behavior support plans that are specialized, individualized, and highly intense. Such plans must be based on information about the nature of the problem behavior and the environmental context in which the problem behavior is observed. The FBA approach provides a systematic and informed means by which targeted interventions can be developed and monitored.

Functional assessment is not new; it can be found in a variety of disciplines (e.g., vocational education, physical therapy, chemistry, physics). In education, however, particularly special education, functional assessment had its beginning in the 1960s in applied behavior analysis (Bijou & Baer, 1961; 1978; Bijou, Peterson, & Ault, 1968; Bijou, Peterson, Harris, Allen, & Johnston, 1969). Initially, research studies and applied applications of the functional assessment technology demonstrated the value of defining variables that maintain a problem behavior prior to constructing an intervention (Carr, 1977; Carr & Durand, 1985; Iwata et al., 1982; Repp & Horner, 1999; Touchette, MacDonand, & Langer, 1985). Although most of this work has been conducted with individuals with severe developmental and intellectual disabilities (Blakeslee, Sugai, & Gruba, 1994; Lohrman-O'Rourke, Knoster, & Llewellyn, 1999), a growing body of research and applications focuses on individuals with mild, high-incidence disabilities (e.g., emotional and behavioral disorders, learning disabilities; e.g., Broussard & Northup, 1995; Dunlap, Kern-Dunlap, Clarke, & Robbins, 1991; Dunlap et al., 1993; Dunlap, White, Vera, Wilson, & Panacek, 1996; Kern, Childs, Dunlap, Clarke, & Falk, 1994; Lewis & Sugai, 1993, 1996a, 1996b; Umbreit, 1995; Volmer & Northup, 1996).

In this section, we provide an overview of FBA, including definition and outcomes, defining features, and major steps, especially in relation to behavior support development and planning.

DEFINITION AND RESULTS

We define *functional behavior assessment* as a systematic process of identifying problem behaviors and the events that (a) reliably predict occurrence and nonoccurrence of those behaviors and (b) maintain the behaviors across time. The purpose of gathering this information is to improve the effectiveness, relevance, and efficiency of behavior support plans (Carr et al., 1999; Foster-Johnson & Dunlap, 1993; Horner, 1994; O'Neill et al., 1997; Sugai, Horner, & Sprague, 1999; Sugai, Lewis-Palmer, & Hagan, 1998; Tilly et al., 1998). Specifically, if we can identify the conditions under which problem behavior is likely to occur (triggering antecedents and maintaining consequences), we can arrange environments in ways that reduce occurrences of problem behavior and teach and encourage positive behaviors that can replace problem behaviors.

Several procedures exist for conducting an FBA (Center for Effective Collaboration and Practice, 1998), but we maintain that any professionally appropriate assessment should conclude with, at minimum, three main results. The first is hypothesis statements that include three key features: (a) operational definitions of the problem behavior(s), (b) descriptions of the antecedent events that reliably predict occurrence and nonoccurrence of the problem behavior, and (c) descriptions of the consequence events that maintain the problem behavior(s). The second is direct observation data supporting these hypotheses. The third FBA result is a behavior support plan. The importance of the link between hypotheses that are derived from FBAs and the development of comprehensive behavior support plans must be emphasized. Behavior support plans provide a summary of intervention manipulations in four areas: (a) setting event strategies, (b) antecedent strategies, (c) behavior-teaching strategies, and (d) consequence strategies. In addition, a comprehensive behavior support plan provides implementation scripts that detail (a) who does what strategies when, where, how often, and why, (b) how emergency or crisis situations will be handled, and (c) how implementation and effectiveness will be monitored.

In sum, FBA is not a set of forms or static products. It is a process of understanding behavior in the context in which it is observed and guiding the development of positive behavioral interventions that are relevant, effective, and efficient. FBA is a best and preferred practice for all challenging behavior, not just for behavioral events that result in suspensions or other disciplinary actions.

PROCESS STEPS

In this section, an overview of the six main steps involved in conducting an FBA and developing behavior support plans is provided (see Table 2). Additional guidelines for

Table 2. Overview of Functional Behavioral Assessment and Behavior Support Planning

Step	Tools/Procedures	Outcome
1. Collect information regarding conditions under which problem behavior is and is not observed and more appropriate behavior is required.	Archival review, analysis of routines, interviews, direct observation	Descriptions of possible setting events, triggering antecedents, problem behavior response classes, maintaining consequences
2. Develop testable (manipulable) hypotheses.	Team analysis of information from Step 1	Testable hypotheses
3. Collect direct observation information.	Direct observations	Verified summary statements
4. Design behavior support plans.	Team development	Specification of (a) desired and acceptable alternative behavior, (b) antecedent strategies and manipulations, (c) consequence strategies and manipulations, (d) strategies for teaching desired and acceptable alternative behavior, and (e) setting event/establishing operation strategies and manipulations
5. Develop implementation scripts.	Team development	Scripts that specify how, when, where, and by whom the behavior support plan is to be implemented
6. Collect information on effectiveness and efficiency of behavior support plan and redesign based on evaluation information.	Team development	Data on student progress and plan implementation; redesign/updated plan

implementing the process are available in O'Neill et al. (1997); Sugai, Lewis-Palmer, and Hagan (1998); and Tilly et al. (1998).

Step 1

Using archival review, analysis of routines, interviews, and/or direct observations, information is gathered regarding the conditions under which (a) the problem behavior is and is not observed and (b) more appropriate behavior is required. Attention is focused on four primary factors: (a) setting events/establishing operations that make the problem behavior worse (e.g., diet, medical conditions/illness, sleep, fatigue, social conflicts), (b) antecedent events that predictably precede and trigger or occasion problem behavior (e.g., task demands, instruction, peer/adult requests), (c) problem behaviors that as a response class or set are maintained by a common function or outcome (e.g., attention, escape/avoidance), and (d) consequence events that predictably follow and maintain problem behavior (positive or negative reinforcement).

For example, when Linda's teacher requested assistance because of problem behaviors in his classroom, members of the school's behavior support team interviewed the teacher, reviewed Linda's behavioral incident records, examined her typical class and activity schedule, and consulted with other adults (e.g., parent, music teacher) who had firsthand knowledge about Linda's strengths and problem behaviors. (The details of this example have been simplified to illustrate the general features of each step.)

Step 2

The information collected in the first step is used to develop testable hypotheses that best describe the conditions under which the problem behavior is most likely to occur. A complete testable hypothesis indicates (a) problem behavior, (b) triggering antecedent events, (c) maintaining consequence events, and (d) influential setting events/establishing operations (O'Neill et al., 1997).

For example, from a review of interview and archival information, the behavior support team determined that when Linda's teacher asked her to redo spelling and grammar errors in her essay (antecedent), Linda verbally protested, failed to follow directions, and used profane language (problem behavior). Her teacher typically removed the essay task and turned his attention to other students (maintaining consequence). Problem behaviors also were more likely to occur and be worse in intensity when she had failed to complete her work during the prior math class or had had an argument with an adult (setting event).

Step 3

After testable hypotheses are developed, direct observation information is collected to verify the accuracy or predictability of these statements. Usually, multiple observations are conducted across multiple settings and situations to determine whether problem behavior patterns occur under hypothesized conditions and contexts. These observations involve the careful documentation of antecedent and consequence variables that are present or absent when problem behaviors are and are not observed.

In cases where hypotheses are difficult to establish or where problem behavior is particularly resistant to intervention, functional "analysis" may be recommended. A functional analysis involves a systematic manipulation (i.e., removal and addition) of factors that are hypothesized as triggering or occasioning problem behavior. These manipulations are designed to trigger problem behavior under one set of conditions and not under others. However, in educational and clinical applications, we do not recommend functional analysis without the direct involvement of an experienced behavior analyst, consent and collaboration by families and caregivers, and existence of structures for maintaining appropriate accountability (e.g., data collection, monitoring of implementation fidelity).

In Linda's situation, the school counselor, Linda's classroom teacher, and the special education teacher conducted direct observations during music, math, and language arts periods. They noted those antecedent and consequence events that were associated with each problem behavior displayed by Linda. They also looked for times when or situations where the problem behavior did not occur. For Linda, direct observation data confirmed the hypothesis statement generated in the previous step.

Step 4

Based on information from verified hypotheses, behavior support plans are developed that specify possible teaching strategies or manipulations for (a) desired and acceptable alternative behaviors, (b) antecedent events, (c) consequence events, and (d) setting events/establishing operations. This plan serves as the basis for defining the actual implementation of the behavioral intervention. Unlike more typical single-dimension interventions that focus on reactive, consequence manipulations (e.g., time-out, behavioral contracts), behavior support plans that are based on FBAs consider intervention components that are (a) instructionally focused (i.e., teaching acceptable and desired replacement behaviors), (b) prevention focused (e.g., neutralizing or eliminating the conditions that trigger problem behaviors or make them worse or more likely), and (c) environmentally based (e.g., rearrangement of the problem context).

For Linda, the behavior team, which included Linda's teacher and father, developed a behavior plan that had the following general elements:

1. Teach Linda to ask for help and/or indicate that the task is too difficult and teach her to self-record at the end of the period whether she "kept her cool" (behavior teaching);
2. Review correction strategies, provide an answer key, and point out what is correct about her

work before asking Linda to make corrections (antecedent manipulations);
3. Provide verbal praise for asking for help or indicating that work is too hard, do first two to three corrections with Linda, check her self-recording, and give her a break from the task if she appropriately begins her work (consequence manipulations); and
4. If she has had a prior conflict with an adult, provide Linda with an opportunity to problem solve the prior conflict and present her with a neutral and simple task before requesting making corrections (setting event manipulation).

Step 5

Implementation scripts are developed to specify how, when, where, and by whom the behavior support plan will be implemented. Contingency plans for responding to emergencies, training staff, and collecting data also are indicated. If necessary, resources and assistance from other support individuals or agencies (e.g., mental health, medical, vocational) are indicated.

For example, Linda's teacher agreed to implement the plan the next day and to keep track of Linda's language arts errors and corrections as a way of determining if the intervention was working. The counselor and special education teacher developed simple checklist scripts to guide Linda's teacher through the implementation of the behavior support plan. Linda's father agreed to provide positive acknowledgments at home if Linda met her goal for each day. If Linda's problem behavior escalated in intensity, the counselor would come immediately to assist the teacher.

Step 6

Information on the effectiveness and efficiency of the behavior support plan is collected regularly, and the plan is redesigned based on an evaluation of this information. A formative (direct, frequent, regular) approach is emphasized. In Linda's example, one or more members of the behavior support team met with Linda's teacher every other day during the 2-week implementation of the behavior support plan. This frequent support was provided to ensure that the plan was working and to provide Linda's teacher with assistance in implementing the plan.

Conclusion

Schools can be great places for students, teachers, related-services personnel, families, human-service practitioners, and community members to work collaboratively to achieve meaningful results for all children and youth. However, limited resources; diverse students, families, and neighborhoods; increases in school violence; and increased social responsibilities have decreased the efficiency and effectiveness of many schools. Although the solution is multi-faceted, schools can make a significant contribution by "working smarter." This approach requires the establishment of proactive school environments (i.e., "host environments") that have the capacity to identify, adopt, and sustain the use of effective policies, systems, and practices.

PBS is an important approach to identifying and organizing effective school practices, especially for students who present significant problem behavior. However, many systems-level challenges remain to be addressed. First, schools need guidelines for making the adoption and sustained use of PBS practices efficient and relevant. Attention must be focused on the policies, environments, structures, and practices of PBS. For example, addressing the needs of students who present significant problem behavior requires personnel with time, highly specialized skills, access to resources, and administrative supports.

Second, balancing efforts and attention between schoolwide and individual student systems is a challenge for many schools. For example, a schoolwide discipline system that operates efficiently and effectively for the majority of students in a school can ease the high costs associated with addressing the intense needs of the relatively small proportion of students who present the most significant problem behavior (Sugai et al., 2000). However, many schools lack the capacity to maintain the efficient and ongoing operation of both schoolwide and individual student systems. Increasingly, partnerships that include schools, community agencies, businesses, and family members offer new pathways for using PBS to change systems (Illback et al., 1998; Sailor, 1996, in press).

Third, as the specialized nature of interventions increases with the increasing intensity of problem behavior, so does the complexity of implementation. Schools need user-friendly ways to use PBS and FBA. Consideration must be given to the unique features (e.g., cultural, geographical, demographic, physical) of a school and its students, families, teachers, and community members.

Finally, Carr et al. (1999) noted that lifestyle results were measured in less than 3% of PBS studies. Schools must develop mechanisms for determining if their efforts at the schoolwide, classroom, nonclassroom, and individual student levels actually are associated with meaningful outcome improvements for students, their families, and the school. Attention to the reduction of problem behavior is understandable; however, the impact of PBS efforts on larger lifestyle results (e.g., peer relations, family functioning, community mobility) also must be considered.

The PBS approach offers students, teachers, and family and community members a process that begins to address these systems-level challenges. The process is based on an established science of human behavior, pays attention to important lifestyle results, works from a systems perspective, and gives priority to research-validated practices. The goal of PBS is to use information from FBAs to guide the design of learning and teaching environments that support and encourage adaptive behavior and lessen the usefulness of problem behavior.

ABOUT THE AUTHORS

George Sugai, PhD, is a professor of special education in the College of Education at the University of Oregon. His primary areas of interest are positive behavior support, emotional and behavioral disorders, applied behavior analysis, functional behavioral assessment, and schoolwide discipline. *Robert H. Horner*, PhD, is a professor of special education in the College of Education at the University of Oregon. His primary areas of interest include applied behavior analysis, positive behavior support, severe disabilities, functional assessment, and instructional technology. *Glen Dunlap*, PhD, is a professor of child and family studies at the University of South Florida. His primary areas of interest include applied behavior analysis, positive behavior support, early intervention, and functional behavioral assessment. *Meme Hieneman*, PhD, is an assistant professor in the Department of Child and Family studies, Louis de la Parte Florida Mental Health Institute, University of South Florida. Her interests focus on behavioral support in school, home, and community settings. *Timothy J. Lewis*, PhD, is currently an associate professor in and department chair of special education at the University of Missouri–Columbia. His primary interests include social skill instruction, functional behavioral assessment, and proactive schoolwide discipline systems. *C. Michael Nelson*, PhD, is a professor of special education in the Department of Special Education and Rehabilitation Counseling at the University of Kentucky. His primary interests are in correctional special education, functional behavioral assessment, and emotional and behavioral disorders. *Terrance Scott*, PhD, is an assistant professor of special education in the Department of Special Education and Rehabilitation Counseling at the University of Kentucky. His primary interests are in functional behavioral assessment, schoolwide discipline, social skill instruction, and emotional and behavioral disorders. *Carl Liaupsin* is a doctoral candidate in the Department of Special Education and Rehabilitation Counseling at the University of Kentucky. His primary interests are in instructional technology, functional behavioral assessment, and schoolwide discipline. *Wayne Sailor*, PhD, is the director of the University Affiliated Program for the Lawrence Campus of the University of Kansas. He is a professor in the Department of Special Education. His primary interests are in functional behavioral assessment; severe disabilities; integrating community services and schools; inclusive education; educational policy; and school, family, and community partnerships. *Ann P. Turnbull* is the co-director of the Beach Center on Families and Disability and a professor in the Department of Special Education at the University of Kansas. Her main PBS interest is in comprehensive lifestyle support for individuals with intense needs. *H. Rutherford*

Turnbull III, LLB, LLM, is professor of special education, courtesy professor of law, and co-director of the Beach Center on Families and Disability, The University of Kansas. He specializes in law, public policy, and disability studies. Donna Wickham, PhD, is a program associate with the Beach Center on Families and Disability and the University Affiliated Program at the University of Kansas. Her research interests include positive behavioral support, severe disabilities, and inclusive education. Brennan Wilcox, JD, MSW, is a legal and policy analyst for the Beach Center on Families and Disability at the University of Kansas. His research interests have focused on the legal and policy aspects of IDEA disciplinary issues and the use of positive behavioral interventions and supports. Michael Ruef is an assistant professor of special education at California State Polytechnic University at San Luis Obispo. His research interests include family support, positive behavioral support, and bridging the gap between research and practice. Address: George Sugai, Behavioral Research and Teaching, 5262 University of Oregon, Eugene, OR 97403-1265.

AUTHORS' NOTES

1. This article is a technical assistance guide that was prepared by the OSEP Center on Positive Behavioral Interventions and Supports, which is supported by a grant from the Office of Special Education Programs, with additional funding from the Safe and Drug Free Schools Program, U.S. Department of Education (No. H326S980003). Opinions expressed herein are those of the authors and do not necessarily reflect the position of the U.S. Department of Education, and such endorsements should not be inferred.

2. The purpose of the Center is to give schools capacity-building information and technical assistance for identifying, adapting, and sustaining effective schoolwide disciplinary practices. The Center has two main activities: (a) broad dissemination to schools, families, and communities about a technology of schoolwide positive behavioral interventions and support and (b) demonstrations at the level of individual students, schools, districts, and states of feasible and effective schoolwide positive behavioral interventions and supports.

3. FBA and PBS are not required in all cases of discipline but, instead, are required only in some clearly specified circumstances.

REFERENCES

Adelman, H., & Taylor, L. (1997). Addressing barriers to learning: Beyond school-linked services and full service schools. *American Journal of Orthopsychiatry, 67*(3), 408–421.

Alberto, P. A., & Troutman, A. C. (1999). *Applied behavior analysis for teachers* (5th ed.). Columbus, OH: Merrill.

Albin, R. W., Lucyshyn, L. M., Horner, R. H., & Flannery, K. B. (1996). Contextual fit for behavioral support plans: A model for a goodness-of-fit. In L. K. Koegel, R. L. Koegel, & G. Dunlap (Eds.), *Positive behavior support:*

Including people with difficult behavior in the community (pp. 81–89). Baltimore: Brookes.

Albin, R. W., & Sandler, L. (1998, May). Contextual fit as a variable affecting the fidelity with which behavior interventions are implemented. Paper presented at the annual meeting of the Association for Behavior Analysis Annual Convention, Orlando, FL.

Baer, D. M., Wolf, M. M., & Risley, T. R. (1968). Some current dimensions of applied behavior analysis. *Journal of Applied Behavior Analysis, 1,* 91–97.

Benson, L., & Harkavy, I. (1997). School and community in the global society: A Neo-Deweyian theory of community problem-solving schools and cosmopolitan neighborly communities in a Neo-Deweyian "manifesto" to dynamically connect school and community. *Universities and Community Schools, 5*(1/2), 11–69.

Biglan, A. (1995). Translating what we know about the context of antisocial behavior into a lower prevalence of such behavior. *Journal of Applied Behavior Analysis, 28,* 479–492.

Bijou, S. W., & Baer, D. M. (1961). *Child development I: A systematic and empirical theory.* Englewood Cliffs, NJ: Prentice Hall.

Bijou, S. W., & Baer, D. M. (1978). *Behavior analysis of child development.* Englewood Cliffs, NJ: Prentice Hall.

Bijou, S. W., Peterson, R. F., & Ault, M. H. (1968). A method to integrate descriptive and experimental field studies at the level of data and empirical concepts. *Journal of Applied Behavior Analysis, 1,* 175–191.

Bijou, S. W., Peterson, R. F., Harris, F. R., Allen, E., & Johnston, M. S. (1969). Methodology for experimental studies of young children in natural settings. *Psychological Record, 19,* 177–210.

Blakeslee, T., Sugai, G., & Gruba, J. (1994). A review of functional assessment use in data-based intervention studies. *Journal of Behavioral Education, 4,* 397–414.

Broussard, C. D., & Northup, J. (1995). An approach to functional assessment and analysis of disruptive behavior in regular education classrooms. *School Psychology Quarterly, 10,* 151–164.

Carr, E. G. (1977). The motivation of self-injurious behavior: A review of some hypotheses. *Psychological Bulletin, 84,* 800–816.

Carr, E. G. (1994). Emerging themes in the functional analysis of problem behavior. *Journal of Applied Behavior Analysis, 27,* 393–400.

Carr, E. G., & Durand, V. M. (1985). Reducing behavior problems through functional communication training. *Journal of Applied Behavior Analysis, 18,* 111–126.

Carr, E. G., Horner, R. H., Turnbull, A. P., Marquis, J. G., Magito McLaughlin, D., McAtee, M. L., Smith, C. E., Anderson Ryan, K., Ruef, M. B., & Doolabh, A. (1999). *Positive behavior support for people with developmental disabilities: A research synthesis* (American Association on Mental Retardation Monograph Series). Washington, DC: American Association on Mental Retardation.

Carr, E. G., Levin, L., McConnachie, G., Carlson, J. I., Kemp, D. C., & Smith, C. E. (1994). *Communication-based intervention for problem behavior: A user's guide for producing positive change.* Baltimore: Brookes.

Center for Effective Collaboration and Practice. (1998). *Addressing student problem behavior: An IEP team's introduction to functional behavioral assessment and behavior intervention plans.* Washington, DC: American Institutes for Research.

Colvin, G., Kame'enui, E. J., & Sugai, G. (1993). School-wide and classroom management: Reconceptualizing the integration and management of students with behavior problems in general education. *Education and Treatment of Children, 16,* 361–381.

Colvin, G., & Sprick, R. (1999). Providing administrative leadership for effective behavior support: Ten strategies for principals. *Effective School Practices, 17*(4), 65–71.

Colvin, G., Sugai, G., Good, R. H., III, & Lee, Y. (1997). Using active supervision and precorrection to improve transition behaviors in an elementary school. *School Psychology Quarterly, 12,* 344–363.

Cooper, J. O., Heron, T. E., & Heward, W. L. (1987). *Applied behavior analysis.* Columbus, OH: Merrill.

Delpit, L. (1995). *Other people's children: Cultural conflict in the classroom.* New York: New Press.

Dryfoos, J. G. (1997). The prevalence of problem behaviors: Implications for programs. In R. P. Weissberg, T. P. Gullotta, R. L. Hampton, B. A. Ryan, & G. R. Adams (Eds.), *Healthy children 2010: Enhancing children's wellness. Issues in children's and families' lives* (Vol. 8, pp. 17–46). Thousand Oaks, CA: Sage.

Dunlap, G., Kern, L., DePerczel, M., Clarke, S., Wilson, D., Childs, K. E., White, R., & Falk, G. D. (1993). Functional analysis of classroom variables for students with emotional and behavioral disorders. *Behavioral Disorders, 18,* 275–291.

Dunlap, G., Kern-Dunlap, L., Clarke, S., & Robbins, F. R. (1991). Functional assessment, curricular revision, and severe behavior problems. *Journal of Applied Behavior Analysis, 24,* 387–397.

Dunlap, G., White, R., Vera, A., Wilson, D., & Panacek, L. (1996). The effects of multi-component, assessment-based curricular modifications on the classroom behavior of children with emotional and behavioral disorders. *Journal of Behavioral Education, 6,* 481–500.

Durand, M. V., & Carr, E. G. (1985). Self-injurious behavior: Motivating conditions and guidelines for treatment. *School Psychology Review, 14,* 171–176.

Eber, L. (1996). Restructuring schools through wraparound planning: The LADSE experience. In R. J. Illback & C. M. Nelson (Eds.), *School-based services for students with emotional and behavioral disorders* (pp. 139–154). Binghamton, NY: Haworth Press.

Eber, L., & Nelson, C. M. (1997). School-based wraparound planning: Integrating services for students with emotional and behavioral needs. *American Journal of Orthopsychiatry, 67,* 385–395.

Epstein, M. H., Nelson, C. M., Polsgrove, L., Coutinho, M., Cumblad, C., & Quinn, K. P. (1993). A comprehensive community-based approach to serving students with emotional and behavioral disorders. *Journal of Emotional and Behavioral Disorders, 1,* 127–133.

Foster-Johnson, L., & Dunlap, G. (1993). Using functional assessment to develop effective, individualized interventions for challenging behaviors. *Teaching Exceptional Children, 25,* 44–50.

Gottfredson, G. D., & Gottfredson, D. C. (1996). *A national study of delinquency prevention in schools: Rationale for a study to describe the extensiveness and implementation of programs to prevent adolescent problem behavior in schools.* Ellicott City, MD: Gottfredson Associates.

Gunter, P. L., Denny, R. K., Jack, S. L., Shores, R. E., & Nelson, C. M. (1993). Aversive stimuli in academic interactions between students with serious emotional disturbance and their teachers. *Behavioral Disorders, 18,* 265–274.

Haring, N. G., & De Vault, G. (1996). Family issues and family support: Discussion. In L. K. Koegel, R. L. Koegel, & G. Dunlap (Eds.), *Positive behavioral support: Including people with difficult behavior in the community* (pp. 116–120). Baltimore: Brookes.

Horner, R. H. (1994). Functional assessment: Contributions and future directions. *Journal of Applied Behavior Analysis, 27,* 401–404.

Horner, R. H., Albin, R. W., Sprague, J. R., & Todd, A. W. (1999). Positive behavior support. In M. E. Snell & F. Brown (Eds.), *Instruction of students with severe disabilities* (5th ed., pp. 207–243). Upper Saddle River, NJ: Merrill/Prentice Hall.

Illback, R. J., Nelson, C. M., & Sanders, D. (1998). Community-based services in Kentucky: Description and 5-year evaluation of Kentucky IMPACT. In M. H. Epstein, K. Kutash, & A. Duchnowski (Eds.), *Outcomes for children and youth with emotional and behavioral disorders and their families* (pp. 141–172). Austin, TX: PRO-ED.

Individuals with Disabilities Education Act of 1990, 20 U.S.C. § 1400 *et seq.*

Iwata, B. A., Dorsey, M., Slifer, K. J., Bauman, K. E., & Richman, G. S. (1982). Toward a functional analysis of self-injury. *Analysis and Intervention in Developmental Disabilities, 2,* 1–20.

Kagan, S. L., Goffin, S. G., Golub, S. A., & Pritchard, E. (1995). *Toward systemic reform: Service integration for young children and their families.* Falls Church, VA: National Center for Service Integration.

Kame'enui, E. J., & Carnine, D. W. (1998). *Effective teaching strategies that accommodate diverse learners.* Upper Saddle River, NJ: Prentice Hall.

Kauffman, J. (1997). *Characteristics of emotional and behavior disorders of children and youth* (6th ed.). Columbus, OH: Merrill.

Kavale, K. A., & Forness, S. R. (1999). Efficacy of special education and related services. Monograph of the American Association on Mental Retardation. Washington, DC.

Kern, L., Childs, K. E., Dunlap, G., Clarke, S., & Falk, G. D. (1994). Using assessment-based curricular intervention to improve the classroom behavior of a student with emotional and behavioral challenges. *Journal of Applied Behavior Analysis, 27,* 7–19.

Kerr, M. M., & Nelson, C. M. (1998). *Strategies for managing problem behaviors in the classroom* (2nd ed.). Columbus, OH: Merrill.

Knitzer, J. (1993). Children's mental health policy: Challenging the future. *Journal of Emotional and Behavioral Disorders, 1*(1), 8–16.

Knitzer, J., Steinberg, Z., & Fleisch, B. (1990). *At the schoolhouse door: An examination of programs and policies for children with behavioral and emotional problems.* New York: Bank Street College of Education.

Koegel, L. K., Koegel, R. L., & Dunlap, G. (Eds.). (1996). *Positive behavior support: Including people with difficult behavior in the community.* Baltimore: Brookes.

Lawson, H. A., & Briar-Lawson, K. (1997). *Connecting the dots: Progress toward the integration of school reform, school-linked services, parent involvement and community schools.* Oxford, OH: Institutes for Educational Renewal.

Lewis, T. J., Colvin, G., & Sugai, G. (in press). The effects of pre-correction and active supervision on the recess behavior of elementary school students. *School Psychology Quarterly.*

Lewis, T. J., & Sugai, G. (1993). Teaching communicative alternatives to socially withdrawn behavior: An investigation in maintaining treatment effects. *Journal of Behavioral Education, 3,* 61–75.

Lewis, T., & Sugai, G. (1996a). Descriptive and experimental analysis of teacher and peer attention and the use of assessment-based intervention to improve the pro-social behavior of a student in general education settings. *Journal of Behavioral Education, 6,* 7–24.

Lewis, T. J., & Sugai, G. (1996b). Functional assessment of problem behavior: A pilot investigation of the comparative and interactive effects of teacher and peer social attention on students in general education settings. *School Psychology Quarterly, 11,* 1–19.

Lewis, T. J, Sugai, G., & Colvin, G. (1998). Reducing problem behavior through a school-wide system of effective behavioral support: Investigation of a school-wide social skills training program and contextual interventions. *School Psychology Review, 27,* 446–459.

Lipsey, M. W. (1991). The effect of treatment on juvenile delinquents: Results from meta-analysis. In F. Losel, D. Bender, & T. Bliesener (Eds.), *Psychology and law* (pp. 131–143). New York: Walter de Gruyter.

Lipsey, M. W. (1992). Juvenile delinquency treatment: A meta-analytic inquiry into the variability of effects. In T. D. Cook, H. Cooper, D. S. Cordray, H. Hartman, L. V. Hedges, R. V. Light, T. A. Louis, & F. Mostellar (Eds.), *Meta-analysis for explanation* (pp. 83–127). Beverly Hills, CA: Sage.

Lipsey, M. W., & Wilson, D. B. (1993). The efficacy of psychological, educational, and behavioral treatment: Confirmation from meta-analysis. *American Psychologist, 48,* 1181–1209.

Lohrman-O'Rourke, S., Knoster, T., & Llewellyn, G. (1999). Screening for understanding: An initial line of inquiry for school-based settings. *Journal of Positive Behavioral Interventions, 1*(1), 35–42.

Luiselli, J. K., & Cameron, M. J. (Eds.). (1998). *Antecedent control: Innovative approaches to behavioral support.* Baltimore: Brookes.

Mayer, G. (1995). Preventing antisocial behavior in the schools. *Journal of Applied Behavior Analysis, 28,* 467–478.

Meyer, L. H., & Evans, I. M. (1989). *Nonaversive intervention for behavior problems: A manual for home and community.* Baltimore: Brookes.

O'Neill, R. E., Horner, R. H., Albin, R. W., Sprague, J. R., Storey, K., & Newton, J. S. (1997). *Functional assessment and program development for problem behavior: A practical handbook.* Pacific Grove, CA: Brooks/Cole.

Patterson, G. R., Reid, J. B., & Dishion, T. J. (1992). *Antisocial boys.* Eugene, OR: Castalia Press.

Peacock Hill Working Group. (1992). Problems and promises in special education and related services for children and youth with emotional or behavioral disorders. *Behavioral Disorders, 16,* 299–313.

Reichle, J., & Wacker, D. P. (Eds.) (1993). *Communicative alternatives to challenging behavior: Integrating functional assessment and intervention strategies* (Vol. 3). Baltimore: Brookes.

Repp, A. (1994). Comments on functional analysis procedures for school-based behavior problems. *Journal of Applied Behavior Analysis, 27,* 208–412.

Repp, A., & Horner, R. H. (Eds.). (1999). *Functional analysis of problem behavior: From effective assessment to effective support.* Belmont, CA: Wadsworth.

Risley, T. (1996). Get a life: Positive behavioral intervention for challenging behavior through life arrangement and life coaching. In L. K. Koegel, R. L. Koegel, & G. Dunlap (Eds.), *Positive behavioral support: Including people with difficult behavior in the community* (pp. 403–424). Baltimore: Brookes.

Rose, L. C., & Gallup, A. M. (1998). The 30th annual Phi Delta Kappa/Gallup Poll of the public's attitudes toward the public school. *Phi Delta Kappan, 80*(1), 41–56.

Sailor, W. (1996). New structures and systems change for comprehensive positive behavioral support. In L. K. Koegel, R. L. Koegel, & G. Dunlap (Eds.), *Positive behavioral support: Including people with difficult behavior in the community* (pp. 163–206). Baltimore: Brookes.

Sailor, W. (in press). *Inclusive education and school/community partnerships.* New York: Teachers College Press.

Sasso, G. M., Peck, J., & Garrison-Harrell, L. (1998). Social interaction setting events: Experimental analysis of contextual variables. *Behavioral Disorders, 24,* 34–43.

Schorr, L. B. (1997). *Common purpose: Strengthening families and neighborhoods to rebuild America.* New York: Anchor Books.

Schwartz, B. (1989). *Psychology of learning and behavior* (3rd ed.). New York: W. W. Norton.

Shores, R. E., Gunter, P. L., & Jack, S. L. (1993). Classroom management strategies: Are they setting events for coercion? *Behavioral Disorders, 18,* 92–102.

Shores, R. E., Jack, S. L., Gunter, P. L., Ellis, D. N., DeBriere, T. J., & Wehby, J. H. (1993). Classroom interactions of children with behavior disorders. *Journal of Emotional and Behavioral Disorders, 1,* 27–39.

Special issue on functional analysis approaches to behavioral assessment and treatment. (1994). *Journal of Applied Behavior Analysis, 27*(4).

Sprague, J., Sugai, G., & Walker, H. (1998). Antisocial behavior in schools. In S. Watson & F. Gresham (Eds.), *Child behavior therapy: Ecological considerations in assessment, treatment, and evaluation* (pp. 451–474). New York: Plenum Press.

Stevens, L. J., & Price, M. (1992). Meeting the challenge of educating children at risk. *Kappan, 74*(1), 18–23.

Sugai, G. (1998). Postmodernism and emotional and behavioral disorders: Distraction or advancement. *Behavioral Disorders, 23,* 171–177.

Sugai, G., & Horner, R. (1994). Including students with severe behavior problems in general education settings: Assumptions, challenges, and solutions. In J. Marr, G. Sugai, & G. Tindal (Eds.), *The Oregon Conference monograph* (Vol. 6, pp. 102–120). Eugene: University of Oregon.

Sugai, G., & Horner, R. H. (1999). Discipline and behavioral support: Practices, pitfalls, & promises. *Effective School Practices, 17*(4), 10–22.

Sugai, G., Horner, R. H., & Sprague, J. (1999). Functional assessment-based behavior support planning: Research-to-practice-to-research. *Behavioral Disorders, 24,* 223–227.

Sugai, G., Lewis-Palmer, T., & Hagan, S. (1998). Using functional assessments to develop behavior support plans. *Preventing School Failure, 43*(1), 6–13.

Sugai, G., Sprague, J. R., Horner, R. H., & Walker, H. M. (2000). Preventing school violence: The use of office discipline referrals to assess and monitor school-wide discipline interventions. *Journal of Emotional and Behavioral Disorders, 8,* 94–101.

Taylor-Greene, S., Brown, D., Nelson, L., Longton, J., Gassman, T., Cohen, J., Swartz, J., Horner, R. H., Sugai, G., & Hall, S. (1997). School-wide behavioral support: Starting the year off right. *Journal of Behavioral Education, 7,* 99–112.

Tilly, W. D., III, Knoster, T. P., Kovaleski, J., Bambara, L., Dunlap, G., & Kincaid, D. (1998). *Functional behavioral assessment: Policy development in light of emerging research and practice.* Alexandria, VA: National Association of the State Directors of Special Education.

Todd, A. W., Horner, R. H., Sugai, G., & Sprague, J. R. (1999). Effective behavior support: Strengthening school-wide systems through a team-based approach. *Effective School Practices, 17*(4), 23–37.

Tolan, P., & Guerra, N. (1994). What works in reducing adolescent violence: An empirical review of the field. Boulder: University of Colorado, Center for the Study and Prevention of Violence.

Touchette, P. E., MacDonald, R. F., & Langer, S. N. (1985). A scatter plot for identifying stimulus control of problem behavior. *Journal of Applied Behavior Analysis, 18,* 343–351.

Turnbull, A. P., & Turnbull, H. R. (1996). Group action planning as a strategy for providing comprehensive family support. In L. K. Koegel, R. L. Koegel, & G. Dunlap (Eds.), *Positive behavioral support: Including people with difficult behavior in the community* (pp. 99–114). Baltimore: Brookes.

Umbreit, J. (1995). Functional assessment and intervention in a regular classroom setting for the disruptive behavior of a student with attention deficit hyperactivity disorder. *Behavioral Disorders, 20,* 267–278.

Vollmer, T. R., & Northup, J. (1996). Some implications of functional analysis for school psychology. *School Psychology Quarterly, 11,* 76–92.

Walker, H. M., Colvin, G., & Ramsey, E. (1995). *Antisocial behavior in school: Strategies and best practices.* Pacific Grove, CA: Brooks/Cole.

Walker, H. M., Forness, S. R., Kaufman, J., Epstein, M. H., Gresham, F. M., Nelson, C. M., & Strain, P. S. (1998). Macro-social validation: Referencing outcomes in behavioral disorders to societal issues and problems. *Behavioral Disorders, 24,* 1–18.

Walker, H. M., Horner, R. H., Sugai, G., Bullis, M., Sprague, J. R., Bricker, D., & Kaufman, M. J. (1996). Integrated approaches to preventing antisocial behavior patterns among school-age children and youth. *Journal of Emotional and Behavioral Disorders, 4,* 193–256.

Wolery, M. R., Bailey, D. B., Jr., & Sugai, G. M. (1988). *Effective teaching: Principles and procedures of applied behavior analysis with exceptional students.* Boston: Allyn & Bacon.

Zins, J. E., & Ponti, C. R. (1990). Best practices in school-based consultation. In A. Thomas and J. Grimes (Eds.), *Best practices in school psychology—II* (pp. 673–694). Washington, DC: National Association of School Psychologists.

Action Editor: Robert L. Koegel

A Schoolwide Example of Positive Behavioral Support

Terrance M. Scott
University of Kentucky

Abstract: Without prevention strategies, schools can expect to observe behavioral difficulties in more than 20% of the school population. Using schoolwide systems of positive behavioral support, schools can decrease the number of problem behaviors by students, providing a clearer focus for intervention on the students with the greatest support needs. This article presents a case example of schoolwide positive behavioral support, including its planning, implementation, and outcomes. The entire process of creating schoolwide teams, determining actions, and developing consensus is described in detail with specific examples. Outcomes of school-selected dependent variables indicate large decreases in the number of students excluded from the classroom learning environment for problem behaviors. Details of specific problems and issues are discussed with examples.

Incidents of violent and disruptive behavior are on the rise in the U.S. public school system. Many of these students' behaviors are challenging to such a degree that they often can consume up to 80% of a teacher's instructional time (Sugai & Horner, 1994). Despite the stereotype that this problem belongs to the inner-city high school, evidence has indicated that students in both urban and rural areas and in elementary, middle, and high schools are equally likely to be involved in violent acts at school (Metropolitan Life Insurance Company, 1999). The degree to which we can have an effect on the most severe of these problems is directly related to our ability to prevent the total number of problems that occur (Nelson, 1996; Scott & Nelson, 1999; Sprague, Sugai, & Walker, 1998; Sugai et al., 2000). In the average school, nearly one quarter of students can be expected to exhibit problem behaviors to some degree, while 3% to 7% can be expected to exhibit chronic problems that will require more directed and individualized efforts (Todd, Horner, Sugai, & Colvin, 1999). This smaller group of students are well known because of their repetitive problems; many more are students who fail because of unclear expectations, poorly planned routines, and/or inadequate physical arrangements (e.g., supervision). In any case, efforts to have an effect on the neediest of these students are complicated by the sheer numbers of students having problems (Mayer, 1995; Sprague et al., 1998; Walker, Colvin, & Ramsey, 1995). To find the neediest students, we must prevent problem behavior from all students.

Positive behavioral support is a team-based, comprehensive, and proactive system for facilitating and maintaining student success across settings (Bambara, Mitchell-Kvacky, & Iacobelli, 1994; Eber & Nelson, 1997; Koegel, Koegel, & Dunlap, 1996; Mayer, 1995; Sprague et al., 1998; Sugai & Horner, 1999). Systems of positive behavioral support involve input and decision making from every adult in the school, identification of predictable problem contexts to develop preventative solutions, and teaching/reinforcing behaviors that predict student success (Nelson & Colvin, 1996). The idea behind behavioral support is that predictable problems are preventable problems. When proactive systems are in place, the number of problem behaviors that occur due to inadequate or poorly designed rules, routines, and/or physical arrangements will be reduced through prevention. Under these conditions, we can predict that in the average school approximately 10% of the students will continue to exhibit problem behaviors (Langland, Lewis-Palmer, & Sugai, 1998; Taylor-Green et al., 1997).

Identifying the neediest group of students and those who are most at risk of school failure represents the first step in a comprehensive and systemic strategy (Scott & Nelson, 2000; Colvin & Sprick, 1999). Having identified these students, we can realistically provide more time-consuming and costly individualized interventions to prevent failure (Foster-Johnson & Dunlap, 1993). The key is prevention; we can't truly know who the needy students are until we provide maximum prevention procedures for all students.

This article presents a case example of the first steps toward implementing a comprehensive system of schoolwide positive behavioral support and describes the initial schoolwide prevention process, including its planning, implementation, and outcomes. Procedures for identifying problems, determining actions, and developing consensus are described in detail with specific examples.

Method

SETTING AND PARTICIPANTS

This schoolwide study was conducted in an inner-city elementary school (Grades K through 5) of about 500 students in central Kentucky. At the time of initial involvement, this school could be described as a school in crisis, ranking 275 out of 285 elementary schools in Kentucky by state academic measures. The student population could best be characterized as high risk with 96% of the students receiving a free or reduced lunch and not a single student reading at the proficient level by state standards. Further, by district count, students in this school exhibited more problem behaviors and were subsequently excluded from classroom learning environments at a rate higher than any other school in the district—including middle and high schools. Adding to this problem is that although minorities made up approximately 17% of the school population, they accounted for nearly 60% of the exclusionary discipline procedures.

POSITIVE BEHAVIORAL SUPPORT PROCESS

This particular school was approached to participate as a positive behavioral support model because of the degree of need, as indicated by the earlier characterization. The initial contact was made through the district's central office and a meeting was arranged between district-level administrators, the school's principal, and the author. At the initial meeting, an overview of positive behavioral support was presented along with a brief plan for how such procedures might be undertaken at this particular school. The principal was interested and took the idea to his staff for reaction. After an initial agreement to consider the proposal, further discussions took place directly between the author and the school faculty and staff.

Obtained Staff Commitment

After three 1-hour staff meetings in May, wherein the procedures for positive behavioral support were discussed in detail, school personnel were asked to vote on whether they wanted to commit to schoolwide implementation. As part of this commitment, the author asked that two conditions be met. First, all school personnel must agree to fully participate in the process, abiding by group decisions and not to sabotage those decisions that are not personally favorable. Second, all school personnel must commit to positive behavioral support systems for the following full school year. At the end of the third meeting, school personnel unanimously voted to adopt positive behavioral support for the upcoming school year.

Identified Predictable Problem Contexts

Because all adults in the school are responsible to some degree for observing, supervising, and enforcing the consequences of student behavior, all school personnel were asked to participate. During the summer, all school personnel (certified and classified) met in a lecture room at the University of Kentucky to begin the process of developing positive behavioral support systems. This process was conducted over one 8-hour day, at no cost to the school. Certified staff were provided with professional development credit and classified staff were paid a small stipend out of the school's training budget.

The author served as the facilitator for the group and, as an initial step, divided the group into several subgroups according to common job responsibilities. All instructional assistants sat together, as did primary teachers; intermediate teachers; specialists; secretaries, custodians, and cafeteria workers; and administrators. Each group was then asked to take 20 minutes and list all the locations, times, and conditions under which problem behaviors they saw were most likely to occur. At the front of the room, chalk boards and chart paper represented each physical location in the school. As each location was presented, group spokespersons listed the problems they saw as predictable and the conditions under which those problems occurred. The end result was a complete listing of the places, times, and conditions under which problem behaviors were predictable in the school.

Brainstormed Prevention Strategies

Once the predictability of problem behaviors was established, groups were again asked to get together for 20 minutes. This time they were asked to spend their time brainstorming simple solutions in terms of rules (student expectations), routines (e.g., timing and number of transitions) and physical arrangements (traffic patterns, physical environment, and supervision). That is, personnel were to ask themselves, "What simple solutions are there that will prevent these problems?" After this brainstorming session, each physical location was again presented and a comprehensive list of proactive strategies was created.

Developed Staff Consensus

During the brainstorming session, personnel were prompted not to make judgments but to submit all ideas so that lists contained a full range of possibilities. Once this was complete, the task of discussion and consensus building was undertaken. For any brainstorming strategy to be a viable proactive solution, the group needed to agree that it was (a) logically calculated to prevent identified problems, (b) practical enough to be consistently implemented, and (c) able to gain consensus (at least 70% vote) from the group. This particular portion of the process definitely was the most time consuming, taking nearly 4 hours to complete. By a process of elimination, a set of agreeable strategies was developed. For each location, the group first deleted those strategies they believed would not result in the desired effect, then those that were not believed to practical enough to be immediately or consistently implemented. Finally, the group had to agree on which remaining strategies were acceptable. This process, the most time consuming, involved a great deal of discussion, negotiation, and compromise by all participants prior to achieving consensus. For each identified area, a set of procedures eventually achieved group consensus.

For example, in the cafeteria, school personnel identified the lunch routine as particularly predictive of problem behaviors including fights, vandalism, and assorted other disruptive behaviors. The identified problems included long lines waiting to be served—inciting pushing and fighting, and resulting in spilled food and abandoned trays with students arguing when asked to clean their area—and too many students up and wandering the cafeteria, making it impossible to sufficiently monitor the area. As preventative strategies, school personnel agreed to revise the lunch schedule to minimize wait lines. They also agreed to provide entire classrooms with reinforcers when the entire table was cleaned (students eat at tables by classroom),

providing students with an incentive to clean and police their own areas. Further, the cafeteria workers determined that they would wear aprons with all necessary utensils so that students would remain seated and raise their hand when in need of assistance. Table 1 presents examples of identified problem locations, contexts, and proactive solutions.

Determined Schoolwide Expectations and Teaching

As a final activity, the group as a whole determined schoolwide expectations by determining what behaviors would be predictive of student success. They further discussed and negotiated these expectations until a consensus was achieved. The end result was a brief list of behavioral expectations for each location in the school. These expectations were positively stated (i.e., what students should do as opposed to what they should not), clearly posted, and taught to the students beginning on the first day of school. Teaching expectations involved teachers and staff accompanying students to each location in the school during the first week of school and specifically and explicitly teaching and modeling the rules (e.g., at the lunch line, go to the left and stay single file; in the stairway go to the right and keep a hand on the rail).

Further, personnel agreed to consistently reinforce students for complying with the expectations and to reteach and/or enforce consequences for students who did not comply with the expectations. While reinforcement is a key component of effective instruction and behavior change, specific schoolwide agreements for reinforcement were neither agreed upon nor monitored. In this particular example, school personnel were only able to agree that they

Table 1. Examples of Identified School Locations, Problem Contexts, and Proactive Solutions

Location	Problem and context	Proactive solutions
Cafeteria	Lunchtime • long lines—pushing and shoving • messes on tables create frequent negative consequences • too many students moving about—difficult to supervise all	• rearrange transition routine to minimize line wait • group contingency—entire table clean = group reward • monitors wear aprons with necessary items, students raise hand for assistance and remain seated
Hallway and stairs	Transition times • congestion—students pushing and shoving—injuries and fights • noise in hall—disrupting classes • too many students in hall at one time—difficult not to bump	• teach students to stay to right in hall • teach students to hold stair rail with right hand (force to right and single file) • teach students to use whisper voice in hallway
Gymnasium	Before school • students use unsupervised restrooms on way to class • students fight and engage in horseplay activities causing injury • students find unsupervised areas and engage in problem behaviors	• teach students to use gym restroom prior to leaving (provide daily prompt before bell) • teach students appropriate games in which to engage • set clear expectations and provide more supervision

would positively acknowledge expected behavior in some manner.

Created Schoolwide Team

Before adjourning, each group was asked to reconvene and select a representative to serve on the school behavior support team. The configuration of the team included a representative from each identified faction plus the principal and a school-based student services coordinator. Any problems identified by individuals in the school would be reported to their representative who would then take those concerns to the team. The team agreed to meet on a monthly basis to look at the data, report back to the school as a whole, and facilitate group discussions of any necessary changes.

DEPENDENT VARIABLES

As part of the regular positive behavioral support process, the school was asked to determine the outcomes they were most interested in monitoring for change. This school was under a great deal of scrutiny from the school district for excluding high numbers of students. In addition, the local Office of Civil Rights was involved and asking that the school address the overrepresentation of minorities in its exclusionary practices. These conditions helped define the dependent variables. The school personnel felt that, if the process were successful, they would have fewer students misbehaving and thus fewer students being disciplined via exclusionary practices.

SAFE Referrals

The acronym "SAFE" stands for "suspension and failure eliminated." The SAFE room is a small area with desks facing the wall around the perimeter of the room. Used in a manner similar to typical in-school suspension models, students are sent to SAFE for predetermined amounts of time for violating school rules or disrupting learning environments. While in SAFE, students are supposed to do academic work. However, repeated observations of SAFE reveal that students are provided with tasks, but typically do not engage in any academic activities because time serves as the only contingency for return to class. All referrals to SAFE were recorded by the SAFE facilitator on a form that also included the amount of time the student was there and each student's race. A summary of these records was required by the district on a monthly basis.

Suspensions

Students were suspended from school for a variety of predetermined disruptive or dangerous behaviors. Suspension was defined as temporarily being sent home from the school—for a period of at least 1 day. All suspensions were initiated by the principal and were recorded as the total number of students and days by race. A summary of this information was also required by the district on a monthly basis.

Results

SAFE REFERRALS

Figure 1 presents the observed changes in SAFE referrals from the baseline year to the intervention year as an average number of student-hours per day. During the positive behavior support year, a decrease was realized during each of the months, with a total decrease in hours of 61% for both the school population as a whole and for minority students alone. This difference can also be expressed in terms of total hours saved during the positive behavior support year with students gaining more than 775 classroom hours through prevention.

SUSPENSIONS

Figure 2 presents the observed changes in suspensions from the baseline year to the intervention year as a total number of days and total number of students by race. A 65% decrease in number of days suspended was realized. In addition, a 75% decrease in both the total number of students suspended and total number of minority students suspended was realized.

Discussion

This article provides an example of the implementation of a schoolwide system of positive behavioral support. The general results of this demonstration indicate that schoolwide positive behavioral support was associated with a decrease in the number of students requiring exclusionary disciplinary actions due to problem behaviors. However, due to the case study nature of this demonstration, causal conclusions cannot be drawn. Further, dependent variables such as hours spent in SAFE and number of suspensions represent the outcomes of problem behavior rather than counts of actual behaviors. Thus, it is possible that problem behaviors decreased in intensity, but not in frequency; or that problem behaviors remained the same, but school personnel chose to handle the problems in a different manner. Further, this demonstration represents a package of strategies including staff consistency, clearly defined and taught expectations, schoolwide appraisal of predictable problems and solutions, and reinforcement for desired behavior. However, there is no solid data on either the fidelity with which any of these procedures was implemented or the relative effect of any single procedure. We can make statements regarding the outcomes only relative to the entire package and must weigh those outcomes against the fact that although the process was definitely initiated as stated, the fidelity of the package components over time is unknown.

One of the defining features of positive behavioral support is its fit to individual contexts, allowing school personnel to determine a school's individual problems and solutions, and the focus and manner in which those solutions will be evaluated. To be certain, a more scientific process could have been developed for evaluating the effects of positive behavioral support. However, the purpose here was to demonstrate an actual implementation of positive behavioral support. The outcomes monitored were those identified by school personnel as most important. Despite the limitations, the fact remains that students at the school were excluded less frequently and spent more time in class.

This school has committed to continuing positive behavioral support and expanding the system to focus on providing specialized interventions for those students who continue to have problems, while refining the schoolwide prevention component. Future studies of this model would do well to look at these students and how systems of positive behavioral support can be refocused to affect the number and types of problem behavior observed. Further, issues related to the relative effectiveness of individual components remain unclear and are deserving of further study. Finally, although this example did demonstrate comparable effects in minorities with respect to the entire school population, it must remain clear that these outcomes do not represent equality for minorities. Research must focus on groups traditionally overrepresented in exclusionary disciplinary policies. Our solutions will be positive and equitable only when the representation of all students in disciplinary procedures is in accordance with their representation in the population.

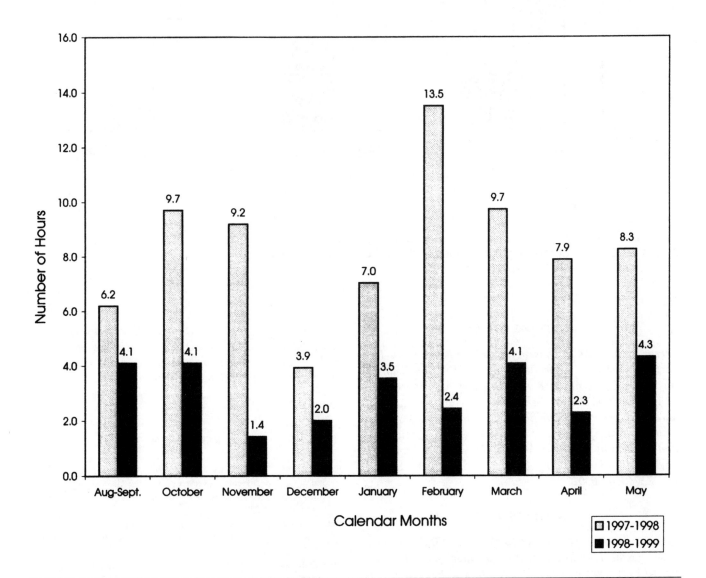

Figure 1. Average number of hours per day spent in SAFE.

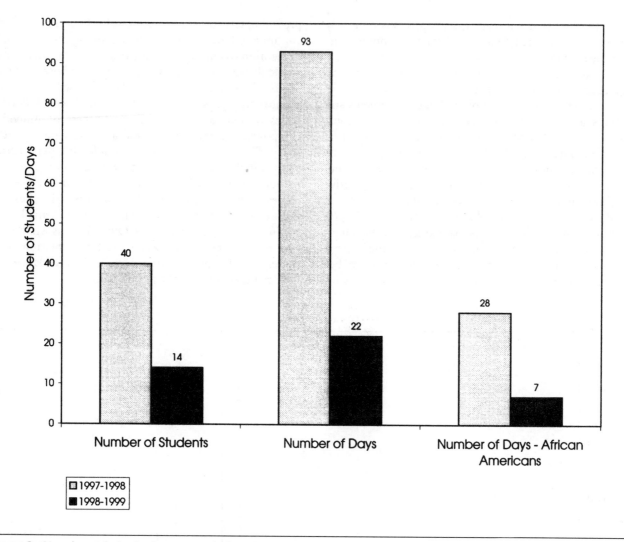

Figure 2. Number of students suspended and number of days suspended.

ABOUT THE AUTHOR

Terrance M. Scott, PhD, is an assistant professor in the Department of Special Education and Rehabilitation Counseling at the University of Kentucky and is a partner in the OSEP Center on Positive Behavioral Interventions and Supports. His interests include functional behavioral assessment, schoolwide discipline, social skill instruction, and emotional and behavioral disorders. Address: Terrance M. Scott, 229 Taylor Education Building, University of Kentucky, Lexington, KY 40506-0001.

AUTHOR'S NOTE

This article was supported, in part, by the OSEP Center on Positive Behavioral Interventions and Supports, which is supported by a grant from the Office of Special Education Programs, with additional funding from the Safe and Drug Free Schools Program, U.S. Department of Education (Grant No. H326S980003). Opinions expressed herein are those of the author and do not necessarily reflect the position of the U.S. Department of Education, and such endorsement should not be inferred.

REFERENCES

Bambara, L. M., Mitchell-Kvacky, A. A., & Iacobelli, S. (1994). Positive behavioral support for students with severe disabilities: An emerging multicomponent approach for addressing challenging behavior. *School Psychology Review, 23,* 263–278.

Colvin, G., & Sprick, R. (1999) Providing administrative leadership for effective behavior support: Ten strategies for principals. *Effective School Practices, 17*(4), 65–71.

Eber, L., & Nelson, C. M. (1997). School-based wraparound planning: Integrating services for students with emotional and behavioral needs. *American Journal of Orthopsychiatry, 67,* 385–395.

Foster-Johnson, L. & Dunlap, G. (1993). Using functional assessment to develop effective, individualized interventions for challenging behaviors. *Teaching Exceptional Children, 25,* 44–50.

Koegel, L. K., Koegel, R. L., & Dunlap, G. (Eds.). (1996). *Positive behavioral support: Including people with difficult behavior in the community.* Baltimore: Brookes.

Langland, S., Lewis-Palmer, T., & Sugai, G. (1998). Teaching respect in the classroom: An instructional approach. *Journal of Behavioral Education, 8,* 245–261.

Mayer, G. (1995). Preventing antisocial behavior in the schools. *Journal of Applied Behavior Analysis, 28,* 467–478.

Metropolitan Life Insurance Company (1999). *The 1999 survey of the American teacher: Violence in America's schools.* New York: Author.

Nelson, J. R. (1996). Designing schools to meet the needs of students who exhibit disruptive behavior. *Journal of Emotional and Behavioral Disorders, 4,* 147–161.

Nelson, J. R., & Colvin, G. (1996). Designing supportive school environments. In R. J. Illback & C. M. Nelson (Eds.), *Emerging school-based approaches for children with emotional and behavioral problems: Research and practice in service integration* (pp. 225–249). New York: Haworth Press.

Scott, T. M., & Nelson, C. M. (1999). Universal school discipline strategies: Facilitating positive learning environments. *Effective School Practices, 17,* 54–64.

Scott, T. M., & Nelson, C. M. (2000). *Effective instruction: The forgotten component in school safety and violence prevention.* Manuscript submitted for publication.

Sprague, J., Sugai, G., & Walker, H. M. (1998). Antisocial behavior in schools. In T. S. Watson & F. M. Gresham (Eds.). *Handbook of child behavior therapy: Ecological considerations in assessment, treatment, and evaluation* (pp. 451–474). New York: Plenum.

Sugai, G., & Horner, R. H. (1994). Including students with severe behavior problems in general education settings: Assumptions, challenges, and solutions. In J. Marr, G. Sugai, & G. Tindal (Eds.). *The Oregon conference monograph* (pp. 102–120). Eugene: University of Oregon.

Sugai, G., & Horner, R. H. (1999). Discipline and behavioral support: Practices, pitfalls, & promises. *Effective School Practices, 17*(4), 10–22.

Sugai, G., Horner, R. H., Dunlap, G., Hieneman, Lewis, T. J., Nelson, C. M., Scott, T. M., Liaupsin, C. J., Sailor, W., Turnbull, A. P., Turnbull, H. R. III, Wickham, D., Ruef, M., & Wilcox, B. (2000). Applying positive behavioral support and functional assessment in schools. *Journal of Positive Behavior Interventions, 2,* 131–143.

Taylor-Green, S., Brown, D., Nelson, L., Longton, J., Gassman, Cohen, J., Swartz, J., Horner, R. H., Sugai, G., & Hall, S. (1997). School-wide behavioral support: Starting the year off right. *Journal of Behavioral Education, 7,* 99–112.

Todd, A. W., Horner, R. H., Sugai, G., & Colvin, G. (1999). Individualizing schoolwide discipline for students with chronic problem behaviors: A team approach. *Effective School Practices, 17,* 72–82.

Walker, H. M., Colvin, G., & Ramsey, E. (1995). *Antisocial behavior in schools: Strategies and best practices.* Pacific Grove, CA: Brooks/Cole.

Action Editor: Tim Knoster

Urban Applications of School-Wide Positive Behavior Support:

Critical Issues and Lessons Learned

Jared S. Warren
University of Kansas

Hank M. Edmonson
Loyola University

Peter Griggs
Stephen R. Lassen
Amy McCart
Ann Turnbull
Wayne Sailor
University of Kansas

Abstract: Researchers and educators have recognized that typical school-wide approaches to discipline and the prevention and management of problem behavior are often insufficient to address the needs of many students in inner-city schools with high base rates of problem behavior. This article outlines critical issues and lessons learned in the planning and implementation of effective and self-sustaining Positive Behavior Support (PBS) efforts in inner-city schools. Among these issues are methods for the facilitation of school–university partnerships, the incorporation of PBS into existing comprehensive school improvement efforts, the maintenance of school-wide PBS efforts, and the formalization of exit strategies and arrangements for subsequent technical assistance. The importance of service integration, family support, youth development, and community development are emphasized in ensuring the effectiveness and sustainability of school-wide PBS efforts in inner-city settings.

Kevin is proud of having accomplished his long-standing goal of passing the sixth grade. This is a significant achievement when one considers that he is the first member of his immediate family to do so. While discussing the family's history of economic and social disadvantage, Kevin's mother remarked, "I wouldn't know what to do with a life that wasn't filled with chaos." Living in an inner-city neighborhood surrounded by poverty, violence, crime, drugs, and gang activity, Kevin has proven relatively adaptive. In spite of numerous life challenges and limited opportunities, Kevin carries high hopes of rising above the disadvantages that characterize his community. Some of Kevin's teachers, however, express little sympathy for his life circumstances as they describe the severity and chronicity of his problem behavior at school. "He needs some serious help," they say, "but so do a hundred other kids at this school."

Cases similar to Kevin's are all too familiar to educators in some urban settings. In inner-city communities characterized by poverty, violence, and disadvantage, schools are met with the challenge of accomplishing their educational goals in the face of many adversities beyond their immediate control. The challenge to schools, as stated by the Car-negie Council Task Force on Education of Young Adolescents (1989), appears especially daunting for schools in disadvantaged communities: "School systems are not responsible for meeting every need of their students. But where the need directly affects learning, the school must meet the challenge" (p. 61). In recent years, a number of inner-city schools have made efforts to address behavioral challenges that impede the learning process through the school-wide application of positive behavior support (PBS). Through the collaborative efforts of educators, researchers, families, and community partners, a number of valuable lessons have been learned that hold important implications for the planning and implementation of school-wide PBS in inner-city schools. This article reviews these important lessons and examines other critical issues relevant to the ways in which urban schools approach systems-level factors that contribute to problem behavior.

Positive behavior support includes a broad range of systemic and individualized strategies for achieving important social and learning outcomes while preventing problem behavior. PBS is intended to enhance quality of life and minimize/prevent problem behavior through the rational integration of (a) valued outcomes, (b) behavioral and biomedical science, (c) empirically supported procedures, and (d) systems change (Carr et al., 2002). School-wide PBS interventions are employed at a number of levels to address the continuum of support required by all students. Universal interventions are used on a school-wide level (i.e., all students participate), whereas specialized interventions are employed for targeted groups and individual students who require more intensive supports (see Figure 1; Lewis & Sugai, 1999; Sugai & Horner, 1999; Walker et al., 1996).

Universal interventions are geared toward primary prevention by including all students. These supports help promote a positive climate and a culture of competence within the school by shifting the focus from exclusively punitive disciplinary approaches to more positive approaches that acknowledge appropriate behavior. These approaches are tailored to the needs and strengths of school systems but typically share a number of core components, including the establishment of a team to guide the school's PBS efforts; the definition of school-wide expectations; the provision of direct instruction to students on behavioral expectations; the establishment of effective systems to acknowledge appropriate behavior and address problem behavior; and the regular use of data to plan, monitor, and evaluate interventions (Colvin, 1991; Colvin, Kameenui, & Sugai, 1993; Cotton, 1990; Lewis & Sugai, 1999; Lewis, Sugai, & Colvin, 1998; Taylor-Greene et al., 1997; Todd, Horner, Sugai, & Sprague, 1999). For schools in which the majority of students demonstrate mild or no problem behavior, universal approaches are typically successful in achieving significant decreases in overall problem behavior within the school and reinforcing a positive school climate (Colvin et al., 1993; Lewis et al., 1998; Taylor-Greene et al., 1997). These improvements in turn provide opportunities for increased attention to students with more chronic and severe problem behavior.

Group interventions (secondary prevention) may subsequently be designed for students at risk for problem behavior and for whom universal supports are insufficient. These interventions are often conducted in individual classroom settings or in other specific settings in the school where a need for improved behavior has been identified (e.g., lunchroom, hallways). These may include more specialized instruction and practice of school expectations as they apply to the setting in question, specific skills training for students, modification of group contingencies, or other interventions based on the patterns of problem behavior observed (Hawken & Horner, 2001; Lewis & Sugai, 1999; Lewis et al., 1998).

Finally, students for whom universal and group interventions are insufficient may be referred for increased individual support (tertiary prevention). As with other forms of PBS, the objective of individual support is not only to decrease the frequency of problem behavior but also to improve the overall quality of life of the student and those in-

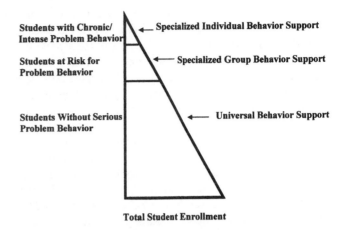

Figure 1. Levels of positive behavior support.
Note. Adapted from material in "Effective Behavior Support: A Systems Approach to Proactive School-wide Management," by T. J. Lewis and G. Sugai, 1999, *Focus on Exceptional Children, 31*(6), pp. 1–24. Copyright 1999 by Love Publishing. Adapted with permission.

volved in the student's life. Using behavioral assessments to generate and test hypotheses related to the function of problem behavior, individual PBS interventions focus on the development of individualized behavior support plans that attempt to address the multiple factors that contribute to problem behavior (Foster-Johnson & Dunlap, 1993; Horner, O'Neill, & Flannery, 1993; Larson & Maag, 1998; Lewis & Sugai, 1999).

Through the effective use of these three levels of support, we expect that schools will be able to adequately address the range of problem behavior that impedes the learning process and that all students will be provided with the support necessary to succeed in school. School-wide PBS efforts have resulted in decreases in problem behavior in a variety of contexts in both elementary schools (Lewis et al., 1998; Scott, 2001; Todd et al., 1999) and middle schools (Colvin et al., 1993; Taylor-Greene et al., 1997). However, few studies have evaluated applications of school-wide PBS in urban schools characterized by severe poverty, community violence, and high base rates of problem behavior. As a result, the bulk of previous research may not adequately take into account the systems-level challenges inherent in some communities that place limitations on the effectiveness of "typical" school-wide PBS interventions.

Along with his peers, Kevin was introduced to the school's "Steps to Success" program, in which the school's expectations (be responsible, be respectful, be ready to learn, be cooperative, and be safe) were defined and taught to all students. Teachers began systematically acknowledging appropriate behavior through "positive behavior tickets," which were given to students and could be entered into a drawing for special prizes and privileges. Kevin and a small group of other students were chosen as case studies for whom intensive individualized supports would be provided, although teachers indicated that a large proportion of students in the school were also in need of intensive support. A functional behavioral assessment was conducted and a behavior support plan was developed for Kevin, and considerable efforts on the part of researchers, school personnel, family members, and community partners were brought to bear in the development of interventions to address problem behavior as well as the quality of life of each of the case study students and their families.

Initial efforts with Kevin were encouraging. Quality-of-life interventions appeared especially relevant in addressing the larger family- and systems-level issues that influenced behavioral outcomes at school. For example, the family had no transportation, no telephone, and no health insurance, and they relied on one adult's minimum-wage income to support four adults and two minors living together in a tiny rental house. In addition to behavioral interventions at school, efforts were aimed at linking the family to resources within the community, and opportunities were made available to secure health insurance, transportation, potential employment, mental health services, and needed material resources. Regrettably, modest improvements in behavior were not maintained, as serious breakdowns in established community supports and severe family stressors seemed to provide continual setbacks. Toward the end of Kevin's eighth-grade year, his home, including all the family's possessions, was destroyed in a fire. Kevin's behavior deteriorated significantly after this catastrophic event, as depression, anger, and social withdrawal increased. Kevin concluded the school year by being suspended for the final weeks of school, failing the eighth-grade, and being socially promoted to high school against his family's wishes.

In most schools, the severe challenges highlighted by this case vignette are fairly rare. In some inner-city schools, they are the rule. Kotlowitz (1998), in describing the disparity between the "two Americas" (suburban vs. inner-city America), used the imagery of a "deep and wide chasm" (p. 4). Similarly, the number and severity of challenges faced by many inner-city schools are very different from schools in more advantaged communities. Youth in the inner city are often raised in stressful and unstable environments where poverty, poor health care, crime, lack of employment opportunities, and fragmented community services can combine to create a culture of chaos and despair (Wang, Haertel, & Walberg, 1994). For students who face dangers walking through their own neighborhood to get to school, being "ready to learn" as they walk into the classroom is not likely to be a high priority.

These stressors may combine to create a school culture in which noncompliance is the norm and where peer reinforcement leads to students' acceptance and expectation of disruptive behavior in their peers. This pattern is supported by data from inner-city schools with which our team has worked. For example, in the first school in which

we intervened, 42% of the student body had received at least five office discipline referrals for problem behavior during the previous year, and 81% had received at least one discipline referral during the previous year (Warren et al., in press). These data suggest that the proportions of students with varying levels of problem behavior in inner-city schools may differ significantly from estimates in the "triangle" model previously proposed (Sugai & Horner, 1999). For example, data provided by Horner and colleagues at the University of Oregon (R. H. Horner, personal communication, June 12, 2001) indicated that for 26 middle schools (15,713 students) in which data were being collected, 76% of students received zero or one office discipline referrals during the school year (students without serious problem behavior), 15% received from two to five office referrals (at-risk students), and 9% received six or more office referrals (students with chronic/intense problem behavior; see Figure 2).

In contrast, data collected from the three inner-city middle schools (1,971 students) with which our team has worked yield very different proportions. In these inner-city middle schools, 38% of students received 0 or 1 office discipline referrals, 30% received from 2 to 5 office referrals, 21% received from 6 to 14 office referrals, and 11% received 15 or more office referrals. These data support the notion that inner-city schools differ from most schools not only in the severity of problem behavior in students but also in the frequency with which it occurs.

Through observing firsthand the severe challenges facing the students and families for whom we provided individualized supports and recognizing the intensity and frequency of problem behavior in the school as a whole, we began to appreciate the monumental task facing inner-city schools in their primary mission to educate students. The realization that hundreds of students in each inner-city school likely required the level of individualized support that we were then providing to a handful of students was sobering. Naturally, we do not expect inner-city schools to be responsible for resolving poverty, crime, unemployment, fragmented community supports, and other problems in their communities. Nevertheless, our team's experiences with PBS approaches in inner-city schools in recent years have yielded a number of valuable lessons that are applicable to future school-wide PBS efforts in urban settings. The following pages highlight some of our experiences with the school-wide implementation of PBS in inner-city schools, provide insight into potential reasons for the disparity between suburban and inner-city schools, and present a discussion of lessons learned and suggestions for future research in urban applications of school-wide PBS.

School-Wide PBS in Wyandotte County

Although the issues presented in this article come from our experience working in several middle schools in Wyandotte County, Kansas, the following case study describes

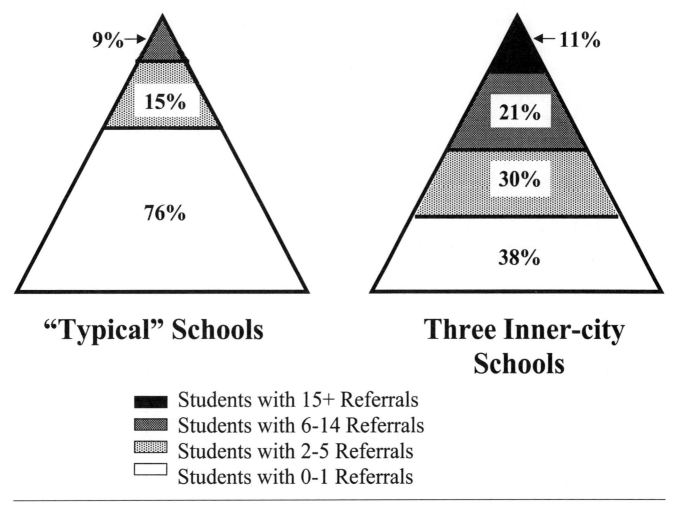

"Typical" Schools   Three Inner-city Schools

■ Students with 15+ Referrals
▨ Students with 6-14 Referrals
▦ Students with 2-5 Referrals
☐ Students with 0-1 Referrals

Figure 2. Proportion of students with varying numbers of office discipline referrals in "typical" versus inner-city middle schools.

some of our experiences in the first school in which we worked.

UNIVERSITY/SCHOOL DISTRICT PARTNERSHIP

The research reported here began with funding from the University of Kansas (KU) portion of the national Rehabilitation Research and Training Center (RRTC) awarded to the University of South Florida. The Kansas research proposed a partnership between the Beach Center on Families and Disability at KU with the Unified School District (USD) 500 in Kansas City and Wyandotte County. The partnership agreement solicited the participation of four middle schools in the district over a 5-year period of project funding (now in Year 4). Support for the ongoing KU/USD 500 partnership to establish school-wide PBS has now expanded to include elementary schools and is funded from a variety of federal, state, and local sources.

SCHOOL DEMOGRAPHICS

We begin with a case study of an inner-city middle school, the first school with which we began our research partner-

ship. As reported by Edmonson (2000), the average yearly enrollment for the school (Grades 6–8) was 724 (1997–1999 school years). Ethnic representation of students in the school was reported as 40% African American, 32% Hispanic, 20% White, 8% Asian or Pacific Islander, and .001% Native American. As a comparison, data indicate that for the state as a whole, approximately 81% of students are White, 8% Hispanic, 6% Asian or Pacific Islander, 4% African American, and 3% Native American (based on the average of 1997–2000). In addition, 90% of the students at this school qualified for free or reduced lunch, whereas the state's percentage of students receiving free or reduced lunch was 31%.

ESTABLISHING "BUY-IN"

Although administrators had agreed to allow our team to work with the school, our attempts to begin school-wide PBS efforts were initially met with skepticism or were generally ignored by many teachers. We learned that approximately 42 programs were already in place in the school that related to student behavior in some manner. Given the large number of initiatives already underway at the school, teachers' initial negative reaction to PBS as "one more thing" was not surprising. As a result, teacher "buy-in" had to be earned incrementally in a number of ways. As a whole, teachers and administrators became more receptive to implementing universal and group supports after our team spent nearly a year building rapport and becoming more familiar with the school's unique culture and, most important, after we achieved positive results with several students for whom individual supports were being provided. Later, the three major components of PBS (universal, group, and individual supports) were used as a framework for understanding what the school already had in place and how efforts could be streamlined. This approach served to increase coordination of resources and decrease duplication of efforts and allowed teachers to see how a PBS perspective served to make their jobs easier, resulting in increased teacher buy-in.

PLANNING FOR SUSTAINABILITY

A crucial component of assuring the sustainability of the intervention was the securing of resources for the school to implement the PBS model. Resources that were identified included staff development for teachers; release time for planning and gathering and organizing data; and coordinating services. The funding for these activities came from several sources. Staff development dollars were identified for providing training and release time for teachers and staff members. The local mental health agency provided "in-kind" coordination of services as a part of a grant that was already in operation. The district's prevention services provided funding for teacher coverage. Some funds were directed from Title I school improvement for this effort. A local business partner also contributed.

Another strategy for improving the likelihood that the school would maintain the intervention was the attempt to incorporate PBS strategies into their plans and requirements for accreditation. As "citizenship" had previously been chosen as one of the school improvement goals, school-wide PBS (called "Steps to Success" by school personnel) was incorporated into the school improvement plan. This was an important milestone in embedding PBS strategies into the school, as the citizenship goal provided the objectives, strategies, resources, and evaluation components necessary to systematically internalize the initial stages of school-wide behavior support. This report and associated data subsequently became the major portion of the school's accreditation report under "school climate."

COMMUNITY SUPPORT STRATEGIES

An important component of any school improvement plan is to have the participation of stakeholders from the community. It seemed apparent that interventions at this level would be most effective in dealing with factors outside of school that contributed to students' success or failure. Both the comprehensive school improvement plan and the state's school improvement guidelines called for increased parent participation. The participation of parents was considered extremely important but was found lacking. The school improvement team, therefore, began to invite parents to their meetings simply to share data and review their input about what was going on in the school that affected their children. The team's next question was, "Who else would benefit from the improvement of behavioral and academic outcomes for students in our school's feeder pattern?" This list grew as time progressed and included, among other participants, local business owners, residents of the community, the federal district's congressman, local religious organizations and churches, school district personnel, regional prevention services personnel, and representatives from the local juvenile justice programs. Representatives from the other 41 programs onsite at the school were also were invited.

The purpose of these meetings was to (a) review current data, (b) identify other data sources that were needed, and (c) identify and solidify members of the support team. In this case, the unit of analysis was the entire school community. The data that were selected were those that could be considered setting events for problems at school (Horner et al., 1993). Through partnerships with the regional prevention services agency, other relevant data were also identified, including the results of surveys given to sixth, eighth, tenth, and twefth graders throughout the county (Graves & Schalansky, 1999). Data were aggregated to identify both protective and risk factors for citizens of the county. For Fiscal Year 1999, the number one risk factor for the county was community disorganization. Conversely, opportunities for involvement in the community were identified as the number one protective factor. This led to the convergence of three interrelated areas: comprehensive positive behavior support, school improvement, and a "community school" approach to community setting events (Lawson & Sailor, 2000).

The next stages involved the development of small-group problem-solving teams in the three target areas, identified through summarization of data covering extended day services for students, mentoring, and community support. Each of these target areas addressed the major setting events that seemed to contribute to the most frequent behavior problems at school.

Via school-wide surveys, teachers identified that most problem behaviors in the school were maintained by attention and avoidance of difficult academic tasks. As a result, the group believed that increased access to mentoring adults would "fill the tank" for students who were low on much needed positive attention. Concurrently, extended day programs would provide the opportunity for academic needs to be addressed in more targeted programs. These extended day services would be tied to the resources of the school (e.g., diagnostic reading programs, teacher expertise).

Community support team members addressed the need for increased access to community resources and activities. For instance, it was pointed out that if students wanted to go swimming during the summer, they would have to drive to the adjacent county (considerably more affluent). This team began to focus on increasing students' access to activities that would improve their quality of life. In all, the community support meetings offered the opportunity for discussing school and community goals, examining data from which a variety of interventions would be based, bringing together diverse groups and agencies from the community to address needs of the school (and needs of the community that affect the school), and reinforcing the sense of shared responsibility to the community by every member present.

Although the strategies described (establishing buy-in, planning for sustainability, facilitating community supports) are inherent to PBS as applied in any setting, these aspects of the intervention were judged to be particularly critical for achieving lasting positive change in this case study. The increased importance of these strategies was underscored by many of the challenges inherent in this inner-city school (i.e., school personnel already feeling overwhelmed with previous initiatives, high rates of staff turnover, high base rates of problem behavior, very little perceived support from parents and community members), which are likely to be shared by schools in many urban settings.

STUDY OUTCOMES

As reported by Warren et al. (in press), the school witnessed a number of encouraging outcomes during the 1st year of full school-wide PBS implementation (Year 2 of the study). For example, the total number of office discipline referrals decreased by 20% from Year 1 to Year 2, "time-outs" decreased by 23%, and, most notable, short-term suspensions decreased by 57%. Reports from teachers and administrators confirmed that the combination of universal, group, and individual supports made a positive impact on the school climate and student behavior in general (Warren et al., in press).

Although these data were very encouraging, several negative trends began to appear the following year (Year 3), when our team began the transition from a direct intervention role to a more consultative role. During several months of Year 3, disciplinary referrals exceeded the reduction in Year 2, and at least 2 months exceeded baseline. For example, in the 3rd year, office referrals were up 32% from October of the 2nd year (602 and 469, respectively). Also, the number of disciplinary referrals for the month of October was 20% higher during the 3rd year than during baseline (613 and 493, respectively).

We identified two primary reasons for the increase in office referrals: the school's implementation of another intervention involving increased punishment and inconsistency in the application of universal supports. As reported earlier, there were at least 42 other programs in place at the time of initial intervention, with more to follow. One programmatic addition, which was implemented by the school outside of the PBS framework, came in the form of required school uniforms starting in Year 3 of our involvement. Students who frequently did not wear their uniform would earn an office referral. At least 15% of the office referrals for Year 3, from August to March, were a direct result of students' not wearing uniforms. Teachers and administrators also reported that the actual number of referrals that could be attributted to the uniforms could be higher. For example, staff reported that when students were out of uniform, they were more likely to be noncompliant and/or disruptive during class. Some of the staff members also reported that conflict regarding uniform compliance led to additional power struggles and subsequent disciplinary referrals. Staff members were in the process of revising their dress-code policies during the latter part of the 3rd year as a result of these data.

A second area of concern reflected a management issue. One of the vice principals requested to be responsible for the school-wide daily drawings for prizes. Unfortunately, the increase in problems associated with school uniforms and other management-related issues took time away from her ability to make sure the daily drawings occurred. As a result, students had less frequent access to identified reinforcers and positive attention from peers and adults from these daily drawings than had previously been provided.

Critical Issues and Lessons Learned

STRUCTURAL ARRANGEMENTS FOR SCHOOL-WIDE PBS

Except for full-service schools and community schools (Lawson & Sailor, 2000), most schools have no formal structures for linking their mission and functions with families and with community service systems. School-wide PBS applications offer the opportunity to begin to establish this expanded structural arrangement by recruiting and implementing a school/family/community oversight committee to offer advice on the process of, and provide an overall sense of direction for, implementation as it affects the three groupings of stakeholders.

It is our opinion that the early establishment of an oversight committee dedicated to the success of the implementation effort will help anticipate and provide a buffer against the "winds of change" that constantly blow across urban schools and that can interact negatively with PBS outcomes. It is important that such oversight committees be ethnically diverse and representative of the patterns of students that make up the population of the school. Diversity on the oversight committee provides the added value of helping ensure that PBS applications are carried out in culturally competent and sensitive ways and that special attention is paid to diverse language backgrounds where needed.

SCHOOL–UNIVERSITY PARTNERSHIPS

The typical relationships that exist between inner-city schools and universities are likely to be insufficient to sustain interventions of the scope and magnitude of school-wide PBS. A substantive systems-change effort of that level requires developing a relationship and joint planning time prior to developing a formal partnership agreement.

Traditional university–school relationships advance because schools have a need for university resources: personnel training and staff development, research-to-practice information, and access to course credit and certification for personnel. Likewise, universities typically need practicum training sites for students and access for research investigations. However, even when schools do take advantage of university resources, efforts at systems-change are often met with considerable resistance by some school personnel. For example, implementing school-wide PBS is likely to imply a change in the culture of the school. Such a change is unlikely to be realized in the absence of significant support from a large sector of the professional and administrative staff of the school.

Inner-city schools are very likely to have site as well as central office administrators who are highly motivated to incorporate evidence-based practices into their schools, particularly when there is evidence that such practices have a high probability of increasing pupil scores on standardized tests of literacy and math skills. Teachers, however, will be less enthusiastic and may even be resistant to adopting new practices if those practices are perceived to be adding "one more thing" to their workloads. The partnership development must confront teacher perception of workload requirements from the outset.

The premise of school-wide PBS is a change of school culture, moving away from coercion as a means of managing difficult and off-task behavior and toward building positive relationships and teaching appropriate responses to school and classroom expectations. As such, it represents a shift from exclusionary practices to inclusionary practices. For example, teachers who are accustomed to referring students out of class for disruptive behavior would, under school-wide PBS, be expected to manage these problems in the classroom. If teachers perceive this change as removing from them their only source of control over students (referral) rather than discarding one practice in favor of a better one, then the enterprise will likely fail for lack of teacher acceptance.

One reason teachers may choose to support PBS is that keeping their students in the classroom can lead to increased student achievement. Student progress as measured by standardized achievement tests is one of the most frequently used measures of the effectiveness of teachers and school resources. One of the best predictors of pupil progress is actual time in instruction. If teachers can manage students' behavior with inclusionary practices, their efforts are likely to be rewarded with improved evidence of pupil progress. If teachers agree at the outset with the premise and are willing to be trained in inclusionary practices, then the basis for a formal partnership is greatly increased. University personnel may need to present skeptical teachers (many inner-city teachers will tell you they've "seen it all") with evidence of school-wide PBS efficacy in schools like theirs. Published reports, videotapes, and CDs are helpful, but our experience has shown us that the most successful initial professional development activity has been to feature presentations by teachers and administrators from similar schools that have undergone school-wide PBS and have become inclusionary school cultures. Inner-city teachers and administrators trust those whom they perceive to be operating under circumstances similar to their own. This usually does not include university faculty.

School-wide PBS implies not only a partnership between the university and the school but also a partnership among the school, its families, and its community service-provider systems. Traditional school–university arrangements do not include important stakeholders such as parents and members of community after-school programs. Teachers and parents may initially feel uncomfortable learning new practices in the company of each other. In inner-city areas, where exclusionary practices have been the norm, family members may feel alienated from the school. Sometimes schools make families feel that they have failed as parents because their children have failed academically or socially. School-wide PBS, however, implies that school personnel, community agency staff, and families can engage in conjoint problem-solving efforts where needed, with each member bringing valuable knowledge and experience to the table. Arranging initial professional development activities to include family and community members from the outset, and to the maximum extent possible, is likely to build a stronger foundation for a formal partnership.

The basis for a formal school–university partnership to achieve school-wide PBS as the outcome is in place when (a) a school, as well as the involved families and community services, is motivated and all or most of the relevant stakeholders understand and believe in the required practices and procedures and (b) a qualified and respected team from the university is willing provide requisite professional development activities to achieve valued outcomes. The formalized partnership's agreement can be written at that point and should include each party's relevant expectations. These expectations are likely to include (a) persons responsible for the coordination of professional development from both the school and the university, (b) the means of implementing professional development activities, (c) the overall length of time of the partnership agreement, (d) the evaluative measures against which the partnership will assess its progress, and (e) the process by which decisions will be made to implement the partnership agreement over time.

At one of our school–university partnership sites, an assistant principal was selected to be the school's coordinator. The university team selected a doctoral student in special education to be its coordinator. The two coordinators worked closely to carry out the terms of the partnership agreement. This school–university agreement took place over a 2-year period. Professional development activities included school-wide inservice days as well as in-school and in-classroom exercises conducted over time. Team members from the university worked within the school team structures and used actual student "cases" selected by the teams, both to engage in joint problem solving and to teach methods of functional behavioral assessment and PBS plan development to team members.

PBS IN THE CONTEXT OF COMPREHENSIVE SCHOOL REFORM

Urban schools are targets of opportunity for entrepreneurs, reformers, grant-getters and government experts, all of whom have ideas for improving student progress. In one of our urban partnership schools, a district administrator explained that we would be under the constraint of making sure that our evaluative data on the application of school-wide PBS would not in any way "interact with or contaminate" the ongoing evaluative database of the district's comprehensive school improvement (CSI) model. This model, which was financed by a local philanthropic foundation as well as the Office of Educational Research and Improvement of the U.S. Department of Education, had a vested interest in positive results reflected in its ongoing internal and external evaluation studies. We elected to seek permission to be nested within the overall CSI treatment model, as a part of the school-wide discipline program at our partnership schools.

By becoming a component of the CSI program, we allowed the CSI developer, an out-of-state education professor, to take credit for any positive increments in the CSI evaluations that might be traceable to our partnership efforts. We also agreed that any negative results would lead to our early departure. We concurred, as a local university, that it was in our own best interest to assist the overall efforts of the CSI developer in our local urban district. In fact, we had confidence in the model and were committed to helping it succeed. If we had chosen to work outside of the CSI model, it is unlikely that the partnership would

have succeeded. We would have been regarded by the schools either as in competition with a program to which they were committed or as adding one more thing to a full plate.

INTERACTION OF PBS AND OTHER INTERVENTIONS

Results from school-wide PBS are likely to be highly interactive with other comprehensive interventions undertaken by the school after PBS has been initiated. For example, as mentioned earlier, one of our partnership schools undertook a major new dress-code policy midway through the term of the school–university partnership. Under the new policy, all students were required to wear uniforms. The authority for and guidelines under which the new policy was implemented, in its 1st year, were undertaken outside of the infrastructure for school-wide PBS. The interactive result was to produce a neat reversal in an otherwise negative (i.e., downward sloping) trend in indicators for exclusionary practices resulting from PBS. Dress-code infractions were treated under policy guidelines as grounds for exclusion from the classroom until the infraction could be corrected. In retrospect, the partnership implementers should have taken steps to ensure that dress-code violations were treated with PBS measures rather than constituting exceptions to the school-wide application.

The administration of another partnership school decided to put into place a novel procedure that one of the administrators had learned about at a conference. This procedure called for the operation of a "reflection room," where classroom teachers could send students to reflect on the reasons that they were excluded from the classroom. Some school personnel felt that this new measure would be consistent with PBS practices because the student would in effect be engaging in a self-conducted functional behavioral assessment and PBS plan development activity while in the reflection room. However, the practice served to suppress the otherwise downward trend of measures of exclusionary practices.

These examples also help illustrate the importance of helping schools truly adopt a PBS mentality in which any number of initiatives can be coordinated to achieve identified goals. Ideally, in these examples, administrators' decisions to implement new strategies should have been made under a PBS framework in which the strategies were adopted by the school as a whole, developed in response to an identified problem, and systematically evaluated. Regrettably, some administrators and teachers in one school continued to view PBS as just one more initiative, rather than a system that incorporates and enhances all behavioral efforts within the school. Schools must be trained and supported in such a way that they understand that multiple interventions need not be viewed as competing against each other when they are implemented within the PBS system.

NO QUICK FIXES

School-wide PBS applied to inner-city, urban schools through university–school partnerships is a long-term commitment for everyone involved. The systems-change element of moving a school culture from coercion to support requires a significant investment in time and resources. We initially estimated that a minimum of 1 year of intensive on-site support would be required to begin to initiate the longitudinal momentum to sustain school-wide PBS as the basis for an inclusionary culture of support for students. However, given the complex systemic challenges facing some inner-city schools, a multiyear plan may be necessary in order to ensure an effective transition.

Our key strategies have been to work within the school site's team structures; to provide ongoing staff and professional development activities in a longitudinal fashion; to share and extend knowledge and practices through an oversight committee; to assist schools in effectively responding to the school site's data summaries on a regular basis in making short- and long-term policy decisions; and to use individual and targeted group supports as teaching vehicles to extend PBS practices across the entire school. The benefit to the university from these sustained partnership efforts is significant. Putting together the mosaic of individual, group, and universal support strategies provides many opportunities for interdisciplinary research and for teacher and other interprofessional training experiences.

When the intensive intervention phase of the partnership activity has ended, it is important that the university not be seen as abandoning its commitment to the process. There is a long history of university students and faculty using urban schools to gather data for various research projects and then disseminating the results in the higher education community, with no information on the studies finding its way back to the schools. University students often use inner-city schools as training sites and then seek and take jobs in more well-financed areas of the city, leaving inner-city schools with vacancies for certified personnel.

Our partnership model emphasizes an intervention phase at each site that is set to run for a predetermined length of time. In our studies, this period has lasted from 1 to 1½ years, but a longer period may be required in some schools to ensure that the PBS approach becomes solidly embedded within the school's philosophy of discipline. Following the intervention phase, there should be a second technical assistance phase of involvement, also set for a predetermined length of time. Both phases of activity are spelled out in a written agreement delineating the terms and expectations of the work of the partnership from the outset. For the university, this provides a clearly defined and agreed-upon exit strategy so that resources are not drained at a single site when there are multiple site requests. For the schools, the agreement helps focus personnel on the constraints imposed by the passage of time and keeps progress on a steady track.

ROLE OF THE DISTRICT CENTRAL OFFICE

Whatever is done at a single school through an urban school–university partnership arrangement will reverberate through, and have repercussions for, all schools in that region of the district, and perhaps throughout the district. There is heavy competition for scarce resources, and many turf battles are underway in urban districts at any given time. If a partnership arrangement at one site is perceived as a significant resource that other sites are not being offered, then requests to extend similar arrangements to other schools will soon be forthcoming. This is particularly the case when word gets out in the district that partnership efforts are leading to demonstrably improved pupil progress and reduced student social problems. The question then arises as to a rational basis for "going to scale."

Because most universities have limited resources with which to implement partnerships to accomplish school-wide PBS, careful thought will need to be given to a plan for expansion within the district. School-wide PBS applications can result in immediate positive outcomes, even in early stages of implementation. In many inner-city schools, positive recognition by school personnel for small increments of social and academic progress by students often turns out to be just about the only positive self-esteem building experience those students receive. Many will respond in dramatic ways. From the outset, university and district personnel should plan how to proceed when things go well at initial sites. From the initial perspective of district administrators, it is likely that school-wide PBS is just one more intervention that may or may not make a difference. District administrators are supportive of efforts to test new, promising programs as long as these are consistent with district and/or state initiatives for which they are held responsible (e.g., CSI models).

We approached the scale issue by responding to a district request to get involved with a particular school that was considered to be at risk for low performance. Through this willingness to engage district priorities, we were able to secure approval for an orderly sequence of interventions over time at multiple school sites through a prearranged site intervention plan. We were also able to secure a state commitment to help support the long-range strategy through use of Title I funding from the state to establish a service center for math and literacy curriculum enhancement, as a part of the broader university–district partnership arrangement.

The most recent piece of the broader puzzle, which is under development as this is being written, is a partnership with the state to develop a mechanism to enable the use of Medicaid dollars to fund school-wide PBS efforts throughout the state. This mechanism, which will be pilot tested in an urban partnership, will enable the university–school partnership to tap federal health-care financing to offset the costs of implementation of school-wide PBS. This partnership will allow PBS applications to be reimbursable as a school health service expense under state Medicaid regulations.

Recommendations

In our experience, the unique challenges faced by many inner-city schools often result in a level of problem behavior for which "typical" school-wide PBS strategies may be insufficient. Although these strategies are vital to making significant improvements in school climate and student discipline, often progress must be made in improving systemic factors before school-wide PBS strategies can be expected to maintain success. The combination of universal, group, and individual supports may only scratch the surface of addressing problem behavior in some schools. With this problem in mind, Turnbull, Allen, and Nelson (2001) recommend the following vital systemic approaches that may help set the stage for successful school-wide PBS implementation in school settings where levels of problem behavior may at first appear insurmountable:

1. Effective service integration must become a reality in schools (Lawson & Sailor, 2000; Sailor, 1996). By providing truly coordinated and/or co-located services for education, mental health, public health, transportation, childcare, social services, recreation, and other community services, families will have greater access to needed supports. In addition, service integration will provide a greater opportunity for service providers to work together to provide a coordinated constellation of supports that best meets the needs of the family.
2. Coordinated efforts for family support must be increased to ensure that resources, services, and information are provided in family-friendly ways. Schools can provide increased support to families by building on family strengths, honoring family preferences, and considering the whole family as the unit of support rather than the individual student.
3. School–family–community partnerships must provide an increased focus on youth development by including young people as partners in the decision-making process, developing their assets and talents in settings both outside and inside the school, and providing opportunities for youth to serve as resources to their communities.

4. Students, families, schools, and other partners must accept a joint responsibility for community development. Naturally, schools are more successful when the communities in which they are located are successful, and vice versa. All partners must focus on strengthening the social networks, economic viability, and physical infrastructure of the community, which will subsequently influence behavioral and educational outcomes in students both directly and indirectly.

As noted by Turnbull et al. (2001), the concepts of service integration, family support, youth development, and community development are not new by any means but have yet to be effectively integrated together in a community setting. Truly, the educational and behavioral outcomes of the effective implementation of these systems-level components has yet to be realized, but the effect is likely to be great. At the very least, it is anticipated that increased attention to these components will lead to school-wide PBS interventions that are more successful and sustainable in inner-city communities.

Kevin remains enrolled in high school at the present time, although his attendance is sporadic and his problem behavior has resulted in numerous suspensions from his new school. Individual supports continue to be offered by university personnel, but his teachers, whose patience with Kevin is apparently exhausted, have been extremely reluctant to invest time and effort in PBS strategies that have proven successful in previous settings. Requests have been made of the school to screen Kevin for special education eligibility, but these requests have essentially been refused, with the explanation that Kevin must first attend class regularly (and not get kicked out) for teachers to evaluate his educational needs and learning style.

The lessons outlined in this article, when effectively applied, could hold many positive implications for Kevin, his family, and ultimately all residents of this inner-city community. For example, the issue of establishing teacher buy-in will be essential in working with those who are currently reluctant to implement PBS strategies with Kevin. This may require strengthening the school–university partnership, providing examples of other teachers who have "been there" to show the usefulness of PBS approaches to skeptics, and helping the school better understand the relationship between behavior and academic outcomes. In addition, a truly integrated system of services would be extremely beneficial to addressing many of the social service needs required by Kevin and his family and would decrease the negative impact of economic, social, and psychological factors that prevent Kevin from coming to school "ready to learn." In contrast to actions by the school system that have served to alienate the family (such as the decision to promote Kevin to high school against his family's wishes), improved family support efforts would provide Kevin's family with increased incentive for cooperating with the school and not seeing teachers as "the enemy." Likewise, increased attention to youth and community development would result in increases in individual and community pride and improvements in Kevin's overall quality of life. The task of addressing many of these issues may appear daunting. However, it is clear that for Kevin, and many others like him, the positive impact of PBS strategies will not be sustainable unless important systemic factors are also addressed.

ABOUT THE AUTHORS

Jared S. Warren, MA, is a doctoral candidate in clinical child psychology at the University of Kansas. His interests include school-based prevention and intervention strategies and stress and resilience in youth. Hank M. Edmonson, PhD, is the special education program director at Loyola University of Chicago. His research activities include teacher preparation, community school development, school improvement, and positive behavior support in urban schools. Peter Griggs, MEd, is a research associate with the Beach Center on Disability at the University of Kansas. His interests are in positive behavior support, effective instruction for persons with severe disabilities, and systems change. Stephen R. Lassen, MA, is pursuing a doctoral degree in clinical child psychology at the University of Kansas and has interests in the prevention and treatment of antisocial behavior in children and adolescents. Amy McCart, MA, is a project coordinator with the Beach Center on Disability at the University of Kansas and is currently completing her doctoral degree in the Department of Special Education at KU. Ann Turnbull, PhD, is co-director of the Beach Center on Disability and a professor in the Department of Special Education at the University of Kansas. Her research focuses on family quality of life, family–professional partnerships, and positive behavior support. Wayne Sailor, PhD, is a senior scientist with the Beach Center on Disability and a professor in the Department of Special Education at the University of Kansas. Dr. Sailor's focus of interests are full integration of students with severe disabilities through school restructuring processes and service integration strategies for health, social, and educational services for all children at the school site. Address: Wayne Sailor, Beach Center on Disability, University of Kansas, 3142 Haworth Hall, 1200 Sunnyside Ave., Lawrence, KS 66045-7534.

AUTHORS' NOTES

1. The preparation of this manuscript was supported by the NIDRR Rehabilitation Research and Training Center on Positive Behavioral Support Grant H133B980005 and the OSEP Technical Assistance Center on Positive Behavioral Interventions and Supports Grant H326S980003 from the U.S. Department of Education. No endorsement by any supporting agency should be inferred.

2. The authors express sincere appreciation to Shelly Beech, Lili Englebrick, Donna Wickham, Rachel Freeman, and Gwen Beegle for their contributions to this work through technical assistance, conceptual help, and direct implementation efforts.

REFERENCES

Carnegie Council Task Force on Education of Young Adolescents. (1989). *Turning points: Preparing American youth for the 21st century: The report of the Task Force on Education of Young Adolescents.* Washington, DC: Author.

Carr, E. G., Dunlap, G., Horner, R. H., Koegel, R. L., Turnbull, A. P., Sailor, W., et al. (2002). Positive behavior support: Evolution of an applied science. *Journal of Positive Behavior Interventions, 4,* 4–16, 20.

Colvin, G. (1991). *Procedures for establishing a proactive school-wide discipline plan.* Eugene: University of Oregon, College of Education.

Colvin, G., Kameenui, E. J., & Sugai, G. (1993). Reconceptualizing behavior management and school-wide discipline in general education. *Education and Treatment of Children, 16,* 361–381.

Cotton, K. (1990, December). Close-Up #9. Schoolwide and classroom discipline. *School Improvement Research Series,* 1–21.

Edmonson, H. (2000). A study of the process of the implementation of school reform in an urban middle school using positive behavioral support: "Not one more thing" (Doctoral Dissertation, University of Kansas, 2000). *Bell Howel,* 9998074.

Foster-Johnson, L., & Dunlap, G. (1993). Using functional assessment to develop effective, individualized interventions for challenging behaviors. *Teaching Exceptional Children, 25,* 44–50.

Graves, B., & Schalansky, J. (1999). *Connect Kansas: Supporting communities that care. Wyandotte County data and planning guide.* Topeka, KS: Department of Social and Rehabilitation Services.

Hawken, L. S., & Horner, R. H. (2001). *Evaluation of a targeted group intervention within a school-wide system of behavior support.* Manuscript submitted for publication.

Horner, R. H., O'Neill, R. E., & Flannery, K. B. (1993). Effective behavior support plans. In M. Snell (Ed.), *Instruction of persons with severe handicaps* (4th ed., pp. 184–214). Columbus, OH: Merrill.

Kotlowitz, A. (1998). Breaking the silence: Growing up in today's inner city. In H. I. McCubbin, E. A. Thompson, A. I. Thompson, & J. A. Futrell (Eds.), *Resiliency in African-American families* (pp. 3–15). Thousand Oaks, CA: Sage.

Larson, P. J., & Maag, J. W. (1998). Applying functional assessment in general education classrooms. *Remedial and Special Education, 19,* 338–349.

Lawson, H. A., & Sailor, W. (2000). Integrating services, collaborating, and developing connections with schools. *Focus on Exceptional Children, 33*(2), 1–22.

Lewis, T. J., & Sugai, G. (1999). Effective behavior support: A systems approach to proactive school-wide management. *Focus on Exceptional Children, 31*(6), 1–24.

Lewis, T. J., Sugai, G., & Colvin, G. (1998). Reducing problem behavior through a school-wide system of effective behavioral support: Investigation of a school-wide social skills training program and contextual interventions. *School Psychology Review, 27,* 446–459.

Sailor, W. (1996). New structures and systems change for comprehensive positive behavioral support. In L. K. Koegel, R. L. Koegel, & G. Dunlap (Eds.), *Positive behavioral support: Including people with difficult behavior in the community* (pp. 163–206). Baltimore: Brookes.

Scott, T. M. (2001). A schoolwide example of positive behavioral support. *Journal of Positive Behavior Interventions, 3,* 88–94.

Sugai, G., & Horner, R. H. (1999). Discipline and behavioral support: Practices, pitfalls, promises. *Effective School Practices, 17*(4), 10–22.

Taylor-Greene, S. D., Nelson, L., Longton, J., Gassman, T., Cohen, J., Swartz, J., et al. (1997). School-wide behavioral support: Starting the year off right. *Journal of Behavioral Education, 7,* 99–112.

Todd, A. W., Horner, R. H., Sugai, G., & Sprague, J. R. (1999). Effective behavior support: Strengthening school-wide systems through a team-based approach. *Effective School Practices, 17*(4), 23–27.

Turnbull, A., Allen, C., & Nelson, L. L. (2001, May). *Meeting the challenges of poverty in urban schools: Phase 2 of school-wide PBS.* Paper presented at the annual meeting of state positive behavior support trainers, Indianapolis, IN.

Walker, H. M., Horner, R. H., Sugai, G., Bullis, M., Sprague, J. R., Bricker, D., & Kaufman, M. J. (1996). Integrated approaches to preventing antisocial behavior patterns among school-age children and youth. *Journal of Emotional and Behavioral Disorders, 4,* 193–256.

Wang, M. C., Haertel, G. D., & Walberg, H. J. (1994). Educational resilience in inner cities. In M. C. Wang & E. W. Gordon (Eds.), *Educational resilience in inner-city America: Challenges and prospects* (pp. 45–72). Hillsdale, NJ: Erlbaum.

Warren, J. S., Edmonson, H. M., Turnbull, A. P., Sailor, W., Wickham, D., Griggs, P., & Beech, S. (in press). School-wide application of positive behavior support: Implementation and preliminary evaluation of PBS in an urban middle school. *Educational Psychology Review.*

Action Editor: Wayne Sailor

Positive Behavior Support:

A Proactive Strategy for Minimizing Behavior Problems in Urban Multicultural Youth

Cheryl A. Utley
*Schiefelbusch Institute for
Life Span Studies
The Juniper Gardens Children's Project
University of Kansas*

Elizabeth Kozleski
*National Institute for Urban
School Improvement
University of Colorado at Denver*

Anne Smith
*U.S. Office of Special
Education Programs
Washington, DC*

Ingrid L. Draper
*Urban Special Education
Leadership Collaborative
Education Development Center, Inc.
Newton, Massachusetts*

Abstract: The social–emotional needs of children in urban school communities place these students at risk for educational failure. For these children, successful teaching and learning models appear particularly complex because they must combine both multicultural approaches and effective positive behavior support (PBS) strategies that promote healthy, prosocial behaviors. This article examines trends in the racial disparity in exclusionary discipline procedures that impact the schooling experiences of urban children, presents a conceptual framework for understanding culturally influenced social behaviors, and discusses ways to incorporate multicultural education into PBS programs.

Eliminating school discipline problems is a major element for improving the nation's schools. In a recent national report, Violence and Discipline Problems in U.S. Public Schools (U.S. Public Schools, 1996–1997), statistics showed that aggressive and violent behaviors are increasing among children and youth in U.S. schools and that school discipline is critical to the prevention of student problems and behavior. Rutherford and Nelson (1998) noted, "Although many children and adolescents occasionally exhibit aggressive and sometimes antisocial behaviors in the course of development, an alarming increase is taking place in the significant number of youth who confront their parents, teachers, and schools with persistent threatening and destructive behaviors" (p. 71). Skiba and Peterson (2000) agreed: "The shocking and tragic violence that has played out in our nation's schools in the last 2 years has elevated

the status of school discipline from an issue of perennial concern to one of national urgency" (p. 335).

The threat and problems of school violence are not restricted to students identified with emotional and behavioral disorders and students residing in inner-city or urban-poverty environments. Recent school tragedies and scenarios of violence throughout the country have affected students across geographical, ethnic, and socioeconomic boundaries. Sugai and Horner (2001) explained, "In schools across the United States, educators and families are engaged in valiant efforts to maximize academic achievement and to create and sustain safe and orderly environments for all students. These efforts are associated with a variety of initiatives, for example, character education, safe schools and healthy environments, proactive schoolwide discipline, drug-free zones, multiculturalism and diversity, and inclusive education" (p. 16). One current schoolwide initiative is positive behavior support (PBS), a systems approach to enhancing the capacity of schools to educate all children, especially those with challenging social behaviors (Kline, Simpson, Blesz, Smith Myles, & Carter, 2001). PBS has a rich, empirically derived database, steeped in applied behavior analysis and, more recently, in the application of functional behavior analysis to solve school-related behavioral issues. Because of careful documentation, researchers can show how the principles of shaping, fading, prompting, and rewarding can help individuals and groups modify and improve their behavior and cognitive processes. However, in reviewing the literature on PBS, the majority of studies included students with a range of disabilities—pervasive developmental disabilities, mental retardation, autism, learning disabilities, and emotional/behavioral disturbances (EBD; Carr et al., 1999).

To improve school success for every student, issues that are not typically considered as part of behavioral education must be addressed by general and special educators. Researchers and practitioners must examine issues related to classroom discipline, cultural diversity, and culturally responsive teaching to develop successful approaches for teaching prosocial skills and reducing antisocial behavior. Sugai and colleagues (2000) noted,

> The use of culturally appropriate interventions also is emphasized in the PBS approach. *Culturally appropriate* describes interventions that consider the unique and individualized learning histories (social, community, historical, familial, racial, gender, etc.) of all individuals (children with problem behaviors, families, teachers, community agents, etc.) who participate in the PBS process and approach. Data-based problem solving and individualized planning processes can help to establish culturally appropriate interventions; however, individual learning histories ultimately can affect how data are summarized, analyzed, and used. (p. 134)

Sugai et al. confirmed, "PBS emphasizes the importance of procedures that are socially and culturally appropriate. The contextual fit between intervention strategies and the values of families, teachers, schools, support personnel, and community agency personnel may affect the quality and durability of support efforts" (p. 136).

In spite of these claims, the use of PBS in diverse, inner-city urban schools has its critics. Critics point to the underlying tensions of who is deciding what behaviors are appropriate, for whom, and under what conditions. More than simply acknowledging that cultural norms may vary among groups, the notion that some types of behaviors are acceptable or not is highly charged since the dominant cultural norms, even in many inner-city schools, are predominantly White and/or middle class. Because the social behaviors of urban at-risk African American and Hispanic/Latino youth are culturally influenced, it is critical that

PBS and multicultural perspectives are infused to increase school success and life choices, academically and socially, for these students. Therefore, the purposes of this article are to (a) examine trends in the racial disparity in exclusionary discipline procedures administered to minority youth, (b) present a conceptual framework to understand culturally influenced social behaviors of urban multicultural children, and (c) discuss how to incorporate multicultural education principles and approaches into PBS programs.

National Trends in Discipline Policies and Procedures

To reduce the incidence of violence in public schools, preventive measures and school disciplinary sanctions known as *zero tolerance policies* have been implemented. These school policies include punitive disciplinary strategies for dealing with disruptive and violent behaviors in schools (i.e., suspension and expulsion), maintaining order in the school buildings, ensuring the school security and the safety of teachers and students, and fostering a school climate to prevent the occurrence of school violence. Yet, a compelling body of research indicates that these "get tough disciplinary measures often fail to meet sound educational principles, and in some cases, their application defies commonsense . . . some of these policies employ sweeping interpretations of the federal law by including violations not intended to be covered by the laws" (Civil Rights Project, 2000, p. 3). Over the counter medicines such as aspirin, Midol®, and even Certs® have been treated as drugs, and paper clips, nail files, and scissors have been considered weapons. Other policies apply the theory of zero tolerance to a broad range of student actions that have no connection to violence and drugs.

National trends indicative of the disproportionate suspension and expulsion of African American and Hispanic/Latino students have been consistently documented and cannot be overlooked (Costenbader & Markson, 1994; Skiba, Peterson, & Williams, 1997; Townsend, 2000). The nondiscretionary punishment guidelines and harsh disciplinary approach promulgated under zero tolerance policies have come under intense scrutiny. During the 1998 school year, more than 3.1 million students (K–12th grade) were suspended, and approximately 87,000 students were expelled in school districts throughout the country (U.S. Department of Education, Office for Civil Rights, 1998). Statistics provided by the Applied Research Center (1999) revealed that African American children, particularly African American boys, are disciplined more severely than children from any other minority group. For example, in South Carolina's public schools, 61% of African American students were charged with a disciplinary code violation, even though the African American student population is 42%. Furthermore, when compared to White students,

African American students were disciplined for minor acts of conduct (e.g., loitering), discretionary offenses (e.g., disrespect for authority), and disciplinary cases in which a school administrator's decision about misbehavior might have been biased (Building Blocks for Youth, 1999). In a similar vein, the U.S. Department of Education (1998) statistics revealed that approximately 25% of all African American boys were suspended at least once over a 4-year period. According to the National Center for Education Statistics (1999), racial disparities in school disciplinary policies have been documented in predominantly African American and Hispanic/Latino school districts. For example, zero tolerance policies addressing violence (85%), firearms (97%), other weapons (94%), and drugs (92%) were more likely to be adopted in urban, minority school districts than predominantly White school districts (71%, 92%, 88%, and 83%, respectively). National data on rates of school discipline and suspension for African American students were between two and three times higher than suspension rates for White students at the elementary, middle, and high school levels (Skiba, Michael, Nardo, & Peterson, 2000). In addition, African American students were more likely than White students to be suspended more than once (U.S. Department of Education, Office for Civil Rights, 1995). More recently, Costenbader and Markson (1994, 1998) reported that African American students are also more frequently exposed to harsher disciplinary strategies (e.g., corporal punishment). When school suspension and expulsion are allowed as punishment for infractions, their use appears to increase (Advancement Project, 2000).

Policymakers, researchers, and educators have expressed their concerns about the disproportionate representation of African American students in special education. National trends indicative of the disproportionate suspension and expulsion of African American and Hispanic/Latino students have been consistently documented and cannot be overlooked (Costenbader & Markson, 1994; Skiba, Peterson, & Williams, 1997; Townsend, 2000). One plausible explanation is that urban multicultural students at risk for school failure are influenced by many social factors including poverty, racism, sexism, family dysfunction, crime and violence, and substance abuse. These living conditions influence six areas of social development, as identified by Morse (1985):

1. A history of poor adult–child relationships with an accompanying need for positive supportive relationships.

2. A tendency to lack a sense of personal efficacy or power and the associated need to experience this by better understanding the learning process and developing a sense of personal responsibility and power.

3. A closely related focus on external factors that influence their behavior and the need to learn to accept responsibility for their behavior and to see how they can control their own learning and behavior.

4. Low self-esteem, especially related to such school behaviors as achievement and peer friendships, and the need to develop and validate a positive self-esteem through positive social interactions and school success.

5. A poorly developed sense of social cognition and inability to understand others' feelings or points of view and take this into account when making decisions and the need to learn to understand others' responses and to work cooperatively with others.

6. Poor problem-solving skills and the need to develop these skills as a means to enhance self-efficacy and self-esteem as well as to develop an important life-long skill. (pp. 1–5)

Gay (1993) remarked that most teachers do not know how to understand and use the school behaviors of these students, which differ from their normative expectations, as aides to teaching. Therefore, they tend to misinterpret them as deviant and treat them punitively. She noted,

> Most curriculum designs and instructional materials are Eurocentric. . . . They are likely to be more readily meaningful and to have a greater appeal to the life experiences and aspirations of Anglo students than to those of ethnic minorities. Thus, when attempting to learn academic tasks, Anglo students do not have the additional burden of working across irrelevant instructional materials and methods. A high degree of cultural congruency exists between middle-class and Anglo students' culture and school culture. These students do not experience much cultural discontinuity, social-code incompatibility, or need for cultural style shifting to adjust to the behavioral codes expected of them in school. (pp. 182–183)

Even though it is true that student behavior is influenced by factors outside the control of the school, studies on school and teacher effectiveness have demonstrated that teachers and schools have a major impact on how students behave and learn and on how they feel about themselves (Darling-Hammond, 1998; Sanders & Rivers, 1996). Therefore, another approach to understanding student problems is to consider the impact of culture on students' social behavior.

Understanding Culturally Influenced Social Behaviors

During the last decade, many educational theorists have become interested in sociocultural theory and multicultural perspectives. These perspectives bring together the disciplines of psychology, semiotics, education, sociology, and anthropology on issues related to language, cognition, culture, human development, teaching, and learning (Garcia, 1994). The implications of multicultural perspectives for general and special educators are that (a) social behaviors are influenced by culture, (b) learning and social interactions are inextricably connected and inseparable from cognition, and (c) both teacher and student are engaged in the process of constructing knowledge through shared social activities and dialogue. Therefore, general and special educators are challenged to (a) interpret the social behaviors of learners from culturally diverse backgrounds, (b) distinguish social behaviors from deficits, and (c) employ effective instructional strategies to help these learners maximize their schooling experiences and acquire the most productive interpersonal skills (Cartledge, Lee, & Feng, 1995).

Consequently, the inclusion of culturally diverse students, particularly those with EBD, requires general and special educators to develop effective and efficient management techniques and interventions. Numerous problems arise when general and special educators fail to consider the role of culture and the experiences students may bring to school. Cultural diversity cannot be ignored in the behavioral assessment of urban students because the social context of learning and the attitudes, values, and behaviors of the family, peer group, and community profoundly influence students' emotional, behavioral, moral, and cognitive development. Therefore, before judging behaviors as deviant, general and special educators must acknowledge culture and social environment as critical factors when developing effective educational practices. Kauffman (1989) noted, "Nearly all behavioral standards and expectations and therefore nearly all judgments regarding behavioral deviance are culture-bound; value judgments cannot be entirely culture-free. In our pluralistic society, which values multicultural elements, the central question for educators is whether they have made sufficient allowance in their judgments for behavior that is a function of a child's particular culture" (p. 212). Because culture influences interpersonal relations and behaviors, study results of children's social competence cannot be generalized outside the culture in which they are obtained. To understand the influence of cultural factors on children's behavior, researchers must conceptually and empirically validate a cultural framework that reflects the dynamic interactions between children and their cultural context.

As members of a cultural group, people interact with the dominant society and become aware of different ways of behaving, different expectations, and they may change their thinking individually or collectively (Shade, 1997). It is understandable that deviant social behaviors (e.g., aggression, violence) are not inherent characteristics of culturally diverse groups. Issacs (1986) identified a host of

external factors that affect the emotional status of multicultural children and youth:

1. Racism and discrimination.
2. Mass media and the way in which ethnic minority groups are portrayed.
3. The strain of acculturation and the migration experience.
4. Legal constraints and strategies for circumvention, such as issues on American Indian reservations.
5. Language and communication pattern differences.
6. Socioeconomic status, especially since ethnic minority groups are disproportionately represented among those defined as living in poverty.
7. The American economy and the availability of employment opportunities.
8. Geographic isolation and resource-poor environments; such environments include urban inner cities, rural areas, reservations, barrios, and other enclaves in which people of color are isolated from the mainstream.
9. Inter- and intra-group conflicts and tensions.
10. Assimilation and the loss of some of the most highly skilled/competent members of ethnic minority groups to the larger society. (pp. 2–4)

In examining social behaviors from cultural perspectives, it is important to understand that culture is integral to every aspect of being, influencing to varying degrees one's thinking and acting, interpersonal relations, and social competence (Cartledge & Feng, 1996; Gay, 2000). A cultural systems approach to education "considers the organization of society, specifically the roles and status assigned to cultural groups within a society as a major determinant of cognitive and social development" (Garcia, 1994, p. 197). Earlier, Ogbu (1991) suggested that the specific social placement of a cultural group within the broader social fabric of society will directly affect the values, perceptions, and social behaviors of members of that group. For several decades, distinct culturally influenced social behaviors have been found between multicultural children and European American children (Cartledge & Milburn, 1996; Rivera & Rogers-Adkinson, 1997). Sidebars 1, 2, 3, and 4 describe culturally influenced social behaviors in African American, European American, Hispanic, Asian American, and Native American children.

Sonia Nieto's (1999) understanding of the concept of culture is critical for understanding urban, multicultural children and youth. Nieto, in citing the work of Brice Heath (1995), pointed out that "urban dwellers in the United States are creating new cultural categories based upon shared experiences because, according to her, these young people 'think of themselves as a *who* and not a *what*'" (p. 45). Nieto further stated, "Multiple identities of

---

Sidebar 1. Comparison of African American and European American's Culturally Influenced Social Behaviors

	African American	European American
Mannerisms/behavior	• Interpersonal skills • Tendency to get involved in heated discussion/debate with others • Tendency to express emotions of anger and hostility	• Impersonal in communication style • Emotionally calm • Tendency to avoid confrontations • Tendency to engage in turn taking in discussion meetings
Communication style	• Expressive or verbal presentation style of communication • Tendency to express opinions in an intense and dynamic way • Tendency to use of concrete, nonabstract words that imply action • Tendency to use personalized experiences, sounds, and images to express oneself • Tendency to use call and response patterns of communication (i.e., back channeling)	• Preference for indirect communication style or concealing one's ulterior motives • Avoids insults or hurting people's feelings • Tendency to engage in conversations using personal information about oneself (e.g., position, residence, occupation)
Social interactional style with adults and peers	• Tendency to engage in body language, looks, gestures, and signals to "tell it like it is" • Tendency to use a nonverbal communication style (e.g., body language) to express feelings, stance, and to send a message of support or nonsupport • Tendency to share personal experiences with others • Tendency to validate knowledge in relation to one's own personal experiences • Tendency to work cooperatively and/or collaboratively • Tendency to have a high degree of social sensitivity to facial expressions and social cues in the environment • Tendency to challenge school personnel based on attributes of strength, generosity, and persuasiveness	• Tendency to work competitively with peers • Tendency to not challenge school personnel because of position and/or credentials
Eye contact	• May not use eye contact in conversations	• Often maintains eye contact in conversations

Note. Based on data from Black Students and School Failure: Policies, Practices and Prescriptions *by J. J. Irvine, 1990, New York: Greenwood.*

youths have important and far-reaching implications for the development and implementation of multicultural education: It is evident that simplistic and bounded conceptions that focus just on specific racial or ethnic groupings fail to capture the realities of many urban youths who live with complicated and heterogeneous realities" (p. 52).

Incorporating Multicultural Approaches into PBS Programs

The behavior management tradition has been characterized by change and the integration of concepts from other models (e.g., cognitive behaviorism, self-management, social skills training; Jones & Jones, 1998). We propose that the PBS model must be (a) characterized by change for the 21st century; (b) grounded in effective, respectful, supportive teacher relationships; and (c) integrated in multicultural education principles and approaches. Grant and Ladson-Billings (1997) conceptually defined multicultural education programs using several different frameworks and approaches, three of which have direct implications for the PBS model. The first approach, *teaching the exceptional and culturally different,* "accommodates students who are considered exceptional or culturally different through the use of teaching strategies or culturally relevant materials that otherwise might be used in pull-out programs for students with special needs" (p. 173). One specific goal of this approach is to help students improve their academic performance and social skills in general education classrooms. The second approach, *human relations,* is designed to promote unity, tolerance, and acceptance within the existing social structure. The school's curriculum program goals are focused on (a) developing positive relationships among students of diverse backgrounds, (b) enhancing personal characteristics (e.g., self-concept/self-esteem), (c) changing stereotyped perceptions, and (d) understanding individual differences and similarities. This approach emphasizes cross-cultural communication strategies, collaboration, and cooperative learning among culturally diverse groups. The third approach, *multicultural education* (MCE), supports the human relations approach by teaching students to learn how to respect each other, how to get along with others, and how to develop positive self-concepts by using a curriculum that is culturally responsive to the culture, language, and learning styles of students.

Multicultural education encompasses the role of cultural pluralism in U.S. education and can be integrated into beliefs about teaching and learning. Gay (1994) noted,

1. Cultural background and ethnic identity are critical determinants of human attitudes, values, and behaviors in all settings, including teaching and learning.
2. Racial, cultural, and ethnic biases permeate schools and society, and thereby minimize individual and social potential.
3. The diversity that characterizes individuals and cultural groups requires a plurality of instructional programs and strategies, if education is to be most effective for all students.
4. The ethnic identity and cultural backgrounds of students are as important as their physical, psychological, and intellectual capabilities in planning and implementing effective educational programs. (p. 49)

Advocates of multicultural education principles have translated general education principles within a conceptual framework of including cultures, experiences, contributions, and perspectives of different ethnic, racial, cultural, and social groups in school programs and practices (see Gay, 1994). As illustrated in Table 1, general education

Sidebar 2. Culturally Influenced Social Behaviors of Asian American Children

Social behavior
- Authority-oriented
- Conforming
- Self-controlled
- Cooperative
- Academically oriented
- Shy
- Low-levels of social communication skills

Self-confidence
- Low assertiveness
- Internalized behavior
- Excessive modesty
- Reluctant to express feelings
- Socialized to be family oriented
- Harmonious relationships emphasized
- Shy
- Conforming

Sidebar 3. Culturally Influenced Social Behaviors of Hispanic Children

Language
- Slow to initiate conversations with peers and others
- Receptive and expressive English skills are minimal

Interpersonal behaviors and peer interaction skills
- Cooperative, quiet, and obedient
- Passive, shy, less socially competent

Verbal behavior
- Difficulty making positive statements about the qualities and accomplishments of others
- Difficulty describing one's feelings or moods
- Difficulty conducting group activities
- Difficulty appropriately responding to cues
- Low level of class participation
- Difficulty expressing opinions

Sidebar 4. Culturally Influenced Social Behaviors of Native American Children

Play behaviors	• Socially active • Formation of same-gender dyads and triads • Spontaneous and creative • Spirit of cooperation and harmony emphasized with peers	Touch	• Public displays of affection are not encouraged • Hand shakes involve a gentle clasping of hands • Young children do not receive gentle touches and hugs
Close friends	• Best friends are close relatives • Respectful of family members	Gestures	• Gestures are used to reinforce main idea of a conversation
Verbal behavior	• Shy/silent in class (Hopi tribe) • Speaks out in class frequently (Choctaw tribe)	Personal space	• Persons converse side by side and not face to face • Prefer to stand 2 to 3 feet from one another
Prosocial behavior	• Value of sense (Navaho Tribes) • Good-natured in interactions with each other • Spirit of belongingness • Spirit of mastery • Spirit of independence • Spirit of generosity	Time	• Regard time on a continuum with no beginning or end
		Speech	• Silence is viewed as a strength • Language is allegorical • Language is spoken in low tones and soft voices
Problem behavior	• Feelings of rejection and alienation • Frustrated by a lack of mastery • Feelings of impotence and lack of self-control • Selfishness	Engaging behavior	• Interruptions are considered rude • Listening skills are taught • Children do not initiate conversations in mixed-aged groups • Observation learning is taught • Internal focus of control • Children are encouraged to be independent • Self-discipline and personal responsibility are emphasized • Group-centered orientation
Eye contact	• Direct open-faced eye contact is avoided (Navaho, Lakota, and Sioux tribes)		
Facial expression	• Feelings and emotions of pleasure, pain, and joy are not expressed	Learning style	• Visually oriented

Note: *Patterns of social behavior are tribe-, age-, and gender-specific. Generalizations about the social behaviors of Native American children should be avoided so as not to perpetuate stereotypes.*

---

principles have been "multiculturalized" and shown to be complementary within a culturally pluralistic framework.

Successful PBS programs for urban, multicultural students require cultural sensitivity, caring and respectful relationships between teachers and students, and a nurturing school environment to create learning communities in schools (Gay, 2000; Obiakor, 1994, 2001; Osher, Woodruff, & Sims, 2000). Accordingly, developing and reviewing codes of acceptable, schoolwide behavior with families, students, teachers, and administrators is an essential first step of using PBS at the schoolwide level. These discussions must be anchored by multiple segments of performance-based evidence such as video clips that show a range of student deportment not only in the classroom but also on the school grounds, in the hallways, cafeteria, and library. By engaging families and students in reviews of actual student performance, the subsequent dialogue leads to a broader agreement on what constitutes acceptable student behav-

Table 1. Multicultural Translation of General Education Principles

General education principles	Multicultural education principles
1. Teachers should build upon and expand the learning potential and style preferences of students.	1. Teaching styles should match the learning styles of different ethnic individual and cultural groups.
2. Education should facilitate the self-acceptance of students.	2. Education should help students accept their ethnicity as an essential component of their personal development.
3. Education is necessary for social consciousness, democratic citizenship, and personal well-being.	3. Knowledge about cultural, racial, and ethnic diversity is needed for citizenship in a democratic and pluralistic society.
4. Education should promote intolerance for all forms of discrimination and oppression.	4. Students should be taught an ethic of social justice for culturally diverse groups and individuals.
5. Relevant teaching methods and materials increase learning.	5. Multicultural content, experiences, and perspectives improve learning for culturally different students.
6. Education should transmit the cumulative knowledge of humankind	6. Students should learn about the contributions that diverse groups and individuals have made to humankind and culture in the United States.

Note. *From* At the Essence of Learning: Multicultural Education, *by Geneva Gay, 1994, West Lafayette, IN: Kappa Delta Pi, International Honor Society in Education. Copyright 1994 by Kappa Delta Pi International Honor Society in Education. Reprinted with permission.*

ior in the school. Critical to this process is the involvement of facilitators who represent the full range of multicultural experiences, backgrounds, and ethnicities within the school community. Of course, this may mean that teachers and other professionals need to moderate their standards of student comportment based on the dialogue and agreed standards of performance. Logically, it means that families and students need to develop a greater appreciation for the difficulty of managing behavior in group situations where the degrees of freedom may not be able to be as broad as they are in family and community settings. Strong facilitation is needed to make sure that the voices of families and students are not overshadowed by professionals (Mehan, 1993).

Fine, Weis, and Powell (1997) stated, "The process of sustaining a community must include a critical interrogation of difference as the rich substance of community life and an invitation for engagement that is relentlessly democratic, diverse, participatory, and always attentive to equity and parity" (p. 250). This dialogue of difference needs to occur at the classroom level, acknowledging the different standards of behaviors that urban, multicultural students bring with them to the classroom. It is critical that we educate one another about how these standards of behavior have been established, their purposes, and the outcomes for groups and individual children. The dialogue must continually be punctuated with specific examples of acceptable and unacceptable behavior so that teachers and their students can come to mutual agreement about what constitutes good citizenship within each classroom. From a multicultural perspective, these opportunities for developing shared standards, norms, and sanctions represent an important step in developing democratic classrooms in which students as well as teachers have opportunities to voice their concerns, opinions, and perspectives publicly.

An ongoing collection and review of information about student behavior is essential to establishing school norms about behavior and improving prosocial teaching and learning. In order for the school community (i.e., students, school staff, parents, community members) to achieve this goal, they must be educated about how to define the norms and how the norms can be used and evaluated. Culturally responsive PBS models must focus on the (a) school's demographic composition of students; (b) students who are referred for chronic, inappropriate behaviors; (c) students who are earning poor grades; (d) students who are not attending school; and (e) students who do not have schooling opportunities to learn. Aggregated student information can be reviewed frequently to (a) uncover potential biases in teaching, (b) discuss antisocial student behavior, and (c) remediate poor academic performance. Through frequent and continuous review of information about student behavior, the school community can continue to hold itself responsible for reaching its democratic goals of "engaged citizenship" for all of its students. These three elements are essential to fostering culturally responsive PBS programs, particularly in schools where students from nondominant cultures (i.e., African American, Native American, Hispanic/Latino, Asian America) are the majority. A shared dialogue and agreement among school personnel about school and classroom norms must be a part of the school culture so that opportunities for democracy and citizenship are created and flourish within schools.

A comprehensive and positive schoolwide model of PBS that is determined by problem type (e.g., students with serious problem behavior, students at risk for problem behavior, students with chronic/intense problem behavior) and intensity of behavior support (e.g., universal interventions, specialized group interventions, and specialized individual interventions) has been developed, validated, and implemented in classroom environments (Sugai & Horner, 1999). There are three levels of support:

1. clear expectations and positive feedback,
2. functional assessment and individualized interventions, and
3. functional assessments and comprehensive services across multiple environments (Turnbull & Turnbull, 2001).

In addition, schoolwide efforts must employ effective instructional programs and interventions that have been shown to have positive benefits for urban, multicultural youth. Highly effective programs (e.g., Success for All; Slavin, Madden, Dolan, & Wasik, in press) and strategies (e.g., classwide peer tutoring, cooperative learning, social skills instruction) have been well-documented in the literature. These interventions focus on improving academic and critical thinking skills and developing prosocial skills (e.g., empathy, getting along, appropriate ways to seek help). For instance, in a multicultural framework, factors such as culture, socioeconomic status, language diversity, peers, family, school demographics, and community play a critical role in defining problem type, intensity of behavior support, and implementation of interventions. Consider the following case:

> Kim was an Asian American student who was truly having problems in school. She was abusive to her peers and not doing well in her classes. In her "good" school, there was the presumption that all Asian Americans were great students. As a result, her teacher did not want her to be tested and placed in special education or alternative programs. Kim's parents thought she needed to see a counselor, and the teacher refused, indicating, "Asian Americans do not have learning or behavioral problems. They are smart minorities who do not need counselors to survive." Kim continued to be exceedingly disruptive, and her teacher never responded. On one occasion, Kim took a knife and stabbed one of her classmates in the hand. It was only then that the school responded and placed her in an "alternative" program where she began to receive counseling. (Obiakor, 2001, p. 90)

This case reveals typical problems that many culturally diverse learners experience. Many Asian Americans suffer in school because they endure psychological problems related to the "model minority syndrome," and teachers downplay the effects that stressors have on their socioemotional well-being. In applying a PBS model, a functional assessment would reveal that Kim had chronic problem behaviors and that specialized individual interventions were needed to change her behavior. The use of culturally responsive interventions approaches was recommended as one solution to ameliorating her behavioral problems (Nevin, Harris, & Correa, 2001; Obiakor, 2001; Utley & Obiakor, 2001). Recommendations included (a) actively listening and communicating with parents, (b) discussing the teacher's biases and her expectations, (c) addressing Kim's socioemotional level of functioning, (d) recognizing

the impact of stressors (e.g., acculturative stress) on her behavior, (e) implementing cultural practices, (f) working with Asian American staff members (e.g., interpreters) on the multidisciplinary team, (g) examining Kim's interpersonal interactions with peers within the school setting (e.g., verbal and nonverbal communication patterns, attitudes, beliefs, and feelings), and (h) providing counseling services.

One essential component of infusing multicultural principles into the PBS model is cultural competence, which involves practitioners having the capacity to respond to the unique needs of populations whose cultures are different from "mainstream" U.S. culture. Cross, Bazron, Dennis, and Issacs (1989) defined *cultural competence* as follows:

> The word culture is used because it implies the integrated pattern of human behavior that includes thoughts, communications, actions, customs, beliefs, values and institutions of a racial, ethnic, religious, or social group. The word competence is used because it implies having the capacity to function in a particular way: the capacity to function within the context of culturally-integrated patterns of human behavior as defined by the group. Thus, cultural competence is defined as a set of congruent behaviors, attitudes, and policies that come together in a system, agency, or amongst professionals and enables that system agency or those professionals to work effectively in cross-cultural situations. (p. 3)

The essential elements of a culturally competent system include (a) valuing diversity, (b) having the capacity for cultural self-assessment, (c) recognizing the dynamics inherent in cross-cultural interactions, (d) having cultural knowledge, and (e) developing adaptations to interventions and service delivery options that reflect an understanding of cultural diversity. Issacs and Benjamin (1991) outlined critical aspects of cultural competence:

1. The concept of cultural competence applies not just to Euro Americans but to all of us who have been born, educated, and live on American soil. Very few things in American institutional structure have prepared us to live harmoniously in a pluralistic and multicultural society. Therefore, every one of us needs to learn and practice from a culturally competent perspective.

2. To bring about a shift in attitudes and behavior, we must learn to accept our own ethnicity and another's without judgment.

3. It is imperative to recognize the importance and acceptability of culture as a viable concept for all ethnic groups.

4. There is no one model or approach to cultural competence and knowledge development. Therefore, in our attempts to become more sen-

sitive to other cultures, we must avoid substituting one set of stereotypes for another.

5. Cultural competence is a dynamic, developmental process and a state towards which we should strive, but it takes a long-term and consistent commitment to achieve.

6. Cultural competence requires ongoing sharing, communication, and dialogue about differences in perceptions and experiences.

7. It should be acknowledged and recognized that cultural competence requires an understanding of the region, size and diversity of the ethnic minority population, and sociopolitical climate within the school system or agency. (pp. 37–38)

Barriers to Implementation: Research to Practice Issues

To implement the suggestions in the previous section, we must examine potential barriers: (a) teacher and principal recruitment, selection, preparation, and ongoing development; (b) issues of measuring and tracking aggregate student behavior performance information; (c) effective family and student involvement in school governance; and (d) epistemological tensions between PBS and multicultural education proponents. In this next section, we explore some of the tensions within each of these issues.

In a recent survey, beginning teachers reported that they feel poorly prepared to deal with issues of classroom management and discipline (Farkas, Johnson & Foleno, 2000). When teachers lack "multiethnicity and reflective nationalism," this problem is exacerbated (Banks, 2001). The most effective preparation of urban teachers has occurred when they are (a) carefully selected (Haberman, 1995; Ladson-Billings, 1995), (b) prepared with a focus on understanding the influence of culture on learning and pedagogy (Trent & Artiles, 1998), and (c) placed as an intern in multicultural school settings (Kozleski, Sands, & French, 1993). Unfortunately, the traditional recruitment practices, the selection of teachers, and the preparation, development, and training diverge from these recommendations and examples of culturally relevant teacher education programs are relatively rare (Cochran-Smith, 1995).

This need for ongoing reflection and discovery about the influence of culture, class, and ethnicity does not end with entry into the teaching profession. Veteran teachers reported that they recognized the need for further education about the impact of culture on teaching and learning (Schultz, Neyhart & Reck, 1996). Similarly, principals reported a lack of knowledge about culturally relevant teaching practices. Without a solid understanding of the relationship between culture and learning, it will be difficult to implement culturally relevant PBS models in schools (Cartledge & Milburn, 1996; Trent & Artiles, 1998; Utley & Obiakor, 2001).

Gathering and interpreting evidence of culturally relevant PBS practices poses a second challenge. Much of current school accountability reform has focused on single measures of student learning, often captured by a standardized test offered once a year. Problems with measurement and the timing of the release of the data complicate school accountability processes. Recommending that culturally relevant PBS co-opt the process of publicly reviewing evidence of student behaviors poses similar dangers if single sets of information are used to make judgments about culturally relevant practice. Helpful evidence comes from a variety of sources, collected over time, and aggregated in such a way that successes and potential problems can be spotted and addressed as needed. Many schools in inner city urban areas lack the resources to collect and aggregate such information.

The scholarly works of Fine, Weis, and Powell (1997), Keith (1996), and Anyon (1995) speak to the complexity of creating serious and thoughtful involvement of families and students in school decision making. This is the third challenge to creating culturally relevant PBS practice. These authors each make the case that much of what passes for participation is reactive and passive rather than active and constructive. For culturally relevant PBS to be realized, professionals, families, and students must all wrestle with achieving interactive, participatory norm setting and resetting to ensure that one cultural perspective does not dominate the rule making, the norm setting, and the curriculum.

The epistemological tensions between behavioral scientists, practitioners, and the social constructivists pose a fourth challenge to achieving culturally relevant PBS practice. The underlying assumptions and perspectives of multicultural scholars conflict with those of the positive behavior support researchers. On the one side, we have pluralistic views of reality that operate simultaneously. Multicultural scholars herald a rich tapestry of ideas, celebrate varying rituals and routines of human behavior, and appreciate diverse languages for the way that they influence the exploration and elaboration of understanding (Banks, 2001; Grant & Ladson-Billings, 1997). From a multicultural perspective, tensions caused by the hegemony of dominant worldviews are eased through the recognition, support, and interest in alternative viewpoints. On the other hand, the PBS paradigm emphasizes reinforcement and consequences to change behavior. Human behavior is objectified, measured, interpreted, and influenced by using change principles that work across settings, individuals, and time. If PBS programs are implemented without considering multicultural pedagogy and practices, a potential conflict arises if the preferred behaviors are reinforced by members of the "dominant" cultural perspective and the values, beliefs, and lifestyles of urban, multicultural children are devalued. Without conscious effort, the dominant viewpoint will prevail, in most situations, and individuals who align themselves with the dominant view will seek to alter and change the behaviors of urban, multicultural children. Culturally relevant PBS models can only occur in contexts that acknowledge and explore these different worldviews and their potential impact on the learning, behavior, and instructional practices.

Conclusion

The racial disparity in discipline procedures continues to be problematic. There is great merit in implementing schoolwide PBS interventions that provide the necessary social, cognitive, and effective conditions for learning to occur. It is critical to understand the mediating effects of culture on the social behavior of urban, multicultural children in order to distinguish what kinds of behavior need to be addressed and what kinds of behavior supports (e.g., interventions) are needed. General and special educators must examine their expectations, broaden their knowledge base, and develop skills so that behavior problems are not based on unidimensional or deficit perspectives. Culturally responsive teaching must be multidimensional and encompass curriculum content, learning context, classroom climate, student–teacher relationships, instructional strategies, and performance assessments that are based on cultural knowledge, experiences, contributions, and perspectives of urban multicultural youth. The implications of this rapprochement are significant in terms of retooling our teacher and school leadership preparation programs and instituting culturally responsive PBS practices in schools.

ABOUT THE AUTHORS

Cheryl A. Utley, PhD, is an associate research professor of special education, Schiefelbusch Institute of Life Span Studies, Juniper Gardens Children's Project. She is also a courtesy assistant professor, Department of Special Education, University of Kansas. Her current research interests include effective academic and behavioral interventions, observational assessment, and multicultural education and special education. Elizabeth B. Kozleski, EdD, is acting associate dean, School of Education, University of Colorado at Denver. She is currently the director of the National Institute for Urban School Improvement at UC at Denver. Her research interests include systemic change in urban schools, qualitative program evaluation methodology, university–school district partnerships, inclusionary practices, nonaversive behavior supports, self-regulation of students with affective and cognitive needs, and communicative competence in individuals who are nonverbal. Anne Smith, EdD, is an education research analyst, Office of Special Education Programs, U.S. Department of Education. Her research interests include the inclusion of students with disabilities in general education classes and education reform initiatives, dimensions of support across the lifespan for individuals with disabilities, diversity and multiculturalism, urban schooling, and inter-national education and inclusion of students with disabilities. Ingrid L. Draper, EdD, is a consultant to the Urban Special Education Leadership Collaborative Education Development Center, Inc. She is also the chairperson of the Leadership Team for the National Institute for Urban School Improvement. Her research interests include urban special educational administration, urban school improvement/ reform and systemic change, systems thinking and collaborative practices, minority issues in special education, and urban communities and school culture. Address: Cheryl A. Utley, The Juniper Gardens Children's Project, 650 Minnesota Ave.– Second Floor, Kansas City, Kansas 66101; e-mail: cautley@ ukans.edu

REFERENCES

Advancement Project/Civil Rights Project. (2000, February). *Education denied: The negative impact of zero tolerance policies.* Testimony before the U.S. Commission on Civil Rights, Washington, DC.

Anyon, J. (1995). Inner city school reform: Toward useful theory. *Urban Education, 30,* 56–70.

Applied Research Center. (1999). *Making the grade. A racial justice report card.* Washington, DC: Author.

Banks, J. A. (2001). *Cultural diversity and education foundations: Curriculum and teaching.* Needham Heights, MA: Allyn & Bacon.

Carr, G. E., Horner, R. H., Turnbull, A. P., Marquis, J. G., McLaughlin, D. M., McAtee, M. L., et al. (1999). *Positive behavior support for people with developmental disabilities: A research synthesis.* Washington, DC: American Association on Mental Retardation.

Cartledge, G., & Feng, H. (1996). The relationship of culture and social behavior. In G. Cartledge & J. F. Milburn (Eds.), *Cultural diversity and social skills instruction: Understanding ethnic and gender differences* (pp. 13–44). Champaign, IL: Research Press.

Cartledge, G., Lee, J. W., & Feng, H. (1995). Cultural diversity: Multicultural factors in teaching social skills. In G. Cartledge & J. F. Milburn (Eds.), *Teaching social skills to children and youth: Innovative approaches.* Needham Heights, MA: Allyn & Bacon.

Cartledge, G., & Milburn, J. F. (1996). Teaching social skills to children and youth: Innovative approaches: Needham, Heights, MA: Allyn & Bacon.

The Civil Rights Project. (2000, June). *Opportunities suspended: The devastating consequences of zero tolerance and school discipline policies.* Cambridge, MA: Harvard University.

Cochran-Smith, M. (1995). Color blindness and basket making are not the answers: Confronting the dilemmas of race, culture, and language diversity in teacher education. *American Educational Research Journal, 32,* 493–522.

Costenbader, V., & Markson, S. (1994). School suspension: A survey of current policies and practices. *NASSP Bulletin, 78,* 103–107.

Costenbader, V., & Markson, S. (1998). School suspension: A study with secondary school students. *Journal of School Psychology, 36,* 59–82.

Cross, T. L., Bazron, B. J., Dennis, K. W., & Issacs, M. R. (1989). *Towards a culturally competent system of care: A monograph on effective services for minority children who are severely emotionally disturbed.* Washington, DC: Child and Adolescent Service System Program (CASSP) Technical Assistance Center, Georgetown University Child Development Center.

Darling-Hammond, L. (1998, February). Teacher learning that supports student learning. *Educational Leadership, 55,* 6–11.

Farkas, S., Johnson, J., & Foleno, T. (2000). *A sense of calling: Who teaches and why.* New York: The Public Agenda.

Fine, M., Weis, L., & Powell, L. (1997). Communities of difference: A critical look at desegregated spaces created for and by youth. *Harvard Educational Review, 67,* 247–284.

Garcia, E. (1994). *Understanding and meeting the challenge of student cultural diversity.* Boston, MA: Houghton Mifflin.

Gay, G. (1993). Ethnic minorities and educational equality. In J. Banks & C. Banks (Eds.), *Multicultural education* (pp. 182–183). Boston, MA: Allyn & Bacon.

Gay, G. (1994). *At the essence of learning: Multicultural education.* West Lafayette, IN: Kappa Delta Pi.

Gay, G. (2000). *Culturally responsive teaching: Theory, research, and practice.* New York: Teachers Press.

Grant, C. A., & Ladson-Billings, G. (1997). *Dictionary of multicultural education.* Phoenix, AZ: Oryx.

Haberman, M. (1995). The dimensions of excellence in programs preparing teachers for urban poverty schools. *Peabody Journal of Education, 70,* 24–43.

Heath, S. B. (1995). Race, ethnicity, and the defiance of categories. In W. D. Hawley & A. W. Jackson (Eds.), *Toward a common destiny: Improving race and ethnic relations in America* (pp. 39–70). San Francisco: Jossey-Bass.

Irvine, J. J. (1990). *Black students and school failure: Policies, practices and prescriptions.* New York: Greenwood.

Issacs, M. R. (1986). *Developing mental health programs for minority youth and their families.* Washington, DC: Georgetown University Child Development Center, Child and Adolescent Service System Program (CASSP) Technical Assistance Center.

Issacs, M. R., & Benjamin, M. P. (1991). *Towards a culturally competent system of care* (Vol. II). Washington, DC: Georgetown University Child Development Center.

Jones, V. F., & Jones, L. S. (1998). *Comprehensive classroom management: Creating communities of support and solving problems.* Needham Heights, MA: Allyn & Bacon.

Kauffman, J. M.(1989). *Characteristics of behavior disorders of children and youth* (4th ed.). Columbus, OH: Merrill.

Keith, N. (1996). Can urban school reform and community development be joined? The potential of community schools. *Education & Urban Society, 28,* 237–268.

Kline, S., Simpson, R. L., Blesz, D. P., Smith Myles, B., & Carter, W. J. (2001). School reform and multicultural learners with emotional and behavioral disorders: Issues, challenges, and solutions. In C. A. Utley & F. E. Obiakor (Eds.), *Special education, multicultural education, and school reform: Components of quality education for learners with mild disabilities* (pp. 118–139). Springfield, IL: Charles C. Thomas.

Kozleski, E. B., Sands, D. J., & French, N. K. (1993). Preparing special educators for urban environments. *Teacher Education and Special Education, 16*(1), 14–22.

Ladson-Billings, G. (1995). Toward a theory of culturally relevant pedagogy. *American Educational Research Journal, 32,* 465–491.

Mehan, H. (1993). Beneath the skin and between the ears: A case study in the politics of representation. In S. Chaiklin & J. Lave (Eds.), *Understanding practice: Perspectives on activity and context* (pp. 241–268). Cambridge, UK: Cambridge University Press.

Morse, W. (1985). *The education and treatment of socioemotionally disturbed children and youth.* Syracuse, NY: Syracuse University Press.

National Center for Education Statistics. (1999). *Indicators of school crime and safety.* Washington, DC: Author.

Nevin, A., Harris, K. C., & Correa, V. (2001). Collaborative consultation between general and special educators in multicultural classrooms: Implications for school reform. In C. A. Utley & F. E. Obiakor (Eds.), *Special education, multicultural education, and school reform: Components of quality education for learners with mild disabilities* (pp. 173–182). Springfield, IL: Charles C. Thomas.

Nieto, S. (1999). *The light in their eyes: Creating multicultural learning communities.* New York: Teachers College Press.

Obiakor, F. E. (1994). *The eight-step multicultural approach: Learning and teaching with a smile.* Dubuque, IA: Kendall/Hunt.

Obiakor, F. E. (2001). *It even happens in "good" schools. Responding to cultural diversity in today's classrooms.* Thousand Oaks, CA: Corwin Press.

Ogbu, J. U.(1991). Low school performance as an adaptation: The case of Blacks in Stockton, CA. In M. A. Gibson & J. U. Ogbu (Eds.), *Minority status and schooling: A comparative study of immigrant and involuntary minorities* (pp. 249–286). New York: Garland.

Osher, D., Woodruff, D., & Sims, A. (2000, June). *Exploring relationships between inappropriate and ineffective special education services for African American youth and their overrepresentation in the juvenile justice system.* Paper presented at The Civil Rights Project, Harvard University, Cambridge, MA.

Peoples, J., & Bailey, G. (1991). *Humanity: An introduction to cultural anthropology* (2nd ed.). St. Paul, MN: West.

Rivera B. D., & Rogers-Adkinson, D. (1997). Culturally sensitive interventions: Social skills training with children and parents from culturally and linguistically diverse backgrounds. *Intervention in School and Clinic, 33*(2), 75–80.

Rutherford, R. B., & Nelson, C. M. (1998). Management of aggressive and violent behavior in schools. In E. L. Meyen, G. A. Vergason, & R. J. Whelan (Eds.), *Educating students with mild disabilities: Strategies and methods* (2nd ed., pp. 71–92). Denver, CO: Love.

Sailor, W. (1996). New structures and systems change for comprehensive behavioral support. In L. K. Koegel, R. L. Koegel, & G. Dunlap (Eds.), *Positive behavioral support: Including people with difficult behavior in the community* (pp. 163–206). Baltimore: Brookes.

Sanders, W. L., & Rivers, J. C. (1996). *Cumulative and residual effects of teachers on future student academic achievement.* Knoxville: University of Tennessee Value-Added Research and Assessment Center.

Schultz, E., Neyhart, T. K. & Reck, U. M. (1996). Swimming against the tide: A study of prospective teachers' attitudes regarding cultural diversity and urban teacher. *The Western Journal of Black Studies, 20,* 1–7.

Shade, B. J.(1997). *Culture, style and the educative process: Making schools work for racially diverse students.* Springfield, IL: Charles C. Thomas.

Skiba, R., Michael, R. S., Nardo, A. C., & Peterson, R. (2000, June). *The color of discipline: Sources of racial and gender disproportionality in school punishment.* Bloomington: Indiana State University, Indiana Education Policy Center.

Skiba, R., & Peterson, R. L. (2000). School discipline: From zero tolerance to early response. *Exceptional Children, 66,* 335–347.

Skiba, R., Peterson, R. L., & Williams, T. (1997). Office referrals and suspension: Disciplinary intervention in middle schools. *Education and Treatment of Children, 20*(3), 295–315.

Slavin, R. N., Madden, N., Dolan, L., & Wasik, B. (in press). *Every child, every school: Success for all.* Thousand Oaks, CA: Corwin Press.

Sugai, G., & Horner, R. H. (1999). Discipline and behavioral support: Practices, pitfalls, and promises. *Effective School Practices, 17*(4), 10–22.

Sugai, G., & Horner, R. H. (2001). Features of an effective behavior support at the school district level. *Beyond Behavior, 11*(1), 16–19.

Sugai, G., Horner, R. H., Dunlap, G., Hieneman, M., Lewis, T., Nelson, C. M., et al. (2000). Applying positive behavior support and functional behavioral assessment in schools. *Journal of Positive Behavior Interventions, 2*(3), 131–143.

Townsend, B. (2000). The disproportionate discipline of African American learners: Reducing school suspensions and expulsions. *Exceptional Children, 66*(3), 381–392.

Trent, S. C., & Artiles, A. J. (1998). Multicultural teacher education in special and bilingual education: Exploring multiple measurement strategies to assess teacher learning. *Remedial and Special Education, 19,* 2–6.

Turnbull, A. P., & Turnbull, R. (2001). *Families, professionals, and exceptionality: Collaborating for empowerment* (4th ed.). Upper Saddle River, NJ: Merrill/Prentice Hall.

U.S. Department of Education, Office for Civil Rights. (1995). *Elementary and secondary school civil rights compliance report: National and state projections.* Washington, DC: Author.

U.S. Department of Education, Office for Civil Rights. (1998). *Elementary and secondary school civil rights compliance report: National and state projections.* Washington, DC: Author.

U.S. Public Schools (1996–1997). *Violence and discipline problems in U.S. public schools.* Washington, DC: Author.

Utley, C. A., & Obiakor, F. E. (2001). *Special education, multicultural education, and school reform: Components of quality education for learners with mild disabilities.* Springfield, IL: Charles C. Thomas.

Webb, R. B., & Sherman, R. R. (1989). *Schooling and society* (2nd ed.). New York: Macmillan.

Action Editor: Wayne Sailor

Young Children with Challenging Behavior:

Issues and Considerations for Behavior Support

Lise Fox
Glen Dunlap
Diane Powell
University of South Florida

Abstract: The critical importance of intervening early to promote the social and emotional development of young children is a recurring theme in several reports commissioned by national organizations and leaders (i.e., Child Mental Health Foundations and Agencies Network; National Research Council of the Institute of Medicine; U.S. Surgeon General). There is an increasing awareness that social–emotional difficulties and problem behaviors in young children are highly likely to continue in school. In addition, young children who show the most chronicity and stability of problem behavior are more likely to be members of families who experience marital distress, parental depression, and poverty. Young children in urban environments who have problem behavior are likely to also face challenges in health, poverty, and access to quality childcare and other services. In this article, the complexity of the urban context is described with a focus on the lives of young children and their families. The authors present a discussion of appropriate practices and research that provides a foundation for the development of effective early intervention programs for young children affected by environmental and developmental challenges. The emphasis of program recommendations is on comprehensiveness in the design of family-centered behavioral support options.

There is an increasing awareness among educators, researchers, and policymakers that many young children are beginning their school experiences without the requisite emotional, social, behavioral, and academic skills that will be necessary for success. Recent national organization and commission reports have emphasized the critical importance of early intervention and prevention in the support of young children who have social–emotional difficulties (Child Mental Health Foundations and Agencies Network, 2000; Department of Health and Human Services, 2001; National Advisory Mental Health Council, 2001; Shonkoff & Phillips, 2000). This phenomenon is sharply evident within urban school environments where many of the students are more likely to be poor, have limited English proficiency, move frequently, and live in one-parent home environments (National Center for Education Statistics, 1996), all factors that have been associated with less successful educational outcomes. Research indicates that many children who have difficulty with the successful transition into kindergarten programs continue to show social and emotional problems throughout their school careers and into adulthood (Huffman, Mehlinger, & Kerivan, 2000).

The alarming frequency in which young children who enter school display severe problem behavior has resulted in an interest in providing early intervention to children in the toddler and preschool years (Department of Health and Human Services, 2001; Shonkoff & Phillips, 2000; Simpson, Jivanjee, Koroloff, Doerfler, & Garcia, 2001). A promising approach for delivering early intervention is through the use of positive behavior support. Positive behavior support has been demonstrated to be effective with individuals with disabilities and students at risk for disabilities in a variety of settings with applications of positive behavior support occurring primarily within school or adult service programs where there are professional program staff and mandates for providing behavior support to address challenging behavior (e.g., IDEA 1997).

In this article, we discuss the issues relevant to providing behavior support to young children with challenging

Journal of Positive Behavior Interventions
Volume 4, Number 4, Fall 2002, pages 208–217

behavior. We describe the nature and course of challenging behavior in young children that necessitates a systematic and comprehensive approach to intervention. We also discuss the complexities associated with providing services to young children in urban environments. The article concludes with a description of the elements that must be considered in the design of behavior support models for young children.

Prevalence, Course, and Correlates of Problem Behavior

Challenging behaviors in young children not only occur at significant rates but are also often precursors to long-term, serious difficulties. Although problematic behaviors in toddlers and preschool-age children have often been dismissed as age-appropriate expressions of developmental change or transient responses to adverse environmental conditions (Campbell, 1995), an emerging body of research supports the robustness of early onset externalizing behavior problems.

Findings from prevalence studies vary depending on the sample characteristics and method used. However, a review of studies with community samples of preschool children found rates of oppositional defiant disorder (ODD) between 7% and 25% (Webster-Stratton, 1997). In a study of 3,860 two- to five-year-old children identified through pediatric visits, 16.8% of the children met the criteria for ODD, with half of the cases (8.1%) considered severe (Lavigne et al., 1996). Rates were highest (22.5%) for 3 year olds and lowest (15%) at 5 years. In this study, attention-deficit disorder was identified in 2% of the participants and was almost always co-occurring with ODD.

Problem rates for children living in poverty appear to fall into the high end of the range. Using the Child Behavior Checklist (Achenbach & Edelbrock, 1991), rates of over 25% for parent reported clinical level externalizing problems (Webster-Stratton, 1997) and rates as high as 39% for teacher reported problems in boys (Kaiser & Hancock, 2000) have been found among children in Head Start. A study using classroom observations found higher levels of physical aggression in children in Head Start compared with children in community childcare, although the community participants displayed higher levels of verbal aggression (Kupersmidt, Bryant, & Willoughby, 2000).

Evidence supports the view that early problems often persist and that the roots of later problems are found in the early years. A review of longitudinal studies revealed that approximately 50% of preschool children with externalizing problems continued to show problems during their school years, with disruptive behavior diagnoses showing the highest rates of persistence (Campbell, 1995). There appears to be remarkable stability in the early years, with 88% of boys identified as aggressive at age 2 continuing to show clinical symptomatology at age 5 and 58% remaining

in the clinical range at age 6 (Shaw, Gilliom, & Giovannelli, 2000) and into adolescence (Egeland, Kalkoske, Gottesman, & Erickson, 1990; Pierce, Ewing, & Campbell, 1999).

Accumulating support exists for an "early starter" developmental pathway for conduct disorders beginning with aggressive, impulsive, and oppositional behaviors in the preschool years, progressing to conduct disorder symptoms such as fighting, lying, and stealing in middle childhood, and the emerging into serious behaviors in adolescence, including interpersonal violence and property violations (Loeber, 1990; Patterson, DeBaryshe, & Ramsey, 1989; Tremblay, Phil, Vitaro, & Dobkin, 1994). Furthermore, it appears that children who display problems at an early age are most likely to develop serious and intransigent antisocial problems in adolescence and adulthood (Webster-Stratton, 1997).

The risk and protective factors that influence the course of a child's development toward emotional and behavioral well-being or problems are complex, synergistic, and cumulative. The more risk factors a child experiences, the higher the risk for poor outcomes, including emotional and behavior problems (Landy & Tam, 1998; Rutter, 1990; Shaw, Winslow, Owens, & Hood, 1998). Risk and protective factors occur at multiple levels and are generally categorized into child factors, family and parenting factors, school-related factors, and community factors. Children living in persistent poverty, especially those living in poor and violent neighborhoods, have increased susceptibility to emotional and behavioral problems both through direct effects on children and contributions of family stress (Brooks-Gunn, Duncan, Klebanov, & Sealand, 1993; Dodge, Pettit, & Bates, 1994; Klebanov, Brooks-Gunn, & Duncan, 1994; Myers, Taylor, Alvy, Arrington, & Richardson, 1992). Family factors are paramount in shaping the development of infants and young children. Chronic family adversity and the resulting disorganized, stressful, and chaotic family environments are demonstrated risk factors. Such family stress may in turn affect levels of maternal depression and other parent psychological states, maternal responsiveness, parent management strategies, marital conflict and degree of maternal support, all factors that have been found to influence the development of disorders in young children (Deater-Deckard, Dodge, Bates, & Pettit, 1998; Huffman et al., 2000; Landy & Tam, 1998; Shaw et al., 2000).

Once children move outside the home setting, negative experiences in preschool and school may further exacerbate their adjustment difficulties. Peer rejection and academic difficulties both contribute to child problems (Arnold, 1997; Patterson et al., 1989), with reading disabilities in particular associated with conduct problems (Sturge, 1982). Poor-quality childcare and ineffective behavior management by teachers in childcare and school settings may also worsen children's problems (NICHD Early Child Care Research Network, 1998; Webster-Stratton, 1997). Although all of these environmental factors are interconnected, their effects are also modulated by child factors involving temperament and cognitive abilities.

Conversely, protective factors can operate at the child, family, school, and community levels to counteract adverse factors and promote social and emotional health. For the individual child, easy temperament and intellectual ability have been the most noted protective factors. At the family level, the presence of two parents, competence of parents, a positive relationship with at least one parent, and social support are significant elements in a child's life. In preschool or school, two important variables are positive relationships with peers and teachers (Huffman et al., 2000; Landy & Tam, 1998; Shonkoff & Phillips, 2000).

Taken together, these findings indicate that disruptive disorders in young children are multicausal, occur at high rates, especially among disadvantaged children, and for a large number of children, problems will persist without intervention.

Complex Context of Early Years and Urban Environments

The daily lives of families in urban environments are replete with conditions that contribute to the known risk factors for emotional and behavioral problems in young children and that, at the same time, offer few resources and supports to families for negotiating the demands needed because of the hazards present in such environments. The everyday stresses on families include financial strain, poor and often overcrowded housing, transience, neighborhood violence and crime, lack of transportation, and social isolation. Welfare reform has added the demands of work to the lives of many single mothers, often in low-paying jobs for employers who make few allowances for the responsibilities of parenting young children. These stressors influence outcomes for young children through direct pathways and indirectly through effects on maternal well-being and parenting capabilities (Brooks-Gunn & Duncan, 1997; McLoyd, 1998). As stated by Hanson and Carta (1995, p. 204), "The stress associated with these societal concerns can sap parents' energy, try their patience, undermine their sense of competence and reduce their sense of control over their lives." Subsets of young children living in families where domestic violence, substance abuse, or maternal depression are present face even greater instability and turmoil in their daily lives.

Immigrant populations in large cities are growing in size and diversity. For these families, language, culture, and intergenerational acculturation issues are added complications in negotiating employment, social services, childcare, education, health care, and other systems within a largely monolingual dominant culture (Washington & Andrews, 1998). Providers of services and supports to families and their young children living in such environments must address the realities of urban life and understand that living in these demanding conditions may well leave families with little extra time and energy to meet the special needs of a child with disruptive behavior.

Serving young children living in urban environments in natural settings presents challenges due to the wide variety of situations in which they spend time. These include early intervention programs and an assortment of childcare arrangements as well as their own homes. Young children living in low income families (> 200 of federal poverty level) whose mothers work are found in center-based care (26%), family childcare (14%), relative care (28%), or with a parent (28%) or baby-sitter (4%; Capizzano, Adams, & Sonenstein, 2000). In addition, 30% of such children receive their regular care in two different arrangements, and 7% receive their care in three or more different arrangements; these multiple arrangements are most commonly a combination of formal and informal care (Cappizano & Adams, 2000). Center-based care includes both private childcare and publicly funded preschool programs such as Head Start and prekindergarten, which have varying mandates and resources for serving children with behavior disorders. Furthermore, the quality of childcare arrangements is highly variable, and providing supports for children with challenging behaviors within such settings requires adapting to a variety of contextual issues. These can include programs of marginal quality with already overwhelmed resources, early childhood education cultures that may view behaviorally based interventions as incompatible with developmentally appropriate practice, and programs with few incentives and little investment in serving children with special needs.

Also, certain populations of identified or at-risk young children are served in a variety of different living arrangements or specialized childcare arrangements. Children eligible for early intervention services through Part C of the Individuals with Disabilities Education Act (IDEA) may be served in segregated or inclusive center-based settings, while children receiving Part B services are found in a variety of school-based classroom settings that often include children with various special needs. Children who have been abused or neglected may live in foster care, in kinship care, or in informal care with relatives. In recent years, many programs for teen mothers and for substance abusing mothers have developed child-focused service components that include center-based childcare. Finally, homeless shelters and domestic violence shelters often have their own childcare programs for resident young children.

Just as young children with behavior challenges are found in a variety of settings across service systems, intervention services for young children and their families are embedded in a number of different systems. An analysis of federal policies and programs that address risk factors for social and emotional problems in young children (Cavanaugh, Lippitt, & Moyo, 2000) identified 29 separate federal programs that affect young children in the areas of health, early childhood care and education, family support and child welfare, mental health and disabilities, child nutrition, and socioeconomic status. Similarly, an examination of the funding streams for early childhood mental health services found 39 different governmental sources of funding (Wishman, Kates, & Kaufman, 2001). These reports note that differing policies, procedures, and disciplinary philosophies among programs create difficulties in coordinating efforts, and despite the multiplicity of programs, services do not reach all children in need. Notably, although there are many federal and state programs that impact young children at risk for, or who have been identified with, emotional or behavior problems, there is no program, system, or funding stream with this population of young children as it sole focus.

The result is a system of programs and services that is fragmented and difficult for families to understand and navigate. In most communities, families do not have access to any visible single point of information about services for young children with behavior issues. Multiple eligibility criteria based on income, diagnosis, test scores, age, geographic area, and specific risk factors create barriers for families trying to access services. In addition, families may lose services or be forced to change providers based on changing circumstances that affect eligibility. Examples include IDEA's Part C to Part B transition at age 3, loss of Part C services if retesting shows improvement above cutoff levels, and loss of Medicaid eligibility and services with rise in income. Finally, families must often seek services from multiple agencies in order to obtain the full range of needed supports.

This complex and fragmented system for serving families and their young children with emotional and behavior problems presents challenges not only to already overburdened families seeking services but also to early interventionists who seek to provide family-centered services within natural settings. The needs of urban families call for a system of supports that provides services within the child and family's natural environments, including childcare, services offered at nontraditional times to accommodate the schedules of working families, providers who can provide information in the family's primary language, a coordination of services among agencies, and changes in program eligibility to ensure a full range of services and program continuity.

Positive Behavior Support and Early Intervention

The complexity of the environments and risk factors of young children in urban environments who have challenging behavior creates a need for comprehensive services that address the ecological needs of the family unit in an effort to influence the behavior and development of the child. In a recent review of the science of early intervention, it was determined that early intervention programs specifically designed to enhance parenting behavior and the development of the child have the greatest impacts (Shonkoff & Phillips, 2000). Thus, in addressing the needs of young children who have problem behavior, it is essential for intervention programs to shift their focus from intervention with the child to supporting the family in securing the resources, skills, parenting skills, and social support needed to provide a nurturing environment for the child (Shonkoff & Phillips, 2000; Simpson et al., 2001).

Positive behavior support (PBS) offers many of the components necessary to address the unique needs of each individual child and family. PBS has been conceptualized as the process that is broadly applied to address the deficient behaviors of the individual and the deficient contexts associated with problem behavior (Carr et al., 1999). The behavior support process includes interventions and supports that are focused on enhancing the ecology of the individual with the ultimate goal of improving people's lives. When young children have problem behavior, comprehensive applications of PBS are necessary to provide the family and other caregivers with strategies to address the child's problem behavior, to teach the child new skills, and to ensure that the family has the resources, support, and knowledge to nurture the development of the child (Dunlap & Fox, 1996).

Although the bulk of research on PBS has addressed the needs of older individuals with challenging behavior, an increasing number of demonstrations exist regarding the efficacy of PBS applications for young children and their families. Research has demonstrated that the implementation of functional assessment, functional communication training, and family-centered behavior support processes result in important outcomes for young children and their families (Blair, Umbreit, & Bos, 1999; Blair, Umbreit, & Eck, 2000; Dunlap & Fox, 1999; Frea & Hepburn, 1999; Galensky, Miltenberger, Stricker, & Garlinghouse, 2001; Lane, Umbreit, & Beebe-Frankenberger, 1999; Moes & Frea, 2000; Reeve & Carr, 2000).

Dunlap and Fox (1999) have described an early intervention model for young children with pervasive developmental disorders and challenging behavior that uses PBS as the framework of services. Their model, the Individualized Support Program (ISP), was designed as an adjunctive program to the child's ongoing services with a goal of helping families and other caregivers address the child's challenging behavior (Dunlap & Fox, 1996; Fox, Dunlap, & Philbrick, 1997). The ISP model provided comprehensive and individualized family support to young children and their families within home and community contexts. The ISP interventionist provided family support, PBS, and served as the support team facilitator for all of the informal and formal service providers in the child's life. Most important, the ISP model focused on assisting the family with the advocacy skills needed to secure resources and services needed by the child and family system.

In the ISP model, the behavior support process began with functional assessment (O'Neill et al., 1997; O'Neill, Vaughn, & Dunlap, 1998) and person-centered planning (Mount & Zwernick, 1988). The functional assessment process provided detailed information on the child's problem behavior, activities, and contexts that were difficult for the child and family; the relationship of the problem behavior to antecedents and consequences; and the function of the behavior. The person-centered planning process provided the family and the child's care providers with the mechanism to articulate the dreams and challenges for the child and the family system. These two processes informed the development of a behavior support plan that addressed problem behavior, ecological supports, and family lifestyle issues. Once the support plan was developed, the interventionist assisted the family and all other caregivers in implementing the plan in all of the child's environments and activities. In addition, the interventionist helped the family in identifying and accessing the additional resources, information, and the social support needed by the family system.

The ISP model provides a demonstration of the efficacy of using positive behavior support to address the challenging behavior in young children who have an identified developmental disability (Dunlap & Fox, 1999). The model has been implemented in several communities and states (Tampa, FL; Connecticut; New Hampshire; Montgomery County, PA), with reports from providers on the success of the approach for young children who have a range of disabilities and who reside in a diversity of communities including urban settings.

Behavior support efforts for young children in urban environments should involve similar components to the ISP model. In addition, the complexities of the lives of urban families would require primary consideration in the provision of behavior support. In these contexts, ecological interventions and systems-change supports would be essential to assisting families in addressing their child's behavioral challenges. The use of PBS as the framework for intervention with young children and their families who live in urban environments will most likely require assisting families in accessing basic resources (financial, housing, medical), the developing of parenting skills, and acquiring social support, as well as the developing and implementing a behavior support plan for the child. Furthermore, behavior support efforts will need to involve all of the child's caregivers within diverse environments (e.g., siblings, grandparents, childcare, home). Behavior support efforts that neglect to acknowledge and assist families with meeting their most basic needs will most likely experience limited success in helping families achieve the lifestyle outcomes necessary to support and nurture their children with challenging behavior.

Key Considerations in the Design of Behavior Support Efforts

In the previous section of this article, we described the use of PBS for addressing the needs of young children with problem behaviors. The following section addresses some issues and challenges that need to be considered by systems and provider agencies as behavior support efforts are designed for individual children and families. These issues tend to focus on the manner in which services are made available, organized, and delivered rather than on the specific intervention and support strategies that compose the behavior support plan. The major point is that the quality of behavior support is essentially irrelevant if systems are not arranged to ensure that young children and their families have direct access to the specific types of interventions and supports that will be of help to them in their particular life circumstances. Thus, the considerations to be addressed in this next section relate to our quest to ensure that the potential benefits of validated approaches are actually received and realized by children and families.

EARLY IDENTIFICATION

A great deal of important research has enabled early interventionists to delineate indicators of serious behavioral disorders when children are young (Campbell, 1995; Reid, 1993; Walker, Severson, & Feil, 1995). In order for this progress to produce value for children and families, early detection and intervention mechanisms need to be activated. Fortunately, the last decade has witnessed encouraging steps in the form of child find and early screening programs. A major contribution of Part C of IDEA has been the implementation of early identification and evaluation systems. Part C, along with other federal and state initiatives (e.g., Early Head Start), has led to significant improvements in the timeliness of detection and intervention. Still, state and local systems of identification and intervention need to improve in many ways.

First, screening and identification systems are not yet universal and, thus, many children are not identified until (or later than) kindergarten and elementary school (Child Mental Health Foundations and Agencies Network, 2000; Department of Health and Human Services, 2001). This is particularly true when children do not exhibit obvious developmental or physical disabilities. For children whose challenges involve learning and/or activity disabilities, or whose environmental circumstances place them at serious risk for behavioral challenges, current screening programs are typically irrelevant or inadequate. An important issue that needs to be confronted is to define behavioral adaptation as a consideration for screening and assessment, independent or in combination with other disabilities.

A second issue involving early identification is what happens after detection occurs. Too frequently, there are lengthy delays between identification and intervention, or the system's capacity to follow through with appropriate and effective intervention is limited (Shonkoff & Phillips, 2000). Early identification without a complementary response is a frustrating and all too prevalent reality in many of our nation's communities.

Another issue closely related to the link between identification and intervention is the early involvement of families. Even when children are identified as being in need of intervention and support, the message may not be communicated effectively with families so that the development of an appropriate program of intervention fails to become a family priority. The involvement of families at an early point in time is a complex topic that relates to numerous variables of family circumstance and the resources and orientation of service systems. Families affected by economic limitations and other competing priorities may find it difficult or impossible to reach out for assistance, especially when the purpose and expected outcomes are vague (Halpern, 2000). Systems of early intervention need to remove barriers and adopt extensive family-friendly outreach practices if early identification is to be matched by functional family involvement (Knitzer, 2000; Simpson et al., 2001).

CULTURAL COMPETENCE

A crucial factor in linking effectively with families to promote early identification and early intervention is cultural competence. Gaining family involvement depends on relating effectively to provide cogent explanations regarding the child's developmental needs and initiating a trajectory of functional support. The process of communicating and developing a functional relationship with the family depends on the ability of the early interventionist to develop rapport, and this often hinges on the interventionist's capacity to relate to the cultural context that defines the family (Hernandez & Isaacs, 1998; Lynch & Hanson, 1998). The establishment of a cultural affinity constitutes the foundation of the relationship and is therefore pivotal in recruiting family involvement and participation (Harry, 1997; Hernandez & Isaacs, 1998; Kalyanpur & Harry, 1999; Lynch & Hanson, 1998; Santarelli, Koegel, Casas, & Koegel, 2001).

A major issue for systems is to ensure that the personnel and programs of early identification, evaluation, and intervention are infused with the cultural competence necessary for connecting with the families residing within the targeted communities. This is especially critical in communities that contain multiple risk factors because it is the families in these communities who are the most vulnerable to competing priorities and distrust of service systems (Halpern, 2000). Systems and provider agencies must assure that culturally competent professionals are consistently available and that programs and service options

avoid inflexible adherence to the assumptions of a dominant cultural perspective.

STRENGTH-BASED AND FAMILY-CENTERED PHILOSOPHY

Family-friendly, culturally competent systems of early intervention are needed to activate behavior support efforts in resolving the challenging behaviors of young children. The essential goal of early intervention services is to help construct a foundation of support and family capacity that will endure and, thus, serve as a longitudinal facilitator of positive development and functional antidote to the later emergence of serious behavioral challenges. As explicated in the previous section on research foundations, effective programs for addressing the challenging behaviors of young children are those that stress parent education and family support. The orientation must be on enhancing the strengths of the family system because it is the family that inevitably, and preferably, assumes the primary responsibility in guiding the child's behavioral development.

Several authors (e.g., Friesen & Stephens, 1998; Lucyshyn, Dunlap, & Albin, 2002; Powell, Batsche, Ferro, Fox, & Dunlap, 1997; Turnbull, Blue-Banning, Turbiville, & Park, 1999) have argued that effective and enduring support efforts eschew the traditional expert-driven model and embrace, instead, a collaborative model of parent–professional partnership. This model, in the case of early intervention, assumes an approach that is fully centered around the family's circumstances, needs, dreams, culture, and specific priorities. The professional's role in this model is to inform, guide, reflect, and join the family as a supportive interventionist with the objective of increasing the family's capacity to achieve their goals (Bailey et al., 1998; Turnbull et al., 1999).

The implications for systems and service providers are dramatic. Efforts need to be undertaken to effect a transition from the expert-driven model to a family-centered orientation. This transition can be very difficult for agency personnel, professionals, and administrators, who have been geared for decades toward the benevolent, authoritative role of the expert. Focusing on family strengths and working in the posture of a facilitating family partner represents a change that can be disconcerting. However, to be optimally effective in the endeavor of family-focused early intervention, such change is vital.

ACCESS TO SERVICES

The manner with which systems arrange for children and families to access services can be facilitative or a massive impediment to early intervention. Following early identification, evaluation, and the development of an individualized service plan, the challenge becomes one of locating and accessing the appropriate types and intensities of services that the plan recommends. Ideally, a seamless process of linkage to qualified, family-centered service providers would occur so that the child and family's needs would be met expeditiously and as intended.

Unfortunately, for children with multiple risks and behavioral challenges, this ideal process rarely occurs. Professional specialization often makes it difficult to match a child and family's idiosyncratic needs to the particular offerings of the local professional community. At the same time, it is common for communities to lack appropriately trained service resources so that finding a suitable provider can be a futile endeavor. This may be especially true for families seeking access to professionals who are skilled in family-centered functional assessment and PBS. Although such providers are becoming more numerous, gaining access can still be difficult.

Children and families affected by multiple challenges and disabilities, and needing a comprehensive and multifaceted intervention approach, can encounter even greater frustrations in accessing services. Service providers and service agencies are usually specialized, and systems are fragmented so that meeting multiple intervention objectives can mean extensive work in tracking down and obtaining the various types of services specified in the intervention plan (Halpern, 2000; Knitzer, 2000). It is not unusual for families with children who have behavioral challenges and multiple risk factors to seek access to five or more different providers and to simultaneously attempt to arrange schedulings, transportation, finances, and some kind of programmatic coordination and follow through. This rapidly becomes a full-time job and beyond the means of all but a few families. To counter this substantial problem of access to appropriate services, systems must find ways to counter the fragmentation and overspecialization that characterizes the field and to implement improved, community-based and family-friendly programs for linking children and families with the services they need.

COMPREHENSIVE ORIENTATION TO SERVICE DELIVERY

An issue closely related to the last point involves the comprehensiveness with which early interventions are provided for children and families affected by problem behavior. Families characterized by multiple risks and stressors have needs for support that transcend the behavioral and developmental disabilities of the child. An optimal approach for enhancing the child's developmental fortunes requires a focus not only on the child's intervention but also on supports for the family system as a whole (Knitzer, 2000; Shonkoff & Phillips, 2000). This perspective is dictated by the reality that the child's progress is inextricably tied to the functioning of the family as a whole. For this reason, a number of authors have asserted that early intervention services must be broad based and evalu-

ated in terms of both child and family functioning (Powell et al., 1997; Weissbourd & Kagan, 1989).

As with the orientation of family centeredness, the notion of providing comprehensive, broad-based supports represents a shift from more traditional services, which tend to be confined to a particular problem or disciplinary purview. The transition to comprehensive supports demands that service systems be increasingly integrated, with flexible funding and a consistent emphasis on family-focused assistance.

PROVIDING FOR A CONTINUUM OF SUPPORTS

The level and type of services that are needed for intervention with children and families affected by challenging behavior vary extensively according to the severity and chronicity of the challenging behavior, the child's developmental functioning, and the resources and circumstances of the family. Although supports should be provided from a broad-based and family-centered perspective, the specific kinds and amounts of support for any child and family system depend on their individual characteristics and situation. Some children and families will need only a little of one type of intervention, but they may benefit greatly from greater concentrations of another service. Some children and families will need minimal support initially but relatively intensive supports later on. Services systems must be arranged in a manner that allows families to access a flexible array of supports that fully meet their needs, including the possibility of intensive supports that exceed typical service allocations.

Summary

In this article, we have described the evidence that clearly indicates a need to provide behavior support efforts to children and their families during the toddler and preschool years. We also describe the difficult and complex circumstances of young children with challenging behaviors and their families who live in urban communities that necessitate the development of a highly flexible, community-based model of both family and behavior support. In our discussion, we provided guidance on how behavior support efforts must be arranged and the considerations needed to develop effective systems of support.

PBS offers a very promising intervention approach with demonstrated efficacy in resolving the challenging behavior of individuals and creating systems of problem behavior prevention and intervention (e.g., schoolwide systems). We believe that positive behavior support has equal promise in addressing the needs of families with young children in urban environments. However, in this article we discuss the unique complexities associated with the delivery of behavior support to young children. It is evident that the delivery of services calls for an integrated and coordinated approach that targets the entire family system for intervention and support services.

We have described an approach to early intervention that is uncommon within most urban communities, although there is recent widespread recognition that this type of service system is necessary for achieving effective outcomes. The approach we describe also stretches the traditional concept of behavior support services. Professionals who are knowledgeable about PBS will be challenged to think deeply about ecological supports, family's access to services, and family unit needs. Families who are stressed by meeting their most basic needs are unlikely to be able or available to provide the intervention and guidance needed to address their child's challenging behavior.

It is reasonable to conclude that the knowledge and technology for achieving behavior change for young children with challenging behavior is known; the challenge that remains is the delivery of those supports in ways that reach the most vulnerable families. Implementing an effective system of behavior support will require the involvement of professionals, practitioners, policymakers, community leaders, and families to develop policies that are effective, arrange service delivery systems in ways that are responsive, and consider new approaches in meeting the needs of young children and their families.

ABOUT THE AUTHORS

Lise Fox, PhD, is a research professor in the Department of Child and Family Studies at the University of South Florida. Her publications and research interests include supporting children with disabilities and challenging behavior in developmentally appropriate environments, positive behavior support, and family support. Glen Dunlap, PhD, is a professor of child and family studies at the University of South Florida, and principal investigator of the OSEP Center on Evidence-Based Practices: Young Children with Challenging Behavior, and the NIDRR Research and Training Center on Positive Behavior Support. Diane Powell, PhD, is an assistant professor in the Department of Child and Family Studies at the University of South Florida. She has experience in service delivery and research in the fields of early childhood mental health and family support and has directed federally funded projects focusing on support for young children affected by violence and parent involvement in education. Address: Lise Fox, Department of Child and Family Studies MHC 2113A, University of South Florida, 13301 Bruce B. Downs Blvd., Tampa, FL 33612.

REFERENCES

Achenbach, T. M., & Edelbrock, C. S. (1991). *Manual for the Child Behavior Checklist and 1991 profile.* Burlington, VT: University Associates in Psychiatry.

Arnold, D. (1997). Co-occurrence of externalizing behavior problems and emergent academic difficulties in high-risk young boys: A preliminary evaluation of patterns and mechanisms. *Journal of Applied Developmental Psychology, 18,* 317–330.

Bailey, D. B., McWilliam, R. A., Darkes, L. A., Hebbler, K., Simeonsson, R. J., Spiker, D., & Wagner, M. (1998). Family outcomes in early intervention: A framework for program evaluation and efficacy research. *Exceptional Children, 64,* 313–328.

Blair, K. C., Umbreit, J., & Bos, C. S. (1999). Using functional assessment and children's preferences to improve the behavior of young children with behavioral disorders. *Behavioral Disorders, 24,* 151–166.

Blair, K. C., Umbreit, J., & Eck, S. (2000). Analysis of multiple variables related to a young child's aggressive behavior. *Journal of Positive Behavior Intervention, 2,* 33–39.

Brooks-Gunn, J., & Duncan, G. J. (1997). The effects of poverty on children. *The Future of Children, 7,* 55–71.

Brooks-Gunn, J., Duncan, G. J., Klebanov, P. K., & Sealand, N. (1993). Do neighborhoods influence child and adolescent development? *American Journal of Sociology, 99,* 353–395.

Campbell, S. B. (1995). Behavior problems in preschool children: A review of the literature. *Journal of Child Psychology and Psychiatry, 36,* 113–149.

Capizzano, J., & Adams, G. (2000). *The number of child care arrangements used by children under five: Variation across states.* Washington, DC: The Urban Institute.

Capizzano, J., Adams, G., & Sonenstein, F. (2000). *Child care arrangements for children under five: Variations across the states.* Washington, DC: The Urban Institute.

Carr, E. G., Horner, R. H., Turnbull, A. P., Marquis, J. G., McLaughlin, D. M., McAtee, M. L., et al. (1999). *Positive behavior support as an approach for dealing with problem behavior in people with developmental disabilities: A research synthesis.* Washington, DC: AAMR.

Cavanaugh, D. A., Lippitt, J., & Moyo, O. (2000). Resource guide to selected federal policies affecting children's social and emotional development and their readiness for school. In *Off to a good start: Research on the risk factors for early school problems and selected federal policies affecting children's social and emotional development and their readiness for school.* Chapel Hill: University of North Carolina, FPG Child Development Center.

Child Mental Health Foundations and Agencies Network. (2000). *A good beginning. Sending America's children to school with the social and emotional competence they need to succeed.* Bethesda, MD: National Institute of Mental Health.

Deater-Deckard, K., Dodge, K. A., Bates, J. E., & Petit, G. S. (1998). Multiple risk factors in the development of externalizing behavior problems: Group and individual differences. *Development and Psychopathology, 10,* 469–493.

Dodge, K. A., Petit, G. S., & Bates, J. E. (1994). Socialization mediators of the relation between socioeconomic status and child conduct problems. *Child Development, 65,* 649–665.

Dunlap, G., & Fox, L. (1996). Early intervention and serious problem behaviors: A comprehensive approach. In. L. K. Koegel, R. L. Koegel, & G. Dunlap (Eds.), *Positive behavior support: Including people with difficult behavior in the community* (pp. 31–50). Baltimore: Brookes.

Dunlap, G., & Fox, L. (1999). A demonstration of behavioral support for young children with autism. *Journal of Positive Behavior Interventions, 1*(2), 77–87.

Egeland, B., Kalkoske, M., Gottesman, N., & Erickson, M. F. (1990). Preschool behavior problems: Stability and factors accounting for change. *Journal of Child Psychology and Psychiatry, 31,* 891–909.

Fox, L., Dunlap, G., & Philbrick, L. A. (1997). Providing individual supports to young children with autism and their families. *Journal of Early Intervention, 21,* 1–14.

Frea, W. D., & Hepburn, S. L. (1999). Teaching parents of children with autism to perform functional assessments to plan interventions for extremely disruptive behaviors. *Journal of Positive Behavior Interventions, 1,* 112–116.

Friesen, B. J., & Stephens, B. (1998). Expanding family roles in the system of care. In M. H. Epstein, K. Kutash, & A. Duchnowski (Eds.), *Outcomes for children and youth with behavioral and emotional disorders and their families* (pp. 231–260). Austin: PRO-ED.

Galensky, T. L., Miltenberger, R. G., Stricker, J. M., & Garlinghouse, M. A. (2001). Functional assessment and the treatment of mealtime behavior problems. *Journal of Positive Behavior Intervention, 3,* 211–224.

Halpern, R. (2000). Early childhood intervention for low-income children and families. In J. P. Shonkoff & S. J. Meisels (Eds.), *Handbook of early childhood intervention* (2nd ed.) (pp. 361–386). Cambridge, UK: Cambridge University Press.

Hanson, M. J., & Carta, J. J. (1995). Addressing the challenges of families with multiple risks. *Exceptional Children, 62,* 201–212.

Harry, B. (1997). Leaning forward or bending over backwards: Cultural reciprocity in working with families. *Journal of Early Intervention, 21,* 62–72.

Hernandez, M., & Isaacs, M. R. (1998). *Promoting cultural competence in children's mental health services.* Baltimore: Brookes.

Huffman, L. C., Mehlinger, S. L., & Kerivan, A. S. (2000). Risk factors for academic and behavioral problems at the beginning of school. In *Off to a good start: Research on the risk factors for early school problems and selected federal policies affecting children's social and emotional development and their readiness for school.* Chapel Hill: University of North Carolina, FPG Child Development Center.

Kaiser, A., & Hancock, T. (2000, June). *Early identification and prevention of conduct disorder in Head Start children.* Presentation at Head Start's Fifth National Research Conference: Developmental and Contextual Transitions of Children and Families, Washington, DC.

Kalyanpur, M., & Harry, B. (1999). *Culture in special education. Building reciprocal family-professional relationships.* Baltimore: Brookes.

Klebanov, P. K., Brooks-Gunn, J., & Duncan, G. J. (1994). Does neighborhood and family poverty affect mothers' parenting, mental health, and social support? *Journal of Marriage and the Family, 56,* 441–455.

Knitzer, J. (2000). Early childhood mental health services: A policy and systems development perspective. In J. P. Shonkoff & S. J. Meisels (Eds.), *Handbook of early childhood intervention* (2nd ed.) (pp. 416–438). Cambridge, UK: Cambridge University Press.

Kupersmidt, J. B., Bryant, D., & Willoughby, M. T. (2000). Prevalence of aggressive behaviors among preschoolers in Head Start and community child care programs. *Behavioral Disorders, 26,* 42–52.

Landy, S., & Tam, K. K. (1998). *Understanding the contribution of multiple risk factors on child development at various ages.* Quebec: Human Resources Canada, Applied Research Branch.

Lane, K. L., Umbreit, J., & Beebe-Frankenberger, M. E. (1999). Functional assessment research on students with or at risk for EBD: 1990 to present. *Journal of Positive Behavior Interventions, 1,* 101–111.

Lavigne, J. V., Gibbons, R. D., Christoffel, K. K., Arend, R., Rosenbaum, D., Binns, H. J., et al. (1996). Prevalence rates and correlates of psychiatric disorders among preschool children. *Journal of the American Academy of Child and Adolescent Psychiatry,35,* 889–897.

Loeber, R. (1990). Development and risk factors of juvenile antisocial behavior and delinquency. *Clinical Psychology Review, 10,* 1–41.

Lucyshyn, J., Dunlap, G., & Albin, R.W. (Eds.). (2002). *Families and positive behavior support: Addressing problem behavior in family contexts.* Baltimore: Brookes.

Lynch, E. W., & Hanson, M. J. (1998). *Developing cross-cultural competence: A guide for working with young children and their families* (2nd ed.). Baltimore: Brookes.

McLoyd, V. C. (1998). Socioeconomic disadvantage and child development. *American Psychologist, 53,* 185–204.

Moes, D. R., & Frea, W. D. (2000). Using family context to inform intervention planning for the treatment of a child with autism. *Journal of Positive Behavior Interventions, 2,* 40–46.

Mount, B., & Zwernik, K. (1988). *It's never too early, it's never too late: An overview of personal futures planning.* St Paul, MN: Governor's Council on Developmental Disabilities.

Myers, H. F., Taylor, S., Alvy, K. T., Arrington, A., & Richardson, M. A. (1992). Parental and family predictors of behavior problems in inner-city Black children. *American Journal of Community Psychology, 20,* 557–576.

National Advisory Mental Health Council Workgroup on Child and Adolescent Mental Health Intervention Development and Deployment. (2001). *Blueprint for change: Research on child and adolescent mental health.* Bethesda, MD: National Institute of Mental Health.

National Center for Education Statistics. (1996). *Urban schools. The challenge of location and poverty.* Washington, DC: U.S. Department of Education, Office of Educational Research and Improvement.

NICHD Early Child Care Research Network. (1998). Early child care and self-control, compliance and problem behavior at twenty-four and thirty-six months. *Child Development, 69,* 1145–1170.

O'Neill, R. E., Horner, R. H., Albin, R. W., Storey, K., Sprague, J. R., & Newton, J. S. (1997). *Functional assessment of problem behavior: A practical assessment guide.* Pacific Grove, CA: Brooks/Cole.

O'Neill, R. E., Vaughn, B. J., & Dunlap, G. (1998). Comprehensive behavioral support: Assessment issues and strategies. In A. M. Wetherby, S. F. Warren, & J. Reichle (Eds.), *Transitions in prelinguistic communication* (pp. 313–341). Baltimore: Brookes.

Patterson, G. R., DeBaryshe, B. D., & Ramsey, E. (1989). A developmental perspective on antisocial behavior. *American Psychologist, 44,* 329–335.

Pierce, E. W., Ewing, L. J., & Campbell, S. B. (1999). Diagnostic status and symptomatic behavior of hard-to-manage preschool children in middle childhood and early adolescence. *Journal of Clinical Child Psychology, 28,* 44–57.

Powell, D. S., Batsche, C. J., Ferro, J., Fox, L., & Dunlap, G. (1997). A strengths-based approach in support of multi-risk families: Principles and issues. *Topics in Early Childhood Special Education, 17,* 1–26.

Reeve, C. E., & Carr, E. G. (2000). Prevention of severe behavior problems in children with developmental disorders. *Journal of Positive Behavior Interventions, 2,* 144–160.

Reid, J. B. (1993). Prevention of conduct disorder before and after school entry: Relating interventions to developmental findings. *Development and Psychopathology, 5,* 311–319.

Rutter, M. (1990). Psychosocial resilience and protective mechanisms. In J. Rolf, A. S. Masten, D. Cicchetti, K. H. Niechterlein, & S. Weintraub (Eds.), *Risk and protective factors in the development of psychopathology* (pp. 181–214). New York: Cambridge University Press.

Santarelli, G., Koegel, R. L., Casas, J. M., & Koegel, L. K. (2001). Culturally diverse families participating in behavior therapy parent education programs for children with developmental disabilities. *Journal of Positive Behavior Interventions, 3,* 120–123.

Shaw, D. S., Gilliom, M., & Giovannelli, J. (2000). Aggressive behavior disorders. In C. H. Zeanah (Ed.), *Handbook of infant mental health* (pp. 397–411). New York: Guilford.

Shaw, D. S., Winslow, E. B., Owens, E. B., & Hood, N. (1998). Young children's adjustment to chronic family adversity: A longitudinal study of low-income families. *Journal of the American Academy of Child and Adolescent Psychiatry, 37,* 545–553.

Shonkoff, J. P., & Phillips, D. A. (Eds.). (2000). *From neurons to neighborhoods: The science of early childhood development.* Washington, DC: National Academy Press.

Simpson, J. S., Jivanjee, P., Koroloff, N., Doerfler, A., & Garcia, M. (2001). *Promising practices in early childhood mental health. Systems of care: Promising practices in children's mental health* (2001 series, Volume III). Washington, DC: American Institutes for Research, Center for Effective Collaboration and Practice.

Sturge, C. (1982). Reading retardation and antisocial behavior. *Journal of Child Psychology and Psychiatry, 23,* 21–31.

Tremblay, R. E., Phil, R. O., Vitaro, F., & Dobkin, P. (1994). Predicting early onset of male antisocial behavior from preschool behavior. *Archives of General Psychiatry, 51,* 732–739.

Turnbull, A. P., Blue-Banning, M., Turbiville, V., & Park, J. (1999). From parent education to partnership education: A call for a transformed focus. *Topics in Early Childhood Special Education, 19,* 164–172.

U.S. Department of Health and Human Services. (2001). Report of the Surgeon General's conference on children's mental health: A national action agenda. Retrieved August 1, 2001, from www.surgeongeneral.gov

Walker, H. M., Severson, H. H., & Feil, E. (1995). *The early screening project.* Longmont, CO: Sopris West.

Washington, V., & Andrews, J. D. (1998). *Children of 2010.* Washington, DC: Children of 2010.

Webster-Stratton, C. (1997). Early intervention for families of preschool children with conduct problems. In M. J. Guralnick (Ed.), *The effectiveness of early intervention* (pp. 429–453). Baltimore: Brookes.

Weissbourd, B., & Kagan, S. L. (1989). Family support programs: Catalysts for change. *American Journal of Orthopsychiatry, 59,* 20–31.

Wishman, A., Kates, D., & Kaufmann, R. (2001). *Funding early childhood mental health services and supports.* Washington, DC: Georgetown University Child Development Center.

Action Editor: Wayne Sailor